MW00559826

American Coin Treasures and Hoards

and caches of other American numismatic items

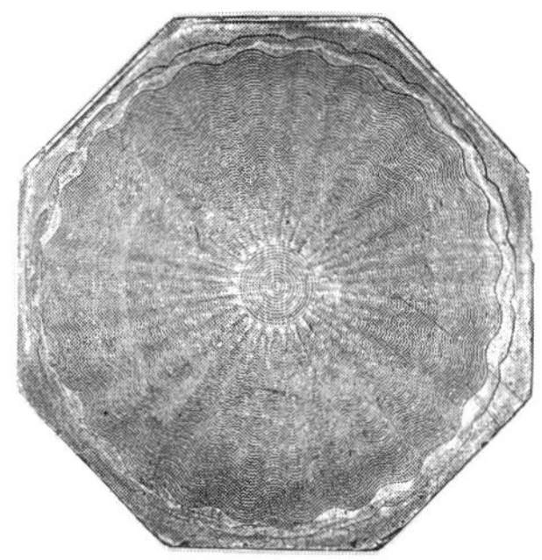

Hundreds of exciting and informative accounts of

FORTUNES LOST! FORTUNES FOUND!
FORTUNES WAITING TO BE DISCOVERED!

A treasury of treasure stories from

Sunken ships
Bank vaults and reserves
Hidden compartments
Buried chests and boxes
Old safes
Pirates and privateers
Cornerstones
Barrels and casks
Mint and Treasury storage
Wrecked buildings
Caves and crevices
Estates
Time capsules
Forgotten collections
Attics and basements
and other places

by Q. David Bowers

with Michael Hodder, *Research Associate*

Foreword by Kenneth E. Bressett

About the Author

Q. David Bowers began his interest in rare coins in 1952 and in 1953 became a dealer while a young teenager. Since that time he has achieved prominence in the field, has handled many important coins and collections, and has written several dozen books, several of which have become classics in the field. His books and catalogues have earned more "Book of the Year" and other honors given by the Numismatic Literary Guild than have the works of any other author.

He is a past president of the Professional Numismatists Guild and the American Numismatic Association and is a recipient of the highest honors given by these organizations, the PNG Founders' Award and the ANA Farran Zerbe Award. He is a recipient of the Pennsylvania State University's College of Business Administration's Distinguished Alumnus Award. With Raymond N. Merena he is an owner of Bowers and Merena Galleries, Inc., in Wolfeboro, New Hampshire.

ISBN — 0-943161-69-X

Published by

Bowers and Merena Galleries, Inc.
Box 1224
Wolfeboro, NH 03894-1224.

Table of Contents

Acknowledgements

The author expresses appreciation to the following contributors who have helped in the ways indicated:

John W. Adams provided an illustration. **David W. Akers** discussed hoards with which he is familiar and made several valuable suggestions; he also reviewed portions of the manuscript and submitted additions and corrections. **Gene and Audra Andries** sent a clipping from the *St. Louis Globe-Democrat* about a 1960 find. **Roy D. Ash** corresponded concerning hoards of Liberty Seated silver coins including the New Orleans find.

Stephanie Bean of Littleton Coin Co. provided photographs. **Ray Bolduc** provided information on gold coins found in California. **Remy Bourne** sent information on several old-time finds. **Roger Boye** provided a list of undiscovered treasures and a map showing various locations. **Kenneth E. Bressett,** president of the American Numismatic Association and editor of *A Guide Book of United States Coins,* wrote the foreword and suggested several areas for inquiry.

Robert Ellis Cahill provided information on pirate treasures and sent a copy of one of his books on the subject. **Winthrop Carner** assisted with an inquiry. **Frank Campbell,** librarian, American Numismatic Society, furnished copies of nineteenth-century auction listings and Economite hoard data. **Lynn Chen,** librarian, American Numismatic Association, provided several catalogues and books for study. **W. Murray Clark** shared recollections of Vermont hoarder Alexander Miller.

John Dannreuther discussed several hoards. **Joe Darnell** submitted a clipping about a find in Valmy, Wisconsin. **Hal Dawson,** of Garrett Metal Detectors and editor of *Searcher,* provided a file of clippings. **Beth Deisher,** editor of *Coin World,* did a computer search of that publication's files, using the word "hoard" as a key, to seek information; many citations were obtained, and from this group over a dozen were used. **Thomas K. DeLorey** provided a citation relative to the Aaron White hoard, related an experience concerning a remarkable hoard of double eagles, another regarding an 1894-S dime, and after reading the manuscript made several valuable suggestions, amplifications, and corrections. **Lou Dieke** provided information on a gold coin cache. **R.L. Dixon, Sr.,** sent a 1901-dated clipping from the *Brunswick* (Maine) *Telegraph,* relating to a find.

John F. Eaves sent a clipping about the cornerstone of the Lutheran Home near Allentown, Pennsylvania. **Bruce Ellis** sent a clipping.

Dr. George Fuld assisted with research, sent copies of several citations, and helped with several clarifications. **Dr. Kathy Helgesen Fuller** reviewed parts of the manuscript and made suggestions.

Jeff Garrett provided several leads for investigation of hoards, notably the gold find in Jackson, Mississippi. **James C. Gray** shared ideas on sea-salvaged gold coins. **Philip D. Greco** furnished information about the cornerstone of the Boston branch of the Bank of the United States and a cache found on Cape Cod.

David Hall furnished information. **James L. Halperin** furnished information about a hoard of 1821 cents. **Thomas J. Hammond** contributed an account of the Alexandria find of Kellogg gold $20 pieces. **David Harper** helped locate information concerning a hoard. **W. Mike Hinkle** shared recollections of foreign hoards of American gold coins. **Wayne Homren** sent several newspaper clippings about varied subjects including the *S.S. Central America,* the supposed find of an 1804 silver dollar, etc. **Mark Hotz** furnished an item associated with the Panama Railroad, commented about the counterstamped quarter dollars of 1815 and 1825, and shared an experience concerning a visit to a numismatically important site on Eden Street, Baltimore. **William M. House** provided a specimen of an Aaron White medal. **Bennie Hutchins** provided information about the Prairie Town, Illinois, hoard.

Don Jensen provided information about a currency hoard.

Arthur M. Kagin shared recollections of various commemorative hoards and other caches he has handled during his long numismatic career. **John M. Kleeberg,** American Numismatic Society, made several suggestions. **Abner Kreisberg** answered an inquiry about gold dollars of the 1879-1881 years.

James Lamb, Christie's, furnished an illustration. **David Lange** shared his research and comments concerning the Cogswell time capsule. **Robert D. Leonard, Jr.,** supplied an inventory of items found in the sea-floor wreckage of the *S.S. Winfield Scott* and much supporting material, including correspondence with various numismatists. **David Lindvall** made several important suggestions.

Janice Marchese read the manuscript and made valuable comments. **Dr. John McCloskey,** Liberty Seated Collectors Club, sent information on several hoards for which he had records. **Wayne Miller** was interviewed and provided information about two hoards, one that came to light in Montana and the other in California. **Karl Moulton** acquainted the author with the Charles White Collection (containing a hoard) and provided a catalogue of it; likewise, the Judge J.P. Putnam hoard information came from him; he also provided a comprehensive historical file as well as his own thoughts and ideas concerning the hoard of 1815 and 1825/3 quarter dollars with E and L counterstamps. **Gerald Murack** sebt a newspaper clipping. **Col. William Bain Murray** discussed coins retrieved from the wreck of the *Arabia.* **Rich Mulcahy** furnished a suggestion.

Eric P. Newman supplied an 1863 advertisement for quantities of copper-nickel cents and provided a recollection of the dispersal of the Stepney Depot hoard from which he obtained a key 1776 Machin's Mills copper. **James ("Jimmy Sierra") Normandi** provided information about several finds in which he was involved during the course of treasure hunting with an electronic detector.

Dean Oakes was interviewed and provided information on several coin and currency hoards including the "Oat Bin" hoard, the Davenport Bank hoard, and the Ella Overby hoard. **Florence Ogg,** Suffolk County Vanderbilt Museum, sent information concerning the *Lexington.* **Dr. Joel Orosz** contributed comments about the Wiley and Rood hoards of numismatic literature and a cache once owned by Henry Chapman; not all of this material was used. **Dan Owens** provided nineteenth-century newspaper accounts of shipwrecks, located modern descriptions and citations about wrecks, and helped in other valuable ways.

Donald Prybyzerski sent several clippings and accounts concerning the 1840 *Lexington* disaster.

Greg Roberts discussed hoards of gold coins. **Jay Roe** provided information about gold coins salvaged from the *S.S. Winfield Scott.* **Bob Ross** provided details of coins found in Glasgow, Kentucky. **Russ Rulau** helped with information concerning the Aaron White hoard and corresponded about various tokens.

Harry E. Salyards, M.D., reviewed the manuscript and made valuable suggestions. **Clifford L. Sayre, Jr.,** sent information concerning steamboat disasters. **Thomas H. Sebring** discussed various shipwreck hoards and made several suggestions. **Daniel Frank Sedwick** provided certain information concerning Spanish-American coins and, separately, the wreck of the *Pewabic.* **Neil Shafer** provided recollections of a cache of coins that may have belonged to nineteenth-century numismatist R. Coulton Davis. **Raymond Shepherd,** curator, Old Economy Village (Ambridge, PA), provided much hitherto unknown information about the settlement there, the coin hoard, the Museum of Curiosities, and other aspects of what seems to have been a veritable financial center in western Pennsylvania in the mid-nineteenth century. **Michael W. Sherman** sent information concerning a vast hoard of Confederate States of America bonds and the disposition of them. **Pete Smith** discussed the Aaron White and Economite hoards and provided information concerning A.M. Smith's remarkable holdings. **Dr. Henry Stevens** sent historical information about the Pennsylvania Hospital cornerstone. **Paul T. Stimmler** sent a newspaper clipping. **David Sundman** sent several old-time newspaper clippings about coin hoards, gave details of the New York subway hoard, provided information about the Miller cache in Vermont, and made suggestions concerning several parts of the manuscript.

Anthony Terranova furnished several suggestions concerning colonial and early American coins. **David E. Tripp** corresponded concerning a gold hoard, a cache of 1927-D Peace dollars, and other treasure matters including several individual pieces described separately in Chapter 21; David and his wife Susan have helped in many research matters over the years, beginning with our association in the sale of the Garrett Collection of U.S. coins for The Johns Hopkins University (1979-1981) and continuing with our sale of the Virgil M. Brand Collection (1983-1984).

Bob Vail suggested several citations from old auction catalogues. **Carolyn van Praag,** Fisher Research Laboratory, sent information concerning finds made by the firm's electronic metal detectors. **Mark Van Winkle** provided information on numismatic hoards. **Doug Veal** furnished an extensive file of clippings from treasure-hunting magazines of recent decades. **Kenneth V. Voss** furnished a 1984 clipping about a Civil War treasure.

Alan Victor Weinberg provided illustrations and a newspaper article relating to the *S.S. Central America* and helped in several other valuable ways including style and proofreading suggestions. **Fred Weinberg** suggested an avenue for further exploration and provided a book. **Randall E. Wiley** suggested sources for Liberty Seated hoard information and answered an inquiry. **Mark B. Wolf** sent a file of clippings and citations. **Ashton R. Woodhouse** made a suggestion. **William M. Wright, Jr.,** sent a story about a hoard of Indian cents.

Keith Zaner discussed 1815 and 1825 quarter dollars with E and L counterstamps.

Michael Hodder, well-known numismatic scholar and author, and research associate on this project, created several entries including accounts of the *Feversham* and *Le Chameau,* furnished numerous citations, proofread the text, and provided certain annotations.

John J. Ford, Jr., reviewed several drafts of the manuscript, made numerous corrections and amplifications, commented on many old-time hoards, provided illustrative and historical material, and was interviewed by Michael Hodder concerning hitherto unpublished details of several hoards of Western gold items.

Sandy Martin, talented artist, illustrator, and photographer of Wolfeboro, NH, was commissioned to prepare numerous pen-and-ink sketches to illustrate this work. The concepts are based upon her impressions of scenarios from reading the text and are each signed by her.

Bowers and Merena Galleries staff credits include: Mark Borckardt reviewed selections from the manuscript and made corrections and additions. **Robin Edgerly** assisted with graphics, reproduction of photographs and etchings, and helped in other ways. **Roberta French** transcribed several accounts and helped with searching for citations in old magazines and books. **Jennifer Meers** coordinated the project, designed the book, and did much of the graphics and layout. **Rosalie Minnerly** helped with research, the gathering of information, coordination of the project, transcription of notes and drafts, and assisted in many other ways. **Douglas Plasencia** took and developed many of the coin photographs.

Other credits and bibliography citations are given in the footnotes.

Style and Production Notes

CAPITALIZATION: For consistency and ease of understanding by present-day readers, coin grades in new and quoted text are capitalized, as in Very Fine, although in original text they may have appeared differently (as very fine, v. fine, VF, etc.).

FOOTNOTES: Sources, amplifications of material, and suggestions for further reading are given in the footnotes. The writer has experienced great frustration during the course of research for this book, in that many if not most accounts of treasures and hoards cite little in the way of supportive material. To the present reader who finds the footnotes to be more plentiful than desired, I suggest that they can easily be ignored. However, if you are interested in pursuing a subject further, the footnotes are there if you want them. Besides, as Michael Korda, John J. Ford, Jr., and others have said or written, to someone interested in a subject, there is no such thing as *too much* information. In the style of Hubert Howe Bancroft (one of my favorite historians, and a person who liked footnotes as much as any author I have read—sometimes his footnotes even had their own extra numbered notes!), the notes are, as stated, *footnotes,* are on or next to the pages to which they refer, and will not require constant paging back and forth to use them (as would, for example, endnotes). Footnotes in quoted material are modern and are by Q. David Bowers or to an attributed source.

ILLUSTRATIONS: Photographs are of the general types of coins found in the hoards mentioned, but unless noted otherwise are "stock" pictures and are not necessarily of specimens directly attributable to the hoards. Indeed, most hoard coins have long since lost their pedigrees. As an example, of the thousands of silver coins in the Economite Hoard that came to light in 1878, not a single piece can be specifically traced today (although a few pieces found later in Economy may be from that source). Illustrations of western mining scenes, ships, railroads, buildings, etc., are primarily from nineteenth-century publications and imprints including proof vignettes from the Continental Bank Note Company, New England Bank Note Company, National Bank Note Company, and the American Bank Note Company; *Harper's Weekly* and *Monthly, Gleason's Pictorial Drawing-Room Companion* (and, *Ballou's,* its successor), *Frank Leslie's Illustrated Newspaper,* and other sources.

ITALIC TYPE: Ship names are given in italics, as *Saxony,* although various sources may have had them otherwise as "Saxony," Saxony, SAXONY, etc. Similarly, book titles are given in italic type.

ORDER OF LISTINGS: Within a typical chapter most entries are listed in approximate chronological order of their discovery (preferably) or first known publication. Ships are listed by dates they were lost.

QUOTED MATERIAL: Some quotations are lightly edited, but in all instances the original meaning has been preserved.

RELIABILITY OF INFORMATION: In instances in which two or more sources, each considered reliable by historians, differ from each other, such differences are mentioned. To the extent that information is available, an effort has been made to give numismatically accurate information concerning various pieces. However, for reasons stated in the Introduction, facts concerning discovered hoards are often scarce. Facts concerning undiscovered hoards are scarcer yet and often include an element of fantasy (if they were *too* factual, they would not remain undiscovered).

POSSIBLE FUTURE BOOK: During the research for this book it quickly became apparent that it could have been doubled or tripled in size without much effort, as virtually every avenue of inquiry brought forth news of some long-forgotten treasure ship, or a purse of old coins brought to a coin dealer by a lady in whose family they had descended, or one or another account. With this in mind, I *may* someday write a sequel to this book. If you have information you wish to share for this purpose, please submit it in writing. The more factual numismatic and historical details you can furnish, the better. Any illustrations should be black and white, sharply detailed, captioned, non-returnable, and dated. "Payment" will be in the form of printed credit and a copy of any future book in which your material is used.

Foreword

by Kenneth E. Bressett

President, American Numismatic Association
Editor, *A Guide Book of U.S. Coins*

This is the story of hidden treasures that have surfaced and become part of the American tradition of numismatic lore and collecting. Most of the stories are true. Some are legendary tales that have come down to us on good authority. Some have been fabricated as hoaxes or to deceive collectors (and are identified as such). All are fascinating pieces of history.

Imagine what it would be like to discover a cache of nearly Uncirculated Massachusetts Pine Tree shillings. That is what a young boy named George Reed did in 1863 while playing near his home in Roxbury, Massachusetts! There were 28 coins in the group which consisted of Oak and Pine tree designs in several different denominations. A ready-made collection so to speak and one that would make any one of us proud and wealthy.

Finding a treasure like that must be a secret dream of every collector. And why not? Don't we all long to find original and untouched coins that may yield new information for our study of numismatics? Don't we all sometimes long for riches and a collection unrivaled by anyone else? There are people who have found such treasures, but most of those stories were generally forgotten or lost in the past.

Now, for the first time, we can relive all of the excitement of treasures rediscovered and preserved for us to collect. The team of Q. David Bowers and his research associate Michael Hodder has made this possible by researching all available material on the subject and presenting it in a condensed and exciting form for your reading pleasure. Do you own an Uncirculated halfpenny of Virginia dated 1773? Do you know the story of the Colonel Mendes I. Cohen hoard that probably contained your coin? This book gives all the details, and in a highly readable and enjoyable style you will not soon forget.

Reading this account of trials and treasures set me to reminiscing about my own experience with fabulous finds from the sunken Spanish ship *Nuestra Señora de Atocha*. When the remains were discovered in 1985 by Mel Fisher he was thoughtful enough to invite me to dive at the site and see first-hand the material that was being located and brought to the surface. The experience was one of the greatest thrills of my life. Piles of pieces-of-eight were everywhere. There were more silver bars, gold chains, and emeralds than I could count. The thrill of discovery far outweighed the longing for actually owning any of the material. Numismatic research is a compelling drive beyond personal gain. I discovered that is the true thrill of recovered treasure. I learned then and there that knowledge of these treasures is nearly equal to actual ownership. Alas, these coins were deposited on the sea bottom long before American coins (the primary subject of the present book) were made, and thus the detailed story of the *Atocha* is to be found elsewhere, although it is mentioned here. Dave, now that you've finished this great book on American treasures, how about writing one about the golden (and silver) era of the Spanish Main? It seems as if you already have a fine start with the information in your Chapter 10.

You will thrill at the tales told in Dave Bowers' account of the hundreds of finds that have been made from sunken ships, bank vaults, hidden chests, buried boxes, and old safes. Some great finds have even been located right under our collective noses in mint and Treasury storage. Caves, crevices, attics, and basements are other likely places to find long forgotten treasure. Perhaps after reading of the successful discoveries of others you too will become a lucky finder. It is not impossible. Not all of these spoils have been unearthed in the distant past.

Many finds are of recent origin. And, there are more to come. In fact, Dave devotes a chapter to important treasures that are yet to be found. You could be the lucky one!

It doesn't seem possible that a group of 11 sparkling 1873 gold dollars could have been found as recently as 1976. They were hidden in a bank safe deposit box, and long forgotten by the family. More recently, in 1984, the sunken *H.M.S. Feversham* was recovered and was the source of 131 Massachusetts silver coins as well as numerous Spanish-American and Dutch pieces. Yes, such treasures are still around for the lucky searcher.

Knowing where and how the hidden wealth of the past has been discovered will be an inspiration for many to try their hand in looking with modern techniques and equipment. What has been done in the past can surely be duplicated now. Will new discoveries bring new coins that future collectors can add to their collections? Undoubtedly that will happen at some not too distant time. What new information will be added to our wealth of numismatic knowledge and lore by future hoards is hard to imagine, but exciting to contemplate.

What we can be assured of is that the wealth of the past is now accurately recorded for posterity in this exciting book. The accounts are not only entertaining and thrilling, but give collectors an insight into the backgrounds of many of the actual coins that they now have in their collections.

You may be astounded to learn that your Uncirculated 1855 half cent can be traced back to when Judge J.P. Putnam, of Boston, took part in a ceremony at the Philadelphia Mint and while there acquired dozens of coins as souvenirs. If you are lucky enough to own a rare 1856 Flying Eagle cent, it was likely once owned by George W. Rice who at one time accumulated 756 of them (today, even finding two or three together at once would be unusual). If you want to learn where your Uncirculated 1925 Fort Vancouver Centennial half dollar was concealed for many years, see Chapter 14 on commemorative coin hoards and see where these and many other similar pieces were hidden away.

There has never been another book like *American Coin Treasures and Hoards.* It is original, entertaining, inspirational and, above all, a valuable contribution to the history of American numismatics. It is a treasure in its own right.

Kenneth E. Bressett

Introduction

Buried treasure! Gold! Pirates! This is the stuff of which dreams are made.

In numismatics there are many stories of coin treasures that have come to light, most often under circumstances a bit less exciting than written in buccaneer lore, but often quite intriguing.

Typically, notices of such finds have been reported first in newspapers or other popular periodicals, often with incomplete or inaccurate information. Then, if a numismatist was consulted, the facts might have come to light. Otherwise, coins were usually spent, sold, or otherwise scattered without any inventory being made of them. The latter is the usual scenario, especially for finds made a generation or longer ago.

Over the years there have been numerous mentions of coin (and sometimes currency) hoards in the *American Journal of Numismatics, The Numismatist, The Numismatic Scrapbook Magazine, Coin World, Numismatic News, Bank Note Reporter,* dealer catalogues, and elsewhere. Remarkably, there has been just one significant effort to compile an anthology, that being Walter H. Breen's "A Survey of American Coin Hoards" in *The Numismatist,* January 1952 (with a continuation in October), which told of 21 different finds. Sydney P. Noe's *Coin Hoards,* American Numismatic Society, 1921, is useful for its general information and philosophy concerning hoards, but not for specific information concerning American issues (for it is primarily concerned with ancient finds and mentions only one American find, the Economite hoard).

The present work by the author, working with Michael Hodder as research associate, brings together in one volume the most famous American coin treasures and hoards along with accounts of many obscure finds and other caches, some of which have never been chronicled before. The grand total amounts to hundreds of entries.

How did hoards come to be? This is a natural question, and one that has many answers.

Some groups of coins were buried in yards or hidden in house partitions by wealthy people in an era when there were no banks or safe deposit boxes to offer secure storage. Many coins, including some fabulous cargoes of gold, went down with ships. Still others were concealed in cornerstones, secret compartments, or basement walls.

Uncle Sam did his share of putting coins away. Bags of sparkling silver dollars were held in Mint and Treasury vaults for many years, to come forth to delight a new generation of numismatists. And then there is the story of crates of patterns hidden in the Philadelphia Mint for many years, only to be revealed and to figure in an exchange of hitherto unknown $50 gold pieces in 1909.

Some hoards known today were concealed years ago to avoid capture by Indians, or by robbers, or by Yankee troops about to overrun a Louisiana plantation. Certain gold and silver coins found in the Midwest and West were taken in holdups or by some other illegal method and concealed in order to permit fast escape. The idea was that the site of the hidden loot would be visited later and under more leisurely circumstances, and the coins or paper money would be retrieved to be spent and enjoyed. Meanwhile, the crooks were killed by posses or the local sheriff, jailed, or met some other end. After reading accounts of railroad robbers, ship pirates, bank holdups, marauding soldiers, one can easily conclude that transporting or even owning a large holding of silver and gold coins a century or so ago was fraught with danger.

Reminiscent of the famous "Purloined Letter" story by Nathaniel Hawthorne, some caches of coins and currency have been hidden—where else?—in bank vaults.

As you read this book, many other reasons why coins were concealed or lost will be revealed. In other numerous instances, no one will ever know who secreted these precious coins or why they did, as those involved died years or generations before their treasures were brought to light. Thus, we do not know now, and may never know, who hid the thousands of 1818, 1820, and other large copper cents that are famous as being from the Randall Hoard (named after a later owner of the pieces). Coins keep their secrets well. Coins tell no tales as to where they have been, what they have seen, and the roles they played.

To qualify for inclusion a hoard or find had to include American coins, paper money, or other numismatic items relating to the United States or its antecedent colonies. Such hoards were mostly found within the borders of our country, but some (the *S.S. Central America* and the "Bank of France" treasures are but two of several examples) were not.

Hoards consisting entirely of foreign coins, but found in the United States, are discussed in Chapter 10, "Spanish-American Coins and Pirate Treasures," where you will find accounts of lost Spanish fleets and related treasures mostly found near or on the Gulf of Mexico and Atlantic coasts.

The present work gives information concerning most if not all of the larger and better-known hoards and a generous measure of other finds as well. The accounts of lost and found hoards and treasures are arranged by categories in 22 chapters. Of all of the treasures discussed in this book, only a few have similar stories.

No listing of hoards can ever be comprehensive, as there are countless thousands of instances in which members of the public have brought long-forgotten rolls, money purses, and other holdings to coin dealers or have otherwise disposed of finds without giving details to the press. Indeed, more than just a few treasure finders have found that publicizing their good luck was just about the worst thing they could have done.

Especially in recent times, the finders of hoards have often made great efforts to keep details secret, what with Uncle Sam, previous property owners, estranged spouses, local authorities, insurance companies and their successors, state revenue officers, former partners, and others often waiting in the wings to claim an interest. The more publicity given, the more numerous and aggressive are the claimants that seem to come out of the proverbial woodwork. It was a sad day in the early 1970s when Thomas Gurr, disgusted with bureaucrats of the state of Florida who threatened and harassed his ship treasure recovery, threw back into the sea various coins and artifacts he had spent much time and effort finding. In the course of research for this book I contacted several manufacturers and distributors of electronic treasure-detecting devices. This reply is probably typical of the sentiments of many who discover valuable pieces: "Most of the people who find coins with our detectors keep the details secret." In other instances—including in contemporary accounts—misinformation has been given out to throw other treasure seekers off the track, as in an 1850s newspaper account of early salvage attempts for the treasure of the *S.S. Yankee Blade.*

Adding interest are accounts of the "hoarders among us," detailing the activities of numismatists such as Virgil M. Brand, George W. Rice, John A. Beck, Col. E.H.R. Green, and others who were collectors, but who enjoyed squirreling away quantities of favorite items. For example, Brand cornered six of the 10 known 1884 silver trade dollars and Col. Green had each and every specimen of the five known 1913 Liberty Head nickels.

Not included in the text are numerous interesting fictional tales related over a long period of years by scribes ranging from Jules Verne and Mark Twain to modern folklorists (except that Walt Disney's Scrooge McDuck is mentioned).[1] Anyone with a love of adventure has but to read Robert Louis Stevenson's *Treasure Island* or Edgar Allan Poe's so-exciting-I-can't-put-it-down "Gold Bug" tale. The latter is said by later historians (see Chapter 21) to have been written on a plantation that was, in time, recognized as a real treasure site! Treasures of bullion (bulk metal and gold dust, not coins) are not treated in this book, save for stamped or assay bars of numismatic interest (as in the case of certain remarkable pieces fished up from the wreck of the ill-fated *S.S. Brother Jonathan*).

Appendix I, "Pseudo Hoards and 'Amazing Finds'," discusses holdings of coins and fantasy pieces that have been questioned and are believed to have been made later than the dates they bear or the eras from which they

---

1 For an overview of tall tales of treasure and hoaxes see Vardis Fisher and Opal Laurel Holmes, *Gold Rushes and Mining Camps of the Early American West*, 1968, chapters 27 and 28; also Hubert Howe Bancroft's nineteenth-century series of histories on the American West. In general, various romanticized accounts of railway and bank holdups, adventures with Wells Fargo stagecoaches, miners' treasures buried beneath cabin floors, etc., contain no meaningful references to specific coins. In contrast, Robert A. Nesmith's book, *Dig For Pirate Treasure*, 1958, has much numismatic lore, but mainly relates to other than United States coins as Captain Kidd and other buccaneers mainly roamed the seas in the days before American coinage became a reality; Nesmith was a numismatist. Another volume that combines numismatic accuracy with lively reading is Thomas H. Sebring's *Treasure Tales,* 1986, but it, too, is concerned with finds of coins antedating the United States series. For the treasure seeker, F.L. Coffman's, 1001 *Lost, Buried or Sunken Treasures,* 1957, gives lists of shipwrecks and estimated values of lost cargo (without regard to the type of cargo carried) and other citations; Coffman stated that he checked over 42,000 treasure reports, of which about 10% had some sort of documentation.

appear to be. Some such "hoards" are not hoards at all, but represent contrived stories—capers and taradiddles, many of which make fascinating reading today.

Appendix II is a handy index in numismatic order of the items of which 10 or more were found and discussed in various finds and hoards.

As you can tell from the many subjects mentioned in passing in these introductory remarks, this volume probably contains enough information for *several* books. Perhaps I should take Ken Bressett's advice in the Foreword, that I write a book on sunken Spanish-American treasures. If so, I'll re-read the aforementioned "Gold Bug" to set the tone for flavor.

While when reading the present book it might be worthwhile to start with Chapter 1 and continue in order to Chapter 22, just as when sampling a smorgasbord you can begin just about anywhere. If you don't have a preference and like to eat your ice cream before your salad, start with Chapter 9.

All in all, it is hoped that the accounts will provide interesting reading, perhaps your own "treasure" of numismatic information and entertainment. Certainly, this book has been a lot of fun to research and write.

Q. David Bowers

October 21, 1996

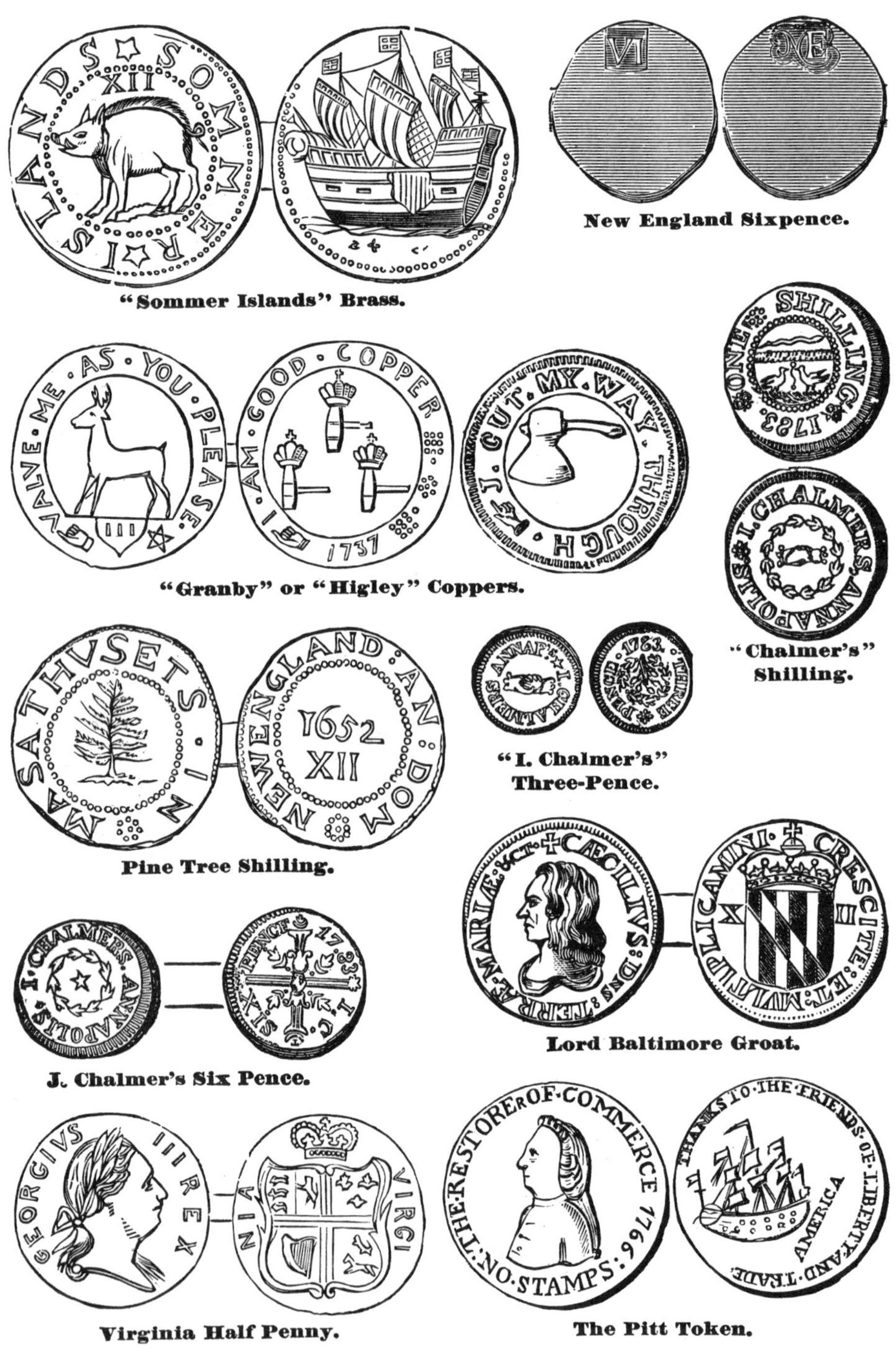

A selection of coins relating to early America (from A.M. Smith, *Visitor's Guide to the U.S. Mint;* similar coins were represented in the Mint Cabinet and were on view at the Philadelphia Mint)

CHAPTER 1

Colonial and Early Coins

Introduction

Many numismatists know that the Philadelphia Mint began operations in 1792. In that year the staff of that facility prepared several varieties of pattern coins, including some copper cents the dies for which were cut by someone surnamed Birch, but whose first name has proven elusive to historians. In the same year, apparently in the cellar of a saw maker named John Harper, some little silver half dismes (an early word for dimes) were struck from official dies, the nearby federal mint not being quite ready to produce such pieces. Unfortunately, 1792 pattern Birch cents are too rare to figure in any accounts of hoards. Indeed, some are known only to the extent of one, two, or three pieces (however, Chapter 18, "Secrets of the Philadelphia Mint," reveals that some traces of 1792 patterns remained at the Mint site for many years thereafter). The 1792 silver half dismes are not known from hoards either. Apparently, the 1,500 or so pieces made were widely distributed at the time they were made.

The first coins struck at the Philadelphia Mint in quantity for circulation were the copper half cents and cents of 1793, followed by the first silver coinage in 1794 (half dollars, and dollars), the first half dimes in 1795 (from 1794-dated dies), and the first gold coinage in 1795 ($5 and $10 pieces). It was not until 1796 that silver dimes, quarter dollars, and gold $2.50 pieces were made for the first time. Quantities were small in comparison to the needs of commerce, and it was not until a decade or more later than enough coins were around to make it possible for significant hoards of federal United States coins to be formed. For this reason, nearly all hoards found in America before the nineteenth century contained foreign coins.

At what time were United States coins—that is, those struck at the Philadelphia Mint—first hoarded? Probably soon after the opening of the facility, and certainly by 1794-1795. Meanwhile, many hoards were formed, not of federal coins, but containing other, earlier coins relating to America and her colonies.

Settlers in Boston in the seventeenth century.

From the time of the establishment of early settlements in Massachusetts, Virginia, and other Atlantic seaboard colonies, circulating coinage consisted primarily of foreign issues, particularly the divisions of the silver 8 reals ("dollars") of Mexico and other Spanish-American areas. Coins of England, Holland, France, and other lands were in wide circulation in America as well. Many such pieces remained legal tender until the implementation of the Act of February 21, 1857. By that time the Philadelphia Mint and its branches—Charlotte (opened in 1838), Dahlonega (1838), New Orleans (1838), and San Francisco (1854)—had produced enough pieces to make America self-sufficient in coinage.

Prior to the opening of the Philadelphia Mint in

1792, several state and private mints in America produced coins, and some facilities abroad made coins with America-related inscriptions to be circulated here. Silver coins of Massachusetts (mostly dated 1652); 1722-1724 Rosa Americana coins made in England to be distributed in the American colonies; Nova Constellatio coppers of 1783-1786; copper coins made by or for the states of Connecticut, Massachusetts, New Jersey, New York, and Vermont in 1785-1788; and various tokens with portraits of General George Washington are examples.[1] Some of these coins subsequently found their way into hoards, this being particularly true of Massachusetts Bay Colony silver issues, which seem to have been ubiquitous in the Northeast at one time.

The gold and silver coins of the Spanish Main and most pieces captured and buried by pirates were not American coins and thus are not a significant part of this chapter, although related accounts concerning the notorious Charles Gibbs, Samuel Bellamy and their ilk will be found in Chapter 10. Captain Kidd, Blackbeard, and other knaves of the sea plundered gold doubloons (Spanish-American 8-escudo coins worth about $16 at the time), the aforementioned silver 8-real coins (worth about $1), and their fractions, although, doubtless, these buccaneers saw their share of Pine Tree shillings.

Thus, the present Chapter 1, although it describes many fascinating caches of coins buried, stolen, or otherwise put away in the years before 1800, could be expanded to the length of several *books* if it included non-American issues. Fortunately, much has been published elsewhere on pirate and other early treasures, and, unlike for hoards of American coins, a veritable bookshelf of already-written volumes can be acquired. Unfortunately, only a very few such texts are accurate from a numismatic viewpoint. To the average "popular" writer, all pirate coins are "doubloons" or "pieces of eight" whether they actually were or not. One particularly uninformed delineator of pirate tales decided that "double eagle" was the correct modern translation of "doubloon," never mind that double eagles or $20 gold pieces were not made until 1850, long after the pirate era had ended! Chapter 10 discusses Spanish-American coins further, in the context that these, too, can be considered American "colonial" coins by virtue of their having circulated here.

The story of early American coin hoards begins, logically enough, with some of the first silver coins to be minted in this country:

A Fabulous Find!

Hidden: 17th or early 18th century
Found: 1737
Treasure: Massachusetts silver

One of the earliest known notices of a hoard of American coins was carried in the *Boston Weekly News-Letter,* July 21, 1737:[2]

> We hear from Salem [Massachusetts] that on Friday last William Brown, Esq., the youngest surviving son of the Hon. Col. Brown, deceased, having had information that some money had been concealed in a place which he owned, caused search to be made for the same, where were found five or six jars full of silver, containing about one thousand and ninety-three ounces of silver of several species, among which were about six thousand New England shillings scarcely discolored.

Most probably—and unfortunately for generations of numismatists yet unborn—these pieces were simply spent in commerce, there being no collectors' premium for them at the time in America. By that time the New England shillings (a general term for Massachusetts silver coins) were only a few decades old.

Interestingly, numismatics as a hobby and historical discipline was slow in developing in America, and by a century after the aforementioned 1737 find—in 1837—the number of serious coin collectors in the United States was probably fewer than two dozen and the Mint Cabinet (formed in June 1838) was still a year away.

---

1 Readers who are not numismatically knowledgeable may wish to consult these two standard references as a guide to most of the American coins mentioned in the present book: *A Guide Book of U.S. Coins,* Kenneth E. Bressett, editor, an inexpensive reference guide (contains prices, is published annually, also contains a list of numismatic newspapers and magazines and other sources for information) and/or *Walter Breen's Complete Encyclopedia of U.S. and Colonial Coins* (henceforth cited as "Breen, *Encyclopedia,* 1988"); contains much historical and technical information, die variety descriptions, etc., but not prices). In addition, many of the books mentioned in the footnotes are available through coin dealers and numismatic booksellers and furnish worthwhile reading.

2 Quoted in the *American Journal of Numismatics,* 1890, p. 31; also *AJN,* 1881, p. 46. Another early citation was in the *Salem Gazette,* July 11/18, 1737. Sydney P. Noe, *Pine Tree Coinage of Massachusetts,* 1952, p. 17, wrote that this find "bears all the marks of gross exaggeration," but does not elaborate upon his opinion.

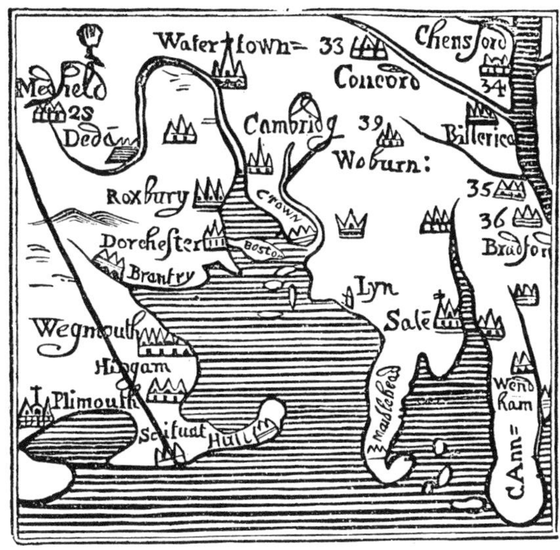

Boston and vicinity as shown in a 1667 map. During this era the Massachusetts Bay Colony produced silver coinage.

Massachusetts Silver Coinage

As Massachusetts silver coins figure prominently in several treasure accounts in the present work it is appropriate to include a few remarks concerning them.

This numismatically fascinating coinage was effected under authority of the General Court of Massachusetts and took place under contract with John Hull and Robert Sanderson who operated a mint in the Boston area. While Pine Tree shillings are the best remembered today, they are only part of a silver coinage that consisted of these main styles, here given with the approximate dates they are believed to have been struck:[1]

NE (New England) coinage, undated, struck 1652. On one side is the stamped impression NE and on the other is the denomination expressed in pence as III, VI, or XII (shown above). Twelve pence (XII) equaled one shilling.[2]

Willow Tree coinage, dated 1652, struck 1653-1660. Threepence, sixpence, and shillings (sixpence shown above).

Oak Tree coinage, dated 1652 (except for the twopence dated 1662), struck 1660-1667. Twopence, threepence, sixpence, and shillings.

Pine Tree coinage, dated 1652, struck 1667-1682 (with the large planchet Pine Tree shillings struck in the earlier part of the range, 1667-1774). Threepence, sixpence, and shillings (large planchet shilling shown above).

NE silver coins are rare, Willow Tree pieces of all denominations are exceedingly rare, and Oak Tree coins are somewhat scarce. The most readily available issues are of the Pine Tree style, especially the shillings. The last-named coins have been the subject of several romantic accounts including a dramatization by Nathaniel Hawthorne.

In summary, denominations include threepence, sixpence, and shillings, undated (in the case of the NE coins) or dated 1652. In addition, 1662-dated Oak Tree twopence pieces were made.

Today, several thousand specimens exist in private and museum collections, and all are highly prized and of significant value.

---

[1] As stated, for example, in Breen's *Encyclopedia,* 1988, pp. 11-15. No records of coinage have survived, and year ranges are simply estimates. See Sylvester S. Crosby, *Early Coins of America,* for original legislation and selected contemporary commentaries.

[2] There were 20 shillings to the British pound. Years later in the 1790s, when United States dollars became a reality, a British pound was worth about $4.85, although exchange rates varied over a period of time.

The Castine Hoard of Silver

Hidden: Late 17th century
Found: 1840
Treasure: Massachusetts silver

On a Rocky Cove

Over a period of time between November 1840 and April 1841, many silver coins (one account says nearly 2,000, another says about 500) were dug up by Capt. Stephen Grindle and his son Samuel on their family farm in the town of Penobscot, near Johnson's Narrows on the Bagaduce River about six miles upstream from the harbor of Castine, Maine.[1] At that point the inlet from the Atlantic Ocean becomes narrow, and the water is of great depth. A small indentation on the shoreline furnished a landing suitable for mooring. The location was on a path that had been used for many years by Abenaki Indians and others and may have been an overland route to Blue Hill (and Bay) and Mount Desert Island on the way to Frenchman's Bay. At the time of the 1840 discovery, the landscape was covered with second growth forest, the original stands of tall pines having been cut about 75 years earlier.

In the waning days of November, 1840, the Grindles were hauling wood down to the shore. Young Samuel saw a coin—a French crown—near a mostly-buried large rock on the side hill about 75 feet from the water. He and his father started digging and clearing away the top of the rock. In short order about 18 to 20 other silver coins were unearthed. How exciting! Dusk came all too quickly, and the pair abandoned their search, resolving to come back the next day to recover more. However, fate intervened, and during the night a severe snowstorm occurred, rendering further exploration impossible.

Treasure Found, Treasure Spent

After the spring thaw in April, the Grindles came back to the site. By removing some alder trees and rooting around the large rock they came across 400 to 500 coins (per Williamson's 1859 report) in a cache, and additional pieces were found downhill some 10 to 12 feet closer to the water. The latter probably had washed away from the original group at some former time.

Unfortunately for numismatics and posterity, most of the coins were paid to a creditor of Capt. Grindle and were subsequently melted into bullion by a silversmith.[2] Although no other coins were ever found at the site, the discovery became known in the area, and during the next 20 years a number of fortune seekers made excavations. Today, the Castine Hoard is one of the better remembered of early American finds, and accounts of it appear in several modern books.

Apart from several dozen Massachusetts silver coins, the Castine Hoard comprised silver issues from England, France, Spain (and Spanish America), Holland, and Portugal—of the types once prevalent in America in the absence of any sizable indigenous coinage.

The latest-dated piece was a 1690 French demi-écu from the Bordeaux Mint. Thus, the hoard was secreted on or after that date, but in any event probably within a few years of that time. Otherwise, later-dated pieces would have been included. However, Sydney P. Noe, of the American Numismatic Society, New York, commented that "the date deduced for the burial of the deposit was about 1704."[3] The 1690s were tempestuous times at Fort Pentagoet, and there were many skirmishes between the local Abenaki Indians and European settlers, resulting in the plundering of homes and killing of those who had sought to

---

[1] The town and surrounding district, earlier known as Fort Pentagoet, was named Castine after Baron Jean-Vincent d'Abbadie de St. Castin (1652-1708), a wealthy Frenchman who was on duty at the fort and later married the daughter of local Indian Chief Madockawando; she took the French name of Mathilde. The fort consisted of a military garrison plus several civilians who in the early years mainly engaged in trade with the Indians. Castine was a focal point in several conflicts, was occupied twice by the British, and at one time was invaded by Dutch pirates (after their spy, John Rhoades, came to the fort and surveyed the possibilities). In 1701 Castin left the area and went back to France.

[2] Although such melting does not seem logical, unless the coins were purchased by the silversmith as a source for metal to make tableware, etc. It seems likely that the French and most related coins could have been spent by the creditor, if desired.

[3] *Pine Tree Coinage of Massachusetts,* 1952, p. 16; he did not state the basis for his deduction. This reference book is also the source for "Noe numbers" assigned to various dies and combinations.

live in this particular section of America. In such parlous times, the Castine Hoard coins could have been hidden for safety by someone who did not live to reclaim them. Finally, peace was established in September 1697 under the Treaty of Ryswick.

At the time the coins were hidden, the Castine district was part of Massachusetts (the state of Maine was not created until 1820). However, there were many disputes among the English, French, and the colonies themselves as to where one political division began and another ended.

Massachusetts Silver Coins

In the Castine Hoard were 1652-dated Massachusetts silver coins described in various accounts as totaling from 30 to 75 pieces. Examples said to have been from this remarkable find passed to Dr. Joseph L. Stevens of Castine, and from this holding 17 coins went to the Maine Historical Society. An examination of the Society's pieces by Sydney P. Noe revealed four different varieties including Pine Tree shillings attributed to his own Noe numbers 2, 25, and 29, and a sixpence. In several W. Elliot Woodward auction sales[1] coins were described as being from this hoard, indicating that pieces apart from the Maine Historical Society specimens may have reached numismatic channels with stories or labels attributing them to Castine.

A variety from the hoard, later known by the attribution Crosby 6-K (Noe-12), was published in *Historical Magazine,* October 1863. It remains unique today and is almost certainly a product of the Boston mint. Eric P. Newman exhibited this specimen at the 1991 Coinage of the Americas Conference at the American Numismatic Society.

The Roxbury Hoard

Hidden or lost: Late 17th century
Found: 1863
Treasure: Massachusetts silver

In late summer 1863, a young boy, George Wilber Reed, son of George P. Reed of Roxbury, Massachusetts, was playing outdoors. Climbing up an embankment made during the recent cutting through of a new street, he put his hand in a crevice of a rock to aid his ascent. He felt something within, and it proved to be a silver 1652-dated Pine Tree shilling of Massachusetts, to which two other coins adhered.

His interest aroused, young George continued prospecting in the crevice and was eventually rewarded by finding 28 Massachusetts silver coins of various 1652-dated denominations plus several 1662-dated twopence.

It was later reported that the 28 coins consisted of one 1652 Oak Tree shilling, seven sixpence of the same design and date, two 1652 Oak Tree threepence, and six 1662-dated twopence. Among Pine Tree coins, all dated 1652, there were six shillings, two sixpence, and four threepence. The latest-made coin was a small-planchet Pine Tree shilling of the type made circa 1675-1682, but bearing the standard 1652 date.

Presumably, the hoard was buried no earlier than 1675, and possibly later—but not too much later, as evidenced by the coins showing relatively little wear.[2]

The Exeter Hoard

Hidden: 17th century
Found: 1876
Treasure: Massachusetts silver

Digging Out a Cellar

In 1876 in Exeter, New Hampshire, an underground hoard was found and is said to have included 30 to 40 Massachusetts silver shillings among which may have been an example of the exceedingly rare and quite valuable Willow Tree shilling type.

---

[1] *E.g.,* April 28, 1863, lots 1870-1873; October 20, 1863, lots 2460 and 2467 (Crosby 6-K shilling with MASASTHVSETS inscription); and March 30, 1864, Lot 13. Woodward, of Roxbury, Massachusetts, was the most erudite numismatic auction cataloguer of the 1860s and 1870s, although his main vocation was that of a pharmacist. His interests were diverse, and he published a two-volume book set on Washington memorabilia, restored old buildings, sold antiques and second-hand items, and enjoyed American history.

[2] Sources: Sydney P. Noe, *Massachusetts Pine Tree Coinage,* 1952, p. 14; Noe's information was from *The Historical Magazine,* October 1863. Walter H. Breen, "Survey of American Coin Hoards," *The Numismatist,* January 1952. W. Elliot Woodward auction catalogues including John F. McCoy *et al.,* June 21, 1864; and the Levick, Emery, Illsley, Abbey sale of October 1864. Woodward, born in Oxford, Maine, in 1825, lived in Roxbury at the time the coins were found, and had been a resident there since 1848.

This remarkable discovery was made when a cellar was being excavated under the extension of a store located close to the town railroad station. The store owner had given the sandy fill to an Irish laborer[1] with the condition that he haul it away. Quite probably, some former owner of the property had hidden the pieces for safekeeping purposes, there being no public security facilities such as banks in the area at the time.

In the process of dumping the sand into a cart, the Irishman saw a Massachusetts silver shilling, then another, then some more. At this point he decided to sift through the earth. In short order he located further specimens as did several bystanders. Also found were the remains of what seemed to be a wooden box, much decomposed, which probably was used to bury the coins at some earlier date when the area was used as a garden for a private residence.

Upon examination all of the pieces were reported to be of the Oak Tree and Pine Tree denominations dated 1652 (as were all shillings made). However, in W. Elliot Woodward's sale of the Ferguson Haines (of Biddeford, Maine) Collection in October 1880, there was a notation that Lot 1084, a rare *Willow Tree* shilling, was pedigreed to "Treasure trove, Exeter, N.H., 1876."[2]

The Boothbay Harbor Find

Hidden or lost: 17th century
Found: 1880
Treasure: Pine and Oak Tree shillings

In a note captioned "Treasure Trove," W. Elliot Woodward in his sale of the William J. Jenks Collection, September 1880, lots 429-432, related that "the four following pieces were found, quite recently, in a small cove in Boothbay Harbor, Maine. The entire find consisted of five pieces, and the finder, hoping to secure more, very judiciously keeps secret the exact place of discovery."[3]

Giving more details is this commentary, signed "W." and probably submitted by Woodward, printed in the *American Journal of Numismatics,* October 1880:

> Milton Ambrose of Boothbay, Maine, several months since, found in Wall's Cove, East Boothbay Harbor, five Pine Tree and Oak Tree shillings. Description of four of these will be found in the catalogue of coins sold by Bangs & Co.,[4] New York, September 1-3, nos. 429, 430, 431, 432; the fifth is now in possession of a gentleman at Boothbay. They have evidently been long in salt water, having lost about half of their original weight and thickness, and are destitute of ring, but are of unquestionable genuineness, being of well known varieties. W.

In a subsequent offering of his own collection, 1884, Woodward described Lot 354 as: "1652 Oak Tree shilling. Found in a little cove with a number of others at Boothbay, Me., where it had lain long under salt water, the action of which reduced its weight nearly one-half. Piece broken from edge."[5] This might indicate that Woodward found the provenance to be suf-

[1] Following the potato famine of 1846 and relief shipments from America in 1847, vast numbers of Irish citizens emigrated to the United States to start new lives in the land of opportunity and plenty. By the 1870s they constituted a significant percentage of laborers on the Atlantic seaboard states and in certain other locations. In the 1860s there were more Irishmen working in the Comstock Lode in Nevada than were men of any other single nationality or native-born Americans (cf. Eliot Lord, *Comstock Mining and Miners,* 1883, appendices).

[2] Sources: *American Journal of Numismatics,* 1877, p. 92; *AJN,* 1878, p. 105 (signed "C.H.B.," probably Charles H. Betts); Sydney P. Noe, *Pine Tree Coinage of Massachusetts,* 1952, p. 16. Walter H. Breen, "Survey of American Coin Hoards," *The Numismatist,* January 1952, commented that the Haines Willow Tree shilling, Noe 11 (dies 30C), later appeared in the C.T. Whitman sale, 1893, Lot 103; later in the Jenks Collection sale, 1921; Mabel B. Garvan; Yale University.

[3] Essentially the same comment appeared in Charles Steigerwalt's *Coin Journal,* September 1880: "A few Pine and Oak Tree Shillings were recently found in a small cove in Boothbay Harbor, Me. The finder hoping to secure more, keeps secret the exact place of discovery." Steigerwalt, of Lancaster, Pennsylvania, was best known for his fixed price lists and catalogues.

[4] Bangs & Co. was a general auction room at which venue various art and collectible objects were offered for bids. Catalogues were prepared by private firms or individuals, including Woodward, who paid a fee to Bangs for the use of their facilities.

[5] Source: Sydney P. Noe, *Pine Tree Coinage of Massachusetts,* 1952, p. 18. Numismatically, such a corroded coin would have relatively little value unless it were a rare die variety. However, the pedigree, if carried along with such a coin as it changed hands over the years, would add value to collectors with an interest in history.

ficiently interesting that he kept one from his September 1880 sale for his own cabinet, or that Milton Ambrose was rewarded by not disclosing the precise location of his discovery, and found some other pieces later, one of which was acquired by the well-known Roxbury dealer.

Talbot, Allum & Lee Coppers

Accumulated: 1795-1796
Sold: 1795-1796
Treasure: Copper one-cent tokens

Thousands of Tokens Ordered

At 241 Water Street in lower New York City, the firm of Talbot, Allum & Lee engaged in the India trade, importing goods by ship. Formed in 1794, the partnership operated only until 1796. Principals included William Talbot, William Allum, and James Lee. This particular district of the city was a beehive of activity with vessels continually arriving and departing. Numerous ships' chandlers, grog houses, cheap lodging places, and other establishments for the convenience of sailors did a lively business.

Copper tokens dated 1794 and 1795, bearing the image of the standing goddess of Commerce on the obverse and a fully-rigged sailing ship on the reverse, were struck to the order of Talbot, Allum & Lee by Peter Kempson & Co., Birmingham, England, and imported into America by the partners. The quantity has been estimated at over 200,000 coins, but no original records have ever been located.

At the time, copper coins in circulation in New York and nearby areas were a curious admixture of issues made by or for various states (Connecticut, Massachusetts, New Jersey, New York, and Vermont), British halfpence, counterfeits, and other pieces. The Liberty Head copper cents made at the Philadelphia Mint beginning in March 1793 were not particularly numerous. Generally, just about any copper coin the size of a British halfpenny (about the same size as an American cent) would trade in commerce at the value of one cent. It was a popular speculation and at the same time a worthwhile advertising scheme to have copper tokens privately struck for a cost of less than a cent apiece, and pay them out at one cent.[1]

In accordance with this practice, Talbot, Allum & Lee tokens dated 1794 were put into circulation where they served at the value of one cent in local and regional commerce. Pieces dated 1795 seem to have been less popular. Apparently, undistributed tokens piled up at the waterfront store. What should be done with the hoard?

Early sketch of the docks in lower New York City.

To the Philadelphia Mint

The answer came quickly. On April 23, 1795, the firm sold 1,076 pounds of the tokens to the Philadelphia Mint for 18¢ per pound, or $193.68. On December 10, 1796, the remainder of the token stock amounting to 1,914 pounds of copper was purchased by the Mint from William Talbot for $319, or 16.6¢ per pound. These tokens weighed in at about 46 to 50 to the pound, equivalent to around 140,000 to 150,000 pieces acquired in the Mint's two purchases.

The coins were a godsend to the Mint, which had been experiencing severe difficulties obtaining copper stock from which to strike half cents and cents. Supplies of this metal were erratic and of uncertain quality

[1] The circulation of private one-cent tokens would reach a peak in 1837-1838 when millions of such pieces flooded commercial channels at a time when silver and gold coins were not being paid out by banks and were hoarded by the public; these are known as Hard Times tokens by numismatists today. During the Civil War, especially in the year 1863, countless millions of cent-size bronze (mostly) tokens again filled a need when specie payments had been suspended by the Treasury Department and banks.

and included such varied sources as copper sheet for roofing and the protection of ships' hulls, and old pots and kettles.

Planchets for United States half cents were cut by punching discs from the Talbot, Allum & Lee tokens, most of which were probably in mint condition. Today it is not unusual to find a 1795 or 1797 U.S. half cent (but not one dated 1796) with faint traces remaining of the token undertype—usually some of the ship's rigging and/or some of the letters around the border of the token. Such half cents are highly prized by numismatists as they are literally two coins in one.

A Later Hoard

Concerning an unrelated holding of such pieces, in 1988 Walter Breen wrote: "Those [Talbot, Allum & Lee tokens] dated 1795 were formerly considered rare, but a hoard found in Britain after World War II yielded many Uncirculated examples, mostly brown to light olive, fewer original red."

Background of the Tokens

While Talbot, Allum & Lee tokens dated 1794 and 1795 and bearing the standing figure of Commerce on the obverse and a sailing ship on the reverse were made as advertisements for the firm, certain other die combinations were not. Included among such *mules* or *mulings,* as numismatists designate them, were pieces combining a Talbot, Allum & Lee obverse die (featuring the goddess of Commerce) with a completely irrelevant reverse, such as one picturing a bird and the inscription PROMISSORY HALFPENNY, another pertaining to the Blofield Cavalry, and one depicting the York Cathedral. Such pieces were a general part of the extensive "conder" token series produced in England in the 1780s and 1790s for use in circulation, but especially for sale to collectors in the British Isles (acquiring them by varieties was a very popular fad).[1]

In 1859 Charles I. Bushnell commented:[2]

> These mules were struck for exclusive circulation in England and were issued at a time when the rage for provincial halfpence extended to a degree almost incredible, threatening at one time even to supersede the national currency. Patronized by the nobility, and encouraged by the wealthy, die sinkers vied with each other in the number they produced.
>
> Obverses and reverses bearing no relation to each other were used for the production of illegitimate varieties, whose only value was their novelty, while impressions even from unfinished dies were bought at extravagant sums, merely for the selfish gratification of having what others had not. Varieties of collar were made to produce varieties of edge; old hubs were ferreted out to multiply specimens supposed to be unique, while worn-out and discarded dies were lapped,[3] and impressions therefrom palmed off upon inexperienced but enthusiastic young collectors as Proofs.[4]
>
> Tokens ridiculing even the collectors themselves were put forth and eagerly bought up as soon as issued by a throng of voracious antiquarians. Of these caustic emissions, the most celebrated was the collectors' halfpenny token, by [Obediah] Westwood, of two varieties of reverse. One of them, bearing a representation of a race between two persons mounted on asses, ridiculed the reckless passion for collecting, in the legend *"Asses Running for Half Pence,"* while the other, being intended as a sarcasm upon the encouragement shown to the production of ridiculous combinations, bore the representation of an ass and a mule in private consultation, with the legend emanating from the mouth of the former, *"Be assured, friend Mule, you never shall want my protection."*
>
> So great was the demand for copper tokens that no less than 600 tons weight were coined in Birmingham alone from the year 1787 to the year 1797. The profit to the publisher on one ton alone, as shown by an estimate furnished by a manufacturer, was no less a sum than £64/13/4. It is not surprising, therefore, that the sale of these pieces was a source of great profit to dealers, and that many of them soon retired with means not only adequate for their support through life, but also amply sufficient for the enjoyment of almost every luxury which they might or could desire.
>
> This mania in England for tokens, which commenced in 1787 and continued until the year 1797, received in that year an effectual check in the issue by the [British] government of 500 tons of copper coined into pennies of an ounce weight each, pursuant to a contract made with the ingenious Mr. [Matthew] Boulton, of Soho.

When Talbot, Allum & Lee tokens and other conder tokens bearing inscriptions relating to America started having significant value to collectors in the United States, beginning in the 1940s, numismatists found that London dealers (primarily Spink & Son, A.H. Baldwin & Sons, and B.A. Seaby, Ltd.) had such pieces in inventory among regular British tokens. Thus, many were sold to Americans. Probably, beginning in the 1940s examples of Uncirculated 1795 tokens became somewhat numerous in United States collector and dealer holdings.

---

1 Birmingham was the primary manufacturing center for such tokens.

2 *An Historical Account of the First Three Business Tokens Issued in the City of New York, N.Y.,* 1859, pp. 17-20. Among the two regular dates, Bushnell considered the 1795 Talbot, Allum & Lee cent to be "by far the rarest, fewer from that die having been struck." This would seem to indicate that 1795 tokens, considered to be fairly plentiful in high grades by numismatists today, were scarce in America in 1859. Bushnell (1826-1880) was one of the first numismatists in America to take a serious interest in tokens. His collection was sold at auction by his nephews, S. Hudson Chapman and Henry Chapman, in 1882 and was considered to be the most extensive offering of United States coins by auction venue up to that time.

3 Lapped (past tense of lap) = resurfacing or repolishing a die, perhaps rusted or pitted, to make it serviceable for further use.

4 "It takes one to know one," it is said, and Bushnell himself had certain fantasy and restrike Hard Times tokens (dated circa 1837-1841) made to his order in the 1850s, around the same time he wrote these comments about creating unusual pieces "merely for selfish gratification."

The writer is unaware of any single hoard such as mentioned by Breen and wonders if this comment may have referred to the general outflow to the United States of such tokens in the 1940s and early 1950s. By 1960, such American-related pieces were not seen in quantity in dealers' stocks in London, although those with British themes were common.[1]

Talbot, Allum & Lee tokens have been desired by numismatists for many years. In his 1858 work, *An Arrangement of Tradesmen's Cards, Political Tokens, also, Election Medals, Medalets, &c. Current in the United States of America for the Last Sixty Years,* the aforementioned Charles I. Bushnell described these tokens. He further noted that the dies for them had been cut in Birmingham, England, and stated that in 1855 at the P. Flandin sale in New York City, a pair of 1794 and 1795 Talbot, Allum & Lee tokens had sold for $2, the purchaser being "Walker."

Since that time these tokens have been featured in virtually every comprehensive reference work on American coins and in countless auction and sale catalogues.[2] While certain die varieties and mulings are rare, common issues of 1794 or 1795 are inexpensive on the numismatic market. Those dated 1794 are usually seen with light wear, while it is not unusual to encounter Mint State specimens of the 1795. Many of the latter have prooflike fields.

The Secret of an Old Desk

Hidden: 1780s
Found: Circa 1844
Treasure: 1783 federal pattern coins

Earliest Federal Coinage

This story begins over two centuries ago, in 1783. In that year a remarkable group of pattern coins was struck: the 5-unit piece, the "bit" of 100 units, the "quint" of 500 units, and the "mark" of 1,000 units. Sylvester S. Crosby, in his landmark *Early Coins of America* book, commented "These are undoubtedly the first patterns for coinage of the United States and

Unique 1783 pattern silver 1,000 units or mark (from the desk of Charles Thomson)

command an interest exceeding that of any others in this class."

John Thomson's Discovery

For a long span of decades the one-time existence of these coins had been forgotten by most numismatists and historians, until circa 1844 the marvelous discovery was made of two specimens in an old desk. The dating of this find to circa 1844 is implied from a commentary by Dr. Montroville W. Dickeson, *American Numismatical Manual,* 1859, p. 91:[3]

> [The two pieces we have described as Figures 2 and 3 on Plate 9] formerly belonged to Charles Thomson—a contemporary and particular friend of Benjamin Franklin-who was a very decided advocate of the just rights of the colonies, and distinguished himself greatly by his uniform patriotism.
>
> They were discovered after the death of his son, which occurred, we are informed, some 15 years ago, near Newark, Delaware, in the secret drawer of an old desk that formerly belonged to the father. They are now in the possession of a gentleman of this city, who values them very highly, not only as memorials of the past, but for their direct association with one of those noble men, whose visions were never obscured by anything that was, or could be, interposed between them and their country.

These two rarities were acquired from the "gentleman of this city," Rathmell Wilson by name, by Philadelphia dealer John W. Haseltine and years later were sold into the Garrett Collection.

In a statement to John W. Haseltine, May 28, 1872, Wilson gave further information concerning the pieces:

> The history of the two coins which you obtained from me, viz. Nova Constellatio 1783, U.S. 1,000, Nova Constellatio, 1783 U.S. 500 is as follows:

[1] General sources include Frank H. Stewart, *History of the First United States Mint,* 1924, pp. 73 (T., A. & L. copper purchases) and others (copper shortages, etc.). Breen, *Encyclopedia,* 1988, p. 102. As late as 1960, there was not a widespread modern interest in England in the collecting of conder tokens; the "asses running for half pence" of nearly two centuries earlier had no counterparts among current numismatists. In that year Robert Bashlow of New York City purchased for sixpence each many thousands of pieces from B.A. Seaby, Ltd.; these pieces had accumulated in the Seaby stock for many years and were not considered to be worth enough for individual tagging and cataloguing. However, soon thereafter in the 1960s British numismatist R.C. Bell wrote widely on the conder series, and in short order the series became quite popular, as, indeed, it remains today.

[2] The definitive study on the series is by George and Melvin Fuld, "The Talbot, Allum & Lee Cents, *Numismatic Scrapbook Magazine,* September 1956. The Norweb Collection auctioned in 1987 and 1988 had a particularly extensive selection of unusual mulings and varieties.

[3] Dickeson's book appeared in later printings as well, then slightly retitled as *American Numismatic Manual.* This folio-size volume represented *tour de force* in the hobby at that time. Even today, it remains impressive, despite much information having been proved incorrect or having been superseded.

> They were the property of Hon. Charles Thomson, secretary of the first Congress. At his death the property was left by will to his nephew, John Thomson, of Newark, state of Delaware. These two coins were found in the desk of the said deceased Charles Thomson, and preserved by his nephew during his life; at his death they came into the possession of his son Samuel E. Thomson of Newark, Delaware, from whom I received them. So you will perceive that their genuineness cannot be questioned; as they were never out of the possession of the Thomson family, until I received them.

1783 500 units or quint from the holdings of Charles Thomson.

Charles Thomson, born in County Derry, Ireland, in 1729, came to America at the age of 11. He became a teacher and merchant in Philadelphia. Interested in politics, Thomson espoused the feeling for independence and was described as "the life of the cause of liberty" in Philadelphia.

From 1774 to 1789 he served as secretary of the Continental Congress, recording with enthusiasm the details of the birth of the United States. It was Thomson who was tapped to inform General George Washington of his nomination as president. Washington later sought to have Thomson appointed to service of the new government, but Thomson replied that he wished to retire. In his later years he lived on his estate and engaged in biblical scholarship. He died near Philadelphia in 1824.

When They Were Made

Among the accounts of the United States, under the category of "Expenditure for Contingencies," between January and July 1783, the following entries appear in relation to coinage and bear upon the Nova Constellatio patterns:

> February 8. Jacob Eckfeldt, for dies for the Mint of North America, $5 and 18/90ths.[1]
>
> March 21. Benjamin Dudley employed in preparing a mint. $75 and 24/90ths.[2]
>
> April 17. John Swanwick, for dies for the public mint $22 and 42/90ths.
>
> May 5. A. Dubois, for sinking, casehardening, etc., for pair of dies for the public mint $72.[3]
>
> June 30. Benjamin Dudley employed in preparing a mint $77 and 60/90ths.

Further circumstances surrounding the issue of 1783 pattern coins were recorded by Robert R. Morris, the financier. His diary noted that on April 2, 1783, "I sent for Mr. Dudley who delivered me a piece of silver coin, being the first that has been struck as an American coin."

On April 16th it was noted that he "sent for Mr. Dudley and urged him to produce the coin to lay before the Congress to establish a mint."

On the following day, the 17th, he "sent for Mr. Dudley to urge the preparing of coins, etc., for establishing a mint."

Morris reported on April 22nd that "Mr. Dudley sent in several pieces of money as patterns of the intended American coins."

On July 5th he noted that "Mr. Benjamin Dudley...also informs of a minting press being in New York for sale,[4] and urges me to purchase for the use of the American Mint."

On August 19th he reported as follows:

> I sent for Mr. Benjamin Dudley, informed him of my doubts about the establishment of a mint, and desired him to think of some employment in private service, in which I am willing to assist him in all my power. I told him to make out an account for the services he had performed for the public and submit at the Treasury office for inspection and settlement.

On August 30th it was reported that "Mr. Dudley brought the dies for coining in the American Mint."

The dies were cut by hand and show numerous irregularities, with the same letters appearing in different configurations on the same coins. The largest denomination, the mark, was punctuated as "1.000" on the coin.

Rarities Today

Of the 1783 mark just one specimen is known today, the example which traces its pedigree to Hon. Charles Thomson and was found in his desk. The ob-

---

1 John Jacob Eckfeldt (1733-1818), patriarch of a long line of Eckfeldts who would become associated with American coinage, especially the Philadelphia Mint (established 1792).

2 A different person from the Dudley who was employed at the Rahway (New Jersey) mint (some citations state he later cut dies for certain varieties of New Jersey copper coinage, but he seems to have been a laborer who worked in other jobs there, was not paid his due, and later sued to collect back wages).

3 This identifies A. Dubois as the die engraver. Presumably, Eckfeldt and Swanwick supplied blank, unhardened dies.

4 It would be interesting to learn the earlier use(s) of this particular coining press. Coins dated prior to 1783 and made in the United States are very few in number (but include, as an example, the 1776 Continental Currency "dollar").

verse displays an all-seeing eye surrounded by rays and stars, with the legend NOVA CONSTELLATIO around. The reverse bears the legend LIBERTAS JUSTITIA 1783, a wreath, and within the wreath U.S 1.000.

Of the quint there are but two specimens known to exist, each of which is a slightly different design. The obverse of one is similar to the mark, but of reduced size, and with the legend NOVA CONSTELLATIO surrounding an all-seeing eye with rays and stars. The second variety has the all-seeing eye with rays and stars, but lacks the NOVA CONSTELLATIO inscription. The reverse of both is from the same die and is similar in concept to the mark, but with the denomination 500.

Of the bit there are three examples known, each with the same obverse and reverse design. There are two treatments of the edge, the Garrett Collection piece having an edge with an olive leaf design, and the Eric P. Newman Collection piece having a plain edge. A third example was discovered in England in the 1980s and was auctioned by Stack's. The obverse and reverse designs are similar to the mark but are of reduced size and bear the denomination 100.

Related to the preceding is a 1783 Nova Constellatio 5-unit copper coin of a similar design, but with the denomination expressed as "...5" on the reverse. This is said to have been in various private collections in England, then the property of an English coin dealer in Paris in 1977, then American dealer Fred S. Werner in the same year, then into the collection of John J. Ford, Jr.[1]

The Fugio Die Find Hoax

Said to have been lost: 18th century
Said to have been found: 1858
Supposed treasure: Coin dies

An Ambitious 14-Year-Old Boy

This is the story of a treasure or hoard that never existed.[2] Nevertheless, it has attracted much attention over the years.

In several nineteenth-century accounts it was related that 14-year-old C. Wyllys Betts[3] visited the site in New Haven, Connecticut, where certain 1787 Fugio copper coins had been minted under federal government contract years earlier. He fortuitously located several original dies from which the so-called "New Haven restrikes" were later made in copper, brass, silver, and gold. These "restrike" coins differed from all originals inasmuch as the linked rings on the reverse were much thinner.

During the last century these pieces were a stock in trade item with many dealers. Later, an account similar to that just given concerning the fortuitous find of C. Wyllys Betts found its way into various modern references including *A Guide Book of United States Coins.*

The Peripatetic Horatio Rust

Reality seems to have been a bit different, and even the following account—which is believed to be closer to the truth—has elements of imagination:

From the 1850s through at least the 1880s Horatio N. Rust (life dates: 1828-1906) was a prominent collector. Augustus Sage, a New York City printer turned rare coin dealer, made a medal with Rust's portrait as No. 8 in his "Sage's Numismatic Gallery" series, 1860. In 1875 Rust was a subscriber-patron to Sylvester S. Crosby's *Early Coins of America* book.

In the 1870s Rust, then living in Chicago, related that circa 1860, while residing in New York City, he resolved to learn more about the Fugio coppers minted in 1787. Realizing that specimens had been struck in New Haven, he decided to spend a day there, investigate the situation, and "if possible find the dies."

After vainly searching in old newspaper files for information, he spent the evening with a coin collector, who, as it turned out, was a fountainhead of information. The 1787 Fugio copper coins had been struck, his host said, by the firm of Broome & Platt, hardware jobbers. Certain of the apparatus still existed and was in the hands of a hardware dealer on Chapel Street. An impromptu visit was arranged. As luck would have it, on the cashier's desk were two original Fugio dies being used as paperweights! During his visit Rust learned that there had been a third die, but it had been loaned to a man in Bridgeport and never returned. (In a later account, Rust changed his recollections to

[1] *Coin World,* January 9, 1980, p. 1; Breen, *Encyclopedia,* 1988, pp. 113, 116.
[2] Appendix I of the present work describes other fantasy hoards.
[3] Life dates: 1845-1887. Betts was criticized for creating fantasy rarities with legends implying the coins were part of the American colonial series. In actuality, it seems that there was no intent to deceive, just to amuse. His master work, *American Colonial History Illustrated by Contemporary Medals* was published posthumously in 1894 and today remains the standard reference on the subject.

finding two *pairs* of dies during his visit and learning about one missing die.) Rust bought the dies on the spot and, in his words:

> [I] took them to Waterbury, Conn., and struck several hundred for cabinet specimens. I had one struck in gold and several in silver and for many years used them as exchanges in collecting coins. I printed an account of finding the dies on a slip, which I gave with each restrike, that all might know what they were. After coming to California I sold the dies to a coin collector in Philadelphia. Recently I noted in an eastern paper that a Ring cent in gold had been found. Probably it is the one I struck in 1860.

Henry Chapman's catalogue of the George Parsons Collection, June 1914, reprinted the text of Rust's paper slip:

> First United States Cent, known as the Ring or Franklin Cent. July 6, 1787, the United States government ordered the minting of its first coin. Messrs. Groome [*sic*] & Platt, New Haven, Conn., did some part of the coinage. About the year 1860 the undersigned found (and still retains) the original dies among their effects in New Haven. The dies were taken to Waterbury, Conn., and a few coins struck for cabinet specimens, the enclosed being one of the restrikes.
> Horatio N. Rust
> Chicago, 1875.

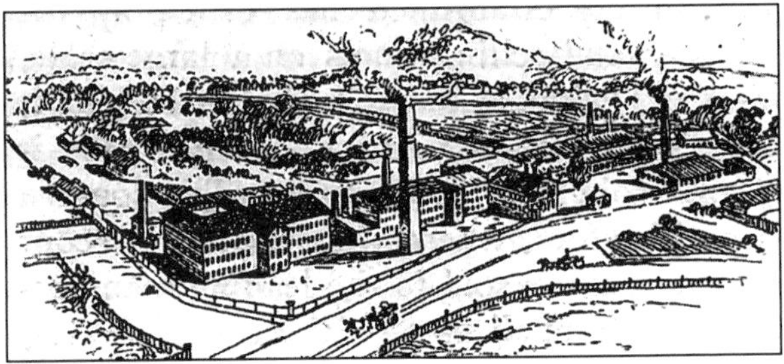

Scovill Manufacturing Co.

Not Quite Accurate

The above scenario is flawed in that certain workmanship of the dies is of a technology not in use in 1787. It seems likely that new "1787 Fugio" hubs were made by the Scovill Manufacturing Company in Waterbury, and from these hubs several new dies were made. These included not only the dies for the "New Haven restrikes," but also for several varieties of rare "Fugio patterns" listed by Sylvester S. Crosby in *Early Coins of America,* pp. 300-301.

Although the facts may be never known, a possibility is that the instigator may have been Charles I. Bushnell, a New York attorney who in the 1850s had Scovill make for him several fantasy rarities similar to circa 1837-1841 Hard Times tokens. Scovill had been a major manufacturer of tokens in the Hard Times era and had the techniques and equipment to make more. The company, still in business today in the 1990s, made many small metal products besides coins and tokens, including Civil War uniform buttons, clothing snaps, etc.

After the 1860s, Bushnell's interest in numismatics waned. After his death (1880) his coins were consigned to his nephews, young Philadelphia coin dealers S. Hudson Chapman and Henry Chapman. The sale of the Bushnell Collection was held in June 1882 and created a sensation, much to the consternation and envy of their gray-bearded, old-time competitors who, presumably, better deserved to have had the collection.

In his time Bushnell was not above being deceptive.[1] It is believed that many of his later Hard Times token fantasy rarities were deliberately oxidized and lightly corroded to give them the false appearance of age. It does not strain the imagination to envision that Bushnell "laundered" several of the new Fugio dies through a New Haven collector who put Horatio N. Rust on to them, or that Rust obtained them from Bushnell and invented the Broome & Platt episode. After all, it was Rust who could not keep his stories straight and at one time said he made "several hundred" restrikes and at another time recalled he had made "a few." Similarly, he was inconsistent in his stories about the so-called 1858 "find" of dies. Paraphrasing Abraham Lincoln, no person has a good enough memory to be an effective liar.

That these may have been "possibly a manufacture of new dies" and not original was suggested by W.C. Prime in his 1860-copyrighted book, *Coins, Medals and Seals.*

How Many Were Made?

The following appeared in the *American Journal of Numismatics,* January 1873, page 72, and gives some mintage figures:

> *Mind Your Business; Ring, or Franklin Cent*
> The first owners of the dies of this cent, as far as we can learn, were Broom [*sic*] & Platt, hardware dealers, of New Haven, Conn. There were three sets of dies; our informant, Mr. H.N. Rust, tells us that he found a single die at Bridgeport, Conn., in 1858; afterwards he obtained the remaining five parts of the dies in the store formerly occupied by Broom & Platt, in New Haven.[2]

---

1 See related comment under earlier account of Talbot, Allum & Lee tokens in which certain Bushnell comments are quoted.

2 This account, yet another version of the "1787 die find," states that Rust first found a single die in Bridgeport and later found five dies in New Haven!

> Mr. Rust sold three of the dies to a dealer in New York City, but who did not succeed in obtaining good impressions from them. Mr. R. had some three or four hundred pieces struck at Waterbury, Conn., in a metal composed of copper and nickel, also a few in silver, and one only in gold.

Today, probably several hundred of the copper and brass pieces (most of which look somewhat alike) exist, a few dozen silver coins, and several in gold.

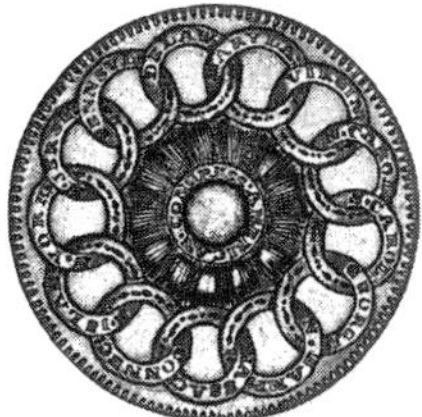

Fantasy "1787 Fugio pattern" possibly made to the order of Charles I. Bushnell.

The related fantasy "pattern" Fugio coppers listed by Crosby and in later references are much rarer and were probably distributed under different circumstances, quite possibly by Bushnell in the 1850s, as Rust does not seem to have been involved with them.[1]

The Bank of New York Hoard

Put away: Circa 1787
Found: Before 1859
Treasure: Fugio copper cents

An Old-Time Keg

The Bank of New York, founded in 1784, came into possession of a keg of original 1787 Fugio copper cents sometime around the time they were manufactured. Over a period of many years, beginning at least by 1859, bank officials passed these out to favored clients and employees and made some available to numismatists. Included were some of the scarce type with UNITED above and STATES below on the label at the center of the reverse (in contrast, most other varieties have these words to the left and right sides).

Walter Breen has written that a keg containing fewer than 5,000 coins was deposited in 1788 at the Bank of New York, 44 Wall Street, and remained unopened until 1856. After this time the hoard became widely known and, among other citations, was mentioned as follows by W.C. Prime in his book, *Coins, Medals and Seals* (copyright 1860, published in 1861):

> Within the past year a keg of these [Fugio] coppers was found in the vault of a New York City bank, in fresh proof condition.[2] This statement has been doubted; but we are indebted to the cashier for fine specimens of the contents of the keg, which abundantly prove the truth of the story. A recent discovery of the old dies, and possibly a manufacture of new dies, or repairing and retouching the old, has made these coins very common in various metals.[3]

Numismatic Commentary

By about 1948 some 1,641 pieces remained in possession of the bank and were numismatically analyzed by Damon G. Douglas. It was learned that the pieces were made from two batches of planchets weighing on average 143 grains and 155 grains respectively. Today, numerous Bank of New York Fugio coppers are in private collections, and a selection is in the cabinet of the American Numismatic Society, New York.[4] The typical piece (such as the plentiful Newman variety 12-X) is somewhat casually struck, lightly defined in certain areas (especially at the bottom of the obverse), and is apt to have carbon streaks or planchet rifts. Coloration is likely to be a blend of original mint red with brown toning.

Anthony J. Terranova examined the remainder of the hoard about 1888 and reviewed 819 coins. These were being kept in a cloth sack. Terranova arranged for their transfer to protective holders. Grades ranged from Red Uncirculated to MS-60, water stained. In addition to the 819 loose pieces, there were 50 or 60 pieces embedded in lucite, which the Bank had done some time ago to present as gifts to favored customers.[5]

---

[1] Sources include Eric P. Newman, *Varieties of the FUGIO Cent, Coin Collector's Journal,* 1952, this being the standard reference in print on history and die varieties; Damon Douglas' unpublished manuscript; Breen, *Encyclopedia,* 1988, p. 147 (source of Rust quotation); *Colonial Newsletter,* December 1968, commentary by James Spilman; *Colonial Newsletter,* May 1976 (Rust correspondence); *American Journal of Numismatics,* January 1873 (attributing the discovery to Rust); *AJN,* July 1887 (obituary of Betts; he is credited with the discovery); Henry Chapman's catalogue of the George Parsons Collection, 1914.

[2] In the 1860s the term "Proof" was not well defined and was often used in various texts, auction catalogues, etc., to refer to Mint State coins that had what today would be called a "prooflike" surface; these coins, of course, in addition to what we know as regular Proofs specifically minted as such.

[3] This is Prime's reference to Horatio N. Rust's Fugio die discovery caper.

[4] Breen, *Encyclopedia,* 1988, p. 147; other sources.

[5] Anthony J. Terranova, conversation, October 26, 1996.

Hoard Remnants? Restrikes?

First minted: 1795
Found: 1850s
Treasure: Washington "Grate Cents"

Is the following account of a hoard? Or, were restrikes being made? The author is inclined toward the first view. These words appeared in W.C. Prime's 1860-copyrighted work, *Coins, Medals, and Seals,* p. 94:

> Another English token was issued with a head of Washington, and on the reverse a [fireplace] grate. This is called the *Washington Grate cent* or token, and was issued by Clark and Harris, a firm whose name it bears.
>
> The die is doubtless still preserved in England, as fine proof specimens are furnished to order in any quantity. It is a coin of little interest or value, and only to be noted as a compliment paid to the American patriot by an English house of tradesmen. The legend around the bust is "G. WASHINGTON, THE FIRM FRIEND TO PEACE & HUMANITY."

Walter Breen attributes the dies for this piece to Thomas Wyon and suggests that they were struck by Peter Kempson & Co. in Birmingham.[1] At least two die varieties exist, one with small coat buttons and the other with large buttons, the former considerably the rarer. There are several variations of the edge treatment, the most often seen being with diagonal reeding.

The Col. Cohen Hoard

Put away: Circa 1775
Found: by the 1870s
Treasure: 1773 Virginia halfpennies

Copper Halfpence to Virginia

In 1773 the colony of Virginia ordered a supply of copper halfpence from the British crown. Examples were struck at the Tower Mint, London, and in due course exported to America.[2] In February 1774 the ship *Virginia,* under Captain Howard Esten, arrived at the York River (which empties into the Chesapeake Bay) with five long tons of new halfpence aboard, equivalent to about 672,000 coins. The coins bore the portrait of George III on the obverse and a heraldic shield on the reverse, the latter side inscribed VIRGINIA.

Distribution of the pieces in commerce was quite slow. Finally, in late winter 1775, Robert C. Nicholas, treasurer of the Virginia colony, published notices that the halfpence were on hand and ready for exchange "either for gold, silver, or any Treasury notes."

As it turned out, the American colonies and Britain commenced war with each other a short time thereafter, less than two months after the availability of Virginia halfpence was announced. Widespread hoarding by the citizenry commenced, as it usually does during times of extreme political and economic uncertainty. Thus, many of the Virginia coins that were distributed were immediately saved, rather than used in everyday commerce. However, enough reached circulation that numerous examples later became lost or misplaced as pocket change (as described under the "Early Coins found at Williamsburg" entry in Chapter 10).

Colonel Cohen

Colonel Mendes I. Cohen (1796-1879) of Baltimore, Maryland, served with distinction in the Mexican War. An inveterate collector in many fields, Cohen acquired art, coins, and other objects. His notable collection of Egyptian antiquities was given to The Johns Hopkins University in Baltimore. Cohen was an early member of the Baltimore Numismatic Society and must have known such notable numismatists as Dr. George Massamore and T. Harrison Garrett. Of all American cities, Baltimore has had many very special numismatic connections over the years, and several of the most memorable cabinets ever formed were assembled within its city limits.[3]

Sometime in the nineteenth century, quite possibly in the 1870s, Col. Cohen acquired over 2,200 bright

[1] *Encyclopedia,* 1988, p. 143. Kempson was a prolific coiner of conder tokens.

[2] Sources include: Eric P. Newman, *Coinage for Colonial Virginia,* 1956, this being the standard reference on these pieces and also the source for die variety attribution information. Walter H. Breen, "Survey of American Coin Hoards," *The Numismatist,* January 1952.

[3] Among these being the Robert Gilmor collection assembled during the early nineteenth century; the Waldo C. Newcomer collection of the early twentieth century, dispersed by B. Max Mehl in the early 1930s; the John Work Garrett collection (built upon the foundation established by T. Harrison Garrett), and the Louis E. Eliasberg, Sr., collection. For many years Frank G. Duffield, editor of *The Numismatist,* maintained his offices and created the publication there; it was printed in Federalsburg, Maryland.

Uncirculated specimens of the 1773 Virginia halfpenny under circumstances not recorded, although in 1952 Walter Breen speculated that they may have been found in a Maryland state government building in Annapolis and may have been in an original wooden keg. By 1988, Breen had modified his theory and forthrightly stated that they were "from a keg found in Richmond before the Civil War and long owned by Col. Mendes I. Cohen...."[1]

On October 25-29, 1875, Cohen's collection was sold at auction by Edward D. Cogan. The offering was remarkable for its quality and included many rare early pieces, an extensive run of United States gold Proof sets, and other treasures. However, Virginia halfpence did not play a notable part. Apparently, most of these sparkling copper pieces were subsequently bequeathed to his nieces and nephews who also received many art objects.

In his January 21, 1880 auction catalogue of properties from various sources, John W. Haseltine gave brief notice of a find of 1773 Virginia halfpennies without mentioning either their quantity or how they were located.

Raymond Acquires Many

The Col. Cohen cache remained nearly intact until 1929 when antiques and other items belonging to Bertha Cohen were auctioned in Baltimore. About 2,200 1773 Virginia halfpennies were sold loosely and in bulk and fetched a few cents each. From that time forward, these pieces have been relatively plentiful in numismatic circles. Apparently, many of these were later resold by Wayte Raymond. About 20 different die pairings were represented in the Cohen hoard.

At least a few hundred of these coins passed to a Mr. Gottschalk of Syracuse, New York, who had groups of these for sale in the 1950s and would bring several dozen pieces at a time to conventions of the Empire State Numismatic Association.[2]

The Knoxville and Easton Finds

Dr. Montroville W. Dickeson, in his 1859 work, *American Numismatical Manual,* commented (p. 84) concerning two hoards of 1773 Virginia halfpence:

> Some few years since, a quantity of these copper coins was dug up from the summit of the hill on which the college now stands at Knoxville, Tennessee; and quite a number were exhumed from a locality near Easton, Pennsylvania, showing that they must have been extensively circulated, and have amply rewarded the projectors.

Little if any other information is known about the Knoxville and Easton finds, the condition of the pieces, where they went, and their relationship (if any) to the Col. Cohen hoard. Apparently, Dickeson did not know of the Cohen holding if, indeed, it existed as early as 1859.

Today, the 1773 Virginia halfpennies are the only colonial (pre-1776) American coins that are readily available in Mint State. Indeed, Mint State examples are more often encountered—and by a large margin—than are pieces with extensive evidence of circulation.

These coins are commonly collected by two major variations in obverse punctuation, with or without a period after GEORGIVS. Relatively few have pursued the series by minute die varieties as described in Eric P. Newman's 1956 study, quite possibly because this monograph has been out of print for a long time. Thus, exceedingly rare die varieties, if found, are apt to cost no more than common ones.

The Natrona Hoard

Buried: 18th century
Found: By 1912
Treasure: Indian peace medals

Medals and a Skeleton

In the eighteenth and nineteenth centuries, as immigrants from Europe and restless citizens of the Eastern Seaboard pushed the frontiers of America west-

[1] The latter from Breen, *Encyclopedia,* 1988, p. 31. A reading of Breen's comments and theories in many areas over the years reveals many of his speculations and ideas became "facts" in his later works, or at least took the form of positive statements without stating that they were opinions. These speculations are most pervasive in his taking certain annual mintage figures from Treasury reports and arbitrarily breaking them down into mintages by types or varieties. What in many instances was pure guesswork by Breen is now accepted as fact in the *Guide Book of U.S. Coins* and many other sources (two of many examples include the division of 1795 silver dollars by Breen into 160,295 of the Flowing Hair type and 42,738 of the Draped Bust style; and the wildly incorrect division of 1856 business strike gold dollars into just 33,660 of the Upright 5 style and the vast quantity of 1,729,276 of the Slanting 5 style).

[2] Recollection of the author, who bought many of these pieces; Jonah Shapiro, who operated the Syracuse Stamp & Coin Co., was also an active buyer.

White men (seated) endeavoring to work out a treaty with Indians. As part of such efforts, peace medals were often presented to chiefs and other important tribe members.

ward, Indians (the true Native Americans, as they are now designated) were continually displaced.[1] Naturally, they were resentful, and numerous skirmishes and incidents resulted. In an effort to promote "peace" various government and private agents and traders presented medals to Indian chiefs and others.

Today, such Indian peace medals are a specialized niche of American numismatic interest. Best known are the medals struck at the Philadelphia Mint in the last century. However, other, rarer, pieces were distributed by the British in the days before the United States declared independence, by fur traders, and by the French. It is British medals given to American Indians that concern us here.

In a 1987 coin auction sale a small and select offering of King George I Indian peace medals was included. This group, never before seen on the market, had been consigned by a Pennsylvania resident who related the following story to the present writer (MJH):

---

1 Text and research for this account is by Michael Hodder. Certain information is adapted from his presentation of these medals for sale as an additional consignment to the Frederick B. Taylor Collection catalogue, Auctions by Bowers and Merena, March 1987. The illustration is of Lot 1131 in that sale and represents an actual specimen from the Natrona hoard.

These medals were found in a little town called Natrona, Pennsylvania, which is about 20 miles northeast of Pittsburgh along the Allegheny River. The group was found about 75 years ago when Penn Salt Manufacturing Company was digging a ditch for a water line which ran across Dr. Bungarner's property at 51 Federal Street, Natrona. Dr. Bungarner's daughters collected them, along with about 2,000 beads and a male skeleton.

Recently, one of the daughters died, and the other gave me [*i.e.,* the consignor] the collection which they had had in their possession for about 75 years. The Carnegie Museum in Pittsburgh tells me that back in 1714 to 1734 Natrona was called "Chartier's Town" and that there was an Indian settlement there.

The skeleton that accompanied these nine medals may very well have been that of the British Indian agent who was carrying them at the time of his death. The cataloguer (MJH) further noted that the conditions of the medals were unusually good, suggesting that they had never actually been awarded. Each medal was looped at the top for suspension, the loops being intact and integral. Grades ranged from Fine to choice Extremely Fine and rivaled any offered at public auction previous to their time of sale.

The cataloguer noted that there were two major types represented in the group, corresponding roughly to Betts-164 and Betts-165.[1] Three obverse dies and four reverse dies were used for the Betts-165 similar pieces. There were three obverse die duplicates among the seven specimens, and two reverse die duplicates (the third specimen being a brockage). The two pieces similar to Betts-164 were from the same die pair. Weights and diameters of the pieces in the hoard were largely heavier and wider than previously seen on similar Betts-165 specimens. One example was an oval medal, an unrecorded state to date, struck from the normal dies used on round pieces.

Prices realized for these medals ranged from $2,900 to a high of $4,800 (not including the 10% buyer's premium), with one piece, very probably a contemporary cast, selling for considerably less.[2]

A Virginia Find

Another find of related medals formed the subject of this item in the *American Journal of Numismatics,* July 1874:

INDIAN PEACE MEDALS

I gladly comply with your request for a fuller explanation of the Indian peace medals in my collection. I was not aware of their rarity. As I wrote you in my previous letter, there is an engraved copy of the medal published in an octavo volume of the *History of the Massacre of Wyoming* [*sic;* apparently *History of Wyoming,* by Miner, was intended] by whom I know not.[3]

The medals in my possession were found in 1859 on the banks of the Ohio River, at Point Pleasant, Va.—the scene of the battle between the Indians under Cornstalk and the Virginia troops under General Andrew Lewis in 1774.[4] The washing away of the banks by the high waters of the Ohio brought to light a great many Indian relics of those days, and among other things thus discovered were the medals in my possession, and also a silver or pewter plate bearing an inscription in French, relating to the encampment of the French at that point on their first voyage up the Ohio River. This plate is supposed to be now in the possession of the Pennsylvania Historical Society. The medals were found by Dr. S.G. Shaw of Point Pleasant, and presented to me. The largest of these is black with corrosion.

No. 1, Obv. Bust of George I, draped and laureated, facing right; legend, GEORGE KING OF GREAT BRITAIN. Rev. Large Indian to the right drawing his bow in the act of shooting a deer, which stands on a hill to the left behind a short tree; flowers and bushes in the background and sun at the top; exergue, blank. Brass, looped, size 26.

No. 2, Obv., bust of George, laureated, facing left; legend, GEORGIUS—MAG. BR. FRA. ET. HIB. REX. Rev., Indian to right, nearly erect, leaning forward under a tree, which follows the curve of the medal, holding a bow at arm's length in left hand, right hand slightly extended beyond his body; to the left, on slightly more elevated ground than the Indian, and under a tree which follows the curve of the medal, a deer is running at full speed; in foreground, a shrub. Brass, looped, size 16

Very truly yours,

Horace Edwin Hayden
Brownsville, Pennsylvania
May 9, 1874

---

[1] C. Wyllys Betts, *American Colonial History Illustrated by Contemporary Medals,* 1894 (published posthumously, Betts died in 1887; Betts also figured in the "Fugio Die Find Hoax" discussed in the present chapter). An early illustration of a somewhat similar medal appeared in Charles Miner, *History of Wyoming,* 1845, plate opposite p. 27. "Wyoming" referred to the Wyoming Valley area of northeastern Pennsylvania; this is an Indian name and is one of several variants, Wyomissing being another. Miner related that in 1814 he had visited the scene of an ancient Indian fortification on the site of present-day Wilkes-Barre, Pennsylvania. "Fortune was unexpectedly propitious to our search, for we found a medal bearing on one side the impress of King George the First, dated 1714 (the year he commenced his reign), on the other, an Indian chief.... It was deposited with the Philadelphia Historical Society." The accompanying description notwithstanding, the illustration in his book is of a medal bearing no date.

[2] Following the appearance of these Natrona hoard medals at auction, Ebenezer Nii Quarcoopome published an interesting study titled "The Indian Peace Medal of George I" in the American Numismatic Society's *The Medal in America* (New York: COAC, 1987).

[3] The reference is to the massacre of settlers in the Wyoming Valley of Pennsylvania, July 3, 1778. Today, the Wyoming Monument in Wyoming (near Wilkes-Barre, Pennsylvania) observes the event.

[4] Now Point Pleasant, West Virginia; the area today known as West Virginia, earlier was a part of Virginia. On June 20, 1863, it joined the Union as a separate state.

A Handful of Copper Coins

Lost: 1780s
Found: 1924
Treasure: Nova Constellatio and other coins

It is not often that a find of copper coins makes news in the general press. This notice told of finding a 1783 Nova Constellatio copper and a few other pieces:[1]

> "Sand hogs" working 80 feet underground on the foundations of the New York Telephone Company building recently, in New York, unearthed several American coins dating back to the latter part of the eighteenth century. An official in charge of the work said 50 feet underground the men found the hulk of an old vessel about the size of a modern canal boat.
>
> While digging out the hulk the men found the coins, which were bronze or copper. One bears the word "Libertas" and is dated 1783. On the reverse side is the inscription "Constellatio Nova." Another coin found is dated 1780. Of the nine coins found no two are alike.

The "Solitude" Hoard

Hidden or lost: 1780s
Found: By 1925
Treasure: New Jersey copper coins

Walter Mould at Solitude

In 1734, on a site well watered and fertile, a lovely house was built which later, due to its secluded location, was named "Solitude."[2] Within a space of a few years, the home became the family seat for justice John Cleves Symmes, a member of the New Jersey Supreme

Court and a very important politician in state affairs.

In 1787, Justice Symmes, along with other influential members of Northern New Jersey's political elite, invited one Walter Mould to reside near Solitude and commence coining New Jersey coppers. Less than one year earlier, Walter Mould, in conjunction with two other Englishmen, had successfully bid for and won a contract to supply the state of New Jersey with a copper coinage. After a falling out among the partners, Mould removed himself to Morristown and placed his operations under the tutelage and political protection of Justice Symmes.

For the next year and a half, Mould struck coins in Morristown, but the venture was not a commercial success, and both he and his backers reaped only substantial losses where they had expected equally large profits. By the summer of 1788, Walter Mould had died on a journey to Ohio, leaving behind a destitute wife and young son. Justice Symmes, in whose entourage Mould had traveled to Ohio, began a successful legal career in the western territories.

Meanwhile, back home at Solitude, Justice Symmes' house was sold and turned into a Tavern named the "Wheatsheaf," run by Captain Benjamin Holloway. Holloway's establishment soon became a favorite stopping place along the Morristown to Elizabethtown turnpike. A copper mine on the site of Solitude (from whence it is believed that Mould obtained the copper for his coins) flooded due to the absence of pumping, and the pond then served as the inn's chief water supply.

A View of the Mint

In the way of further background we quote this related commentary concerning the Symmes house from a letter dated August 8, 1855, from W.C. Baker of Morristown, New Jersey, to numismatist Charles I. Bushnell:[3]

---

1 *The Numismatist,* March 1924, p. 243, quoting an unidentified press clipping. The 1780 piece was not of American origin, as no indigenous copper issues bear that date.

2 Text and research for this account are by Michael Hodder; also see his article, "When Morristown Made Coins," *The Numismatist,* August 1993, pp. 1099-1102, 1159-1162.

3 As quoted in Sylvester S. Crosby, *Early Coins of America,* 1875, p. 282. Crosby also quoted early information about several other New Jersey mint locations. The mentioned book, *The Hole at the North Pole,* treated the "theory of concentric spheres," which proposed that another civilization existed beneath the surface of the earth as we know it, and could be accessed via an opening in the Arctic.

> There were two mint-houses in this state, one located in Morristown, and the other in Elizabethtown. The mint-house in the former place, which is still standing, was the residence of John Cleve Symmes, chief justice of the state of New Jersey, uncle to John Cleve Symmes, author of *The Hole at the North Pole,* and father-in-law of Gen. Wm. H. Harrison, president of the United States.
>
> The residence was called "Solitude." It was at one time occupied by a Mr. Holloway, and is known by some as the "Holloway House." The mint here was carried on by Walter Mould, an Englishman, who previous to his coming to America, had been employed in a similar way, in Birmingham. In the coinage of the New Jersey coppers, a screw with a long lever was employed. This information is vouched for by Mr. Lewis Condict, of Morristown, who saw the mint in operation.

Wheat Sheaf Farm

In 1897 a German immigrant, Gustave Kissel, bought the old place and renamed it "Wheat Sheaf Farm." At some later time Kissel or his heirs sold the farm to Edwin S.S. Sunderland, who commenced renovations to the property. During one of these efforts, Sunderland discovered behind an old mantelpiece a series of New Jersey coppers of the large planchet type, which had been sealed behind the wall for over a century. In addition, at least one other coin was discovered in the garden during the course of landscaping. These coppers, numbering 30 or more pieces, were placed into the pages of a National Coin Album and proudly shown to visitors.[1]

In 1955 Edwin Sunderland published *A History of Old Wheat Sheaf Farm, formerly "Solitude."* In the book, on page 13, Sunderland mentioned the 30 coppers that he had found while doing restoration work on the house and in the grounds. This was the first notice that came to the attention of specialists in New Jersey coppers that any pieces had been found on the old site of Walter Mould's New Jersey mint. By 1964 several collectors had traveled to Sunderland's home to see the coins.

In October 1964, Everett T. Sipsey published his narrative account of the examination of the coins he had made in Sunderland's house. By the time Sipsey had seen them there were only 17 pieces left, and they had clearly been mixed up out of their places in the National Coin Album page, as some notations underneath the openings no longer corresponded to the coins contained in those apertures. It is clear that at some point someone had attributed these coins to their particular Maris varieties, but that, over time, the coins had been taken out and put back so many times by inexperienced collectors that attributions underneath each slot no longer corresponded to the coins contained therein.

Sipsey did note that eight of the coins included were large planchet pieces, and that one variety, the popular PLURIBS reverse, which was noted as having been found in 1925, was missing from the group. Sipsey noted that it was no longer possible to be sure exactly which large planchet coins had been plowed up in the garden, discovered behind the fireplace or, perhaps, added later to augment the collection. However, Sipsey suggested that all Maris numbers, 59-o through 67-v, could confidently be attributed to the Morristown Mint based upon their large planchet size.

While the "Solitude Hoard" was not an important find in terms of either individual coin values or overall numismatic content, for New Jersey specialists it marked a turning point. As the site was known to have been where Mould's mint was located in Morristown, and as coins discovered on site, and confidently datable to the late 1780s, were large planchet varieties, it could safely be assumed that the large planchet pieces were Mould's products and not those of the Rahway Mint.

---

[1] National brand cardboard coin albums with celluloid slides were made in Shippensburg, Pennsylvania, by M.L. Beistle and marketed by Wayte Raymond of New York City.

The Stepney Depot Hoard

Hidden: 1788 or later
Found: 1950
Treasure: 18th-century copper coins

A detailed report of this find was given by Walter H. Breen in 1952, based upon his examination of it in 1951:[1]

Some excavations during 1950 on a pre-Revolutionary War estate in Stepney [Depot], Fairfield County, Connecticut, brought to light an old iron kettle apparently filled with earth. The kettle was of eighteenth-century vintage, was undamaged and probably had lain undisturbed since its burial next to one of the posts in the old barn (built 1760) whence it was unearthed. It proved to contain some 200 coins, encrusted, which the owners subsequently sold to Stack's in New York. The encrustations were cleaned off without damage to the coins, and some pieces were sold (reportedly including eight Uncirculated Vermont cents of the portrait types and 20-odd Connecticut cents in the same condition). I later had the opportunity to study the remainder of the hoard.

What I saw included 181 coins, as follows:

One was a 1787 Nova Eborac; three were Vermont cents (two having the BRITANNIA. reverse, the third being Ryder 27); 72 were counterfeit halfpence, all with correct legends (*i.e.,* no bungtowns); the remainder were Connecticut cents 1785-1788, mostly in Mint State or almost as fine, though many were poorly struck.

The Connecticuts were just as noteworthy for variety as for condition. Fully 74 different die varieties, including some extreme rarities, were represented. Among these I might mention 1786 Miller 4.2-G (unlisted muling), 5.2-H.1, 5.2-L, 5.8-F, 5.11-R, 5.14-S, 33.13-Z.1, and 33.40-Z.2—all Rarity 5 or 6; all represented by one to three specimens.[2]

Probably of equal importance are the quantity and character of the counterfeit halfpence. Sixteen of the 72 were dated 1778-1787, *all* being in Mint State, all on planchets of the same fabric, all having identical letter and figure punches and die workmanship. Three of the 1787s have the identical die for a reverse that was later used with Vermont obverse to make Ryder-13, the BRITANNIA variety; this die is attributed to James F. Atlee and the coins to Machin's Mill near Newburgh, New York. One of the three 1787 counterfeits has both obverse and reverse the same as that illustrated by Howard Kurth as "Machin's Halfpenny" in his introduction to Richardson on Vermont cents (May 1947 *Numismatist*). These Machin-made halfpence will be further discussed below.

Early farm scene. In rural New England, many coins were hidden for safekeeping.

Some of the conclusions that can be drawn from this hoard follow, the complete catalogue of the contents being omitted for lack of space:

1. The hoard was buried in 1788, unless most of the Connecticuts of that date were predated. I would suspect it was fairly early in the year, too, inasmuch as the 1788-dated coins are extremely few in proportion to the 1787s, and all of the 1788s are choice Mint State. There are only four 1788 Connecticuts, but 75 1787s, 13 1786s and eight 1785s. Purely negative evidence seems to confirm this; there are no late Machin issues such as the GEORGIVS III REX / INDE ET LIB pieces, Immune Columbias, or "emergency" issues overstruck on earlier pieces such as Nova Constellatios or half pence.

2. Since coppers passed current then at six to eight for a penny, the whole current value of the hoard at time of burial cannot have exceeded two Spanish dollars (even allowing the maximum number of specimens to have been sold from the hoard before I saw it), and probably did not even equal one dollar. The answer to the natural question, "To whom would this junk have seemed treasure worth burying?" immediately suggests itself: this was a small boy's hoard, made up of his acquisitions of a few coppers at a time, gathered over a period of a couple of years (hence the great diversity of varieties). This hypothesis incidentally provides one of two possible explanations for the great number of counterfeit halfpence: either it was a child's ignorance of base coin, or else false halfpence really circulated in those times as if genuine—or both.

3. In any event, this hoard provides an extraordinary illumination of the kinds of currency of low value that passed in Connecticut and the surrounding area in that period. Compare the account in S.S. Crosby's *Early Coins of America* (pp. 291-292) which applied to New York, but is largely confirmed by this hoard buried only a few miles east of the New York-Connecticut border. There is one anomaly for which no explanation seems satisfactory, however: the complete absence of Massachusetts, Fugio, or New Jersey coppers.

4. The base halfpence mentioned above, dated 1778 and attributed by implication to Atlee and Machin, were certainly *predated,* judging both by condition and by the fact that stylistically they are connected with 1788 Connecticuts and halfpence—not to mention the identity of letters and

---

1 Walter H. Breen, "Survey of American Coin Hoards," *The Numismatist,* January 1952. Here edited.

2 Attributions of Connecticut copper coins are to Henry Miller's numbers as published in *State Coinage of New England,* American Numismatic Society, 1919.zzz. Hillyer C. Ryder's attributions for Vermont and Massachusetts coppers are included in the same book.

figure punches. This confirms a conjecture of C. Wyllys Betts (*Counterfeit Half Pence,* p. 16) that they were so made. I suspect that the "1778" was an error for 1787.

5. The "base coins in similitude of British half-pence" repeatedly mentioned by Crosby (pp. 291, 172-174) were these counterfeits, both Birmingham-made (circa 1736-1776, as in this hoard) and Newburgh-made (1778-1787-1788). They were mostly certainly NOT the so-called "Pennsylvania coppers" or bungtowns. Strictly speaking, a *bungtown* is a bogus British copper of halfpenny or farthing size, with legends (such as GLORIOVS IER VIS, CORNWALLIS IND., GEORGE RULES, GREGORIVS III. PON., etc.) designed to evade drastic British anti-counterfeiting acts—and, at worst, to deceive the illiterate. These are better termed "evasions" and left completely out of the American colonial series, as most of the legends have been shown to refer to [British] historical events of the period 1789-1805, making it absurd to say that they circulated in Pennsylvania in 1781-1788. (See J.D.A. Thompson's article "Evasions," No. 373, *Seaby's Bulletin,* June 1949, for evidence.) There is plenty of evidence both inside and outside of the Fairfield County hoard that counterfeit British halfpence with correct legends circulated in the colonies. There is, however, NO evidence (other than Dr. Maris's conjecture quoted by Crosby, pp. 172-173) that these *evasions* ever did; and there is some evidence, namely the present hoard, that they did not circulate in quantity, if at all—for there is not a single specimen in evidence. I suggest therefore that the coins suppressed in Pennsylvania were simply British counterfeits of the kind which form a good part of the present hoard, and that the Maris conclusions otherwise were based on too little evidence.

Another conclusion (perhaps weakened by my lack of metallurgical experience) that might be drawn from this hoard is that the same source apparently supplied copper for both the Machin halfpence and many of the Connecticut coppers of 1787-1788, as the fabric and finish are identical. If the conclusion that these latter were made in Machin's Mill be correct, then the statement on Crosby's p. 202 (concerning the insignificantly small output of the Newburgh manufactory of hardware before 1789) will need revision—especially as the false halfpence are fairly common. There was also, apparently, a good bit of shipping of dies from one mint to another.

I may also briefly mention here that there were several hubs or head-punches used concurrently among obverse dies of Connecticuts, Vermonts, and halfpence. One was the Mailed Bust seen on Connecticut 1785 obverses 7 and 8; 1786 types 4 and 5.1, 5.3, 5.6; and Vermont obverses of Ryder 10, 11, and 15. Another was the Draped Bust used for Connecticut obverses of 1787, numbers 16 to 56 and all of the 1788 Draped Busts. Still another was the hub found on Vermont coppers attributed as Ryder 1, 14, 20, 21, etc., and some others, and also on a GEORGIVS III REX obverse listed as Ryder 31. A fourth was that seen on 1787 Connecticut obverses 9 and 15; 1788 obverses 7, 8, 10, 11, 12, and 13.

Walter Breen went on to accomplish much in numismatics, with the capstone of his career being the publication by Doubleday in 1988 of *Walter Breen's Complete Encyclopedia of U.S. and Colonial Coins.*

It is believed that many of the Stepney Depot Hoard state copper coins went into the collection of Edward Hessberg.[1]

Eric P. Newman's
1776 Machin's Mills halfpenny.

A key piece in the Stepney find was a 1776 Machin's Mills imitation halfpenny, the variety today known as Vlack 76 B-9, which Eric P. Newman used as the center point to his 1958 article, "A Recently Discovered Coin Solves a Vermont Numismatic Enigma," in the *Centennial Publication of the American Numismatic Society.*

Recently, Newman recalled the purchase of this piece and made a few other comments:[1]

> I bought this coin from Stack's, with Walter Breen handling the matter for them. There were about 10 to 12 Machins I bought from the group sent me and only one offered me was in Mint State. This was in May 1951 according to a recent article by John Kleeberg in *The Colonial Newsletter,* January 1996, page 1608. Walter knew I was working on the matter.
>
> While Walter may not have known the full significance of the 1776 coin he sold me he did note in his 1952 *Numismatist* article that the head punch matched some Connecticut and Vermont pieces, as stated in your adaptation of his article.
>
> I believe you should correct some of his erroneous guesswork. He makes it appear that Bungtown was an English name for evasive legend halfpence. When I wrote this up in 1976 to show it was strictly an American word for counterfeit halfpence he helped and was later delighted with the Shakespearean association. When I wrote more in 1991 on Shakespeare's bunghole usage, Walter was responsible for the filthy Rabelais tie in.
>
> Walter's comment about "six to eight for a penny" is an error or mix up. There were six to eight shillings to a Spanish dollar in money of account, but before rejection of halfpence there were 14 to 18 coppers to a shilling and after rejection never more than 60.

---

[1] Norman Stack related to Michael Hodder that a client of Stack's, Edward Hessberg, happened to visit the firm when Norman was examining some of the Connecticut coppers, and said, "I'll take the lot." The coins Breen examined were those owned by Hessberg. (Michael Hodder, commentary, July 1, 1996)

[2] Letter to the author, August 7, 1996, after reviewing a draft of this account.

The Umpqua River Hoard

Buried: 19th century
Found: 1950s
Treasure: 1820 North West Co. tokens

The North West Company

The North West Company was one of Canada's premier trading outfits, running a profitable business buying beaver and other furs from Indians across the length of Canada. The company had a near monopoly on trade with the Indians in the northwest territories of Canada and the United States, the areas that later became the provinces of British Columbia and the states of Washington and Oregon. By the first decade of the nineteenth century, however, the North West Company had lost its control of the western fur trade to the bigger and more aggressive, Hudson's Bay Company. By 1820, the North West Company was no longer capable of directing its own business affairs, and one year later, it was forced to merge with its rival.

At some time prior to 1820, the North West Company decided to follow its rival's lead and issue brass tokens which would entitle the bearer to one prime beaver pelt's worth of trade goods at one of the company's forts. These tokens bore a male head on one side, possibly that of George IV, and the inscription TOKEN 1820. The other side showed a beaver, indicating the token's value in trade, and the inscrip-

Colony of beavers, whose fur was a prime staple in trade in the Pacific Northwest.

tion NORTH WEST COMPANY. These tokens may have been made by John Walker & Company, or by Cotterhill, Hill & Company, both of which firms were located in England. The tokens appear to have been holed at the time they were made, so they could be stored strung on leather cords at the company's stores and carried easily by Indians. A couple of tokens are known not holed.

Demise of the North West Company

This account was printed in 1840 and told of the end of the North West Company:[1]

> The mercantile rivalry of the two great British corporations, the Northwest [*sic;* spelled North West in many other accounts and on the tokens] and the Hudson's Bay Company, which had been long strengthening, now began to rage in the wilderness, and in 1814 had broken out into actual war. A colony of Scotch highlanders had been established upon the Red River[2] by Lord Selkirk, in virtue of a grant of the country from the Hudson's Bay Company. On the other hand, the Northwest Company denied the validity of that grant, and it was of great injury to the last-named body, as their posts had been almost entirely supplied from the Red River lands. In consequence, numerous acts of violence ensued, and in 1814 the Scotchmen were driven away, their houses demolished, and the colony subverted.
>
> It was re-established, however, during the following year when the hostilities were renewed, the posts retaken and burned. On the 19th of June, 1816, a more formidable battle was fought between the rival traders; the Scotchmen were routed, and their governor, Mr. Temple, and five others, were killed.
>
> These facts having been brought before the British Parliament, an act was passed on the 2d of July, 1821, uniting the two companies by the name of The Hudson's Bay Company, under a charter giving to them the privilege of trading in the Indian territory claimed or belonging to Great Britain for the period of 21 years....
>
> The system of the Hudson's Bay Company is one calculated to further the exercise of its despotic power.... The trade of this company at the west is prosecuted by a resident governor, agents, factors, and clerks, some of whom have a share in the profits of the trade; also by a more active class of agents, the hunters, voyageurs,[3] and trappers, consisting of French Canadians, half-breeds, and Indians, who are paid a small salary with the promises of future advancement according as they shall render themselves of value to the trade. They are allowed only a small share of miserable food, and are kept by promises in a state of entire subjection to the will of the company.
>
> The furs which are collected are procured mainly from the Indians, in exchange for manufactured goods, which are imported into the country free of duty....

Use of the Tokens

Presumably, these brass tokens were used in the district at least circa 1820-1821 by the North West Company, and possibly even later by the Hudson's Bay Company after its assumption of the former firm.

By the late nineteenth century the North West Company tokens were considered to be rare and were of special interest to those collecting numismatic specimens of Canada. In 1894, P.N. Breton, in his landmark book, *Illustrated History of Coins and Tokens Relating to Canada,* illustrated the piece as his No. 925 and commented:

> The North-West Company was organized in Montreal about the year 1785. It carried on operations until about 1821 in the district south and west of Hudson Bay. This coin was good for a beaver skin. It is now very rare, not over five or six specimens being known, of which four are to be found in the collections of Mr. Thomas Wilson of Clarence, Ontario;[4] Rev. Father Michaud, C.S.V., of Montreal; Mr. W. Bastian, also of Montreal; the last one in the Ottawa government's collection.

In time, collectors south of the Canadian border took a fancy to this token as well. Today it is listed in *A Guide Book of United States Coins* and is firmly on the "want lists" of many stateside numismatists.

Caches

In the present century, several caches of North West Company tokens came to light in the Columbia River and Umpqua River valleys of Oregon, including 26 highly oxidized tokens unearthed with a copper kettle (which had contained the pieces) and a skull in a burial mound along the Umpqua River near the coast in central Oregon. Twenty-two of these were consigned to the writer's company and were sold to collectors.[5] Concerning the other four pieces in the find, one was donated to a museum, and three were so extensively corroded that their edges were crumbling.

Other hoards of North West Company tokens have been variously reported. One consisting of 14 pieces is currently in a western museum. Others have been excavated from the ruins of western forts, including two pieces shown by Steve Bibler at the October 28, 1954, meeting of the Seattle Coin Club, which were excavated from the ruins of Fort Vancouver.[6]

---

1 "The American Fur Trade," *Merchants' Magazine and Commercial Review,* New York, 1840, Vol. III, pp. 199-200.

2 Now in Manitoba, Canada.

3 Voyageur: Traveling (often by canoe) fur-gathering agent, woodsman, and trader who visited various remote sites. A voyageur is depicted as part of a standard reverse design on many Canadian silver dollars from the 1930s onward.

4 Thomas Wilson's collection was later purchased *en bloc* by William W.C. Wilson, of Montreal, whose cabinet was auctioned by Wayte Raymond in 1925; some of its rarities later were in the Norweb Collection sold in 1996 (the catalogue of which reprints biographies of both Wilsons).

5 Via a listing in *Rare Coin Review* No. 31, 1978, p. 11.

6 Fort Vancouver formed the subject for a U.S. commemorative half dollar in 1925; the fort is mentioned in passing in the present book in Chapter 11 under the account of the fate of the *S.S. Brother Jonathan.*

Cache of Kentucky Tokens

Put away: 1790s
Found: 1996
Treasure: "Kentucky" tokens

In June 1996 a small hoard of about 25 gem Mint State Kentucky tokens with lustrous red surfaces was found in England and sold to an American dealer.[1] Doubtless, these had remained in the British Isles since the time of their coinage, circa 1792, in Birmingham.

These tokens feature an obverse inscription that includes UNANIMITY IS THE STRENGTH OF SOCIETY and OUR CAUSE IS JUST. On the reverse is the legend E PLURIBUS UNUM and a pyramid made of 15 letters abbreviating states' names, with a K, for Kentucky, at the top. Hence the popular name of Kentucky token. Kentucky, the 15th state, was admitted to the Union on June 1, 1792. The 16th state, Tennessee, was admitted on June 1, 1796. Thus, it is presumed that the Kentucky tokens were minted sometime between the summer of 1792 and the summer of 1796. In the writer's view, few if any of these tokens ever circulated in America.

Such pieces are part of over a dozen different America-related conder tokens, a vast panorama of copper halfpenny-size token designs struck in the 1780s and 1790s to create varieties for collectors in England (there being no significantly developed numismatic activity in the United States at the time). Other conder tokens with American themes include Talbot, Allum & Lee cents of 1794-1795, the 1794 Franklin Press token, and several pieces relating to George Washington.

Walter Breen stated that Kentucky tokens, struck as part of the conder token series, "circulated widely along the Eastern Seaboard, while the floundering Philadelphia Mint's cents remained unfamiliar curiosities," certainly a different opinion of the history of this piece.[2] He further suggested that they were ordered from England by "New York or Philadelphia merchants."

An Old-Line Family's Treasure

Put away: Beginning in the 17th century
Disclosed but not distributed: In recent years
Treasure: Massachusetts silver coins

In the seventeenth century or early eighteenth century it is said that an old-line Massachusetts family saved the best part of 100 newly-minted examples of 1652-dated large-planchet Pine Tree shillings and some other Massachusetts silver coins. It is further said by two contributors to the present book,[3] that these pieces still exist today, are kept in a Boston safe deposit box, are very much appreciated by their owner for their historical and numismatic value, and that there are no immediate plans to distribute them.

To add to the collection the owner acquired in recent times through an eastern dealer a silver undated NE shilling and a Willow Tree shilling, two important rarities.

When fully described in numismatic publications in the future—as may happen—this magnificent holding will certainly enchant the growing community of specialists in the colonial series.

---

[1] Anthony J. Terranova, letter, October 15, 1996, stated that he had personally viewed this group.
[2] Breen, *Encyclopedia,* 1988, p. 129. See expanded information about conder tokens under Talbot, Allum & Lee tokens earlier in the present chapter.
[3] Neither of whom wanted to receive printed credit.

CHAPTER 2

Hidden Here and There

Introduction

Rare coin treasures are where you find them, and that can be just about anywhere! Over the years there have been many unusual places where valuable coins have been located, often as much by chance as by intention. However, as some of the accounts about "coinshooting" relate, some checking of old maps and other planning can increase the chance of success.

The finds in this chapter cover a wide range of coins and circumstances. Descriptions of hundreds more were encountered during research for the present book, but only those with a degree of numismatic information were among those selected for inclusion. It is truly amazing how many popular accounts in newspapers of hoards go on and on for paragraph after paragraph-and tell about the weather, the age and a brief biography of the person making the find, and just about everything else—and give no facts at all concerning the actual coins discovered! Is an "old cent" a common 1910 Lincoln cent or a rare cent of 1799? We may never know.

Mint Reports issued over a long period of years tell of half cents, large cents, early half dollars, gold coins, and other items that have been turned into the Treasury Department for redemption. It is amazing to note that these records indicate that only a few half cents (minted from 1793 to 1857) have ever been redeemed, that tens of millions of 1793-1857 large cents are still missing, as are untold millions of nickel, three-cent pieces, Liberty Seated coins, and other issues. Thus, the potential is immense.

Mrs. Rea's Birthday Present

Hidden: 1795
Found: By the 1860s
Treasure: 1795 half dimes

In 1795 a Roxbury, Massachusetts, lady named Rea is said to have received a "little hoard" of glittering new half dimes of this date as a birthday present. She kept these for many years—possibly until the early 1860s—at which time the hoard was sold to a numismatist, the identity of whom is not known today.

The quantity has been estimated at from a dozen or so up to 100 pieces. Specimens attributed to this lightly documented cache are of Valentine die varieties 4, 5, and 6, with most being V-4 or V-6.[1]

---

[1] A specimen (Valentine-2) appeared in W. Elliot Woodward's John F. McCoy Collection sale, May 1864, Lot 609. In later years Woodward suggested that the hoard may have been sold by Ms. Rea in the 1860s *or* 1870s, but the latter decade seems improbable given the sale of one in 1864 (how easy it is to forget!). See Breen, "A Survey of United States Coin Hoards," *The Numismatist,* January 1952, but information there differs greatly from what the same writer had to say in his, *Encyclopedia,* 1988, p. 276 ("about 100"; there the date of the find is given as 1880 and it is called the Wadsworth-Rea hoard; in his 1952 work the "Wadsworth" find is used to describe 1794 half dimes). Wadsworth-Rea nomenclature is also used in a commentary in Breen's half cent *Encyclopedia,* 1983, p. 38. Valentine attributions are to Daniel W. Valentine, *The United States Half Dimes,* American Numismatic Society, 1931.

An old mill as photographed in the nineteenth century, an ideal possibility for a hoard location.

The circumstances surrounding this little hoard are as mysterious as the answer as to what happened to all of the coins.

Judge Putnam's Souvenirs

Put away: 1864
Disclosed: 1885
Treasure: Half cents of 1855

In 1864 and again in 1868, 1871, and 1877, Judge J.P. Putnam of Boston journeyed to Philadelphia to participate in the annual Assay Commission ritual. Putnam was a numismatist and a personal friend of Roxbury (Massachusetts) dealer W. Elliot Woodward.[1] To participate in Woodward's November 1862 sale of "Selected Specimens from the American Portion of the Finotti Collection," the first major auction held by Woodward in New York City, Putnam made the trip from Boston to attend in person.[2] He was in good company in the sale room and must have visited with such numismatic luminaries as Charles I. Bushnell, Edward Cogan, Charles Betts, William Harvey Strobridge, and John F. McCoy, each of whom purchased lots in the same section of the auction.

Traveling in style in Massachusetts in the nineteenth century, quite probably as Judge Putnam might have done.

Under the Assay Commission procedure, the various mints (at the time these being Philadelphia, Carson City,[3] and San Francisco) set aside samples from quantities of silver and gold (but not copper) coins struck. These were sent to the Philadelphia Mint and reserved for the Assay Commission, which met early the following year to review the preceding year's precious-metal coinage. Thus, on Monday, February 8, 1864, the commission members gathered to review coins bearing the date 1863.[4]

On hand in 1864, by virtue of their offices, were Hon. Judge Cadwalader (judge of the U.S. District Court for the Eastern District of Pennsylvania), George A. Coffey (United States attorney for the same district), and William B. Thomas (collector of the Port of Pennsylvania). These men had served in meetings of earlier years as well. In addition, a group of officers were attended from the Mint itself: James C. Booth (melter and refiner), John G. Butler (chief coiner), Jacob R. Eckfeldt (assayer and numismatist), Henry R. Linderman (secretary of the Assay Commission and a numismatist), James B. Longacre (chief engraver), and Archibald McIntyre (treasurer).[5]

From the quantities of sample coins on hand, random pieces were selected by the commissioners. These were weighed to determine their compliance with coinage statutes. Some pieces were also assayed to determine their percentage of silver and gold (authorized at 90%) with 10% copper alloy.

Undoubtedly, Judge Putnam enjoyed being a part of the 1864 ceremony, for it was considered an honor to be named to the select group. Apparently, while he was there he sought to acquire some souvenirs of his visit, and obtained a few bright Uncirculated copper half cents bearing the date 1855. Coins of this denomination had not been made at the Mint since early 1857, and all supplies on hand had been melted shortly

---

1 Putnam-Woodward connection courtesy of Karl Moulton, letter, September 10, 1996, with enclosures.

2 This sale was originally scheduled to be held in September or October, 1862, but was delayed. The sale date of November 11-14, 1862, was pasted as a correction on the front page of the catalogue. The auction venue was the sale room of Messrs. Bangs, Merwin & Co., Irving Buildings, 594 and 596 Broadway. Among Putnam's purchases at the event were Lot 1596 (Boston Latin School medal displaying "rod with wings and serpents" on the obverse, silver), $1.75; and Lot 1598 (with motif of "book and pens crossed, 'The Gift of Franklin,'" etc., in silver), $1.50.

3 Coins were first struck in Carson City in 1870; first reviewed by the Assay Commission in 1871. In 1863 (the year for which coins were being reviewed by the Assay Commission in 1864) there were two active mints, Philadelphia and San Francisco.

4 Certain information is from Francis Pessolano-Filos, *The Assay Medals, the Assay Commissions, 1841, 1977,* pp. 155, 159, 162, and 168.

5 Several of these individuals are well known today in a numismatic context. Information about them can be found in the *Coin World Almanac, U.S. Mint and Coinage* (Don Taxay), and *American Numismatic Bibliographies* (Pete Smith), among other texts. Booth was one of the most talented individuals on the Mint staff and was primarily responsible for determining metallic compositions and proportions (including for the 1856 Flying Eagle cent). Eckfeldt was a long-time employee and a competent numismatist (and was associated with the Mint Cabinet over a long period of time). The rascally, but very intelligent Dr. Linderman would later serve as Mint director and would enjoy having restrikes and other special pieces made for his personal numismatic cabinet. James B. Longacre served as chief engraver at the Mint 1844-1869, passing away on New Year's day of the latter year.

afterward.[1] However, the Mint acted as a depot for citizens, banks, and others seeking to redeem the obsolete copper cents and half cents of years before, and, quite probably, someone had recently brought these sparkling little copper 1855 half cents to the facility. One of the numismatically interested people on the staff—Jacob R. Eckfeldt is a good candidate—set them aside, rather than consigning them to the melting pot.

Certainly, such inexpensive pieces would make nice mementos for friends back home in New England, Judge Putnam may have reasoned on that cold February 1864 day.

Nearly 20 years later, on December 16-18, 1885, W. Elliot Woodward offered for sale the A.W. Matthews Collection and other properties, to which certain coins from the former holdings of Putnam, now deceased, had been consigned.[2] Described as part of Lot 1761 and following offerings were these items:

> **Lot 1761:** 1855 [half cents] Bright red Uncirculated. In 1855 Judge J.P. Putnam, of Boston, was a member of the Mint Assay Commission; he bought these half cents from the Mint, and parted with them only just before his death. All are perfect, and nearly all are selected for fineness of impression, as well as other qualities. Another lot so fine probably does not exist. 10 pieces.
>
> **Lot 1762:** 1855 Another lot; of the same perfect quality.[3] 10 pieces.
>
> **Lot 1763:** 1855 Another lot from the same source and equally fine. 8 pieces.
>
> **Lot 1764:** 1855 Red Uncirculated. 6 pieces.
>
> **Lot 1765:** 1855 Perfectly Uncirculated, a handsome lot; one I think is a Proof impression. 10 pieces.
>
> **Lot 1766:** 1855 Very fine to red Uncirculated. 13 pieces.[4]
>
> **Lot 1767:** 1855 Very fine lot. 18 pieces.

The same sale continued with quantities of 1856 and 1857 half cents, including 19 Uncirculated examples of the last date of the denomination.

The number of gem Mint State 1855 half cents in the Putnam hoard was most certainly the sum of Lots 1761 through 1763—these being specifically cited as having been acquired by Putnam at the Mint. Using this total, the Putnam hoard would have amounted to 28 coins. If Lots 1764 through 1767 are added (although it is unclear if these were from Putnam's acquisition at the Mint), the total swells to 75.

A Sag Harbor Physician

Hidden: 1836
Found: 1880
Treasure: 1836 half dollars

It must have been a free-for-all among collectors on Long Island, New York, in 1880, by which time Capped Bust half dollars (minted 1807-1836) had long since disappeared from circulation. In fact, such pieces had not been generally seen since the early 1850s, when many if not most remaining pieces were melted down for bullion when the price of silver rose on international markets.

The story is told by this item in the *Evening Transcript,* August 20, 1880:[5]

> A gentleman of Southampton, Long Island, writes that a great deal of curiosity has been excited by the sudden appearance in circulation of a large number of silver half dollars, all bearing the date of 1836, and as bright as when they came from the Mint.
>
> The mystery is thus explained:
>
> An old resident of Sag Harbor, formerly well known as a practicing physician, but who for several years has led a comparatively secluded life, at the time of the panic of 1836 [*sic*] hoarded 1,500 half dollars of that date. He kept them in total disregard of interest or premium until the present time. He has now put this hoarded treasure into circulation.

Actually, it was the Panic of 1837, not the Panic of 1836, but in early 1837 (when by May 10 financial problems had increased to the point at which most leading eastern banks stopped paying out coins) anyone seeking a large quantity of silver coins might likely have found them to be dated 1836. At the time the half dollar was the largest currently minted silver coin of the country, silver dollars having been last minted

---

1 Those stored at the Mint were melted by spring 1857, per an account of Director James Ross Snowden in *A Description of Ancient and Modern Coins in the Cabinet of the Mint of the United States.* Philadelphia: J.B. Lippincott, 1860 (this excellent book was mostly researched and written by George Bull, who was then curator of the Mint Cabinet, and William Ewing DuBois).

2 Citation suggested by Bob Vail. Copy of Woodward's sale catalogue furnished by Karl Moulton.

3 Apparently Woodward had forgotten his immediately preceding comment, "Another lot so fine probably does not exist." Logic was never a major precept in auction catalogues of this era. Moreover, it took some modern-day digging in reference books to determine that Putnam was on the Assay Commission for the first time in 1864 and that he neither served in 1855 nor obtained his cents as a commission member at that time, as the Woodward catalogue seems to imply.

4 It is not clear whether all the coins in this and the following lot were Uncirculated, or whether some were in the grade of Very Fine.

5 As quoted in the *American Journal of Numismatics,* October 1880, p. 43.

in large numbers in calendar year 1804 (and bearing dates of 1803 and earlier). About 1,600 1836-dated Gobrecht silver dollars were made, but these were primarily placed into circulation in Pennsylvania and would not have been available in quantity to anyone seeking a bag or any other notable quantity of them at a bank in distant Long Island.

Today in the 1990s no 1836-dated half dollars are known with specific pedigrees to the Sag Harbor physician, but probably some of them did reach numismatic channels at the time of their release.

An Obscure "Celebrated" Find

Hidden or lost: Circa 1795
Found: Before 1884
Treasure: 1794 half dimes

In his catalogue of the Heman Ely Collection, January 8-10, 1884, W. Elliot Woodward offered Lot 356, a silver half dime dated 1794 described as a "splendid Proof, from the celebrated Wadsworth find in Hartford." What seems to be the same coin was subsequently offered as Lot 897 of Woodward's December 16-19, 1885, sale of the A.W. Matthews Collection.

However celebrated the Wadsworth find may have been to Woodward and to his knowing readers in 1884, little else has been heard of it in numismatic circles. Certainly, the find could not have been acclaimed solely for this solitary 1794 half dime. Thus, it must have contained other notable pieces. Wadsworth is a well-known Hartford surname, and the Wadsworth Athenaeum is one of the city's leading institutions.

Wadsworth Athenaeum in Hartford as shown in a nineteenth-century engraving.

In 1988 Walter Breen suggested that about 15 Mint State 1794 half dimes were saved "as first of their kind," but there is no mention of the Wadsworth hoard in reference to this date. Instead, the Wadsworth name is used for a group of *1795* half dimes (see "Ms. Rea's Birthday Present" above).[1]

It is worth noting that any cache of 1794-dated half dimes could not have been secreted earlier than 1795, for that is the year that this denomination was first struck at the Mint (those made early in the year were from dies dated 1794).

The Ill-Fated Donner Party

Hidden: 1846-1847
Found: 1891
Treasure: Silver coins

Seeking the Fastest Route West

One of the most chilling (literally) and gruesome accounts of western migration is that of the Donner Party, stranded in the high Sierras near the California-Nevada border.[2] In spring 1846 a group of 29 adven-

[1] Citation from Bob Vail. Also see Walter H. Breen, "Survey of American Coin Hoards," *The Numismatist,* January 1952; Breen, *Encyclopedia,* 1988, p. 276.

[2] Adapted from several sources, especially and extensively H.H. Bancroft, *The History of California,* Vol. V, Chapter XX; the numismatic portion and inventory are from Philip W. Whiteley, "Coin Find Reveals Pioneer Money Usages," *The Numismatist,* August 1963. Dr. Whiteley is often remembered for assembling a particularly notable set of 1900-1901 Lesher "dollars" (not related to the Donner situation) which was later sold to Abe Kosoff, the author, and then to William Henderson.

turous people gathered at Springfield, Illinois, to plan a trip by wagon westward to the Pacific Coast. This group, the Reed-Donner Party, would later be joined by others to form the Donner Party, of which more will be said.

At the time, yellow metal had not yet been discovered on the American River, and the Gold Rush was a couple of years away. Still, California represented a land of opportunity for many hundreds easterners who in the 1840s sought to better their lives, including perhaps as many as 500 who came to California in 1846 by land through the high Sierra Nevada mountains, the "Truckee route" through Nevada.[1] Many others went to north to the Oregon Territory and other points in the Pacific Northwest.

Typically, adventurers would form in wagon trains at a jumping-off spot near the Mississippi River. The Donner Party chose Independence, Missouri, the most popular point of assembly before the journey west. From May to July, 1846, about 2,000 emigrants left Independence to take various routes west. For mutual protection and convenience, the travelers assembled into large groups, chose a leader, and made other communal arrangements. The name of the leader was assigned to each group, such as the Boggs, Cooper, Donner, Jacob, and Ritchie parties, among numerous others. In such wagon caravans family groups usually remained together, but sometimes loners would switch from one party to another.

At the time the routes to the West—especially to California—were uncertain, poorly marked, and fraught with hazards. Many discussions were held as to which way was the fastest and, to a lesser extent, which route offered the most safety. There was no one main way to go. The Donner Party was convinced it would save several hundred miles by taking a divergent trail at the so-called Hastings Cutoff, a route that had been partially explored by John Frémont years earlier, but whose characteristics were not completely known. Bancroft wrote that "Hastings, in his partisan zeal, supported by the proprietors of [Fort Bridger in Wyoming] for their own interests, exaggerated the advantages and underrated the difficulties of the new route; but though not a very wise counselor in such matters, he doubtless acted according to his judgment honestly."

The sandy and alkali plain areas in Utah and Ne-

Wagon-train party of emigrants to California shown in the Rocky Mountains, apparently in the area before the Great American Desert (as it was often called) began. The Donner Party traveled under similar circumstances. Coins were carried aboard the wagons, but were often hidden to prevent embezzlement by fellow travelers or, worse, capture by marauding bandits or Indians.

[1] Bancroft, p. 526, notes that he located the names of about 200 male immigrants and supposed that there may have been another hundred, plus families, for the trans-Sierra route circa 1845-1848; this number is lower than the many thousands noted in some overviews of the subject. Many others took alternate routes. After the discovery of gold, emigration west became almost continuous and numbers reached into the many thousands.

vada—known as the Great American Desert—were particularly barren, desolate, and hostile, but this was usually learned of only when passing through them. In 1846 there were no reliable guides for emigrants across those trackless wastelands. Even if there had been, not many eager travelers would have paid attention.

Guided personally by Hastings, the Harlan and Young parties preceded the Donner Party across the vast empty stretches on the way to California, encountered many problems, lost much livestock in the Great Salt Lake desert country, but succeeded in crossing the Sierra Nevadas in late 1846.

Composition of the Donner Party

On July 20, 1846, under George Donner, a party of 87 people formed a group at Little Sandy stream. In the Donner Party train of ox-drawn covered wagons were 36 men, 21 women, and 30 children, the latter including five infants. The travelers were composed of the members of four families surnamed Green, Donner, Graves, and Murphy. Their origins were various and included members of the Reed-Donner Party from Springfield, Illinois; 10 from Keokuk, Iowa; and others.

Important to the present account, the caravan included Franklin W. Graves, his wife Elizabeth, sons William C., Jonathan B. (age 7) and Franklin, Jr. (age 5), daughters Mary A., Eleanor, Lovina, Nancy (age 9), and Elizabeth (infant), his son-in-law Jay Fosdick and his wife Sarah (née Graves). Together with a fellow named John Snyder, the 12 members of the Graves clan had come from Marshall County, Illinois.

The backgrounds of the Donner Party members were varied and included those of American, Irish, and German extraction and of such religious inclinations as Catholic, Mormon, and Protestant. Their economic status ranged from rich—in the case of George Donner who took with him a stock of merchandise to sell when he reached California and, apparently, quite a bit of money—to poor, which characterized the majority of the travelers. All shared the hope that California would be the Promised Land.

Difficulties Along the Route

On July 28, 1846, the Donner Party set out for the West, only a few days behind a party guided by Hastings. Soon after their departure, they received a letter from Hastings, who advised that great difficulties had been encountered in the Weber Cañon, and that another route should be taken.

Seeking to learn more, the party dispatched James Reed and two others to catch up with Hastings. This took a week or more, after which the Donner group continued on another trail. The new way proved to be very difficult, and it was not until early September that Great Salt Lake was reached. The season was becoming late. On the 3rd of the month the first casualty occurred when Luke Halloran, who had come from Missouri, died of consumption at the southern reaches of the lake.

From September 9 through 15 the Donner Party traveled through the alkali flats and desert areas, headed in a northwest direction. With virtually no grass and no untainted water, many of the cattle perished. One family lost all of its oxen. Wagons had to be abandoned for the lack of motive power.[1]

Finally, a clear stream—a part of the headwaters of the Humboldt River—was reached. However, food and other provisions were seriously short, and two of the party—William McCutchen and Charles T. Stanton—volunteered to ride ahead on horses to obtain relief. With cold weather approaching and the trail difficult, this was a long shot, but in the absence of any other ideas it was deemed best. Increasingly, those remaining in the Donner Party realized they were in great danger.

Around the end of September, the group found the old emigrant trail along the Humboldt, and began following it westward, down the river and toward the Sierra Nevada range.[2] On October 5, James F. Reed (of Springfield, an organizer of the original Reed-Donner Party) became involved in a violent argument with fellow traveler John Snyder and killed him, which led to Reed's expulsion from the remaining group. Reed went ahead, taking with him Walter Herron, also from Springfield, in the hope of finding some provisions to bring back to his wife and children, who stayed with the party.

On October 12, Indians stole 21 head of cattle. By this time, several families had neither oxen nor cattle and were plodding westward on foot. Hardcoop, a Belgian immigrant in the party, became sick and was left behind to die. Wolfinger, one of several Germans in the group, also was abandoned, under circumstances suggesting foul play on the part of his fellow countrymen.

---

[1] This happened to numerous travelers on other routes as well. It was not unusual for westward emigrants to burn their abandoned wagons, so as not to help "competitors" who might otherwise have an easier trip to California, but there is no record of the Donner Party doing this.

[2] The Oregon Trail, most of which was to the north of the several routes followed by emigrants by land to California, was used by several thousand travelers during the 1842-1845 years. Its dangers were better recognized than were those of the southern paths to the Pacific Coast.

On October 19, advance man Stanton returned to the Donner Party, having gone ahead to Sutter's Fort near Sacramento, California, an outpost established in 1839 by John Sutter, a Swiss. His fort included shops for provisions and repairs, and serviced the surrounding agricultural industry. Stanton, accompanied by two California Indians, Luis and Salvador, brought seven mules, five of which, laden with flour and other provisions, were a great help. McCutchen, who had gone with Stanton, became ill and remained in California. Stanton's return to the distressed Donner Party was all the more remarkable and altruistic in that he had no family members in the group.

In the region of what is now Reno, Nevada, the travelers stopped for several days to rest. On October 23, the journey westward was resumed. Within the week they arrived at a lake in the Truckee region. Snow was falling, and at higher elevations the accumulation reached several feet. Obviously, travel across the Sierras was now impossible.

For the next several weeks the party members were in chaos. Some tried to set out on their own through the snowy mountains, only to meet with failure and return to camp. Most of the remaining cattle and oxen strayed. Meanwhile, a week-long storm brought an estimated 10 feet of snow to the areas of higher elevation, rendering impossible any escape from the area. With little food and only primitive shelter, the situation went from bad to worse. By February 19, 1847, when a small relief party reached the camp, many had died, and the remains of some had been eaten by the survivors. The leather shoelaces from a pair of boots had furnished New Year's dinner for some.

In the spring, several other relief parties set out from California to seek the survivors. One group of nine men left on April 13 under the charge of William Fallon and reached the Donner Party site on the 17th As an inducement, the group had been promised half of the value of anything that could be saved. Fallon eagerly looked forward to divvying the large amount of money that George Donner was reported to have with him. Upon arrival, he found that Donner had died from privation, and that Mrs. Donner had been killed, apparently by Louis Keseberg, who was said to have stolen her money. Keseberg,[1] when threatened with being hanged, surrendered some coins that he claimed Mrs. Donner had given him to care for on behalf of her children.

By the spring of 1847, of the 87 people originally in the Donner Party, 22 men, five women, and 12 children—or a total of 39-had died. Later, the remains of those who could be located were given burials. Their

Typical camp of emigrants on the way to make a new life in the American West.

[1] Keseberg had come to America from Germany two years earlier. His wife Philipine and their two children, Louis, Jr., and Ada, were also traveling with the Donner Party. Keseberg later went to trial. Bancroft, pp. 541-543, discussed the alleged murder in detail, citing oft-repeated and probably exaggerated tales of Keseberg having a thirst for human blood, eating human flesh when beef was still available, etc., and concludes that this unfortunate incident served as the focal point for writers who wanted to dramatize even further the hardships of the Donner Party. Although the truth will never be known, Bancroft stated it was his view that Keseberg was not guilty.

campsite came to be known as Donner Lake and the nearby gap in the mountains as Donner Pass.

Many Years Later

In 1891, Edward Reynolds, a prospector from Sierra Valley, was poking around the Donner Lake area when he found a handful of dollar-size silver coins. Digging in the earth, he found many more pieces. Seeking to return at a later date, he reburied the treasure and joined several other miners with whom he was exploring and went back to Truckee. Later, he and a friend returned and dug up the cache of silver coins amounting to about $146 in face value.

It was subsequently determined that the pieces had been carefully hidden in holes bored into the undersides of cleats mounted on the floor of the wagon of Elizabeth (Mrs. Franklin W.) Graves, who, realizing that she might never cross the Sierras, took the coins from the wagon and buried them. By this time the remains of her husband had been consumed as food by the survivors. Mrs. Graves, too, would die.

An inventory of the coins revealed these pieces (per published listing):

Argentina 8 reals: 1835.
Bolivian 8 reals: 1836.
French "dollar" with Louis Phillippe portrait.
French 5-franc pieces of the Republic: year 8 • year 11 (2 pieces) • year 13.
French 5-franc pieces: 1806 • 1808 (3) • 1809 • 1811 • 1812 (10) •1814 (2) • 1816 • 1818 • 1819 • 1820 • 1822 (2) • 1823 • 1824 • 1825 • 1827 (2) • 1828 • 1829 (2) • 1831 (3) • 1832 (2) • 1833 (3) • 1834 (2) • 1837 • 1838 (2) • 1839 • 1840 • 1841 (2) • 1844.
Mexico City silver 8 reals: 1805 • 1810 (2) • 1812 • 1821 • 1826 • 1827 • 1828 (2) • 1830 • 1831 (2) • 1832 (3) • 1833 • 1834 (4) • 1835 (3) • 1836 (4) • 1837 (3) • 1838 (3) • 1839 (3) • 1840 (3) • 1841 (5) • 1832 (4) • 1843 (2) • 1844 • 1845 (2) • additional coin, date not completely readable, but from the 1830s.
Saxony 5 marks: 1835.
Spanish silver 4 reals: 1800 • 1805.[1]
United States half dollars: 1810 • 1813 • 1815 • 1817 • 1818 (3) • 1822 (2) • 1823 (2) • 1824 (2) • 1825 (2) • 1826 (3) • 1827 (2) • 1828 • 1829 (6) • 1830 (6) • 1831 • 1832 (6) • 1833 (3) • 1834 (2) • 1835 (3) • 1836 (4) • 1837 (4) • 1838 (2) • 1839 (3) • 1840 • 1841 (3) • 1842 (3) • 1843 (4).

From a numismatic viewpoint today, the coins do not appear to represent a cross-section of pieces in circulation in America circa 1845 (the latest date on a coin). Apparently, it was desired to acquire large denomination silver pieces, perhaps to facilitate counting and handling. For some reason, no silver dollars were included, although they actively circulated in the early 1840s. Perhaps the source(s) for the coins had none on hand. Neither French 5-franc nor Mexican 8-real coins were in active circulation to any extent, but some were stored in banks. Most popular in use in general commerce and trade were Spanish-American two-real silver coins worth about 25¢.

Others in the Donner Party had coins, including the group's unfortunate leader, but no description of them has been located.

The Collins Find

Hidden or lost: 1828
Found: By 1894
Treasure: 1828 half cents

Many Half Cents

In his catalogue of the Allison W. Jackman Collection, June 28-29, 1918, Philadelphia dealer Henry Chapman inserted this commentary after Lot 879, a rare *1811* half cent, to shed light on the ready availability in Uncirculated grade of 1828-dated half cents, the variety with 13 obverse stars:

> This [1811] coin was discovered in 1884, being brought by an old colored woman of Alexandria, Va., to Mr. Benjamin H. Collins of Washington, to whom she stated she had a bag of them! He, thinking there was not any mistake about the hoard, sold it [*i.e.*, the 1811] to S.H. & H. Chapman for $3! with the remark, "How many more will you take?"
>
> We said the lot.
>
> The woman subsequently brought him the bag, but to his astonishment they were all 1828 13 stars! and it has always been a mystery to me that an 1811 equally fine as the 1828s should have been in with the later date, and that her pick at random should have alighted on the only 1811 in the bag! It was subsequently sold in the Warner Sale, $67, and there bought by Mr. Jackman.

How Many Coins Were There?

The preceding account has a number of inaccuracies and requires some amplification and modification including the following:

B.H. Collins of Washington, D.C., specialized in early copper coins, especially cents, and was known for the fine specimens he handled including several

[1] Probably actually Spanish-American coins such as from the Mexico City Mint.

notable pieces imported from Europe. However, in 1884 he was an employee of the Treasury Department. It was not until the 1890s that he became a rare coin dealer. Thus, the date of the hoard is moved up a decade to 1894. The 1811 half cent was sold by Collins to Chapman for $18, not $3. Further, the Warner and Jackman specimens were two different coins. The number of 1828 half cents in the hoard was stated to be 50 by Collins in a conversation with John F. Jones in December 1899.

It is not known how many 1828 13-stars half cents were in the Collins Find, and the figure of 50 may be correct, but probably is not. Many more than that are known today. In 1988 Walter Breen commented that the hoard "apparently originally numbered 1,000; as late as 1955 a remnant containing several hundred pieces was in the holdings of F.C.C. Boyd."[1]

Later Distribution

In confirmation of the preceding, in 1996 John J. Ford, Jr., stated that many of these pieces were owned by David U. Proskey, who sold them to Boyd along with other material. In the early 1950s about 200 to 300 bright red coins were sold by Boyd to New Netherlands Coin Co.[2]

Fact-finding concerning hoards is never an easy task, and absolute definition is often impossible.

The typical Collins Find specimen seen today is bright orange-red with spotting.[3]

The Woodpile Find

Hidden: 1862 or later
Found: February 6, 1900
Treasure: Large cents and other coins

On February 6, 1900, George Norwood of Dalton, Michigan, found a "rare collection of old coins, presumably stolen," and believed to be quite valuable. The pieces had been concealed in a woodpile in a stand of trees next to the C.K. & S. Railway. The pile had been stacked in 1899, and it was presumed that the pieces were hidden at that time, perhaps "the loot of some distant robbery."[4]

Dr. George F. Heath, founder (in 1888) and editor of *The Numismatist,* learned of the find and passed the information along to George W. Rice, a Detroit collector who today is best remembered for his unprecedented hoard of 756 specimens of the famous 1856 Flying Eagle cent (dispersed into the market in 1911). For many years Rice stood ready to buy from collectors, dealers, and at auction any example of this coin in any grade. Rice is noticed in Chapter 19, "Dealer and Collector Hoards," in the present work.

An inspection of the woodpile find by Rice revealed these coins:[5]

1803 U.S. copper cent.
14 various U.S. cents 1819 to 1854.
92 Canadian coppers (presumably tokens) 1844-1862.
Prince Edward Island token, 1857.
English coin dated 1822, not otherwise described.
German pfennig, not described.
Chinese cash, one specimen, not described.
Netherlands coin, not described.
Two coins worn smooth, not described.

Rice summarized that there was "a total of 119 pieces, all in ordinary condition from Fair to Good, which could be duplicated for about $2.50."

Thus, upon inspection the group, rather than being a "rare collection of old coins," was instead a miscella-

---

1 Boyd's obituary, by Elston G. Bradfield, appeared in *The Numismatist,* October 1958, p. 1180. Boyd died on September 7, 1958, at the age of 71. The notice observed that he had been an executive of the Union News Company (a subsidiary of the American News Co.). Further, "One of America's prominent numismatists, Boyd was Life Member No. 5 of the American Numismatic Association and a fellow and benefactor of the American Numismatic Society.... In 1937 and 1938 he was an appraiser of the Col. Green Collection. At one time he owned an outstanding collection of United States coins, territorial and pioneer gold coins, tokens, medals, and paper money.... Several years ago most of his collection was sold at auction, although most of his pattern coins were disposed of through private sales. Many of the latter found their way into the King Farouk Collection." In actuality, "several years ago" was in 1945 and 1946 when the Numismatic Gallery (Abe Kosoff and Abner Kreisberg) auctioned Boyd's holdings under the title of "The World's Greatest Collection." The same dealer duo bought many of his other coins—including patterns—privately and sold them to King Farouk of Egypt, who in the 1940s was the best customer of the firm.

2 Conversation with the author, June 27, 1996.

3 Walter H. Breen, "Survey of American Coin Hoards," *The Numismatist,* January 1952, modified by his comments in the same journal, October 1952, p. 1010 (pointing out inaccuracies in the Chapman account, this new information having been gained by Breen from old-time numismatist John F. Jones, who had known and visited Collins); Breen, *Encyclopedia,* 1988, p. 169.

4 George F. Heath, "Editorial," *The Numismatist,* February 1900, p. 62.

5 George F. Heath, "Editorial," *The Numismatist,* March 1900, p. 89.

neous accumulation presumably gathered by 1862 and for some unknown reason removed to a woodpile in 1899. Quite possibly the coins were brought to Michigan from Canada—not distant from the place of discovery—as there were few copper-nickel cents, but quite a few large copper cents. In 1862 there was a glut of United States copper cents north of the border.

Fooling an English Dealer

Exported to England:
18th and 19th centuries
Found: Early 1900s
Treasure: Rare early copper coins

In the late eighteenth and early nineteenth centuries quite a few United States coins emigrated to England as souvenirs in the pockets of returning travelers and as specimens desired by British numismatists who collected coins of the present and former British colonies.

A 1905 newspaper account told of a New York City coin dealer, name not disclosed, who visited a well-known London dealer, name also not given, who "thoroughly versed as he is in every phase of the old coin business, still he is not well up on American rare coin values" Quite possibly, the London dealer had acquired some old "American souvenirs" that in the meantime had acquired significant numismatic value:[1]

> The English dealer brought out about 25 specimens of early American copper coins, the greater part of them dating from 1793 to 1800. They were all in superb condition, and every one of them was a rare variety.[2]

The story went on to relate that the Englishman asked $75 for the lot, which figure was eagerly accepted. Upon returning to the United States the other dealer "in less than a month disposed of the whole lot, realizing a total profit of nearly $1,500." Upon learning of this, his British counterpart advised the American dealer never to darken his doorway again.

The Chapman Hoard of Half Cents

Hidden or lost: 1806
Found: Circa 1906
Treasure: 1806 half cents

Sometime around 1906 Philadelphia dealer Henry Chapman found a hoard of 1806 half cents (the variety today known as Breen-4, Cohen-4) variously estimated to contain from about 200 pieces up to "many hundreds."

Most of these seen today have generous areas of original mint red, but are spotted. Examples are always weakly struck at the upper part of the wreath.[3]

Cornerstone of the Bank of the U.S.

Sealed: 1824
Opened: Circa 1912
Treasure: Various mementos

A Rare Gold Medal

On April 24, 1990, R.P. Durkin & Co. offered for sale the contents of the cornerstone of the Boston branch of the Bank of the United States, which had been chartered in Philadelphia in 1816. The stone had been opened years earlier, about 1912.

Encased in a flat glass bottle was an engraved silver plaque marking the laying of the stone on July 4, 1824, "being the 48th anniversary of American Indepen-

[1] From an account, "Europe Hunting Place For Coins," in the *Boston Sunday Herald,* April 30, 1905, furnished by David Sundman, Littleton Coin Co.

[2] It seems unlikely that the group was comprised entirely of rarities; such is the nature of popular accounts in newspapers.

[3] Breen, *Encyclopedia,* 1988, pp. 165-166, *Henry Chapman* and the 200 estimate. Alternatively, Breen's half cent *Encyclopedia,* 1983, p. 276, places the number as "many hundreds"; there as *Chapman brothers.*

dence," and the inscription: "This Building erected by order of the Parent Bank for accommodation of its Office of Discount Deposit in this City of Boston A.D. 1824." The sum of $1,500,000 had been appropriated for the conduct of the branch.

Other contents included a biography of Israel Putnam by S. Swett, a certificate of membership in the Bunker Hill Monument Association and three battle maps of the skirmish there, various marine documents, and, important to the present text, a medallion of James Otis, described as weighing 11.9 grams and being struck in pure gold. Otis, a Boston lawyer, had argued against the policies of tyrant King George III.

Cape Cod Hoard

In the same auction sale, but from a different source, were a 1787 Massachusetts cent and United States large cents of 1816 and 1818, these apparently "part of a small hoard of coins found in a bag on Cape Cod," and in company with a group of 14 early Swedish coins described as: "Christian I 1634; Charles IV, 1667 and 1668; Christian V 1670; Charles XII 1715; Adolphus Frederick 1763; 1/2 shilling of Charles XIV of 1822." These appeared as Lots 109 and 110 in the auction.

A Curious Find In Arizona

Hidden: 19th century
Found: 1924
Treasure: Political tokens, etc.

Any numismatist who has studied American monetary history knows that in old-time Arizona, citizens and strangers liked "hard money," and that money was silver or gold. Copper coins were not in circulation until late in the nineteenth century, and even then they were not plentiful. Thus, this 1924 account is rather curious:[1]

> Ted Spencer, of the First National Bank of Flagstaff, has a treasure of 80 copper coins, found by a Mexican highway laborer under a large rock. The containing leather sack was almost rotted away. One of the coins, bearing the head of George I of England, is dated 1723. The others are mainly of American manufacture, running down to 1850, some of them apparently struck for political purposes and others the issue of private firms, who used them as tokens.

The "Bank Holiday" and Related Hoards

Hidden: 19th century
Found: 1930s
Treasure: 1833 and 1835 half cents, 1853 cents

Half Cents Found

In the 1930s the Guttag Brothers, New York City securities brokers and rare coin dealers, discovered a large hoard of 1833 half cents. During the same era, dealer Elmer Sears found a hoard of 1835 half cents, "probably a bag of 1,000 pieces, possibly more than that. They were in spotty mint red Uncirculated state."[2] This was an era in which times were hard, the Depression was pervasive, and long-held cash assets were often liquidated, including some possibly from bank reserves (see below).

The total for both half cent dates was in the thousands of coins. Most were bright red, usually with some tiny black flecks. During the 1930s these sold for about 25¢ each on the market. In the mid-1950s the remainder coins were distributed in New York and sold for several dollars apiece. Some of the 1833 half cents

---

1 Adapted from an account in the *El Paso* (Texas) *Herald* reprinted in *The Numismatist*, November 1924, p. 709, "Old Coins Found at Flagstaff, Ariz." Someone numismatically knowledgeable must have examined the coins, for the copper issues of George I were marked "GEORGIUS" with no Roman numeral suffix I, as it was not known that there would be later Georges on the throne (later issues under different reigns were noted as II and III). Although copper coins did not circulate widely there in the early days, the Arizona Territory was an important producer of copper ore.

2 Walter Breen, half cent *Encyclopedia*, 1983, p. 338.

were prooflike and were offered as Proofs. For several years thereafter, half cents of these two dates were fairly plentiful in dealers' stocks, but with the great boom in numismatics that took place in the 1960s, most became widely scattered.[1]

A Keg of 1853 Cents?

Walter Breen commented that certain large cents of the 1850s are common in numismatic circles because of caches which came to light in this era:[2] "Some of these hoards appear to have come from banks' cash reserves during the 1933 Bank Holiday, when examinations of bank vault assets yielded quantities of obsolete coins. There may have been a full keg or more of 1853 cents, which would mean at least a ballpark figure of about 14,000 coins."

Cent varieties mentioned as coming from these hoards include 1850 Newcomb-7, 1851 N-2, 1852 N-3, 1853 N-25, 1855 N-5, and 1856 N-14.

A.C. Gies, Bigger than Life

Put away: Circa 1854
Dispersed: Circa 1935
Treasure: Uncirculated 1854 half cents

Fantastic Holdings

August C. Gies, a jeweler and numismatist of Pittsburgh, Pennsylvania, was said to be a hoarder *par excellence,* and it is has been related that he had bank-wrapped rolls of most bronze, nickel, and silver coins after about 1900. And, apparently, he did have some, but they were nearly all of smaller denominations. As an example of a story that grew in the telling, he is traditionally assigned the ownership of one roll each of such rarities as the 1901-S and 1913-S quarter dollars. After a few more retellings he was said to have quantities of just about *everything.*[3] However, John J. Ford, Jr., who in the early 1940s personally worked with many of the Gies coins, later stated that accounts of Gies putting away rare rolls of higher denominations were "pure hogwash."[4]

Gies was born on January 29, 1855, and spent his life in the Pittsburgh area. In 1879 he moved to East Liberty and gained employment with a jeweler. In 1883 he opened his own jewelry business, and remained active in the trade until 1941. Along the way he collected coins and, as noted, saved some bank-wrapped rolls of coins of smaller denominations. Gies died in 1944.

Half Cents of 1854

Circa 1935, A.C. Gies happened upon a marvelous group of 1,000 half cents dated 1854, each coin being a bright orange-red, typically with some minor spotting. The 1930s seemed to be a good decade for finding such things, as other half cents came to light elsewhere. These 1854 half cents were distributed in numismatic channels in due course and provide the source for most pieces seen today.

In 1941, as his first job when working for Joe and Morton Stack, young John J. Ford, Jr., had to catalogue cents and other coins from the Gies holdings. Thomas L. Elder may have been involved in the transaction as well. At the time Ford was given the opportunity to buy some bright red 1854 half cents for $1 each, which he did. These several coins were consigned by Ford to the Bowers and Ruddy Galleries auction of the Seller Collection and other properties in 1980 and realized between $2,000 and $3,200 apiece, not a bad investment return![5]

---

[1] Breen, *Encyclopedia,* 1988, p. 171; also personal recollection of author concerning the availability of the coins in the 1950s.

[2] *Ibid.,* p. 211.

[3] Breen, *Encyclopedia,* 1988, spread the word about Gies. On p. 323 he related concerning Barber dimes that he "obtained rolls of all of them;" on p. 358 he credited Gies with having rolls of all Barber quarter dollars; on p. 410 he said the same thing about Barber halves. William Pukall and Wayte Raymond were also credited with having most or all Barber coins in roll form, also a highly unlikely scenario.

[4] Ford, conversation with the author, June 27, 1996; Ford worked for Stack's, New York City, circa 1941-1942 and saw the Gies coins at that time.

[5] Breen, *Encyclopedia,* 1988, p. 173; related information is in Breen's half cent *Encyclopedia,* p. 450. John J. Ford, Jr., conversation, June 27, 1996. Seller Collection, March 1980, lots 3056-3059, there stated to have been from Thomas L. Elder, and illustrated on the cover of the sale catalogue. Additional 1854 half cents of somewhat lesser quality, but from the Ford holdings, appeared in the Bowers and Ruddy sale of the Park Forest Collection and other consignments, October 1980, lots 2061-2064.

The Boston Hoard of Half Cents

Hidden or lost: 1800s
Found: Circa 1935-1937
Treasure: 1800 half cents

In the 1930s a hoard of several dozen or more 1800 half cents (the variety known today as Breen-1b, Cohen-1) turned up in Boston. Specimens from this holding display mint red, but are usually spotted. Estimates of 30 to 100 pieces have reached print. Where had they been hidden? Who found them? No one knows.

Other 1800-dated half cents of the same variety, typically with lustrous brown surfaces, are said to have come from another hoard discovered in New England. This other cache is believed to have been found before 1910 and to have contained "hundreds of pieces."[1]

A Little Bag in an Old Safe

Hidden: 1855
Found: 1940s
Treasure: 1855 half cents

Long Hidden Coins

This is another story about half cents, seemingly an ideal denomination for hoarding purposes. No doubt the low face value of such pieces was a factor in their having been put away—and once put away, not readily spent. There was little temptation to cash in a handful. Thanks to such hoards, numismatists today can avail themselves of attractive Mint State examples of several different varieties of half cents. This is another story of such a find:

In the 1940s Charles French, a hobby shop operator and rare coin dealer in Troy, New York, purchased a small cloth bag containing 500 bright red half cents, each bearing the date 1855. The coins had been found in a small metal safe of the type painted black with a scene on the front, as were commonly used in the late nineteenth and early twentieth centuries.

Fearing a reduction in their numismatic market value, French said little about the coins at the time, but parceled them out to clients and, in small groups to dealers. By about 1960 most or all were gone.[2]

Mr. and Mrs. French

Charlie and Arline French are still remembered today by old timers in numismatics. Charlie, who had changed his surname from Lehrenkraus (in the 1930s a few coin leaflets were issued under this name by him), did business from a basement-level hobby shop in Troy, typically trading as "A. French" or "French's." Probably his sales of model airplanes, stamp kits, and other hobby supplies paid the rent and heating bills, while his first love, coins, occupied most of his attention.

Charlie and Arline conducted 113 auctions from 1939 to 1976. Now and then their catalogues turn up today, although they are not common as circulation was small and relatively few were saved. They are rather simple affairs, but those of most of their competitors in the 1950s were rather light reading as well.[3] A typical listing for a certain half dollar might be something like "1879 Proof."

I recall attending several of their sales and, having looked at the lots beforehand, selecting some nice pieces in competition with a small roomful of bidders. These events were staged in the glory days of the Empire State Numismatic Association, which held small conventions—more like informal gatherings-each year. Such coin—collecting greats as Fiore Pipito, John

---

1 Breen, *Encyclopedia,* 1988, pp. 165-166. Breen, half cent *Encyclopedia,* 1983, p. 201, gives the find date as "sometime between 1935 and 1937" and notes that estimated quantities have ranged from 30 to 100 pieces; further, "there was an earlier (before 1910?) hoard of darker specimens, variously graded as About Uncirculated or brown Uncirculated; this must have included hundreds of pieces." Some mentions of hoards in the Breen half cent *Encyclopedia* (for example, the 1796 With Pole, p. 162; the 1804 B-7 Spiked Chin, p. 245; 1804 B-11, p. 252, etc.) are highly inferential; Breen suggests that just because multiple Mint State specimens exist today, "there may have been a small hoard" (cf. p. 245). The present book omits such supposed hoards.

2 Charles French, conversation with author.

3 Detailed, numismatically authoritative cataloguing of United States coins presented at auction had its beginning with the 1952 American Numismatic Association Convention sale, in the portion written by John J. Ford, Jr., of New Netherlands Coin Co.

Jay Pittman, Charles W. Foster,[1] Jonah Shapiro, Jake Cheris, Jasper Robertson,[2] Dave Nethaway, and Ken Sartoris—to give just a short list—were on hand, and all had a good time. Among the "youngsters" often attending were Jim Ruddy, Bill Vanco, Les Zeller, and the present writer.

Old-Time Troy

Troy was and is a town with many traditions. Numerous old commercial buildings remain. It requires but little imagination for the traveler to envision what the city must have been like in the nineteenth century when Troy was one of the leading manufacturing centers of the state, horses were clip-clopping with their carts down the streets, and Hudson River steamers were discharging passengers and cargo from New York City.

Fortunately for numismatic posterity, several manufacturers and tradesmen advertised via copper tokens, these being highly collectible today. Bucklin's Interest Tables, as an example, were contrived by Troy schoolteacher Isaac B. Bucklin, who decided that advertising their availability via copper tokens would be worthwhile. The N. Starbuck & Son machine shop also put out tokens as did the dry goods firm of Carpenter & Mosher. More than is the case for tokens from any other city of the 1830s and 1840s, nearly all with a Troy imprint were made from amateurishly-cut dies and were crudely struck. From a collecting viewpoint, such naiveté makes them especially interesting to study today. By the 1940s and 1950s such pieces had for the most part long since disappeared, but now and then a local resident would bring a handful of old tokens, large cents, and other coins into Charlie French's shop. It is not difficult to imagine that the safe containing the sparkling little 1855 half cents that he bought had rested comfortably in some dusty old attic or room in Troy for the best part of a century.

Charlie French's best retail customer was Ellis H. Robison, who lived locally and conducted a drug wholesaling firm. Robison had all of his purchases checked by French, who had to put his stamp of approval on each. His goal was to acquire one each of the various coins listed in the *Guide Book,* and he certainly gave it a good try. Later, the Robison collection was auctioned by Stack's.

Each month for *Hobbies* magazine Charlie French conducted a question and answer column. In 1967 some of this material was incorporated into the *American Guide to U.S. Coins,* a paperback distributed in bookstores.

Hidden in an Old Woodstove

Lost: Early 20th century
Found: 1954
Treasure: Gold and silver coins

Bob Ross tells of an interesting treasure that started him in the hobby of numismatics:[3]

> The year was 1954. The location was in my pool room, which I had just opened in Glasgow, Kentucky.
>
> A man walked in and wanted to sell some gold and silver coins to me. They all looked like they were just minted, and some were over a hundred years old. I settled on a half dollar minted in 1850 and paid him four dollars. I was afraid word would get out I had paid someone four dollars for a half dollar and they would put me in the loony house.
>
> The man I bought these from had been on a construction site when a bulldozer pushed an old shack and the contents into a 20 foot dug water well. He spotted some coins on the path to the well and picked them up. The owner of the property arrived shortly afterward and found enough one-dollar gold coins to make his wife a necklace. He picked up several other gold and silver coins as well. Apparently, the coins were dropping out of an old wood stove that years

[1] Foster is little remembered today by numismatic historians, but in his time he was one of the most admired people in the profession. His integrity was of the highest order, and he had a warm personality. His advertisements and listings were sometimes titled "Suitcase Specials," reflective of his carrying part of his inventory to conventions in a small traveling bag.

[2] Jasper Robertson, M.D., of Hoosick Falls, New York (located only a few miles from Troy, on the road to Bennington, Vermont), is one of many numismatists of the era of the 1930s to the 1950s who assembled a fine cabinet of coins, but whose activities were never chronicled in print. In the 1950s Jim Ruddy and I, then trading as the Empire Coin Co., Johnson City, New York, acquired via Dave Nethaway the Robertson collection of copper, nickel, and silver coins. As I recall, most of the coins from 1880s onward were gems, as were many earlier pieces. Years later, the Robertson gold coins were sold at auction by Mid-American Rare Coin Galleries (Jeff Garrett and Ron Guth).

[3] Letter to the author, August 1996, here slightly edited; additional information sent on September 4, 1996, this including copies of certain pages of the book, *Barren County Heritage,* 1980.

earlier had been used to heat the now long-abandoned building. It was later learned that any time the old black man, Stephen Landrum ("Uncle Steve"), who lived there, received money he would exchange most of the bills for coins. The story was that most of the coins are still down at the bottom of the well. Maybe yes or maybe no.

In a book of our county's history, Landrum's attorney, E.H. Smith, commented:

"One time I helped him in his negotiations to purchase a building in Glasgow for which he was to pay $4,500. The deed was drawn and ready for delivery, and it was time for 'Uncle Steve' to pay. 'Just wait a little while and I'll be back,' he said.

"He was gone some 15 or 20 minutes, and when he returned he had exactly $4,500 in a little split-bark basket with a napkin over the money. There was nothing larger than a $10 bill in the basket, and there were many ones and several hands full of silver."

Landrum was further described as a generous man who carefully managed rental properties, bought houses for his relatives, provided for needy blacks, and was a benefactor of the Ratliff Industrial Institute and Teachers Normal College.

I still have the 1850-O half dollar and it's not for sale.

That started me on the road to collecting coins for the next 10 years. Then I gave up interest, but I started again about a year ago. The hobby surely is different now.

There have been two other "finds" here that I have heard about. Back in the 1940s a man was plowing a garden in his backyard and unearthed a jar of gold coins. The other "find" was from a fireplace in another section of town. I have not been able to learn anything specific about either of these hoards.

An Elderly Druggist

Saved: Early 20th century
Revealed: 1954
Treasure: Two-cent pieces

During the early part of the twentieth century a druggist whose store was on the west side of Market Street, Kingston, Pennsylvania, thought that bronze two-cent pieces (minted 1864-1873) were curious. Whenever he received one in change, he set it aside in a cigar box.

In 1954 he saw an advertisement placed by young Q. David Bowers, who at the time had recently begun his numismatic career. Dave was invited to come and inspect the several hundred pieces he had accumulated. Dave did this—and bought them on the spot. Most of the two-cent pieces were dated 1864 and 1865, but there were some of all other dates through 1872. The typical grades were Good to Very Fine.

Half Dollars on a Sandy Beach

Lost: 1840s
Found: 1950s
Treasure: 1841-O and 1843-O half dollars

Coins in the Sand

In the 1950s, when Grover C. Criswell and his brother Clarence were partners in the rare coin and Confederate currency business, the author met with them in their hotel suite one evening at a coin show. These were the days when theft was not a problem at such events, and guarded "security rooms" were not provided for the safekeeping of collectors' and dealers' coins.

Displayed before me were several 1843-O Liberty Seated half dollars, not a rare date (2,268,000 were minted), but one not often seen, then or now, in high grades such as Mint State. I bought one or two and also purchased some Proof Barber dimes of the 1892-1915 years that the Criswells had as part of their stock.

Upon inquiring about the 1843-O coins, I was told that a few months earlier a beachcomber in the St. Petersburg, Florida, area had stumbled upon a small metal can or container in the sand, and in it were between a dozen and 20 of these 1843-O halves, all Mint State and all of the same general appearance—indicating that they had been kept together for a long period of time. As I recall, the coins were fairly brilliant and lustrous and had no evidence of saltwater etching.[1]

1841-O Halves at an Old Fort

Somewhat related may be a group of 1841-O half dollars mentioned in *Walter Breen's Complete Encyclo-*

[1] The viewing of these coins was probably circa 1955-1957.

pedia of U.S. and Colonial Coins, p. 395, here paraphrased: "1841-O A hoard of this (possibly 40 Uncs.) turned up in Clearwater, Florida, before 1957."[1]

More information is found under Lot 2166 of Coin Galleries' mail bid sale of November 9, 1988, where an example of an 1841-O is described as being Mint State, of a better strike than usual, "a handsome specimen from the 'Clearwater Hoard' of 40 pieces found in Florida on the site of the former Fort Harrison and presumably buried by a soldier on duty there at about the time of issue."

Put Another Nickel (or Penny) In

Hidden: 19th century onward
Found: 1950s onward
Treasure: Interesting cents and nickels

Time was when coin-operated amusement and entertainment devices were omnipresent in the United States. The Mills Novelty Co., of Chicago, published a booklet, *The Poor Man's Club,* noting that a person of modest means who could not afford to belong to a country club or other social gathering place could certainly have a lot of fun in a room full of coin-in-the-slot machines. In the first two decades of the twentieth century, Mills sold such devices as Cupid's Post Office (the deposit of a one-cent piece would yield a "love letter"), the World Horoscope machine (your fortune for a penny), and other amusements. The Mills Violano-Virtuoso, a mechanical violin-playing machine operated via a paper roll, was billed as one of the eight greatest inventions of the decade, based upon acclaim it received when exhibited at the Alaska-Yukon-Pacific Exposition in Seattle in 1909; a nickel in the slot would yield a tune.

Mills as well as numerous other manufacturers—and such names as Caille and Watling come to mind—made slot machines that in the early days had a spinning disc mounted on the front (the three-reel type became popular later, especially in the 1920s and 1930s). These were often equipped to take nickels or quarters, but some were outfitted with dime or, rarely, cent or half dollar slots.

Regina disc-changing music box made in Rahway, New Jersey, at the turn of the twentieth century. Upon receipt of a nickel it would play a tune selected by the patron from a program of 12 pieces.

Coin-operated music was the order of the day for a long time, from the 1890s when the Regina Music Box Co. of Rahway, New Jersey, began marketing music boxes that used metal discs to pluck steel "music combs," and upon deposit of a nickel or cent would

[1] Walter Breen kept extensive notes on U.S. coins for many years, only to have many of them stolen or misplaced in the 1970s when he was working in New York City. Thus, some of his thoughts were lost forever, others were recalled quite accurately, and still others were incorrectly remembered by the time he wrote his 1988 *Encyclopedia,* which today stands as his masterwork, and justifiably so. Most probably, at an earlier time he had more information concerning these 1841-O coins.

play *In the Good Old Summertime, At a Georgia Campmeeting,* or *Swanee River.* Particularly elegant Regina models stored 12 discs like pieces of toast in a rack, and permitted the patron to choose the tune desired. Later in the decade, the Rudolph Wurlitzer Co., of Cincinnati (and later with a factory in North Tonawanda, New York), introduced its first coin-operated piano, the Tonophone. A Liberty or Shield nickel in the slot in 1899 would produce a cascade of rippling melodies. Wurlitzer went on to greater things including the manufacture of orchestrions (coin-operated pianos with drums, xylophone, pipes, and other orchestra instruments) and theatre pipe organs.

"DROP A NICKLE IN"

TO HEAR THE LATEST DANCE AND SONG HITS
AS PLAYED BY A

"THE BEST NICKLE PIANO IN THE WORLD"

Wyoming Valley Music Co.
Wilkes-Barre, Pa.

Card advertising a Link "nickle" piano in the 1920s. Such a notice was intended to be placed near a Link coin-operated piano to invite an inflow of five-cent pieces.

In Binghamton, New York, in the 1920s, Edwin A. Link kept busy making nickel-in-the-slot pianos, many of which had the accompaniment of a xylophone or a couple ranks of pipes, and sometimes a drum or two. The inventive Link also made theatre organs which were widely acclaimed in their day. By 1929 the coin piano and theatre organ business was waning, what with the popularity of the radio and the phonograph. Link turned his talents elsewhere, and using player piano parts he made the world's first automatic aviation flight trainer, a project that later developed into a huge manufacturing firm. Important to the present book is another of Link's loves and pursuits: deep-sea submersible vehicles. While Ed never found an extensive coin treasure first-hand, he was on the scene in Florida to view some notable discoveries, led an underwater survey of the sunken city of Port Royal[1] (with his 164-ton *Sea Diver* ship as the base of operations), and was one of the best-known and most-liked figures in his

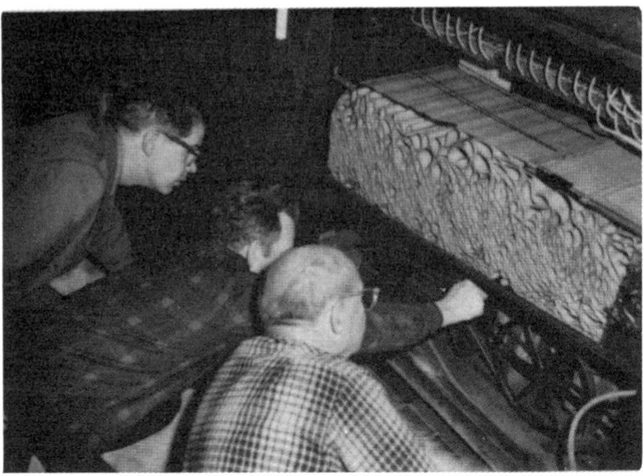

Ed Link—maker of coin operated pianos, aviation training devices, and undersea exploration devices—shown in 1965 in photographs taken in the Link home in Binghamton, New York. Top: Ed Link holding an interior part of a Link Style 2E coin-operated piano. Middle: Harvey Roehl and Ed Link examine the Link piano. Bottom: Dave Bowers, Murray Clark, and Ed Link explore the innards of the instrument.

[1] Destroyed by an earthquake on June 7, 1692, at about 11:42 a.m. (the hour time is according to a watch recovered by Link on the site; the hands had stopped at that point).

field.[1] *History Under the Sea,* by Mendel Peterson, Smithsonian Institution Press, 1965, bears this dedication: "To Edwin A. Link. Inventor and Underwater Pioneer. Whose financial support and kindly guidance have made possible the experience upon which this publication is based."

Elsewhere around the map, in Chicago the J.P. Seeburg Co., the Marquette Piano Co., and the Operators' Piano Co. each turned out some really nice coin-operated pianos and orchestrions. The Exhibit Supply Co. took a chapter from the Mills Novelty Co. book and produced a large line of arcade machines including fortune tellers and "iron claw" grabbers.

Other types of coin-operated machines included gum vendors, jukeboxes (which became the sensation of America beginning in the early 1930s; brands included Wurlitzer, Mills, Seeburg, Rowe, and AMI), Mutoscope and other penny-in-the-slot peep shows and flip card machines, and more.

Now to the "treasure" part of all this:

From the 1950s onward, the collecting of such old-time devices has been a very popular pursuit. And, well it should be. There is something fascinating about putting a nickel in the slot of a Seeburg coin-operated piano and hearing music exactly as it was played in 1915, or inserting a penny into a "Grandma's Fortunes," watching the wax figure sweep her hand over an array of playing cards, and then reading the printed fortune card dispensed in the slot below.

During the restoration process for such machines, many interesting old coins—particularly cents and nickels—have been found. Harvey Roehl, of Vestal, New York, discovered an 1857 Flying Eagle cent in the bottom of an old Seeburg coin piano that took nickels. Apparently, someone (obviously not a numismatist!) sought to make it play by putting in one of these old copper-nickel cents. The unwanted cent was rejected by the coin chute and fell into the bottom of the piano, where it remained until found in the 1960s.

The author, when examining the innards of a Seeburg Style G orchestrion (piano, mandolin, two ranks of pipes, drums, etc.) found a well-worn 1921 Mercury dime, one of the scarcer dates. It had been put into the unit instead of the required nickel (perhaps it was the only coin the patron had), and, rejected, it fell to the bottom.

A crank-operated Mutoscope which displays flip-cards so rapidly that they look like a movie, and which took in many Indian cents when it was used in New Orleans from about 1905 to 1915, was found to contain a handful of such pieces when it was taken apart for restoration in the early 1960s; no rare dates, however.

Many other such coin finds could be described. In fact, just about any restorer of such devices has a few coins on hand that have been found this way.

Maine Half Dollar Hoard

Hidden or lost: 1830s
Found: By 1963
Treasure: Early half dollars

John J. Ford, Jr., told of a group of about 2,000 Capped Bust half dollars of various dates, as well as some earlier pieces, but mostly dated in the 1820s and 1830s. The hoard was brought to him at New Netherlands Coin Co., 1 West 47th Street, New York City. The seller was Canadian dealer Fred Samuels, who said that the hoard had come from Maine, where it had been hidden for over a century, but did not provide specific details. Ford speculated that the coins might have been hidden by someone fearful of banks circa 1837-1838 during the financial panic.

Some of these halves—but not the best ones—were catalogued and appeared as part of "a splendid run of half dollars" in New Netherlands' Sale 57, December 10-11, 1963, there mixed with material from other consignments. The catalogue made no mention of any hoard.

About 150 to 200 of the Maine hoard half dollars were "absolute gems" and were reserved for the New Netherlands Coin Co. inventory. Many if not most of these selected pieces remained with Charles M. Wormser of New Netherlands, and in the 1980s were sold by Wormser's widow, acting on the advice of dealer Lester Merkin, to a West Coast dealer. The best of

[1] I knew Ed Link over a long period of years from the 1960s to the 1980s and interviewed him for material included in the books *Put Another Nickel In* (1966) and *The Encyclopedia of Automatic Musical Instruments* (1972). When my third son, Andrew, was one or two years old, circa 1980, Ed Link visited New Hampshire, and I photographed him with Ed. Sometimes when browsing through my library at home I will drop a nickel into my restored Link Style 2-E coin piano with xylophone and listen to it play.

these coins were dated 1831 and were sold into the market in various transactions.[1]

Meanwhile circa 1963, about 1,000 coins averaging EF and AU were wholesaled by New Netherlands to Philadelphia dealers Harry J. Forman and Ruth Bauer, who paid $15 apiece and later sold many of them to New York dealer Edwin Shapiro. In turn, Shapiro consigned them to New Netherlands 66th Sale, July 21-22, 1976, by which time the firm was operated solely by Charles M. Wormser, Ford having retired. Beginning with Lot 28 and ending at Lot 747, the pieces appeared in singles as well as multiple-coin lots under the title of "Extraordinary Collection of Bust Half Dollars—Possibly the Largest Ever Offered at Public Auction," again with no specific mention of the Maine hoard.

The present description represents the first time detailed information concerning this cache has reached print.[2]

An Array of Sparkling Half Dimes

Hidden or lost: 1835
Found: 1960s
Treasure: 1835 half dimes

In the 1960s the writer purchased a quantity of lustrous gem Mint State 1835 half dimes from a California numismatist who had obtained them from some source not revealed to me. Perhaps the explanation is that given years later (1988) by Walter Breen:[3]

> The 1835 Small Date with Small 5 C. has become [the commonest variety of the year in Mint State] owing to a hoard of at least 100 specimens found in a Boston bank in 1969 and dispersed by Q. David Bowers.

If the pieces were indeed found in a Boston bank, it seems likely that they were in someone's safe deposit box, not a part of a bank's cash assets. I had never thought to ask Walter Breen the source of his information.

Church Cornerstone Yields Rarities

Hidden: 1877
Found: 1972
Treasure: Coins dated 1877

In 1877 the First Methodist Church was built in Lynn, Massachusetts. At the start of construction a metal box was placed in the cornerstone. Among the contents were current coins.

As events would prove, 1877 was indeed a fortunate numismatic year, for Proofs of this year included key issues in the Indian cent, nickel three-cent, Shield nickel, and other series.

Nearly a century later in 1968, the First Methodist Church merged with St. Paul's Methodist Church to form the present-day Christ Church. In 1972, the old First Methodist structure burned. The cornerstone box with its many books, documents, papers—and 1877 Proof and other coins—was recovered unharmed.

The numismatic contents proved to be a mixture of issues of the 1877 year including a number of rarities:[4]

> 1877 Indian cent: prooflike Uncirculated.
> 1877 nickel three-cent piece: Proof.
> 1877 Shield nickel: Proof.
> 1877-S (San Francisco Mint) Liberty Seated dime: Uncirculated.
> 1877-S Liberty Seated quarter dollar: Uncirculated.
> 1877-CC (Carson City Mint) Liberty Seated half dollar: Uncirculated.
> 1877 trade dollar: Uncirculated.

---

1 Many if not most of the 1831-dated coins had small, mostly triangular marks on the lower third of the obverse, particularly on the bust, perhaps artifacts of some type of coin-ejecting device used at the Mint. Since that time the author has kept an eye out for other 1831 halves with these marks and has seen them on many other Mint State examples.

2 Recollection of John J. Ford, Jr., conversation, June 24, 1996; also New Netherlands Coin Co. auction catalogues as cited.

3 Breen, *Encyclopedia,* 1988, p. 280.

4 Information from an American Auction Association sale (Q. David Bowers and James F. Ruddy), February 7, 1974, lots 10-16.

The Cogswell Time Capsule

Sealed: 1879
Opened: April 1979
Treasure: Silver coins

The Many Successes

Once each month members of the Cogswell Society gather at one saloon or another in Washington, D.C., to lift their glasses to the memory of Dr. Henry Daniel Cogswell (March 3, 1820-July 8, 1900) and his *failure*.[1]

Cogswell, a San Francisco dentist active in the 1870s, made a small fortune as a securities and real estate trader. This was his success. But, many people had successes of this sort, and this was hardly worthy of camaraderie and celebration among beer drinkers of a century later. Similarly, Cogswell College, a trade school he founded in San Francisco, went on to success and, in fact, is still highly esteemed.

Now, about his seemingly important failure:

You see, Cogswell did not like alcohol. In fact, he detested it. He came up with a novel idea to combat demon rum: for every 100 saloons in a town, he would donate a drinking fountain to dispense water. Not every city wanted such a reminder of temperance, but enough did that some 20 fountains were erected at his expense, including about half this number scattered around San Francisco, a place with more than its share of rum sellers and grog shops.

One such fountain was put up in Washington Square in San Francisco, and was topped with a statue not of the Father of our Country, but of Benjamin Franklin, who, presumably, was seen as epitomizing the virtues of abstinence or some other virtue. This particular dispensary of *aqua pura* was also outfitted with a time capsule, which was placed there in 1879 to be opened a century later.

Other fountains, often surmounted by the effigy of Cogswell himself, were installed in San Jose, California; Dubuque, Iowa; Buffalo, New York; Rockville and Willimantic, both in Connecticut; Pawtucket, Rhode Island; and Washington, D.C. Several efforts to remove the Washington, D.C., statue have been resisted over the years by the aforementioned Cogswell Society.

What a Time Capsule Revealed

Years passed, and in 1979 the long-sealed capsule in San Francisco's Washington Square was opened, to reveal many souvenirs, messages, and other memorabilia placed by quite a few donors. Cogswell himself inserted a number of items including a letter warning future readers of "Irish Catholic hoodlums." Relevant to the present text, a handful of United States coins came to light along with several medals and foreign coins. Nearly all showed wear, indicating they were probably taken from pocket change at the time. Exceptions were the half dimes, dimes, and silver dollars, each of which was lightly toned Uncirculated. Federal issues included these:

1851 silver three-cent piece.
1873-S half dimes (9 pieces, all Uncirculated).
1877-S dimes (9, all Uncirculated).
1876-S quarter dollar.
1877-S quarter dollar (2).
1878-S quarter dollar (2).
1875-S half dollar.
1879-S Morgan silver dollars (2, both Uncirculated).
1873 Open 3 gold $1.

The Single Failure

Cogswell was an easterner who departed Philadelphia on May 9, 1849, aboard the *Susan G. Owens,* and after a long journey arrived in San Francisco in October. There, while he was drinking water, just about everyone else, so it seemed, was drinking whiskey, wine, and other alcoholic beverages, often to excess. Cogswell went from one dental, real estate, and stock market success to another, because his mind was never clouded. Thus was born his temperance crusade, apparently his only *failure,* as there was no measurable decrease in alcohol consumption following the erection of his statues.

Back to the meetings of the Cogswell Society:

Lift your glasses high! Here's a toast to the memory of Henry Cogswell!

[1] Adapted from David W. Lange's article, "Henry D. Cogswell and His Curious Time Capsule," *Calcoin News, Summer* 1984, courtesy of the writer.

Scenes of the Cogswell Fountain, located in Washington Square in San Francisco, California. Shown above is the statue of Benjamin Franklin which tops the fountain. The photo at right shows the inscription regarding the time capsule. (Photos courtesy of David Lange)

Silver Coins Aplenty

Hidden: 1951 or later
Found: 1979
Treasure: Thousands of silver coins

An old whisky still![1] Sealed jugs of liquor! Such were the surprise discovered in an old grocery store building in Pontiac, Michigan in 1979. The business had been owned for a long time by Joseph Polasek, who had died eight years earlier. Apparently, during Prohibition in the 1920s the facility was used for certain less-than-legal activities. Now in 1979, the premises at 534 Franklin Street were being dug out to make a cellar for the Gethsemane Bethel Apostolic Church.

As demolition and excavation work continued, crane operator Brad Bronkhorst of the Jonkisch Excavating Company cracked open a large crockery pickle jar, one of many leftover store items that were of no use to anyone and were destined to be hauled to the dump. You can imagine his surprise when out poured a cascade of silver coins in the form of quarters, half dollars, and silver dollars dated from 1879 to 1951! Silver, silver everywhere! The staggering total eventually reached $9,000 face value! Workers had wondered if more whiskey would turn up, but no one suspected a treasure of coins was in the offing.

The coins were loaded into two large garbage cans that became so heavy that it took four men to carry each one.[2] The cache was taken to the Police Department to be stored and inventoried. Meanwhile, word of the find spread around town. The prospect of finding free coins drew fortune seekers from far and wide, and caused several traffic jams. Equipped with metal detectors, rakes, and shovels, latecomers poked further around the site and found about $200 more in coins.

As of the time a report was filed on the matter, the coins had been transferred to the Pontiac State Bank, and a protracted court session was expected as the present as well as previous property owners each filed claims. No numismatic inventory was published.

The New Orleans Excitement

Hidden: Early 1840s
Found: October 29, 1982
Treasure: New Orleans Mint silver coins

Pandemonium!

On October 29, 1982, a few minutes past noon, excitement prevailed in the French Quarter in downtown New Orleans as earthmoving equipment brought to light a vast treasure of silver coins.[3] The site, scheduled to be used for a new Meridien Hotel, may have secreted a long-forgotten bank reserve.

Passersby grabbed what they could in a frantic free-for-all. In the melee no accounting was ever made of what was found. However, it is estimated that over 1,000 (perhaps *well* over) silver pieces were found, including large numbers of Spanish-American silver coins. Apparently, these had been buried in three cedar boxes. A report of the scramble by James H. Cohen noted:

> Visualize, if you will, businessmen in Brooks Brothers suits, women executives dressed in high heels and stockings, and laborers in their work clothes all on their hands and knees in mud at times up to their waists, digging with their bare hands for buried treasure.

How Many Coins Were Found?

Among large denomination United States silver coins, various half dollars from about 1811 to 1837 were registered as was a solitary 1798 dollar. However, most attention by numismatists was centered on a remarkable cache of Liberty Seated quarter dollars struck at the nearby New Orleans Mint in 1840 and

---

[1] Adapted from Carrie Dolan, "Found: $150,000 Silver Coin Cache," *Oakland* (Michigan) *Press,* reprinted in *Treasure Magazine,* October 1979; copy furnished by Doug Veal.

[2] $1,000 face value in silver weighs about 56 pounds.

[3] Sources include *Coin World,* November 24, 1982, account by New Orleans dealer James H. Cohen, "New Orleans Hoard Yields O-Mint Treasures"; this is the source of the specifically quoted commentaries. Also Breen, *Encyclopedia,* 1988, p. 346; personal recollection of the author.

Artist's conception of the free-for-all in New Orleans on October 29, 1982 (Sandy Martin illustration).

1841, many if not most of which were Mint State! A few of the 25-cent pieces were of the 1840-O No Drapery variety, but most were 1841-O With Drapery.[1] The exact quantity of 1840-O and 1841-O quarters found has been a matter of conjecture ever since. In 1988 Walter Breen suggested about 40 of the most plentiful variety, 1841-O, but the present writer believes that several multiples of that number were found. Indeed, Larry Briggs in his book, *The Comprehensive Encyclopedia of United States Liberty Seated Quarters,* notes that of one die variety of 1841-O alone, more than 200 coins are known from this hoard.[2]

The latest-dated coin in the New Orleans hoard was an 1842 quarter dollar, which dealer James H. Cohen graded as "About Uncirculated, which indicates that the hoard was buried shortly thereafter."

The typical coin was blackened from 150 years of immersion in damp soil. Many were cleaned soon thereafter, judiciously and otherwise, by numismatists. Today, survivors from this hoard can be identified by having a somewhat matte-like surface (not lustrous mint frost), usually with some traces of gray or black in areas.

Reflective of today's world and its thinking is this commentary:

> While quite understandable from an insurance viewpoint, but most unfortunate for the numismatic fraternity, the hotel owners promptly put a police guard around the site. This prevented people from coming in after hours with metal detectors and possibly being injured in the process. Additionally, the construction company accelerated its schedule and has poured concrete into the treasure hole, thus making the balance of the coins forever inaccessible.

The Ash Interviews

Additional information on this fascinating find is revealed in these personal interview notes by James D. Ash, taken with New Orleans coin dealers and collectors and an investment broker who was on the scene; also a later (September 16, 1986) interview with New Orleans dealer James Cohen:[3]

> The coins were found in three cypress [*sic*] wood boxes. The first was broken open, and the coins were mingled with mud and dirt. Many passersby entered the excavation area to gather the coins, stuff them in their pockets, etc.; this was the account that was widely publicized. Some of these coins were later purchased by collectors and dealers.
>
> The second box was picked up at the scene by two individuals and loaded into a pickup truck. They left the scene quickly without opening the box at the time. So far as is known, the contents of this box never came on the local coin market.
>
> The third box was more systematically distributed at the scene, and numerous specimens from it were traded and sold on the local market. For several years thereafter these could be purchased without difficulty. I recall buying about a dozen quarters from James Cohen in the late 1980s. I also recall seeing an interesting pair of matched gem brilliant Uncirculated 1841-O quarters in a frame. One had a gem obverse, but a severely corroded reverse, while on the other the reverse was gem and the obverse was corroded. Together, with their best sides up, they made a nice display. This pair was offered to me for $650, but I passed. These had come from the third box.
>
> I was able to learn from witnesses that boxes one and three each contained two cloth bags filled with silver coins, possibly weighing about 50 pounds per bag, and estimated to contain about $1,000 face value per bag. Considering that a $1,000 bag of silver dollars weighs about 56 pounds, this estimate may have been close to the mark. Later, there were some rumors that box number two had gold in it, but this is probably not true.
>
> I understand that all verified coins were dated 1841 or earlier, although there were rumors of an 1842 quarter. The coins were 80% foreign and 20% United States. Most of the foreign pieces were Spanish-American silver 2-real and 8-real pieces. The United States coins were all quarters plus a few higher denominations. I heard of no half dimes or dimes. If each of the three boxes contained about $2,000 worth of coins, or a total of $6,000, it might be reasonable to assume that perhaps $800 this was in quarters, or 3,200 pieces. Most I have observed were of the 1841-O, and more than half of these were from a slightly doubled obverse die.

Years from Now

Here is a treasure for the future. The Meridien Hotel will not stand forever, and perhaps in the distant future when it, too, succumbs to "progress," someone will dig out a dusty old copy of this book and learn that beneath the broken-up concrete foundation are more silver coins.

Coins Found in a Ghost Town

Lost: Late 19th and early 20th centuries
Found: 1992
Treasure: Various coins

In the summer of 1992, Mr. and Mrs. R.L. McGrew decided to replace the old and quite deteriorated

[1] Chris Pilliod reported in *Gobrecht Journal*, March 1992, pp. 44-45, that of the 21 specimens of 1841-O he studied, 11 were of the doubled obverse variety (Breen-3946).

[2] Published by Larry Briggs Rare Coins, 1991. Various die combinations of the era are discussed, and several comments are made concerning those found in the New Orleans hoard. The variety of which more than 200 are known is Briggs' 2-C.

[3] Roy D. Ash, letter, August 26, 1996; notes edited and adapted to reflect material not already given.

wooden walk in front of an old false-front stone building they owned in the ghost town of St. Elmo, Colorado.[1] Mr. McGrew had been a coin collector since 1959 and thus was in a position to give a numismatic description of what happened.

Upon removing the rotting boards another, older boardwalk was discovered under several inches of dirt below it. In the soil was found a variety of old coins including an 1898 Indian cent; 1867 Shield nickel; dimes of 1875, 1900, 1903, and 1908-O; and numerous early Lincoln cents.

The St. Elmo area is said to have yielded many Liberty Seated and Barber dimes as finds by tourists over the years, these coins sometimes coming to light after being washed out of the soil by rain.

Kept in the Family

Set aside: Circa 1824
Brought to market: 1992
Treasure: Capped Bust half dollars

On Tuesday, June 23, 1992, at Sotheby's sale rooms in New York City, coins described as "The Property of a Gentleman" crossed the block.[2] Offered were 37 examples of Uncirculated (mostly) half dollars bearing dates from 1820 to 1824. The catalogue noted:

> This collection of half dollars was assembled in the years in which they were struck, by an ancestor of the present consignor. Not only is it unusual to find a group of coins assembled over a century and a half ago, but the quality and freshness of all of the coins is extraordinary.

The following half dollars were included, all Mint State except as noted:

> 1820/19, Overton-101[3] • 1821 O-103, nearly Mint State • 1821 O-105a • 1822 O-104 • 1822 O-106 (2 pieces) • 1822 O-106a (late die state; 4 pieces) • 1823 O-103 (3 pieces, two nearly Mint State and one full Mint State) • 1823 O-105 (3) • 1823 O-106a • 1823 O-108 • 1823 O-108a (2) • 1823 O-112 (5) • 1824 over 1 O-101 (9 including three later die states) • 1824 O-104 • 1824 O-108.

Under the Mast of the *U.S.S. Constitution*

Deposited: 1979
Found: 1992
Treasure: Various coins

For many years the venerable *U.S.S. Constitution*, launched in 1797, has been a tourist and historical attraction at the naval shipyard on the Charles River in Charlestown, Massachusetts, not far from Boston and within sight of the Bunker Hill Monument.[4] On September 16, 1992, the three masts were removed ("unstepped") to facilitate removal of the hull to a drydock for reconditioning. Known as "Old Ironsides" from an encounter with the British warship *H.M.S. Guerriere* in the War of 1812, the ship has an illustrious naval history. Its first rebuilding occurred in 1833.

Beneath the mast were found 165 coins (mainly) and medals including a copper cent of 1797. The mystique ends with the revelation that the masts are unstepped every 20 years or so, and most of the coins were placed there in recent times. The 1797 cent had been donated in 1979 by Joseph Kent, who at the

---

[1] From R.L. McGrew's letter to the editor, *Coin World,* March 22, 1993.
[2] Information from David E. Tripp, cataloguer of the sale.
[3] Attributions to the die variety description in Al C. Overton's book, *Early Half Dollar Die Varieties 1794-1836,* 1990 edition (edited by Donald Parsley).
[4] Adapted from William T. Gibbs, "Coins, Medals From Warship on Display," *Coin World,* October 5, 1992.

Naval action between the *U.S.S. Constitution* (foreground) and the *H.M.S. Guerriere* in the War of 1812, as shown in a nineteenth-century engraving.

time owned the Badge Coin Shop in Charlestown.

During the repair of the ship beginning in 1992 the extracted coins were placed on view in the nearby Constitution Museum.[1] Seemingly, here is a treasure location that can continue to be "discovered" on a regular basis in the future!

Surprise in a Dog Pen

Hidden: Circa 1916
Found: 1996
Treasure: Gold and silver coins

In July 1996, Betty Brauer struck it rich! Until that time her greatest stroke of luck was finding a $5 bill while shoveling snow.[2] The Valmy, Wisconsin, lady had been pulling weeds around a pen she was preparing for her beagles near the home she and her husband had owned for 33 years. There, exposed in the earth, was a gleaming treasure, hidden years earlier in a fruit jar, which upon inspection was found to consist of 21 gold and 29 silver coins! Dealer Mike Worchek, of Card & Coin Corner in Green Bay, examined the coins and pronounced them to be worth more than $7,000.

George Evenson, president of the Door County Historical Society, conjectured that the coins had been buried there by frugal former owners who did not trust banks. A thrifty couple had lived there, had a couple of cows, and sold milk locally. From the dates on the coins the pieces had been put away at least 80 years before, which would place the date at 1916 or earlier. Betty Brauer remembered that there had been a hint of such a find years ago when her sons dug for night crawlers for fish bait and found some old silver dollars.

Perhaps displaying more sense than the earlier owners of the house, Mr. and Mrs. Brauer quickly took the coins to a safe deposit box for security.

An Old Cornerstone Is Opened

Sealed: 1897
Opened: 1996
Treasure: Various coins

On July 26, 1996, at a ceremony at the Topton (Pennsylvania) 100th Anniversary Day Fair, the cornerstone of Old Main was opened.[3] Sealed in the late 1890s by Uriah P. Heilman, president of the Lutheran Home there, the cornerstone's contents proved to be quite varied. Amid old Bibles and a list of 2,000 patrons who had donated $1 each to the building were found some old coins. Among these were an Indian cent and Morgan silver dollar dated 1897 (each showing slight wear), a 1799 Draped Bust silver dollar in Very Fine grade, and an 1800 silver dollar in similar preservation.

Treasure Hunting Electronic Style

Hidden: 19th century onward
Found: 1970s-1990s
Treasure: Interesting old coins

Coinshooting

From the 1970s to the present time, seeking coins with electronic metal detectors has been a great hobby for thousands, many of whom belong to clubs and subscribe to magazines. "Coinshooting," as it is called, is often practiced on beaches, vacant downtown lots, city parks, and other places where people gathered years

---

[1] The display included certain numismatic and historical information provided by Frank Van Valen.

[2] Adapted from an article, "Woman Discovers Some Buried Booty," by Jesse Garza, Milwaukee *Journal-Sentinel,* August 11, 1996; submitted to the author by Gerald Murack and, separately, by Joe Darnell.

[3] Account adapted from the *Allentown* (Pennsylvania) *Morning Call,* July 27,1996; submitted to the author by John F. Eaves.

ago. Old cellars and foundations are fertile spots as well. Ghost towns offer obvious possibilities.

Panning, dredging, and otherwise looking around for gold nuggets has also brought forth some coins that must have been lost in western streams a century or more ago by fishermen or an earlier generation of prospectors.

The typical experienced coin hunter in the American West is likely to have found a few silver dollars and, perhaps, one or two gold coins, plus an array of old-time loose change. In the Eastern United States coins are more apt to be bronze or smaller silver denominations, but anything can and has happened.

Electronic devices bearing such names as Fisher, Garrett, and White—and there are others as well—can mean many happy hours for the treasure hunter. To avoid problems, precautions must be taken before "coinshooting." Some type of a written agreement from the land owner granting permission to explore is a necessity. Such a document should give, in a general way, a description of what is sought (old coins, artifacts, or whatever), the time limits for the search, and the "consideration" or reward to the land owner, the latter expressed as a flat fee or a percentage arrangement. Various brochures issued by the manufacturers of metal-detecting devices often give suggestions. For best protection, have an attorney draw something up.

Coinshooting on National Historic Sites is nearly always forbidden, and obtaining permission to look for hidden things in city parks, school grounds, and other publicly-owned places often involves a lot of red tape. For this reason, many treasure seekers do it on an informal (read *illegal*) basis, not from desire, but from frustration. This is not to suggest that "thou shall go and do likewise," but is simply an observation.

Here are some accounts of coinshooting. First, are some individual stories, then some interesting finds as reported to the Fisher and Garrett companies:

The Springhouse Find

The time is in the early 1990s and the place is *somewhere* in the United States.[1] The printed account of this particular find gave no geographical information at all, but some leafless trees suggested it took place in an area which has both deciduous trees and a winter season. This eliminates, for example, the Mohave Desert and the state of Florida. Often, treasure accounts do not include specifics as to locations, lest a modern-day Gold Rush ensue as soon as the magazine reaches readers! And, if anything really valuable is found, claimants will materialize from just about everywhere.

Anyway, Roy Zeper had memories from his childhood when he used to go by a large estate, perhaps on a square mile or more of land. "No Trespassing" signs and guard dogs forbid youthful exploration of the property and getting close to the grand mansion on it.

One day many years later, the adult Roy Zeper drove by the old estate only to find that the landscape had been torn apart by a developer, and now there were new streets and new houses on the property. However, one corner of the land, near a low-lying marshy spot, remained undisturbed from the early days. Probably, the soil was too wet to permit building. There, barely standing, was an old springhouse in decrepitude. Years earlier it had been used to store milk, meat, and other things in cool surroundings.

Equipped with a Fisher 1265-X metal detector, Zeper and his wife asked permission to prowl around. After finding a few pull-tabs from modern soda cans, the device picked up a strong signal near the base of one of the interior stone walls. Zeper used a hand trowel to loosen a likely rock, then pulled it free, to reveal a muddy Mason jar filled with coins!

Inspection soon revealed Indian cents, bronze two-cent pieces, nickels, dimes, quarters, half dollars, and many silver dollars! The oldest coin was a Capped Bust half dollar of 1812 in what seems from a photograph to be in Extremely Fine grade. Apparently, one of the workers who used the springhouse had an interest in old and unusual coins and hid them there years earlier. Perhaps he forgot about them, perhaps he moved to a distant place, perhaps he died unexpectedly. As is often the case, the story probably will never be completed.

It Paid to Look Further

Another account with no geographical information given related the experience of Tom Collins and Judi Miyasaki in 1992.[2] The pair had been exploring a city demolition site where a $20 gold coin had been found

[1] Adapted from Roy Zeper, "The Springhouse Cache," *Western & Eastern Treasures Magazine,* February 1992; copy furnished by Doug Veal.
[2] Adapted from "Gold Coin Cache," *Western & Eastern Treasures Magazine,* March 1993; copy furnished by Doug Veal.

recently. Luck was with them, and another $20 was found in short order, followed by four more all stuck together, followed by even more.

On the first day 14 double eagles were found, three the next day, and another a few days later. Along the way an 1899 $10 piece was found as well. A coin dealer subsequently advised that all but one coin was Mint State. A photograph accompanying the printed account revealed that the $20 coins were dated from 1877 to 1906, suggesting that the coins had been secreted on or after 1906.

A Bordello in the Desert

Somewhere in the vast Mojave Desert there was once a house of prostitution.[1] Perhaps there were several such houses in that desert, or even a lot of them. In any event, in the 1970s one was sufficiently defunct that only its old foundation remained. The madam and her ladies of the night had long since departed.

Russ Dieffenbaucher, a treasure hunter from Bakersfield, California, poked around the place with his electronic metal detector and found five $5 gold pieces, a $10 gold coin, and 40 silver dollars in an old Mason jar, perhaps remaining from the receipts of decades earlier. The $5 pieces were attributed as 1881-S, 1892-S, 1901-S, and two of 1909-D. The $10 was a 1902-S.

Dieffenbaucher had long experience in hunting for coins, and in other places he turned up 60 or 70 Indian cents over a period of years, assorted gold coins, and other pieces. His oldest find was described as an 1819 copper cent so worn that he had to soak it in catsup until the date "was finally raised" so it could be seen.

The "Goat Doctor" Find

In the same state as the bordello foundation, but in a canyon in the foothills of the Sierra Mountains, the aptly—named "Jimmy Sierra"—actually the nickname of James Normandi, one of the West's best-known treasure hunters-equipped with a White's 6000/D Series 2 metal detector (a brand which he distributes) had a streak of luck one day in October 1980. Accompanying him were Ed Milota, Ray Bolduc, and Don Arthur.

He first found a "large Wells Fargo bag containing over 2,000 silver dollars," then in the same place a year later dug up a rusted strongbox stuffed with $2,500 in Silver Certificates and more silver dollars and half dollars.[2] The silver face value alone amounted to over $15,000, ranking this as one of the greatest hidden treasures ever found buried on land in the United States!

The site was an old orchard that formerly belonged to a so-called "goat doctor," otherwise described in the account as a faith healer and self-taught chiropractor—perhaps of the specialty of using extracts from goat glands to cure various afflictions of his coin-laden patients. Whatever he did, customers were willing to pay in silver, and plenty of it! Over a period of many years from about 1920 to 1950, his customers handed over a wide variety of coins that would prove to be treasures. One cannot help but wonder why the "goat doctor" never recovered his earnings. There must be a story.

Good Times on Dollar Creek

It was the dry season in Utah, and although there was enough water for fishing in the creek, the level was far below normal.[3] Dan Davis and his sons were enjoying the day, and one of the boys was idly tossing

[1] Adapted from Dr. Richard M. Fales, "Ill-Gotten Gold Uncovered!" *Treasure Found Magazine,* Winter 1977; copy furnished by Doug Veal.

[2] Unfortunately, the silver dollars were stolen from the finder in a burglary in February 1982 (James Normandi, letter, October 3, 1996, enclosing articles on the find as published in the spring 1981 and March 1982, respectively, in *Treasure Found* and *Treasure Magazine*).

[3] Adapted from Boyd M. Jolley, "Found: $1,000 Silver and Gold Coin Cache," *Treasure Found Magazine,* Summer 1978; copy furnished by Doug Veal.

Jimmy Sierra with some of the fabulous items hidden by the "goat doctor" many years ago. (Courtesy "Jimmy Sierra" Normandi)

rocks into the water. One hit a black rock. No! It was actually a little pile of blackened coins! Upon close inspection, 136 silver dollars and 87 other coins were found, including one struck in gold!

Dan shared the good news with his friend Boyd M. Jolley, who gave the place the nickname "Dollar Creek" after he went there with his Daytona-brand detector and found 21 more coins including five silver dollars, one a low-mintage 1885-CC.

Did they get them all, or are there still more to be found?

Coin Hunting in Westchester County

In New York north of Manhattan in the residential area known as Westchester County, John V. Dimaio sought treasure for 15 years.[1] Although it could be argued that it might have been cheaper and easier to have bought his coins from a dealer, no doubt he had a great deal of fun in the thrill of the hunt. Perhaps buying such pieces from a professional numismatist would be analogous to a fisherman buying a "catch" at a seafood store.

His biggest find came from an area with a 20-foot perimeter, where coins must have been scattered or hidden in the 1880s or later. An inventory listed $5 gold pieces of 1881 and 1881-S; $10 coins of 1848-O, 1880, and two dated 1882; an 1822 Spanish gold coin and an 1874 German coin in similar metal; and United States half dollars of 1818/7, 1842-O, 1859, 1871, 1876-CC (2), and 1877 (3). In addition he found an 1877 Liberty Seated quarter and an 1853 English shilling. Quite a varied group!

Good Luck at Crescent Peak

Randy Grantham of Las Vegas, Nevada, and his friend Scott Hardow were new to treasure hunting in the 1980s. They sniffed around with their electronic detectors and in parks and schoolyards found some old pocket change. Seeking bigger things, they headed into the Crescent Peak area.

Before long they came upon the littered landscape of what seemed to be an old mining site, long since abandoned. Amid old bottles, rusted scraps of metal and the like, Randy got a promising signal, dug about six inches into the dry soil, and found a silver dollar!

This was just the beginning, and in short order the remains of a broken glass jar were found to contain two $5 gold coins, two $10 pieces, and three of the $20 denomination, the latest dated 1906. Silver dollars from 1878 onward were found—159 in all! Also found on the same trip was a rattlesnake, but little was said about that critter. There are some things that treasure hunters to not want to find!

Silver Coins in California Streams

Collector Duwayne Statzer related that in the 1980s he talked with two friends who had bought some Liberty Seated coins in central California from people who had panned and dredged for gold. An 1859-S dime found in a small creek was in VF to EF grade, but was heavily oxidized. In another location a dredging operation yielded dimes of 1867-S and 1869-S, both quite corroded, and a dark 1855-S half dollar rarity,

[1] Adapted from "Gold & Silver Coins Cache," *Western & Eastern Treasures Magazine,* March 1990; copy furnished by Doug Veal.

but in better preservation than the dimes. A half dozen or more other dimes from the area were all found to be so oxidized that neither the dates nor the mintmarks (if any) could be discerned.

Perhaps the best find was a rare 1874-CC dime found by a gold panner. Although well worn and somewhat oxidized, it graded Fine-15.[1]

Coinshooting Successes (Fisher)

The following items are a few of many success stories printed in *Fisher World Treasure News,* various issues 1992-1996, published by the Fisher Research Laboratory. The company was founded in the 1930s by Gerhard Fisher, who was a German immigrant who studied electronics at the University of Dresden and later had many varied accomplishments, including flying more than 35,000 miles in the airship *Macon*. Today the firm is located in a sprawling factory in an industrial park in Los Banos, California.

Quantity and, we hope, quality: During one month Dick and Nancy Waters with their Fisher 1210-X and 1260-X metal detectors found an incredible total of 2,490 coins! A photograph indicates that this was a varied lot, but no numismatic information was given. An account such as this can be replicated many times, for just about anyone with an electronic detector and a well populated beach can report some degree of success, perhaps not 2,490 pieces, however.

An 1838 campsite: Richard Procyk located an 1838 Florida campsite of the Tennessee Volunteers who fought in the Seminole Wars. Muscat balls, knives, buttons, and other items were mentioned, including some lead discs thought to be gambling tokens (if so, here is a possibility for an article in the *Token and Medal Society Journal*). Joining him in the search near the lake shore outside the town of Fort Jupiter was Bob Carr, staff archaeologist for Dade County.

Mexican Army treasures: Clive Cussler (novelist who wrote *Raise the Titanic* and other works and who is mentioned in Chapter 9 in a note concerning the *Lexington*) was one of 20 volunteers who had been spending some time in Texas in January of each year when the San Antonio River was drained. Group members were searching for cannons used to defend the Alamo. "Ten of the 22 artillery pieces used to protect the 189 Alamo defenders during the 13-day siege by Mexican General Santa Anna's army of 2,000 men are believed to lie at the bottom of the San Antonio River, dumped there by the Mexican army after the capture of the Alamo," an account commented. Among those on the team, Tommy Worsham, found a "Spanish coin minted in April 1790 near Vera Cruz, Mexico." Also found was a "sixteenth century Spanish coin."

Two for two: David Crasep of Carmel Valley, California, found two gold coins on two consecutive days by using a Fisher CZ-6 electronic detector, one being an 1847-D $5 piece and the other an 1829 gold two escudos from Peru.

Included some old coins: James Mane was searching the banks of the Guadeloupe River near San Antonio, Texas, with a Fisher 1280-X equipped for underwater exploration. Near the base of a dam he found over $200 in change, including "some older coins."

Slave hire badges: In Charleston, South Carolina, in the early nineteenth century, owners of slaves had to register them with local authorities and pay a yearly tax or fee. Each slave was then given a copper badge to wear, upon which was stamped his main occupation such as PORTER, FISHER, CARPENTER, etc. These are sometimes called "slave hire badges." From time to time, these have caused attention in numismatic circles, as when Michael Hodder catalogued two important groups of them for Stack's, and when Rich Hartzog offered many pieces for sale. Using a Fisher detector, Rudy Wyatt of Charleston has achieved great success in finding them, and an article in the 1996-1997 edition of *Fisher World Treasure News* showed an impressive display of 30 pieces he had located.

Rare dime: Ron Attansasio discovered an 1874-CC Liberty Seated dime, grade not stated, with the Fisher CZ-6 detector, which became the "Find of the Year" for the *Western and Eastern Treasures* magazine. Ron lived near Lake Tahoe, California, and had started up a Fisher dealership, Metal Detectors of Northern Nevada. Unfortunately, Ron, age 46, died of a heart attack on December 19, 1992, and did not live to see his coin glamorized in print. The grade of the piece was not stated.

Another "jar find": Old coins are often found in jars, as with a small jar found on the shore of Lake Tahoe at an old home site. Upon inspection, a dozen $2.50 and $5 coins were found, all dated before 1900.

Those Spanish treasure fleet coins keep turning up: Richard A. Small of Sebastian, Florida, turned up a number of cob-type silver pieces with his Fisher 1280-X treasure detector while looking around the beach.

No time for girl-watching: Lee Worthy, prospecting a Southern California beach CZ-6 treasure detector during two weeks of stormy weather–which washes the sand–found three diamond rings (one appraised at $4000), three gold rings, four silver rings, three watches, six bracelets, one Canadian silver dollar, and 542 other coins.

Coinshooting Successes (Garrett)

Hal Dawson, editor of *Searcher,* published by Garrett Metal Detectors, whose motto is "Nobody knows treasure like Garrett," sent a file of interesting clippings, some excerpts from which are given below. Editor Dawson commented the "perhaps the most valuable coin ever found with a metal detector was the colonial Pine Tree threepence."

Liberty Seated coins found: In Bonham, Texas, Rickey Kirk, armed with his Garrett Freedom Plus detector, found an 1845 silver dime and an 1854 half dollar. "A longtime history buff and active participant in the Fannin County Historical Society, Rickey hoped that searching with a metal detector would enable him to discover items from Bonham's past.... Rickey has searched old home places and the sites of old houses. He always requests permission from the owner of the property and has been turned down only twice in two and one-half years. His 1854 half dollar from the New Orleans Mint was found six inches deep beneath the dining

[1] *Gobrecht Journal,* March and November 1986.

room of a house.... Rickey's greatest success came in scanning on the site of what had once been a saloon in downtown Bonham. When the current building was being remodeled, Rickey sought permission to hunt and was told he could work after the floor had been ripped out. However, he was limited to a period of only three hours before a new floor was to be installed. 'The area was dark because it was inside a building,' Rickey remembers, 'but it turned out to be a regular treasure hoard.' In a space roughly 30 by 65 feet he found 20 old coins and a broken saloon token. Among these coins was an 1845 dime and a 1941 Mercury dime. Most of the coins were nickels, dimes, and half dimes. 'They tell me that these coins were popular in saloons,' he explains, 'because a glass of beer cost a nickel.'"

A lucky find: Daniel Coutre of the Calgary (Canada) Metal Detecting Club related: "We were hunting a site that had been used as a Bible camp since the turn of the century.... As usual, I was using my trusty Garrett Master Hunter 7. During the first few hours many good finds were made, including some silver coins from the turn of the century. I had my share, which included a 1920 Standing Liberty quarter, a Canadian 1910 quarter and a Canadian 1917 silver five-cent piece, all in good condition. After lunch, I decided to go over an area that had already been searched that morning.... I found the pickings limited indeed there, and I decided to move on after that proverbial "one last sweep." And, what a sweep it was! I got a faint, but a consistent, signal. When I saw the coin that came from the hole, I had to ask some other club members to confirm that I wasn't dreaming. My heart started to pound when I realized I'd found one of the scarcest of all Canadian coins, ***a 1921 five-cent piece—in extremely good condition!*** I have had the coin graded by several coin dealers and their consensus is that it is in VF to EF condition. The current retail trend value for such a coin is approximately $4,000. Only about 400 of these coins are known to exist. Who said that metal detecting doesn't pay off?"

That Pine Tree coin: Tom Brown, of Hudson, New Hampshire, who used a Garrett Master Hunter CX detector, was searching in a farm field near the Merrimack River, and here's what happened: "'When I uncovered it about three inches down in the sandy soil, I didn't know exactly what I had at first,' he explains. 'I didn't know I had a coin. When I got home and carefully washed off the dirt, I saw the date 1652 and knew it was an important find.' The New Englander said he figures the coin, which gets its name from the crude outline of a pine tree it carries, is worth about $5,000. 'It's a coin collection in itself,' he says. 'I look at it every day.' With the new Garrett detector he has discovered large cents, two-cent pieces, Indian Head cents, a Civil War token and an 1818 Spanish-American real, a coin that was used throughout the U.S. in the nineteenth century. Mr. Brown has concentrated his searches in old towns, which gives him numerous opportunities in New England. Before he turns on his detector, Mr. Brown heads for the local library and 'a bit of detective work.' He searches records for old meeting sites, such as churches. 'If it's all pavement, you're out of luck,' he said. But, when Mr. Brown finds an open field, he heads 'for the oldest tree and begins searching there.' And, some of his best finds have come under old trees."

Silver coins found: Bill Callahan told this story: "It was early on a Sunday morning last fall, when my partner Vic Benamati and I started out to do our usual weekend thing—go metal detecting. Vic uses a GTA 1000, and I hunt with a more expensive model from a competitive manufacturer. Here in Northern California we generally stay within about 50 miles of home. We started slowly, and after looking in a couple of yards I had only a 1942 Mercury dime and some clad coins to show for my efforts while Vic had yet to come up with a single piece of silver. But, this was about to change in a likely looking yard where we asked a nice lady for permission to hunt. When she said, 'Yes,' away we went. We recovered several clad coins when Vic shouted from where he was looking between the sidewalk and street that he had a half dollar signal. 'Dig it!' I yelled back, and he did. 'I've found a treasure,' Vic exclaimed. And, what a treasure it was! Vic showed me two half dollar coins and one quarter, all Liberty Seated. The quarter was dated 1857, and the halves were 1862 and 1871, all minted in San Francisco. Vic had found them stacked on top of each other just as if they were placed exactly that way on purpose. The coins were in excellent shape and would grade about Extremely Fine."

Glass jar yields treasure: With Garrett detector in hand, James E. Brewer of Illinois enjoys treasure searching. On one particular day he looked through a 1938 plat book of Livingston County to find the sites of long-demolished schools. Here is what happened at one location: "'I began scanning near the old foundation and found many items, such as square glass ink wells, green copper conduit pipes and lightning arresters. But no coins!' Then, his luck changed. 'Scanning at the corner, I received a very strong reading. The cursor indicated a dollar-size object but after digging nine to 10 inches I recovered a fruit jar full of someone's unfortunate loss. Now, a quart jar is quite a find to me, and my heart almost stopped when I dug it up.' Brewer found its contents included 70 Indian Head cents, the oldest being 1866 and worth $250 Uncirculated; six silver half dollars, the oldest being an 1875 Liberty Seated; 37 silver dimes, the oldest being 1853; two half dimes, nine silver quarters and one 1921 Morgan dollar. Quite a find for one day!"

CHAPTER 3

Hoarders and Misers

Hoarding coins has been a popular thing to do since ancient times. In America there have been some famous hoarders—Aaron White is an example—as well as obscure personalities (Charles White). Hoards assembled by numismatists who primarily bought their coins from dealers (rather than finding them in the hands of the general public) are discussed separately in Chapter 19, "Dealer and Collector Hoards."

Charles White: Banker, Numismatist, Hoarder

Gathered: Early 19th century
Dispersed: 1886-1887
Treasure: Early quarter dollars, etc.

A Bank Cashier

Charles White, cashier of the Northampton Bank in Massachusetts, is little remembered today.[1] However, the masterwork by James A. Haxby, *Standard Catalog of United States Obsolete Bank Notes 1782-1866,* Vol. 2, p. 936, illustrates $1 (series of May 27, 1863) and $2 (alteration) notes of the Northampton Bank bearing White's inked signature. This institution in 1865 became the Northampton National Bank, Charter 1018.

Charles White, who apparently later moved to New York City, was also a coin collector, and like many numismatists he could not resist some hoarding, too. Little survives in print about his hoard(s). However, what does is fascinating

Harlan P. Smith, of 269 West 52nd Street, New York City—himself a first-rank collector—catalogued the White cabinet in 1886 and offered it for sale. Smith, born on March 18, 1839, was in the wholesale fruit business up to about the time of the White sale, but had a coin dealership on the side. The Charles White auction took place in a well-known gallery rented for the purpose. Smith's introduction to the offering noted:

> The cabinet of Mr. Chas. White of New York City, comprising a remarkably fine and full series of U.S. silver and copper coins, with few medals, to be sold at public auction, without reserve, on Tuesday, March 9th, 1886, at two o'clock, p.m., by Messrs. Bangs & Co., Auctioneers, 739 and 741 Broadway, N.Y.

What Was In the Hoard?

The flavor of this long-ago event is gained by reprinting some of the catalogue descriptions beginning with Lot 121, the prices in brackets being those realized. Note in particular Lot 128 which gives a hint of a hoard of a particular date, but which, unfortunately for present-day aficionados in the early quarter dollar field, leaves much unsaid. How many were there? Where were they found. What happened to the others?:

---

[1] The world of numismatics is full of surprises. And, such a surprise was furnished by Karl Moulton, book dealer and collector, who acquainted the author with White and furnished copies of the two auction catalogues quoted.

QUARTER DOLLARS:

Lot 121: 1796 Very Fine, bold impression; slightly touched by circulation; a handsome piece [Price realized at the sale: $9.25]

Lot 122: 1804 Very Good [$2.00]

Lot 123: 1805 Uncirculated, except for two minute nicks in field: beautiful sharp impression generally: few stars flat: surpasses my own specimen and all others I've seen. [$2.87]

Lot 124: 1806 over '5; Good. [$0.60]

Lot 125: 1806 Fine; perpendicular crack across obverse die [$0.90]

Lot 126: 1807 Uncirculated: splendid impression: excels the 1805 in some points: a very desirable specimen: in the Randall sale Lot 558 brought $90: that piece claimed to be the only Uncirculated specimen existing; this proves the contrary. [$26]

Lot 127: 1815 Uncirculated: sharp impression. [$2.90]

Lot 128: 1818 Uncirculated: sharp: rev. die cracked across; this is the last specimen of the hoard discovered by Mr. White, while cashier of the Northampton Bank; he naturally reserved the best specimen for his collection. [$1.40]

Lot 129: 1818 Uncirculated: sharp: *plain edge;* only specimen known. [$1.20]

Lot 130: 1819 Very Fine, sharp impression: barely touched by circulation: Reverse with colon after the "25 C:," the "5" engraved twice; desirable in this condition. [$1.40]

Lot 131: 1820 Uncirculated; sharp impression [$2.40]

Lot 132: 1821 Uncirculated; sharp impression [$2.30]

Lot 133: 1822 Uncirculated; stars flat; seldom equaled [$3.10]

Lot 134: 1823 over '22; Good for date; the most difficult date to obtain, except '27. [$30.00]

Lot 135: 1824 Very Fine, but little circulated. [$5.00]

Lot 136: 1825 Uncirculated; sharp impression. [$2.80]

Lot 137: 1828 Very Fine; rubbed only on highest points. [$0.65]

Lot 138: 1831 Uncirculated. [$0.45]

Lot 139: 1832 Uncirculated; desirable so perfect. [$0.95]

Lot 140: 1833 Uncirculated. [$0.70]

Lot 141: 1834 Uncirculated; sharp [$0.90]

Lot 142: 1834 Uncirculated; sharp; lacks the period after "25 C." [$0.40]

Lot 143: 1835 Uncirculated; cracked die. [$0.50]

Lot 144: 1836 Very Fine; cracked die. [$0.40]

Lot 145: 1837 Uncirculated. [$0.50]

Lot 146: 1838 Uncirculated. [$0.55]

Lot 147: 1838 Liberty Seated; Uncirculated. [$0.45]

Lot 148: 1839 Very Fine. [$0.40]

Lot 149: 1840 Uncirculated; draped elbow; "O" mint; splendid specimen. [$0.75]

Later in the catalogue a half dollar was described as follows, an overdate not known to numismatists today:[1]

Lot 218: [Capped Bust half dollar] 1820 over '18 Fine, and now first described; only specimen I've seen. [$2.00]

Also of interest is an 1840 Liberty Seated half dollar:

Lot 246: [1840 Liberty Seated half dollar struck at New Orleans, but lacking an O mintmark] Fine: large lettered reverse; this appears to be the same die used in the New Orleans Mint in 1839, and re-engraved; this variety seldom found.[2]

These were the cradle days of American numismatic information. As part of the description of Lot 182, an 1879 Uncirculated Liberty Seated quarter (which brought $0.45), cataloguer Smith noted concerning issues from that year through 1885: "None issued for circulation."

A similar comment was found under Lot 293, an 1889 Liberty Seated half dollar (which realized $0.75), part of a listing continuing through 299, mostly *Uncirculated* pieces, also bearing this note: "Of this and all following dates, none were issued for circulation."

It is known that business strikes were indeed made, and contemporary *Mint Report* issues mention them. Curiously, such pieces were made to prevent the dates becoming rare (as they would have been had only Proofs been struck). Inasmuch as the Mint and certain of its officials were exploiting the numismatic community for all it was worth, this in retrospect seems to have been a curious motive.

With regard to the remark, "none were issued for circulation," it could have been the case that by the time that when these were auctioned in 1886, the relatively restricted business strike mintages of these dates were still in storage and were not generally available, although the offering of "Uncirculated" examples indicates that at least a few got out.

A gratuitous comment concerning trade dollars appeared before Lot 353, the first coin in a set of Proofs by date from 1873 through 1883 inclusive. Harlan P. Smith, apparently no fan of trade dollars, was incorrect in his information as, in fact, trade dollars were heavier than regular silver dollars. The introduction read as follows:

---

1 This may have been the 1820/19 overdate—one does not know in retrospect—but, on the other hand, it probably was not. Harlan P. Smith was an accomplished numismatist and was familiar with the 1820/19, not a rare variety, and also knew well the *Type Table* published by John W. Haseltine in 1881, which listed known varieties. This "1820/18" captured his attention and quite possibly represented a variety that awaits rediscovery by a new generation of specialists. Here is a "treasure" possibility for the alert half dollar specialist.

2 As cataloguer H.P. Smith stated that the variety is "seldom found," this would imply that he had seen at least a few others. Relevant to the Charles White Collection coin, Thomas K. DeLorey, letter, September 26, 1996, commented: "This is most likely Wiley-Bugert #101 as listed for the 1840-O, struck from a leftover reverse die of the Capped Bust type of 1838-1839 on which the mintmarks were on the obverse. See their article in the Coinage of the Americas Conference proceedings for 1987. Apparently, credit for the original publication of this should now be given to Harlan P. Smith."

It will be noticed that Mr. White wasn't an advocate of the lightweight dollars, which must eventually be recoined; as they are actually tokens.

A mini-hoard of sorts followed Lot 474, a collection of 1864-1873 two-cent pieces, Uncirculated except for the 1872 and 1873 which were Proofs. Then were presented four separate offerings of Proof 1873 two-cent pieces—the rarest date in the series.

And That Was Not All

On April 15, 1887, Part II of the Charles White Collection was offered by Harlan P. Smith, who by this time had exited the wholesale fruit business and was devoting much if not all of his time to being a coin dealer. The 1887 catalogue bore these introductory comments:

Having concluded to dispose of the balance of the White Collection, the reader will find described in the following pages many very choice specimens of the U.S. coinage. The exceptionally fine condition of so large a number of pieces will be found worthy of attention of the most prominent collectors.

In this second sale, in remarks preceding Lot 134, the cataloguer noted this in connection with an offering of silver Proof sets:

Prices of Proof sets are now as low as they possibly can get, and now would be the opportunity for parties desiring an investment to obtain a series which will undoubtedly greatly increase in value in a few years.

Interestingly, Lot 162 was described as a set of "1884 brilliant Proofs, no trade," while Lot 163 was described as "1885 brilliant Proofs," with no mention of a trade dollar being either absent or present. This would seem to indicate that in 1887 cataloguer Harlan P. Smith was aware of the existence of an 1884 trade dollar, but realized that there was not one in this particular 1884 Proof set. Otherwise, there would have been no reason to have noted its absence. However, the numismatic community at large did not know of silver strikings of the trade dollar until 1907 when John W. Haseltine and Stephen K. Nagy made known the existence of 10 pieces, although the rumor of silver 1884 trade dollars had surfaced earlier, and some copper impressions had appeared on the market.

Beginning with Lot 315 in the second sale, quarter dollar listings included the following. Note that Lot 320 alludes to White's hoard of quarters, implying via "of this period" that dates other than 1818 may have been included:

QUARTER DOLLARS

Lot 315: 1796 Strong, sharp, brilliant impression; entire surface Proof: 6 in date almost touches bust; I believe this to be the finest known specimen; a gem for any collection. [$57.00]

Lot 316: 1796 6 more distant from bust: Fine, strong impression; everything sharp except centers of stars on left; hair clear and well defined; eagle's head perfectly struck up (more so than in preceding); it has seen but the slightest, if any, circulation. [$44.00]

Lot 317: 1796 Broken die; Very Fair. [$1.20]

Lot 318: 1807 Uncirculated; all sharply struck except for a few stars; mint lustre still retained; one of the finest specimens known; that in Randall's sale sold for $90. [$42.00]

Lot 319: 1815 Barely circulated; clear, bold impression. [$2.10]

Lot 320: 1818 Uncirculated, brilliant and sharp; nearly all the extra fine quarter dollars of this period came from Mr. White's hoard, as he seems to have paid more attention to this series than any other. [$2.10]

Lot 321: 1819 Very slight trace of circulation; strongly struck; very desirable in this condition. [$2.10]

Lot 322: 1820 Large O; Uncirculated. [$3.20]

Lot 323: 1821 Uncirculated. [$2.10]

Lot 324: 1822 Very Fine specimen; barely circulated; desirable in this condition. [$3.10]

Lot 325: 1824 Very Fine for this date, in fact, I think it the best I have seen; very desirable. [$14.00]

Lot 326: 1825 over '22; Uncirculated; sharp. [$1.80]

Lot 327: 1828 Uncirculated; sharp. [$1.65]

Lot 328: 1833 Very faint traces of circulation; sharp, bold impression, and equal to any I ever saw. [$1.60]

Lot 329: 1834 Handsome impression. [$0.40]

Lot 330: 1837 Uncirculated. [$0.60]

Lot 331: 1840 Draped Elbow; Uncirculated. [$0.75]

Lot 332: 1842-O mint; fine. [$0.60]

Lot 333: 1852 Uncirculated; sharp. [$1.20]

Lot 334: 1853 Without arrows; Uncirculated; very desirable specimen. [$12.25]

Lot 335: 1863, '4 Brilliant Proofs, 2 pcs. [$0.55 each]

Lot 336: 1865 Brilliant Proof. [$0.60]

Lot 337: 1867, '8 Brilliant Proofs. 2 pcs. [$0.65 each]

Lot 338: 1873 Without arrows, '72, '75; brilliant Proofs, 3 pcs. [$0.37-1/2 each]

Lot 339: 1880, '3, '5, '6 Brilliant Proofs, 4 pcs. [$0.40 each]

Lot 340: 1881, '2, '4, '6 Uncirculated, 4 pcs. [$0.50 each]

The commentaries after lots 339 and 340 no longer mention that 1880 and 1881 quarters were not released; possibly by 1887 they had been. Also of interest was Lot 421, described under patterns as:

1877 Copper Fifty Dollars: large head of Liberty left, by Barber, 13 stars surrounding. Reverse similar to double eagle but enlarged: FIFTY DOLLARS below: fine broad planchet (size 32); fine Proof. A prominent Philadelphia dealer recently had one of these and held it at $300, which alone will give an idea of the great rarity of this remarkable piece: this fact, however, has not influenced the owner to place any limit whatever on the piece, which will be sold on its merits solely; *first and only one ever offered.* [$20]

Several later lots are representative of the eclectic nature of Charles White's holdings:

Lot 436: Original steel hub die for California octagonal $50 gold piece (1850): eagle on a rock, with upraised wings, long ribbon in beak: shield, arrows, olive branch in talons; perfect.[1] [$2.20]

Lot 437: Hub die for pattern $10 (or a Half Do.), head in circle of stars; unfinished.[2] [$1.00]

Lot 438: Hub die for small bust of Franklin, perfect.[3] [$0.25]

Harlan P. Smith's Later Career

As it turned out the second part of the Charles White Collection was the last of Harlan P. Smith's catalogues under his own imprint. Later in the same year, 1887, he joined forces with David U. Proskey in the New York Coin & Stamp Company. In due course the pair handled many fine collections at auction, among which were numbered the cabinets of R. Coulton Davis, Lorin G. Parmelee, Francis Worcester Doughty, and George D. Woodside.

Davis, a Philadelphia druggist, had close ties to the inner circle of coiners at the Mint and thereby acquired many interesting rarities, especially in the pattern series, for which he wrote the first numismatic check list. The holding of Boston bean baker Parmelee crossed the block—or at least some of it did, as the owner bought quite a bit back—in June 1890 and at the time was considered to be the most complete cabinet of United States coins ever formed (second was the collection of the late T. Harrison Garrett, of Baltimore). Doughty was a writer of children's fiction, student of large cents (in particular), and a couple of decades later would become a screenplay author. Woodside, whatever his vocation may have been, was a hobbyist of refined numismatic tastes who acquired many gems.

Harlan Page Smith departed this earthly sphere on March 2, 1902. His private collection was auctioned a few years later in May 1906 by the Chapman brothers and, among other things, included an 1822 half eagle, one of just three known to exist. The next month the same cataloguers offered the balance of Smith's coins, after which Samuel Hudson Chapman and Henry Chapman dissolved their partnership which had been formed in June 1878. Later, both brothers conducted many illustrious auctions separately. Samuel Hudson Chapman, born on July 15, 1857, retired in 1929 and died on September 22, 1931. Henry, born on October 18, 1859, died on January 4, 1935, and remained in the coin trade until his final days. Among his last commissions was the appraisal (with Burdette G. Johnson) of the vast numismatic estate of Virgil M. Brand (1861-1926).

"Never Keep a Paper Dollar In Your Pocket Till Tomorrow"

Hidden: 1860s
Found: By 1888
Treasure: Thousands of U.S. coins

The Panic of 1857

Aaron White, a New Boston, Connecticut, lawyer, had a deep and abiding dislike of banks, financial in-

[1] This may have been a hub created by Charles Cushing Wright in New York City to create dies shipped to San Francisco for the 1851 (*sic*) $50 coinage of August Humbert, United States assayer of gold. Alternatively, it could have a connection to Francisco engraver Albrecht Küner, who cut some later (circa 1852-1853) $10, $20, and $50 dies for the U.S. Assay Office of Gold, using various size punches. A different punch for a $50 piece by Küner is in different relief and is signed with his name (unlike the punches used in the early 1850s) and was employed much later to create souvenir impressions for the 1915 Panama-Pacific International Exposition; this particular punch would have been in existence during the 1880s when the White Collection was sold.

[2] This would have been a U.S. Mint hub die, era unknown, except that in 1838-1839 certain pattern half dollars (but no known $10 gold coins) were made with a Liberty head and stars; about this same time the coinage of $10 pieces, suspended since 1804, was resumed utilizing a Liberty head by Christian Gobrecht.

[3] This could have been any one of various Franklin busts or even a Civil War token obverse die later (circa 1900-1910) believed to have used by Stephen K. Nagy to create impressions by flattening the obverses of copper cents dated in the 1840s and 1850s, this latter piece listed as No. 14990 in Gregory Brunk's *American and Canadian Countermarked Coins* and also illustrated with a full-page photograph (specimen from the present author's collection) on p. 202.

Scene in Wall Street, New York City, during the height of the Panic of 1857.

stitutions, and paper money. It is said that he may have sustained losses in the bankruptcies and financial difficulties of 1857. At least the date 1857 figured prominently in his thinking.

Early in that year the country was riding a wave of feverish speculation in real estate and in railroad stocks, the latter comprising the vast bulk of the most actively traded issues on the New York Stock Exchange. Railroads were America's growth industry, lines were expanding rapidly including to the West, and profits could be immense. However, not all was well with banks, insurance companies, and financial markets.

On August 24, 1857, the New York City division of the Ohio Life Insurance & Trust Company failed, followed by its parent company shortly afterward.[1] Following the August announcement, "conditions in the money market rapidly approached a state of panic."[2] This triggered a wave of financial crises. Banks in some larger eastern cities stopped paying out silver and gold coins, and by year's end several thousand companies were bankrupt. A later government report, *Condition of Banks in 1857,* revealed that throughout the year most banks in America issued paper money equal to many multiples of the amount of coins on hand to redeem such notes if they were offered. During the same year, railroad shares fell precipitously, examples being the January to October crash of Michigan Southern stock from $88 to $15 and Illinois Central from $123 to $79.

Concerning New York City banks, the report noted that on January 1, 1857, banks had liabilities of $43,974,000 and held $6,557,000 in specie (gold and silver coins). By June 6, specie had increased sharply to $14,370,000, but liabilities had increased far more dramatically, to $127,703,000. Thus, although there were more coins in banks' hands, wild speculation in railroads, lands, and other areas put many bank assets in non-liquid form.

Banks began to noticeably weaken on September 4, when a broker protested a non-payment of just $250. Two more small protests occurred with other banks on the 12th and 15th. This precipitated a call for redemption of paper notes in coins, and accelerated a trend that had been increasing each month since June. Toward the end of September, three leading banks failed in Philadelphia, and the other leading banks there suspended specie payments. By October 1, more than 30 banks had failed in New York state.

On October 13, 1857, all banks in New York City, with the single exception of the Chemical Bank, stopped paying out silver and gold coins.[3] Most banks remained solvent, but not liquid. Paper currency is-

[1] Ohio Life's main business was banking, and its bills of exchange were accepted in virtually all parts of the United States.

[2] Margaret G. Myers, *The New York Money Market,* Vol. I., 1931, p. 142. This work also gives many details about the worsening conditions of banks during the year and the high ratio of paper money and credit in relation to coin reserves (specie). Myers' detailed account of the Panic of 1857 does not mention any losses of gold coins en route from California.

[3] The Chemical Bank was severely criticized by its competitors for not suspending; shortly afterward, Chemical Bank's privileges at the New York

sued by insolvent private banks became worthless or for a time sold for pennies on the dollar, later to become valueless as well.[1] Meanwhile, notes of solvent banks sold at various small discounts in terms of cash, although some clothing merchants and others took the opportunity to advertise that they would accept currency at par in exchange for merchandise.

Following the suspension of specie payments, banks in New York (mainly) and New Orleans accumulated unprecedented amounts of coin, of course to the detriment of the value of their circulating paper. On November 7 the first steps were taken for solvent banks to resume paying out coins, and this was accomplished on December 11. In New York state certain obligations, particularly of inland banks, were allowed to be paid out via a time schedule, these and other arrangements to be administered by the state banking superintendent, James M. Cook. New England banks were generally more solvent than those in New York state, and in the southern United States there was little problem at all.

Didn't Like Paper Money

It may have been that Aaron White was left holding the paper money of a failed bank or otherwise suffered depreciation of his assets during the uncertain times of October and November 1857. Whatever the reason, he later issued a satirical medal depicting on one side a sow hanging from a hook, and the inscription 1837-1857 SUS PENDENS[2] (probably a reference to banks' suspension of specie payments in 1837 and again in 1857) and NEVER KEEP A PAPER DOLLAR. The reverse continued the inscription with IN YOUR POCKET TILL TOMORROW. Depicted on the reverse was another sow, this one rooting in a jar inscribed 10, and the inscriptions DI OBOLI, DEUX SOUS, and SUS TOLL ENS.[3] At a later date dealer W. Elliot Woodward stated that "these tokens were suppressed by the government and are now very rare."[4]

Back to the Past: 1837

By 1857 the Panic of 1837, also alluded to on the medal, was a distant memory for most American citizens, but apparently not for White. Following widespread land speculation combined with reckless issu-

The Merchants' Exchange in New York City was an important financial center in the 1837 era and was depicted on a Hard Times token.

ance of paper money by banks with questionable assets, New York City and many other eastern banks suspended specie payments on May 10, 1837. Coins were hoarded, and few federal issues were to be seen in general circulation. To fill the need for a commercial medium a wide variety of what today are called Hard Times tokens were minted. Depreciated currency of the era, known then as wildcat notes and shinplasters and today as broken bank notes, are also of great interest to numismatists. As is the case with the 1857 financial difficulties, Aaron White's specific involvement in the 1837 monetary scene is not known today.

Hoarder *Par Excellence*

While most hoarders who disliked paper money preferred gold, White had a penchant for copper and nickel coins. Copper-nickel 1862 and 1863 Indian cents were bought by him directly from the Mint and stashed. Old half cents, large cents, colonials, and other copper coins were squirreled away as well. Gold and silver coins were very few by comparison. All told, the American pieces in the hoard seem to have amounted to around $2,000 or so in face value, but as most coins were of smaller denominations the *quantity* was vast.

After White's death his hoard was taken to the attic of a warehouse where it remained for years. Later it was examined by dealer Édouard Frossard, who disposed of the majority of pieces privately and offered the rest in an auction on July 20, 1888, billed as "18,000 American and foreign copper coins and tokens selected from the Aaron White hoard."

Clearing House were revoked! Such was the nature of competition in America at the time.

[1] The financial difficulties of 1857 are mentioned in the section of Chapter 11 devoted to the *S.S. Central America* and its treasure. An excellent account is found in R.M. Devens, *Our First Century*, pp. 644-652.

[2] Sus = sow; pendens = suspended or pendant.

[3] Di oboli = two oboli, a small Greek copper coin; deux sous = two sous, a small French copper coin; toll ens = rooting. Perhaps White intended to convey the sentiment that paper *dollars* were worth *two cents* each in terms of coins.

[4] Woodward's comment in his May 1884 J.N.T. Levick Collection catalogue. Levick was arguably America's leading collector of tokens in his era. Today, the White tokens are still considered somewhat scarce. All seen by the writer have been with mirror Proof surfaces.

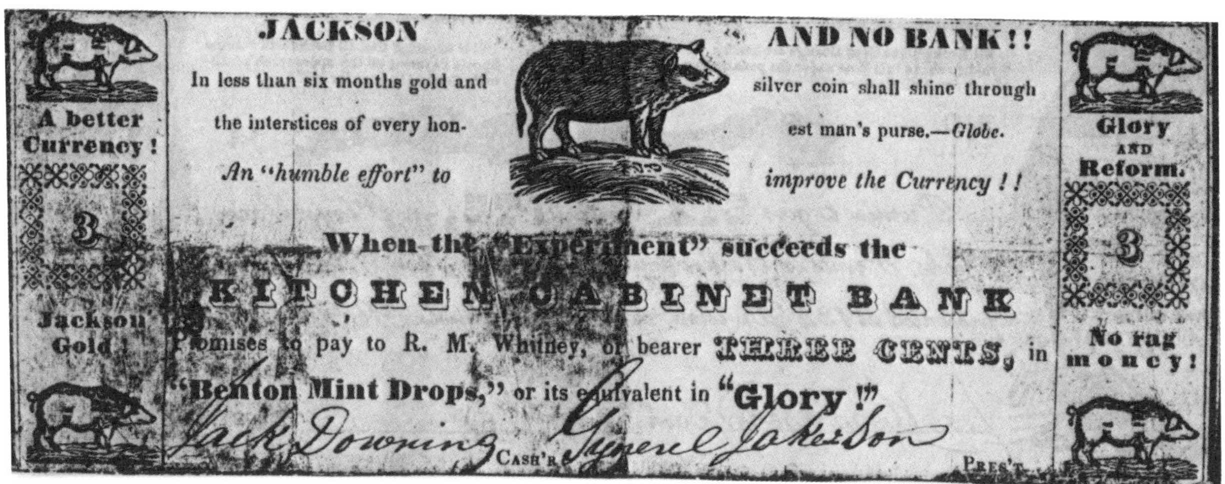

Aaron White was not the only satirist of the American monetary situation. These privately-issued notes appeared in the 1837-1840 era. (Courtesy of Russell Rulau)

What Aaron White Had

Benjamin P. Wright, an early student of tokens and medals, summarized certain of White holdings as follows:

250 colonial and state copper coins.
60,000 copper large cents [which were mainly "rusted" and spotted; 5,000 of the nicest ones were picked out and sold for 2¢ each].
60,000 copper-nickel Flying Eagle and Indian cents [apparently most dated 1862 and 1863].
5,000 bronze two-cent pieces.
200 half dollars.
100 silver dollars.
350 gold dollars.
20,000 to 30,000 foreign copper coins.

The Frossard auction catalogue omitted the bulk coins and concentrated upon those of numismatic value. That listing included the following federal coins:

Half cents dated 1800-1855: 945 pieces.
1795 plain edge copper cents: 19.
1795 lettered edge cents: 2.
1796 Liberty Cap cents: 2.
1797 cents: 26.
1800 cents: 14.
1802 cents: 34.
1803 cents: 42.

1804 cent (altered date): 1.
1805 cents: 23.
1806 cents: 16.
1807 cents (including some 1807/6): 34.
1808 cents: 24.
1809 cent: 1.
1810 cents: 29.
1811/0 cent: 1.
1811 cents: 6.
1812 cents: 65.
1813 cents: 18.
Miscellaneous cents 1795-1813, "worn, holed, stamped": 471.
Cents 1816-1856, Poor to Very Good: 3,902.
Copper-nickel cents: 338.

And these miscellaneous items adapted from the original catalogue descriptions; modern commentary in brackets:

Early American coins: 47 Wood's halfpence, 1723, low grades; 1 Rosa Americana coin, not described; 7 Nova Constellatio coppers; 41 Fugio cents; 56 Connecticut coppers; 29 New Jersey coppers; 42 Massachusetts coppers; 1 1787 Nova Eborac copper; 5 Vermont coppers dated 1788; and 7 North American tokens dated 1781.

Hard Times tokens: 174 pieces.

Civil War tokens: 534.

Brass tokens with inscription including CONTRAHENDO ET SOLVENDO, etc.: 559. [This legend translates approximately to: "I drag (or pull) together and loosen up," apparently a reference to pants suspenders, a punning allusion to the suspension of specie payments. Today these are known as Rulau Y-3, Y-3C, Y3E, and Y3G.[1] Y-3 is described as brass, 27mm. diameter, with obverse legend: CONTRAHENDO ET SOLVENDO / PUN. GO. / SEM. PAR. Russell Rulau theorizes that SEM. PAR may refer to Semper Paratus ("always prepared") if, indeed, the abbreviations are Latin. The reverse is inscribed SUSPENDER BUTTONS / TWO / CENTS / 1837 1857. The planchet is perforated with two "buttonholes." Y-3C is smaller, 19mm., and has the obverse inscription CONTRAHENDO ET SOLVENDO / S.P.[2] enclosing the numeral 2 flanked by two small circles in imitation of buttonholes. The reverse legends are: SUSPENDER BUTTONS / 1837 / (two small circles) / 1857. Y3E, 19mm., has an obverse similar to the preceding, but a reverse inscribed THURSDAY at the top and 1863 below. Y3G, also 19mm., has an obverse similar to the preceding. The reverse is that found on a token attributed to Cuba and has YNGENIO ECUADOR above, 1864 below, and a palm tree at the center. These relate to the Ecuador ("Equator" in Spanish) sugar estate, Camaguey Province, Cuba, and translate to Equator Sugar Mill.[3] This same palm tree die is found muled with at least a half dozen patriotic Civil War token dies, indicating that the Aaron White-related token may have been struck simply as a novelty for collectors.]

White's own NEVER KEEP A PAPER DOLLAR, etc., tokens: 105 in copper, 147 in brass, one in white metal.

Brass calendar medals of the type sold in 1863 by White: 16. [The obverse displays a calendar of seven columns and six lines headed CALENDAR / FIG. DAY / CHANGE YEARLY. On the same side of the medal are far-ranging inscriptions including EMANCIPATION / JAN. 1, 1863, INDEPENDENCE / JULY 4, 1776, and CONSTITUTION / MARCH 4, 1789. In reference to the year at hand is the notation EQUINOXES / MAR. 20 SEP. 23. The reverse gives life dates of men from history: Franklin, Jefferson, Washington, and Lafayette. The medal is signed at the bottom: AARON WHITE, / NEW BOSTON CONN. / JAN. 1, 1863. PRICE 25 CTS.][4]

Proof strikings of a token, COLONEL PERCIE CLARK, etc.: 191. [Russell Rulau advises that Frossard, a careless cataloguer, should have referred to Percie Kirk, a figure from British history. Kirk, a major-general by 1688 and remembered by historians as being a very cruel man, led the relief of Derry in 1689; Aaron White's tokens depict a bust facing left, presumably that of Kirk, with the inscription COLONEL PERCIE KIRK around. White's token obverse was copied from or inspired by a 1796-dated British evasion halfpenny, Atkins-64 (but which had a different reverse, pertaining to North Wales. On the reverse is a seated figure copied from the Britannia of British minor issues, with the date 1686 below, and the inscription BRITONS OWN HAPPY ISLE. The whole affair is reminiscent of one of the satirical "bungtown" British halfpence produced in the late eighteenth century, but in this instance of a generally later appearance. In fact, it bears a stylistic resemblance to Alfred S. Robinson's NON DEPENDENS STATUS fantasy token dated 1778, created circa 1862-1863.][5]

An examination of the foregoing Frossard listing shows it is not particularly valuable for present-day research inasmuch as certain coins (*e.g.*, cents of 1798, 1801, and 1814) must have been grouped or sold sepa-

---

[1] *Standard Catalog of United States Tokens 1700-1900,* pp. 271-272. Russell Rulau suggests these tokens "were apparently struck by the Thomas Kettle firm in Birmingham, England," but this does not seem likely to the present author.

[2] L.B. Fauver, *Exonumia Symbolism & Classification,* 1982, pp. 205-208, illustrates and gives theories concerning these pieces, suggesting that the abbreviation "S.P" means "slave power" and referred to the burning political and humanitarian issue of the day. However, S.P. could just as easily have referred to SEM. PAR., as discussed above. PUN. GO. and SEM. PAR. quite probably were abbreviations of Latin phrases, as White seems to have preferred this language for certain inscriptions.

[3] Information from Russell Rulau, letter, August 12, 1996, who pointed out that such past numismatists as Fonrobert and Eklund had unknowingly attributed them to the country of Ecuador. For further reading and sources upon which Rulau drew see his book, *Latin American Tokens,* Krause Publications, 1992, p. 333.

[4] This medal was described and illustrated by George and Melvin Fuld in *The Numismatist,* June 1959.

[5] For information about Robinson, who (significantly?) lived in Hartford, Connecticut, and must have known White, see Richard D. Kenney, *Struck Copies of Early American Tokens,* 1952, pp. 3-6. Robinson, a man of many business interests—including the sale of rare coins—enjoyed making fantasy pieces. The NON DEPENDENS STATUS dies are said by Kenney to have been cut by George H. Lovett; if this is so, Lovett probably also cut the PERCIE KIRK dies for White. Biographies of G.H. Lovett are found in Leonard Forrer, *Biographical Dictionary of Medallists*,1904, *Vol.* III, pp. 480-483, and the *American Journal of Numismatics,* April 1894, p. 104 (obituary).

rately, no dates are given for the copper-nickel cents, and so on.[1] However, Frossard's descriptions of White's token productions open the door to a veritable fun house of modern numismatic research possibilities!

It Was Just Pocket Change

Buried: 1900s onward
Disclosed: 1975
Treasure: Various coins

In 1975 Wayne Miller was a fledgling in the coin business in Helena, Montana.[2] He would become well known in the field, particularly so with his landmark *Analysis of Morgan and Peace Dollars,* released in 1976, followed by *The Morgan and Peace Dollar Textbook,* published in 1982. Along the way he would handle quite a few silver dollar bags from the famous Treasury dispersal of 1962-1964 and the Redfield Hoard of 1976. However, that is not the thrust of this account.

As Wayne relates the story:

I received a telephone call from a couple who had some coins for sale. They invited me to their home in the Helena Valley. As I parked my car I noticed a most unusual dog house—it consisted of three bales of hay! The husband was an ex-Marine in Army fatigues, over six feet tall. His wife was Chinese and at least a foot shorter.

The interior of their home consisted of narrow pathways to the kitchen, bathroom, and bedroom, and a very constricted view of a television set in the living room. The rest of the house was crammed from floor to ceiling with an assortment of newspapers, magazines, old appliances, car parts, etc. Glancing at what must have been many tons of worthless junk, my expectations for their coin collection plummeted. However, when the first coin I saw was a nice Uncirculated 1916-D half dollar, my heart raced!

As I examined the somewhat dusty group (they had been buried loose in their dirt floor basement and had been removed when there was a threat of flooding). I noticed that the latest dated coin was from 1948. The wife explained that she was the eldest daughter of a Chinese family that had moved to Helena in the early 1900s. (Helena had a sizable Chinese population because of its beginnings as a mining town in 1864.) It was the family's custom to set aside extra money and pass it on to the oldest daughter in each generation.

After I sorted the pieces I was amazed at their high quality. There were virtually no worn or circulated coins! This was no ordinary coin collection!

The wife said that for many years her family would put extra money into a jar. What I was looking at was pocket change from 1916 to 1948. No one in the family was numismatically knowledgeable; no effort was made to find or save anything rare, or unusual.

After looking through about 135 marginal to gem brilliant Uncirculated 1916-S Mercury dimes, I realized why I had never bought a single 1916-D dime from the local public. If there had been any released in Helena, surely some would have been in this hoard. Obviously, when Mercury dimes were sent to Helena around 1916 and 1917 they came from the San Francisco Mint, not from the closer mint in Denver.

There were several dozen high-grade 1916-D half dollars, several hundred Denver Mint Washington quarters from 1932 to 1939 (including 30 or more of the rare 1932-D), and many other Denver and San Francisco coins. However, there were only a few silver dollars, and there were no Indian cents or Buffalo nickels. These had been sold earlier to another "coin dealer" at double face value!

My generous offer for their 1,500 coins delighted them. They thought that the most they would be able to get would be twice their face value!

About six months later the couple brought in their gold coins. Included were about 20 $20 double eagles, 50 $10 pieces, 90 $5 coins, and 200 $2.50 pieces. Most of these were quite nice. There were also about 100 gold dollars, but most had been damaged or used as jewelry, including about 30 that had been holed and put on a chain. The gold coins realized another $15,000 for the owners. Of course, the coins were worth a lot less in 1975 than they would be today.

About a year later the couple called again: Would I know anyone who would buy sapphires? We met at the bank. They handed me a quart fruit jar full of raw sapphires (one of the largest sapphire deposits in the world is about 20 miles east of Helena, on the banks of the Missouri River.) The jar contained over 20,000 carats of sapphires!

After disposing of the silver coins, the gold, and the sapphires, I waited for the next call. But I never saw either of them again. Too bad—I had come to expect the unexpected from this unusual couple.

---

1 Benjamin P. Wright, "American Store or Business Cards," serialized in *The Numismatist,* 1898-1901; this token is Wright's no. 1230. John F. Jones, "The Aaron White Hoard of Coins," *The Numismatist,* February 1938 (Jones interviewed Frossard who told him of the hoard contents and of 5,000 copper cents sold for 2¢ apiece). Walter H. Breen, "A Survey of American Coin Hoards," *The Numismatist,* October 1952. White's tokens are described in the Hibler-Kappen text, *So-Called Dollars,* as HK-829, 830, and 831. A satirical medal related in concept is Betts-115 (C. Wyllys Betts, *American Colonial History Illustrated by Contemporary Medals,* 1894), of 1720, with a legend that translates to "credit is as dead as a rat," and showing (per Betts) "a man lying dead on rocky ground grasping a winged caduceus in his right hand, and in his left a packet, inscribed ['letters of exchange'], his cocked hat has fallen near him."

2 Adapted from an interview with Wayne Miller conducted by the author in Denver, Colorado, August 16, 1996; reviewed and edited by Wayne Miller, letter, September 26, 1996.

Two Tons of Coins—Really!

Put away: 1950s onward
Found: Circa 1983
Treasure: Various coins

Wayne Miller, the aforementioned Montana professional numismatist, has had his share of unusual properties, but few matched a hoard that came to light in the early 1980s.[1] Here is the story as adapted from his own account:

> Sometime in 1983 I received a call from a fellow tenor in the Helena Symphony Chorale. He told me that his father had recently passed away and left him a coin collection. He was a bit vague describing its contents, but he was sure that it weighed over a ton. I was skeptical, but intrigued.
>
> About a month later I traveled to Los Angeles to meet my friend at a storage facility. He ushered me into a room measuring about 16 feet square. I was stunned by the sight of a gigantic pile of coins measuring about two feet high in the center and spreading out to the walls!
>
> My friend explained that he and his late father had been estranged for 20 years. His dad had been a Greek merchant who ran a neighborhood grocery store. For over 30 years he saved every unusual coin that came his way. At the end of each week he would package these in penny-candy bags and take them home. The son had not seen his father for a long time and had never visited his home. Upon opening the front door to his father's house he found a well-worn trail leading to the kitchen, bedroom, and bathroom. The entire rest of the house was piled to the ceiling with newspapers, magazines, broken appliances, and other things.
>
> [Sound familiar? See the preceding "It Was Just Pocket Change" story—Wayne Miller seems to have a way of stumbling on such places!]
>
> It took my friend 45 days to clear all the debris away. As he did this, he came across the little bags of coins and set them aside. There were about 1,600 sacks, each with varying amounts of pieces therein. After he had sorted the loose and bagged coins from the tons of newspapers and other worthless junk he called me.
>
> It took four people four 12-hour days just to empty the little bags and divide the coins by denominations. There were about 200,000 wheat-back Lincoln cents, 35,000 silver dimes, 15,000 silver quarters, 12,000 silver half dollars, 2,000 or so silver dollars, 22,000 Eisenhower dollars, and about 5,000 assorted world coins. The accumulation had been started about 1950 and continued until the father's death in 1983. Imagine an accumulation of nearly 300,000 coins weighing over 4,800 pounds, assembled from 1950 to 1983. One would assume such a hoard would contain hundreds, even thousands of scarce coins. But there was virtually nothing exciting at all. So much for the numismatic desirability of Los Angeles pocket change!
>
> My friend's father also had a hoard of countless filled liquor bottles upstairs over his business, in a stifling hot, unventilated, upper room. The wine had of course deteriorated, but the whiskey was okay. The retail value was easily $100,000. These bottles were sold for $15,000 as a lot.

Under the Schoolhouse Floor

Put away: 1946 onward
Found: 1996
Treasure: Various coins and tokens

Living in a Remote Town

Alexander K. Miller, who lived in the isolated village of East Orange, Vermont, was a peculiar sort of fellow.[2] Miller and his wife Imogene moved there from New Jersey in 1946 to retire and, as it turned out, remained for the rest of their lives. The town, reachable only after traveling several miles on unpaved roads, is sufficiently remote that it has no zip code and was not included in the 1990 United States census. It was the ideal place for privacy, it seems. With only a few exceptions, people in the outside world did not know of the Millers, nor would they during their lifetime. However, in 1996, that would change dramatically!

The Miller house in East Orange, Vermont, as photographed in the summer of 1996. (David Hewett photograph, copyright *Maine Antique Digest*).

---

[1] *Ibid.*

[2] Information from David Sundman (president, Littleton Coin Co.), letters, September 7 and 13, 1996; Christie's catalogue of the Miller automobiles, September 1996; Article in the Manchester, NH *Union Leader*, September 6, 1996, "His Mystery Was Vintage Cars, Collection of Vermont Man Estimated at $1.24 M," by Anne Wallace Allen. Other sources are subsequently cited.

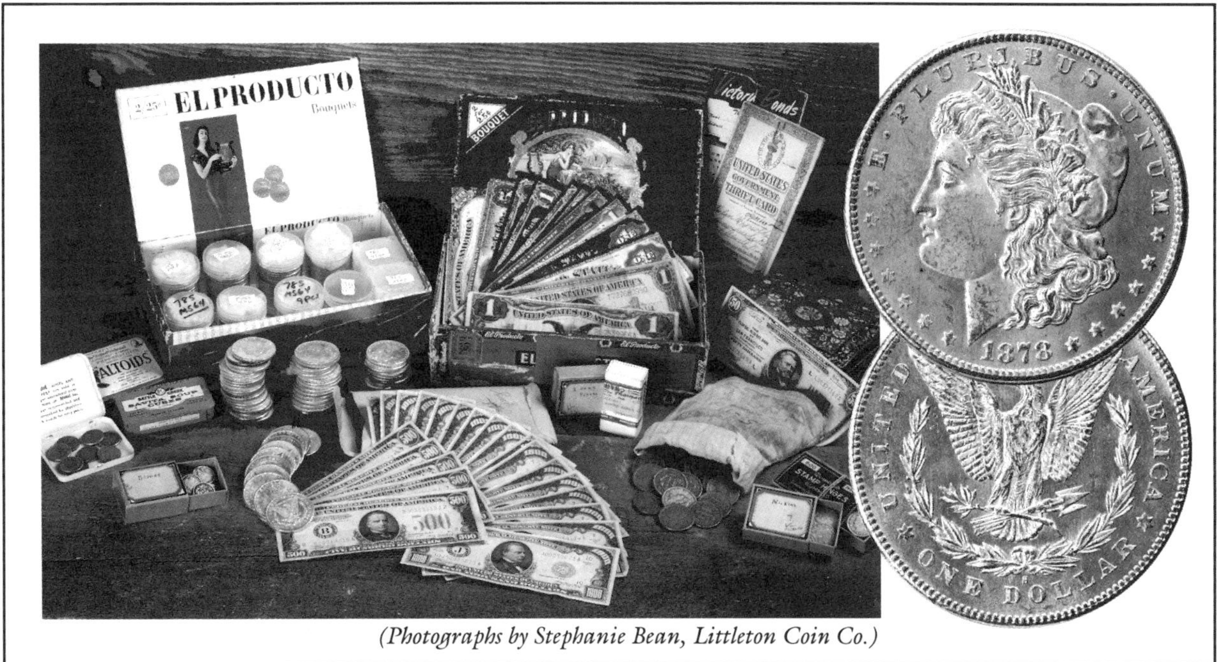

(Photographs by Stephanie Bean, Littleton Coin Co.)

Born on July 14, 1906, the only child of Edward S. and Jane Kennedy Miller, Alexander spent much of his early life in Montclair, New Jersey. He became a collector of license plates by age 16. In the 1930s he engaged in "expert automobile repairing" and offered Miller's Flying Service for "aeroplanes rebuilt and overhauled," according to one of his old business cards. In World War II he served in the Royal Canadian Air Force. He maintained his interest in aviation, as evidenced by his acquisition of an old World War I biplane which for a time he stored in a barn on his Vermont farm, after which he sold or traded it away.

After moving to East Orange, Alexander and his wife did very little socializing. They kept to themselves, and rarely discussed their interests or affairs. However, he must have reached out now and then, as his next-door neighbor remembered him as treasurer of the local church for two decades. He was a student of the Bible and often quoted verses from it. In 1957, Alexander's father, a prosperous New York merchant and securities dealer, died and left his son a substantial amount of money. Apparently, some or much of this was converted into "hard assets" such as coins.

In Vermont, Alexander K. Miller kept active with automobile repairing, but no longer on a commercial basis. Rather, he collected and restored cars that interested him—and that included just about everything from classics to rusted modern junk. Along the way he accumulated many parts—seemingly far more than he could ever use.

In addition to his cars, he enjoyed other old methods of transportation including pedaling around on a 1903 Eureka bicycle. Miller would often trade cars or other items with other collectors. He gave the impression that he had no telephone (but he did), and engaged in protracted negotiations via letters and postcards, often demanding gold, silver, or cash in payment. Other times he would have a check made out to one of his favorite religious organizations. Obviously, Alex was a generous man.

W. Murray Clark, owner with his family of Clark's Trading Post, Lincoln, New Hampshire, recalled communicating with Miller over the years and visiting him upon occasion in East Orange.[1] At one time Miller had some Indian cents, and Clark had some brass lamps and other auto parts. A trade was to be arranged. The two met on the first floor of the Miller home, but after some give-and-take discussions, Clark came to the conclusion that the Vermonter wanted high retail prices for his coins, but wanted to acquire the auto parts below wholesale. End of transaction. Murray Clark also had the impression that Miller had brought many of his various coins with him from New Jersey, and had acquired relatively few after his move.

Alexander Miller relished his surroundings and remained there until his death from a fall from a ladder while installing storm windows, in autumn 1993 at age 87. His wife Imogene, age 78, died in Montclair, New Jersey, in February 1996.

---

[1] Conversation with the author, October 11, 1996. The Clark family members have been fine personal friends for many years.

A Great Surprise!

Upon the passing of Imogene Miller, the couple's assets were nearly entirely intended to go to religious groups. When administrators visited the property, they were amazed at what they found on the rundown farm. Cars, antiques, gold and silver ingots, coins, and other items were estimated to be worth about $3 million!

Underneath an old schoolhouse and other outbuildings on the property was found $82,000 in silver coins, including a small but interesting cache of 1878-S Morgan dollars. Some $100,000 worth of gold coins is said to have been located as well. However, most of his gold was in bullion form—about $900,000 in large ingots. Silver was in 70-pound ingots that a representative of Christie's later said "resemble loaves of bread." About $200,000 worth of stocks and $700,000 in promissory notes were also located.

The tin-roofed house in which the Millers lived had not seen serious repair or renovation for a long time. Mrs. Miller scrimped, and instead of buying raincoats she made them from plastic bags. Apparently, both husband and wife scraped by with just the barest of essentials in their personal life. They were good people, if a bit eccentric.

A pack rat deluxe to outsiders, and perhaps a clever buyer in the view of his fellow collectors, over a period of time Alexander Miller accumulated about 40 old automobiles, some of which had great collectors' value. On May 24-26, 1996, Archie and Joshua Steenburgh sold at auction the first group of accumulations from the Miller buildings.[1] About 600 to 700 people were on hand, a combination of serious bidders and curiosity seekers. Among the items crossing the block were typewriters, furniture, mechanical gadgets, and music boxes. Murray Clark recalled that prices were quite high the first day, but after the novelty wore off, there were some excellent values to be had—including for a half dozen or more antique sewing machines Murray acquired for his collection.

By this time the state of Vermont had filed claims totaling nearly $900,000 against the Miller estate, Uncle Sam was in there with a demand for $7,300,000 (noting that the Millers neither had Social Security numbers nor had ever filed tax returns), and 50 other claims had been recorded!

Dispersal of the Treasures

At a sale held by Christie's auction house at the Vermont farm in September 1996, such marques as a 1935 Stutz Bearcat and, from more recent times, a 1962 Rolls Royce Silver Ghost Piccadilly Roadster crossed the block. Stutz had been Miller's favorite brand, and he had quite a few stored in old, but well maintained buildings around his property. If one has to have a favorite marque of old car to buy in quantity, fewer names are better than Stutz, the Indiana manufacturer that went out of business before World War II.

For the first day of Christie's sale, September 7, about 3,000 people crowded into East Orange. Most had come to look around, but quite a few registered as bidders. Highlight of the car auction was a 1916 Stutz 4C Bearcat which fetched $173,000. The Rolls Royce went to a new home for $129,000. On the other hand, "Volkswagens sold for pocket change; one brought $23 (the buyer was an eight- or nine-year old boy bidding with his allowance money and his dad's approval), and another brought $12.08."[2]

Littleton Coin Company, which seems to always be on the lookout for quantities of interesting things to sell, latched on to the 1878-S Morgan silver dollars found under the schoolhouse floor, and in September 1996 began to offer them for sale. Thus, before long quite a few collectors around the country will have a bit of Vermont folklore to go with the coins they buy.

Miss Drury's Little Tokens

The Miller holdings included another surprise, not necessarily valuable, but quite interesting.

In the early years of the present century, continuing into the 1920s, Miss Millie J. Drury operated a retail business and, later, a lunch room in the lower level of the Grange Hall in Williamstown, Vermont.[3] The building later burned, and today no trace of it remains, although the local historical society has an old-time photograph showing part of her sign there.

---

[1] David Hewett, "Three-Day Auction Disperses First Part of Miller Estate," *Maine Antique Digest,* October 1996. The sale was held under the supervision of a court-appointed asset management team, the Stratvest Group.

[2] "Miller Auto Trove Exceeds Wildest Expectations; Brings $2.18 Million," *Maine Antique Digest,* October 1996. Certain information also from John R. White, "A Car Auction of Legend," *Boston Globe,* September 14, 1996.

[3] Information from David Sundman, letters, September 18 and 20, 1996; certain information also from the Williamstown Historical Society; subsequent footnote information from the Rulau *Standard Catalog of United States Tokens 1700-1900.* Also R.G Dun's credit report of July 1909.

In 1909 her business consisted of selling "fancy goods," toys, and novelties. At the time, fancy goods were generally defined as including small items that added to the enjoyment of life, such as clocks, vanity mirrors, binoculars, china plates, etc. Her business was not particularly well financed, and in 1909 it was said that her assets were less than $500.[1] Of course, in that era, such an amount went much further than it would today.

Sometimes when a business or person is long gone and largely forgotten, a numismatic memento will serve as a souvenir to excite the curiosity of a later generation of collectors. Among the Alexander Miller treasures a cache of 48 aluminum cent-size tokens was found. Each one bore on the obverse the inscription MISS M.J. DRURY / WILLIAMSTOWN / VT., with the reverse reading GOOD FOR ONE 5¢ CIGAR.[2]

Used in the early twentieth century, such pieces were probably stored in the payout slot of a trade stimulator and given as prizes in an era when cash rewards were prohibited. Such mechanical devices were made by the Mills Novelty Co., Exhibit Supply Co., Watling, Caille Brothers, and others, and usually were placed on top of a store counter, often near the cash register. Upon the deposit of a cent, wheels would turn, or dice would be shaken, or another game of chance would be activated. If a lucky combination was hit, a token would be dispensed. This token could be exchanged for merchandise, in this case a cigar.

Somewhere along the line this little group of 48 tokens, most showing signs of use, was preserved and acquired by Alexander Miller, to be purchased in 1996 by Littleton Coin Co. These pieces have relatively nominal numismatic value in the overall scheme of market prices, but like many tokens, they certainly have an interesting history!

---

1 R.G. Dun's *Mercantile Agency Credit Report,* July 1909.

2 The reverse of this Vermont token is similar to those listed by Russ Rulau in his *Standard Catalog of United States Tokens,* pieces described as having been issued by the Brooks News Company, Jamestown, New York (Brooks was a printer and also operated a news company and sold news and cigars, circa 1900-1902); also a token issued by Meile Yund, Mill Grove, New York (who kept a store at the turn of the century in this small Erie County town of 257 people, per the 1910 census); a token bearing the imprint of. O. Dimick, of Newark Valley, New York (who operated a hotel, circa 1900-1914); and a token issued by S.A. Wright, of Ouaquaga, New York (Samuel A. Wright's business flourished circa 1900-1920 in a town which by 1918 had 100 people, a wagonmaker's shop, Wright's General Store, and a grocery). In a conversation with David Sundman, September 17, 1996, Russell Rulau commented that the Drury token is the only variety known to him that has the word "Miss" as part of the name of its issuer.

Domestic tranquillity (presumably) in the era of large cents—as illustrated in a nineteenth-century engraving.

CHAPTER 4

Those Old Copper Cents

Today, few series are more avidly collected than old copper "large" cents minted from 1793 to 1857. Some of these can be pedigreed to old-time hoards. Interestingly, although the Nichols Find and Randall Hoard have been known for a long time and mentioned extensively in literature concerning cents, little is known of the circumstances of their original concealment.

In the nineteenth century the copper cent was the most ubiquitous of all American coins. After 1857, when these were redeemed by the Treasury Department, many millions of coins remained unlocated. Most probably disappeared one at a time during the era in which they were used. But—who knows—perhaps a few hoards are yet to be discovered.

The Nichols Find

Hidden: 1797
Found: By 1859
Treasure: Cents of 1796 and 1797

Benjamin Goodhue on the Scene

Chances are excellent that if you encounter a Mint State 1796 or 1797 copper large cent, it will be linked by pedigree to the famous Nichols Find (also known as the Goodhue-Nichols Find).

According to numismatic tradition, these pieces came from an original bag of cents obtained in late 1797 or early 1798 by Benjamin Goodhue, who was born in Salem, Massachusetts, in 1748 and died there in 1814. Goodhue, a Federalist, was a representative to Congress 1789-1796 and a senator 1796-1800.

If Goodhue obtained the pieces at the Mint, it would probably have been after November 21, 1797, for during 1797 coins were only delivered by the coiner to the treasurer from November 22 to December 18. Blank planchets had been imported recently from Matthew Boulton of Birmingham, England, such planchets being remarkable for their high quality (in sharp contrast to those made within the Mint which were often irregular or of uncertain purity). As a result, coins in collections today and attributed to this hoard, are apt to have particularly smooth and glossy surfaces.

It is believed that Goodhue gave the coins to his daughters, from whom they descended in the family. Eventually, they were distributed from the Salem area.

One account (Breen, 1952) quotes a rumor that the coins came from Major C.P. Nichols of Springfield, Massachusetts.

David Nichols of Gallows Hill

In any event, by 1858-1859, the numismatic community was aware of the coins, at which time they traded for about $1 each. By 1863 all of the pieces had been dispersed—apparently by David Nichols—by which time they had a market value of about $3 to $4 apiece.

Another account (*Penny Whimsy,* p. 189) suggests that they were dispersed to collectors, "perhaps just prior to 1863," and that "David Nichols of Gallows Hill, near Salem, passed them out at face value."

The assigning of the quantity of 1,000 pieces to the hoard is assumed from Mint records that show in 1797 that the Mint regularly issued cents in bags of 1,000 and boxes of 5,000 coins. As at least several hundred specimens are known to exist today, the 1,000 estimate may be reasonable.

Varieties Included

Today, the typical Nichols Find cent is apt to be glossy brown with somewhat prooflike fields, toned a medium brown. Varieties attributable to this source include 1796 Sheldon-119, 1797 S-123 and 135, and, to a lesser extent, 1796 S-104 and 118; 1797 S-122(?), 136, and 137.

Specimens of 1798 S-154, not in the Nichols Find, appear to have been struck on planchets from the same Boulton lot and were probably made very early in 1798, possibly as part of a shipment arriving from England on the *H.M.S. Adriana* in spring 1797.[1]

The Randall Hoard

Hidden: Circa 1830s
Found: By 1869
Treasure: Thousands of large cents

Beneath a Railroad Station Platform

Of all nineteenth-century American coin finds, the most famous is the so-called Randall Hoard, named

Railroad of the 1830s—of the type associated with at least one account of the Randall Hoard.

after a later owner of the cache. Even today, mention of the Randall Hoard recurs with frequency in auction catalogues and sale lists. Probably just about any numismatist who has collected large copper cents for more than a few weeks has heard of it.

Among United States large cents of the early years of the Matron Head design, nearly all are very elusive in Mint State, except for the first five years, 1816 through 1820. Today, many of these exist, with 1818 and 1820 being the most numerous. Such coins are commonly attributed to the Randall Hoard. Cents dated 1816 are in the minority and are not even mentioned in some historical accounts of the hoard and may be from another source.[2]

While notices about the Randall Hoard differ in some details, it seems to be the consensus that a *small* wooden keg (or perhaps more than one keg) filled with Uncirculated copper cents was found beneath a railroad station platform in Georgia after the Civil War, but before autumn 1869.

The cents may have been hidden during the 1861-1865 Civil War to prevent discovery, or they may have been stored in such a railroad facility before that time, possibly as early as the late 1830s.[3] Alternatively, the hoard may have had nothing to do with any railroad

---

[1] Sources include Walter H. Breen, "A Survey of American Coin Hoards," *The Numismatist,* January 1952; Breen, *Encyclopedia,* 1988, p. 189; Dr. William H. Sheldon, Dorothy I. Paschal, and Walter Breen, *Penny Whimsy,* 1958, pp. 189-190. Breen (1952) lists these further sources: Breen, *Copper Coinage Figures Revised,* in the May-June 1951 *Coin Collector's Journal;* George H. Clapp and Howard R. Newcomb, *U.S. Cents 1795-6-7-1800,* p. 17; Adam Eckfeldt, "Cent Book," 1796-1803, bound ms. volume in R.G. 104, Treasury Section, National Archives, Washington, D.C.; same source, treasurer's receipts for copper coins; Joseph N.T. Levick, "Reminiscences of Coin Collecting," *American Journal of Numismatics,* December 1868 (the reference there to "Mr. C." is to Edward D. Cogan); Dr. W.H. Sheldon and Homer K. Downing, *Early American Cents,* 1949, pp. 11, 173-175, 183, 190-192; various W. Elliot Woodward auction catalogues including October 1864 (Levick, Emery, Illsley, Abbey), lots 620-622, December 1866 (Jencks and Paine), Lot 316, January 23, 1882 ("Elmira") Lot 972, January 8, 1884 (Ely), Lot 673 and photographic plate in front of the catalogue, January 21, 1889 (Stetson), Lot 15 (Breen: "The accounts in the 'Elmira' and Stetson catalogues vary slightly, but the substitution of Nichols for Goodhue in the last-named was probably a slip of memory; W.E.W. was then very old, nearly blind, and generally declining. All of his late catalogues were put out with help from younger dealers, and many show rambling reminiscences not seen before 1879 except in rare tantalizing fragments").

[2] However, in most modern references and citations the 1816 is included; *e.g.,* John D. Wright, *The Cent Book,* 1992, p. 4, concerning 1816 Newcomb-2: "Possibly a few thousand Mint State examples survive from the Randall Hoard circa 1867."

[3] The 1830s represent the first decade of growing popularity of the railroad. This is only relevant if, indeed, a railroad platform was involved. Atlanta, settled in 1833, was founded in 1837 at the end of the Western & Atlantic Railroad and at first was named Terminus. However, there were many other Georgia cities and towns antedating the railroad, that could have received a keg of copper cents in the 1820s, shortly after their manufacture. However, it is likely that no railroad platform was involved (see later footnote).

platform (as usual, hard facts are scarce).

Walter Breen related that in the 1816-1820 period the Philadelphia Mint reused wooden kegs that had been obtained from Boulton's establishment in Birmingham, England, from whom the Mint bought blank planchets.[1] These kegs typically held about 14,000 cents or cent planchets, although Mint records exist of kegs containing 12,000 to 18,000. However, as the Randall Hoard coins were described as being in a *small* keg, quite possibly the number was less, perhaps on the order of 5,000 to 10,000 coins. Again, hard facts are lacking.

An early citation (given below) indicates that some 1825-dated cents were included as well, but for a long time specialists (*e.g.,* Walter Breen) considered this unlikely as Mint State cents of that date are very rare and have been for a long time. In his sale of August 16, 1887, under Lot 654, W. Elliot Woodward, stated the Randall Hoard contained cents from 1817 to 1856, but the latter date was probably a typographical error or a slip of memory.

What the Hoard Contained

The knowledge we have today of the hoard is due in large part to the publication in 1869 of an answer to a correspondent. Ebenezer Mason, Philadelphia coin and stamp dealer, published this in his magazine:

> L.M. Troy. Beware of bright pennies of old dates. Buy them as restrikes, but not as originals. We can send 1816, 1817, 1818, 1819 (large and small dates) and 1820 U.S. cents for 25 cents each, or fair ones for 2 cents each.

This evoked a response from veteran dealer Edward D. Cogan, who wrote this to Dr. Charles E. Anthon, for publication in the *American Journal of Numismatics.* The date was January 11, 1870:

> My Dear Sir:—
>
> When I presented to our Society, through my friend Mr. Betts, at the last meeting, the cents of 1817, '18, '19, and '20, I did so upon the full conviction that they were from the issues of the U.S. Mint, struck in the years of which they bear the date. Judge, then, of my surprise to find in Mason & Co.'s Magazine, of this month, a caution against buying these pieces as being re-strikes.
>
> I believe all these pieces were purchased of Mr. J. Swan Randall, of Norwich, in the state of New York, and I immediately wrote to this gentleman, asking him whether he had any idea of their having been re-struck from the original die, and herewith I send his reply, which exculpates him from having reason to believe that he was offering anything but original pieces; and from his statement I must say I believe them—as I have from the time I purchased them—to have been struck at the Mint in the years of their respective dates.
>
> Yours faithfully,
>
> Edward Cogan.

Randall's letter, datelined Norwich, January 7, 1870, is given herewith:

> Edward Cogan, Esq.
>
> Dear Sir:—
>
> I should not sell coin that I knew or believed to be re-strikes without letting it be known. The bright, Uncirculated cents I have sold of 1817, 1818, 1819, 1820, and 1825, I am very sure ***are not re-strikes.*** I bought them of Wm. H. Chapman & Co., dry goods merchants of this village, and the head of the firm, W.H.C., informed me that he got them of a wholesale merchant in New York, who informed him that he got them from a merchant in Georgia; that he took them as a payment on a debt, and that the Georgia merchant wrote him that they were found since the war in Georgia buried in the earth.[2]
>
> Mr. Chapman said to me that he was in New York about the time the cents were received there, and that the merchant who had (ditto) thought they were too large to use, and did not know what to do with them; and that he

[1] Walter H. Breen, "Survey of American Coin Hoards," *The Numismatist,* January 1952.

[2] Thus negating the "railroad platform" theory mentioned by others later, unless the hoard was beneath a railroad platform ***and also*** buried in the earth.

(Chapman) thinking that his customers here would be pleased with bright cents, offered ninety cents a hundred for them, which was immediately taken.[1]

Chapman & Co. commenced paying them out here, and their bright appearance and old dates made many think they were counterfeits, and they were called "Chapman's counterfeits," and the firm stopped paying them out.

I then went to the store and asked W.H. Chapman if he had disposed of many of his bright cents. He replied, "No. I made a bad bargain," and laughed about their being regarded as his counterfeits.

I then offered to take them at the price he paid—ninety cents a hundred—and he was very willing to let me have them. They were loose together in a small keg,[2] and the great mass of them were of 1818; and a great many, though apparently Uncirculated, were more or less corroded or discolored. I enclose herewith one of the 1817 and 1818, discolored on one side and bright on the other, From this statement, you will see that there can be very little doubt about their being the genuine issues of the United States Mint of their respective dates.

Very respectfully,
John Swan Randall

Randall passed to his final reward on January 1, 1878. Shortly thereafter, on May 6-9, 1878, Edward D. Cogan offered the remaining coins at auction, comprising 85 pieces dated 1817, 1,464 of 1818, 67 of 1819, and 500 "various dates," presumably including many dated 1820.

Becoming Elusive

The typical specimen seen today with a Randall Hoard pedigree is a mixture of bright original red with flecks and stains of deep brown or black. Few if any are pristine (uncleaned, undipped) full mint red.

According to Walter Breen's research sponsored by Wayte Raymond in the 1950s, the most readily available variety attributable to the Randall Hoard is 1818 Newcomb 10, followed by 1820 N-13.[3] Curiously, both of these varieties are usually seen with die breaks linking the stars and date. Then follow in descending order of rarity the 1817 N-14, 1816 N-2, and the 1819 N-9 and N-8 are encountered.

However, by 1988 Breen revised his thoughts and stated that 1816 N-2 and 1819 N-9, although traditionally ascribed to this hoard, were from other groups, and that the Randall Hoard included specimens of 1825 N-9.[4] Inasmuch as a few nineteenth-century commentaries did not mention 1816, but did include 1825, perhaps this is nearer the truth, if not fact.

As late as the 1950s it was not unusual to see groups of Randall Hoard coins in dealers' stocks. By the 1990s the supply had become widely dispersed, and when seen such coins were apt to be as single specimens.

In Retrospect: Not Plentiful in 1859

In 1859 in his *American Numismatical Manual,* Dr. Montroville W. Dickeson wrote of the cents of various years, but at this time the hoard was not known, nor would it be, apparently, until after the Civil War. Thus, in 1859 the 1820 was viewed as being rare. Extracts from Dickeson:[5]

1816 cent: They are quite plenty, and can be procured looking as fresh as when they first came from the Mint.

1817: The metal of which they were composed is well milled and very hard, which protects the face of the coin. They are hence in a good state of preservation.

1818: Plenty and well preserved.

1819: Equally plenty, and in good order with the preceding emission out.

1820: The slight milling of the edges of these coins render good specimens difficult to be obtained.[6]

The Mansion House Cornerstone

Hidden: 1809
Found: By 1871
Treasure: Cents dated 1809

Thomas Birch & Sons' June 21, 1871, sale of the M.W. Nickerson consignment offered as Lot 183 an 1809

[1] At the time one-cent pieces were legal tender only to the amount of 10¢. Although they normally circulated at par and probably could have been spent at par in the 1860s, from time to time, including for a period in the 1840s and 1850s, cents were in oversupply in certain commercial channels (such as in New York City from 1841 through 1853) and traded at a discount for face value.

[2] Significant contemporary mention that they were in just one keg, and it was small. The hoard "grew" as later stories of it reach print, these being by people not involved in the original find or distribution.

[3] Rarity information is from Walter Breen, *United States Minor Coinages 1793-1916*, p. 11.

[4] Breen, *Encyclopedia*, 1988, p. 202.

[5] Pages 211-212.

[6] Dickeson suggests that the "milling of the edges"—the rim on the coins—is not sufficiently raised to protect the surfaces from contact marks and undue wear.

large cent, "One of nine taken from the cornerstone of the Mansion House, Philadelphia; extremely rare."[1]

Years earlier the Mansion House, located at 122 South Third Street, was considered to be one of the leading stopping places in the city, with its well-known contemporaries including the U.S. Hotel (opposite the Bank of the United States), City Hotel, National Hotel, Washington Hotel, and Congress Hall.[2]

Today, 1809 is considered to be the scarcest date among United States large cents of the 1808-1814 Classic Head design. It would be interesting to learn more concerning the opening of the old cornerstone and what else, if anything, was found there.

The Hidden Find

Secreted: Early 19th century
Found: before 1889
Treasure: Large cents

In his catalogue of the Charles Stetson Collection, January 21, 1889, W. Elliot Woodward offered as Lot 26 an 1802 large cent, not otherwise attributed, described as: "One of the few known as the Hidden Find, discovered many years ago in Rhode Island."[3]

As A. Conan Doyle did in his Sherlock Holmes detective stories with mysterious references such as the "giant rat of Sumatra," Woodward and his contemporaries printed many asides in their catalogues, some of which were probably recognized at the time by the knowing ones, but most readers probably had no clue as to the meaning of the references. A certain William E. Hidden was a well-known antiquarian and numismatist around the turn of the twentieth century (his collection was sold by Thomas Elder in 1916); could he have been associated with the Hidden Find?

Of course, if the coins had been concealed prior to their finding, this group could be referred to as the hidden Hidden find (not to be confused with the Hoard Hoard; see Chapter 12)!

A Copper-Filled Stump

Hidden: 19th century
Found: before 1914
Treasure: Many large cents

A acquaintance of Walter B. Gould, of Winterport, Maine, related years later in 1914 that:

> [Gould] had copper cents ever since he was a small child, and before he knew what money was, or copper was, and thinks that copper is to him a magnet, or that he possesses a magnetism for coppers.
>
> At one time in the Maine woods several miles from any habitation he kicked several hundred of the U.S. copper cents out of an old rotten stump where they had been for a great many years. This find was advertised at the time, but no one ever claimed the coins. He never knew, then, who owned the land the stump was on that held the coins.
>
> Most of these cents from that stump were dated before 1849 [although a listing showed some dated as late as 1855],

[1] Citation furnished by Bob Vail.

[2] *The Traveller's Guide Throughout the Middle and Northern States,* G.M. Davison, Saratoga Springs, New York, 1834, p. 69.

[3] Citation suggested by Bob Vail

and a few were so much worn that the date cannot be seen. For years friends who had seen the cents he had in a showcase in his store would contribute now and then one or more as they happened to get them, and he received some from Eastport (Maine), Oregon, California, and many other places.

Anyway, he has kept all that came to him and bought large lots, until he has now about two bushels altogether of this one kind of coin. For the past two weeks Mr. Gould and his family have worked spare time sorting dates and dies....

In the Gould hoard of many thousands of large cents somewhat over 80 to 100 pieces were found with counterstamps by certain merchants (for example, USE G.G.G. & G.G.G.G., a patent medicine) and were believed to be of special interest and value. In 1914, Gould offered to exchange such counterstamped cents to anyone "for most any relic or coin worth a few cents." The eventual disposition of this vast hoard of copper cents, most of which were not counterstamped, was not recorded.[1]

In the same era George C. Arnold, proprietor of the Arnold Numismatic Company, Providence, Rhode Island, made a specialty of buying old large copper cents in quantity and had thousands of them on hand.

A Sleepy Tramp?

Lost: 1897 or later
Found: 1910
Treasure: Miscellaneous coins

Sometime in 1897 or soon thereafter, a tramp or other itinerant may have fallen asleep on the Boston Common, the large park-like area in the downtown of that Massachusetts city.[2]

A few years later in 1910, workmen "unearthed over 75 coins, not to mention various badges and a gold ring." Although it seems unlikely that such a large number of items would have been lost casually,

Boston Common as it appeared in the nineteenth century.

[1] Certain information is from Bowers, *The Strange Career of Dr. Wilkins: A Numismatic Inquiry,* 1987, pp. 11-12, with the quotation about Gould being from *Collector's Blue Book,* May 1914.

[2] Adapted from an account by Howland Wood, "Buried Coins," *American Journal of Numismatics,* October 1910, pp. 156-157. This is how numismatic "facts" are created; Howland Wood had no way of knowing whether these were unconsciously deposited or that they "rolled out one by one," etc.

Howland Wood, a prominent numismatist, seemed to think so and wrote this:

> The recent excavations furnish an instance of hidden treasure unconsciously deposited by man, for these pieces rolled out one by one from the pocket of someone lying down to rest, and were lost for the time as surely as if they had been purposely buried.
>
> The coins found were of various dates from 1779 to 1897, many of them being old cents of our fathers, struck between 1800 and 1852. Quite a number of foreign coins as well were exhumed.

If such coins were in the pocket of a snoozing citizen, he or she must have been carrying the family coin collection, for by 1897 (the latest date) copper large cents of the 1800-1852 era had long since passed from circulation, to say nothing of other coins dated as early as 1779.

The New Bedford Coin Blast

Hidden or lost: 1798 or later
Found: 1914
Treasure: Various coins

New Bedford, Massachusetts, is a storied town and figures prominently in American maritime history, particularly in the annals of the whaling industry. In the early nineteenth century square-rigged sailing ships departed from there and were often gone on voyages lasting up to a year or two seeking oil for lamps that illuminated homes across the nation.

However, years later, for a short time in 1914, the community received attention of another sort. An account datelined New Bedford, January 9, tells the tale:[1]

> Granite workers preparing for a blast near the road between this city and Fall River dug up a bag of coins, some of them dated before the Revolution and none of them dated later than 1798. All were of copper, and it took considerable cleaning before they could be deciphered.
>
> Of the 11 coins two were of the famous old Liberty pennies, dated 1797 and 1798 respectively, and there is one King George [English] penny dated 1774.
>
> As interesting and peculiar as any of them, however, are the old Fugio pennies. These pennies have on one side a design of the sun and below it a sundial. Under this design is the date, 1787, and the legend "Mind Your Own Business," while the Latin inscription, "Fugio," is printed on the edge.[2]
>
> On the reverse are 13 links in a circular chain, emblematic of the 13 original states. These Fugio coins were manufactured in Connecticut by a citizen there, and under a special act of Congress in 1786 and 1787, and there was but a limited number to the issue. They are rare now and eagerly sought by collectors.

No great treasure here, it seems. However, the unidentified newspaper writer at least had access to a numismatic book telling about Fugio cents.

The South Shore Hoard

Hidden or lost: 19th century
Found: By 1910
Treasure: Large cents

In the catalogue for the Allison W. Jackman Collection, sold June 28-29, 1918, Philadelphia dealer

1 Published in the *Boston Herald,* January 10, 1914. Citation provided by David Sundman, Littleton Coin Co.

2 The actual motto is MIND YOUR BUSINESS (with no "OWN"); the inscription, "Fugio," meaning "I fly"—a reference to the rapid passage of time—appears on the obverse of the coin, not the edge, but it is near the rim. Congress awarded a contract for their coinage in 1787.

Henry Chapman, in the offering of various lots from No. 762 intermittently to 772, presented 42 "bright Uncirculated" United States large cents. These were said to have been from the South Shore Hoard once in the possession of Boston dealer H.E. Morey.

Born in Malden, Massachusetts, on April 21, 1848, Morey became fascinated with coins at a young age in 1857 when the old copper "large" cents were discontinued. Although he graduated from the Massachusetts Agricultural College in 1872 and pursued other lines of work, his interest in coins was maintained, and at one time he was offered the curatorship of the Mint Cabinet.

In 1890 he became a professional numismatist and bought out the interests of Boston dealer Henry Ahlborn, who had published coin premium lists since at least 1875. Morey seems to have conducted a business based upon the widespread sale of his coin-buying catalogue, a forerunner of what B. Max Mehl would do in the next century. Along the way Morey bought many things from the public.[1]

A Cache of Large Cents

Hidden: 19th century
Found: By the early 1940s
Treasure: Cents dated 1826

The late Oscar G. Schilke, lived on the shore of Dodge Pond in Niantic, Connecticut, in the 1950s and 1960s. Prominent on the numismatic scene for many years beginning in the early 1930s, he would often set up exhibits in banks. These displays served to attract customers to the financial institutions, and for Oscar it mean getting leads which often resulted in his acquiring choice pieces for his collection.

On one particular day a gentleman told him that in the course of doing some work in the Boston harbor area, he came across what was left of an old building which was once the office of a customs agent or toll-taker of some kind—the informant wasn't sure. In any event, cemented into the floor of the structure was a little metal vault or strongbox which, through an opening, appeared to contain a bunch of old coins.

Oscar went to Boston with the gentleman in question, and after some effort pried the top off of the box, to reveal an early-day version of a piggy bank. All in a heap were dozens of large cents dated 1826, and no others. Grades ranged from worn nearly smooth on up to lustrous Uncirculated, or close to it. Apparently, some long-forgotten person once took a fancy to this particular date and each time an 1826 cent was found in the course of commerce it was dropped through a slot in the floor into this tiny chamber. As large cents did not circulate much after 1857 and not at all after the summer of 1862, presumably this cache was formed in the 1840s or 1850s, after which it was untouched for the best part of a century.

Perhaps the original depositor passed away and never told anyone about the cents, or perhaps he realized that their value was insufficient to warrant tearing up the floor. For several years afterward, Oscar Schilke had a good trading stock of cents of this date![2]

The Boston Cornerstone

Hidden: 1821
Found: 1981
Treasure: Cents dated 1821

In 1821 a building was constructed in Boston, and to memorialize the event at least seven new copper cents were placed in its cornerstone. In 1981 the structure was razed, and the long-forgotten pieces came to light.

These coins were attributed as two specimens of 1821 Newcomb-1 and five of 1821 N-2. Both N-1 coins were called Mint State-63 by the cataloguer, while four of the five examples of N-2 were graded MS-63 and the fifth MS-60.

---

[1] Citation suggested by Bob Vail. Certain information about Morey is from *American Numismatic Biographies,* Pete Smith, 1992. It has been suggested that the profits earned by Morey, Mehl, and other issuers of premium catalogues were primarily from the sale of the catalogues, not by profits from rare coins purchased by catalogue holders.

[2] Recollection of Oscar G. Schilke to the author.

Adding to their appeal was the appreciation of the 1821 cent as the second (after 1823) scarcest of the later-date large cents. Sold at auction by New England Rare Coin Galleries in 1981, six of the pieces went to Gary Fitzgerald and one to Roy E. Naftzger, Jr.[1]

A Remarkable Find of Large Cents

Hidden or lost: 19th century
Found: 1996
Treasure: Large cents

In 1996 a feature article by Burnett Anderson in *Numismatic News* told of "a remarkable hoard of 4,700 large cents" that came to light in New Jersey and was acquired by Stephen K. Ellsworth, a Clifton, Virginia dealer.[2]

"It appears to have been untouched by two or three generations, and may go back to the 1880s," Ellsworth was quoted as having said.

Grades of the coins are said to range from Good to Very Fine. Among the pieces were a number of scarce issues, including two of the rare 1799 (but none of 1793). The hoard was acquired through New Jersey numismatist Robert W. Miller, who first learned of it from a friend.

It was related that 3,500 of the cents were dated from 1816 to 1839, about 600 in the range of 1794 through 1814, and the balance from 1840 through the end of the series in 1857. The hoard was assumed to have come from somewhere in "eastern Pennsylvania."

A later account in *Numismatic News* reiterated that the hoard had more than 4,000 coins, but 3,559 were from the period 1816 through 1839.[3] The name "Butternut Hoard" had been assigned to the group, from owner Ellsworth's business, Butternut Coins.

---

[1] John D. Wright, *The Cent Book,* 1992, pp. 81-82. James L. Halperin, letter, July 1, 1996. New England Rare Coin Auctions, October 1981 Long Beach Sale, lots 58-64.
[2] July 2, 1996, "Large Cent Hoard Discovered."
[3] September 17, 1996, "Large Cent Hoard Departs from Expected Pattern."

CHAPTER 5

Those Small Cents, Too

Flying Eagle cents (1856-1858), Indian cents (1859-1909), and Lincoln cents (1909 to date) have come in for their share of hoard stories, too. In fact, just about every family in America is apt to have a "hoard" of Lincoln cents at this very moment, if all of the pieces in piggy banks, drawers, shelves, purses, and other places are put together in a pile!

Here are some interesting and quite varied accounts of hoards from the past:

Dry-goods store in the nineteenth century. Illumination was by gas lamps. The hoarding of coins in summer of 1862, continuing through 1863, caused many hardships for those in the retail and service trades.

The Collapsing Floor

Stored: 1862
Treasure: Copper-nickel cents

Lots of Indian Cents

By early 1862 the outcome of the Civil War was uncertain, and the public began to hoard "hard money." At first, gold coins were saved and then silver.

By early summer 1862, Liberty Seated half dimes, dimes, and other silver issues were nowhere to be seen in commerce. The only federal coins in general circulation were copper-nickel cents. These cents had been minted for circulation since 1857, when the Flying Eagle cents made their debut, to be followed in due course by Indian cents in 1859.

In order to making handling of cents easier, many people wrapped them in paper rolls or put them up in packets of 25, 50, or 100 coins, to later use them in trade. American financial historian Neil Carothers told what happened:[1]

> Bus companies, theatres, and restaurants accepted these rolls everywhere. A retail store in New York received so many that the floor of the room in which they were stored collapsed.

By the second week of July, 1862, no federal coins of any kind were to be seen in circulation in the larger eastern cities. Even the once plentiful copper-nickel cents had disappeared. The lack of cents caused great difficulty with ordinary transactions such as paying for barber services, newspapers, and public transportation.

[1] Neil Carothers, *Fractional Money,* 1930, p. 187. Citation suggested by Michael Hodder.

Several types of substitutes arose including printed cards or "chits" valued from 1¢ upward, postage stamps glued to cardboard or put in paper envelopes, postage stamps in brass frames ("encased postage stamps"), federal Postage Currency notes, and, especially, private tokens.

Cents at a Premium

Copper-nickel Flying Eagle and Indian cents continued to be hoarded, probably as late as December 1863, if an advertisement in the December 1 number of *Thompson's Bank Note & Commercial Recorder* is any indication. At that time, there must have been some demand for these at a premium, enough to warrant this notice:[1]

> NEW PENNIES
> U.S. Pennies for sale in bags from Ten to One Hundred Dollars, at Ward's Shirt Manufactory, 387 Broadway, N.Y.

Unfortunately for numismatists, such vast hoards of what must have been several tons of copper-nickel Flying Eagle and Indian cents are not known to have been preserved, and likely as not, most of the coins were back in general circulation by spring 1864, by which time the shortage of small change had eased.[2]

A Remarkable Hoard of Indian Cents

Hidden or lost: 1862
Found: before 1918
Treasure: 1862-dated cents

On January 25 and 26, 1918, Thomas L. Elder, New York City, conducted an auction featuring the Robert Hewitt and B.C. Bartlett collections. Included was a remarkable hoard of 1862-dated Indian cents.

Lot 318 was described: "1862 C. Nickel. Bright. Unc. 125 pcs." This was followed by lots 319 to 323, each described as "Bright Unc." and each containing 100 coins.

Then came Lot 324, also of 100 coins, "Unc. red." Apparently, these were toned. Lot 325 featured 50 specimens, "Unc. Bright." To this point 775 pieces of Mint State 1862 cents had been offered. Then followed three lots of 100 coins each, described as containing mixed cents dated from 1857 to 1862, each including "many" 1862 cents, but without the number specified.

Accordingly, it is probable that the Elder hoard consisted of about 1,000 specimens of this date.[3] After July 1862, any cents released by the Mint—which was coining them in large quantities—were apt to be hoarded. Perhaps the Elder hoard of about a thousand coins remained intact from this pivotal era in American history.

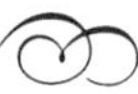

The Endicott Hoard of Cents

Put away: Early 20th century
Disclosed: 1950s
Treasure: Rolls of Lincoln cents

In the late 1950s a gentleman who lived in Endicott, New York, located a cache of bank-wrapped Uncirculated rolls of Lincoln cents, mainly of the dates 1910 through 1915. These were all from the Philadelphia Mint, with not a Denver or San Francisco coin in the lot. Each coin was sparkling, brilliant Uncirculated, virtually as nice as the day of mintage, save for a trace of natural light toning.

Many dozens of these rolls were eventually sold to the Empire Coin Company (Q. David Bowers and James F. Ruddy) and in due course were distributed into numismatic channels.[4]

---

1 Citation furnished by Eric P. Newman.

2 History repeats itself, and an article in *Coin World,* July 22, 1964, told of a sagging (but, apparently, not collapsed) floor. "Braden Coin Hoard Set For Sale" related that $60,000 in coins had been located in the lodgings of the late Clarence Braden, of Jefferson, Texas, who was described as a frugal professor. The coins, of which perhaps $3,000 worth were numismatically valuable, were "found in shoe boxes and cigar boxes under Braden's bed and in a closet; weight of the coins caused the apartment's floor to sag."

3 Catalogue copy furnished by Frank Campbell, American Numismatic Society, New York City. Citation suggested by Bob Vail.

4 Recollection of the author.

"This Is Your Life" Dr. Kate

Gathered: 1954
Treasure: Millions of cents

Stories about caches and accumulations of Lincoln cents have filled coin magazines, newspapers, and popular journals for many years. However, possibly the Lincoln cent hoard to end all Lincoln cent hoards was one described by television producer Ralph Edwards, a friend of the author, who in 1992 responded to a letter about an earlier campaign he started nationwide to gather these coins. In his words:

> I presented "THIS IS YOUR LIFE, DR. KATE PELHAM NEWCOMB" on March 17, 1954. Dr. Kate was a country practitioner serving patients in 300 miles of wilderness in the north woods of Woodruff, Wisconsin. She ministered to wounded hunters, trappers, injured lumberjacks, and Indians. She revived half-drowned vacationers and trudged miles on snowshoes through frozen woods to deliver babies by the light of a kerosene lantern. She was called "an angel on snowshoes."
>
> Dr. Kate Newcomb was born on July 26, 1885, in Wellington, Kansas, daughter of Thomas Pelham and Kate Callahan Pelham, country school teachers. After her mother's death when Kate was three years of age, she went to live with her grandparents in Leoti, Kansas. When her father remarried, she moved to Buffalo, New York, to live with him and his new wife.
>
> Dr. Kate opened her medical practice in Detroit, and in 1920 married a husky auto plant employee, Bill Newcomb. Bill became seriously ill, and Dr. Kate left a thriving medical practice to move to Crandon, Wisconsin (south of Lake Superior), where Bill recovered. An elderly Dr. Torpy pleaded with Dr. Kate to assist him on an emergency case. That was the last case Dr. Torpy was able to take, which left the backwoods without a doctor. Therefore, Dr. Newcomb met the challenge of becoming the country doctor in a remote wooded area with no hospital within a 300 mile radius.
>
> After the show, I told the television audience of the hospital Dr. Kate had dreamed of building which would be opened formally the next Monday morning. I said to the viewers: "It takes a lot of pennies to build and equip a hospital. There's still a construction debt to pay off, and there's a lot of equipment to buy *before* it can truly fulfill its mission. And that'll take a lot of pennies, too. We thought maybe you folks in our audience would like to share in Dr. Kate's great work...."
>
> Over $250,000 worth of pennies was received in Woodruff, Wisconsin, for the new hospital."

This $250,000 in face value translates to 25,000,000 "pennies," far eclipsing any other hoard of these coins that has come to our attention.

Several Other Lincoln Cent Hoards

Additional examples of Lincoln cent hoards include:

In 1979 Edwin Rommel, of Cold Brook, New York, deposited in his bank one million cents that he had gathered over a period of 20 years. The stash filled 200 cloth bags and weighed three and one-half tons.[1]

In the 1990s a front-page article in *Coin World* was captioned: "Adage 'a penny saved is a penny earned' becomes lifestyle for 70-year old Ohioan. Eight million cents fill 40 large cans." Ray Amoroso, collection manager for the Steel Valley Bank in Dillonvale, Ohio, age 70, had been collecting cents since he was five years old. Talk about a long-term interest!

Possibly even more prevalent in the press than accounts of deliberately acquired accumulations of cents are stories of "spite" quantities in which someone who disliked paying a debt, such as taxes, fulfilled the obligation with a bucket or wheelbarrow full of Lincoln cents.

The latter concept is hardly new, as is evidenced by an article, "Cents as Legal Tender," in the October 1846 issue of *The Bankers' Magazine:*

> In a case pending before the Baltimore County Court, sitting as a court of appeals, Judge Purviance presiding, a question arose as to whether cents are a legal tender. From the evidence, it appeared that the appellant had tendered, in payment of a debt amounting to upwards of $20, bags of cents, which were refused.
>
> On the part of the appellee it was contended, upon the authority of a decision of the Supreme Court of South Carolina, that cents are not legal tender in payment of any debt amounting to more than four cents, as the smallest silver coin is a half dime or five-cent piece, and as the Constitution of the United States uses only the words gold and silver.
>
> For the appellant it was maintained that the Act of Assembly of Maryland, 1812, makes the coins of the United States current money, which may be tendered in payment of debts in Maryland, and that cents are as much the coins of the United States as any coins issued from the Mint.[2]

[1] "Turns In Cent Hoard," *Coin World,* January 31, 1979, p. 60.

[2] It may be of interest to note that in the nineteenth century, New Hampshire decreed that all transactions, to be legal, had to be expressed in the British system of pounds, shillings, and pence. In 1950 an alert state legislator noted that this law was still in effect! It was promptly changed, and from 1950 to date, Uncle Sam's dollars have been legal tender in the state.

In the course of the evidence it appeared that the tender was not made to a person authorized to receive it, and therefore the case passed off upon this point. The learned judge, however, in the course of his opinion, intimated that no difficulty could exist as the fact of cents being a legal tender, and in support of his opinion referred to a note to *Greenleaf on Evidence,* page 436, an able work, sanctioned by the approbation of the late Judge Story, in which it is declared "copper cents and half cents are established as part of the currency, and by implication made a legal tender, by statute in 1792, Chapter 39, Section 2."

Indian Cents in a Virginia Mansion

Hidden or lost: 1880s
Found: 1970
Treasure: Indian cents

Around 1970, James F. Ruddy purchased a large group of common-date Indian cents that had been found in the attic of an old mansion in Virginia. Nearly all were dated in the 1880s—nothing rare here. Each coin was Mint State, indicating that the group had been put away decades earlier, quite possibly at the time of issue.

Upon careful examination, two of the 1888 Indian cents were determined by Jim to be overdates, 1888/7, a variety previously unknown to numismatists. Publicity was given to the issue, and every expectation was that additional pieces would turn up. However, years went by, and the variety remained rare. Today in the 1990s these two specimens remain the finest known of their kind, although further examples have been located (in worn grades).[1]

[1] Account from James F. Ruddy, circa 1970.

CHAPTER 6

Fabulous Silver Hoards

This is the story of two hoards of silver coins, one of which is fairly well documented, but which retains a share of mystery. The other is known by inference from occasional specimens seen today, but its origin and dispersal remain enigmatic, although several speculations and theories have reached print.

Thus, while the following pages tell much, there is still abundant opportunity for research and new discoveries concerning each.

The Economite Treasure

Hidden or lost: 1830s or later
Found: 1878
Treasure: Many silver coins

The Village of Economy

One of the most remarkable of all nineteenth-century coin hoards is the so-called Economite Treasure (or Hoard) found in 1878 at Economy, Pennsylvania.[1] The coins had been gathered by "Rappites" of the Harmony Society, a utopian work-share commune which followed the teachings of their spiritual leader, German immigrant George Rapp, who in turn was guided in certain decisions (such as church design) by an angel, it was said.[2] After Rapp's demise his leadership was assumed by others.

The Economy community prospered during the mid-nineteenth century and can be said to have been a financial center of western Pennsylvania. At one time the Rappites loaned money to the city of Pittsburgh to aid with the building of a water works. On another occasion the fledgling state government of Indiana was given financial assistance. Nicholas Biddle—one-time president of the Bank of the United States and for a long time the pre-eminent banker in the East—dealt directly with the Harmony Society, so important was its patronage.

At least two popular accounts have it that this fabled trove of silver coins—the Economite Treasure—was secreted in a cellar in 1863 to avoid capture by Confederate raider General John Hunt Morgan.[3] However, it seems much more likely that these coins and other money were sealed in vaults by bricks and mortar at some other time, by the end of the year 1836. By this time the Harmony Society had tens of thousands of dollars' worth of silver, and within a decade the amount would top $500,000. If, indeed, any coins

---

[1] Today, Ambridge, a town named for the American Bridge Co., is on most of the original land, although a small part of the original village is preserved as a historical site.

[2] Arthur E. Bestor, *Backwoods Utopias*, 1970, described selected all-for-one, one-for-all socialistic settlements in the United States, most of which flourished in the nineteenth century. Numerous other texts have been published on the subject. Well-known examples include Brook Farm, Amana, Oneida, Ephrata Cloisters, various Shaker villages, early Mormon settlements (such as in Ohio), etc.

[3] Morgan may have buried his own treasure seized in other raids against the Yankees, per W.C. Jameson, "General John H. Morgan's Buried Treasure," *Buried Treasures of the Ozarks and Appalachians*, pp. 293-297.

Old Economy Village in Pennsylvania as seen circa 1880. The building which housed the Cabinet of Curiosities, including the rare coin collection, is the large structure seen to the right. On view were many marvels of history, nature, science, and manufacture, for the enjoyment and education of visitors. The facility was established by 1827 and added to over the years. In 1846 a theft occurred, but those responsible were caught shortly thereafter and at least some of the coins were recovered. What happened to them in later years is not known. (Old Economy Village Archives, courtesy of Raymond Shepherd)

were quickly hidden in advance of Morgan's anticipated depredations, they must have been other than those forming the Economite Treasure discussed here. These particular silver coins had long since been hidden away by the time the Gray challenged the Blue.

It seems probable that at one time there were three substantial caches of silver (primarily) and gold coins stored in as many vaults. The Economite Treasure of silver coins here discussed was taken from one of these hiding places. What happened to the contents of the other two is not known.

While the single vault in question seems not to have been added to after 1836, deposits of silver and gold coins in the other two chambers continued well past that date—at least into the 1840s—and in 1838 included newly-acquired gold English sovereigns.[1]

The coins in the 1878 Economite Treasure discovery were mostly United States silver issues from 1794 onward, but some foreign pieces were present as well. The pieces were blackened from being stored in damp surroundings for over 40 years, and after their discovery were all cleaned to remove tarnish.[2] It seems that earlier issues dated from 1794 through the next two or three decades showed evidence of wear, but it is likely that many coins struck in the 1820s through 1836 were Uncirculated.

Hoard Described in 1878

The *Sharon* (Pennsylvania) *Herald,* December 22, 1878, printed this account:[3]

> The Economites of the time of Morgan's raid buried $100,000 in coin of 50-cent pieces, bearing dates from 1804 to 1835, which coin was recently dug up and sold to western banks. On last Monday there was $10,000 worth of it paid to workmen on the P. & L.[4] and on Saturday some of the same coins were paid at the Westerman Iron Co.'s office. They looked bright and clean as the broken backed duck coins[5] can do, and some of the men were a little suspicious of them, but coming from "Davy" they knew it was all right. We note this to show how rapidly the medium will "circulate."

Content of the Economite Treasure

Another early account of this find, published in the March 1881 issue of *The Coin Collector's Journal,* is more numismatically detailed:

> THE ECONOMITE TREASURE
>
> Our worthy correspondent, Mr. Jos. M. Lippincott, has furnished us with particulars concerning the long secreted treasures of the Harmony Society at Economy, Pa., of which we have written an odd line heretofore, but lacking positive information we could say but little. The aforesaid gentleman has kindly obtained for us all the points to be desired, in particularizing just what kind of coins and their number, which will be of great interest to all collectors. When we consider the many years during which the quantities were being amassed, especially during the earlier years of the Mint, we may safely judge the rarity of the respective dates by the quantity of each discovered in this vast amount.
>
> Mr. Lippincott had the pleasure of examining the entire lot soon after its recovery from the underground vault, in the latter part of 1878; where it had been secreted during the Morgan raid. Its discovery by that wily general would have added greatly to the success of his band of rebels, as there were perhaps greater quantities of United States securities concealed with it. When the silver was brought to light it was black or tarnished from oxidation, and our correspondent says, "sore fingers were plenty in Economy" from cleaning the coins, as all were scrubbed before sold or circulated. Before their great value was discovered, two half dollars of 1796 and one of 1797 and several other dates were paid out at face value.
>
> Mr. Morrison, cashier of the Economy Savings Institution, furnished our correspondent with the information; consequently we regard it as authentic. The amounts are as follows:[6]
>
> **Quarter Dollars**
>
> 1818 to 1828: 400 pieces.
>
> **Half Dollars**
>
> 1794: 150
> 1795: 650
> 1796: 2
> 1797: 1
> 1801: 300
> 1802: 200
> 1803: 300
> 1805 over '04: 25
> 1805: 600
> 1806: 1,500
> 1807: 2,000
> 1815: 100
> Common half dollars 1808-1836: 111,356 pieces

1 Raymond Shepherd, curator, conversation of October 10, 1996.

2 Sources include Walter H. Breen, "Survey of American Coin Hoards," *The Numismatist,* January 1952; *Coin Collector's Journal,* March 1881; and Sydney P. Noe, *Coin Hoards,* American Numismatic Society, 1921 (primarily derived from the *CCJ* account of 1881). A modern commentary is found in "Another Visit to Economy, Pennsylvania," John Kovach, *John Reich Journal,* July 1993.

3 As cited by Chuck Erb in the *John Reich Journal,* April 1993; this article and other information had been located in 1992 by Lawrence Dzuibek while perusing the January 1926 number of the *Western Pennsylvania Historical Magazine.*

4 Pittsburgh & Lake Erie Railroad, of which the Economites were the primary stockholders. Jacob Henrici, third president of the Economy Society, was at one time president of the line. More information appears subsequently in the present account.

5 The term "broken-back duck" to describe the eagle on the reverse of the Capped Bust half dollar is, to say the least, quite innovative. It is quite possible that many of the "bright and clean" Economite Treasure coins were Uncirculated at the time they were secreted.

6 Here presented in edited form. It is obvious that most of these numbers have been rounded off and are only approximate.

Silver Dollars

1794: 1
1795: 800
1796: 125
1797: 80
1798 Small Eagle reverse: 30
1798 Large Eagle reverse: 560
1799 5 stars facing: 12
1799: 1,250
1800: 250
1801, '02, and '03: 600

Foreign silver (French, Spanish, and Spanish-American), total face value: $12,600.

Total face value of the hoard: $75,000.00

A well known dealer purchased the scarce dates, $4,000.00 face value, for $6,500, and the 1794 silver dollar for $22.00.

Our readers here have all the facts; the coins are now scattered all over the country, and it may be safe to say that less remain in Economy than at any other point.

Where They Went

Unexplained in the preceding account is the absence of coins dated after 1836, especially in view of the theory of their having been secreted in 1863 to protect them from Morgan. As noted, the author believes that the Economite Treasure was a separate group and had been hidden circa 1836. Morgan had nothing to do with it.

It is likely that the dealer who bought the coins was none other than Capt. John W. Haseltine of Philadelphia. On January 30-31, 1885, Haseltine catalogued and sold through the offices of Lyman H. Low, B. Westermann & Co., 888 Broadway, New York City, a number of the Economite Treasure pieces. Sample descriptions and prices realized include these:

Half dollars:

1794 Star pierces the curl. Very Good, nearly Fine. H and D lightly scratched in field. Rare. $4.00. [Lot 193a in the sale; these initials may pedigree this coin if it can be located in a collection today]

1795 varieties. Fair to Good. (Total: 6 pieces) $0.60 per coin.[1] [Lot 194]

1975 Fair to Good. (Total: 4 pieces) $0.60 each. [Lot 195]

1795 16 and 17 berries on wreath. Very Good. (Total: 2 pieces) $0.60 each. [Lot 195a]

1803 Very Good. $0.55. [Lot 196]

1803 Very Good. $0.55. [Lot 197]

1803 Very Good. $0.52. [Lot 198]

1803 Good. $0.52. [Lot 199]

1803 Good. $0.52. [Lot 200]

1803 Varieties. Large and small 3. Good. (Total: 2 pieces) $0.55 each. [Lot 201]

1803 Fair to Good. (Total: 8 pieces) $0.53 each. [Lot 206]

1803 and 1805. Fair and Good. (Total: 6 pieces) $0.55 each. [Lot 207]

Silver Dollars:

1795 Flowing Hair. Curl over the star. Rev. 13 berries. Very Fine. $1.45. [Lot 108]

1795 The same. Very Fine. $1.30. [Lot 109]

1795 Curl touches one point of star. Rev. 19 berries. Fine. $1.20. [Lot 111]

1795 Long Head. Stars near date. Rev. 17 berries. Good. $1.20. [Lot 112]

1795, 1798, 1799 and 1800. Good and Very Good. (Total: 4 pieces) $1.16 each. [Lot 117]

1795, 1798, 1799 and 1800. Good to Fine. (Total: 20 pieces) $1.16 each. [Lot 126]

1795, 1798 and 1799. Good to Fine. (Total: 20 pieces) $1.16 each. [Lot 127]

1795, 1798 and 1799. Good and Very Good. (Total: 23 pieces) $1.75 each. [Lot 128]

1799 All without berries on olive branch. Good and Fine. (Total: 5 pieces) $1.15 each. [Lot 146]

1799 The same. Good and Fine. (Total: 10 pieces) $1.15 each. [Lot 147]

Old Economy Village

The following history of the Economy settlement is paraphrased and edited from information received from Raymond Shepherd, curator of the museum complex there, and from related material:[2] Along the way the reason for the dispersal of the aforementioned Economite Treasure in 1878 will be revealed.

The Old Economy Village was the third and final home of the Harmony Society, a nineteenth-century Christian communal society best known for its piety and industrial prosperity. The group, indeed, believed in economy—careful use of time, material, and labor. The Pennsylvania settlement was referred to differ-

---

1 "Per coin" added; at the time prices realized in various sales, including bulk lots, were given on a per-coin basis, not the actual total realized. Additional modern comments are given in brackets.

2 Information from Mr. Shepherd per conversation, October 10, 1996, and material subsequently sent including *A Guide to Old Economy*, by Daniel B. Reibel; "Old Economy Village," a brochure issued by the Pennsylvania Historical and Museum Association; "Harmonie Herald," by The Harmonie Associates, Ambridge, Pennsylvania; and copies of historical records, museum accession records, financial and coin-deposit data, and other information. Excerpts from three books by Karl J.R. Arndt, who for 60 years (1934-1994) was the primary person with access to the Harmony Society files, were also sent: *George Rapp's Harmony Society 1785-1847* (Rutherford: Fairleigh Dickinson University Press, 1965); *George Rapp's Successors and Material Heirs 1847-1917* (Rutherford, 1971); and *George Rapp's Years of Glory: Economy on the Ohio 1834-1847* (New York: Peter Lang, 1987). Certain information concerning the Rappites in Indiana is from John E. Faris, *The Romance of Forgotten Towns*, 1924, which discusses the formation of the movement and quotes accounts by Robert Dale Owen, son of Robert Owen, purchaser of the Indiana tract from the Rappites.

ently in various documents over the years. Names included Economy, Harmony, OEkonomie, Harmonie, Harmony Village, and Economy Village. Harmony may have been the most used in the early years, Economy the most used in later times including today. In 1851, Harmony Village was set off separately from Economy.

In 1804 the Harmonists (later also called Economites) emigrated to America from Ipptingen (near Stuttgart) in southwest Germany to seek religious and economic freedom. Nearly 800 farmers and craftsmen followed leader George Rapp (1757-1847), first to Butler County, Pennsylvania, then to Posey County, Indiana. They stayed at each of these locations (both called Harmony) for 10 years. The actual, official title of the Harmony Society was Georg Rapp mit Gesellschaft, which translates to "George Rapp and Company." All of the property was in the name of his son, Frederick.

The towns were designed by Frederick Rapp (1775-1834), adopted son of the founder. In the final settlement in Pennsylvania, the plan was primarily in the form of rectangular blocks separated by streets, with brick communal factory and other work buildings in the center and with houses on the periphery. Most (but not all) Harmonists adopted celibacy in 1807 in order to purify themselves for the Millennium or Christ's 1,000 year reign on earth.[1] They worked for the good of the Society and received what they needed to live simply and comfortably.

Rapp claimed to have a special connection to God and His messengers, including the angel Gabriel (who, it was said, visited Rapp personally and left two footprints in a stone preserved at Harmony, Indiana).[2] On another occasion, the design for the church building was revealed in a dream. George Flower[3] described the church building as being 120 feet long and being supported by 28 pillars "of walnut, cherry, and sassafras, varying in circumference from five to six feet, and in height from 21 to 25 feet."

Apparently there was some unrest about the sharing of property, and in 1818 George Rapp burned the book containing the list of original contributions to the Society, to help quiet the problem.

In May 1824 the Harmony Society returned to Beaver County, Pennsylvania and built "OEkonomie" ("Economy") overlooking the Ohio River, this being the site of the famous coin hoard. Their vacated Indiana facility was assumed on January 3, 1825, by Robert Owen, a wealthy Scottish cotton manufacturer, who established the utopian community of New Harmony there, to explore his "New Moral World."[4] Owen paid the Harmony Society $150,000 for the facilities.[5]

Robert Owen's son, Robert Dale Owen, described the Harmonists' settlement in Indiana as it was in 1824, immediately prior to the Rappites' move to Pennsylvania:

> The [work-share community] experiment was a marvelous success in a pecuniary point of view; for at the time of their immigration [from Germany] their property did not exceed $25 a head, while in 21 years a fair estimate gave them $2,000 for each person—man, woman, and child—probably 10 times the average wealth throughout the United States, for at that time each person in Indiana averaged but $150 of property, and even in Massachusetts the average fell short of $300 for each adult and child.
>
> Intellectually and socially, however, it was doubtless a failure; as an ecclesiastical autocracy, especially when it contravenes an important law of nature [having children], must always be. Rapp was absolute ruler, assuming to be such in virtue of divine call, and it was said, probably with truth, that he decided to sell Harmony because life there was getting to be easy and quiet, with leisure for thought; and because he found it difficult to keep his people in order, except during the bustle and hard work that attended a new settlement.
>
> When my father first reached the place, he found among the Germans—its sole inhabitants—indications of plenty and material comfort, but with scarcely a touch of fancy or ornament; the only exceptions being a few flowers in the gardens, and what was called The Labyrinth, a pleasure ground laid out near the village with some taste, and intended—so my father was told—as an emblematic representation of the life these colonists had chosen. It contained small groves

[1] The Millerites, active in the 1830s and 1840s, placed the arrival of the Millennium at the forefront of their beliefs, but unlike the Rappites, the Millerites are remembered by historians as not being very industrious and, in fact, often relaxed or lazy while they awaited the return of Christ. The Harmonist or Rappites are said to have been as close to the Lutheran doctrine as any branch of Protestantism, but they had their own set of practices. The practice of celibacy was taken from the teachings of St. Paul, who believed that celibacy was better than the state of being married.

[2] Faris, p. 166. One non-believer suggested that these footprints had been hewn from a rock quarried near St. Louis.

[3] Who visited Harmony in 1819 and who is remembered as the Englishman who founded Albion, Illinois. Flower was a friend and business associate of Rapp, and it was he who went to England to visit Robert Owen to try to interest him in buying the Indiana Harmony village. Cf. Faris, pp. 165-166, 168. Albion = the Latin designation for England.

[4] Owen wrote a book of this title. The foundation of utopian (Utopia was a fictional island created by Thomas More) and work-sharing societies forms an interesting part of nineteenth-century American history. Among the better known facilities were Oneida (New York) and Amana (Iowa) in addition to those mentioned here. Various Shaker and Mormon settlements also had work-sharing aspects. The New Harmony, Indiana, settlement under Owen lasted briefly; he left in 1827, and in 1828 its organization as a utopian society ended. Oscar Wilde once commented: "A map of the world that does not include Utopia is not worth glancing at."

[5] Doubtless, this payment became part of the Harmonists' cash reserves and was employed to build the new facility in Pennsylvania. Owen had many ideas including a 10-hour work day (which was a shorter day than most people worked at the time), schools for the children of workers, etc. Owen had made his fortune as the owner of a cotton mill at New Lanark, Scotland.

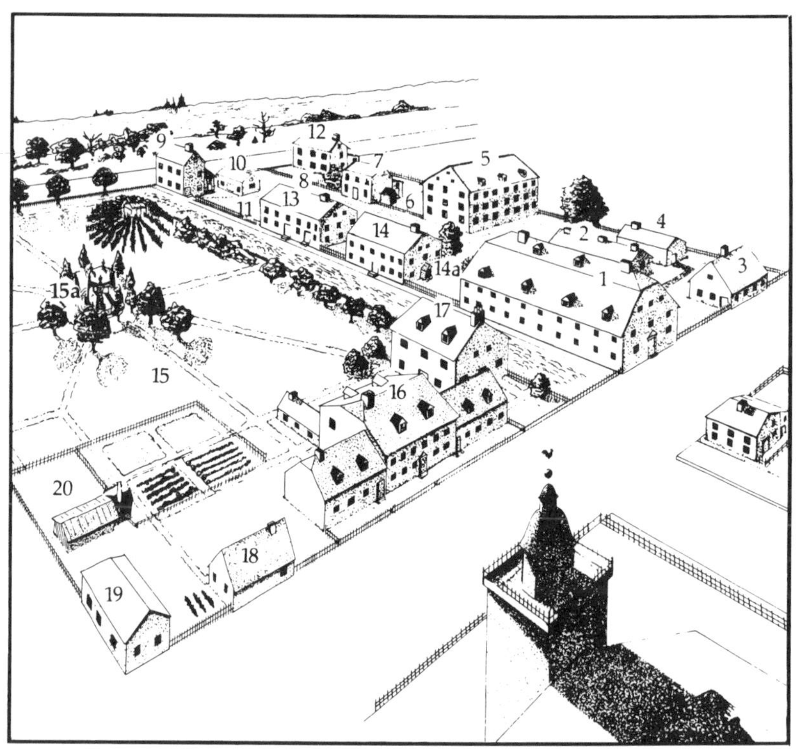

(Map and descriptions of buildings from the brochure for Old Economy Village)

#1: Feast Hall was a Natural History and Fine Arts Museum, first open to the public in 1826. The Library and adult education classrooms for the Society members are also here. Six times a year, all the Harmonists gathered in the 100 by 50 foot hall on the second floor to celebrate their anniversaries, hold their love feasts, and celebrate the Last supper.

#16: George Rapp House described in 1826 as the "principal building two stories high, with two lower wings standing in the same line" along Church Street. George Rapp furnished his house with objects made at Economy. He lived here with his wife, daughter-in-law, and granddaughter.

#17: Frederick Rapp House added to the rear of Father Rapp's House around 1828. Adopted by George Rapp, Frederick was a co-founder of the Society, an architect, stonemason, and businessman. He was the Society's principal representative in the outside world. He furnished his house with stylish objects, many purchased in Philadelphia or Pittsburgh.

The George Rapp House. (Photo courtesy of Raymond Shepherd)

Museum Building. Within these walls the Cabinet of Curiosities was established in the mid 1820s, complete with a display of rare coins.

George Rapp House. Vault in basement for the community's semi-secret cash reserves of silver and gold coins. (Photos on this page courtesy of Raymond Shepherd)

Frederick Rapp House. Basement stairway and vault. Hundreds of thousands of early American coins were stored here.

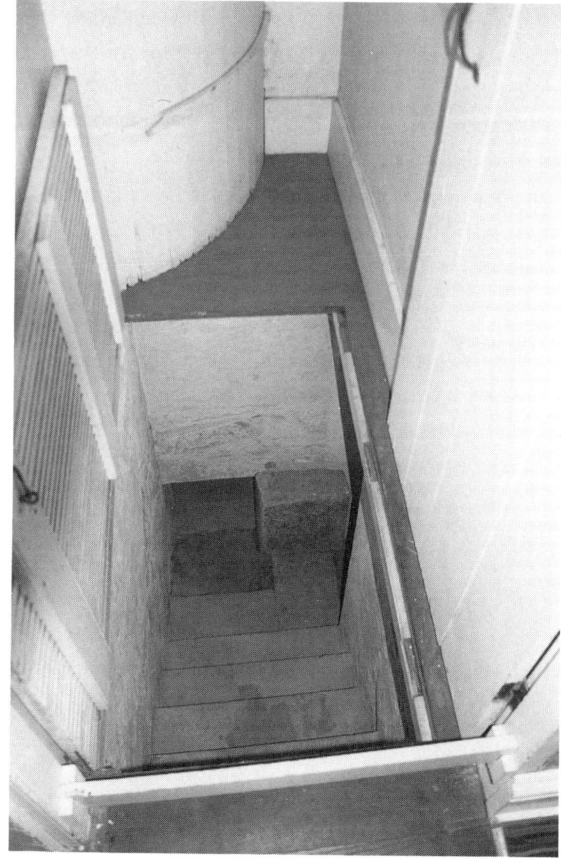

and gardens, with numerous circular walks enclosed by high beech hedges and bordered with flowering shrubbery, but arranged with such intricacy that without some Daedalus to furnish a clue, one might wander for hours and fail to reach a building erected in the center.[1] This was a temple of rude material, but covered with vines of the grape and convolvulus, and the interior neatly fitted up and prettily furnished. There George Rapp had sought to shadow forth to his followers the difficulty of attaining a state of peace and social harmony. The perplexing approach, the rough exterior of the shrine, and the elegance displayed within, were to serve as types of toil and suffering, succeeded by happy repose.

The toil and suffering left their marks, however, on the grave, stolid, and often sad German faces. They looked well fed, well clothed, and seemed free from anxiety. The animal had been sufficiently cared for. A shelter from life's wearing cares is something—but a temple typifies higher things, more than what we shall eat, and what we shall drink, and wherewithal we shall be clothed. Rapp's disciples had bought these too dearly—at the expense of heart and soul.

Now, It Was Robert Owen's Turn

Robert Owen's followers numbered about 800 and soon were settled in the Harmony village, now renamed New Harmony, in the buildings and surrounding 20,000 acres of land. Owen proceeded with "the redemption of the human race from the evils of the existing state of Society." As were the Rappites before them, the incoming Owenites were called Harmonists.

Now it was Owen's turn to use this verdant patch of Indiana landscape to bring joy and comfort into the lives of souls seeking new inspiration and direction. Hopefully, everyone would have a happy face, not like the recently departed Germans.

Apparently, Owen's precepts were diametrically opposed from those of the Rappite order, for Owen, in an address arranged to the assembled members of the U.S. Congress in Washington, avowed, among other things, that "the principles usually recognized in the pursuits of trade and commerce must be renounced as degrading and pernicious." Owen brimmed with enthusiasm as he envisioned an earthy equivalent of heaven.

In his *New Moral World* book, Owen proposed abolishing the family as the basis of life and training and to replace it with "scientific associations" with 500 to 2,000 people, to act as "magnified families" and to offer more services and benefits than any husband and wife could possibly ever give their children. Ruling was to be done by a council comprised of all members of the community who were between the ages of 30 and 40. To insure behavior, "all members must act as rational physical and mental beings or be removed to an asylum." Presumably, the asylum was on somebody else's land.

Robert Owen went back to England to attend to his business affairs, intending to come back in late autumn of 1825. However, he did not reckon with the canal system across southern Pennsylvania being frozen shut, and delays of over a month in travel occurred.

Finally returning to New Harmony toward the end of January, 1826, he was delighted to see the wonderful progress that had been made by his followers and others who had come to bask in the anticipated glow of education, science, and happy community living. Several well-known persons in the sciences and arts had come there, including among their number Constantin Rafinesque (student of fishes and other fauna), Charles Albert Leseur (likewise), Thomas Say (a founder of the Academy of Natural Sciences in Philadelphia), Gerard Troost (mineralogist), and William McClure (known as The Father of American Geology and president of the Philadelphia Academy of Sciences). Innovations in the teaching of children had been developed. A museum (based upon one formed in the community in a fortress-like building by George Rapp) and a library had been instituted, a common dispensary of tools and implements had been set up, and other amenities had been put into place. What happened to the Rappites' large brewery was not stated, as the Owenites were forbidden to drink liquor.

However, there was trouble in paradise. It soon developed that the inhabitants were not able to govern themselves effectively, and the council of 30- to 40-year-olds was replaced by another system then another. In about a year, Owen's experiment collapsed. The editor of the *New Harmony Gazette* reflected that Owen had placed too little consideration upon the great privations and anti-social circumstances his followers had experienced before joining his group, and too much emphasis on the untried aspects of harmony and idealism. The abilities, motivations, ideas, feelings, and aspirations of the various settlers proved to be too diverse for working together as a single unit.

Owen, who had suffered great financial loss with the venture, sold off land and buildings in New Harmony to those who wanted them, and the philosophy of the New Moral Order lapsed into history.

---

[1] Daedalus = the Greek architect of the Labyrinth on the island of Crete in the Mediterranean Sea. The way out of the Labyrinth was gained by Thesus by following a *string*—for which Greek word we have today the word *clew* or *clue*. Ornamental gardens with labyrinthine walks were very popular elsewhere in the early nineteenth century and were seen in England, Virginia, and other places, where they offered a social diversion. In the 1980s such gardens enjoyed a revival in Japan, where amusement parks featuring these puzzles were set up for the amusement of anyone caring to pay the requisite admission fee.

Prosperity in Pennsylvania

Meanwhile, the Rappites worked quickly on the banks of the Ohio River in their new community near Pittsburgh, and by winter 1825 the Harmony Society members had constructed cotton and woolen factories powered and heated by steam and had developed centralized steam laundries and a dairy. Among their number were blacksmiths, tanners, hatters, wagonmakers, cabinetmakers, wood turners, linen weavers, potters, and tinners.

The Harmonists developed new technologies for their daily needs and in due course also made quality industrial products, the latter being sold into American commerce. Their high-quality silk received gold medals during exhibition competitions in Boston, New York, and Philadelphia.[1] In addition to whatever awards the group may have received, their output of silk, cotton, and wool goods achieved an outstanding reception in the marketplace.

Silver (especially) and gold coins poured into the coffers of the Society, and in due course some of this treasure was cached in various places, including, it is said, in the bedroom of the founder, and, later, in three brick vaults. Most probably, a goodly amount of wealth was also on hand from the earlier and quite prosperous days in Indiana.

In 1832 about one-third of the members of the Harmony Society left under the leadership of Count de Leon, a self-proclaimed prophet also known as the Lion of Judah and the Archduke Maximilian von Este, among other cognomens. When he was at Economy he was known to his fellow members as Bernhard Müller. His real name may have been Bernard Proli, but this has never been confirmed. A new settlement named Monaca, a.k.a. Phillipsburg, the "New Jerusalem," was built by Proli and his entourage. The 1818 burning of the Society's records was cited as an excuse to escape, and those who decamped demanded cash settlements for what they thought they had deserved or put into the Society. The sum of $105,000 was decided upon, to be paid in three installments. Two payments were made, but as signed releases could not be obtained from some of the secessionists, the third payment was denied. An angry mob of former Harmonists returned to Economy to demand their due, but were repelled by militia. A mill was later destroyed in the village in what was believed by some to be a case of arson, quite possibly by the dissidents. Apparently, Proli later converted some of the $105,000 payment to his own use.

The Society members did not have a bank, but employed their own system of credits, loans, deposits, bills of exchange, etc. This served the community well. Over a period of time, a cash reserve of coins was built. Following the payments to Proli and his followers, George Rapp established a special fund to provide for any such future withdrawals. He told Romelius L. Baker[2] to assemble $500,000 in specie, and the latter brought in large quantities of silver coins and a lesser amount of gold. The money was stored in the Great House (Frederick Rapp House).

An 1826 Deposit of Silver Coins

Records show that on June 5, 1826, the first deposit of coins may have been made to the "treasure," this being in addition to many funds that were constantly being received and paid out.[3] These were mostly silver issues, denominations not known—but probably mostly half dollars, and consisted of the following:

10 boxes of silver coins, each containing $1,000, or $10,000

Plus these additional boxes:

1 box containing $1,065
1 box containing $1,065
1 box containing $1,056
1 box containing $1,025

[1] In the mid-nineteenth century and extending to later times as well, gold medals were "awarded" to many entrants as a thank you for their participation. Such entrants could then use these awards in advertising. Early bestowers of awards included the American Institute (New York) and the Massachusetts Charitable Mechanic Association (Boston; Christian Gobrecht designed its award medal; certain of these impressions seem to have been struck illegally in the Medal Department of the Philadelphia Mint, by Chief Coiner Franklin Peale, who was later fired for this and other dereliction of duty, according to an 1853 government report)—today the Old Economy Village preserves examples of both of these types, awarded in the early nineteenth century. After the Crystal Palace (New York, 1853), large fairs became the leading venue for such medals. Years later, at the 1904 St. Louis World's Fair gold medal distribution ran rampant, and there were so many such "awards" that *copper* medals inscribed GOLD MEDAL were given out! Today, reproductions of many early awards are still seen on liquor and condiment bottles.

[2] Baker managed the Society's store. Later, he became head of the Society, to in turn be followed by Jacob Henrici. Baker exhibited great ability in shepherding the Harmonists' assets. Life dates: 1793-1868.

[3] Furnished by Raymond Shepherd, curator, October 11, 1996.

1 box containing $1,035
1 box containing $1,000
1 box containing $1,075
1 box containing $1,020
1 box containing $1,050
1 box containing $1,005
1 box containing $1,020
1 box containing $1,025

The above separate boxes totaled $12,441 plus "1 bag of gold" worth $3,567 plus the first group of ten $1,000 boxes, for a total deposit of $25,008. In the absence of any records to the contrary, the author assumes that the $3,567 in gold coins represented United States issues, probably $3,567.50, for there were no $1 or $3 gold coins at the time, and the total would have included some $2.50 gold pieces.

The above items are the stuff of which numismatic dreams are made. One can imagine that the boxes containing $1,000 face value in silver were filled with newly minted half dollars (most likely), old silver dollars, or quarter dollars. And for the gold coins, wow! *Anything* in the group would be a rarity today, and any pieces dated in the 1820s would be major rarities! Whether any silver coins in this specific group were a part of the Economite Treasure that was revealed years later in 1878 is not known.

Forming the Coin Hoard

Information extracted from the Harmony Society's records was put into book form by Karl J.R. Arndt, 1987, in *George Rapp's Harmony Society 1785-1847.* These excerpts tell of the secret formation of the vast coin hoard. The Economite Treasure of silver coins disclosed in 1878 probably included some of the deposits made in 1836 and before, from the larger list below:[1]

General Jackson's veto of the Bank of the United States Charter in 1833 created a panic in the money market and had an unhappy effect on the mercantile world, particularly the wool dealers. Through one firm alone in Philadelphia the Harmony Society lost "upwards of $10,000." For a time, R.L. Baker later testified, there was serious apprehension of the stability of the republican form of government. John Quincy Adams himself, on the floor of Congress, uttered his fear that the "Spartan sponge" would be applied. This was later done in part by the suspension of specie payments by [many] banks all over the land [on May 10, 1837]; the effects of the bankruptcy law caused the Society to suffer heavy losses.

In view of this situation George Rapp, after the veto of the bank charter, decided to free himself of dependence on uncertainties of politics and the fluctuations of business and businessmen. He was also moved by an interest in the security of the congregation and "according to the old German habit of having some hard money in the purse," as Baker stated it, he directed the gathering of specie.

For some reason he set a goal of half a million dollars which was to be collected and put away at Economy, without the knowledge of the members of the Society, in order that this fund could be closed, too, and that the elect would not be found wanting in the matter of having invested their talents wisely. By the fall of 1845 the church fund of half a million in silver and gold had been collected. R.L. Baker reported that the specie [silver and gold coins] had been gathered in the following time and manner:

1834, November 20, from the branch of the Bank of the U.S. at Pittsburgh	$14,000
1835, January 10, from the same branch	26,000
1835, November 21, from the same branch	19,026
1835, September 4, from Bank of Pittsburgh[2]	10,000
1841, August 2, from Bank of Pittsburgh	18,000
1843, May 20, from Bank of Pittsburgh	35,036
1843, August 23, from Bank of Pittsburgh	22,156
1845, June 27, from Bank of Pittsburgh	25,000
1838, October, from Bank of the U.S. at Philadelphia	110,000
1840, April, from Philadelphia Bank at Philadelphia	85,738
1841, May, from Philadelphia Bank at Philadelphia	50,759
1842, April, from Philadelphia Bank at Philadelphia	25,426
1844 from Louisville, Kentucky	1,500
Specie on hand June 1834, at Frederick Rapp's death	20,000
Aggregate	$462,641
+1826 [possibly the first deposit]	25,008
Total	$487,649

The difference between this total and $510,000, to the best of Baker's recollection and knowledge and belief, was taken in at Economy in small sums, between the years 1834 and 1846. In a letter of November 6, 1837, Father George Rapp through Baker told his friend and agent J.P. Solms in Philadelphia:

"It is my plan to obtain silver or gold for this as soon as the banks disappear. For you have yourself informed me that at the next session of Congress the government will do all in

[1] Pages 573-576.

[2] Any silver deposits up to this point furnish possibilities for the Economite Hoard formed 1836 and earlier and revealed in 1878. As 1836-dated coins were included, there would have been some coins from later deposit(s) as well.

its power to put through its system. If that is done I do not hope for good times for the United States, and it then becomes every man's duty to look out for himself, as even the government itself is setting the example. Who would have thought that Van Buren, contrary to all better advice, would follow in the footsteps of Jackson and would do more wrong than he?[1] I must admit that I had hoped for more statesmanly wisdom from Van Buren that he has shown until now.

"When one reads the speeches in the Senate by Webster, Clay, King, Tallmadge, etc., carefully and considers how sincere these men are and how they advise what would be right and good for the land, and when nevertheless the majority of the Senate in spite of all that has confirmed the Sub-Treasury system, I cannot help but think and believe that this is a sign of the time to which our attention has been directed by Scripture: 'For God hath put in their hearts to fulfill his will, and to agree, and give their kingdom unto the beast, until the words of God shall be fulfilled.' (Rev. 17:17.)"

R.L. Baker made an interesting report to Father Rapp on April 25, 1838, from Philadelphia, stating that the Bank of England had sent close to two million sovereigns to New York to exchange these for bills of exchange "and with the intent of making a little speculation in this." This caused a sudden rise in exchange to England and was unfavorable to the Society's plan to import sovereigns.

Baker, however, was able to persuade Mr. [Nicholas] Biddle to pay the Society's deposit of $50,000 in the Philadelphia Bank in sovereigns at $4.85 (per sovereign) six months later. Sovereigns then were worth $5.00 in U.S. paper. On making this promise Mr. Biddle demanded that the matter be kept quiet. This secret deal in foreign exchange was inspired by Rapp's distrust of Jacksonism.[2]

This unique combination of good business sense and religious mysticism was the reason why the Harmony Society stood firm and sound as a rock during the Panic of 1837. While bank after bank went under, while towns in the West collapsed,[3] while Americans were starving because of unemployment, the Harmonist "fanatics" enjoyed the blessings of their well-tried "American system."

All the specie collected under orders of Father Rapp was put away in a vault and later moved from that vault to a drier one, but Baker was not informed, nor did he inquire, where the money had been placed. Neither he nor Jacob Henrici[4] ever had access to the vault because this matter was considered the exclusive affair of Father Rapp. Baker states in this connection "that neither myself nor any other true member would interfere in business belonging to him exclusively, without his knowledge, permission or direction."

After this fund had been gathered and put away in a vault to which only the Father George Rapp and George Fleckhammer[5] had access, he wanted it forgotten that the amount existed. An account book kept by Baker containing the record of the half million was burned in 1845 at the direction of Father Rapp, and Rapp also ordered that that amount was not to be recorded on the accounts to be rendered. The fund was a closed matter, and since Father Rapp had directed it so, Baker considered it his duty to leave the item off his accounts, especially since he was satisfied from Rapp's fidelity to the Society, in all respects, and not only in this one, that he had the purest motive tending to the welfare of the Society in so leaving out this amount.

The "church fund" of half a million in gold and silver thus hidden away in a vault in Father Rapp's house and apparently under his bed, was not disturbed during Father Rapp's lifetime, nor did its presence at Economy disturb any of the members of the Society, for these consecrated men had full confidence in Father Rapp and their leaders. They asked no accounting of them, for their minds and hearts were directed heavenward from whence they fully expected the coming of the Bridegroom [Jesus' Second Coming] to whom they had been faithful and for whom they had prepared all these years. The Panic of 1837 and the security of the members of the Society in a tottering world only confirmed them in their faith.

Business Aspects of Economy Village

Around 1846 the money was moved to a vault under the late Frederick Rapp's house, to stay there until the 1870s. The now-coinless vaults under the Rapp house exist today and are arched structures of brick, about six feet high, six feet deep and four feet wide. One of the stones in a wall is removable, just big enough for a man to crawl through. It is known from two court cases that when the chests of money were put in the vaults that the stone door was mortared in and looked just like the rest of the wall. Apparently there was one damp one, but all three are dry now.

As noted in the preceding account the Economites' hard assets had been entrusted to Jacob Henrici and the steward of the Great House, George Fleckhammer. George built new chests of black locust wood when the original ones rotted. The Society purchased a safe in Pittsburgh to hold its papers and small amounts of cash. It was opened with a key, and had a trick lock so that the key would not work unless the rivets were in a certain position. The safe, made by the John Delano

[1] The reader interested in the tumultuous political and banking situation of 1837 will find it richly reflected in copper tokens privately issued as part of what today is called the Hard Times token series; many satirical bank notes and paper items were issued as well. Martin Van Buren, elected in 1836, served as president from 1837 to 1841 and unsuccessfully sought re-election in 1840 and 1848. His "illustrious predecessor" (as the inscription on a Hard Times token stated) was Andrew Jackson, who served from 1829 to 1837.

[2] *Economy on the Ohio*, pp. 373 and 374, reprints a German note—not translated—from R.L. Baker to George Rapp, November 7, 1838, concerning the safe transfer of gold coins (British sovereigns) from the United States Bank to Economy Village. Rapp wrote to say that these would be shipped by canal on a passenger boat and would be disguised as machinery! (There are many printed accounts of canal travel in western Pennsylvania during this era, one of the better known being Charles Dickens' *American Notes for General Circulation,* 1842).

[3] Actually a reference to ***planned*** towns; land speculation was rampant. The "West" referred to part of what today is known as the Midwest and generally included western Pennsylvania, Ohio, Indiana, and Illinois, among other locations.

[4] Life dates: 1804-1892. Henrici joined the Society after its move to Pennsylvania; in time he became in charge of financial matters, the talented and worthy successor to R.L. Baker.

[5] Fleckhammer, chief gardener of the community, was very close to Father Rapp and shared many confidences and participated in numerous decisions.

& Son Co. of New York City, and purchased from Abishhai Way Company, was shipped by canal boat, and is still in the possession of the Association.

Baker and Henrici were responsible for the books. Baker was given the key to the safe after George Rapp's death in 1847. The $510,000 in the vault was never accounted for to its members again. It came to light in the Nachtreib court case in 1851, and Baker spoke of it as a reserve or "church fund."

Meanwhile, with nearly all Harmonists practicing celibacy and with few new members coming in from the outside, the average age of the members advanced. Youthful vitality was gone. By the mid-1850s, production of silk, cotton, and woolen goods had diminished to just a fraction of what it had been two decades earlier.

After George Rapp died in 1847 the Harmonists turned to new ventures including—years later—railroads, oil, and building Beaver Falls and its industrial complex.

In 1874 a group of promoters tried to develop a railroad along the Ohio River near Beaver Falls, but achieved little success. Jacob Henrici became interested, and the course of progress changed.

Emergence of the Economite Treasure

What we now know as the Economite Treasure, publicized in 1878, was probably a small part of a very large group of silver coins brought out of hiding in the late 1870s to provide financing for the railroad. Karl J.R. Arndt, later historian of the Society, related:[1]

> Before 1876 transportation conditions in Pittsburgh and surrounding areas were rather primitive. A committee of people from that city was created in 1874 to plan relief. The Baltimore & Ohio Railroad was approached, but no support was forthcoming.
>
> In 1876 another committee promoted building a line from Pittsburgh to Youngstown (Ohio) in order to connect with the Lake Shore and Southern Michigan Railway (which later became part of the New York Central) and Atlantic & Great Western Railway (which later became part of the Erie Railroad). Both of these had tracks going to the Great Lakes as well as going through New York and Chicago. On December 21, 1876, a prospectus for the Pittsburgh & Lake Erie Railroad was issued, noting that it would cost about $4 million.
>
> "We believe it will be more profitable than our best bank stocks," the promoters suggested, "but what is vastly more important to us all is the great supply to our business. With rents reduced, houses empty, mills idle, and our strongest firms struggling against the low freights given to other cities and the exorbitant freights taken from us, this becomes a paramount importance." Much of the land intended for the railroad right-of-way belonged to the Harmony Society, which gave free access to the railroad's top entrepreneurs, and also signed up for $650,000 worth of bonds. The Harmony Society was also active in the management, with Jonathan Lenz, who at that time was a fellow trustee of Jacob Henrici, in constant contact. Monetary shortages arose, and Jacob Henrici tapped the church reserves.
>
> It will be remembered that Henrici had been George Rapp's trusted agent and assistant at the time when he was determined to collect and bury the fund which he believed he should have on hand as part of the Appropriation of the Second Coming of Christ. Henrici would not have touched this religious fund without the inner conviction that the building of this railroad was a link in the chain of events that would bring on the glorious day when man would be restored to the original image in which God had created him.
>
> Accordingly, Henrici had the money which Father Rapp had buried for that special purpose brought up to the directors' meeting in the Monongahela House. The boxes containing the money were emptied of their contents in the center of the room, forming a large pile of silver, all of which had to be cleaned before it could be put back into circulation.
>
> From January 12, 1881, to January 14, 1884, Henrici was president of the railroad the Harmonists had helped build by their investments, but the obligations of his office were very hard on him. On January 14, 1884, the Vanderbilts took over the railroad and the Harmony Society sold its interests to the new owners for $1,150,000.

The Museum

The Harmonists' village in Pennsylvania had many fine facilities including the Great Hall or Feast House, the second floor of which was given over to Love Feasts held several times a year in celebration of various holidays or simply as occasions for good cheer. The first floor was devoted to the Museum.

The Museum was formed at the Economy Village in 1825-1827 and added to for many years later. Intended for the education and instruction of adults, it contained many interesting and valuable items including oil paintings (signed by Rubens, Mengs, and Florens, and such American artists as Peale, Doughty, and Otis), a collection of plants, mechanical devices (such as an air pump and a static electricity generator), an exhibit of butterflies, and other man-made and natural curiosities. Included in the Cabinet of Curiosities within the Museum were items crafted of precious metals and a fine collection of rare coins.

Marquis de Lafayette visited the Museum in May 1825 during his tour of the United States.[2] At the time

---

1 *George Rapp's Successors and Material Heirs,* 1971, pp. 66-68:

2 His visit began on August 15, 1824, with his arrival in New York and ended with his departure down the Chesapeake Bay and then to France on September 8, 1825. On the way to Pittsburgh, Lafayette and his entourage were aboard a steamship, *Mechanic,* on the Ohio River near Louisville, Kentucky. Just past midnight the ship snagged and sank, but in relatively shallow water. No lives were lost, and Lafayette and his entourage suffered nothing more than temporary discomfort including wading ashore in the rain and spending the night under a dripping tree until another steamer came along at 9:00 the following morning.

he was particularly interested in viewing some of the industries in the Pittsburgh area. Rudyard Kipling and Charles Dickens were among the many other distinguished guests who paid calls to the Harmony Society.

This extract from James Silk Buckingham's *The Eastern and Western States of America* (London, 1842)[1] gives a first-hand view of this Englishman's visit to the Museum at Economy, although without mention of the rare coins:

> The physician of the settlement, Dr. Feucht, or Feight, as it is pronounced, waited on us after dinner with a message from Mr. Rapp (to whom our arrival had been made known on the previous evening by one of the elders, Mr. Henrici, to whom I had brought letters from Pittsburgh), saying that as he understood we were to leave the Settlement tomorrow, when we should require all the former part of the day to see the manufactories, he would be glad if we would devote the afternoon to an inspection of the Museum, before the second service of the church began, which would be at three o'clock and after that, he invited us to come and pass the evening with his family in a social party; observing that though they respected the Sabbath as a day of worship and of rest, they were not so rigid in their own observance of it as to exclude all enjoyment of innocent pleasures at the same time.[2]
>
> We accordingly visited the Museum in company with Dr. Feucht. The building in which this is placed is the largest in the town, being in its external dimensions about 130 feet long, by 80 feet broad, and 70 feet high. The lower story is divided into two series of apartments, with a central passage dividing them, running down the whole length of the building; and in one of these series the present collection is placed, the other being reserved for future accumulations.
>
> In natural history there are many specimens of native quadrupeds, from the elk to the wild cat, well preserved; of birds, native and foreign, a still greater number, from the eagle to the bird of paradise; reptiles in abundance, from the alligator to the rattlesnake; fishes in great variety, and butterflies and insects in full proportion.
>
> Among the minerals to be found almost every kind furnished by this continent; and a large piece of native gold, from the gold region of North Carolina. Of philosophical instruments,[3] they have but few—an air pump and an electrical machine being among the number. Among the curiosities is an antique ironbound chest, with a most comprehensive yet orderly arrangement of drawers and recesses within it, which belonged to William Penn; and in which his celebrated Treaty with the Delaware Indians was kept by him while he remained in this country.
>
> The pictures are more numerous than valuable, and present a strange mixture. An extensive series of Chinese drawings of costumes occupy a large portion of the walls; and a series of American historical portraits, from Columbus and Americus Vespucius, fill another section. Some better engravings of Col. Trumbull's historical pictures, such as the Declaration of Independence[4] and others, follow; and some highly interesting religious subjects are appropriately mingled with them. But the effect of these is strangely marred by their being found in close juxtaposition with some very inappropriate and unworthy associates; such as tawdry French prints, representing Venus and Cupid, one as "L'Amour supplicant," and the other as "L'Amour triomphante," and a still more tawdry English caricature in the "Portrait of Tim Bibbin."
>
> Like every other museum that I have yet seen in this country (excepting only the Chinese collection at Philadelphia), this would be greatly improved by weeding and pruning; and if the articles were reduced in number, the whole collection would be improved in value. The actual cost incurred in forming it, independently of the building, has been only 3,000 dollars; as very many of the articles have been presented and others collected by members, without expense.
>
> In a separate apartment, on the opposite side of the ground floor, is a large painting, about 15 feet by 10, representing the great assembly of the Israelites at the foot of Mount Sinai, while Moses went up to receive the law, amid the thunders and the lightnings that then enwrapped his venerable head. The painter was a young Frenchman, Mr. Louis Cortambert, an enthusiastic traveler, who had been much among the Indians in their wilds and prairies, and who was a visitor here some time since. As a work of art it has no merit, but the conception is grand; amidst all its defects of execution, the whole effect of the picture is striking.
>
> Above the Museum is the large Social Hall, running the whole length and breadth of the interior of the building, about 120 feet by 70, with a lofty arched roof, well lighted and ventilated, abundantly furnished with tables and forms; and well warmed with several central stoves. The Hall is devoted exclusively to the general meetings of the community, of which they have four in each year; one being to commemorate the anniversary of their foundation, the 25th [handwritten note says 15th] of February, 1805; another being about the period of Easter; a third at the gathering in and completion of their harvest; and a fourth at Christmas; so that gratitude and devotion are the leading sentiments that direct these festivities. They then all dine together in the Social Hall, and devote the remainder of the day to music and social enjoyment.

A Coin Theft in 1846

In the summer of 1846 the Curiosity Cabinet was burgled of some of its coins.[5] Certain facts were learned by A. Bimber, who described himself as a friend of the

---

[1] Vol. II, pp. 205-234.

[2] The observance of the Sabbath (Sunday) or lack of observance furnished a focal point for many written commentaries in the mid-nineteenth century. Christians who were especially pious were apt to do without artificial lighting, recreation, or other amenities and enjoyments. Elected officials of certain towns would not receive distinguished visitors, nor would there be festivals, parades, or other civic activities. Likely as not, those who were very pious had very little tolerance for anyone whose views were different from theirs. The Harmonists took a liberal view, as noted here.

[3] Term for machines or devices requiring a measure of science and knowledge to construct.

[4] A print of one of John Trumbull's (painter of American historical scenes; life dates: 1756-1843) better-known images; later reproduced on the reverse of a large medal by Charles Cushing Wright and the back of the 1976 U.S. $2 bill among many other places.

[5] These accounts are adapted from correspondence reprinted in *Economy on the Ohio*, pp. 992-996, 1060.

Society, possibly a spy for them. He had eavesdropped on a conversation of the thieves.[1] Bimber, seeking to have no link to his involvement in the investigation, communicated his findings in a letter dated August 14, 1846, signed simply as "A. BR," and addressed to John Dreher, near Economy, with the knowledge the message would be quickly passed to R.L. Baker, who was postmaster. Bimber forget to maintain the confidentiality of the addressee and referred to "Mr. Baker" in the letter:

> This noon George Schanbacher and Heinrich Hahn came to the sawmill. I immediately also discovered that they wanted to talk with Götz, so I immediately got out of their way, saying to Götz that I had to go to the blacksmith shop to tend to some business there, and that he, that is Götz, should rest meanwhile until I returned.
>
> But I did not go to town, instead, however, I walked through the mill to my room, where the following conversation took place between these three. Götz said to Schanbacher:
>
> "Fellow, one ought to beat you for committing such folly as to break into the Museum and take things that are of no value to you, and to them as well as to strangers they are of great value, for there were among these which soon will be 1,000 years old, and they are of no value to you, and your brother wears the silver ring which also was in the box."
>
> Götz further asked Schanbacher where he had left the box, the latter said that he had thrown it into an elderberry bush at the pig pen on the right side of the hill. Mr. Baker, this as well as what I wrote to you earlier and will write you later I can with a good conscience prove, and I am also ready to do so, but under my present circumstances it would not please me, for this spring when I began my business I was forced to borrow some money from J. Wagner, and if now anything should happen that I should have to bear testimony against this band, he would immediately give me notice, and I would get into difficulty. I will, therefore, give you my advice in order to get back into possession of your stolen goods without great difficulty.
>
> Have a letter written, or write one yourself in Böhm's name to me about these things. The letter must quite on its own seem to originate from Böhm as if no one else but Böhm knew about it; namely, Böhm must tell me in this letter that
>
> 1. These things were stolen from there.
>
> 2. That the windowpanes and the box were found in that place and that a neighbor of yours on the same evening when the things were taken had seen George Schanbacher, for he was there on foot and
>
> 3. That you can call upon evidence that Schanbacher took the things, and that he, Böhm, is therefore writing to me in confidence, so that the witness should not get into great embarrassment; he hoped, however, that I would not betray him (Böhm) in Economy because no one knew a thing about this letter but he and most of the people in Economy knew nothing of the theft. With a letter written in this style I believe I will be able to replace everything without further circumstances.
>
> Do as you like–I ask for a quick reply. When you write sign yourself as "Schaustion."
>
> Your most devoted
>
> A. BR

In an letter dated August 22, 1846, Eduard Acker wrote to R.L. Baker to order a double wool carpet of first quality and included $7 as payment. He expressed appreciation that the thieves of the coin collection had been caught so quickly—apparently within a matter of days from Bimber's letter.

However, it seems to be the case that certain coins were still missing:

Many months later, on April 19, 1847, Bimber wrote to Baker of Economy stating that his neighbor, Jacob Smith, had found 18 to 20 silver coins and three gold coins while repairing a fence. Bimber believed that these were from the group that had been stolen by George Schanbacher from the Harmony Society's Museum. No doubt, they were part of the Curiosity Cabinet.

In Later Years

The economic vitality of the settlement continued to wane as its members aged. By 1880 the average age was 70. Many if not most had simply run out of energy.

By 1890 the Society was experiencing severe financial difficulties. Jacob Henrici died in 1892, after which John Duss (1860-1951) was in complete charge. During this time, most assets "disappeared."[2] The state of Pennsylvania endeavored to take over the remainder of the property in 1894, and after protracted litigation became heir in 1916.

Duss resigned his post in 1903 and turned over management of the Society's affairs to his wife. In 1905 the Society was dissolved, by which time there were only three members still alive. As was the case with virtually all work-share societies that practiced celibacy and at the same time attracted very few new members from the outside, there was no real hope that the dreams of George Rapp and his immediate heirs would extend beyond a few decades. The "silver years" of the Society in its Economy, Pennsylvania, location seem to have been from about 1825 to 1850.

The village, acquired by the state in 1916, today is a 16-acre site administered by the Pennsylvania Historical and Museum Commission. Structures built between 1824 and 1830 house over 16,000 Harmonist objects which are exhibited and can be viewed on self-guided tours.

Today in the 1990s the Economite Treasure is long forgotten except by scholars. Not a single coin in a

---

[1] Arndt, p. 992, called him a "spy" for the Society.

[2] Daniel B. Reibel, *A Guide to Old Economy,* p. 9.

collection today can be positively attributed to the 1878 hoard. Curator Raymond Shepherd advised the author that impressive plans are being formulated for the museum complex, and that this will include expanded information on the Economite Treasure, pieces later found, various award medals, and more.

This numismatic exhibit will be part of the partial reconstruction of the Cabinet of Curiosities. Unfortunately, parts of it were stolen in 1846, as earlier noted, and the balance disappeared years later. The Economy Collection (to give it a name) must be added to a register that includes only a few important cabinets known to have been formed in America prior to 1850 and fewer yet before 1830. Unfortunately, no inventory of the original numismatic exhibit has been located. One can only speculate as to what it might have contained. As the Harmony Society members acquired high quality items in other disciplines, it can be assumed that the coin holding was an impressive one in its time.

At present the Old Harmony Village Museum has the following half dollars, the gift of Ms. Christiana Knodeler in 1975: 1817, 1818, 1819, 1821, 1823, 1826 (2), 1827 (2), 1828, 1833, 1834, 1835, and 1836 (2).[1]

Although there are no specific records, it is believed that these half dollars were kept locally over a long period of time and are survivors from the 1878 Economite Treasure.

The Mysterious Quarter Dollars

Hidden or lost: 1825 or later
Found or distributed: Sometime 1825-1881
Treasure: 1815 and 1825 quarters

Who Made Them and Why?

One of the greatest unsolved mysteries, at least for lovers of numismatic esoterica, has to do with a hoard of certain United States silver quarter dollars of the Capped Bust type.[2] The identity of the hoarder is not known today, although in the 1880s some information must have been available to the knowing ones. It is possible, although not particularly probable, that the aforementioned Harmony Society may have had something to with it. Or, perhaps Latin and English school prizes are relevant to the enigma. Then there is the matter of Lafayette and with—or perhaps separate from—the Erie Canal.

1815 quarter dollars, one with an E counterstamped over the head of Miss Liberty and the other with an L.

Sound confusing?

Well, it is—and has been for a long time.

These curious quarter dollars bear the dates 1815 (one die variety, known to specialists as Browning-1)[3] and one of the three die varieties known of 1825 (B-2, the 1825/3 overdate).[4] During the 1815-1825 period many different die varieties of quarter dollars were coined, but only these two varieties bearing two different and widely separated dates concern us here.

Certain of these two varieties are known today with one or the other of two letters, E or L, carefully

---

[1] Inventory from Raymond Shepherd, letter, October 11, 1996.

[2] Sources include Karl Moulton, letters, August 22 and 31, 1996, enclosing historical citations and extensive numismatic commentary, part of his research for a long-term book project on the large-size quarter dollars of 1796-1828; Kenneth E. Bressett, conversation, August 19, 1996; Breen, *Encyclopedia,* 1988, pp. 340-342; correspondence with Mark Hotz; several conversations, July 1996, with Keith Zaner of *Coin World,* who was preparing an article on the topic (which appeared in the issue of August 26, 1996, "Theories Galore"); and the author's long-time interest in the subject. Gregory Brunk, *American and Canadian Countermarked Coins,* mentions these on p. 65 and among other observations quotes Frank G. Duffield's commentary on them (*The Numismatist,* 1919, Duffield nos. 1345-1346).

[3] Ard W. Browning, whose book, *Early Quarter Dollars of the United States, 1796-1838,* was published by Wayte Raymond in 1925, is himself the center of a numismatic mystery. The obviously talented Mr. Browning apparently published no earlier or later works on coins, but arose in full bloom in 1925 to present the collecting community with a first-class reference book on this rather specialized series. Perhaps a computer analysis of Browning's word usage and writing style (and a handwriting analysis too, if holographic materials can be found) might reveal if the work was actually written by someone else, a la the Shakespeare-Bacon debate. Wayte Raymond has been suggested as the possible real author. Tracing the ownership of the pieces illustrated by Browning would be another avenue of inquiry.

[4] 1825 B-3 is also mentioned in the literature including the Breen update of Browning's 1925 work, but has not been verified by any observed photographs or recent inspections of coins (cf. Karl Moulton, letter, August 31, 1996).

counterstamped above and close to Miss Liberty's head. Most often seen are 1815 quarters with the E counterstamp.

The letters are both from related punches—thin cross members and uprights and each with light serifs—and, in view of their relative consistency of impression and location were probably all done by the same person(s) at the same time. Moreover, as only two die varieties are known, and as, presumably, hundreds or more pieces were originally counterstamped, the coins must have been taken from groups of Uncirculated coins that had been accumulated or stored somewhere, and counterstamped no earlier than 1825. If coins had been retrieved from circulation, other dates such as the large-mintage 1818 and issues through 1824 surely would have been involved. Further, among 1825 quarters there would have been some of the Browning-1 and 3 variety in addition to the counterstamped B-2 examples known to exist of that particular date. Thus, a hoard consisting of Uncirculated coins is indicated.

Debut at a Haseltine Sale

Karl Moulton, who has been studying these counterstamps carefully, reports that the first auction appearance he has been able to find in an extensive search of catalogues beginning with those published in 1859 was in a Capt. John W. Haseltine sale of December 12, 1881, offering an 1815 quarter dollar with an E counterstamp, the coin described as Uncirculated. From that time onward, examples in sales were numerous, and nearly 20 pieces crossed the block in 1882 and 1883. This is rather curious, considering their absence earlier.

It should be noted that John W. Haseltine's *Type Table,* said to have been written with the assistance of J. Colvin Randall and essentially an auction sale conducted on November 28, 1881, did not include any E or L counterstamps.[1] On the other hand, the present writer—who has collected counterstamps of various sorts, but mostly large copper cents, since 1955—recalls that as recently as the 1950s and 1960s, quarter dollars with these letters were considered to be "mutilated." Thus, while a specialist with an academic bent might have taken an interest, the casual buyer was apt to ignore one of these in favor of acquiring an "undamaged" piece. Over the years I have catalogued my share of quarter dollar collections, and only infrequently has a specialist been interested in counterstamped pieces.

Accordingly, it is *possible* that 1815 and 1825 quarter dollars with E or L counterstamps were known in numismatic circles prior to the 1880s, but they were considered to be unworthy of notice in auction catalogues.

Such words as *possible, maybe,* and *perhaps* have been attached over the years to most discussions of these curious counterstamps.

Woodward Takes Notice

Indeed, the philosophy of viewing these counterstamped pieces as being mutilated or damaged was hardly new when I first learned of such pieces in the 1950s. In his auction of the Blanchard Collection, December 11-12, 1882, W. Elliot Woodward—coin dealer, druggist, and historian who lived in Roxbury, Massachusetts—suggested that such counterstamped quarter dollars were from a "recent, mutilated find."

Further, Woodward in his October 16-18, 1882, sale of the Prof. J. Grier Ralston Collection, Lot 323, mentioned the hoard tangentially: "1815 [quarter dollar]. Barely circulated; it will be noticed that this is not one of the inexhaustible lot, stamped with the letter 'E' or 'L' above the head; rare."

Thus, as an "inexhaustible lot" certainly implies a hoard, these interesting quarter dollars of 1815 and 1825 are included in the present book.

By the way, Woodward was as good an iconoclast as the best of them. Then, and sometimes now, if a particular rare coin dealer didn't think of something first, or felt he was upstaged, the result was "sour grapes," Aesop's early equivalent of today's "not invented here" syndrome. Presumably, if the "recent, mutilated find" had come to Woodward first, the commentary would have been different. Recall (see Chapter 1, "The Boothbay Harbor Find") that in 1880 Woodward expressed some degree of enthusiasm in handling Pine Tree shillings that were found in a cove on the seaside, and had been corroded to the extent that they had lost half their weight. Quite possibly, if Haseltine had handled them, rather than Woodward

[1] At the time Haseltine's store was at 1225 Chestnut Street, Philadelphia, and Randall was at 1905 Chestnut Street, a separation of seven blocks (punctuated by the U.S. Mint at Chestnut and 13th). In *Numisma,* January 1880, Ed. Frossard noted: "Messrs. Haseltine and Randall of Philadelphia are now engaged in a descriptive list of the United States silver dollars, half dollars, and quarters, a work for which their long experience and thorough knowledge of the subject eminently qualifies them. Mr. Haseltine informs us that the work will describe minutely all the known varieties...." In March 1880 Frossard noted that Haseltine commented the work was "progressing favorably, and that orders for copies are coming in from every quarter." The "Catalogue of John W. Haseltine's TYPE TABLE..." bears on the cover the notation, "catalogue by John W. Haseltine" with no mention of Randall.

himself, these would have been candidates for the "mutilated" adjective.

As it was, the estimable cataloguer from Roxbury continued his animus toward these counterstamps, even stretching the truth a bit and also denigrating the counterstamp *in absentia,* as in his sale of June 29, 1885, Lot 560, a quarter dollar: "1815 Unc.; the obnoxious letter E or L stamped above the bust on all other known quarters of this date is happily wanting on this." In actuality, there were many other 1815 quarters without either an E or an L. In his sale of June 28-29, 1886, the absent counterstamp received a similar knock: "Lot 348: 1815 The obnoxious letter is absent over the head; very good, scarce."[1]

Modern Times

In more recent times counterstamped coins have come into their own due to enlightenment and interest on the part of many people, the expansion of the Token and Medal Society, and the publication of a reference book on American and Canadian counterstamps by Dr. Gregory Brunk.

Today there are many instances in which a counterstamped coin is worth more than an unstamped one, sometimes *much more.* However, with regard to the 1815 and 1825 quarter dollars with the stamped E and L letters, these tend to sell for a bit less than their unmarked cousins.

Among numerous auction offerings of recent decades, honors for quantity are tied between the Bowers and Ruddy Galleries sale of December 1977 and the Stack's sale of June 1996, both of which featured four counterstamped quarter dollars, the former with one of 1815 and three of 1825/3, and the latter with two of each date.

Theories

If the counterstamps on the quarter dollars of these two dates had been intended to advertise a person or business or to commemorate an occasion, certainly something more than a single initial or letter would have been used. A quarter dollar with an E or L would have no meaning to someone encountering it later. However, it could have been used as an admission check or identification of some type.

For many years it was suggested that these were notations to identify the weight of the coins, with L meaning the coin was *light,* E referring to *extra* or *excess* weight.[2] The only problem with this theory is that careful weighing of such counterstamped coins does not disclose any significant deviation from the standard, and E-stamped pieces are not heavier than L-marked coins.

Best in School and Other Theories

Walter Breen in his *Encyclopedia,* p. 340, suggests that they may have been school prizes, "E = English, L = Latin, which would account for the high grade of survivors; they were kept rather than spent." However, what about school subjects such as arithmetic and reading? For my part, I will dismiss the prize idea, although I will be the first to stand corrected if any documentation should ever be found.

Other related E-L letter-word pairs could be devised and have been suggested by numismatists, as Early-Late (or Earlier-Later, such as seating times in a dining hall or aboard ship), Elephant-Lion (attractions at a circus), etc.

Another idea concerning the counterstamped quarter dollars: The E and L letters could have indicated ownership, possibly by two family members, if the coins were stored for a long time. In that way if some were stolen, they could be easily identified. This idea is not as foolish as it might seem at first consideration. Realize, for example, that James Vila Dexter (1836-1899) boldly counterstamped his surname initial D on the reverse of his most prized coin—an 1804 silver dollar—to give it permanent identification.[3]

Mark Hotz Commentaries

The *John Reich Journal* carried two articles by Mark Hotz in 1987 and 1990, the first accompanied by a separate, related commentary by Bill Subjack.[4] In 1987 Hotz examined existing theories and proposed one of his own: that in order to improve the quality of strike, coin presses were adjusted "Left," "Right," or no ad-

---

[1] A virtually identical "obnoxious" description was used for Lot 958 in the same cataloguer's sale of October 25-27, 1886.

[2] Another counterstamp on these quarters, the letter R, was occasionally mentioned years ago, but it seems to have been recalled incorrectly as no pieces have been located by modern scholars. Sometimes it was said that R meant *regular* or *regulation* weight.

[3] Also see Heritage's 1996 ANA Convention Sale, Lot 7059, which mentions a theory by Karl Moulton that the E and L could have been reference marks relating to star and date placement and alignment. Concerning counterstamping rare coins for numismatic identification, very few collectors if any would want to do this today; the procedure is hardly recommended.

[4] Mark Hotz, "Mint Counterstamped Large Size Bust Quarters 1815 & 1825," December 1987; Bill Subjack, "E & L Counterstamps—Another Theory," December 1987; Mark Hotz, "Those Darned Counterstamped Bust Quarters—The Saga Continues," October 1990. Also see commentary by Q. David Bowers under Lot 1121 in the Harold A. Blauvelt Collection Sale, February 1977.

justment ("Even"). The same writer observed that "the counterstamped issues are at least 15 times rarer than the same dates without counterstamps," which would seem to infer that in W. Elliot Woodward's era of the 1880s there had been a flood of counterstamped pieces on the market, thus making non-counterstamped pieces seem rare, but in the century or more since then, the true rarity ratio has become apparent.

In the same 1987 venue, Bill Subjack mused that the E and L could have referred to changes in the minting technique: "Could the E stand for 'Edge collar die reeding?' Could the L mean 'Lathe' application of the same reeding?"

In 1990 Mark Hotz re-explored the subject. R.W. Julian had advised him that in the 1890s assistant treasurers of the United States "did stamp gold and silver coins with an L to indicate light weight." This may shed light on the origin of the old and now largely discounted theory that the E meant "Extra" or "Excess" weight and L referred to "Light." After discussing several other ideas, the writer remarked that the weight and school prize theories did not seem logical with regard to the 1815 and 1825 counterstamped quarters, the mystery still remained.

Contemporary America

I suggest that the answer may lie in American history, and that the counterstamping was done either to identify these coins at a later date (for example, if they were stolen or fell into the hands of an enemy—much as the HAWAII overprints on World War II currency—thus they could be declared invalid), or to serve as a pass or admission check for use at a one-time event (25¢ being a popular price for certain amusement and transportation services at the time).

In 1824-1825 Marquis de Lafayette, French hero of the American Revolution, revisited the United States and was declared by Congress to be "The Nation's Guest." Celebrations were held in many eastern cities. Could the L be related?

One would need to find an E connection as well. Of course, (E)conomy, the Harmonists' settlement in Pennsylvania, springs to mind as a juxtaposition of L and E. (L)afayette visited there toward the end of May, 1825. Besides, the Economists just might have had wooden boxes filled with Uncirculated quarter dollars dated 1815 and 1825. Vast quantities of coins were stored for long periods of time at Economy, and it is an easy supposition that coins the Harmonists had marked in 1825 could have been stored for decades in wooden boxes, and then brought to light for the first time in 1881.

Lafayette's arrival in New York City in August 1824, the start of a visit that lasted until September 1825 and included parades and receptions in dozens of towns and cities.

Per contra, although E could have been used for Economy, the town was also called Harmony (or Harmonie) in the mid-1820s, although the Harmony name was usually reserved for the two other communities the Rappites established before moving to their final location in 1824.

In 1825 the 360-mile Erie Canal from Albany to Buffalo, New York, was opened amid much celebration and fanfare. Could the E be related? One would need to find an L connection as well. Donald Davis has noticed that E and L are the first and last letters of (E)rie Cana(L).[1]

In June 1825 Lafayette visited that waterway and traveled some distance on two vessels, the *Rochester* and the *Governor Clinton*. Special notice was paid by Lafayette to Lockport, which had recently been constructed and already boasted a large hotel and a newspaper. Thus we have an Erie-Lafayette connection and also an Erie-Lockport pairing.

Seemingly, it is possible to go back and forth on the E-L situation all day long!

Before leaving Lafayette, it may be of interest to note that E and L counterstamp speculation aside, his 1824-1825 visit to America did have many provable numismatic connections. Hundreds of large copper cents were counterstamped with his image on one side and that of George Washington and the others, as were a lesser number of half dollars and some other denominations as well. On June 17, 1825, he was the hon-

[1] As related by Davis to Pete Smith, August 1996; Smith, letter, September 8, 1996.

Illustration of an 1824 United States half dollar counterstamped (by persons unknown) as a souvenir during Lafayette's 1824-1825 visit to America. From the Roach, Witham, and author's collections.

oree of the Bunker Hill Monument Association at the Revolutionary War battle site near Boston, this being the 50th anniversary of the military engagement. Lafayette, with tens of thousands in attendance, participated in the laying of a cornerstone which contained, among other things, "Coins of the United States" (per an 1825 program); Comitia Americana medals of George Washington (two varieties), John Egar Howard, and John Paul Jones; medals of Benjamin Franklin, Thaddeus Kosciuszko, and Christopher Columbus; and "specimens of old Continental money."[1]

What Do We Know or Assume?

The observable realities seem to be as follows:

1. The counterstamping was done at a single time by one or more persons in 1825 or later.

2. A hoard of several hundred or more Uncirculated quarter dollars from 1815 and 1825 was on hand when the counterstamping was done. The estimate of several hundred is assumed as an extrapolation of the dozens of auction appearances of the counterstamps over the years. Karl Moulton reported that there have been about 100 auction offerings since World War II and, of course, many before that time.[2]

3. Nearly all known pieces described in the literature and known to several interested numismatists are in higher grades such as Extremely Fine, AU, and Uncirculated.[3] On the other hand, most known 1815 and 1825 quarters without E or L are in lower grades from Good to Very Fine (although higher grade pieces exist, they are in the minority). This suggests that counterstamped coins may not have been released into general circulation in 1825 or immediately following years, but were kept in storage until circa 1881 and then distributed via numismatic channels.

4. Several hundred or more are estimated to be known today, indicating that at least this many were counterstamped. Such would have required a considerable amount of effort and time. Thus, there must have been a purpose for the counterstamping, but that purpose was not to advertise a person or business or event.

5. No quarter dollars were made for circulation with the date 1826, and apparently 1827 quarter dollars were mostly if not all Proofs for collectors. Thus, the next large production for circulation was 1828. Perhaps, this would suggest a date range from 1825 to early 1828 for the marking to have occurred. However, if these pieces first came to light in 1881, the stamping could have been done anytime between 1825 and that date.

6. These pieces were not generally known to numismatists until late 1881, after which time offerings became numerous.

What is the answer? At present, no one knows.

What are your ideas?

Sherlock Holmes, where are you?

---

1 From an account in *A Complete History of the Marquis de Lafayette,* "by an officer in the late Army," Hartford, 1847, pp. 497-498. The Bunker Hill Monument was not completed until 1842.

2 Letter to the author, September 10, 1996.

3 Kenneth E. Bressett, conversation, August 19, 1996, commented that he had never seen a well-worn one in many years of making notes about the counterstamps. Most pieces offered in the auctions in the 1881-1883 era studied by Karl Moulton were Uncirculated. (Per contra, it could be argued that well-worn pieces were of insufficient value in the nineteenth century to merit auction descriptions.)

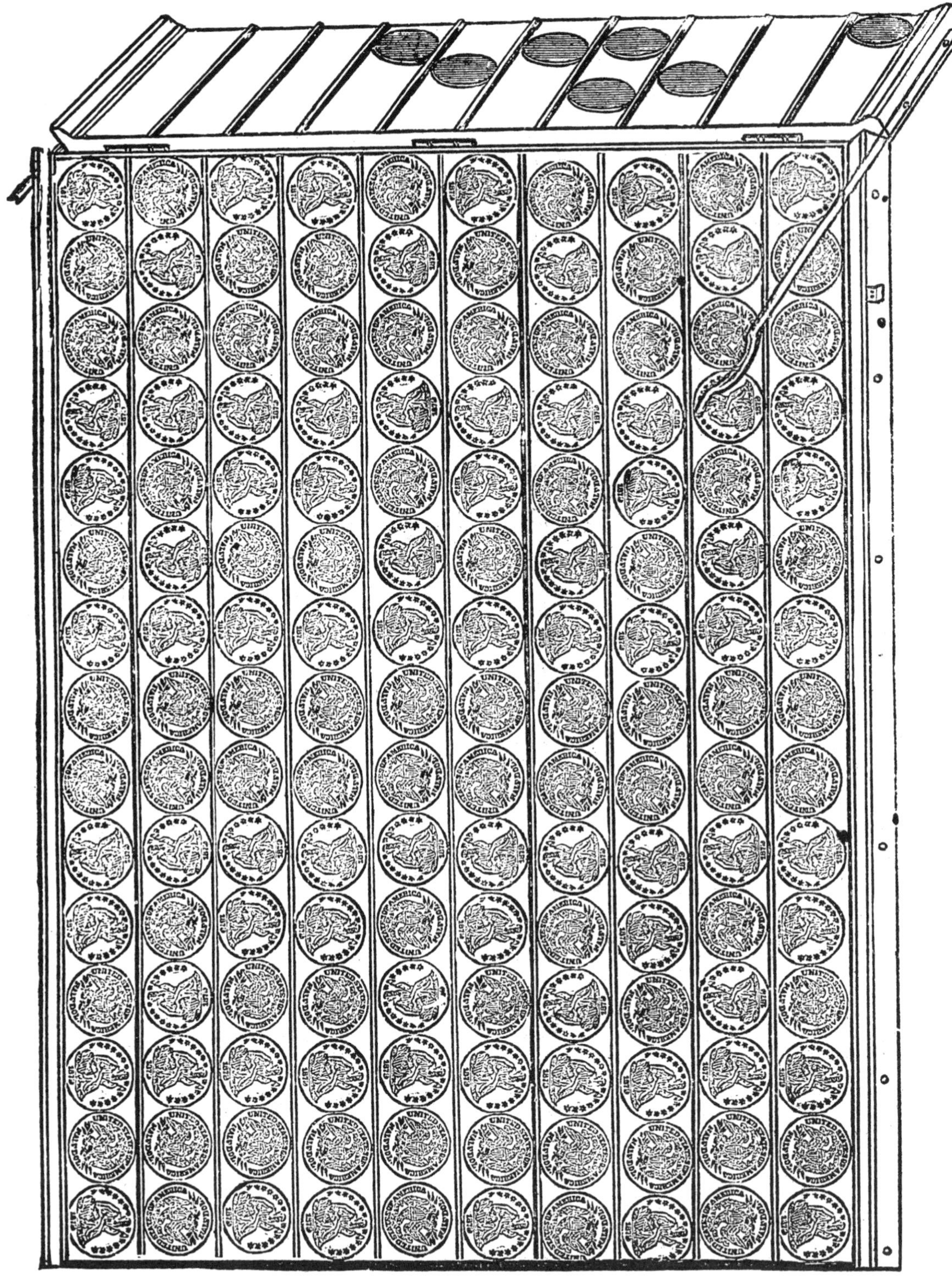

Counting board for Liberty Seated half dollars as used at the Mint in the late nineteenth century. In actuality, the coins would have been randomly arranged, not oriented with their obverses and reverses all facing in the same direction. (Artist's conception from A.M. Smith's *Coins and Coinage, the United States Mint, Philadelphia,* 1881)

CHAPTER 7

Silver Coins Go to Other Lands

Over the years many silver coins minted in the United States have been shipped to and later found in foreign lands. Often such pieces return to America to delight numismatists. In other instances no one is sure what happened to them.

The American Silver Nuisance

Exported: 1858-1870
Treasure: U.S. silver coins

Too Many Liberty Seated Coins!

Today it is impossible for a numismatist to conceive of tons of United States Liberty Seated silver coins being a *nuisance,* but that is exactly what a great surplus of them was called in Canada in 1870.[1] There were simply too many of our half dimes, dimes, quarters, and half dollars (but only a few silver dollars) in circulation north of the border.

The story begins in British North America in the early nineteenth century, in the area that would later be called Canada. In the absence of a native mint in Canada or the production in England (the mother country) of coins especially for Canada, commerce in that territory was largely conducted in foreign coins. Among silver issues most were old Spanish-American coins and various United States denominations, with a lesser number being English pieces. It was not until 1858 that Canada had its own coinage, which consisted of 5-, 10-, and 20-cent pieces in addition to an issue of bronze cents. However, these coins were far short of the amount needed to sustain commerce. Beginning around that time, vast quantities of United States silver coins were imported.

American coins continued to come into Canada. After December 28, 1861, when the New York banks suspended specie payments and in 1862 when the Treasury Department did the same and newly-minted gold and silver coins were no longer in circulation in the United States, there was an overabundance of them north of the border. Historian Neil Carothers wrote:[2]

> From 1858 to 1862 a steady stream of subsidiary silver [coins of less than the $1 denomination] went across the border. After the [newly-issued U.S.] greenbacks fell to a discount in 1862, the profit on export to Canada became large, and in a short while Canada was over-run with United States silver. When the saturation point was reached in the fall of 1862, the Canadian market was wiped out....
>
> Before the end of 1862, United States silver was at a discount of 3% in Canadian gold. The *Detroit Advertiser* said that the city treasurer of Toronto had half a ton of U.S. silver coins that he could not dispose of. In this country [the United States] a greenback dollar would buy about 80 cents in subsidiary coin. Across the line a Canadian paper dollar would buy $1.03 in the same coin.

[1] Sources include: William Weir, *Sixty Years in Canada,* 1903; Weir was the secretary of the Tariff Reform Association of 1858 and the government agent for the exportation of American silver coins in 1870. Neil Carothers, *Fractional Money,* 1930, pp. 217-218, 259-260. A related commentary appears in the *American Journal of Numismatics,* March 1870, p. 87, under "A 'New Dominion' Coinage."
[2] *Fractional Money,* p. 218.

Some Canadian merchants would receive United States silver coins only at a discount. No one wanted to ship them back to their country of origin and exchange them for paper notes of uncertain value. For a period of years during the 1860s it was estimated that in the city of Montreal alone there were 30 or more brokers who derived most of their income from trading in United States coins in bulk at the rate of more than $80,000 per day.[1]

As United States silver coins had no fixed values in Canadian commerce and traded at varying discounts, they were complained of by the public, as those holding such coins were always fearful of sustaining losses.

What To Do With Them All

In 1869 William Weir, an agent of the Canadian government, made arrangements with merchants to export $2 million worth of American silver coins to New York City to be sold to brokers there. A January 27, 1870, proposal by Sir Francis Hincks, government finance minister, to fix the rates of United States coins at a 20% discount was circulated to various merchants and bankers.[2] This resulted in an

> official proclamation, February 12, which fixed April 15, 1870, as the last day of grace for 'the old lady with the broomstick' and other barbarisms of the United States Mint. After that date our half dollars must take forty cents for themselves or give up passports, and all the other coins, even to five-cent pieces, in the same ratio.[3]

In 1870 over $3,500,000 in United States silver coins went from Canada to brokers in New York City, causing a glut there, after which additional pieces were said to have been shipped to England as bullion.[4]

Old Silver Coins Reappear

However, quantities remained in Canada and a few Latin American countries to which coins had "fled" in the 1850s and early 1860s. Carothers takes up the story in 1877, by which time the United States government had been minting record quantities of silver coins and had recently exchanged about $36,000,000 face-value worth of them for paper money:[5]

> Further exchanges of newly-minted silver coins for paper notes were brought to a complete stop by an unexpected and dramatic development. In the winter of 1877 there suddenly reappeared in circulation literally hundreds of millions of the silver three-cent pieces, half dimes, dimes, quarters, and half dollars that had as suddenly departed in 1862. They streamed in from Canada, from Central America, from South America, and from the West Indies. A small quantity, probably, was brought out from domestic hoards. With the value of silver going down and the value of greenbacks rising toward parity with gold a point had been reached where these long absent coins were worth more at home than they were in foreign countries.
>
> The most interesting feature of this unexpected homecoming was the information it afforded as to the fate of the coins in 1862. It showed that they had not been melted or exported to Europe as bullion, although there was a definite profit in melting the coins at that time. They had gone to Latin America, served as local currency for 15 years, and then returned. Sen. John Sherman in 1880 estimated the value of the coins returned in the preceding two years at $22,000,000, and a large amount came back after that time.

Where Are They Now?

No numismatic connection with specific Canadian, Latin American, or related hoard pieces is known today, and, presumably, most of the coins were melted in the 1870s and later. However, the occurrence at one time of large numbers of United States silver coins in Canada—a situation that persisted well into the twentieth century, but to a lesser degree than in the 1850s and 1860s—accounts for specimens found there from time to time.

It is appropriate to mention that in the 1860s, when old copper "large" cents were no longer common in general circulation in the United States, there was a glut of these, too, in Canada, where countless thousands were in commercial channels along with various copper tokens issued by Canadian banks and merchants. Devins & Bolton, Montreal druggists, counterstamped many of these cents with their advertisement during the same decade.

Half Dollars in Guatemala

Exported: Circa 1853-1864
Found: By 1942
Treasure: Half dollars

This hoard is described by John J. Ford, Jr., as follows (also see "Half Dollars in Guatemala—Again" account later in this chapter):[6]

---

1 Weir, p. 138.

2 Weir, pp. 151 ff.

3 Quoted commentary from the *American Journal of Numismatics,* March 1870, p. 87. The "old lady with the broomstick" was a whimsical description of the Liberty Seated half dollar, the "broomstick" being the liberty cap and pole.

4 Weir, p. 159. At the time London was the world's premier market and price arbiter for gold and silver.

5 *Fractional Money,* pp. 259-260, here slightly edited.

6 Breen, *Encyclopedia,* 1988, p. 401. Breen was an employee of the New Netherlands Coin Co. in the 1950s including 1956. Later, he went to work for Lester Merkin, and still later for Stanley Apfelbaum (First Coinvestors).

About 1942 the Stack's dealership [Joe and Morton Stack] in New York City bought a tremendous hoard of Liberty Seated half dollars. These were somewhat oxidized and were said to have been dug up in Guatemala. Perhaps they were buried during the Civil War. Dates ranged from 1853 to about 1864. I remember that there were a lot of San Francisco coins, especially 1861-S, but there was no 1855-S.

I studied the lot carefully and was the first, I believe, to notice that the S mintmarks from this era came in three different sizes. These coins were retailed to customers, including in price lists I wrote in 1942.

After the spring of 1862, silver half dollars were no longer paid out in the East by the Treasury Department. The New Orleans Mint had last minted half dollars in 1861, after which time it was in the hands of the Confederacy. On the West Coast the San Francisco Mint produced half dollars and other coins which, unlike the situation in the East, went readily into the channels of commerce.

In California, paper "greenback" notes were not used, and silver and gold coins continued to be employed, despite the suspension of specie payments in the East. Many of these pieces were exported from San Francisco as payment in international transactions. Presumably, the half dollars that went to Central America as late as 1864 were part of some type of foreign exchange.

Trade Dollars Come Back from China

Exported: 1873-1878
Found: 1940s onward
Treasure: Trade dollars

The Trade Dollar Era

From 1873 to 1878 many millions of silver trade dollars were shipped to China from the United States. Minted at Philadelphia, Carson City, and (mainly) San Francisco, the pieces weighed 420 grains each, or slightly more than the 412.5 grains of a standard silver dollar. Merchants in China preferred silver coins to gold or any other form of payment. The slightly heavier weight of the American trade dollar made it a formidable competitor to several other varieties of silver "trade" coins issued by various countries, most notably the Mexican silver pesos.

While going from hand to hand in China, trade dollars were usually privately stamped with Chinese figures called "chopmarks," to indicate that they were made of good silver and were acceptable in commerce. American trade dollars were extraordinarily popular in China in 1873-1874, and the West Coast mints (San Francisco and Carson City) could not keep up with the demand. However, by 1876 they were plentiful there. Many of the trade dollars sent to China were later sent to India in payment for opium, and in India were melted.[1]

Trade dollars were legal tender in the United States until July 22, 1876, after which they were used only for export purposes. Domestically, trade dollars sold after that time at prices based upon their bullion or melt-down values which in all instances was less than face value.

In 1887 and later years the United States redeemed many trade dollars for face value, under a new law, but those pieces with chopmarks were not accepted. The trade dollars taken in by the Treasury Department were melted and mostly recoined into silver dollars (of the current Morgan design). As an example, many 1891-O (New Orleans Mint) Morgan dollars were made from melted-down trade dollars, although most numismatists today are not aware of this historical connection.

Numismatic Considerations

Large quantities of United States trade dollars remained for many years in Hong Kong and other Chinese cities. Meanwhile, in America there was very little numismatic interest in the trade dollar denomination. As a result, few pieces were retained in cabinets, and even the Proofs of the 1873-1883 dates, which by Mint

[1] Sources include *American Journal of Numismatics*, April 1875, pp. 90-91; April 1876, p. 87; January 1876, p. 66.

policy were included as a part of silver Proof sets of those years, were often spent by collectors who were thus forced to buy them.[1]

Decades later in the 1940s there developed a strong collector market for trade dollars among United States numismatists, and many thousands were brought back to this country. The reasons for the new interest include the listing of the denomination by date and mintmark in Wayte Raymond's *Standard Catalogue of United States Coins* beginning in the 1930s and, starting in 1946, Richard S. Yeoman's *Guide Book of United States Coins.* With such coins illustrated and described, a desire to acquire them arose.

While most of the repatriated trade dollars had chopmarks, many did not. At the time it was felt that those with chopmarks were more valuable, as they "told a story" and showed evidence of having been circulated in China—the intended purpose of such pieces. By the 1950s the situation had changed, and in America trade dollars without chopmarks were considered to be more valuable.

Trade dollars continued to be imported by the thousands through at least the 1960s, after which most supplies ran out. Later finds were mostly of a few hundred or so coins. Perhaps the "re-opening" of mainland China in coming years will disclose additional supplies. The world of numismatic hoards and treasures is ever-changing, and surprises are bound to occur.

The San Francisco Silver Mystery

Although the story of the trade dollar is well known, relatively unchronicled is the vast departure of other silver coins from San Francisco from the 1850s through 1872, the latter year being just before the advent of the trade dollar.

Beginning in the early years of the Gold Rush there developed an extensive sea trade with China. As noted, merchants and banks there preferred payment in silver. Gold coins were not popular, and no one would hear of payment in any kind of paper. It was an era of "hard money" deals, and the money wanted was to be in the form of silver coins.

During most of the decade of the 1850s, merchants in San Francisco bought Mexican silver 8-real "dollars" from bullion dealers and brokers, paying a premium for them. These were readily accepted in China, but the premium added to the cost of doing business. In 1859 the shipping firms of the city petitioned the San Francisco Mint, which had opened for business a few years earlier in 1854, to make silver dollars. Accordingly, in 1859 some 20,000 Liberty Seated dollars were struck for export purposes. What happened to all of these 1859-S dollars remains a mystery, as very few have ever been found in the Orient. Quite possibly, many were melted down or shipped to India (which demanded silver from China in exchange for opium), the same fate that befell many of the later 1873-1878 silver trade dollars.

Quite probably, most other Liberty Seated dollars made in later years through the early 1870s also were used in the export trade. Most of these later dates were struck at the Philadelphia Mint (continuously) with some others in Carson City, New Orleans, and San Francisco.

Even more of a mystery is what happened to what is believed to be the vast majority of other silver coins minted at San Francisco in the 1850s, denominations from the dime to the half dollar (half dimes were not made there until 1863). Most probably, much of the 1855-S half dollar coinage went there, but what happened to most of them after that is not known. Some circulated in China and were affixed with merchants' and bankers' chopmarks.[2] Apparently, half dollars after 1855-S were not as actively used for hand-to-hand transactions, for examples are not seen today. The Irving Goodman holding of United States half dollars found in China, described subsequently, sheds some light on the matter, but did not include an 1855-S. The discussions in this chapter of half dollars found in Guatemala are relevant as well.

---

1 To a lesser extent, Proof Morgan dollars were not popular, and many were spent. In the 1870s and 1880s a dollar had great purchasing power and thus were not retained casually. Numismatists who collected American silver coins usually retained just the smaller denominations, and were interested only in Proofs. Mintmarked issues were ignored as were large-denomination Proofs.

2 An article by David Helfer, "1855-S half dollars in the China Trade," *Gobrecht Journal,* July 1993, included this comment and is one of the very few numismatic citations seen on the subject: "It is my opinion that in all probability a substantial number of these pieces were shipped to China to purchase goods in the China trade. In the Far East these coins would have been viewed as merely bullion and traded to the Chinese by American ship captains." Four examples of counterstamped 1855-S half dollars were illustrated.

Half Dollars in Guatemala (Again)

Exported: 1850s-1860s
Found: 1956
Treasure: Half dollars

This hoard is described by Walter Breen as follows:[1]

> [Half dollar] dates from the San Francisco branch (and to a lesser extent 1863-1865 from Philadelphia) were formerly believed scarce or rare. However, about 1956 unidentified individuals discovered an immense hoard in Guatemala, reflecting massive wartime shipments of coins as bullion.
>
> The Guatemala hoard coins are readily recognizable: they are dated between 1859 and 1865 Philadelphia Mint, and between 1860 and 1865 San Francisco Mint, most often 1861-1862 from either mint, ranging from VF to nearly Mint State, all cleaned with baking soda or some other abrasive.
>
> There were many hundreds of each date, possibly a couple of thousand of 1861-1862. As there were no later date coins in the part of the hoard I saw (at New Netherlands Coin Co., 1956), most likely the hoard was buried about 1865 or early 1866. Either there were no 1866-S No Motto coins, or they were fished out beforehand; but I have seen nothing matching the hoard coins.

From a numismatic-historical viewpoint there seem to be some flaws in the above account. Beginning in 1862, the federal government stopped paying out silver coins at par, and Philadelphia Mint coins struck after early summer 1862 and continuing until after 1865 (the latest date seen in the hoard) never circulated. Thus, it is virtually impossible that such pieces, if buried in Guatemala in 1865 or 1866, could have been worn down to the "Very Fine" level.

San Francisco Mint silver coins, unlike the Philadelphia issues, were circulated at par in the 1860s. Probably, most were shipped to China, but some could have gone to other places such as Guatemala.

It seems unlikely that half dollars minted at San Francisco from 1860 to 1865 (the years of the S-Mint coins mentioned by Breen), even if they had circulated on the West Coast, would have been worn so much that they would be only Very Fine. Perhaps there is some other explanation.

Note: Also see the somewhat similar "Half Dollars in Guatemala" (1942) account earlier.

Half Dollars from Hong Kong

Exported: 19th century
Found: 1960
Treasure: Half dollars

Half dollars were shipped in quantity to China in the nineteenth century, but, unlike for trade dollars shipped to the same place, numismatic accounts of such pieces are seldom encountered. A pleasant exception is provided by Superior's sale of May 1996, Lots 977, 985, and 1000, comprising the Irving Goodman holding of Liberty Seated half dollars brought back to America from Hong Kong in the early 1960s.

All coins were described as being "either cleaned or damaged." A few were chopmarked, but most were not. The offering included the following:

> 1843 • 1843 (chopmarked) • 1846 (chopmarked) • 1848-O • 1849 • 1854 • 1855-O (2 pieces) • 1856 • 1857-O • 1858-O (2) • 1858-S (2) • 1859 • 1859-O • 1859-S • 1860-S (4) • 1861 • 1861-O • 1861-S (19) • 1862-S (20) • 1863-S (15) • 1863-S (chopmarked) • 1864-S (4) • 1864-S (chopmarked) • 1865-S (8) • 1866-S With Motto (9) • 1867 • 1867-S (2) • 1868-S (5) • 1869-S (4) • 1870 • 1870-S (6 pieces • 1871 (2) • 1871-S • 1871-S (20) • 1872-S (2) • 1873 Closed 3 • 1875 (2) • 1875-S (2) • 1876 (6) • 1876-S • 1877 • 1877-S (7) • 1891 • 1895-O (3).

From a numismatic-historical viewpoint this offering is quite significant. Among other things, it reflects that many San Francisco Mint half dollars were shipped to the Orient, that Philadelphia Mint coins of the 1862-1873 era (when the Treasury Department was not paying them out, but was keeping them in vaults or selling them at a premium for export) were scarcely used in the Orient, and that of the half dollars used there, only a few were chopmarked.

---

1 Breen, *Encyclopedia*, 1988, p. 401. Breen was an employee of the New Netherlands Coin Co. in the 1950s including 1956. Later, he went to work for Lester Merkin, and still later for Stanley Apfelbaum (First Coinvestors).

Quite possibly, the sample represents coins sent to the Orient over a long period of years. In general, prior to the advent of the of the United States trade dollar in 1873, larger quantities of American half dollars and other silver coins were shipped to the Orient than were sent in later years. In addition to pieces sent across the Pacific for commercial purposes, large numbers of silver coins were brought back to China by natives who had worked for several years or more in the United States (such as on track-laying gangs for railroads) and who returned to China to visit or to remain home. As recited in our earlier account of trade dollars, the Chinese strongly preferred silver as a store of value and disdained gold.[1]

In Mexico? On the West Coast?

Hidden, lost, or exported?: 1874
Found: By 1949
Treasure: 1874-S quarter dollars

Where Were They Found?

In the 1960s Lester Merkin, New York City dealer, acquired several dozen choice Uncirculated 1874-S quarter dollars, many of which were sold to the writer. These examples were mostly brilliant with light silver-gray and iridescent toning and of a quality that in a later time (when grading by numbers became popular) would be an easy call at MS-65 or MS-66. The story was told that these pieces turned up in Mexico.[2]

In 1988 *Walter Breen's Complete Encyclopedia of U.S. and Colonial Coins* was published and contained this brief comment (p. 355) indicating another origin:

> A hoard of 80 to 100 Uncirculated 1874-S quarters turned up in a West Coast bank about 1949; they were dispersed one at a time, more frequently after 1974, to dealers and type collectors, so as not to depress prices.

Presumably, these are the same coins as those distributed by Lester Merkin, but one never knows when it comes to hoards, for factual information is often scarcer than the coins themselves.

Update

To permit readers of the present book to be part of an unfolding scenario, we mention that a draft of this article was sent to John J. Ford, Jr., a consultant to this volume who shared many recollections. Thus, here is the latest update and probably the most accurate account, per Ford's commentary:[3]

> I bought the hoard of 1874-S quarters from Henry Christensen for New Netherlands [Coin Co.]. You remember Henry; his office was in New Jersey. He had 300 or 400 of them in the early 1960s, which he had bought somewhere in Latin America. Mexican, Central American, and South American coins were his specialty, and somewhere along the line he stumbled on to these Liberty Seated quarters.
>
> After Lester Merkin sold the Helfenstein large cents in the summer of 1964,[4] he had some extra money and bought 15 or 20 of the quarters from New Netherlands. We kept selling them various places, including to you. Some later appeared in stocks and auctions of your company and Superior Galleries. By the time I left New Netherlands in 1971 there were still 30 or 40 in stock. I think some of these ended up in [my former business associate] Charles Wormser's estate.

---

[1] There was a shift in preference, and in later years, including in the present era, gold is very much appreciated by the Chinese—this in addition to the traditional silver.

[2] Recollection of the author.

[3] Conversation with the author, June 27, 1996.

[4] Louis Helfenstein Collection auction held August 1964. The sale, with a "scenic" color cover featuring partially opened cabinet drawers laden with large cents, created a sensation in the numismatic community at the time and gave a great boost to his auction business. Merkin, a long-time private collector, was a professional musician. From the late 1950s to the 1970s he conducted 32 auction sales. George F. Kolbe auctioned his library in 1984, and after his 1992 death, Stack's auctioned his coins.

CHAPTER 8

Gold Is Where You Find It

Hoards and treasures containing gold coins have always had a certain mystique. Years ago many who contemplated hoarding coins selected gold. Such pieces offered the possibility of storing a large amount of value in a small space. The story of Silas Marner, the weaver of Raveloe, who spent his evenings gloating over and enjoying his hoard of gold guineas is well known to readers of the works of George Eliot.[1]

Here are several accounts of finds whose contents were of that precious yellow metal.

Gold! gold! gold! gold!
Bright and yellow, hard and cold,
Molten, graven, hammered, and rolled;
Heavy to get, and light to hold;
Hoarded, bartered, bought, and sold;
Stolen, borrowed, squandered, doled;
Price of many a crime untold-
Gold! gold! gold! gold![2]

Panning gold in a California stream circa 1850.

Rare Double Eagles

Hidden: Early 1850s
Found: 1854 or 1855
Treasure: Rare double eagles

Ballou's Pictorial Drawing-Room Companion, Volume VIII, 1855, page 286, recounts this:

> A rag picker in San Francisco, while tearing out the lining of an old trunk that had been thrown from the Crescent City Hotel, discovered twenty $20 gold pieces snugly stored upon their edges. Some former owner of the trunk had doubtless placed them there for concealment.

By this time in 1855 the San Francisco Mint had been making double eagles for only a short while. Presumably much more numerous in circulation were the private issues of Moffat & Co., the United States Assay Office of Gold, Kellogg & Co., and others. As this trunk was discarded in early 1855 or perhaps in 1854, it is possible that the 20 double eagles bore some of these names. Today, how rare and desirable they would be!

---

[1] George Eliot was the pen name of British writer Mary Ann Evans. Silas Marner, published in 1861, is perhaps the consummate piece of fiction relating to the hoarding of gold coins.
[2] H.A. Wise, *Captain Brand of the Centipede, a Pirate of Eminence in the West Indies*, 1864, p. 138.

The South Mountain Treasure

Hidden: Early 18th century
Found: 1857
Treasure: Gold coins

Ballou's Pictorial Drawing-Room Companion, January 31, 1857, p. 79, printed this account:

> About one thousand dollars in old Spanish and American gold coins and French silver was found by a servant girl in the smokehouse of Peter Texter, South Mountain, Bucks County, Pennsylvania.
>
> The house has been used every day for many years, without any suspicion of the treasure. It is supposed to have been hidden away by some of Mr. Texter's ancestors, who died without revealing its existence.

In 1857 there was very little numismatic interest in gold coins—even very early ones—and it can be supposed that the pieces were spent or sold to a bullion exchange.

A Mysterious Gold Coin Treasure

Hidden: 1860s
Found: 1880s
Treasure: Gold coins

Did this treasure exist? Apparently so. Was it discovered? That is the question. The following is adapted from an account, in the September 14, 1890, issue of the *New York Times:*[1]

During the days when the famous Confederate raider John Morgan was slashing into southern Ohio with his troop of irregular cavalry, attacking the fat farms of the Union's breadbasket, there lived in Summit County a wealthy farmer named William Huddleston. War prices made farming profitable, and Huddleston, wary of any sort of paper money in unsettled times, put his savings into gold, which was then at a high premium. He had accumulated $6,000 in gold when Morgan's Raiders began to pillage farms in his region.

Sensibly mistrusting banks or bonds or other ventures based on conventional commerce, Huddleston buried his treasure somewhere on his land.

The war ended, leaving the resourceful Huddleston still farming his property. Content that he had buried enough gold to fall back on in case of misfortune, he never bothered to dig up the hidden hoard. He shared the secret of the gold's location only with his wife. His children scattered as soon as they grew up, and one of them, Elizabeth, wound up in Cleveland, where she managed to earn a good living.

The elder Huddlestons died, and the farm passed into other hands. A Clevelander, Charles F. Brush, acquired the property, but he immediately rented it out to a series of tenant farmers.

One of these, a man named Wilkinson, unearthed the gold while plowing his rented acres in the 1880s. He spread the news of his windfall widely,[2] and it came to the attention of Elizabeth Huddleston, who was still living in Cleveland. She could not remember the location of the hoard, but she clearly remembered that her father had asked her to gather a number of empty oyster cans, in which he buried the coins. She immediately took steps to recover the treasure.

Discovering that Judge Timballs of Akron had been retained by Wilkinson to help him clear his title to his find, Elizabeth Huddleston consulted another judge named Marvin, and asked him to investigate the Wilkinson claim and her own rights in the treasure matter.

To Miss Huddleston's chagrin, Marvin returned from his conference with Timballs and informed his client that he could tell her nothing without violating the confidence which obtains between lawyers and those who retain them. Said Judge Marvin, "All lawyers have secrets which they must

1 As cited by B.A. Tompkins, *Treasure,* 1979, p. 160. From Samuel Taylor Coleridge.
2 When it comes to finding gold treasures, "silence is golden," as the saying goes, and may be just as valuable as the discovery of the gold coins

keep, and Timballs could not tell me what he knew. All that I know positively is that a large amount of money was found."

The canny Wilkinson, when questioned, would say nothing about the matter except that he had found "a few bogus dollars." Defeated by the legal fraternity, which almost certainly shared in the Wilkinson windfall, Miss Huddleston made a last effort, going the rounds of the banks to try and find out if Wilkinson had made any large deposit recently. In this attempt she ran square into the protocol of the banking community, which guards its secrets as carefully as do the lawyers. The bankers smugly told her nothing.

Presumably Wilkinson died rich. As for Miss Huddleston, deponent sayeth not.

"Bring Down the Stocking"

Hidden: 19th century
Found: 1894
Treasure: Gold coins

In 1894 an agent of the Mutual Life Insurance Co. of New York had been soliciting a prospective client for some time on the isolated Canadian island of Newfoundland, but to date had achieved no success.[1] Then this happened, as described in his report to the firm's home office:

> Dear Sir:—
>
> We are apt to receive a good many kinds of money in some of the remote places here in Newfoundland. Having canvassed one man until I had almost given up, on his plea that he had "no money," he said at last (turning to his wife), "You may as well bring down the stocking," and when that stocking came with its shining mass of stuff poured out on the table, I wondered if I could tell whether I had enough for the premium or not.
>
> Attached please find memo different kinds of specie paid me for the premium. I hardly knew whether I had $30 or $60. I invested in a small pocketbook to put the premium in, to show the friends how business is done here. Will keep it until I return.

The memorandum showed a variety of world coins including a solitary American gold coin, a $2.50 piece of 1851. Among Canadian coins there was an 1870 Newfoundland $2 gold piece. Most of the others were Spanish-American gold, with the largest being a 1788 doubloon. The latest-dated coin was 1887.

A later numismatic writer, R.J. Graham, suggested that the pieces may have been acquired via trading with a foreign fishing fleet.

The Secrets of Old Buildings

Hidden or lost: 19th century
Found: By 1907
Treasure: Gold coins

Secrets of the Flower Pots

Contractors in the business of building demolition often find strange and valuable things. An unsigned account in the *Boston Herald,* September 17, 1907, featured an interview with a New York City contractor, who regaled the reporter with many interesting stories.[2]

"A short time ago," apparently in 1906 or 1907, "an old woman died of starvation in her home in the Bronx, and afterward it was discovered that she had hidden gold pieces in flower pots concealed under the stairs," the man related.

Unfortunately, the numismatic content of these flower pots was not revealed, but even if there were only two flower pots, and they were small ones—the logical minimum in this account—there must have been many hundreds of gold coins.

themselves in terms of legal fees saved, etc. (not a recommendation, but merely an observation).

1 Adapted from "An Old Newfoundland Savings Hoard," R.J. Graham, *Canadian Numismatic Journal,* July-August 1986, reprinted from the *Transactions of the Canadian Numismatic Research Society,* summer 1986.

2 Citation furnished by David Sundman, Littleton Coin Co.

Run-down buildings near the docks in the lower part of Manhattan.

Prisoners of Long Ago

In the same 1907 article, another find was described as follows:

> The most interesting of the many finds made in tearing down old houses was unearthed in the old Sugar House, at Rose and Duane streets, New York, built in 1763, and transformed during the Revolution into a military prison. When the baseboards were torn away many old coins were found. They were discovered in little piles and were of different mints—Spanish, Swedish, English—as if each prisoner had put his money away for safekeeping and there had been a feeling that one prisoner should not interfere with another.
>
> Many of these prisoners were shot, many others died there, and so there was none to claim their little hoards of money and none to know about them. Year after year they stayed there until a blow of the hammer revealed them.[1]

A Counterfeiter

Another account by the same contractor told of an old residence on Bleecker Street in which he found "a complete counterfeiter's outfit for making silver money. It is illegal to have anything of that kind in your possession, and we destroyed it as soon as possible."

The home had been occupied by a "man and woman of quiet ways, who never visited or received anyone." Finally, the couple moved away, after which the building was closed up, until it was demolished.

A Ghastly Find

Worthy of Edgar Allan Poe is the 1907 story of tearing down a number of adjacent houses on Water Street near the docks in lower Manhattan, in the same area where the firm of Talbot, Allum & Lee had been located in the 1790s.[2] Below the cellar of one building was found a sub-cellar, "and in one of these a chain and some bones were disclosed." It was theorized that this was evidence of some nefarious acts by smugglers. Further:

> A number of underground passages from one house to another, or leading direct to the river, have been found. We also found secret panels and sliding partitions that opened to allow a person to pass from one room to the next without being detected. Just how many people were done to death through the use of such passages will never be known.

But Somebody Did Find It

Hidden: 19th century
Found: February 1907
Treasure: Double eagles

The first decade of the present century was a good time to find gold $20 pieces in the Midwest, it would seem. The *Granite State News,* March 2, 1907, told of this hoard:

> Norfolk, Nebraska. February 20, 1907:
>
> Over $4,000 in gold, all in double eagles, has been found in the barn of William Boche, the miser, who died several weeks ago. Boche did not believe in banks, and when he got any money he hid it, and told his wife he had hid his money where no one could find it.

What happened to miser Boche's 200 or more golden double eagles? No one knows. Perhaps some were saved to be examined by collectors, but likely they were cashed in at a local bank.

---

[1] To the present author it seems unlikely that British prisoners of war held by Americans would have retained valuable coins. There is probably another explanation as to the origin of this hoard.
[2] See Talbot, Allum & Lee account in Chapter 1.

Meanwhile in Nearby Iowa

Hidden or lost: 19th century
Found: 1907
Treasure: Gold coins

During the same era gold coins were found in the state to the east of Nebraska. The *Granite State News,* July 20, 1907, printed this:

> Iowa City, Iowa:
> While John Curry, a farmer living near here, was plowing, he turned up three gold pieces, a $20 piece and two of $5 each. All three had dates in the early '50s. The land on which the treasure was discovered was entered by Byron Dennis in the '40s.

The Alexandria Hoard

Hidden: 1867
Found: 1908
Treasure: 1854-1855 Kellogg $20

Abernathy and Bennett

The following narrative by Thomas J. Hammond was contributed for use in the present book:[1]

A gold hoard, lost in 1867, was found at the turn of this century, but its present whereabouts remains a mystery.

The rush for gold is usually associated with western expansion. We have visions of rugged pioneers, ambitious souls blazing trails west through a trackless wilderness. Rarely do we hear stories of those pioneers of the 1850s who returned eastward, having already found that idyllic dream of monetary wealth in the West. This is the story of such a case, a man named William Abernathy who converted his bright yellow dust into gold coin and headed east to Nebraska to homestead a ranch with a man named Joseph Bennett.

This is the story of the "Alexandria Hoard" of Kellogg $20 gold pieces which is only briefly mentioned in a couple of numismatic books and periodicals. Unfortunately, as is the case with much research, it is not the full story, and some questions remain.

My research took me to Thayer County, Nebraska, a fertile valley which was described in the nineteenth century as "surrounded by as fine an agricultural and grazing country as is found in Southern Nebraska."[2] It remains so today. The Little Blue River meanders through thick stands of cottonwood trees. Wild berries and underbrush abound. Ripening August corn hugged the river road which led to the old Abernathy and Bennett homestead. The thickness of vegetation, combined with recent rains, stifled the air. This river bottom land is notoriously fertile. The Oregon Trail passed by this area, and many travelers settled this land instead of traveling farther westward through the "Great American Desert." This land was the setting for a tragic event in 1867.

A Tragic Tale

I discovered that Joe Worrell, a printer and publisher who settled in Thayer County in 1871, collected this story from first-hand witnesses of the time. An expanded account was printed for a larger audience by Mr. Clarence S. Paine of the Nebraska Historical Society, who interviewed Mr. Worrell. An identical account was also published by Erasmus M. Correll, editor of the *Hebron Journal.*

William Abernathy was a rancher-miner who had been in California during the Gold Rush. Authentic ranchers recognize that money is only temporary

---

[1] Sources used by Thomas J. Hammond: Q. David Bowers, *The History of United States Coinage,* 1979. Vi Bruning, personal interview, August 8, 1994. "Find of $1,160 in Kellogg & Co. Double Eagles." *The Numismatist.* January 1915, p. 27. "Found Sack of Old Gold." *Hebron Journal.* November 20 1914, p. 1. *History of the State of Nebraska.* 2 volumes, Chicago: Western Historical, 1882. Donald H. Kagin, *Private Gold Coins and Patterns of the United State,.* Pricing Supplement, 1982. Anne McBride, personal interview. August 8, 1994. *Nebraska History Magazine,* April-June 1933, p. 136. Wayte Raymond, *Private Gold Coins Struck in the United States, 1830-1861,.* 1931. Russell H. Renz, *Private Gold Coinage of the United States,* 1938. Jackie Williamson, personal interview, August 8, 1994. R.S. Yeoman (Kenneth E. Bressett, editor), *A Guide Book of United States Coins,.* 47th edition, 1993. Photographs were supplied by Thomas J. Hammond.

[2] *History,* p. 1450.

The fertile fields of the Little Blue River Valley. Farming and ranching thrive on Abernathy and Bennett's ranch today. A thick field of milo borders a pastureland for cattle.

The Little Blue River in August. Low water levels at this time of year create the sandbars where May and McFarland made their discovery many years ago.

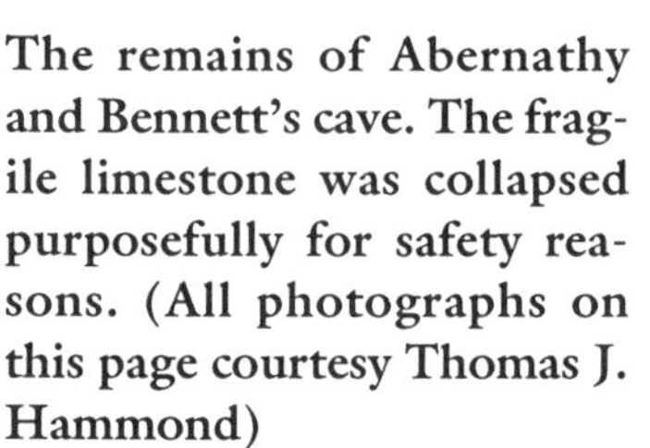

The remains of Abernathy and Bennett's cave. The fragile limestone was collapsed purposefully for safety reasons. (All photographs on this page courtesy Thomas J. Hammond)

wealth, but the wealth of the land is eternal.[1] Perhaps it was this wisdom that brought Abernathy back to Nebraska with at least $1,160 face value in Kellogg & Co. gold $20 pieces, minted in San Francisco in 1854 and 1855, to become partner with Joseph Bennett on a ranch bordering the Little Blue about four miles east of Hebron in Thayer County.

Indian attacks in this valley were numerous and destructive. Only the Otoe tribe lived in consistent peace with white settlers. Reports are graphic and perhaps even biased in their depiction of the slaughter:[2]

> All alike were made to feel [the Indians'] cruelty.... No mercy was shown. No captives were taken but women, and death was preferred to the captivity that awaited them. Could the Eastern philanthropists who speak so flatteringly of "the noble red man of the West" have witnessed the cruel butchery of unoffending children, the disgrace of women, who were first horribly mutilated and then slain, the cowardly assassination of husbands and fathers, they might, perhaps (if fools can learn), be impressed with their true character.

This was the wrath which faced Bennett and Abernathy in August of 1867. A band of Pawnee attacked almost every homestead along the river valley and the bluffs which bordered it. Erasmus Correll, writing in *History of the State of Nebraska,* described the event with less prejudice than most:

> When the helpless and innocent fall into the hands of such monsters, their fates are too terrible for pen to relate. Of what fearful metal are their natures made, how basely turned, and what a multitude of sins their unfeeling bosoms hold! And yet we must admit that among the white men there are natures kindred to these, whose crimes are more revolting when we consider their advantages of civilization—education and nurture in pious homes.... From what an altitude, by comparison, have they fallen, or to what loathsome depths.

This early account addresses the fate of Abernathy and Bennett:

> The Indians proceeded to the Abernathy and Bennett ranch. A cave in a limestone bluff bordering the Little Blue River was converted into a dwelling by the construction of an extended front of logs. The thick underbrush in front of the cave provided the Indians the advantage of surprise. After a short battle, the Indians eventually set fire to the front of the dwelling, and Bennett and Abernathy were killed. The Indians were later overcome about 20 miles east in Superior by a militia of soldiers including A.C. Ring of Hebron.

A group of soldiers commanded by Captain L.P. Luce found the bodies of Abernathy and Bennett "in so charred and mutilated a condition as to be scarcely recognizable."[3]

The cave was quickly sealed. In 1869 or 1870 a portion of the bones was buried. A skull and bones of one of the victims was taken to Davenport, Iowa, as a museum donation.

Settlers knew of Abernathy's missing gold, and the cave was supposedly ransacked. Many suspected their neighbors of theft, but no solid reports were made in the remainder of the nineteenth century.

A Remarkable Find

In August of 1908, two boys named James McFarland and John May were swimming in the Little Blue River. While resting on a small sandbar near the limestone bluff, John May kicked up a gold coin. It turned out to be a Kellogg and Co. $20 coin minted in San Francisco during the Gold Rush. John, an orphan who lived in Belvidere, was able to rake two more coins from the sand near the bluff.

John lived with a man named Spaulding who confiscated the coins and demanded to know where they were found. According to the *Hebron Journal,* the boys refused to tell Spaulding and returned to the bluff the next day. James McFarland found a small hole near the old mouth of the cave and retrieved a sack containing $1,100 in Kellogg $20 gold coins. "The spot where the coins were said to be found was a little south and east of the old Leland Mill where the stream flows to the southeast and then to the north in a bend, two miles north and two and one half miles west of Gilead...."

Evidently, the seemingly heartless Spaulding, who was not John May's legal guardian, kept John's three Kellogg coins. The whereabouts of the coins are unknown today. Spaulding has no known living relatives in the area at the present time.

Reports indicate that the remaining $1,100 in Kellogg $20 coins was deposited into a bank in Geneva, Nebraska . The coins were received into a general account identified as a cash deposit, so tracing the coins has become quite difficult.[4]

---

[1] QDB note: This philosophy would come to the fore in the 1896 presidential election campaign pitting William Jennings Bryan (with his famous "Cross of Gold" speech showcasing the farmer) against William McKinley.

[2] Quoted from *History,* p. 1443. This was written in an era in which the Indians were generally viewed as being savages, while white settlers were seen as virtually blameless.

[3] *The Numismatist,* p. 27.

[4] Breen, *Encyclopedia,* 1988, p. 651, not stating a source, states that "many Uncirculated survivors dated 1854 came from the Thayer County hoard."

The Abernathy-Bennett Site Today

Today, the site of the find has been destroyed, pushed in years ago for safety reasons. The limestone bluff is fragile, and the residents feared a cave-in. The rocks surrounding the exact location show black stains, probably left from many smoking fires.

Much is left to be discovered. Is more gold buried in that limestone bluff? What happened to the 58 $20 coins? How were they disbursed, and who has them now? Or were they melted decades ago? The beauty of research and the enjoyment of numismatics often come not from the actual acquisition of a coin or a bit of information, but from what occurs during the search for discovery. It is through the search that we learn, grow, and share. The contemplation today of an actual specimen of an 1854 or 1855 Kellogg & Co. $20 gold piece becomes all the more interesting when one considers the coin's history—how it was minted and what its later experiences may have been.

A Sketch of Kellogg & Co.

These Kellogg gold pieces filled a definite need in California in the mid 1850s. Today they are elusive, but the record shows that at one time they were numerous.

John Glover Kellogg worked for Moffat and Company after his arrival in San Francisco in the autumn of 1849. He teamed with G.F. Richter, who worked for the U.S. Assay Office prior to its being discontinued in December 1853. San Francisco suffered from a lack of sufficient coin after the Assay Office closed. As private firms ceased striking gold, much of the private gold was melted or shipped out of California, and the San Francisco Mint had not started production.

Curtis, Perry & Ward, the partnership that once operated the U.S. Assay Office, took control of Moffat and Company. In early 1854 the firm signed a contract with the government and sold its building machinery to be used as the San Francisco Mint.

During the coin shortage in early 1854 a group of bankers and businessmen persuaded Kellogg and Richter to issue gold coins on a private basis, assuring the partners that the coins would meet a warm reception in commerce. It took only 10 days for Kellogg & Co. to answer the plea with production of $20 gold pieces. The first Kellogg coins were issued February 9, 1854, about two months before gold coins were made at the new branch mint operated by Uncle Sam.

Kellogg and Richter dissolved in late 1854, reorganizing as Kellogg and Humbert, the new partner being none other than Augustus Humbert, who formerly carried the title United States Assayer of Gold, California, and whose imprimatur had appeared on the well-known octagonal $50 gold pieces of 1851 and 1852. Production was limited at the new branch mint because of copper shortages and problems with refining, although quite a few 1854-S $10 and $20 pieces cascaded from the presses. Only a few 1854-S $2.50 and $5 coins were made, and today these are recognized as extreme rarities. Meanwhile, Kellogg pieces helped fill the vacuum and were produced in greater quantity in 1855 than in the preceding year. An article in a San Francisco newspaper in May of 1855 stated that Kellogg & Co. was supplying over 50% more coins than the government mint.

These 1855 Kellogg issues proved to be the last coins struck, although the partnership lasted until 1860. The company produced about six million dollars in $20 coins. Edgar H. Adams in *Private Gold Coinage of California, 1849-1855,* commented that a large number of these were lost "by the sinking of a steamer in the Pacific on its way from San Francisco to New York.[1]

Kellogg pieces were universally accepted and many banks sent bullion to Kellogg and Richter to be converted into gold coins. A run on banks in 1855 was stayed by $400,000 in gold supplied by Kellogg and Co.

A Teakettle Filled With Gold

Hidden or lost: 19th century
Found: December 9, 1907
Treasure: $20 gold coins

The scene now shifts to the East Coast. The *Granite State News,* December 28, 1907, included this:

[1] QDB note: However, few if any treasure steamers went from San Francisco to New York City as the time-value of the money was too important, and it was easier to go from San Francisco to Panama, transit land there, and connect on another ship to New York. This was especially convenient after the Panama Railroad was opened in January 1855 (See Chapter 11). Could Adams have been referring to the *S.S. Central America* which sank in 1857 on its way from Panama to New York?

New Milford, Connecticut, December 10:

$3,000 in $20 gold pieces were dug up late yesterday by T.T. Jones on his farm in the Merryall district while he was digging a trench. Mr. Jones was formerly a New York businessman and then about a year ago bought the farm of Edgar Peet. The gold was in a teakettle, and Mr. Jones states that it is evident the kettle had been buried for many years.

Tobacco Farm Gold Cache

Hidden or lost: Civil War era or before
Found: 1926
Treasure: Gold coins

For two brothers a fortunate find paid for an automobile. The year is 1926 and the location is Kentucky:[1]

$675 in Gold Found on Tobacco Farm

Buried gold has interfered with tobacco planting on the edge of Stewart County, Tennessee, a few miles from the Kentucky town of Hopkinsville. Two youths told the story when they came to Hopkinsville to buy an automobile with part of the treasure they had found buried.

Ernest Roberts, 20, and his brother Austin, 18, made the find. The boys were setting out tobacco on the farm of their uncle, William Thweatt, when one picked up a five dollar piece. When they made another row of tobacco, they found a twenty dollar coin. Thereafter the tobacco planting languished while the youths searched for treasure. Before long they had uncovered $675 in gold of a coinage antedating the Civil War. They took their treasure home, where they told their mother about the finds.

Coin collectors are offering premium prices for some of the gold pieces. Seven of the five dollar gold pieces, dated 1834, are worth $15 each, it is said.[2] The finders say the gold was scattered about with the remains of a glass jug which had been buried just under the surface and had been broken, letting the coins fall out. It is believed that the money was buried during the war to hide it from one side or the other of the fighting forces.

No steps have been taken by anyone else to claim the money, so the boys will get their auto.

Some *Really* Rare $20 Gold Coins

Hidden or lost: 19th century
Found: May 22, 1926
Treasure: $20 gold coins

In 1926 numismatists and others were startled when they read this Associated Press dispatch datelined Demopolis, Alabama:[3]

Aided by old papers his father left him, Gayus Whitfield, of Middleboro, Ky., has unearthed buried gold valued at more than $200,000 on the Whitfield farm, near here. Discovery of the treasure came as the result of a search which began May 22. Directions for locating the gold were contained in papers left his son by C. Boaz Whitfield, member of one of the oldest and most aristocratic families of Alabama and descendant of the pioneer general, Nathan Bryan Whitfield.

When Gayus Whitfield began his search 35 Negroes were employed to uncover an old boundary stake on the Shady Grove farm, 18 miles from Demopolis, near Jefferson. For a

1 From a 1926 account in the *New York Times* quoted by B.A. Tompkins, *Treasure*, p. 163.

2 There were two main types of $5 gold coins minted in 1834. The rarer pieces are those with the motto E PLURIBUS UNUM on the reverse, minted prior to the summer of the year. Pieces minted in August and later, bearing the so-called Classic Head portrait by Chief Engraver William Kneass, lack the motto. These were made in much larger numbers and most probably represent what the two boys found.

3 The account appeared in many places including in the *New York Times,* June 1, 1926; also quoted in *The Numismatist,* July 1926, page 397, "Finds $200,000 in Gold Coin Buried by Father." The editor of *The Numismatist* could not resist adding: "If any of those $20 gold pieces minted in 1850 'and before' ever reach the auction room, we predict a small-size riot among collectors for front seats at the sale."

week the large force worked without results, but today a large cache of gold coins was discovered. They consist of $20 gold pieces, minted in 1850 and before, buried by the wealthy Boaz Whitfield during Civil War days.

While news of the discovery was confirmed tonight, the exact amount involved was not divulged. There are eight heirs who may put in claims for the gold, all of them sons and daughters of the four Whitfield brothers, born in Civil War days, themselves sons of General Nathan Whitfield.

Other gold coins had been found on the old Whitfield place prior to today's discovery, but the matter of instituting an active search for buried treasure was never given much attention by the Whitfield family until the ancient key left by C. Boaz Whitfield was found in Kentucky. Citizens here expressed the belief that Boaz Whitfield buried the gold to prevent its seizure by Union forces during the Civil War. Similar instances were recalled by older inhabitants of the region, but in no case has so large an amount been involved.

Later Associated Press dispatches from the same location stated that the value of the coins was much less than that originally stated. Numismatists were still left wondering, however, about all of those $20 pieces "minted in 1850 *and before,*" as 1850 was the first year such coins were made for circulation.[1] Such are the "facts" about treasure troves in the daily press.

Readers who want to know more about mythical double eagles minted *before* 1850 will find the next account, "The Secret of the Dump," to be likewise amusing.

The Secret of the Dump

Hidden or lost: 19th century
Found: August 1927
Treasure: Gold coins

In August 1927 there was quite a commotion in downtown Philadelphia at the dump at the eastern end of the Spring Garden Street bridge. It seems that an old house was torn down at Fifth and Noble streets, and the debris was hauled to the disposal site.

Among the dirt, mortar, and other rubble some gold coins, including an "1843 double eagle," were found. Word spread, and before long hundreds of citizens were scrambling among the litter.

"Gold coins only, of all denominations, are reported to have been found, nearly all of which are dated prior to 1850," one account related. Estimates of the amount of money recovered varied widely. And, as numismatists know, there is no such coin as an 1843 double eagle, as the first patterns were made in 1849 and the first coins for circulation in 1850.[2]

On September 7, 1937, F.D. Langenheim of Philadelphia summarized the find:

> Late reports are that some $3,000 in gold coins have been found. An old lady, 86 years old, living near Fifth and Noble streets, says that a French doctor lived in the house being torn down, who died some forty or fifty years ago. He attended many Quaker families living near the Fifth and Noble street Meeting House and was probably the one who hid the gold.

Under an Old Gambling Hall

Lost: Late 1890s
Found: 1929
Treasure: Gold coins

During the wild and woolly days of the late 1890s, Seattle was the jumping-off spot for treasure seekers

[1] A few pattern $20 pieces were made at the Philadelphia Mint in 1849. In 1849 the Mormons in Salt Lake City made a small number of $20 coins, but these never circulated in Kentucky or Tennessee.

[2] Adapted from a report in *The Numismatist,* October 1927, p. 626, "Philadelphians Find Gold Coins Among Debris." The editor of *The Numismatist* gently remarked that the 1843 double eagle story "may easily have been a typographical error." Such inaccuracies in the popular press were common, as in an unrelated account in *The New York Times* which told readers about United States gold dollars minted in 1847 (numismatists know that the first such gold dollars were dated 1849).

going "north to Alaska" (as the popular song went). All of America eagerly read accounts of the excitement as laborers, city slickers, and even novelist Jack London went to Skagway and over the Chilkoot Pass (at one time littered with the bodies of 4,000 dead horses) to the land of the midnight sun.

Many of the fortune hunters on the way to the Klondike or on the way back stopped at the M&N Saloon at the corner of Washington and First Avenue South in Seattle to live it up, lift a bottle or mug, roll the dice, and perhaps make the acquaintance of a lady for the evening.

Apparently, the floor boards in the M&N had a few cracks between them, and every now and again a gold coin, nugget, necklace, or other item would fall through.

Fast forward to December 1928:

> A gold rush stopped street repairing operations at Washington street and First Avenue South, Seattle, Washington, for several hours when a workman turned up a gold nugget with his shovel. Jobless onlookers saw him make the find, and the stampede was on.
>
> Over the site of what once had been the M&N saloon and gambling house, a Mecca for returning prospectors during the Klondike gold rush, fighting crowds of men reenacted the scenes in the North of 30 years ago on a miniature scale. The muddy streets yielded gold nuggets, gold chains, gold coins, South American currency, rings, lockets, necklaces and brooches, and brought Christmas to that part of town where December 25 is just another day without work. Old-timers suggested that the treasure uncovered was lost by patrons of the M&N three decades ago and probably had slipped through floor cracks and become buried in the mud under the building.

As is often the case in such situations, no coin collectors were on hand, or if they were, no specifics were given.[1]

A Double Handful of Gold

Hidden or lost: 19th century
Found: 1931
Treasure: Gold coins

The following account appeared in a Wisconsin newspaper in 1931:[2]

> Near the foot of an old willow stump, Martin A. Born, town of Oconomowoc, Wis., unearthed a cache that netted him perhaps a thousand dollars more or less. He declines to state the exact amount. With the exception of one silver dollar it's all gold—$10 and $20 pieces. He and his uncle, Herman, live on an 80-acre farm, that once was the property of the late Patrick Olwell and adjoining Henry Rosenow on the east.
>
> Down at the edge of the pond, Martin Born was plowing for corn a few days ago. Every inch that could be turned into possible productive land was upturned by the plowman. Close to the stump the plowshare brought up pieces of leather and an innumerable quantity of what appeared to be buttons. Partial cleaning revealed the "buttons" to be gold pieces, genuine American coined money, in all as much as could be held in his two hands.
>
> The following morning he went back to the cache and put the gold and single silver dollar into a satchel, thoroughly sifting the earth through his fingers to make certain he had all the gold. He carried his find to the house, cleaned the coins and then headed for Milwaukee, where he made a deposit in the National Bank of Commerce.
>
> How the money came to be in the stump Mr. Born has no means of knowing. His one guess is that it was hidden away in an old leather boot and placed in the base of the tree by someone who left that section during the Civil War days, and who never returned to reclaim his hidden treasure. He said one coin bore the date of 1847 and another that of 1863.

In 1931 gold coins could be paid into or received from any bank. Presumably, they were not scanned by a numismatist prior to being cashed in.

---

1 Adapted from a press account in *The Numismatist,* February 1929, p. 68, "Workmen Dug Up Coins and Jewelry."
2 Undated article from the Oconomowoc *Enterprise* quoted in *The Numismatist,* July 1931, page 527, "Gold Coins Dug Up in Wisconsin."

The Illinois Gold Rush

Hidden: Circa 1880
Found: July 14, 1931
Treasure: Hundreds of gold coins

On July 14, 1931, all work came to a standstill in downtown Buffalo, Illinois, in a later-day version of the Gold Rush. A contemporary account noted:

> Employers and employees dropped whatever tools they were using and made haste to be the first to peer into a narrow airway between two buildings when it was learned that workmen on the property of Alex M. Booth had unearthed two ancient jugs containing more than $6,000 in gold coins. The coins, believed to have been hidden nearly fifty years ago by a pioneer physician, Dr. Peter Leeds, dated back to 1810. Many children saw their first gold money and some grown-up residents saw their first gold dollar. Older residents stood in groups and reviewed stories heard during their childhood of the strange, almost mythical "Doctor Leeds."
>
> Mr. Booth claims ownership of the money because it was found buried on his property. He has another point in his favor—actual possession—for the money has been placed in his safety deposit vault.
>
> On the other hand, Edward Jack and James M. Rogers, two workmen who unearthed the gold, feel that they should come in for a share. Jack and Rogers were digging a drainage ditch from a new building erected by Mr. Booth, when they uncovered the two old jugs.
>
> Still other claimants appeared today in the person of relatives of Dr. Peter Leeds, recluse of the 'eighties, who is generally believed to have buried the money. Dr. Leeds' relatives live in Lincoln, Clinton and California, and today two granddaughters, Miss Anna and Miss Jennie Leeds, of Lincoln, hired attorneys to protect their interests.
>
> Threats of litigation over the find indicate that by the time the final disposition of the gold is made, much of it may be dissipated in attorney's fees and court costs.[1]
>
> The money was counted only hastily the day it was found, and a recount was made the following day, some of which were badly weathered, in the belief that the total may run close to $7,000. Numismatic authorities also were to be called in to check the pieces in the belief that some of the which date back to 1812 [*sic;* earlier, the date 1810 was given] may have a value for collectors far higher than their actual value.
>
> The hoard was taken to the bank, where Ed McCann, cashier, and G.F. Lester, assistant, began the task of counting it. One of the coins dated as far back as 1812 and the most recent one was 1880, about the time the money is believed to have been buried. The coins ranged from $1 to $20 gold pieces.
>
> Mr. Lester counted a total of $6,028.50. Included were 228 $1 gold pieces. There were 159 $20 gold pieces and $2.50, $3, and $5 gold pieces.

Although in 1931 most of the $20 pieces may have been worth just face value, all $1 and $3 coins sold for a premium, and $2.50 pieces commanded a slight premium regardless of date.[2]

Two Hundred Men Dig 'Em Up

Hidden or lost: 1880 or later
Found: 1932
Treasure: Gold coins

In the vacation resort of Saratoga Springs, New York, on July 25 and 26, 1926, there was what was described as a "gold rush on state property."

In an area famous for its natural springs, a foundation was being excavated for a new "drink hall." Workers found scattered old coins, word spread, and by the afternoon of the second day, "200 men with shovels and picks were delving into the earth." No casual treasure hunt, this!

One man was said to have found $300 in gold coins in a milk bottle (probably a soda water bottle), others found silver and gold coins in tin cans, preserve jars, and other containers. Denominations ranged from silver three-cent pieces to $20 gold double eagles. The latest date seen was 1880.

State Attorney General Bennett was a spoil sport, and when he learned of the frenetic activity, he ordered New York state troopers to put an end to the free-for-all. What, if any, coins were found later (by the state troopers?) was not recorded.[3]

---

[1] Again, this is precisely why only a small percentage of hoards have ever been reported over the years.

[2] Adapted from *The Numismatist,* September 1931, p. 642, "Many Gold Coins Unearthed at Buffalo, Illinois."

[3] Adapted from *The Numismatist,* September 1932, p. 583, "Rush for Buried Coins at Saratoga Springs, N.Y." At one time this town had many different bottlers and sellers of mineral water.

Gold Hidden in a Baltimore Cellar

Hidden: Circa 1856
Found: August 31, 1934 and later
Treasure: Gold coins

On August 31, 1934, two young boys, described as poor and underprivileged, were playing in the cellar of a house at 132 South Eden Street, East Baltimore, owned by Elizabeth H. French and Mary Findley and rented by the father of one of the boys.

Henry Grob, age 15, and his companion, Theodore Jones, 16, came upon a cache of gold coins. After a brief discussion as to what should be done, the lads took the treasure to the local police station and turned the find over to the authorities. Later, the boys said that they had "held out" some of the pieces, and these were subsequently added to the first group. One newspaper account put the amount as 3,558 coins with $11,425.50 face value. All were dated before 1857. Meanwhile, at the police station some of the patrolmen "tried their hand at cleaning them with coal oil [kerosene] and vinegar," a procedure definitely not recommended by numismatists!

How had the coins been hidden and by whom? One story had it that they were secreted by a sea captain of a ship in the coffee trade between Brazil and the port of Baltimore, who lived in the house with his two sisters. Another story suggested that "the coins may have been buried in April 1861 by a resident who was frightened by the passing of federal [*sic*] troops through the city; the house is located close to the depot at which the troops landed in Baltimore."[1]

Multiple claims were filed for ownership. For the rest of 1934 and into May 1935 the matter was in the courts. Meanwhile, although the gold coins were to have remained undisturbed pending the outcome, the family of one of the finders sold $185 worth for face value. Judge Eugene O'Dunne of the Second Circuit Court of Baltimore eventually awarded proceeds from the entire find to the two teenagers, negating an offer by the two ladies who owned the house to give the boys 24%. To finally settle the matter, the court mandated that the coins be sold at auction.[2] The sale was held on May 2, 1935, at the Lord Baltimore Hotel downtown, with Perry W. Fuller serving as auctioneer. About 100 attended including a few out-of-town dealers and many local curiosity seekers. Grouped into 438 lots and casually described (most pieces were simply called "very fine") in a printed catalogue, the hoard realized $19,558.75.

The star of the sale was a "very fine" 1856-O double eagle at $105 which went to a Virginia numismatist. An 1849-O $10, also "very fine," commanded $45, while an 1841 $5, "fine, scratch on date," found a buyer at $26, and an 1847-O of the same denomination, "fine," fetched $22. In an era in which there was very little numismatic interest in gold coins of higher denominations, most pieces sold for double face value.

A copy was later studied by Walter Breen, who created the following inventory from it. Comments in brackets are by the present writer [QDB]:

GOLD DOLLARS (listings apparently omit mintmarks): 1849: 95 pieces [first year of the denomination] • 1850: 78 • 1851: 452 • 1853: 976 • 1854 Type I: 215 [curious that the next two are also 215] • 1854 Type II: 215 • 1855: 215 • 1856: 296 • Various damaged coins 1849-1856: 39.

$2.50 GOLD COINS: 1834: 2 [First year of Classic Head design] • 1836: 5 • 1839-D: 1 [First Dahlonega Mint quarter eagle issue] • 1843: 1 • 1843-O: 4 • 1843-C: 1 • 1847-O: 1 [highest mintage of its immediate era, 124,000] • 1848-D: 1 • 1850: 4 • 1851: 5 • 1852: 11 • 1853: 14 • 1854: 7 • 1855: 3 • 1856: 4.

$5 GOLD COINS: • 1834: 15 [First year of Classic Head design] • 1835: 2 • 1836: 12 • 1837: 3 • 1838: 6 •

[1] *The Numismatist*, October 1934, page 677, "A Large Quantity of Gold U.S. Coins Unearthed." Actually, Baltimore was allied with the Union, and federal troops were not an uncommon sight.
[2] *The Numismatist*, April 1935, page 237, "Baltimore Hoard of Gold Coins to Be Sold at Auction."

1838-C: 1 [First Charlotte Mint half eagle issue] • 1839: 1 [First year of Liberty Head or Coronet design] • 1840: 8 • 1841: 1 • 1842-D: 1 • 1843: 12 • 1843-O: 5 • 1843-C: 2 • 1843-D: 1 • 1844: 6 • 1844-O: 6 • 1844-C: 2 • 1845: 10 • 1845-O: 3 • 1846: 4 • 1847: 20 [mintage 915,981, the highest figure up to this time] • 1847-O: 1 • 1847-C: 1 • 1847-D: 1 • 1848: 8 • 1848-C: 5 • 1848-D: 1 • 1850: 5 • 1850-D: 2 • 1851: 13 • 1852: 20 • 1852-C: 5 • 1852-D: 2 • 1853: 12 • 1853-C: 3 • 1853-D: 3 • 1854: 11 • 1854-O: 1 • 1854-D: 6 • 1855: 15 • 1855-C: 3 • 1855-D: 1 • 1856: 1.

$10 GOLD COINS: 1839: 2 • 1840: 1 • 1841: 1 • 1842: 2 • 1842-O: 1 • 1844-O: 1 • 1845: 1 • 1845-O: 1 • 1846-O: 1 • 1847: 13 • 1847-O: 7 • 1848: 5 • 1848-O: 3 • 1849: 10 • 1849-O: 1 • 1850: 6 • 1850-O: 2 • 1851: 1 • 1851-O: 3 • 1852: 1 • 1853: 4 • 1853-O: 3 • 1854: 1 • 1854-S: 1 [First San Francisco Mint issue] • 1855: 7 • 1856: 3.

$20 GOLD COINS: 1850: 92 [First year of issue of the denomination] • 1850-O: 5 • 1851: 79 • 1851-O: 10 • 1852: 47 • 1852-O: 2 • 1853: 27 • 1854: 12 • 1855: 6 • 1855-S: 12 • 1856: 1 • 1856-O: 1 [prized as a rarity] • 1856-S: 23.

Meanwhile, the Baltimore cellar had been visited by hundreds of curiosity seekers, many with shovels, who sought to find other coins, but with absolutely no success.

However, in May 1935, the same month that the auction took place, the same two young boys revisited the site after one said he was "feeling lucky." In due course over $8,000 face value of additional gold coins was found! This find, too, went to court, and meanwhile an unauthorized sale of $2,500 face value took place (for $3,005, the buyer being Yale Merrill and his brother) about September. No numismatic inventory of the second find is known to have been made.[1]

Unfortunately, the young lads did not receive long-term benefit from their good fortune. The Grob boy died in 1937, by which time the other had been sentenced to reform school.[2]

The Fearful Guest

Hidden: 1854 or later
Found: 1935
Treasure: Gold coins

Workmen tearing down an old hotel in Tuskegee, Alabama, found $185 face value in gold coins dated from 1834 to 1854 when they pried a mantle from a wall. It was conjectured that a "fearful guest" hid the money there during the Civil War (1861-1865). No account of the coin denominations or specific varieties was given.[3]

[1] Yale Merrill's son became a rare coin dealer many years later; Mark Hotz, who became a dealer in his own right, was once in his employ. Hotz visited 132 South Eden Street in Baltimore a few years ago to see what remained on the site, but found that the gold-bearing house was long gone and that the entire block was occupied by two commercial warehouses (cf. Mark Hotz, letter, September 16, 1996).

[2] *The Numismatist,* June 1935, page 374, "Baltimore Hoard of Gold Coins Sold." Walter H. Breen, "Survey of American Coin Hoards," *The Numismatist,* January 1952.

[3] From an unattributed press clipping reprinted in *The Numismatist,* July 1935, p. 420, "Possibly Some Rarities Here." Never mind that the Civil War did not begin until 1861, and the latest coin was dated 1854.

A Strange 1861-S Gold $20

Hidden or lost: 19th century?
Found: 1937
Treasure: Gold coins

In 1937 numismatists were startled to learn of a very strange 1861-S $20 gold coin that came light with a few other United States gold pieces under an old barn in Hull, Texas.

This particular 1861-S was unlike the regularly-seen double eagle in that the letters in UNITED STATES OF AMERICA and TWENTY D. on the reverse were in letters taller and narrower than usual. The editor of *The Numismatist* consulted a copy of the 1912 work on pattern coins by Edgar H. Adams and William H. Woodin and found a somewhat similar piece listed, but as a pattern made in Philadelphia. There was no mention of an 1861-S coin. He concluded that the 1861-S was a new variety of pattern made—possibly by inadvertently using a pattern die—in San Francisco, as evidenced by the tiny "S" mintmark.

As time went on, coin collectors searched their holdings, quantities of $20 gold coins became available from Europe, and numismatic interest increased in $20 coins. It was found that the 1861-S Paquet Reverse $20, as it became known, was rare, but hardly unique. Today in the 1990s several hundred are known, most of which grade in the Very Fine to Extremely Fine range.

What other varieties of gold coins were found in Hull, Texas, in 1937? The information remains unpublished to this day.[1]

Dozens of Double Eagles

Hidden: Before the 1930s
Found: 1938
Treasure: Gold coins

In 1938 Robert K. Botsford of Nescopeck, Penn-

sylvania, reported that a hoard of gold coins was unearthed in nearby Bloomsburg when workmen were digging out the cellar of a house. The hoard, no numismatic details of which were given, was said to have consisted mainly of $20 gold pieces with a total face value of about $3,000. At the time of the report, ownership was being contested in court.[2]

An Eccentric Kentuckian

Hidden: 1911 or later
Found: 1942
Treasure: Gold coins

William H. Cooper had lived in Hodgenville, Kentucky, for nearly all of his life, including from 1898 until his death in October 1932 in a house he had purchased there.

"He was a splendid citizen, but eccentric: what we would term a peculiar man," the administrator of his estate wrote. "Mr. Cooper retired from active business in 1923 and spent practically all of his time at his home. He was a great lover of game chickens and spent much of his time with them. He did not confide in anybody and kept his business strictly to himself. He left a will in which he provided that no inventory should be made of his estate, leaving his property to his wife for her life, and at her death to be equally divided between her people and his people."

By the time of his death, Cooper had suffered memory loss and was in failing health. His wife and

---

[1] *The Numismatist,* March 1937, page 199, "A $20 Gold Coin with Pattern Reverse." Walter H. Breen, "A Survey of American Coin Hoards." *The Numismatist,* January 1952.
[2] *The Numismatist,* April 1938, page 333, "Hoard of Gold Coins Found in Bloomsburg, Pa."

heir, who had not been told where the deceased kept his investments, sought to identify his assets. She found a small sum of money in a local bank. Believing there was more, she started a search and in due course located $3,500 in another bank in a nearby town and several thousand dollars in still another bank in Louisville. Meanwhile, she razed the chicken house that her husband had used for his game fowl.

In 1937 Mrs. Cooper, too, passed away. The real estate passed to a man named Hubbard, who lived there through the early 1940s, except for a four-month period when he was an Army officer stationed at Fort Knox rented the property. The property was then sold to a man who had not moved in by 1942.

In 1942, Otis Enlow, who had been employed by a neighbor, Mr. Routt, to cultivate land for a garden, ran his plow over the old chicken house site and struck gold! Enlow scooped up $600 in $10 and $20 gold coins, and neighbor Routt found $360 worth. The coins, the dates of which ranged from 1850 to 1911, were taken to the Lincoln National Bank, at which point they were intercepted by Judge Handley, who had handled the estates of the Coopers.

The matter went to court in LaGrange, Kentucky, with claims presented by the finder and the administrator of the two Cooper estates. Judge Ballard Clark reviewed the evidence and concluded the coins must have been hidden by the late William H. Cooper sometime around 1911 or later and thus belonged to his heirs. What if anything went to the finder was not stated in the account seen.[1]

The Loxahatchee River Bayou Find

Put away: 1930s
Found: 1950s
Treasure: Gold and silver coins

In the early 1930s a man lived aboard a houseboat in a bayou near the outlet of the Loxahatchee River near Jupiter, Florida.[2] Distrustful of banks, he kept gold and silver coins in an iron kettle which he dangled over the boat rail by a wire. A hurricane came up, the boat was tossed about, and the kettle was lost in deep water.

Years later in the 1950s, Dr. Body, a graduate of the Heidelberg University in Germany, now retired and operating a general store, learned of the missing kettle and contacted F.L. Coffman, who operated a treasure salvage business in West Palm Beach. After one hour and 45 minutes of effort, Coffman located the kettle with an electronic device, brought it to the surface, and found to the delight of Dr. Body and himself that each would be sharing in $7,920 face value worth of rare coins!

The treasure, not numismatically described, was said to consist of the following:

$50 gold: 6 pieces.
$20 gold: 111 pieces.
$10 gold: 309 pieces.
$5 gold: 388 pieces.
Silver $1: 217 pieces.
Silver 50¢: 306 pieces.

Upon reflection today, this was a rather remarkable cache, as $50 gold coins never circulated in Florida or anywhere near it, and in any event, it would have been unusual for anyone to have had such pieces as non-numismatic holdings in the early 1930s. $50 gold coins were produced in California in the early 1850s and circulated in that state. In addition, some 1915 commemorative $50 coins were produced for the Panama Pacific International Exposition in San Francisco that year.

Moreover, the number of $10 coins in this hoard is remarkably large. Typically, a hoard of gold coins saved for their bullion value is found to be oriented toward pieces of the $20 denomination.

Perhaps the houseboat owner had been a numismatist? This would explain the presence of $50 gold pieces. If so, storing $50 gold coins, silver dollars, and other specimens in salt water would have been a very curious way to keep them!

As is the case with many treasure stories, much is left unanswered.

---

[1] Adapted from a report by Judge L.B. Handley, who administered the estates of Mr. and Mrs. Cooper, as published in *The Numismatist,* June 1943.
[2] Coffman, pp. 139-149. The same writer said that he and Dr. Body subsequently found $18,000 in gold coins hidden in the wall of a house, but no details were given.

Hidden in a Staircase

Put away: Early 20th century
Revealed: 1957
Treasure: Gold coins

Raymond Shepherd, curator of Old Economy Village (see the Economite Treasure in Chapter 6), told of a cache of gold coins within his own family:[1]

> My grandmother, Katherine Matlack, called me to her bedside just days before she died late in November of 1957. I was home from college for the Thanksgiving holiday. She was very frail, and I was rather sad to see her in her condition. But, she was happy to see me and asked me to stay when the nurses left.
>
> She motioned me to come closer to whisper in my ear, "Raymond, I want you to go into my sewing room and go to the closet. Under the sheets on the fourth step–pull it toward you–it will come out. In the cut out you will find something for you! Bring it to me!"
>
> To my surprise I only found a cloth bound by a ribbon and something hard inside. However, upon opening it I saw a 1924 $20 gold coin of the Saint-Gaudens design, three Liberty Head $10 gold coins dated 1899, 1900, and 1907, and a gold dollar of 1853. She said they were for hard times and hoped I never had to use them. Happily, I still have them in my safe deposit box.
>
> My grandfather, William Shepherd, had also had retained gold pieces in spite of their possibly being seized. He had given them to my father, as he collected coins as a young boy in the 1920s. When I was 21 my father gave them to me including a $2.50 Indian Head, a $5 Indian Head, and four Liberty Head $10.

Gold Dollars in Baltimore

Put away: 1880s
Found: 1950s-1960s
Treasure: Rare gold dollars

A Popular Speculation

Beginning in 1879 there was a popular speculation in certain United States coin series, especially the gold dollar, but to a lesser extent the silver trade dollar and the $3 gold denomination.

Large quantities of gold dollars bearing the dates 1879, 1880, and 1881 were bought by a Baltimore investor, whose identity is not known today, although it has been suggested that T. Harrison Garrett, an heir to the Baltimore & Ohio Railroad fortune, is a likely candidate. If so, these gold dollars were not transferred to The Johns Hopkins University in 1942 when Garrett's coins were gifted to the institution by one of T. Harrison Garrett's sons, John Work Garrett.

A glance at mintage figures reveals enticingly low production quantities for business strike gold dollars of these three years:

1879: 3,000 pieces minted.
1880: 1,600.
1881: 7,620.

By this time gold dollars, first minted in 1849, had ceased being a meaningful part of the American commercial coinage system, and examples mainly reposed in bank vaults. In contrast, years earlier in 1853, gold dollars were struck to the extent of 4,076,051 examples and were common sights in business transactions.

In the 1950s and 1960s, glittering prooflike gem gold dollars of 1879, 1880, and 1881 began appearing on the market in quantity, especially through the offices of Abner Kreisberg in California and through Thomas Warfield of Baltimore. It was generally acceded at the time that the source for these coins was a Baltimore bank vault, but no other details were given. Recently, Abner Kreisberg recalled that he had purchased some of his coins from old-time dealer Joe Block (who also had large quantities of 1938-D Buffalo nickels).[2]

The writer was involved in the numismatic distribution of these pieces and acquired examples to the extent of many hundreds of each date. If memory serves, there were more of 1881 than of the other two. Today, high-grade gold dollars of all three dates are often encountered and are highly prized for their quality and their low mintage.[3]

A Cache of 1889 Gold Dollars

Also worthy of mention is a small hoard of a couple

1 Letter, October 12, 1996.
2 Letter to the author, June 25, 1996.
3 Breen, *Encyclopedia,* 1988, pp. 480-481, gives Charles E. Green (Chicago dealer) and Horace L.P. Brand (of Chicago, a brother to super-collector

hundred or so 1889 gold dollars, each coin frosty and lustrous (not prooflike), the writer bought from Maurice Storck in the 1950s. These had turned up in a safe deposit box in a bank in Maine.

He Liked Gold!

Accumulated: 1930s
Found: 1960
Treasure: Gold coins

On Wednesday, March 30, 1960, the normally quiet Chicago suburb of Mount Prospect was thrown into a dither, according to a story which broke in the *Chicago Daily News* and immediately was sent out on the wires by the Associated Press.[1]

It seems that the recently deceased (December 25, 1959) Stanley R. Pierce, a wealthy Chicago investment broker, liked gold. However, he kept his liking secret. When his estate had been appraised at $500,000, the valuers were not aware of any gold coins. But, indeed, there were quite a few!

The circumstances of the find were not revealed, nor was it said why appraisers of his estate (who had valued it at $500,000) did not know of the cache earlier. However, he left a map behind in a safe he owned, which was found by representatives of the executor, the Continental-Illinois Bank. Thus, on one memorable day in early spring the coins, said to "total nearly $100,000," were unearthed in his yard where they had been buried beneath two fruit trees. This was no old-time hoard, but, instead, had been secreted by Pierce within the preceding 10 years (his home was built in 1950), although, apparently, the coins had been accumulated by him in the early 1930s.

Pierce, a widower, left no children, and his entire estate went to his alma mater, the University of Chicago, where in 1913 he had been a star fullback on the football squad. Unfortunately, no numismatic details of the cache appeared in the popular press, and it is not known if the $100,000 represented the face value or an appraised numismatic worth.

Four Double Eagle Rarities

Put away: 1931 or later
Disclosed: 1960
Treasure: Rare 1931-D $20 coins

In 1960 a Sidney, New York, businessman took from his bank safety deposit box four "ordinary" $20 pieces and brought them to a coin dealer, for he had heard there was a premium above face value for all gold coins.

The dealer glanced at them, found they were all of the extremely rare 1931-D variety and in blazing gem Mint State, showed him the listing in *The Guide Book,* and expected that the finder would be delighted. Just the opposite occurred. Uncertainty set in—what were they *really worth?* Could they be sold for more elsewhere? Maybe they shouldn't be sold after all.

Back into the safe deposit box the rare 1931-D $20 pieces went. Had they been common dates they would have been sold for the current market value at the time, which would have been between $40 and $50. Such is the life of a dealer![2]

Virgil Brand and co-heir of the fabulous Brand estate following Virgil's death in 1926). If Brand was the source, further information can be found in the extensive Brand archives in the library of the American Numismatic Society, New York. Brand was numismatically active from the 1880s until his death, but probably not as early as 1879-1881, for he was still a teenager then and it is unlikely that he would have bought gold dollars in large quantities.

[1] Adapted from an Associated Press dispatch, "Map Leads to Buried $100,000 Gold Coins," datelined Mount Prospect, Illinois, and published in the *St. Louis Globe-Democrat,* March 31, 1960; clipping furnished by Gene and Audra Andries.

[2] Personal experience of the author. Today it is estimated that fewer than 50 specimens exist of the 1931-D. What happened to the four specimens mentioned is not known.

Pyramid Lake and its namesake as shown in an early engraving depicting explorer John Frémont.

Long-Hidden Gold Coins

Hidden or lost: Early 20th century or before
Found: 1965
Treasure: Gold coins

In Amity, Arkansas, J.C. Bean was clearing a lot preparatory to building a new house. While his bulldozer was scraping out the foundation area a hoard of $538 face value worth of gold coins was revealed.

After the coins were counted, onlookers pressed forward, and two observers "made off with several of the coins during the confusion," reducing the remaining hoard to $438. No list of dates and mintmarks was made available to the press.[1]

Soldiers' Gold at Pyramid Lake(?)

Hidden or lost: 19th century
Found: 1967
Treasure: Gold coins

In 1967 members of the Nicon Tribal Council, Pyramid Lake Indian Reservation, near Reno, Nevada,

[1] "Arkansas Worker Finds Gold Hoard," *Coin World,* January 27, 1965, p. 41.

found a cache of "gold coins dating back to 1814 with a face value of $3,500."[1]

The coins were taken to Nick Jackson, a shop owner in Reno, who inspected them and pronounced that "many are quite valuable." He conjectured that the coins might have been left from a military encampment in the area during the Second Pyramid Lake Indian War.

Gold in Beverly Hills

Stored: 1916
Found: 1970s
Treasure: Gold coins dated 1911 and 1916

Sometime in the 1970s the writer received a call from a trust officer at the Beverly Hills branch of the Bank of America on North Beverly Drive in that town. The John Estate was being sold, and investigation revealed of a cache of gold coins that had been hidden in a vault for decades.

Upon visiting the bank I was greeted by the sight of three white cloth bags, with mint inscriptions on the outside of each, one containing 500 1916-S $10 gold pieces—considered to be a somewhat scarce date—and 500 each of 1911-S and 1916-S $20 gold coins. Each coin was brilliant and lustrous. A deal was struck, and the coins were mine. These were subsequently advertised, and were completely sold out *within four hours* of the time our offering appeared![2]

Gold in a New England Bank Vault

Hidden: 1873 or later
Found: By 1976
Treasure: Gold dollars

There is a romantic link between numismatics and New England, the latter representing the source not only of many coins in our history (beginning with the 1652 Massachusetts silver coinage), but also collections, accumulations, and hoards.

Further, the undisclosed contents of safe deposit boxes are always fascinating to contemplate. Any old bank vault is likely lined with scores of such steel-faced boxes, imprinted with numbers, within which may lurk all sorts of treasures.

Thus, when an old safe deposit box in a New England bank yields a treasure, so much the better for romantic and historical purposes. Seemingly, finding a cache of coins in a bank vault in a modern shopping center in Delaware would have less appeal. Anyway....

It was circa 1976 when a box was opened in New England and disclosed 11 different specimens of 1873-dated United States gold dollars, not a rare date, but an issue usually found one at a time. Grades ranged from AU to choice Uncirculated. Nine of the 11 were from an obverse die with a raised die line on Miss Liberty's neck. All coins were toned alike and showed evidence of having been kept together for a long time.[3]

A Long-Buried Snuff Pot

Hidden: Circa 1910
Found: Spring 1977
Treasure: Gold coins

It is not often that museum curators, the custodians of many valuable coins, themselves find a numismatic treasure first hand.[4] However, it has happened, and this account is of such an instance:

In late spring 1977 Donald R. Touhy, a curator at the Nevada State Museum, Carson City, had a singular stroke of good fortune. Excavation was to be done at Lovelock, Nevada, for the right-of-way for the Interstate 80 highway. Chinese laborers had lived in the area in the late nineteenth and early twentieth centuries, and it was felt that the site, which had yielded some artifacts, should be professionally explored be-

---

1 "Indians Locate Gold Coin Hoard," *Coin World,* July 19, 1967.
2 Recollection of the author.
3 Sold at auction by Bowers and Ruddy Galleries, June 20-22, 1977, lots 3422 to 3432.
4 Adapted from Mark Richards, "Found: $26,000 Coin Hoard," *Treasure Found Magazine,* summer 1978; copy furnished by Doug Veal.

fore construction crews came in with heavy equipment.

Curator Touhy was digging in the basement of what had once been a house, when he came across a crockery pot of the type that had been commonly used as a snuff container. Upon inspection, the container was found to contain gold coins dated from the late nineteenth century through to 1910, with a total face value of $1,800. The coins, which became the property of the Nevada State Museum, were appraised as having a numismatic worth of about $26,000. Details of denominations, dates, and mintmarks were not published, but the information was not lost, as the pieces were placed into protective containers and stored in a vault to await preparation for exhibition.

The Nevada State Museum is housed in the impressive stone building that was home to the Carson City Mint. Wonder if any of those buried gold coins had CC mintmarks? If so, they came back home.

Gold in the American River (Reprise)

Hidden: 1850s
Found: 1979
Treasure: Gold coins

Historians know well that the American River was the site in January 1848 of the fabulous discovery of gold by John Marshall.[1] An employee of John Sutter, owner of a wood-sawing mill on the American River, Marshall saw some gleaming yellow gold flakes in the tail race. This set in motion the great California Gold Rush, the ensuing arrival of the 49ers, and, eventually, the development of the West as we know it today.

At some later date an individual, whose identity is not known today, put part of his personal fortune in a little sack, dug a hole about two feet deep, and buried it on the North Fork of the American River where it joins with Indian Creek. This small stash consisted of San Francisco Mint gold coins dated in the 1850s, mostly $20 pieces but two $5 piece coins as well. Also included were three Kellogg $20 gold pieces of the 1854-1855 style.

The scene changes to 1979, when Joe Soule was looking for gold nuggets with a dredge on the North Fork of the American River.

Voila! Under a couple feet of gravel and enclosed in what remained of an old sack were found a handful of the long-hidden $20 pieces, the two aforementioned $5 half eagles, and some gold nuggets. As good fortune would have it these were sold into numismatic channels and today they quite probably rest in a number of different collections with the owners not being aware of their romantic history, a "second find" of gold on the American River!

Four Nice 1852-C $5 "Peas"

Hidden or lost: 1852 or later
Found: 1982
Treasure: Four rare gold coins

David W. Akers described this little cache:[2]

> If four pieces can be called a "hoard", I once saw (and bought several of the coins) four choice Uncirculated, non-saltwater 1852-C $5 that were reportedly buried in a jar. They all looked like the proverbial "peas in a pod," so the story may have been true.

[1] Information provided by Ray Bolduc, letter, August 1996.

[2] Letters, June 22 (quoted here) and July 7, 1996, the last verifying the date of the transaction as 1982.

A Society Lady's Security

Acquired: 1933
Dispersed: Early 1980s
Treasure: Gold coins

In early 1933 it seemed that the United States government would place stringent restrictions on the ownership of American gold coins.[1] Hearing rumors to this effect, a prominent eastern lady, possibly with the cooperation of her mother, decided to acquire and set aside some pieces for the comfort and financial security they seemed to represent in that troubled economic time.

Years later her heirs enlisted numismatist David Enders Tripp to assist with their sale into the numismatic market. The group was found to contain the following pieces, a valuable informational find for scholars, as it shows typical gold coins that could be acquired at banks in early 1933. The earlier-dated coins were for the most part worn, while some of the later pieces were gem Mint State, the 1927 $20 pieces being in the latter category.

In his 1988 *Encyclopedia,* Walter Breen erroneously attributed certain of these pieces to the Virgil M. Brand estate, as in this example: "1923-D $20. Manfra, Tordella & Brookes handled a hoard of over 1,000 Uncs. including many from the Brand estate 1981-1982." As is seen in the inventory below, the number of 1923-D $20 pieces from this source amounted to 154 coins, hardly a quantity to be sniffed at, but not a serious challenge to the 1,000 figure mentioned by Breen.[2]

GOLD DOLLARS: 1850 • 1852.

$2.50 GOLD COINS: 1843-O (2 pieces) • 1845 • 1845-O (2) • 1846-O (2) • 1847-O (2) • 1850 (4) • 1851 (7) • 1852 (14) • 1852-O (2) • 1853 (19) • 1854 (7) • 1854-O (2) • 1855 (2) • 1856 (8) • 1857 • 1857-S • 1859 • 1859-S • 1861 (15) • 1862 • 1871-S (2) • 1873 (12) • 1878 (21) • 1878-S (8) • 1879 (13) • 1879-S (3) • 1887 (2) • 1890 (4) • 1893 (2) • 1895 • 1896 (2) • 1897 (2) • 1898 (3) • 1899 (6) • 1900 (12) • 1901 (22) • 1902 (23) • 1903 (48) • 1904 (43) • 1905 (56) • 1906 (56) • 1907 (88) • 1908 (51) • 1909 (11) • 1910 (2) • 1911 (17) • 1912 (3) • 1913 (6) • 1914 (7) • 1914-D (11) • 1915 (10).

$5 GOLD COINS: 1834 Classic Head (2) • 1836 (3) • 1838 (2) • 1839 (2) • 1839-C • 1840 • 1843 • 1844-O (2) • 1845 (6) • 1846 (4) • 1847 (7) • 1848 (3) • 1849 • 1851 • 1852 • 1853 • 1854 (holed) • 1855-S • 1856-S • 1857 • 1861 (8) • 1863-S • 1874 (3) • 1877-S • 1879-S (3) • 1880 (5) • 1880-S (8) • 1881 (9) • 1881-S (5) • 1882 (11) • 1882-S (2) • 1884-S • 1885-S (2) • 1886 • 1886-S (11) • 1887-S (3) • 1888-S (2) • 1893-S (4) • 1895 • 1897 (5) • 1897-S (3) • 1898 (2) • 1898-S (8) • 1899 • 1899-S (5) • 1900 (10) • 1900-S • 1901-S (12) • 1902-S (4) • 1903-S (8) • 1904 • 1905-S (6) • 1906-S • 1906-D (5) • 1907 • 1907-D (5) • 1908 Indian (17) • 1908-S (22) • 1909 (6) • 1909-S (5) • 1910 (8) • 1911 (9) • 1911-S • 1912 (8) • 1913 (7) • 1913-S • 1914 • 1915 (6).

$10 GOLD COINS: 1840 • 1842-O (2) • 1844-O • 1845-O • 1847 (3) • 1847-O (3) • 1849 (4) • 1850 (3) • 1852 (2) • 1853 • 1854-S (2) • 1856-S • 1857 • 1879-S (2) • 1880 (7) • 1880-S (4) • 1881 (9) • 1881-S (7) • 1882 (11) • 1882-S • 1883 • 1884-S • 1885 (2) • 1885-S • 1886-S (2) • 1887-S (6) • 1889-S (2) • 1890 • 1892 (3) • 1893 (3) • 1893-S • 1894 (2) • 1894-O • 1894-S • 1895-O • 1896-S • 1897 (12) • 1897-S (5) • 1898 (3) • 1898-S • 1899 (6) • 1899-S (5) • 1900-S • 1901 (11) • 1901-S (10) • 1902 • 1902-S (2) • 1903 • 1903-S (2) • 1905 (2) • 1905-S (5) • 1906 • 1906-D (15) • 1906-S (3) • 1907 Liberty Head (4) • 1907-D Liberty Head; • 1907-S Liberty Head (2) • 1907 Indian (29) • 1908 (7) • 1908-D (2) • 1909 (2) • 1909-D • 1909-S (2) • 1910 (2) • 1910-D (3) • 1910-S (5) • 1911 (5) • 1912 (6) • 1912-S (2) • 1913 (4) • 1914 • 1914-D (2) • 1915 (4).

$20 GOLD COINS: 1878-S • 1879-S • 1890-S • 1895 • 1904 • 1907-D Liberty Head (99) • 1923-D (154) • 1927 (14).

---

1 Information furnished by David E. Tripp, letter, August 1996; he appraised the coins and assisted in their sale.

2 Clearly Breen's assumption that the coins in the present inventory were from Virgil M. Brand is erroneous, as proven by the presence in the hoard of 14 1927 double eagles, considering that Brand died on June 20, 1926.

Four Teenagers Strike Gold

Hidden: 1897 or later
Found: 1984
Treasure: Gold coins

In 1984 four teenagers were remodeling the home of Robert Poehling in LaCrosse, Wisconsin.[1] The house had been built circa 1864. In the basement beneath the kitchen was found "a hidden hoard of late nineteenth-century United States gold coins." The pieces were contained in an iron pot.

Upon inspection the treasure was found to contain $5, $10, and $20 denominations dated from 1870 to 1897. It was theorized that a former owner, local merchant Mons Anderson, who died in 1905, had secreted the coins. Previously wealthy, Anderson was poor at the time of his death, deepening the mystery of why the gold coins remained there.

Help Me Find the Missing $5 Gold Coin

Hidden: 1876 or later
Found: 1984
Treasure: $20 gold coins and others

Bob Van Camp, owner of Comstock Metal Detectors, Chico, California, received a call for assistance.[2] A lady had lost a gold coin from her necklace while rototilling her garden. The necklace itself had been found. In all probability, the missing coin, a $5 gold piece, had been plowed under somewhere in an acre of freshly turned earth. Help!

Van Camp switched his detector on and began searching in the area where the chain part of the necklace had been found. A few signals indicated "nails," but to be sure he was not missing the valuable $5 gold coin, he turned over a few spades of dirt. Nothing particular turned up.

A few minutes later, Eureka! There was a tremendous blast in the headphones. The missing $5 had been found, according to the "gold" setting on the meter. Bob dug to extract it, but, what was this? He found a *$20* gold piece! Bob Van Camp showed it to the waiting landowners and was told that in recent years a few other gold coins had been turned up here and there during the rototilling season. Excited about the possibilities of finding a cache, Bob asked questions and found that an old stage line had once passed nearby. A deal was made to split any find, and Van Camp went to work. Soon he found another $20 gold piece, then another, then still another! By day's end a $5 coin (but not the necklace specimen) and six $20 coins had been found, the last including an 1875-CC with a scar from the rototiller blade.

The next day he was on the site early, and in short order found two $10 pieces stuck together, perhaps indicating that he was near the original spot where the coins had been buried. Some more looking disclosed the remains of an old iron pot and some more coins. The following day brought still more. Then, the finds stopped.

When all the coins were counted, the total stood at 44 gold pieces, of which 35 were of the $20 denomination. The oldest coin was a rare 1839 $10 piece, while the most recent was a $20 with the date 1876. And, oh yes, the missing $5 coin from the necklace was found, too.

A Hushed-Up Find in Jackson

Hidden: Circa
Found: mid-1980s
Treasure: Gold coins

In the mid-1980s a glass jar filled with gold coins is said to have been unearthed in Jackson, Mississippi

[1] "Wisconsin Hoard Yields 19th Century U.S. Gold," *Coin World,* April 11, 1984, p. 57.

[2] Adapted from Bob Grant, "Treasure Hunter Hits Gold Coin Bonanza," *Treasure Magazine,* November 1984; copy furnished by Doug Veal.

(or Tennessee).[1] Land was being graded in preparation for the building of a parking lot (said to be the greatest of all civic improvements and at the same time the nemesis of interesting old buildings). A bulldozer dug up a glass jar filled to the rim with glittering gold coins, mostly from the Charlotte and Dahlonega mints. Dealer Jeff Garrett reported that "the workers all jumped in, and the coins were scattered among several individuals. I had the opportunity to examine many of the pieces and they were all of very high quality."

Apparently, the finders of the hoard wanted to keep all information confidential. Today, apart from a few coins that have come on the market now and then and which have been said to have come from Jackson, little is known. Among the coins was a rare 1856-D quarter eagle.

The Chicago Double Eagle Hoard

Hidden: Circa 1929-1933
Found: July 1986
Treasure: $20 gold coins

Thomas K. DeLorey tells the story of this remarkable group:[2]

> In July of 1986 I received a call at the coin shop in Chicago where I was working at the time (having since moved to Harlan Berk's firm in the same city), to ask if we would be interested in doing an appraisal on "some gold coins at a bank." Naturally, I said yes and made an appointment to meet the lady who had them.
>
> At the bank I met the owner. While she went to get the coins for me to view, I waited in a conference room. After some time she returned with a vault attendant who was pushing a heavily laden cart. I noticed that the bank employee left the cart with the coins, as this was easier than having to lift the box off of it. After he departed, the owner opened the box and began pulling out some 10-inch by 10-inch sheets of purple felt sewn into squares, checkerboard fashion, five rows of five squares each. There were 43 of the sheets.
>
> The owner produced a pair of scissors and handed them to me and said that the gold coins were inside the cloths. I carefully began cutting the felt along one side of a sheet, and removed five double eagles from the five pockets in the row thus exposed. Every pocket in each sheet contained a double eagle, for a total of 25 coins per sheet.
>
> As I spent the next few hours carefully opening the sheets, I noticed a definite pattern in their contents. One sheet might have 25 ordinary mixed-date Very Fine to Extremely Fine Liberty Head or Saint-Gaudens double eagles, while the next one might have 25 absolutely gorgeous specimens all of the same date and mint. The Uncirculated coins all had a deep rich patina with a hint of green in it, which I assume was from prolonged contact with the felt, and were remarkably free of bagmarks due to their protection by the felt and the fact that they had never been subjected to an ocean voyage to a Swiss bank and back. Most would grade MS-65 or *better* by today's standards.
>
> In chatting with the owner, I learned that her grandmother, who had been born and raised in the "old country" and had married a successful businessman after emigrating to America, did not trust banks and was in the habit after the stock market crash of 1929 of taking $500 in cash to a bank every so often and converting it into double eagles. She then took the coins home where she sewed them into the squares that made up each cloth sheet. Whatever the bank happened to have a particular day—and there may have been more than one bank involved—was what she received.
>
> Approximately 40% of the pads contained circulated Liberty Head $20s, and there were two or three pads of circulated Saint-Gaudens pieces from the 1907-1916 period. There were no pads of mixed circulated Liberty Heads and Saint-Gaudens coins, which might mean that banks routinely separated the two, though it could just as easily mean that she just happened to draw on one bag of each from two different banks.
>
> Among the Uncirculated pads, there were two or three that were Liberty Head coins dated 1907 and five or six of the 1907-D, plus one to five each of the Saint-Gaudens varieties such as 1907, 1908 No Motto, 1911-D, 1914-D, and 1923-D, and perhaps one or two common dates from the 1920s. The 1923-Ds were exceptionally nice.
>
> All of these pads were of solid dates, except for one exceptional pad which yielded one each of the extremely rare 1927-S, 1929, 1930-S, 1931, 1931-D and 1932! I was astounded, to say the least, when I saw this pad filled with great rarities, and opened the last 10 or so pads hoping to find a legendary 1927-D or even a 1933, but the pattern reverted to normal. Once my pulse reverted to its regular rate, I completed the appraisal and carefully repacked the coins in plastic tubes cushioned with a lot of tissue paper.

[1] Information from James C. Gray, letter, August 13, 1996. As is so often the case with treasure finds, actual facts are scarce. This led to an inquiry to Jeff Garrett, who responded on September 5 and 6, 1996, with recollections and suggestions for further investigation. One source suggested the find might have been in Jackson, Tennessee.

[2] Letter to the author, September 23, 1996.

Eventually we purchased the collection, and it was dispersed at the 1986 ANA convention in Milwaukee.

I have no idea how this hoard happened to have six rare dates in it. Perhaps one of her bankers, in the interest of keeping an important customer happy, arranged to get them for her. Perhaps she just got lucky. In the early 1930s little numismatic attention was paid to these almost-current dates, so it was probably simply the luck of the draw.

Several years later, as I was telling this story to another Chicago area coin dealer, he told me that he had purchased a smaller but similar lot from another heir, who had implied that there was yet another such group in existence. However, his purchase did not include any rare dates, and mostly consisted of 1923-Ds. I do not know if the other group referred to was the one we had bought, or if there is a third (or fourth?) lot still out there.

I would have loved to have seen the entire group in its original hiding place—wherever that was—so that I could have recorded the dates of the strata as they were laid down in the 1930s, but the coins must have been moved several times during the process of distribution to the heirs. However, it is interesting to note that several different original bags of pre-World War I dates must have been in place in Chicago banks in the 1929-1933 period, and not just common Philadelphia Mint double eagles bearing such often-seen dates as 1924 through 1928.

Abe Kosoff once told me how he had assisted a few clients in having bags of U.S. $20s shipped to Swiss banks before the Gold Surrender Act of 1933 took effect, and I take it he was not alone in this endeavor. Perhaps this outflow of $20s caused a shortage of that denomination in this country, which in turn caused the Treasury in Washington and/or the Denver Mint open its vaults of older dates long held in storage, similar to what was done with silver dollars in the 1962-1964 period. Of course, this is speculation on my part.

Forgotten Gold Eagles

Hidden: 1932
Found: 1989
Treasure: $10 gold coins

It is said that in 1932 a sea captain living on a rocky inlet on Penobscot Bay on the coast of Maine liked gold. As in gold coins.

In that year he obtained from his bank 61 freshly-minted $10 gold eagles of the same date and put them in a place for safekeeping. There they remained forgotten for many years, until a descendant came across them and showed them to a leading eastern dealer in art and antiques, who contacted a rare coin dealer. The coins proved not to be rarities, for 1932 is one of the more plentiful issues of the Saint-Gaudens Indian Head design. However, nearly all were particularly nice choice or gem Mint State examples, and when they were auctioned in 1989 there was a wild bidding scramble as collectors competed to acquire them.[1]

A Leather Pouch

Hidden: 1856 or later
Found: Early 1990s
Treasure: Dahlonega Mint gold coins

Jeff Garrett recalled a significant find of gold coins located in the early 1990s:[2]

> About five or six years ago a hoard of southern gold was discovered somewhere in North Carolina. The coins were found in a leather pouch and included a quantity of Dahlonega gold coins. The hoard ended up with a dealer in Atlanta. Al Adams, who saw the coins, said the quality was fantastic. I have heard from other people that the group contained many examples of 1856-D half eagles.

This is a short but numismatically sweet account, as 1856-D $5 gold coins are highly prized no matter what the grade. And, these were only *part* of the find!

---

[1] Sold in the catalogue of the Auctions by Bowers and Merena sale of the Kissel and Victoria Collections, September 1989, lots 556-606.

[2] Letter to the author, September 6, 1996.

CHAPTER 9

Down with the Ship

Introduction

Over the years shipwrecks on American inland and coastal waters have numbered in the tens of thousands. Doubtless, just about any vessel that departed from a United States river, lake, or ocean port and later sank took with it at least some pocket change. Thus, a complete enumeration of shipwrecks with coins or coin possibilities would, in effect, be a multi-volume listing of American shipping history.

That said, there are several notable shipwrecks that are mentioned here (and others in the next two chapters). Certainly, the *Feversham* and *Le Chameau* are numismatically important by any standard. The *Arabia* is representative of many inland steamer incidents and is a wreck that has yielded only assorted pocket change. The tragedy of the *Lexington* is one of many nautical disasters that may in some future day yield specimens of numismatic value, but for the present the coins remain lost.

Possibly more than in any other area of numismatic treasure research, published references concerning lost and sunken ships are apt to differ widely in details, possibly because later writers often romanticized and embellished their accounts. Because of this, the author has listed multiple sources in many instances and has pointed out some differences in details.

The Wreck of *H.M.S. Feversham*

Lost: October 7, 1711
Location: Scatari Island, Nova Scotia
Found: 1984
Treasure: Massachusetts silver

Feversham Lost

During one of the seemingly endless series of colonial military conflicts between England and France—this one called Queen Anne's War—the British government in America decided to mount an attack against the fortress at Quebec, in 1710. Accordingly, a large fleet was assembled in Boston, which sailed for Quebec City in August 1711. On August 14 of that year, the fleet was wrecked in the St. Lawrence River, eight ships being lost along with 900 men. The admiral of the fleet, Sir Hovendon Walker, decided to abandon the venture and retire to Nova Scotia.

H.M.S. Feversham, a 32-gun frigate built in 1696, had earlier been sent to the southern colonies to pick up food and naval stores in support of the ill-fated expedition. During the disaster that befell Walker's fleet in the St. Lawrence, *H.M.S. Feversham* had been on station in the south, and luckily escaped the August 14, 1711 tragedy.

Realizing that his efforts against fortress Quebec had to be abandoned, Admiral Walker sent letters by fast dispatch to New York, advising the governor there to have *H.M.S. Feversham* wait upon Walker's return, and not venture north, as there was no longer any need for her to do so. Unfortunately, Admiral Walker's letters reached New York one day after the *Feversham* had sailed. On September 17 the *Feversham* together with three transport ships carrying more than a thousand barrels of pork, as well as bread, flour, butter, pease, rum, and tobacco, sailed for Quebec City.

While she was in New York Harbor, the *Feversham* also replenished her stores of coinage, which had been exhausted by purchases of supplies in the southern colonies. According to published sources, on September 4 the *Feversham's* purser (*i.e.*, "chief financial officer" of a naval vessel) applied for and received from the New York Office of the British Treasury some 569 pounds, 12 shillings, and 5 pence sterling in coin.

On Sunday, October 7, 1711, *H.M.S. Feversham* was blown onto the rocky shore of Scatari Island, Nova Scotia, during a fierce storm. Of the 150 or so officers and seamen aboard, about 49 survived, the others being drowned. The three transports that accompanied *H.M.S. Feversham* on her doomed voyage north also foundered and sank, with loss of life.

Salvage operations commenced in the summer of the following year, when *H.M.S. Saphyr* was dispatched to Scatari Island to attempt to recover the *Feversham's* cannons and stores. The *Saphyr's* captain stated, however, that he had no opportunity to salvage anything from the bottom of the bay as the weather and the rocks were too dangerous to allow for such operations. No further salvage attempts were made for 250 years.

Feversham Found

Starting in 1984, and continuing for the following several years, salvage operations were undertaken by a private venture group which successfully located and recovered *H.M.S. Feversham's* cargo, including a number of coins she had originally taken on in New York City in 1711. With the approval of the Canadian government, and after having obtained the appropriate legal licenses for export and sale, coins from the wreck of the *Feversham* were first offered to the public by Christie's in February 1989. A further parcel of coins from this wreck was sold by Jeffrey Hoare Auctions, Inc., in February 1993. This latter portion, however, was restricted to purchases by Canadian citizens only, as none of the lots were allowed for export out of the country.

The importance of the treasure recovered from the wreck of *H.M.S. Feversham* cannot be overstated. In strictly numismatic terms, the number of important American coins found marks this wreck as one of the most significant dating to colonial times. In terms of numismatic history, however, the hoard's importance becomes overwhelming. As *H.M.S. Feversham* put into New York in September 1711, and as published records at the time show that she took on coins in that city to replenish her stock, we know that whatever was found in her wreck represents exactly what was in common circulation in New York City at that time. When one considers the number and types of the coins discovered in the wreck, one can see immediately a nearly perfect cross-section of the types of coins one might find in daily circulation in a major colonial eastern seaboard metropolis.

Moreover, the find reflects that the British Treasury paid out silver Massachusetts shillings, having accepted same as a medium of exchange. Various numismatic-historical accounts have suggested that the coinage of Massachusetts was inimical to the interests of the British crown, the date 1652 was maintained on coins minted into the 1680s so that the British authorities would not be aware that pieces were made after 1652, etc. Gradually, certain aspects of this "conventional wisdom" are undergoing revision.

Massachusetts Silver Aboard

Found in the wreck of *H.M.S. Feversham* were 131 Massachusetts silver coins, broken down into the following types:

New England shillings: 1 (Noe 3-C).

Willow Tree shillings: 4 (Noe 1-A, 3-D, 3-E, unidentifiable).

Oak Tree shillings: 35.

Oak Tree sixpence: 1.

Pine Tree shillings: 75.

Pine Tree sixpence: 1.

Cut quarters and halves of Pine Tree shillings, to make small change: nine (four half-shilling segments and five quarter-shilling segments).

In addition, there were numerous Lion daalders of the Netherlands, primarily seventeenth-century strikes; numerous Spanish colonial silver cobs (1/2 to 8 reals), mostly of the reigns of Philip IV through Charles II (1621-1700), and a small quantity of British silver coins. The number of British coins was so small as to pale into insignificance when compared to the number of Spanish colonial pieces, and even the number of Massachusetts silver coins, showing quite graphically exactly how coinage-poor the mother country intended to keep her American colonies!

From the viewpoint of the numismatist interested in American coinage history, what was most important in the find of the wreck from the *H.M.S. Feversham* were the Pine Tree shillings which had been deliberately cut into half and quarter shilling segments. Clearly, there was a considerable need in colonial New York City for small change, denominations smaller than a shilling. While both the Pine and Oak Tree series were struck in large numbers and included many of the smaller sixpence and threepence and some twopence denominations, clearly the number of these lesser coins was not sufficient to meet the needs of the general populace. Accordingly, an expediency was resorted to whereby shilling pieces were carefully cut into quarters or halves to supply the need for sixpenny and threepenny pieces for daily transactions. The cutting of coins into segments was hardly a new idea and had been practiced with Spanish-American silver 8-real coins. Some of these were literally "pieces" of eight. In 1728 this commentary appeared, reflective of the practice:[1]

> CUTTING COIN IN AMERICA
>
> I have been told, that among some of our poorest American colonies upon the continent, the people enjoy the liberty of cutting the little money among them into halves and quarters, for the conveniences of small traffic.

Before the recovery of the fractional pieces from the wreck of the *H.M.S. Feversham*, some, scattered examples of cut fractional Massachusetts silver pieces had been known in the numismatic trade, but these had always been looked upon with some concern, for it could not be determined with any degree of certainty exactly when the host coin had been cut into pieces. As we know that *H.M.S. Feversham* took on her coins in September 1711, we therefore know that her cut fractions must have been nearly contemporary with the 1652-1682 (conjectured) dating of the entire Massachusetts silver coin series.

It is interesting to note, on the other hand, that while Massachusetts silver coins may have been in common circulation in New York City in 1711, exactly 31 years later they were curious enough to be offered at auction sale in London! The earliest recorded auction appearance of any Massachusetts silver coin can be traced back to Christopher Cox's sale in Covent Garden dated March 18, 1742, where Lot 55 included six Massachusetts shillings, two threepenny pieces, and one twopenny piece, all of which were sold for 11 shillings. When it is realized that the face value of the coins in this lot amounted to 6 shillings and 8 pence, it is clear that a considerable premium had been paid for these pieces, which by then must have been both curious and collectible.

The Wreck of *Le Chameau*

Lost: August 26, 1725
Location: Off Port Nova Island
Found: Circa 1965
Treasure: French-American colonial coins

During the night of August 25-26, 1725, the French 600-ton, 48-gun transport, *Le Chameau,* foundered in high winds on the rocks of Kelpy Cove, off Port Nova Island, Nova Scotia, Canada, just 12 miles from her destination of Fortress Louisbourg.[2] The vessel went down taking all hands and passengers, including Guillaume de Chazel, the newly appointed governor of Trois Rivières and Intendant Begon's successor. Salvage operations commenced from Louisbourg late in 1726,[3] but the main gold and silver treasure the vessel carried was not recovered until 1965 when Alex Storm and his associates achieved success, al-

---

[1] *The Intelligencer, No. XIX,* December 2, 1728, as given in Dean Swift's *Works* (quoted in *Historical Magazine,* February 1869, p. 117). Presumably, this referred to Spanish-American silver, but it could have pertained to Massachusetts silver coins just as easily. "Notes on Coins," by William Kelby, in the same issue of *Historical Magazine,* p. 115, notes that the 1652 Massachusetts silver coinage arose in part from the need to convert large amounts of captured Spanish silver brought to New England by buccaneers in 1651.

[2] Portions of this text appeared earlier in Michael Hodder's study, "Guide to Coins of Nouvelle France," which appeared in *Canada's Money,* edited by John M. Kleeberg, Coinage of the Americas Conference at the American Numismatic Society, New York, November 7, 1992 (subsequently published New York: ANS, 1994), pp. 1-35. Thomas H. Sebring, *Treasure Tales,* 1986, pp. 98-101, gives an excellent account of the wreck. The high winds were probably remnants of a tropical hurricane. The illustration is of a 1724-K (Bordeaux Mint) louis d'or recovered from *Le Chameau.*

[3] During the eighteenth century (and earlier), undersea treasure salvage operations typically involved the use of a diving bell, or inverted barrel-like wooden (usually) container filled with air, with an open bottom. A man within the bell could work on a limited area below it. The bell was suspended by a cable from a ship above. As an example, two such bells—apparently open-bottomed barrels heavily laden with weights—were used in Boston harbor in 1642 by Edward Bendall to salvage items from the *Mary Rose* (cf. Edward Rowe Snow, *Sea Disasters and Inland Catastrophes,* pp. 237-244

though a few coins from the wreck had been found in 1914. The first coin identified by Storm was a 1724 Louis XV silver écu. After a division of the recovered treasure, which amounted to over 4,500 silver and gold coins and many artifacts, a large part was sold by Parke Bernet Galleries in December 1971 and realized nearly $200,000.

Le Chameau carried more than 82,000 livres tournois of gold and silver coin, which were meant to supply the colonial governors the funds to pay administrative and military expenses. French Canada had been traditionally coinage poor, a deliberate act on the part of the mercantilist government in Paris. Thus, French colonial finances in Quebec were in disarray. In fact, matters had gotten so bad that the Army was paid with what has been called "card money," which were simply promissory notes printed on the back of playing cards! The gold and silver coins shipped to Canada on board *Le Chameau* were meant to replace the card money, bring French colonial finances onto a better footing, and restore the Army's confidence in the civilian government. The loss of *Le Chameau,* therefore, must have been a tremendous blow not only to finances, but also to the morale of the French colonial citizenry.

No complete inventory listing of all the coins recovered from the wreck has ever been published. The most accessible one remains the auction catalogue entries (the Parke Bernet Galleries auction sale, December 10-11, 1971), which the numismatic scholar will find useful for the gold, but unsatisfactory for the silver coins.

The ill-fated vessel carried gold Louis d'or mirlitons dated 1723 to 1725, including both reverse varieties (long or short fronds), struck at some 24 different mints. In some cases, the coins salvaged represent the majority of the survivors of their particular mintages. The silver écus aux huit L appear to be dated 1724 and 1725, the majority being from the seaboard mints of Bordeaux and La Rochelle. A handful of older French coins, sixièmes, was also recovered.

The auction catalogue included photographs of some representative examples, primarily placed for type. Auction descriptions were laconic per the firm's usual style, but the introductory material was, and remains, extremely useful. The historical information presented has not been supplanted since, and the inventory listing of the coins to be included in the sale can still be used. That enumeration shows that some 109 gold coins were dated 1723, 323 were dated 1724, and only 62 were dated 1725.

While the French coins shipped aboard *Le Chameau* were of royal types struck for circulation within mainland France, the fact that they were shipped to Quebec has been considered sufficient justification to include them among the ranks of French colonial coins, an admittedly broad category, but, unfortunately, one which is not better circumscribed. Some numismatists go so far as to suggest that, since the preponderance of some issues was shipped to Quebec, those issues should be considered exclusively French colonial. The author (Michael Hodder) would not venture to take this leap, but does feel that the coins from *Le Chameau* belong in a special category, neither exclusively French colonial, nor exclusively French metropolitan.

The *Lexington* Tragedy

Lost: January 13, 1840
Location: Off Eaton's Neck, Long Island
Treasure: Gold and silver coins

A Cruise in Long Island Sound

On the night of January 13, 1840, the 488-ton steamer *Lexington* was en route from New York City to Stonington, Connecticut, with about 160 people aboard and a cargo of about 150 bales of cotton. She caught fire at sea in sub-zero weather, and in the ensuing tragedy all but four people died.[1] Still at the bottom of Long Island Sound among the wreckage may be $18,000 worth of silver and gold coins.

This particular ship disaster launched Nathaniel Currier into the Pantheon of American iconography.

in the 1990 Snow anthology, *Disaster at Sea*). The corpus of Snow's works consists of dozens of sea and treasure stories penned by him over a long period of years from 1935 onward. While there is little in the way of solid numismatic information included, a reading of even a few of them will impart a sense of adventure. Charles Tomlinson, *Cyclopædia of Useful Arts and Manufactures,* 1852, Vol. I, pp. 503-510, describes several devices including a diving bell invented by a Dr. Halley before 1721, which permitted the occupants to remain 60 feet underwater for an hour and a half. The question as to who invented the diving bell and other sustained-immersion apparatus seems to be undecided, with many claimants.

[1] William M. Lytle, *Merchant Steam Vessels of the United States 1807-1868.* Passenger accounts and other information in S.A. Howland, *Steamboat Disasters and Railroad Accidents in the United States,* 1840, are the basis for several later stories of the wreck. A dramatization of the final hours of the *Lexington* appears as Part 1 in Clive Cussler, *The Sea Hunters,* 1996, and relates the Longfellow anecdote.

The man who was later a partner with James Merritt Ives in Currier & Ives published a hand-colored print of the disaster, titled *Awful Conflagration of the Steam Boat LEXINGTON In Long Island Sound on Monday Eve'g, Jan'y 13th 1840, by which melancholy occurrence, over 100 PERSONS PERISHED.* In an era in which most newspaper accounts were not yet illustrated with black and white engravings, let alone color, the Currier print with its dramatic perspective of raging flames and smoke reaching high into the sky was a sellout, and it had to be reprinted several times.[1]

A Harrowing Account

The steamer *Lexington* left its pier on Manhattan's East River for Stonington after 3:00 o'clock, possibly as late as 4:00, on Monday afternoon, January 13, 1840, with eager passengers who looked forward to arriving at their destination early the following morning.[2]

As fate would have it, Henry Wadsworth Longfellow (1807-1882), whose poem, "The Wreck of the Hesperus," would be published the next day, desired to make the trip, but missed the boat. Things like that happen. Thus, the world today can enjoy "Hiawatha," "Evangeline," and other epic poems that later flowed from his pen, and a generation of scholars at Bowdoin College in Maine could enjoy the benefits of his instruction there.[3]

Those aboard the *Lexington* settled comfortably in their chairs and on benches awaiting entertainment soon to be provided by Charles Everle and Henry J. Finn, two actors from Boston who were going to present a variety show.

About half past 7:00, when the ship was about 50 miles out of the port of New York City and four miles off Eaton's Neck, on the north shore of Long Island, the woodwork and casings about her smokestack were discovered to be on fire.

Pilot Stephen Manchester,[4] who was at the helm, later related:

> My first movement was to step out of the wheel-house and look aft. I saw the upper deck on fire all around the smoke-pipe and blazing up two or three feet, perhaps, above the promenade deck. The flame seemed to be a thin sheet and, apparently, but just commenced. The blaze seemed to follow up the smoke-pipe and was all around it.... I thought from my first view that it was a doubtful case whether it could be extinguished....

Captain George Childs (of Narragansett, Rhode Island), who had been below deck, came into the wheel-house and placed his hand on the wheel, at which time the drive-rope connected to the rudder gave way. Smoke was so intense that the post had to be abandoned.

An alarm was immediately given, and a small hand-pumped fire engine was brought out, but only two or three buckets could be located, although there were supposed to be several dozen aboard. It was soon found that fighting the fire was futile as the flames roared toward the sky. With much effort the *Lexington* was directed at full speed toward the Long Island shore in the hope of beaching her, but two or three miles away from land her engine stopped and she was dead in the water. Meanwhile, the forward motion of the ship had served to fan the flames to great intensity.

Pilot Stephen Manchester's testimony continued:

> In my opinion, the fire originated from the heat of the smoke-pipe, which was communicated to the woodwork. I have frequently seen the smoke-pipe red hot, and saw it so on the last night. I do not know whether the red heat extended to the flange or not. The cotton was piled within perhaps a foot of the steam chimney.

Shortly after the fire was discovered, the single lifeboat and two smaller boats were made ready, but the lifeboat was smashed when it came into contact with one of the two 23-foot-diameter paddlewheels. As if that was not enough, according to later testimony the two small boats were swamped "by mismanagement in lowering them into the water crowded with passengers." One of the small boats was filled with about 20 passengers and then lowered toward the sea, when someone cut the forward tackle, making her go into

---

[1] Engraving drawn on stone by William K. Hewitt. Published by N. Currier, 2 Spruce Street, New York. Many copies were printed as extras to the New York *Sun*. Four different versions of the print are known to collectors today and are described in *Currier & Ives: A Catalogue Raisonné,* Gale Research Co., 1984, p. 35.

[2] The following account is adapted and paraphrased from the original 1840 *Extra Sun* story as published by Currier; John H. Morrison's *History of American Steam Navigation,* 1903; and testimony given before the Twenty-Sixth Congress. Certain other information is from Jeannette Edwards Rattray, *Ship Ashore!* 1956.

[3] Another bad news-good news "missing the boat" account appears in Chapter 11 under the discussion of the *S.S. Central America,* relative to a passenger who arrived at the dock in Havana after the ship had sailed.

[4] On coastwise ships the pilot, who was familiar (or supposed to be) with shoals, reefs, and other hazards to navigation directed the course of the ship, while the captain was in charge of the crew and passengers. Rates for pilotage into and out of harbors and estuaries were published in various navigation guides and were usually based upon the draft of the ship and its size, and the difficulties presented. As a ship neared the harbor it would raise a small flag or pennant to signal the need for a pilot to come out to meet the vessel. On extended voyages such as along a coast, pilots remained aboard as a member of the crew. If a ship arrived outside a harbor late in the day, it would often wait until a pilot could come aboard the next day (as was the case, for example, when Marquis de Lafayette arrived in New York City harbor in August 1824).

the water bow-first and flooding the interior. Essentially the same thing happened to the second small boat. Meanwhile, the sea temperature was about at the freezing point and the air remained below zero,[1] hardly conducive for unprotected survival even under the best of circumstances.

Captain Childs rigged a small raft "from a spar and flagstaff with a portion of the bulwarks; also throwing overboard four baggage carts after being emptied of their contents, with a line attached." Some of the cotton cargo was pitched into the water as well. The flames increased their intensity, and before long there was no place of safety remaining on the ship. The *Lexington* remained afire until about 3:00 a.m., when the largely gutted hulk slipped beneath the waves, apparently carrying with it the bodies of passengers who had preferred death by fire to death by freezing—an awful choice.

For the passengers who had jumped overboard, the only hope for being saved was to cling to floating cotton bales or other objects, "but none of them succeeded except a passenger (known as Captain Chester Hilliard or Hillard),[2] pilot Stephen Manchester, Charles Smith (one of the firemen), and a passenger who had been picked up and taken to River Head, and who was so far gone as not to be able to disclose his name. It was believed, however, that he would survive." This last-mentioned passenger was David Crowley, who was later identified as the second mate.

Captain Hilliard first went to the improvised raft, then moved to a bale of cotton, to which he clung until 11:00 am on Tuesday when, after having been in the water about 15 hours, he was taken off by the sloop *Merchant,* under Captain Meeker, which had sailed out from Southport. The *Merchant* had jettisoned some of its cargo to permit it to be in shallow water during the rescue. The same sloop saved two more passengers who were clinging to a wood fragment of the since-departed *Lexington.* The bodies of two others were likewise taken from the wreckage on which they had perished from cold.

Another vessel, the steamer *Statesman,* on Thursday picked up one body and 13 luggage trunks. The bodies of Cortland Hempstead (the chief engineer) and Sands (the head waiter in the ship's dining room) were also recovered.

On shore, William S. Mount, a Stony Brook, New York, artist of some renown, witnessed the scene.[3] He later recalled that two rescue boats with eight men had left the shore to row out to the *Lexington,* but the flaming ship stopped coming toward the shore, and with its rudder jammed, steamed around in a tight circle. One of the rescue boats went about two or three miles out from land, but did not reach the steamer.

The Inhuman Captain Terrill

The *Extra Sun* (Nathaniel Currier's color-illustrated print) commented:

> The number of passengers on board is not known with any degree of certainty. It is most probable, however, that they numbered about 80—of whom but two were rescued alive. The boat's crew numbered 30 of whom also two were saved....
>
> Among the passengers were the wife and two interesting children of Russell Jarvis, Esquire, formerly of Boston, more lately editor of the *Philadelphia World,* and at present, editor of the *Evening Tattler* in this city [New York]. Captain Hilliard, whose penchant had been attracted to this interesting and charming family at their table, saw Mrs. Jarvis was clinging with one of her children in her arms on a bale of cotton. The other child had leapt overboard, as had also a great many other passengers—some 20 of whom had life preservers on. When observed by Captain Hilliard, Mrs. Jarvis was frantically calling upon the persons in the water to preserve her child and bring it to her on the bale. Mother, children, passengers and all, however, sunk to a common grave.
>
> The steamboat *Statesman* on Friday repaired to the scene of the disaster, and returned on Saturday, bringing five bodies, one of which was that of Mr. Stephen Waterbury of this city, and another of Mr. Philo Upson of South Egremont, Massachusetts, two others, those of Benjamin Leadden and Silas Thorborn, hands on board the steamer, and the fifth that day, a boy of five years of age.... [All bodies recovered were frozen, partially covered with ice, and many with char marks from the fire aboard.]
>
> On Friday night Captain Comstock dispatched a letter to the city, in which he says that:
>
> "Captain William Terrill, master of the sloop *Improvement,* was, with his vessel, within four or five miles of the *Lexington* at the time she commenced burning, and thinks if he had immediately repaired to her assistance, he could have saved a great number of lives. The reason he gives for not doing so is, *that he would have lost his tide over the bar,* at the port to which he was bound, and accordingly he pursued his inhuman course, leaving upwards of 100 persons to die the worst of deaths.[4] The circumstances of this unparalleled cruelty will hereafter be more clearly exposed, and I trust he will receive his merited deserts."

---

[1] Alternatively, cold, but not as cold as usual for the season; accounts varied.

[2] There were at least three other captains aboard as passengers: E.J. Kimball, B.D. Foster; and Ichabod D. Carver (who was soon to be married).

[3] One of his works—a farmer with corn—was used as a vignette on bank notes of the era. Mount's brother was also a well-known artist. Mount was the subject of an article in *American Heritage,* August 1960, and a 1965 monograph-leaflet, "Popularity of Wm. S. Mount's Art Work on Paper Money 1838-1865," by John A. Muscalus.

[4] Italics per the original account. Captain Terrill was counting on high tide to carry his ship over a sand bar, otherwise he would have had to wait until the next high tide, thus causing a delay and diminishing his profits. Terrill reappears as captain of the Missouri River steamer *Arabia* in a subsequent account in the present chapter.

This conduct of Captain Terrill has elicited a universal burst of indignation against him in this city, and for his safety's sake we advise him not to venture too much in public here.

Besides the bodies, the *Statesman* brought 30 pieces of luggage and the life boat of the *Lexington* but little injured. We understand that a great number of the trunks, etc., which had floated to shore, have been broken open and rifled, and that the trunk of the Reverend Doctor Fallen [Follen][1] was found in the woods, some distance from the shore, rifled of everything but papers.

The head cook was Joseph Robinson whose name was reported among the lost, but as it turned out was not on board because he was detained at his home by sickness. His place was supplied by the second cook, Howell, and Isaac Putnam (colored) supplied the place of Howell.

An Inquiry into the Tragedy

Hearings were held to determine the circumstances of the ship's demise. Testimony related:

[The boat was built as a wood-fired steamer by Bishop & Simonson, New York, for Cornelius Vanderbilt in the latter part of 1834 and beginning of 1835] of the best possible materials and bolted and fastened together and secured in the strongest possible manner without regard to cost or expenses....

She was 205 feet long on deck from stem to stern, 22 feet wide and 40 feet across the wheelhouses from side to side. She was launched in April 1835, and her first trip was in June of 1835. Her timbers were part oak and part chestnut, with planks of oak as far as the waist and then of pine.... About two months before the accident she was repaired in drydock and some new copper and other fittings were put in. Vanderbilt owned her until 1838 and then sold her to the Providence & Rhode Island Steamboat and Transportation Company.

The ship was the only boat that had navigated Long Island Sound for four or five years and never stopped because of weather or lost a trip.... Instructions to the captain were never to stop while they could see to go ahead, he had so much confidence in her strength.

The *Lexington* was first built to burn wood and then converted to burn anthracite coal when the ownership changed. No reference as to whether the boat had ever caught fire from sparks, but such minor fires were common incidents.[2]

The *Lexington* had recently been converted from burning wood to burning coal in her boiler, and there were still problems to be worked out. Coal burned with a much more intense heat, and certain precautions as to insulation and spacing from combustible materials needed to be taken. There had been trouble with the new fuel on a recent trip, and she had been laid up for repairs to the two 36-inch blowers, powered from a shaft on the main engine, that forced a draft in the fire box that became far too hot. The steam engine, built by the West Point Foundry, had a 48-inch cylinder that operated with an 11-foot stroke.

Continuing the testimony:

Captain Hilliard said that when he came out of the cabin and saw the fire he thought three buckets of water would have put it out. Instead of doing that, the crew went to check the engine, and the fire got ahead. Hilliard said that there were two to four dozen buckets on board. Hilliard went to the pilot room and told the pilot that the boat was on fire. The pilot said he knew it, and was steering for shore....

It was said that the boiler was in the center, and the woodwork came within an inch of the chimney. There was a space of eight inches filled with steam around the chimney. The fire could have originated from a spark below. There could have been a little hemp in some of the woodwork in which a spark might have fallen.[3] However, in boats built for burning wood there is no more danger than boats built for burning coal. The smoke pipe is surrounded by a case filled with steam eight inches wide and above her the promenade deck and into the hold. Under the boiler is 18 inches of brick and then a layer of cast iron plates filled with water and that covered with sheet iron. Hilliard stated that changing from wood to coal didn't make it any more dangerous.

In the hearing, Captain William Comstock was examined. He lived at 2234 East Broadway, 53 years old, general agent and superintendent of the New Jersey Steam Transportation Company, formerly called the Boston & New York Transportation Company, charter obtained from the New Jersey Legislature last year. The company had five boats on the line called the *Massachusetts, Rhode Island, Narragansett, Providence* and *Michigan*. They run from New York to Stonington to Providence.

Comstock related that Robert Schuyler, then president of the company, purchased the *Lexington* from Vanderbilt for $60,000, and with additional expenses it cost $70,000 [or $72,000] before her first trip for our company.... Further: "I can't say whether or not that money was to induce Captain Vanderbilt to take his boat off that station, such a boat as the *Lexington* is worth $60,000.[4] She had not been running in opposition to us at the time she sunk, but when first she came on the line she ran in opposition to us...."

Comstock testified that the ship burned about 10 to 13 tons of anthracite coal [on a typical trip] going from New York to Stonington and then from two to three cords of wood. She ran on about eight to 13 inches of steam and could go 12 to 14 miles an hour. Goods were carefully stowed. "You never saw any goods stowed nearer than three or four feet of the casing of the steam chimney, although no danger would be found if it was stowed against the steam chimney."

The *Lexington* had two quarter boats about 22 feet long both in excellent order plus a lifeboat at least 21 feet long capable of saving 40 people, although the builder said 60.

---

[1] Dr. Charles Follen was intended. A street in Cambridge, Massachusetts, is named for him.

[2] Actually, the ship had caught fire on January 2, 1840; a small box ignited and was quickly extinguished.

[3] Hemp (of which ropes were made) and tar were used on wooden ships to fill cracks and crevices to prevent leakage.

[4] It was Vanderbilt's practice to exact tribute from his competitors to induce him to stay away from a route or to keep rates high. Vanderbilt also did this years later in the 1850s in connection with ship service from New York City to San Francisco with an overland crossing in Central America. The *Lexington* was Vanderbilt's first large-scale venture into Long Island Sound freight and passenger traffic, although he had operated the *Nimrod* from New York to Bridgeport for a short time.

> The boats were hanging on the quarter. The lifeboat was forward near the wheel house on the promenade deck which was covered with painted canvas.

Soon after the disaster, Col. Harry A. Hunt, editor of the Sag Harbor *Corrector,* called the event a "willful, savage, horrid murder," further observing: "There was not an officer on the boat who did his duty–each acted for himself only. The Master [captain] was one of the first to desert his post."[1]

Some cotton bales washed ashore along Long Island Sound. From one or more of these, "Lexington shirts" were woven and hawked as mementos of the disaster. Thus, Nathaniel Currier with his prints was not the only person to profit from the tragedy.

Coins Aboard

The account also included the information that among the passengers was:

> Adolphus S. Harnden of the Boston and New York Express Package Car Office, having with him about $18,000 in specie [coins], and $70,000 or $80,000 for brokers in eastern money.

The $18,000 in specie would have consisted of silver and/or gold coins. "Eastern money" probably refers to private paper money of Eastern banks. While coins would have held up to immersion in the water of Long Island Sound for years thereafter, the paper money would have deteriorated quickly. Stephen Manchester testified that Harnden was trapped on the forward deck by the flames and was one of the last to remain aboard the ship.

The January 1840 *Extra Sun,* published by Nathaniel Currier, also mentioned the coins in its account of the disaster:

> Captain Manchester, the pilot, is now at Southport and is slowly recovering. He states that he remained at the wheel until he was actually burnt out. He descended, and got into the air-deck where Mr. Harnden of the Express Line, Mr. Hoyt, baggage master, and two or three others were. They succeeded in getting out the lifeboat and lowered it into the water, and he threw his pea jacket into it.
>
> Unfortunately at this time the painter [rope attached to the prow] gave way and the lifeboat was sucked under the wheel thus depriving those who looked for safety in this boat of all hope. Flames now advanced rapidly to the aft part, and to prevent its progress, the pilot and others broke open some specie boxes [filled with coins], and emptied them of the worthless dross, used the boxes [as fire buckets] to keep off the flames and prevent their progress.
>
> Finding this in vain, Captain Manchester, taking his clasp knife from his pocket, jumped overboard to a cotton bale he saw near the vessel. Endeavoring to get on it, he found another man already sustaining himself on it. In his attempt to get on, both fell into the water. Captain Manchester rose, and supported the man until he could get on. Then using his knife, he cut holes in the bale by which he supported himself. Captain Manchester's companion died in the course of the night. The pilot was picked up on the bale as has been stated.

Another account, this written a year after the disaster, commented on the coins, here called "dollars":[2]

> Everything which could hold water was seized upon. The boxes containing specie were broken open, the dollars poured out and trodden under foot as worthless, whilst the boxes were used to throw water on the devouring flames.

So far as the author knows, none of these coins have ever been recovered from Long Island Sound, although an attempt was made as early as 1842.[3] By now, any silver coins would probably be mostly impaired by action of the salt water, but gold coins would still be intact, although with "seawater" etching.

In 1983, the *Lexington,* described as a "plush" passenger vessel, was said to have been found in about 80 feet of water off Port Jefferson, New York, by the National Underwater and Marine Agency.[4] Susan Wynne, spokesperson for the Agency, commented that "the ship could be raised but is in about three pieces, sitting upright in the bottom, amazingly well preserved." It was not stated whether positive identification of the *Lexington* had been achieved, nor was there any mention of the hull being charred.

Numismatist John J. Ford, Jr., recalled that as a

---

[1] As quoted by Dr. Clarence A. Wood, *Long Island Forum,* 1950.

[2] Charles Ellms, *The Tragedy of the Seas; or Sorrow on the Ocean, Lake, and River, from Shipwreck, Plague, Fire, and Famine,* copyright 1841; edition of 1846, imprint of Loomis & Peck, Philadelphia, p. 422, as part of a chapter, "The Burning of the Steamboat Lexington."

[3] *The Atlas of Ship Wrecks & Treasure: The History, Location, and Treasures of Ships Lost at Sea,* by Nigel Pickford, 1994, called the *Lexington* an "American luxury liner," stated that $800 in specie was recovered at the time of loss. The same writer stated that the ship was wrecked on November 19, 1846. The "luxury" term is in several modern accounts, but the author has not encountered it in any nineteenth century narratives.

[4] Long Island *Newsday,* October 12, 1983; copy furnished to the author by Donald Prybyzerski. The group of treasure hunters had been founded by Clive Cussler, a well-known novelist (*Raise the Titanic, Dragon, Cyclops, Inca Gold, Treasure,* and other stories), who by that time had found 34 significant wrecks. Cussler's 1996 book, *The Deep Sea Hunter,* gives a description of the finding of a ship said to be the *Lexington* and commented that it furnishes a potential site for modern-day divers, although conditions can be dangerous. Relics from the wreck are on display at the Vanderbilt Museum on Long Island.

young man living on Long Island, he would sometimes visit an old cemetery at the corner of Merrick Road and Ocean Avenue in Lynbrook (on the south shore and not close to the north shore wreck site) and seeing an overgrown patch of weeds and brush within which he discovered a modest size monument designating the burial sites of victims of the *Lexington*.[1]

The Wreck of the *Metis*

Another nautical disaster in Long Island Sound has a numismatic connection, this being the wreck of the passenger steamer *Metis,* which was wrecked off Watch Hill, Rhode Island, on August 31, 1872, after having transited most of the Sound. In the following year, Congress voted that a medal be created and awarded to those who assisted with the rescue efforts. In due course, the father and son engraving team of William and Charles Barber collaborated on the production of the medal.[2]

A Mysterious Treasure Ship

Lost: Late 1850s
Location: Off the East Coast
Found: Before 1974
Treasure: Gold coins

From an Unknown Wreck

The sea tells no tales, and, indeed, the majority of old wooden shipwrecks in American coastal waters are not identified as to name of the ship, owner, or time sunk. Such may be the case for an unknown wreck which yielded some highly important coins:

Any specialist in United States gold coins will sooner or later encounter specimens of $2.50 and $5 pieces, mostly dated in the 1850s, bright and sharp, but having a grainy, minutely etched surface instead of frosty lustre. David W. Akers, student of the American gold series, has termed these "seawater Uncirculated."

Writing in 1988, Walter Breen said this:[3]

> Many [$5 gold coins] surviving from Southern branch mints (notably 1853-O, 1853-C to 1855-C, and 1852-D to 1855-D) show full mint sharpness but dull matte surfaces; these are known as "seawater Uncs." They were retrieved from a wrecked ship, said to be a Confederate transport, sometime before 1974. Details have not yet become available, but the hoard also included double eagles and probably other denominations....

However, as the latest coins were dated 1855, and as if a "Confederate transport" were carrying coins it could not have done so prior to April 1861 (when the Civil War started), the Breen comment, while not necessarily needing to be rejected out of hand, seems to bear further study.

Some Possibilities

Most likely the ship in question went down in 1855 or very early 1856 after having visited a southern port such as New Orleans, Savannah, or Charleston. Such a scenario would at once account for the dating of the coins as 1855 or earlier and for the presence of significant numbers of Charlotte and Dahlonega issues. Possibilities for shipwrecks with gold coins aboard, minted in Charlotte, Dahlonega, and New Orleans, and dated before 1856, include these, among many others. The 1855 and January 20, 1856, entries seem to have greater possibilities for having all coins dated prior to 1856:

> **1855, December 6. *Crescent City.*** On this date the *Crescent City,* which had been in the New York to Chagres (Panama) service in 1851 and 1852, was stranded on Matanilla Reef or Shoal off the northwest end of Grand

---

[1] Conversation, October 8, 1996; note October 14, 1996.

[2] J.F. Loubat, *The Medallic History of the United States of America,* 1776-1876, published in 1878, devotes much space to the accounts of several shipwrecks for which life-saving and related medals were awarded. The sister steamers *Electra* and *Metis* left Pier 27 on the North River, New York City, on alternate days, bound for Boston (cf. *Wood's Illustrated Handbook to New York,* 1873 [obviously, with old information!], p. 200)

[3] Breen, *Encyclopedia,* 1988, p. 529. Similar information is found in Douglas Winter, *Charlotte Mint Gold Coins: 1838-1861,* 1987, pp. 113, 117.

Bahama Island in the Atlantic Ocean about 70 miles east of the coast of Florida.[1] However, she was on the way from New York City to New Orleans via Havana, and had no particular reason to carry coins predominantly from Southern mints. (This ship is included because it has been suggested as a possibility for the origin of the above-mentioned coins, but its itinerary would seem to remove it from serious consideration.)

1855, November 5. *Inca.* Under Captain Dennison this ship was en route from New Orleans to New York City, but the voyage was cut short when she was wrecked on Riding Rock, south of Cat Cay in the Bahamas.[2]

1856, January 20. *Valparabo.* With Captain Runnells in charge, this ship was on her way from New Orleans to Liverpool, England, when she went down close to where the *Inca* had sunk two months earlier

1856, May 17. *Peterhoff.* On the way from Charleston to Havana, the *Peterhoff,* Captain Peabody at the helm, was lost near Abaco Island in the Bahamas.[3]

1856, September 24. *Lizzie Lord.* On this day this ship, en route from Savannah to New Orleans under Captain Kendall, went down in the Bahamas.[4]

Another possibility is that these Charlotte, Dahlonega, and New Orleans Mint gold coins could have been lost on a small coastwise sailing vessel or steamer out of one of many southern ports. There were so many small ships wrecked that standard sources on sailing ship or steamship history omit mention of nearly all of them. The only way to track down such wrecks is to peruse contemporary newspapers published at Charleston, Savannah, New Orleans, and other ports.

Alternatively, the coins could have been buried or otherwise deliberately hidden on the shore of some bayou or inlet or on a coastal strand where the groundwater was brine.

With regard to the quality of the coins recovered from this mysterious wreck, David W. Akers commented that the $2.50 and $5 pieces are generally more heavily etched than are "seawater" 1854-S, 1855-S, and 1856-S $20 pieces from this era (see following entry).[5] Thus the "double eagles" mentioned by Breen must not have been San Francisco pieces of the dates indicated. If, indeed, any $20 pieces were included, it seems more likely that they would have been New Orleans issues from 1850-O (first year of the denomination) to 1855-O; yet, Breen does not mention any such O-Mint "seawater" coins. Perhaps the answer will become known in the future if someone involved with the discovery of the $2.50 and $5 coins comes forward.

Coins from Another "Mystery Ship"

Hidden or lost: 1856 or later
Location: Off the Florida coast
Found: Early 1970s
Treasure: $20 gold coins

Double Eagles from the Sea

In the early 1970s hundreds of $20 gold coins dated 1854-S, 1855-S, and 1856-S came on the market. The 1855-S and 1856-S double eagles, judging from their appearance, seem to have come from a separate source from those of 1854-S. The 1856-S pieces were the most numerous.

Many of the 1855-S and 1856-S double eagles were sold through WorldWide Coin Investments of Atlanta and were said to have been from a "sunken treasure ship off the coast of Florida."[6] However, the principals of WorldWide did not know where the pieces had been salvaged as they had been acquired via an intermediary.

---

[1] Tony Jaggers, *A Shipwreck Guide to the Bahamas, Turks and Caicos 1500 to 1990,* Volume I, p. 56. John Haskell Kemble, *The Panama Route, 1848-1869,* 1943, p. 223, attributes the demise of the *Crescent City* to being stranded "on a reef in the Gulf of Mexico in 1856," which shows how accounts can vary widely. The ship had been built in 1847-1848 by William H. Brown, New York, for the New York to New Orleans route (New Orleans being called the Crescent City) in the days before the Gold Rush. Alexander Grant was one of the survivors of the *S.S. Crescent City;* later, in September 1857 he was a survivor of the foundering of the treasure-laden *S.S. Central America.* Cedric Ridgely-Nevitt, *American Steamships on the Atlantic,* 1981, p. 124, states she ran aground on Little Bahama Bank on December 7. Her captain was A.G. Gray.

[2] Kemble, p. 92.

[3] Jaggers,, p. 18.

[4] Kemble, p. 238.

[5] Letter to the author, June 22, 1996.

[6] WorldWide Coin Investments (John Hamrick and Bob Harwell) created a great deal of attention in the early 1970s by purchasing such formidable rarities as the 1913 Liberty Head nickel, 1894-S dime, and 1804 silver dollar. The firm was the first professional rare coin dealer to automate its accounts and records by using a computer, in this case one made by Burroughs. Stock in WorldWide was publicly traded (as were the stocks of several other rare coin companies in the 1970s including First Coinvestors and Schulman Coin & Mint).

Bringing the Coins to Market

The writer was among those who handled dozens of pieces obtained from that source. My first purchase was a few dozen coins, all of which were quickly sold save for 18 coins, advertised in *Coin World* in 1973:

> TREASURE GOLD!
> 1856-S Double Eagles
> We have remaining from a rather remarkable purchase, 18 gold coins which were recovered from a sunken treasure ship off the coast of Florida. The group consists of 1856-S double eagles. Each coin is full, sharp Uncirculated grade, with a matte-like surface from immersion in sea water for over 110 years....

Where Were They Found?

Quite possibly, the several hundred 1855-S and 1856-S double eagles with seawater etching are from a ship that went down in the latter year or very early in 1857, possibly carrying an even greater amount of $20 gold coins aboard. As is evidenced by large mintage figures, inventories of found treasure (as, for example, from the *S.S. Central America*), and other reports, the $20 denomination was the coin of choice when transporting quantities of minted gold over long distances. By using the $20 denomination—the largest being struck at the San Francisco Mint—less time and effort were needed to produce the coins and, later, in the handling and counting of them.

United States Sub-Treasury in lower Manhattan. In this facility vast quantities of $20 coins, ingots, and other gold from California were stored.

At the risk of interjecting still another theory in an area (treasure hunting) where theories are a dime a dozen, I suggest that these 1855-S and 1856-S $20 coins were cargo on a steamer or sailing vessel bound out of San Francisco or connecting from Panama, thus accounting for S-mintmarked coins in Uncirculated grade. Possibly the wreck was found somewhere other than off the coast of Florida, but the location was kept secret to avoid enriching attorneys and their clients instead of the treasure salvors.

No related "seawater Uncirculated" 1855-S or 1856-S coins of other gold denominations have been seen, thus suggesting that the $20 pieces may have been part of a bulk treasure cargo. If these had been "passenger gold" (general term for coins carried on board by passengers, and not listed as part of the cargo manifest), they would have been of various denominations, dates, and mintmarks. It was the practice of the San Francisco Mint in the late 1850s to pack $20 gold coins in tight rows in wooden boxes and ship them by sea to Panama, connecting on the Atlantic with other ships going to New York, New Orleans, or elsewhere. Large quantities were also shipped to Liverpool, England.[1]

What is the identity of the ship? Possibilities include vessels headed for Panama (the most likely choice), China, New York (clipper ship) or Liverpool out of San Francisco, or ships connecting at Panama or Nicaragua that might have been lost in the Caribbean Sea or Atlantic Ocean. As vast quantities of these $20 pieces do not seem to have been located, there would either be a large number of other coins remaining to be discovered on the sea bottom, or else the few hundred pieces found were part of some miscellaneous commercial shipment. A likely time for the wreck would have been 1856 (my first choice) or early 1857.

The Matter of the 1854-S $20s

It is the writer's opinion that the 1854-S $20 coins which show very *light* etching by salt water came from a different source than the 1855-S and 1856-S coins, which show considerably heavier etching. In general,

[1] Chapter 11, "Gold from the Briny Deep," discusses San Francisco Mint coin shipments in detail.

the 1854-S $20 pieces are highly lustrous, but the other two dates are sufficiently etched that the mint lustre or frost was removed, although the sharpness of design details was largely preserved. The 1854-S $20 coins are said by some to have been retrieved from the *Yankee Blade* and are the subject of an account in Chapter 11.

The Snagging of the Steamer *Arabia*

Lost: September 5, 1856
Location: Missouri River
Found: 1987
Coins found: Pocket change

Early Career of the *Arabia*

This is not the story of a fabulous cache of rare coins brought up from the bottom of the Missouri or any other river. It is, instead, the tale of a handful of pocket change found on a steamship *buried in a cornfield.* In treasure hunting, just about anything can and has happened! That said, here is the story:

The steamer *Arabia* was constructed in Brownsville, Pennsylvania, in 1853 at the shipyard of John Snyder Pringle.[1] The Pringle yard, located on the Monongahela River not far from Pittsburgh, was well known and highly regarded in its time. Many boats slid down its ways and saw service on the Ohio, Mississippi, Missouri, and other rivers. Measuring 171 feet (or 181 feet, accounts differ) long, the *Arabia* could carry up to 222 tons of freight. Power was by two engines that turned a pair of 28-foot paddlewheels. As was the case with most inland steamers, cordwood was used as fuel, this being readily available at various ports where it was often loaded on to the wide deck. The *Arabia* under full steam could gobble up 30 cords of wood per day.[2]

After her launching, the *Arabia,* sometimes called the *Great White Arabia,* saw service on inland waters including on the Missouri captained by John S. Shaw, of St. Charles, Missouri. Owners included Shaw and Adam Jacobs, a Brownsville investor.

In spring 1856 she was sold to Captain J. William Terrill and George W. Boyd, both from St. Louis. Terrill was likely the notorious, inhuman Captain Terrill who figured in the *Lexington* disaster in 1840 when he ignored aiding that burning ship so he could adhere to his published schedule.[3]

In the Papers in 1856

Under its new ownership in 1856 the *Arabia* was noticed in newspaper accounts several times.

Steamers on a Western river in the mid-nineteenth century, as illustrated on a National Bank Note Company vignette.

---

[1] Investigation of this ship was suggested to the author by Col. William Bain Murray. Information is largely adapted from the masterfully done monograph, *The Treasures of the Steamboat "Arabia,"* David C. Hawley, 1995. Other sources of information included Frederick Way, Jr., *Way's Packet Directory,* 1848-1983 (Ohio University, 1983); Way's information is used on a secondary basis in the present account as it contains a number of obvious inaccuracies (such as giving the sinking date as August 10, 1856). Similarly, William M. Lytle, *Merchant Steam Vessels of the United States 1807-1868,* 1952, gives her sinking date as September 1, 1856.

[2] A cord of wood is a pile measuring two feet deep by four feet high by eight feet wide (although in commercial practice, measurements often varied slightly). Moreover, wood had differing qualities of suitability as fuel. A cord of dried hardwood generated more heat than a cord of pine.

[3] His surname was misspelled in several contemporary 1840 (*Lexington*) and 1856 (*Arabia*) accounts. Variations included Terrel, Terrell, and Terril.

About the 12th of March a plot to transport about 100 Sharps rifles as "carpenter tools" to anti-slavery forces in Kansas was discovered, and a pro-slavery mob charged the ship and successfully demanded possession of the weapons. These were troubled times in Missouri and Kansas, both considered to be "border states" with pro- and anti-slavery sentiments running high, with much violence resulting. During the general period 1854-1859 the territory was known as "Bleeding Kansas."

On March 18 the *Daily Missouri Democrat* reported that the *Arabia* grounded her stern, swung around and hit a rock, lost her rudder, and flooded her cargo hold with two feet of water.

In April it was stated that one of the ship's steam engine cylinder heads had burst, and the *Arabia* had to return to St. Louis for repairs. Fortunately, a dozen or so other trips were completed without incident.

The St. Louis *Republican,* April 1, 1856, carried this advertisement soliciting trade for the ship:

> *Arabia* for St. Joseph
>
> The good and staunch steamer *Arabia,* Captain Terrill on deck and Mr. Boyd in the office, will leave for St. Joseph this morning at 10:00 o'clock. The *Arabia* has excellent accommodation for passengers and the officers are the right sort of men. Go aboard the *Arabia* and be at home.

Snagging

Submerged tree trunks were among the great hazards of the inland river system, and the captain of the *Arabia* had to be constantly on the lookout for them, as did other helmsmen.

The muddy waters of the Missouri and other rivers ceaselessly carved into earthen banks on one side of a bend and deposited sand and soil downstream at another. In the process, the rivers slowly but constantly changed their courses as the sinuous loops of water literally moved through the landscape. Over a period of time, what was river became dry land, and dry land became part of the river bed. In the process, large trees along the banks of the river had soil washed away from their roots and fell into the water. With the top end of the tree oriented downstream, the root structure remained at the point of catching and was usually just slightly under the surface of the water, where it could snag or even impale a passing steamer. "Snagging," as it was called, on submerged trees was a constant danger for shipping. One account told of a tree trunk piercing the bottom of a steamer and tearing apart a passenger cabin. On the Mississippi, several snagboats (as they were called) with hoists did nothing but remove trees from river channels. However, thousands of trees remained undetected or unremoved, and others were constantly falling away from where they had grown on shore.

United States government snagboat, the *U.S.S. Snag,* in action in the nineteenth century. Snags—as tree trunks were called—were the cause of many steamship wrecks.

Snags caused the downfall of many ships, accounting for two fifths of all steamboat accidents on Western rivers in the 1840s.[1] For the several years since 1850, a *partial* list of lost steamers on the Missouri includes the following. Snagging was a prime hazard, but there were other dangers as well:

1850. ***Little Missouri*** (other accounts say 1848) Snagged and sunk at Glasgow, Missouri, at a place later known as Little Missouri Bend.

1850, March 12. ***Rowena.*** Snagged and sunk at Penn's Bend above St. Charles, Missouri.

1851, April 11. ***Anthony Wayne.*** Snagged above Liberty Landing, Missouri. She had a steam whistle that, apparently, was very memorable. Multiple ships bore the *Anthony Wayne* name.

1851. ***St. Anthony.*** Burned near St. Charles.

1852. ***Saint Paul.*** Steamer snagged and lost at Mokane

[1] Louis C. Hunter, *Steamboats on the Western Rivers,* 1949, p. 193, as part of a detailed discussion about snags and the boats built to remove them. For steamers on Western rivers during the period 1811-1851 causes of accidents were as follows (Hunter, p. 272): collision 4.5%, fire 21.0%, explosion 32.0%, and snags and obstructions 42.5%.

Bend on the river (one account gives the year as 1857).

1852, April 9. *Saluda.* About 37 were killed and many more wounded as a boiler explosion ripped the ship.

1853: *Fire Canoe.* Several ships had this name, derived from the Indians' description of a steamer; accounts have one lost in 1853, another in 1858 and further one in 1861.

1853. *Plow Boy* (or 1848, or there may have been two ships). Snagged above Providence, Missouri.

1854, March 10. *Duroc.* Sunk on the *Mississippi River* at Natchez. However, she is included in the present list of *Missouri River* wrecks as she was snagged at St. Charles Bend in the Missouri in 1852, sunk, and later raised and refloated.

1854, August 26. *Timour II.* Her boiler exploded during a stop to get fuel at a wood yard three miles below Jefferson City, Missouri. There were 17 to 19 killed including the pilot, master, and clerk; the safe was thrown through the air by the force of the blast and landed amid passengers on shore who were picking wildflowers; decades later in 1927, during low water, the wreck was exposed in the river).

1855, April 10. *El Paso.* Snagged and sunk at Franklin Island near White's Landing, near Boonville, Missouri.

1855, May 11. *Georgetown.* It was the second time around for this steamer when she sank at Bellefontaine Bluffs with a cargo of U.S. Army supplies. Earlier, on October 12, 1853, she had been snagged and sunk, to be refloated for later service.

1855, August 10. *Ben West.* This 241-ton steamer, built in Brownsville, Pennsylvania, in 1849, struck a bridge and sunk near Washington, Missouri.

1855. *Commerce.* Lost on the Missouri River.

On to Sioux City

On Saturday, August 30, 1856, at 4:00 p.m. the steamer *Arabia* departed St. Louis and headed up the Missouri River for scheduled stops at many points along the way including, per a newspaper advertisement, Kansas, Weston, St. Joseph, Council Bluffs, and Sioux City, the last being a frontier town deep in the interior.

As usual, George W. Boyd was clerk and tended to the receipt of cargo and passengers, while J. William Terrill was at the wheel. By the appointed hour, over 200 tons of freight were aboard. Included, per later accounts, were 400 barrels of premium quality Kentucky bourbon whiskey, obviously a good story. In any event, at least 10 barrels of some sort of whiskey were indeed aboard, consigned to merchant G.W. Brown of Iowa Point. A complete sawmill and its fixtures were on its way to R. Zimmerman & Co. of Browby Landing; a cook stove was destined for the steamer *Ben Bolt* at Linden; a barrel of ale was headed for Hall & Baker of Nebraska City; and two disassembled wooden *houses* were marked for Tracy & Papin of Logan. Beyond that there were hundreds of "packages" and much lumber.[1]

One Fateful Night

A few days later the *Arabia* had progressed many miles up the Missouri River. All was going well—until the night of September 5. In the swirling current, not far above the town of Kansas (later known as Kansas City) at Quindaro Bend, the *Arabia* snagged on the trunk of a tree. The impact ripped open the hull of the steamer, and nearly immediately she and her freight went to the bottom of the muddy water.

This terse notice appeared in the *Kansas City Enterprise,* September 6, 1856:

> The Steamer *Arabia,* bound for Council Bluffs, struck a snag about a mile below Parkville last night and sunk to the boiler deck.—Boat and cargo total loss.

More details were later given by a passenger, Abel. Kirk:[2]

> I had just been married near Peoria, Illinois, and was on my way to Nebraska with my bride. We embarked on the boat in St. Louis and had been on the water about 10 days.[3] The boat was heavily loaded with freight, but did not have a large number of passengers.
>
> One evening when many of the passengers were at supper the boat struck a snag. We felt the shock, and at once the boat started sinking. There was a wild scene on board. The boat went down till the water came over the deck, and the boat keeled over on one side. The chairs and stools were tumbled about and many of the children nearly fell into the water. Several of the men on board seized the life boat and started for the shore, but they came back and the women and children were put in the boat. They called for a small man to go with the boat and I was small and I got aboard.
>
> The river bank at the point where we landed had been carving off and was very steep. I climbed out and pulled the women ashore. Horses and wagons came down from Parkville and took us to the hotel there that night. Many of the trunks and valises were taken off the boat and stacked up in the woods near the river. That night they were broken open by thieves and all the valuables were taken out.[4] We were taken on the steamboat, *James H. Lucas,* and when we went aboard all that could be seen of our boat was the top of the pilot house. That sank out of sight in a short time.

Salvage Efforts

Such disasters were so common that the typical steamer plying the route above St. Louis often had a

[1] According to a list of lost freight published in the *Daily Missouri Democrat* on September 11, 1856.

[2] As quoted in Hawley, 1995, p. 12.

[3] Actually, it was just seven days. Time must have been passing slowly on their honeymoon.

[4] Unfortunately, such depredations of the possessions of unfortunate shipwreck victims seem to have been *standard procedure* in many wrecks—a sad commentary on human nature. For example, see earlier note concerning the trunk of Reverend Dr. Follen washed up from the sinking of the *Lexington* and the later account (Chapter 10) of what local citizens did on a Delaware beach in September 1785 after the wreck of the *Faithful Steward.*

useful life of only a few years. Accidents and sinkings were reported in newspapers along the route, and soon forgotten, especially if there had been no loss of life. There was no feasible way in September 1856 to salvage the sunken hulk or even see it in the silted water. Even if part of a ship remained above the water level, impact by floating objects and the pressure of the current soon pushed a typical wreck into the river depths.

As years passed, the *Arabia* slipped from the memories of most people. However, a few treasure hunters seemed to remember something about hundreds of barrels of that premium Kentucky bourbon which—who knows?—might now be better aged and flavorful than ever! To some, this was a treasure better than gold.

Some years later several enterprising men from St. Joseph loaded a few oak barrels of whiskey aboard a flatboat, went to the point in the Missouri River where the *Arabia* was believed to have gone down in 1856, and hid the barrels along the river bank. A few weeks later, in broad daylight with onlookers nearby, they "discovered the treasure of the *Arabia.*" It is said that the old-but-really-new whiskey was forthwith sold at a premium by local saloonkeepers! Then, as now, romantic stories help sales.

In July 1877 Robert Treadway and a crew of five, financed by wealthy Kansas City tobacco merchants Henry and William Tobener, sought the whiskey of the *Arabia.* Treadway had kept track of the shifting course of the meandering river and thought he knew where the hulk could be found. Luck attended his efforts, and after much digging the derelict steamer was located. Four months later, after finding nothing but some old hats—and not a single drop of whiskey—efforts were abandoned. As time went on, mud and dirt filled the excavation, and the *Arabia* was once again forgotten—almost.

In 1897 a group of men meeting in a tavern in Holt, Missouri, under the leadership of "Dad" Henson, formed the Holt Syndicate to give the *Arabia* whiskey cache another try. After the men spent much effort digging about 16 feet into the earth, water began to fill the large hole they had created. A steel caisson or casing was made to keep the water out, and after much more difficulty and great expense the wooden deck of the *Arabia* was reached. Some exploration resulted in finding some lumber cargo but-again-not a drop of precious whiskey. Another hole was dug, the caisson placed in it, and this time some boots and shoes were found. A third hole produced nothing but sand and pebbles. After months of effort, it was now March 1898, and the Missouri River was rising, raising the water level in the excavation area. The treasure seekers left, resolving to come back when conditions were better. They never did.

The Secret of the Cornfield

The scene moves forward to July 1987, when David Hawley, who had done quite a bit of historical research, used a magnetometer to locate the *Arabia,* now buried 45 feet below the surface and a mile from the river's edge, in the cornfield of the Norman Sortor farm. After the corn was harvested that year and other preparations were made, excavation commenced on November 7. On the 26th one of the ship's paddlewheels was exposed. Then began a recovery that continued to February 11, 1989. Tens of thousands of pounds of equipment, cargo, and artifacts were brought to the surface to be cleaned and carefully preserved for posterity.

On November 13, 1991, the Arabia Steamboat Museum opened its doors to the public at 400 Grand Avenue, Kansas City, Missouri. Showcased there are ship parts, tools, and salvaged cargo, much of it excellently preserved, thus giving visitors a window to the past—a view of what it must have been like to have been aboard the vessel in 1856.

The salvage of the *Arabia* will never loom large in the annals of American numismatic hoards and treasures, for the only coins reported totaled a face value amounting to 26 cents: two dimes, one half dime, and one 1856 copper cent. But, what stories these coins could tell!

Sinking of the *Republic*

Lost: January 24, 1909
Location: Near Nantucket Island
Treasure: Gold coins

In recent years divers have been exploring the waters off the coast of New England in search of sunken ships and their treasures. One object of desire is the 585-foot, 15,378-ton White Star ocean liner *Republic.*

Out of New York City on her way to stops in the Mediterranean Sea including Genoa and Alexandria, this British ship crashed into the 5,018-ton steamer *Florida* on January 23, 1909. In response to one of the earliest radio distress messages in the annals of transatlantic ships, the "C-Q-D" (popularly translated as "Come Quick, Danger") was heard by the White Star liner *Baltic* and by the *Furnessia,* both of which came to the scene and helped offload stricken passengers who had been taken aboard the *Florida.*

The U.S. revenue tugboat *Gresham* took the damaged *Republic* under tow, but lost her in 45 fathoms, ostensibly shallow enough for recovery, but in a region of strong and changing currents With her was lost an estimated $3,000,000 worth of large denomination United States gold coins. The final death toll included two first-class passengers aboard the *Republic* and four crew members of the *Florida.*

Although this wreck is well known and numerous salvage attempts have been made, no success has been reported.[1] One can imagine that if the cargo included a mixed assortment of $10 and $20 gold coins—these being the two highest denominations in use at the time—perhaps 20,000 coins or so would have been involved. How exciting this may be to a future generation of numismatists!

Shoreline view of Sacramento, California, during the nineteenth century.

Other Unrecovered Sunken Treasures

Many Historical Wrecks

The number of shipwrecks worldwide in the past several centuries has amounted to hundreds of thousands, if smaller vessels are included. One estimate places the total at close to a million.[2]

Some years ago, in 1943, Edward Rowe Snow, New England's best-known chronicler of things nautical and interesting, published a list of 1,119 wrecks of larger ships, mostly of the nineteenth and early twentieth centuries, that had wrecked off the coast of just the *southern part* of New England.[3] Well over 7,000 documented wrecks of larger ships are known on the Great Lakes.[4] A listing of wrecks on the Mississippi and tributary river system would also reach into the thousands. Countless additional ships have been wrecked in the Atlantic Ocean off Cape Hatteras, North Carolina. Sometimes a couple dozen or more ships have been lost in a single disaster, as in port fires in Sacramento and St. Louis. The list goes on.

Likely candidates for having United States coins aboard are wrecked ships said to have contained specie, and on ocean voyages that *originated* in the United States, especially after about 1820. All commercial ships on inland waters are additional possibilities.

Specie cargoes before about 1820 are likely to have contained Mexican-American or other non-United States coins. These, of course, are still of importance to the numismatist and are discussed later in this chapter.

Fortunately for shippers of years ago, but unfortunately for numismatic historians, coins carried as ship cargoes were rarely identified as such. As noted in Chapter 6 as part of the description of the Economite Hoard, the Harmonists located at the village of Economy, near Pittsburgh, Pennsylvania, had tens of thousands of dollars' worth of gold coins shipped to them by canal boat from Philadelphia and listed as *machinery* on the manifest. It was popular in the eigh-

---

1 Charles Hocking, *Dictionary of Disasters at Sea During the Age of Steam,* 1969, p.586. Robert Ellis Cahill, *Finding New England's Shipwrecks and Treasures,* Chandler-Smith Publishing House, 1984. pp. 48-49.

2 Coffman, p. 4.

3 *Storms and Shipwrecks of New England,* Yankee Publishing Co., 1943, pp. 348-354 (set in almost microscopic type!). List furnished to Snow by Miss E.E. Freeman of Wellfleet, Massachusetts, who examined the records of the United States Engineers at Newport, Rhode Island.

4 Coffman, pp. 5 and 122, notes that federal records document 7,167 ships lost in the Great Lakes from 1679 through 1951, with over $300,000,000 in cargo lost in each of Lakes Erie, Huron, Michigan, and Superior. In the 20 years from 1878 to 1898 some 5,999 ships were wrecked or lost on the Great Lakes. Another guide places the number at over 10,000.

In the nineteenth century the harbor of Baltimore was one of America's most active ports.

teenth century to designate coins as *hardware* when shipping them from one place to another by stage or ship. Thus, from historical records we will not gain numismatically informative descriptions of what was aboard the thousands of ships that were wrecked in or near American waters.

A Few Words about Terminology

While just about every sunken hulk within the territorial limits of the United States is apt to have at least some pocket change aboard—as did, indeed, the aforementioned *Arabia*—the listings here are for ships believed to have had significant amounts of gold and silver coins aboard, sometimes referred to as "specie" in cargo manifests and, in particular, accounts the accounts of survivors.[1] Ships whose manifests made no mention of specie were sometimes later described in newspaper stories as having had many gold and silver coins aboard.

To the cognoscenti, *specie* refers to minted gold and silver (but not copper or nickel) coins. In popular practice, the term has been used with reckless abandon and is apt to mean just about anything from gold dust to pearl necklaces! In one account some emeralds were referred to as specie!

Also misused in many accounts including nineteenth-century reports of shipwrecks and robberies is the term *gold dust*. The correct definition of gold dust is native (unrefined) gold metal loose in the form of tiny flakes as recovered from a stream or alluvial deposit. In popular usage the term has been expanded to include gold coins, nuggets, and even gold ingots.

Thus, early accounts referring to a ship's treasure of "gold dust" probably include very little if any gold in flake or dust form, but probably refer to minted gold coins and ingots. Accounts referring to "specie" may or may not indicate a cargo of minted silver and gold coins.

This is given as a caveat, as some of the accounts from which the following were taken simply noted that "gold dust" or "specie" was aboard.

Value Estimates and Reality

In virtually all printed accounts of marine treasures, estimates of the value of coins aboard are apt to be

[1] Sources include: Charles Hocking, *Dictionary of Disasters at Sea During the Age of Steam,* 1969. Frederick Way, Jr., *Way's Packet Directory 1848-1983,* 1983. Nigel Pickford, *The Atlas of Ship Wrecks & Treasure, The History, Location, and Treasures of Ships Lost at Sea,* 1994. William M. Lytle, *Merchant Steam Vessels of the United States 1807-1868,* 1952. John Haskell Kemble, *The Panama Route, 1848-1869,* 1943. Cedric Ridgely-Nevitt *American Steamships on the Atlantic,* 1981. Other publications and periodicals.

wild guesses supported by little in the way of facts, especially by information of a useful numismatic nature. Nor, is it usually stated how such estimates were derived. Some estimates (such as for the aforementioned *Republic*) are based upon contemporary statements of how much gold or other cargo was lost. In such instances, today's coin values would be considerably higher.

For example, a common $20 gold coin in a worn grade lost in 1909 on the earlier-mentioned *Republic* would today in the 1990s be worth about 20 times as much, or about $400. Thus, if $3,000,000 in large denomination United States gold coins happened to be aboard, today those coins would be worth at least 20 times as much, or $60,000,000. However, there are many $10 and $20 pieces that have additional value—sometimes exceptional—if they are either rare varieties or in very high grades, or a combination of both.

Also important in any well-reasoned estimate of present-day values of coins sunk on ships is the state of preservation of the coins. As a fictitious example, if a bag of $50 face value in 1909-S V.D.B. Lincoln cents, amounting to 5,000 coins, had been hidden in a bank vault on dry land in 1909 and discovered today, there would be great cause for numismatic excitement. If in gem preservation the coins would be worth more than $1,000 each, making the $50 bag worth $5,000,000 or more. However, if the same bag were lost aboard a ship in the ocean in 1909, and recovered today, the salt water would have acted upon the coins so as to dissolve them nearly completely or, at the very least, to corrode them to the point that their value would be very little—perhaps a few dollars each as souvenirs.

Silver coins do not fare well in salt water either, while gold coins are sometimes quite resistant to such effects. Curiously, if silver coins are immersed in salt water in contact with iron (ship's nails, boiler supports, etc.), the electrolytic action of the salt water will oxidize the iron first and preserve the silver virtually unharmed. However, this fortuitous juxtaposition of iron and silver has occurred with only a few coins on only a few wrecks.

Water in lakes and rivers is kinder to coins, but still a large amount of oxidation will take place on copper and silver coins over a period of time.

Given information as to the face value of coins lost in a wreck a century or more ago, anyone wishing to evaluate the potential treasure today can do no better than make estimates. If a numismatist is involved in such estimates, the figure may have some semblance to reality. Otherwise, the sky's the limit for wild guesses.

Further, the realistic possibilities are narrowed by what a given ship carried as its main cargo. While passenger vessels are likely in most instances to have had money aboard as travelers' belongings, and while some few ships had treasure or other coins aboard as commercial cargo, most ships were used to transmit merchandise or commodities. It is highly unlikely that a wrecked freighter with a cargo of lumber or fertilizer will ever yield anything significant in the way of rare coins. Indeed, most veteran explorers of underwater wrecks have never found much in the way of numismatically valuable specimens, despite inspecting dozens of wrecks over a long period of years. Clive Cussler, who has salvaged several dozen wrecks and who has written extensively on the subject, recently[1] commented that except for the *Atocha* and *S.S. Central America* recoveries, very few undersea efforts have ever yielded a profit to their discoverers.

Unsalvaged Wrecks with Coins Aboard

For every numismatic treasure that has been found, doubtless dozens or even hundreds remain undiscovered. Perhaps some future chronicler will tell of the finding of rare silver and gold coins of the 1820s in sandy dunes of Long Island—the lost treasure of the *Vineyard*. Or, perhaps some diver will find a carpet of $10 gold coins in the sand of Long Island Sound—relics of the *Lexington* tragedy. And, while underwater treasure hunting has yielded relatively little profit for the majority of modern adventurers, hope springs eternal, and the thrill of finding something special remains a powerful attraction. Besides, there is something incredibly romantic about a ***treasure coin***.

Meanwhile, here are some potential sources for interesting coins as gleaned from several thousand treasure and nautical accounts.

1679, September. *Griffon.* In the water off Hessel, Mackinac County, LaSalle's (Robert Cavelier, Sieur de LaSalle) ship *Griffon* may include gold coins intended for use to purchase furs. This ship departed Green Bay, Wisconsin, on September 18, 1679, and was never heard from again, thus creating one of the most tantalizing mysteries in Great Lakes nautical lore.[2] Any coins aboard would of necessity be foreign, perhaps including French provincial intended for Canada, although it is not impossible that some New England silver coins could have been among them as well.

1799. *Defense.* This privateer is said to have sunk off the coast of Stonington, Connecticut, with $500,000 in captured booty, of which some might have been American coins.

---

[1] In his 1996 book, *The Deep Sea Hunter.*

[2] Robert F. Burgess, *Sinkings, Salvages, and Shipwrecks,* 1970, pp. 150-152, among other sources.

The *Royal Tar* in distress in Penobscot Bay off the coast of Maine. The ship had a menagerie of African animals and other beasts aboard, most of which perished. Six horses jumped overboard, three apparently swam to shore, and the others died while swimming in circles around the flaming ship.

Any United States coins which could be recovered today, if in reasonably good condition, would have immense value.

Early nineteenth century. Unknown name. A schooner with a cargo of gold bullion is said to been wrecked in the early 19th century off the point of Little Bay de Noc near Escanaba in Lake Michigan.[1] Possibly this is the same as an unidentified vessel sunk off Poverty Island, Big Bay de Noc, Delta County, Michigan, mentioned in another source.[2]

1820, January 17. *Midas.* Lost off Boston, Massachusetts, incoming from Santo Domingo. A large quantity of specie was supposedly aboard, and if so, this ship certainly had an appropriate name! Whether this was in the form of United States coins is not known, but it seems somewhat unlikely, but you never can tell.

1823, February 8. *Tennessee.* A steamer of 416 tons built in Cincinnati in 1819, the ship departed New Orleans one day with 300 or more festive passengers aboard, who had pulled away from the shore in a party mood, shouting and waving.[3] What fun!

Soon it was nightfall, the sky and river were dark, and at a bend above Natchez the steamer snagged. One passenger grabbed a skiff, rowed slightly away from the stricken steamer, implored a passenger aboard to throw him his saddlebags which were filled with money; this effort in lieu of his working to save others. The engineer of the ship was given the opportunity to board a small yawl and go to safety, but he elected to remain aboard in an effort to run the *Tennessee* onto a sandbar so the passengers could be saved. The ship went down in the swirling current, taking with it the noble engineer, who was in the steam-engine room, and about 30 others.

1827, January 15. *Panthea.* Wrecked on the east side of Holyhead harbor, England, inbound from New York City. Cargo said to have included specie, some of which was salvaged soon after the disaster. One cannot help but wonder if the cargo might have contained United States gold coins. If so, here is an immense treasure even if only a few coins are found. All American gold coins minted prior to 1827 are exceedingly valuable today.

1836, October 15. *Royal Tar.* Of all maritime disaster accounts of this era, the account of the 400-ton steamer *Royal Tar* is one of the most curious.[4] Departing from St. John, New Brunswick, Canada, headed to Portland, Maine, the ship carried Macomber, Welsh & Company's traveling menagerie with its many exotic beasts said to have been personally captured by the owners in the wilds of the African jungle. Traveling with the animals were two separate sideshows or attractions, the Burgess Collection of Reptiles and Dexter's Locomotive Museum. The latter must have been a special novelty, for trains had been a reality in America for less than a decade. As for the reptiles, who knows? Just about every self-respecting reptile sideshow of the nineteenth century had a rattlesnake, for starters.[5]

---

1 Coffman, pp. 123.
2 Thomas Penfield, 1952.
3 Account adapted from Ellms, pp. 345-346; Lytle, and other sources.
4 Adapted from Ellms, 1841, pp. 295-307; the *Royal Tar* is noticed in various subsequent accounts as well.
5 At the risk of straying too far from the subject at hand, I mention that such were usually of the species *Crotalus horridus horridus,* popularly known as the timber rattlesnake. Rattlesnakes of various species were popular coin motifs of the era including on Mexican issues and 1837 Feuchtwanger one-cent tokens.

While crossing Penobscot Bay along the rocky coast of Maine, and within about a mile of Fox Island,[1] the coal-fired boilers of the *Royal Tar* became red hot as the water in them had boiled away! Soon, nearby timbers smoldered, then around two in the afternoon the wood erupted into flames.

Fire on shipboard is one of the greatest terrors of the sea. Panic soon spread among the passengers, and the animals raised a fearful din. All efforts to extinguish the spreading blaze were ineffective, and it was quickly realized that the only hope to preserve life was to abandon ship. Captain Reed was one of the first off the ship in a lifeboat, with three male passengers. In this particular instance—unlike all too many other accounts of sea disasters—his quick departure was altruistic, as will be related.

Remaining passengers quickly learned that two of the other three lifeboats supposed to be aboard had been put ashore at St. John in order to make room for the menagerie animals and their cages. The second and only other lifeboat was filled with 15 people, who rowed to shore. The flames raged through the sails and rigging, the heat intensified by a strong gale. Matters went from bad to worse, then to worse yet. Men, women, and children jumped overboard. Mogul the elephant at first put his fore feet upon the rail, crushing it and plunging into the sea carrying with him several passengers who were clinging nearby.

Meanwhile there was some good news: By rowing back and forth in his lifeboat, Captain Reed succeeded in rescuing many who were swimming or holding on to objects, although he was in continuous fear of being swamped by too many coming aboard at once. To obviate this and to restore order, he commanded that anyone who wanted to be rescued must first grab on to an oar he proffered, and then he or she would be drawn into the small boat.

By this time the *Royal Tar,* a roaring inferno, had drifted about four or five miles off Fox Island. Helpless people were stranded fore, aft, and amidships, but with no way to communicate with each other.

In a curious turn of events, a government revenue cutter that had put out from the nearby port of Castine[2] drew close the stricken *Royal Tar* to assist in the rescue efforts, but seeing Mogul the elephant frantically swimming in the waves, pulled away lest it climb aboard. However, a small boat was launched from the cutter once the apparent elephantine danger had subsided, and some passengers were saved. Mogul eventually drowned.

Relevant to the inclusion of this story in the present book, an old account noted:

"One man, having secured a quantity of silver dollars to his person, lowered himself to the water's edge, with the intention of seizing a spar, but no sooner let go his hold, than, owing to the weight of the silver, he sunk to rise no more.... Men, women, and children were seen taking their last farewell of each other; some lashing boxes to their backs, loaded with dollars, and some casting their property into the sea."

Six of the menagerie horses leaped overboard, three of which swam toward shore, probably successfully, while the remaining steeds circled the ship in confusion and no doubt perished. Lions in their cages were incinerated as was a Bengal tiger that had been raised from a cub, a gnu, a leopard, two dromedary camels, and other beasts, not to overlook the entire display of reptiles, rattlesnakes presumably included.

The flames continued their work, and as night fell the glow from the burning ship lighted up the sky. Finally, around 9:00 the night grew black, and it was supposed that what was left of the hulk slipped beneath the waves. When the toll was counted, of 85 human passengers aboard, 20 men and eight women had perished, and four members of the crew had lost their lives as well.

1837, May 8. *Ben Sherrod.* This 393-ton steamer, built on the Ohio River at New Albany, Indiana, in 1836, departed the levee at New Orleans at about 10 o'clock on Sunday morning, May 6, 1837, under the command of Captain Castleman. Many women and children were among the passengers who disported about the decks and cabins and looked forward to their 10-day springtime trip up the "Father of Waters." The *Ben Sherrod* was what was known as a "Tennessee cotton boat," with cargo of 1,500 to 2,000 bales of cotton piled up and filling nearly all of the lower outside decks. On this particular day there was a full load of cotton, several rigs of horses and carriages, and other commercial goods. The trip was going well, and all were having a good time. Time passed quickly.

A passenger later recalled:

"On Tuesday evening, the 9th of May, 1837, the steamboat *Prairie,* on her way to St. Louis, bore hard upon the *Ben Sherrod*. It was necessary for the latter to stop at Fort Adams, during which the *Prairie* passed her. Great vexation was manifested by some of the passengers, that the *Prairie* should get to Natchez first.

"This subject formed the theme of conversation for two or three hours, the captain assuring them that he would beat her anyhow. The *Prairie* is a very fast boat, and under equal chances could have beaten the *Ben Sherrod*. So, soon as the business was transacted at Fort Adams, for which she stopped, orders were given to the men to keep up their fires to the extent. It was now a little after 11 p.m.

"The captain retired to his berth, with his clothes on, and left the deck in charge of an officer. During the evening a barrel of whiskey had been turned out, and permission given to the hands to do as they pleased. As might be supposed, they drew upon the barrel quite liberally....

"As the *Ben Sherrod* passed on above Fort Adams, towards the mouth of the Homochitta, the wood piled up in front of the furnaces several times caught fire, and was once or twice imperfectly extinguished by the drunken hands.... As the boat was booming along through the water close in shore—for in ascending the river, boats go as close as they can to avoid the current—a Negro on the beach called out to the fireman that the wood was on fire. The reply was, 'Go to hell and mind your own business,' from some intoxicated hand.... As the vessel rounded the bar that makes off from the Homochitta, being compelled to stand out into the middle of the river in consequence, the fire was discovered. It was about one o'clock in the morning."

A passenger saw the flames and tried to grab a bucket to fill with water, but found it was locked in place and unusable. The captain was awakened, by which time the main deck was aflame. The pilot of the ship, high on the hurricane deck, saw

---

1 The Fox Islands group primarily consisting of North Haven and Vinalhaven, about 14 or 15 miles by sea from the port of Castine.

2 Of Castine Hoard fame; see Chapter 1.

the sheets of flame and tried turn the ship toward the shore, but the fire burned through the pulley ropes and the *Ben Sherrod* became helpless in the middle of the Mississippi River in fast current. She spun around a couple of times, then hit a sandbar. The excursionists woke from their dreams to find a fiery hell, perhaps even the same hell that the drunken deck hand had recently told the black man on shore to visit.

Some of the passengers tried to get away in boats, but their craft capsized. Others jumped into the water. Two other steamers came into view, the *Columbus* and the *Statesman,* and saved many. However, the death toll amounted to somewhere between 72 and 200 persons (estimates vary), among whom were Captain Castleman's father and one of the captain's children. The cargo is said to have included a large quantity of gold and silver coins consigned to banks in Tennessee as well as much "passenger gold."[1]

1837, June. ***Aurora,*** a schooner sailing under the American flag, was on the way from Havana to New York City when she sunk in the Atlantic close to shore off North Carolina. The weather was moderate, and with some effort the captain and crew were able to struggle ashore, unharmed. Lost on board was a shipment of gold coins consigned in Havana to Don Francis Stoughton, the Spanish consul in New York City. Richard Sheridan, captain, was later arrested and charged with fraud. Authorities stated that he, in cahoots with two of his crew members, had staged the wreck. The cargo including 264 doubloons valued at $4,000 (for once, the computation seems to be about right; doubloons were worth about $16 each) was secretly taken by the owners from the ship at the time she went down and, later on shore, converted by them into United States coins. Sheridan was ordered to pay restitution amounting to $4,919, including costs, and was clapped into jail.[2]

There are so many coastal shipwrecks off North Carolina it is said that on a calm, sunny day an observer from the air can see dozens of dark hulks littering the sea bottom within a mile of the shore.

1840, July 25. ***North Carolina.*** This steamship of 370 tons was built in 1838 in New York. On the way from Wilmington, North Carolina, to Charleston, South Carolina, she was sunk off Cape Fear after a collision with the *Governor Dudley.* Gold and silver coins belonging to a passenger were lost and are said to have been worth $15,000.[3]

1841, March 11 (departure date). ***President.*** Ship of 1,863 tons belonging to the British & American Steam Navigation Company. Lost with 136 aboard in mid-ocean on the way from New York City to Liverpool, the latter being the leading British port. Specie said to have been worth $30,000 was aboard, belonging to stage actor and comedian Tyrone Power, ancestor of the film actor of the same name. A message from Power, "President sinking fast," was found in a bottle many weeks later, this being the only message known from the missing ship. Her captain, Richard Roberts, had expressed the sentiment that the vessel was jinxed and had presciently called her "the coffin ship" before departure. Following the loss of the *President,* the company that owned it went into bankruptcy.

One cannot help but wonder if in the North Atlantic Ocean in March the *President* might have encountered an iceberg, an early-day counterpart to the *Titanic* disaster over 70 years later.

1841, February 22. ***Creole.*** Steamer of 192 tons built in Pittsburgh in 1839. Burned on the Mississippi River at Torras, Louisiana, on the way from New Orleans to Natchez, with the loss of 34 lives, $100,000 in coins, and many bales of cotton.[4]

1841, August 9. ***Erie.*** Built in Erie, Pennsylvania, in 1837, she was a steamer of 497 tons, first berthed at Presque Isle. The ship burned in Lake Erie off Silver Creek, New York, 30 to 35 miles from Buffalo, on a voyage from that port to Chicago. The loss of an estimated 242 lives marks this as one of the most tragic nautical disasters ever associated with the Great Lakes.

Gold and silver coins said to have been worth about $200,000 were salvaged in 1856 (another account says $2,000 in 1854) when the wreck was raised, but there may be more specie on the lake bottom. When the derelict hull was being towed it sank in 11 fathoms of water about four miles from shore, possibly containing some treasure. One estimate published in 1957 suggested that the original treasure was worth $100,000, and some remains unsalvaged. In 1960 a group of divers found an estimated $1,200 worth of English sovereigns, kroner, and rubles.[5]

1843, July 1. ***Columbia.*** British ship of the Cunard Line, 1,138 tons, one of four vessels (the others: *Acadia, Britannia*[6] and *Caledonia*) on hand when the line was started by Samuel Cunard in 1840. She was wrecked in strong currents and heavy fog in the Bay of Fundy, off Devil's Limb Rock, about a mile from the coast of Cape Sable Island, Nova Scotia, Canada, without loss of life. The ship had departed from Boston and was on the way to Nova Scotia. A considerable value in specie was said to have been aboard, much of which was salvaged along with luggage and cargo shortly after the disaster. However, some may remain in the derelict hull.

1846, June 11. ***Lexington.*** Sunk in Lake Erie off Point Mouille, near Ashtabula, Ohio, with $300,000 in gold aboard.[7]

1850. ***Anthony Wayne.*** Sunk in Lake Erie near Buffalo, New York, with $60,000 in gold aboard.[8]

---

[1] Ellms, 1841, pp. 343-354 (includes passenger recollection); Lytle, pp. 18 and 219; other sources.

[2] David Stick, *Graveyard of the Atlantic,* 1951, pp. 22-23.

[3] David Stick, *Graveyard of the Atlantic,* 1951, pp. 42-44, source of $15,000. Lytle, pp. 77, 140 and 221; other sources. The *Governor Dudley,* built in New York in 1838, survived the impact; about 17 years later she was renamed the *Catawba.*

[4] Lytle, pp. 42, 222; Nina and William Anderson, *Southern Treasures,* 1987, p. 142.

[5] Coffman, p. 125; Burgess, p. 152, stated that original records are "reputed" to have placed the treasure at $100,000, further noting that the passengers were mainly German and Norwegian immigrants. Probably, no accounting was ever made of the passengers' money. Burgess also furnished information about the 1960 recovery.

[6] An Atlantic voyage of the *Britannia* is noted in Chapter 11 under the account of the *S.S. Central America.*

[7] Coffman, p. 127; also Penfield, 1952. Lytle lists seven steamers named *Lexington,* but not this one.

[8] Coffman, p. 127. Lytle, pp. 10, 220, 235, gives conflicting information, listing the ship as 390 tons, made in Perrysburg, Ohio, in 1837, and wrecked at Vermilion, Ohio, on April 28, 1850, with a loss of 22 lives; also listed as 400 tons, built in Trenton, Michigan, 1849, and also lost at the

1850, March 4. ***Orline St. John.*** This steamer of 349 tons, built in Louisville in 1847, was wrecked in the Alabama River at Bridgeport, about four miles south of Montgomery, Alabama, with 41 lives lost. Colonel Rodman was aboard and is said to have been in charge of about $250,000 worth of "gold dust." Salvage efforts took place shortly thereafter, and it is not known what might have been recovered or missed.[1]

1851, June. ***Salle Fearn.*** En route from New Orleans to Liverpool, she caught fire and was lost about 36° 40' N 70° 45' W. The cargo of cotton and about $120,000 worth of gold was partially salvaged soon thereafter. One might speculate that many New Orleans Mint gold coins could have been aboard.

1852, August 19-20. ***Atlantic.*** Sidewheel steamer of 1,155 tons, built in Newport, Michigan, in 1849. Collided with the *Ogdensburg* in Lake Erie about six miles east of Long Point Island, Ontario, on the well-traveled route from Buffalo to Detroit.[2] The wreck took a toll of about 150 lives. Gold, silver, and various artifacts were recovered in recent years by the Mar Dive Corporation, Los Angeles, and are said to have been worth over $200,000,000, although no numismatic confirmation of such a large figure has been seen by the author.

1854, September 17. ***Arctic.*** Launched on January 28, 1850, this large and well-appointed steamship was built by William H. Brown for the New York & Liverpool U.S. Mail Steamship Company, familiarly known as the Collins Line. On September 27, 1854, in heavy seas about 50 miles off of Cape Race, she was rammed by the *Vesta,* a small French steamer. Those aboard the *Arctic* little thought they had cause to worry and even launched a lifeboat to assist the *Vesta.* Soon thereafter, despite assurances of the captain and crew that there was no problem, it was learned that the *Arctic* was taking on water and was in serious danger. Nonchalance changed to tragedy as lifeboats became swamped in the high waves. Three-hundred twenty-two people lost their lives. Meanwhile, the *Vesta* limped into port in Newfoundland under its own power. Echoes of this disaster resounded for many years thereafter, and until the *Titanic* went down over a half century later, this was the best-known of all passenger shipwrecks.

In his *American Numismatical Manual,* 1859, pp. 76-78, Dr. Montroville W. Dickeson discusses a prime rarity, the 1733 Rosa Americana pattern twopence, noting he knew of the existence of only four, now only three, specimens: "The fourth was purchased in England for the sum of £7, or $35, for Charles Bushnell, Esq., of New York City, unfortunately placed on board the steamer *Arctic,* to be transmitted to him, on her last and fatal voyage, and its pigmy proportions are now added to the vast accumulations that lie imbedded in the sands of the Atlantic Ocean." Also lost with the ship was Jacob G. Morris, one of America's best-known numismaitsts, who lived in Philadelphia. Thus, while the *Arctic* may not have had a cargo of treasure aboard, the loss is significant in the annals of numismatics.

1854, September 30. ***Eliza Thornton.*** Lost at Pedro Branco off the coast of China, approximately 22° 50' N, 115° 20' E, this American brig was on the way from San Francisco to Hong Kong and is said to have carried quite a bit of gold (although silver seems more likely, as the Chinese preferred this metal). Some passengers laden with coins jumped into the water to save their lives and their treasure, but lost both.

1856, October 29. ***Superior.*** This 567-ton steamer was built in Perrysburg, Ohio, in 1845. She is said to have had a goodly amount of specie aboard when she was stranded off Grand Island on the way from Niagara, New York, to Lake Michigan. Thirty-four lives are were lost.

1858, May 7. ***Ostervald.*** Wrecked in the Caribbean Sea about 50 miles off the coast of present-day Belize, this ship was on the way from New Orleans to Liverpool with $45,000 or so worth of specie aboard, much of which was salvaged shortly thereafter.

1858, October 15. ***Water Witch.*** Lost off St. Thomas Island in the Virgin Islands on the way from St. Thomas to Maracaibo, this vessel had specie aboard, but whether this included United States coins is not known. Put this in the "maybe so, maybe so, but probably no" category. *Water Witch* was a popular ship name and it recurs throughout nautical history.

1859, November 14. ***Heidelberg.*** Lost off the coast of Florida on the way from New Orleans to LeHavre, France, the ship contained specie, some of which was recovered at the time. Ships departing with specie from New Orleans in the 1850s are prime candidates for having had New Orleans Mint coins aboard.

1860, November 10. ***Dakatah.*** Sunk in Lake Erie near Long Point, Ontario, with $60,000 in gold aboard.[3]

1862, July 12. ***Phantom.*** This American clipper ship was on the way from San Francisco to Hong Kong when she was wrecked at North Dongsha Qundao, China. Her treasure, said to have been worth slightly over $50,000, was largely salvaged at the time, but, perhaps not all was recovered.

Clipper ships under full sail and in a good wind could handily outdistance steamers. These ships had their glory days in the 1850s and 1860s.

1862, November. ***Black Hawk.*** This brig, laden with a cargo including stained glass and specie, was lost in Lake Michigan about four miles north of Frankfort, Michigan. The stained glass would have little value today, as the state of the art in that field progressed rapidly after 1862, but the coins, total value at the time unknown, might just include some interesting United States pieces.

---

same place and date. Such confusion is in part the result of multiple ships having this popular name. There were various formulas for computing tonnage (the weight of water displaced) by using various measurements of length, breadth, and depth, and the same ship often appeared with different weights in different accounts.

[1] Not to be confused with the *Orline St. John,* a bark built in 1848 and owned by William Bradstreet of Gardner, Massachusetts. That ship went down off Cape Hatteras on February 21, 1854, under circumstances that would prove very distressful to the survivors, who had to practice cannibalism (cf. David Stick, *Graveyard of the Atlantic,* 1951, pp. 48-49).

[2] The 352-ton *Ogdensburg,* built in 1852, survived the *Atlantic* collision, but was star crossed and met her end in another collision, with the schooner *Snow Bird,* on September 30, 1864.

[3] Coffman, p. 126. Also spelled as *Dakotah* and *Dacotah.*

1863, August. ***Georges Sand.*** This ship, named after the pseudonym used by a famous female writer,[1] was on her way from San Francisco to Hong Kong, when she was wrecked on a reef off Dongsha Qundao, China. Rumors of a great value in gold coins aboard circulated, some estimates crossing the $1 million mark, but the actual worth was probably considerably less than that.

1865, August 9 (or 12). ***Pewabic.*** Built in 1863 in Cleveland, Ohio, this 738-ton steamer under Captain George P. McKay (of Toledo, Ohio) was wrecked in Lake Huron about two miles off Thunder Bay Island, Michigan, when she collided with the *Meteor.*[2] About 180 passengers were aboard plus her crew, of which about 125 are believed to have died She was said to have had a cargo of copper metal in her hold and $50,000 in gold coins in a strongbox in the captain's cabin. One account places the value at $200,000.[3]

It is somewhat incongruous for a copper ship to have had a significant value in gold coins as cargo, but stranger things have happened. The copper part of the cargo was salvaged in 1917 as was the strongbox. The latter proved to contain a mass of decomposed paper currency notes, a solitary gold dollar, and a couple of rings. Perhaps some "passenger gold" remains today in the wreck.

In 1990, Daniel Frank Sedwick marketed souvenirs, not numismatic, described as follows:[4] "From the steamer *Pewabic,* sunk 1865, in Lake Huron, Michigan. A piece of Michigan native copper mounted on a 6" section of a wooden stave of the actual barrel in which the copper was packed. The two pieces form a plaque, with an account of the wreck appended."

1865, November. ***Westmoreland.*** Sunk in Lake Michigan north of North Manitou Island with $100,000 in gold aboard.[5]

1868, September 15. ***Parkersburg.*** This ship, with much specie aboard, was lost in the Bay of Fonseca, Honduras, while on the way from Panama. Much was salvaged shortly thereafter.

1868, December 21. ***Estrella.*** In a situation similar to the wreck of the *Water Witch* described above, this steamer had departed St. Thomas in the Virgin Islands, and in the present instance was headed to Curaçao in the Netherlands Antilles off the coast of Venezuela. Her cargo evidently included specie, some of which was salvaged shortly thereafter.

1870, February 22. ***Golden City.*** Steamer of 3,374 tons built by William H. Webb, New York City, and launched on June 24, 1863. On the night of February 21, 1870, on the run from San Francisco to Panama, she encountered heavy fog. After 6:00 the next morning the ship, still in zero visibility conditions, ran on a sandbar with great force, about 10 miles north of Point Lazaro (a.k.a. Cape San Lazaro) at Magdalena Bay, about 225 miles north of the tip of Baja California.

Her 400 or so passengers and the crew went ashore and remained there until February 25 when the *Colorado,* on her way north, was seen, but was not able to take the stranded people aboard at that point on the coast. After much difficulty during which the castaways had to walk to a landing point about 25 miles away, and some became lost, everyone eventually reached safety and at least some of the treasure was recovered.[6] However, one account says she burned and $300,000 in treasure was lost.[7]

1871, February 9. ***Crescent City.*** This 2,039-ton vessel owned by the Liverpool & Mississippi Steamship Company was on the way from New Orleans to Liverpool when she was wrecked near Galley Head, Ireland. Her cargo was said to have included 40 boxes of gold and/or silver coins valued at over $100,000, of which some 20 boxes were salvaged shortly thereafter.

1871, February 12. ***Republic.*** Traveling from Port-au-Prince, Haiti, to Cape Lookout, North Carolina, this ship was said to have had a large amount of specie aboard when she was wrecked 60 miles offshore shortly before reaching her destination.

1871. ***Yangtze.*** On the way from New York City to Fuzhou, China, this elegant clipper ship was wrecked at the Paracel Islands. Her cargo is said to have included specie, presumably intended for the purchase of tea.

1871, October 17. ***R.G. Coburn.*** Sunk in Lake Huron off Harbor Beach with $105,000 in gold aboard.[8]

1872, August 24. ***America.*** This large, 4,560-ton sidewheel steamer owned by the Pacific Mail Line was en route from California to Yokohama, Japan, and was burned in the destination harbor, perhaps due to an incendiary, but this was never proved. On board were several hundred Chinese, primarily returning from California. Most passengers were taken off safely, but 60 to 70 perished. The latter are said to have been lost because they refused to leave the burning ship without taking their heavy wooden boxes filled with coins with them.

The ship was afire for all of the following day and was a hazard to navigation, despite attempts of the Italian corvette *Vettor Pisani* to sink her with howitzer fire. Gold and Mexican coins variously said to be worth from about $400,000[9]

---

[1] George (Georges in French) Sand = the French novelist and playwright Amandine Aurore Lucie Dupin, the Baroness Dudevant (1804-1876), remembered by the literati for her novels including *Lélia* (1833) and *Consuelo* (1842). Interestingly, of the dozens of detailed listings of ships the present author has reviewed, virtually none give the iconography of ship names, although they reflect a rich cross-section of American and European history, geography, biography, literature, and the arts, among other subjects.

[2] The *Meteor* was a steamer of 417 tons built in Louisville, Kentucky, in 1857 (cf. Lytle; if this is the same ship). Coffman, p. 124-125, described salvage attempts.

[3] Thomas Penfield, *Wild Bill Hickok Guide to Lost Treasures,* Rand McNally, 1952.

[4] Daniel Frank Sedwick, letter, October 3, 1996, enclosing description.

[5] Coffman, p. 126; also Thomas Penfield, 1952.

[6] Heyl, 1953, pp. 185-186.

[7] Coffman, p. 263.

[8] Coffman, p. 126. However, one must be very cautious of accounts of specie lost in Eastern and Midwestern domestic commerce during the general period from 1862 to 1876, as gold and silver coins were not being paid out by the Treasury Department, and none were in general circulation. However, such coins did circulated in the West at that time.

[9] Hocking, p. 28, drawing upon Lloyd's insurance information, suggests 400,000 Mexican silver dollars.

to $1,600,000 were aboard, although it seems that there was probably a lot of "passenger silver" (the Chinese preferred this metal) that was not accounted for, among which were likely San Francisco Mint half dollars. At least some of these coins were said to have been stored in an iron-lined compartment with wooden braces extending through the corners. The heat was so intense that much liquid metal ran through the brace holes. About $300,000 worth of metal was salvaged.[1] Whether any coins escaped being melted is not known.

1872, December 5. *Sacramento.* Steamer of 2,682 tons built by William H. Webb, New York, in 1864. On the night of December 5, 1872, she was running about 10 miles offshore near Port Antonio, Baja California, and hit an uncharted reef. The *Montana* took off many passengers on December 11, but the captain and 20 crewmen stayed aboard to guard the cargo. There was no loss of life. Gold valued at up to $2,000,000 may have been aboard.[2]

1873, September 21. *City of Detroit.* Steamer of 682 tons built in Marine City, Michigan, in 1866. She was lost in Lake Erie two miles north of Port Barcelona, New York, with $100,000 in gold aboard.[3] Another account mentions the ship as being sunk in Saginaw Bay near the treasure-laden schooner *Fay.*[4]

1874, December 17-18. *Japan.* This 4,351-ton American sidewheel steamer, under the flag of the Pacific Mail Steamship Co., was on the way from San Francisco to Hong Kong when she was burned at approximately 22° 50' N, 113° 42' E. Her cargo is said to have included $365,000 in specie plus additional gold, of which over $180,000 was recovered by 1878.

1877, February 6. *Bavaria.* British steamer of 2,300 tons sailing under the flag of the Dominion Line. Burned at about 31° 14' N, 78° 42' W, while traveling from New Orleans to Liverpool. Specie valued at about $260,000 was aboard and is said to have been at least partially stolen by the crew at the time of the wreck, possibly as the conclusion to a dastardly plot hatched beforehand, a scenario that happened now and then (as with the *Vineyard,* the account of which is related in Chapter 10).

1889, November 20. *Manhattan.* En route from New York to West Point, Virginia, this 1,585-ton steamer collided with the four-masted schooner *Agnes Manning,* who was on her way from Baltimore to New York. In recent times the ship's safe was raised and found to contain a "treasure" consisting of Norfolk (Virginia) Transit System tickets and 99 coins, not numismatically described, with a face value of $8.04.[5]

1892, January 31. *Eider.* Lost near Atherfield, Isle of Wight, England, on the way from New York City to Bremen, Germany. Specie said to have been valued at about $500,000, perhaps mostly salvaged shortly thereafter.

1893, October 11. *Dean Richmond.* Owned by the Western Transportation Company, this 1,257-ton steamer, built in Cleveland, Ohio, in 1864, was wrecked about a mile off Van Buren Point in Lake Erie near Dunkirk, New York, en route from Toledo to Buffalo. The cargo included gold valued at $141,000 and additional treasure in the form of silver coins.[6] Not far away on the lake bottom is said to be the *City of Detroit.*[7]

1897, March 8. *Ville de St. Nazaire.* Under Captain Jaqueneau, this 2,640-ton French ship operated by the Compagnie Générale Transatlantique departed New York City with nine passengers and 74 crew members and headed toward the West Indies. On the first day out she sprung a leak. Upon due consideration the breach was not deemed sufficiently serious to warrant returning to port. On the next day the leak worsened, and on the following day the ship ran into an unexpected hurricane in that treacherous area known as the "Graveyard of the Atlantic" off Cape Hatteras, North Carolina. As her compartments filled with sea water, the captain ordered the ship to be abandoned, and all took to the lifeboats. While many were later rescued, 34 died from exposure. The cargo is said to have included gold.

1898, November 27. *Portland.* Operated by the Portland Steam Packet Company, this 2,284-ton wooden sidewheel paddle-steamer under Captain H.H. Blanchard left the India Wharf at Boston, bound for Portland, Maine, on the evening of the 26th. The weather was uncertain, and for a time Blanchard considered postponing the voyage, but decided to adhere to the scheduled 7 p.m. departure. Meeting schedules was all-important to the image of any passenger line. At sea the weather proved to be much rougher than anticipated, and heavy waves from an especially fierce gale damaged her superstructure. At the same time there was much destruction from waves smashing the New England coast. It was truly a forbidding night to be out in the open sea.

Around 9:00 the next morning, Captain O.S. Fisher of the Cape Cod Life Saving Station saw a large paddlewheel steamer of unknown name, but possibly the *Portland,* offshore, and heard four blasts from the ship's siren. The weather closed in, visibility decreased to near zero, and the ship was not seen again.

By midnight of the same day, cabin furniture, personal effects, and many bodies had washed ashore on Cape Cod, giving mute testimony that a disaster had occurred at sea, but not a single soul lived to tell what had happened and no messages or other clues were ever found. It was supposed that the *Portland* broke up around 9:00 that evening about 10 to 15 miles north of the cape. Her cargo valued at several hundred thousand dollars or more is said to have included jewelry and specie.[8]

---

1 Per an account in the *New York Herald,* November 2, 1872.

2 Heyl, 1953, p. 373; Coffman, p. 70 (source of $2 million figure).

3 Coffman, p. 126. Lytle, pp. 33, 275, there as fate unknown.

4 Thomas Penfield, 1952 (who, separately, places the *City of Detroit* as being near the *Dean Richmond;* see latter entry).

5 Gary Gentile, *Shipwrecks of Delaware and Maryland,* 1990, pp. 104-107. Mentioned here as coins were recovered. No significant treasure was known to be aboard. However, as the ship went down within 15 minutes after the collision, there may be some coins belonging to the crew still to be recovered.

6 Coffman, p. 126, gives the sinking date as August 19, 1893. Lytle, pp. 46 (as 1,083 tons), 268 (different date of loss, given as burnt on October 29, 1871.

7 Thomas Penfield, 1952.

8 Coffman, p. 183, values the cargo at $3,000,000; on p. 247 of the same book it is valued at $200,000.

Nineteenth century. ***Templeton,*** a steamer said to have been laden with treasure, was sunk off South Manitou Island, Leelanau County, Michigan.[1]

1901, February 22. ***City of Rio de Janeiro.*** This American passenger steamship had left Yokohama on February 2, 1901, crossed the Pacific without incident, and by the wee small hours of February 22 was within San Francisco Bay, tantalizingly close to her intended destination dock.[2] She was about 2,000 feet off Fort Point, just a few miles from the amenities of the City at the Golden Gate, when she ran into pea-soup fog. Visibility was absolutely zero.

What to do? Captain William Ward had been warned of the dangers of proceeding, even slowly, in such conditions, but in his eagerness to reach port he disregarded such advice. Just past 4:30 in the morning the ship struck rocks. With a hole below her waterline she continued under steam for nearly 20 minutes before sinking. Down to the bottom of San Francisco Bay plunged a fortune in coins and cash, of which over $2 million is said to have been recovered. The death toll included Captain Ward and 103 to 128 others (estimates vary). Only 81 people survived. So near, yet so far.

1909, December 8. ***Clarion.*** Built in 1881, this 1,712-ton ship was operated by the Erie & Western Transport Company of Canada. She caught fire and was lost off Point Pelee, Lake Erie, Ontario. Her cargo included specie.

1911. ***R.J. Cochrane.*** Sunk off Angel Island in San Francisco Bay with a cargo of $96,000 in gold.[3]

1911, May 12. ***Merida.*** This passenger ship on a run from Havana to New York City was rammed by the ***Admiral Farragut*** in the Atlantic Ocean off the Virginia Capes, and sunk. She was said to have been carrying much treasure from Mexico, but several visits to the site by diving crews have yielded nothing in this regard.

1917, February 25. ***Laconia.*** This Cunard Line steamer of 18,099 tons, Captain Irvine at the helm, was torpedoed by a German submarine about 160 miles WNW of Fastnet, Ireland, while on the way from the United States to England. The hit occurred just after 9 p.m. on the ship's starboard side near the engine room. Damage was done, but the attack was not fatal. Twenty minutes later another torpedo slammed into the engine room on the same side and spelled the ship's doom. She sank in the darkness about 10:20 p.m. Of the 292 people aboard, 12 were killed. She was said to have had 132 boxes of specie aboard, amounting to over a million ounces of silver. The ship was located by salvors shortly thereafter, but no report was given of any recovery of the coins.

1917, March 21. ***Healdton.*** This 4,489-ton American tanker was torpedoed by a German submarine in the North Sea off the Netherlands. Some rumors had it that $3 million in gold was aboard.

1918, June 25. ***Atlantian.*** On her way from Galveston, Texas, to Liverpool, she was lost about 110 miles WNW of Eagle Island, Ireland. Her cargo is believed to have included gold and silver.

1931, September 11. ***Columbia.*** This steamship sunk off of Port Tasco, Mexico, with about $800,000 in coins aboard. Shortly thereafter the Merritt, Chapman & Scott Salvage Corporation retrieved about $705,000 worth, and Lieutenant Harry E. Rieseberg, a California treasure hunter of renown, found more about two decades later, but the rest may still be there.[4]

---

[1] Thomas Penfield, 1952.

[2] Sources include Jim Gibbs, *Disaster Log of Ships: A Pictorial Account of Shipwrecks, California to Alaska,* 1971: pp. 12 and 40; Hocking, p. 147. As she was inbound to the United States from Japan, presumably relatively little of the specie aboard was in the form of United States coins.

[3] Coffman, p. 260.

[4] Coffman, pp. 118-119. Merritt, Chapman & Scott also investigated the wreck of the ***DeBraak*** (see later entry) in 1932.

A selection of Spanish-American silver coins showing milled coinage plus (as No. 2) a cob-type piece. Such coins were widely used in the United States. (From A.M. Smith, 1881)

CHAPTER 10

Spanish-American Coins and Pirate Treasures

Introduction

Most of the hoards and finds discussed so far have been found here and there as a matter of chance and have involved coins minted in the United States. Even the preceding nautical accounts have emphasized American coins. Finds have been mostly by happenstance.

In contrast, a veritable industry has arisen in recent decades, formed of treasure seekers employing sophisticated equipment and selecting sites based upon careful study and historical research. In no area of undersea treasure has this been more successful than with the search for Mexican, Central American, and South American silver and gold coins from sunken Spanish galleons.

Dozens of firms and partnerships and hundreds of people have engaged in well-organized searches. Many other people have played a part by sitting on the sidelines and writing checks to buy stock or other investment shares. Readers of *National Geographic Magazine,* viewers of Public Broadcasting System television shows, and visitors to bookstores have enjoyed many thrilling accounts. Treasure finding is an ever-popular subject for readers and viewers.

Many explorers and some investors in such ventures have had their dreams come true. Mel Fisher and his *Atocha* treasure, mentioned by Kenneth E. Bressett in the Foreword to this book, is perhaps the most highly publicized success story, but there are numerous others. In Florida several museums have opened to showcase such finds. While some United States coins have been found here and there, by far the greatest emphasis of searchers off the Florida coasts has been Spanish-American coinage. Such form the subject of this chapter.

The Author's Interest

My own interest in hoards and treasures came about in a related way. In 1961 while on an automobile trip to Florida, I decided to take the Overseas Highway south of Miami, ending at Key West. Along the way at Plantation Key I saw a sign advertising the Museum of Sunken Treasure, about which I knew nothing. Curious, I stopped to see what it contained. After about a half hour of conversation with the proprietor, Art McKee, I became fascinated with the idea that millions of dollars' worth of Spanish gold and silver coins were buried in the sandy sea bottom off the coast of Florida, just waiting to be discovered. In fact, Art McKee had discovered more than a few of them (from the sunken fleet of 1733) and had silver and gold pieces on exhibit in his museum.

Ever eager to do more searching, but well aware of the tremendous costs involved, McKee asked me if I wanted to be an investor in his next expedition. Having much enthusiasm, but not a great amount of discretionary income at the time, I declined, perhaps unwisely.

A few years later I was visiting Amon G. Carter, Jr., in his office in the Fort Worth (Texas) *Star-Telegram* building. Amon's office was filled with all sorts of interesting memorabilia including dozens of shovels that he and his father had used in various ground-breaking ceremonies, and souvenirs of American Airlines (which his father had co-founded and of which Amon, Jr., was a director). A door in his office led to a built-in vault where he kept his 1884 and 1885 trade dollars, 1804 silver dollar, and other rarities plus some small hoards of favorite United States, Canadian, and Mexican scarce issues (the 1925 Canadian nickel five-cent piece being an example).

Amon, Sr., had begun his interest in numismatics when, at a Rotary Club meeting in Fort Worth in the 1930s, local dealer B. Max Mehl had given him as a gift an 1879 $2.50 gold piece, 1879 being the year of Carter's birth. His imagination piqued, Carter asked what other 1879-dated coins existed, and soon thereafter purchased a rare $4 gold coin of that year. He went on to become Mehl's single most important customer. After his death his collection passed to his son, Amon, Jr., who added to it in several different areas.

Beginning when I was a youngster in the coin business, Amon G. Carter, Jr., was very nice to me. During a convention in the 1950s he brought over his prized 1804 silver dollar and suggested that I put it in my display of coins for sale. He did not want to part with it, but felt it would attract attention and provide some good publicity for the other things I was offering. I replied that I did not have enough insurance to cover this valuable rarity, whereupon he said that if it were stolen, that would be his problem, not mine (and said that he did not have any insurance on it either). The coin, indeed, did attract a lot of attention.

Anyway, during one particular visit to Amon Carter's office in Fort Worth I was poking around his coin vault when I heard him receive a telephone call. The name "McKee" drifted through the air, and I listened more attentively. The conversation was about treasure hunting! When he hung up the phone I mentioned my earlier visit with McKee. Amon said something to the effect that he did not know McKee from Adam, but McKee had heard that Carter had a lot of money, was interested in coins, and might be a good backer for an expedition. "What the hell," said Carter. "I've invested in just about everything else in my life, why not try a treasure hunt!" Whether or not Carter and McKee ever collaborated I do not know. If so, I hope that both did well.

My earlier meeting with McKee in 1961 prompted me to do several things: to begin acquiring books on the subject of shipwrecks and sunken treasures, to learn more via numismatic references about Spanish-American gold and silver coins, and to be aware of new discoveries of treasures as they reached the popular periodicals as well as the hobby press. As it turned out, the 1960 decade brought many exciting finds to light, primarily by Kip Wagner who carried out explorations off the east coast of Florida. Wagner's 1966 book, *Pieces of Eight*, was well received, widely circulated, and did much to stimulate interest in treasure hunting.

In further connection with the present book it would not be remiss to again recall that I had a number of enjoyable visits over the years with the late Edwin A. Link, pioneer in submersible undersea exploration devices, who has been well chronicled in literature on diving and, to a lesser extent, treasure exploration in Florida. As noted in Chapter 2, my connection with Ed Link was not with treasure hunting, but because of his association with coin-operated automatic musical instruments. Edwin took over from his father the Link Piano & Organ Company, Binghamton, New York, which was well esteemed and highly successful in its time, flourishing in the 1920s.[1] "If dollars are hard to get, go after profitable nickels," Link once advertised.

Ed Link had a handful of Spanish-American coins from treasure wrecks, but I do not recall him saying that he had found them himself. A very likable person, Ed might have received them from another diver. He did offer me for $1,500 a cannon he had pulled up from a Florida wreck, but I did not buy it, again perhaps unwisely missing an opportunity to get further involved in such treasures in what turned out to be the very formative decade of the 1960s.

The unforgiving sea claims ships and treasures, and it claims lives, too. Ed Link lost a beloved son who was trapped in the dark depths in a diving device,[2] and treasure hunter Mel Fisher suffered a similar irreplaceable loss when a ship used by his recovery crew foundered.

In the years since my visit with Art McKee in 1961 I have had the opportunity to buy, sell, and offer at auction or private sale quite a few Spanish-American treasure coins including showcasing at auction many pieces brought up off the coast of Florida by Capt. Thomas Gurr, the Real Eight Company, and other salvors. All of this has been quite enjoyable.

A "Bit" of Coinage History

Coinage produced in the American colonies or struck elsewhere with inscriptions relating to what is now the United States of America began with the silver New England, Pine Tree, and other issues of Massachusetts made from 1652 through 1682, and continued with pieces related to Virginia (1773), copper coins of the states (1785-1788 coinage of Connecticut, Massachusetts, New Jersey, New York, and Vermont), and other such coins. The mintages continued with federal issues and private gold coins. Notwithstanding this seeming deluge of minted discs, most

[1] A curious footnote in American business history is that the International Time Recorder Co., which later became known as the International Business Machines Corporation, had its beginning in Binghamton, New York, in a building earlier used by the Link Piano Co.

[2] This was a tense touch-and-go situation, the proceedings of which were carried live on national broadcast media.

commerce in the United States in the early nineteenth century and earlier times was done via Spanish-American silver coins made in Mexico City, Lima, Potosi, and elsewhere south of the Rio Grande. These silver issues were popularly known as "bits" and "dollars," although neither term was official.

Even the Eastern Seaboard colonies, under English domination in the mid-eighteenth century, used more Spanish-American coins than they did pieces minted in "mother" England! Recall the commentary (by Michael Hodder) in the preceding chapter, where he noted that coins brought up from the *British* ship *Feversham* consisted mostly of *Spanish* colonial pieces.

Many such Spanish-American coins were legal tender in the United States until the implementation of the Act of February 21, 1857, by which time the federal government figured that there were enough United States coins on hand, and foreign coins were no longer essential. From the beginnings of copper half cents and large cents in 1793, of silver coins in 1794, and the first gold coins in 1795, this took many years to do. Early coinages were small, and many coins were melted, exported, or met other fates.

The Spanish-American Coinage System

The Spanish-American coinage system was based on divisions of eight. Silver coins of the largest or 8-real size (real = "royal") were equivalent to one dollar. The first Continental Currency notes issued by the American Congress in the 1770s were denominated in "Spanish milled dollars," there being no United States silver dollars struck by that time (nor would there be until years later in 1794).[1] The 8-real or "dollar" denomination was divided into eight parts, commonly known as "bits."

Very early pieces are found on crude planchets, rarely even close to full round outline, and are known as "cobs." The planchets for these were sliced off the ends of long silver or gold bars. If a planchet was too heavy, a piece or two would be clipped from its rim. The edges of such pieces are plain (without ornamentation or reeding). The cob pieces were struck by hand, with a sledgehammer or mallet used to impress the planchet between obverse and reverse dies. Cobs were irregular in appearance, both as to outline or profile of the planchet and as to the depth and strength of the inscriptions and designs. The uncertain outline invited later owners of such coins to do their own clipping to further reduce weight, in the hope that the lightened coin could be passed along without anyone noticing. This practice was known as "clipping." Various typical "cob" issues bore crosses, royal coats of arms, and inscriptions as their motifs. (See expanded description under "The Salvaged Treasure Fleet of 1715" below.)

Beginning in the 1732 at the Mexico City Mint and later at other Spanish-American mints, coins were made on planchets punched from thin strips of metal, much as a cookie cutter punches cookie "planchets" from flattened dough. This permitted the outline to be round. In addition, ornamentation was applied to the edge (as the coin is viewed edge-on). This deterred clipping. These later issues are known as "milled" coins and are more consistent in appearance and quality of striking. The most famous "Spanish milled dollars" are the early issues showing on the obverse two globes and the Pillars of Hercules. For many years the illustration of such a coin, a "Pillar dollar," has been the frontispiece of *A Guide Book of United States Coins.* Later milled coins depicted the head of the ruler of Spain, with inscriptions in Latin, such as CAROLUS III for Charles III.

The Spanish-American milled dollars (but not the earlier cob-type coins) were made legal tender and receivable in payment for government debts by the Act of February 9, 1793 (effective date, July 1, 1793). Also made legal tender were French silver crowns and various gold coins of France, Great Britain, Portugal, Spain, and Spanish-America. When received by the government, such foreign silver coins were usually melted and recoined into United States denominations, a handy procedure as in the early years there were no significant silver mines within the United States.

For a period of many decades, the annual reports of the director of the Mint reveal that domestic gold and silver coins were mostly produced from bullion derived from Spanish-American, French, English, and other foreign issues.

Spanish-American silver coins were issued in the following denominations:

8 reals = $1 U.S. funds, called a "dollar"; equal in value to eight bits.
4 reals = 50¢, called "four bits."
2 reals = 25¢, called "two bits" (this term is still popular).
1 real = 12-1/2¢, called a "bit."[2]

---

[1] Sources for information include Daniel Frank Sedwick, *The Practical Book of Cobs,* 3rd edition, 1995 (a highly recommended guide to the entire subject of earlier-dated silver and gold issues); Oscar G. Schilke and Raphael E. Solomon, *America's Foreign Coins,* 1964; and Chester L. Krause and Clifford Mishler, *Standard Catalog of World Coins,* 1991 edition. In addition, there are many specialized texts available.

[2] My personal preference is to use "real" when referring to a 1-real coin or as an adjective (such as an 8-real specimen), and use reals as a stand-alone plural, as in 8-reals, 4-reals, etc. I do not care for "reale" as the singular. However, in numismatic circles there is no agreement on this subject. The

1/2 real = 6-1/4¢, called a "medio" or, sometimes, a "picayune."

Of all Spanish-American silver coins, the most ubiquitous in circulation in the United States were the 2-real pieces. The 4 reals denomination seems to have been little used. Apparently, 8-real coins were mostly used in large transactions, not in everyday purchases.

Spanish-American gold coins were based on a similar system of eighths:

8 escudos = $16 U.S. funds, called a "doubloon."
4 escudos = $8, called a "half doubloon."
2 escudos = $4.
1 escudo = $2.
1/2 escudo = $1, called in some accounts a "gold dollar"; these were not made as part of the cob coinage, but only as part of the later milled coinage beginning in 1738.

The coinage of Spanish America is rich and varied, and a comprehensive treatment would require many hundreds of pages. In general, such coins are attributed today by numismatists as to their:

Denomination: Expressed as reals or escudos and fractions thereof.

Date: On later issues this appears in full, as 1782, but on seventeenth-century "cob" coins it is in abbreviated form, such as 84 for 1684. As fully-dated coins and coins bearing the dates expressed as only the last two or three digits do not generally overlap with each other within the same denominations struck at the same mints, the numismatist will quickly find that dating is not a problem. Milled coins of the later era are fully dated.

Mintmark: A letter or monogram noting the place the coin was struck. The most often seen is Mo for Mexico City, typically expressed as a capital "M" with a tiny "o" tucked into the top indentation of the M letter. Other letters and combinations identify coins from Lima (Peru), Potosi (Peru), over a dozen other mints in Mexico, Bogota (Colombia), and other sites.

Assayer: The function of the assayer at a Spanish-American mint was to be sure that each coin contained the correct weight and quality of gold or silver. If there was a consistent shortfall, woe to the assayer whose initial appeared on the coins; death might be the punishment. As an example of an assayer notation, certain Mexico City Mint coins dated circa 1677-1705 bear the letter "L" for assayer Martin Lopez.

Cob and other earlier coinages have related designs no matter at which mint they were struck. As time went on and various countries gained their independence, they typically retained Spanish denominations and other practices (such as indicating the assayer), but developed different motifs ranging from portraits to eagles to trees to ranges of mountains.

The plurality of mints in Mexico, amounting to 14 over a long span of time (but mostly in the nineteenth century), is explained by the desirability of siting a minting facility close to a silver mine. Thus, ore could be processed in the immediate vicinity of an ore deposit and quickly converted into coin, facilitating security and transportation processes.[1]

Sometimes, silver 8-reals or other coins were cut into halves or other fractions, thus literally creating "pieces of eight." The collector of early American tokens knows well the quarter-section, resembling a slice of pie, cut from a silver 8-reals to create a "piece" of 2-reals value, and stamped with a "PB" hallmark in script letters, quite possibly by the Planters Bank of New Orleans circa 1811-1815 (and withdrawn circa 1815-1817), which certified that such a 2-real piece was, indeed, genuine.[2] The practice of cutting Spanish-American coins into fractions invited cheating, such as cutting five "quarters" from a single coin, or making the pieces slightly underweight.

Used in North America

Countless millions of silver and gold coins made in the Spanish possessions were used in commerce in North, Central, and South America. Within the United States they were commonly seen through the late 1850s and occasionally after that time. In the American West, long after Mexican coins had disappeared in the Midwest and East, these coins still were an integral part of commerce. In the 1860s and early 1870s, bullion dealers in San Francisco held quantities of Mexican 8 reals and sold them at a premium to merchants engaged in the export trade, who used them to buy goods in China. In the 1870s certain Western banks paid out and received checks and drafts specifically denominated in Mexican dollars.

In the 1785-1787 period, as in other times of the era, the Spanish-American 8 reals had different values in different states, including this table in which the 8 reals or "dollar" was equivalent to the following in terms of paper denominated according to the British system:[3]

Connecticut: 6 shillings.
Delaware: 7 shillings 6 pence.

---

monetary system of "eighths" is still in use today in the securities business, as on the New York Stock Exchange where quotations are in eighths of a dollar.

[1] In the United States a similar mine-to-mint practice was followed: the San Francisco, Carson City, Denver, Dahlonega, and Charlotte mints were built close to sources for precious metals.

[2] Cf. Russell Rulau, *Hard Times Tokens,* 1832-1844, 6th edition, 1996, p. 37. This represents current thinking as to the attribution of the "PB" punch; earlier, the firm of Puech, Bein of New Orleans was generally thought to have been the originator of the pieces.

[3] Schilke-Solomon, p. 14, quoting various sources dated 1785, 1786, and 1787. Also a nod to Thomas K. DeLorey for commentaries by letter, October 15, 1996.

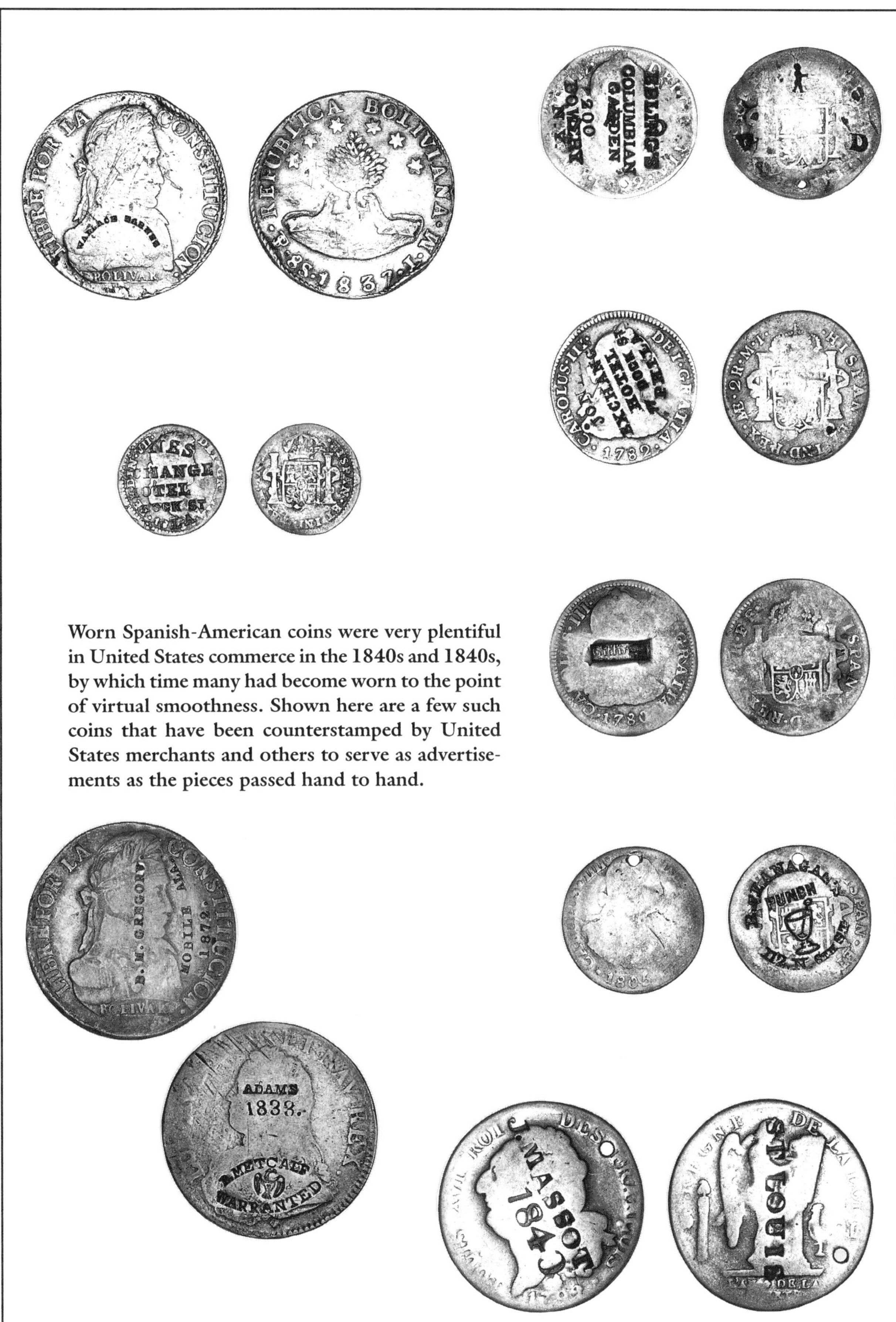

Worn Spanish-American coins were very plentiful in United States commerce in the 1840s and 1840s, by which time many had become worn to the point of virtual smoothness. Shown here are a few such coins that have been counterstamped by United States merchants and others to serve as advertisements as the pieces passed hand to hand.

Georgia: 6 shillings.
Maryland: 7 shillings 6 pence.
Massachusetts: 6 shillings.
New Hampshire: 6 shillings.
New Jersey: 7 shillings 6 pence.
New York: 8 shillings.
North Carolina: 8 shillings.
Pennsylvania: 7 shillings 6 pence.
Rhode Island: 6 shillings.
South Carolina: 6 shillings.
Virginia: 6 shillings.

A United States Senate report dated January 11, 1830,[1] commented in part:

> There are very few Spanish dollars and not many Spanish half dollars now in our circulation; and of those now in use, [only] a few have the weight thus requisite to make them legal money.... Almost all the Spanish dollars now in this country are collected in the commercial seaports, where they are held rather as articles of merchandise, than as circulating coins. The minor coins and especially the quarters, eighths, and sixteenths of the Spanish dollar, are in active circulation in all parts of our country....
>
> Our great supply of Spanish coins has always been derived from the American countries formerly Spanish and now independent; and the Spanish dollar and its parts now current in this country were coined by the mints of Mexico, Peru, and other American countries while those countries were subject to the domination of Spain....
>
> To depend on foreign coins for our ordinary domestic use is unworthy of ourselves and our condition. We have all the reasons of policy which induce nations to establish and coin money for themselves; we have all the means for coining our own money; our own system of money; our own mint and our own coins, are no longer in their infancy, and the just pride of national character should now discard the foreign coins which were from necessity, adopted and used in the country in its colonial state.

In later years many other reports and legislative acts addressed foreign coins, their quality, use, and valuation within the United States. If you had made a purchase amounting to a dollar or two in Philadelphia (where the main mint was located) in 1853, chances are excellent that the silver part of the transaction would have involved more Spanish-American coins than those of the United States! Part of this was due to the well-known law that "bad money drives out good." As Spanish-American coins became more and more worn and thus lost weight, these were more quickly spent than freshly-minted United States coins of heavier weight and higher value. It became profitable at certain times for speculators to melt United States silver and gold coins for their bullion content, while no such activity would have been profitable with lightweight foreign coins.

Finally, the Act of February 21, 1857, mandated the end to the circulation of Spanish-American coins, and within the next two to three years they disappeared from commerce in the area from the Atlantic coast to the Rocky Mountains.

Today, the one-time omnipresence in the United States of Spanish-American silver coins is demonstrated by many records such as newspaper notices, invoices, trade tokens, and bills of account thus denominated.

Because of this, the vast majority of early coin hoards and caches found in the United States before the early 1800s were found to consist mostly of Spanish-American coins, sometimes with French, British, Dutch, and other European issues and a few American coins such as Massachusetts Pine Tree shillings. There was scarcely any numismatic interest in the United States for such coins until the present century. Thus, the writer has encountered not even a single early account of a find that was numismatically described as to denomination, date, mintmark, and assayer, including several stories in the *American Journal of Numismatics* (which were mostly reprinted from newspaper clippings). What a shame!

In recent decades the situation has changed dramatically. Today, Spanish-American coins are widely studied and collected worldwide, but especially in the Western Hemisphere. Many fine reference works have been published concerning them.

Recovered Coins

Spanish-American coins found in old-time hoards, from pocket change descended in families, etc., if not subjected to moisture, are apt to be in such grades as Very Good to Very Fine. Some coins, especially of the 2 reals denomination, are often seen worn nearly smooth, indicating that they stayed in circulation a long time. Coins approaching Mint State are virtually unknown from such sources.

On the other hand, coins dug from the earth are typically highly corroded and oxidized, and silver coins brought up from the sea are even more corroded. The elements did not affect gold coins as much, and these, when found, tend to be better preserved.

Relative to the one-time circulation of these pieces in the United States, treasure hunter Thomas A. Kays has written that 1/2- and 2-real silver coins have been unearthed in significant numbers in sites that were active in American colonial days, such including Charleston, South Carolina, and the low-lying areas of Virginia.[2] The account primarily dealt with coins

---

[1] Senate Document 19, 21st Congress, 1st Session, pp. 9-12, 14. More extensively quoted in Schilke-Solomon, pp. 41 ff.

[2] "More Observations by a Relic Hunter," Thomas A. Kays, edited by Gary Trudgen, *The Colonial Newsletter,* September 1996.

found one at a time, representing pieces that were probably lost or misplaced (rather than multiple-coin hidden caches). He found that the most popular denominations, in order of their finding, were 1/2-, 2- and 1-real pieces. Silver 8-real "dollars" and gold coins are rarely found by treasure hunters, possibly because they were more valuable and were less easily misplaced, or because fewer were used.

Thomas Kays further related the following types of copper coins have been found with some regularity by treasure hunters in Virginia: British halfpence (authentic as well as counterfeit) and, in descending order of frequency, 1773-dated Virginia halfpence, 1722-1724 Wood's Hibernia coinage, 1785-1788 Connecticut coppers, and 1786-1788 New Jersey coppers. In Virginia, new soil accumulates at a rate of about four inches per century, he observed. Thus, coins lost 200 years ago are apt to be found an at average depth of about eight inches below today's surface.

Early Coins Found at Williamsburg

Relative to copper, Spanish-American silver, and other coins circulating in America prior to the establishment of the Philadelphia Mint in 1792-1793, Eric P. Newman gave an accounting of examples found decades ago during the restoration of Colonial Williamsburg in Virginia: [1]

> 1773-dated Virginia halfpenny (40 pieces). This is evidence that many of these circulated in Virginia, although many others were hoarded by the citizenry.
>
> Circa 1695-1701 William III British halfpenny, date apparently not readable.
>
> 1722 Rosa Americana penny (2 pieces).
>
> 1722 British regal copper halfpenny (2 pieces).
>
> George II British copper halfpence, various, only two with dates readable, these being 1738 and 1740 (5 pieces).
>
> George II Irish copper halfpence, circa 1737-1760, dates not readable (2 pieces).
>
> George III copper halfpence, all counterfeits, one dated 1774, another 1775, with the balance being unreadable (5 pieces). Such British issues were widely imitated including by counterfeiters in England as well as in the United States, the latter activity perhaps concentrated at Machin's Mills, Newburgh, New York, where coppers bearing inscriptions of Connecticut, Vermont, and other entities were also struck.
>
> Charles II Scottish sixpence, circa 1677-1679, date not readable.
>
> 1785 Danish 2 skilling of Christian VII.
>
> 1763 Hungarian 1 poltura, Maria Theresa.
>
> Mexico City Mint silver coins of the eighteenth century, various (7 pieces).

The preceding coins were found scattered over a wide area at Williamsburg and thus do not represent hoards, but, instead, finds. The distribution indicates that Spanish-American silver coins—in this case, all from the Mexico City Mint—dominated the larger coins in the monetary system in Virginia during this period.

Pirates and Privateers

The "Golden Age"

The so-called "golden age" of sea pirates took place beginning around the 1690s and continued to the early years of the nineteenth century. The dastardly behavior of Charles Gibbs circa 1815-1830, discussed below, was somewhat unusual for the time. Most pirates had long since gone to their various rewards including rotting away in chains in public exhibits of their corpses. However, "nests" of buccaneers remained in the Caribbean through at least the 1820s, and there are scattered accounts after that.

Typically, pirates maintained a "den" in an inlet or sheltered cove where their moored vessels could not be observed by coastwise ships. Captured "prizes" (as seized vessels were called) could be hidden easily in such places—pending their stripping, surface alterations and name changes, prior to offering them for sale. Headquarters buildings in such coves ranged from large buildings made of masonry, to rude wooden shacks, and were always heavily fortified. Likely as not, arrangements had been made with local officials so as to prevent any snooping or interference by law enforcers. For example, although pirates were not officially allowed in Cuba, many flourished there.

Privateers

In addition to "bad" pirates, there were "good" pirates, these being called privateers. This latter breed received the official sanction of the American, French, English, or other government and could sally forth in quest of any ship bearing the flag of an enemy or, as was often the case, any vessel that was suspected of having a remote connection to such. As the Americans, English, French, Dutch, and Spanish—allied in various combinations—were often at war with each other, the possibilities for "honest" nautical plunder were virtually limitless. Some of America's leading families sponsored privateers and shared in their spoils.

American privateers were hardly new by the Revolution. Marine historian Samuel Eliot Morison noted:[2]

---

[1] Newman, *Coinage for Colonial Virginia,* 1956, pp. 33-34. Inventory is from Newman, comments following each coin are by the present writer with certain adaptations from Newman.

[2] *The Maritime History of Massachusetts,* 1921, p. 20.

> A typical Massachusetts-built vessel of the larger class, subject of our unique pre-Revolutionary ship portrait, was the *Bethel,* owned by the Quincy family. Armed with 14 guns and carrying 38 men, she captured in 1748 by sheer Yankee bluff a Spanish treasure ship of 24 guns and 110 men, worth the better part of one hundred thousand pounds sterling. So congenial, in fact, did our provincial seamen find privateering, that many could not bear to give it up once peace was concluded. In consequence, not a few were hanged in chains on Bird Island or Nix's Mate [both in Boston harbor], whereby every passing seaman might gain a moral lesson.[1]

In England, corpses of pirates were strung up along the Thames for the same educational purpose. On both sides of the Atlantic, public executions of pirates were apt to draw large crowds of cheering spectators. One Boston lady reported that from a half mile away she could hear shouting when the noose tightened around a particular buccaneer's neck. Of course, one country's brave and patriotic privateer was in the eyes of another country a dastardly low-life pirate scum.

An oval gold medal issued in 1760, apparently in connection with a privateer-pirate incident in the colonies in America, was described by C. Wyllys Betts as his catalogue no. 434:[2]

> Obverse: A brigantine under full sail bearing seven guns, sailing to the left, and displaying the banner of England.
>
> Reverse (engraved inscription): THIS MEDALL / GIVEN BY THE UNDERWRITERS / TO THE BEARER CAPTAIN JAMES / WEIR OF THE MARS FOR HIS / BRAVE DEFENCE AGAINST / TWO FRENCH PRIVATEERS / APRIL & JULY / 1760.

Revolutionary War Privateers

It may be of interest to readers to include some information about American privateers, during the Revolutionary War. While it was the practice of the privateers to capture the ships as "prizes" and receive a share of their worth as determined by a proceeding known as an admiralty court, doubtless some quantities of early American coins were involved in the cargoes taken. Coins aboard early ships were rarely mentioned in contemporary shipping notices or cargo lists, lest security be violated. (Recall the comment in the preceding chapter about coins being shipped as "machinery" and "hardware.")

The importance of privateering in the 1770s and 1780s is recounted by Ralph M. Eastman:[3]

> It is safe to say that had it not been for our privateers the Stars and Stripes would have been, for all practical purposes, completely swept from the seas during the Revolutionary War. It was the astonishing development of this form of maritime warfare that enabled the struggling colonists to hold their own on the ocean. The following figures are rather interesting as showing the number of privateers and guns carried during the years of the war:
>
> 1777: (73 privateers in service), 1778 (115), 1779 (167), 1780 (228), 1781 (449),[4] and 1782 (323).
>
> Unfortunately, many of the cruises and actions of these craft have not been recorded. Numerous battles were fought, daring raids on the enemy's coasts were made, and many heroic incidents occurred that might well fill a volume with most valuable historical reading. As these vessels sailed, however, merely in a private capacity, most of their logs have been lost and the information that has been preserved is, as a rule, meager and fragmentary. Enough is known, nevertheless, to show that these private ventures were fraught with thrilling incidents and were most important in their bearing on the results of the war. They carried miscellaneous cargoes in privateering days—missionaries in the cabin, and rum and tobacco in the hold—and everybody was aware of this condition, as it was the custom of the period.
>
> A noticeable feature of the extraordinary development of privateering in this country was the rapid increase in the size and efficiency of the craft thus engaged. In the earlier part of the Revolutionary War any vessel, old or new, that could possibly be converted into a war craft was eagerly seized, a few guns mounted on her, and she was sent to sea, in some cases with the most curious assemblage of men imaginable. Physicians, lawyers, army officers, politicians, staid merchants, and even ministers of the Gospel were found in their complements. All, seemingly, were carried away by the craze for privateering.
>
> The officers and crews of the vessels commissioned by General George Washington received the same pay as officers and privates in the Continental Army, and in addition one-third part of the value of every vessel and cargo taken, after condemnation in the Courts of Admiralty. If the vessel were armed, one-half, instead of one-third, was given as prize money. As afterwards construed, this meant sufficiently armed to attempt resistance, and not a mere technical armament. Of this prize money the captain received six shares, the first lieutenant five shares, the second lieutenant four shares, the master two shares, the master's mate one and a half shares, the gunner the same, and the mariners each one share.

The following commentary published in 1814 tells more:[5]

> The success of the American privateers, during the year 1777, in the capture of English merchantmen, was extremely great. Their daring spirit and boldness was unparalleled. Their enterprises were no longer confined to the American seas. The coasts of Europe were now covered with them. The shores of Great Britain were insulted by these privateers, in a manner their hardiest enemies had never dared to attempt. Even the coasting trade of Ireland was rendered insecure.

---

1 Also see discussion of undiscovered Massachusetts treasures in Chapter 22.

2 *American Colonial History Illustrated by Contemporary Medals,* 1894, p. 194. This work is a rich source for descriptions of the cover subjects, most of which have fascinating histories.

3 *Some Famous Privateers of New England,* 1928.

4 With numbers such as this it is easy to imagine that the East Coast of the United States was fairly crowded with privateer ships!

5 Thomas Clark, *Naval History of the United States,* 1814, p. 81.

Into so great a state of alarm were the linen merchants thrown, that they petitioned for, and obtained a convoy for the linen ships, between Newry and Dublin, and Dublin and England. This was a circumstance before unheard of. The British merchants were forced to adopt the mortifying expedient of chartering foreign vessels, particularly French, to transport English goods to the continent of Europe.[1] Thus was the immense naval force of Great Britain rendered incompetent fully to protect her own shipping, by the privateers of a country that possessed not a single sail of the line, and that had been only a year in existence as a nation.

The countenance given to American privateers by the French court alarmed the English ministry. The *General Mifflin* privateer had committed great depredations along the English coasts.[2] On entering the port of Brest, she saluted the French admiral. After the deliberation of an hour and a half, the admiral returned the salute in form, as to the vessel of a sovereign and independent state. Lord Stormont, the British ambassador at the court of Versailles, was much irritated at the procedure. He threatened to return to London, if they should continue thus to countenance the Americans. In consequence of these representations, an order was issued, requiring all American vessels to leave the ports of France. Notwithstanding this order was positive, yet so many evasions were practiced, and the execution of it was so relaxed that the American ships still continued to frequent the French ports, and to equip and refit in them.

Regarding privateers of another war in another era, the famous escapades of Captain Raphael Semmes and the daring Confederate raider *Alabama* are noted in Chapter 13.

Pirates (Again)

Havana was a particularly popular port for buccaneers of the non-privateer kind, and it is said that some piracy went on within the harbor itself, close to the docks. Ships taken as prizes found a ready resale in the harbor, with no questions asked, and with quick payment in cash. Spain, which owned Cuba, made some half-hearted efforts to suppress piracy, but most authorities on the island were all too willing to look the other way, especially if their palms were crossed with silver reals or gold escudos. As late as the 1820s the Baltimore newspapers suggested that the American government send troops to Cuba and forcibly occupy the island, if that was what was needed to stop this trade.

The various islands in the Bahamas off the eastern coast of Florida served as other pirate roosts. A copper halfpenny token issued for the Bahamas by the Soho Mint in 1806 bears on the reverse a sailing ship and the notation, in Latin, that pirates have been expelled and commerce restored.[3] However, this was wishful thinking. Pirates lingered there for years afterward.

Today in the late twentieth century there is said to be some piracy going on in remote areas of Southeast Asia, and closer to home there are occasional modern accounts of expensive private yachts being captured off the coast of Florida. Perhaps piracy runs in the blood of human adventurers. Certainly, a multitude of stagecoach robbers (see Chapter 22) were "land pirates."

Piracy Off the Coast of Florida

In nautical, shipwreck, and pirate lore there are many stories of dastardly deeds. The following brief excerpt is edited from the first-hand account of a traveler aboard a sailing ship in 1823, whose experiences were related in the *American Monthly Magazine*, February 1824.[4] The narrative is particularly interesting in that it tells how coins and currency notes—quite possibly those of the United States (considering the

"The pirates torturing the crew of the schooner *Mary,*" from Thomas Carey's 1825 book on piracy.

[1] The use of sending merchandise, war supplies, etc., under a flag of neutrality became a popular practice and extended to include World Wars I and II, among many other conflicts. It is curious to observe that during the American Revolution, France was a friend of the United States, yet her ships were available to help British interests escape American depredations.

[2] Ship named for Thomas Mifflin (1744-1800), Revolutionary War soldier who later was president of the Continental Congress (1783-1784) and governor of Pennsylvania (1790-1799; a county in that state is named for him).

[3] The Bahama (without an S at the end of the word) issues of 1806 were made in business strike and Proof formats. Most of the latter seen today are restrikes from circa the 1860s and some have gilt surfaces. Business strikes and original Proofs have engrailed edges while plain edge pieces are restrikes as are 1806 engrailed edge pieces with gilt surfaces. Krause and Mishler in the *Standard Catalogue of World Coins* list an 1807 engrailed edge in Proof, but the writer has never seen one. There was none in the C. Wilson Peck Collection when it was examined by the writer in the early 1960s, and Peck's 1806 piece was a gilt Proof restrike. This obverse die for the 1806 Bahama "pirate halfpenny" restrike was also used on restrikes of British regal coins. It is presumed that the 1807 halfpennies were struck by W.J. Taylor circa 1860s, and that no originals bearing this date were ever made. Also refer to C. Wilson Peck, *English Copper, Tin and Bronze Coins in the British Museum, 1558-1958,* British Museum, London, 1960, page 379.

[4] As quoted in Thomas Carey, *The History of Pirates Containing the Lives of Those Noted Pirate Captains,* compiled in 1825, pp. 261-267.

port of debarkation)—were hidden aboard ship to avoid their falling into the wrong hands:

> In the early part of June [1823] I sailed from Philadelphia in the schooner *Mary*, on a voyage to New Orleans. My principal object in going round by sea was the restoration of my health, which had been for many months declining.[1]
>
> Having some friends in New Orleans whose commercial operations were conducted on an extensive scale, I was charged with the care of several sums of money in gold and silver, amounting altogether to nearly $18,000. This I communicated to the captain, and we concluded to secure it in the best manner our circumstances would admit.
>
> A plank was accordingly taken off the ribs of the schooner in my own cabin, and the money being deposited in the vacancy, the plank was nailed down in its original place, and the seams filled and tarred over. Being thus relieved from any apprehension that the money would be found upon us in case of an attack from pirates, my mind was somewhat easier.
>
> What other articles of value I could conveniently carry about with me, I did so. I had also brought a quantity of bank notes to the amount of $15,000. Part of these I caused to be carefully sewed in the left lapel of my coat, supposing that in case of my being lost at sea, my coat, should my body be found, would still contain the most valuable of my effects. The balance was carefully quilted into my black silk cravat.
>
> Our crew consisted of the captain and four men, with a supply of livestock for the voyage, and a Newfoundland dog, valuable for his fidelity and sagacity. He had once saved his master from a watery grave when he had been stunned and knocked overboard by the sudden shifting of the boom. I was the only passenger on board.
>
> Our voyage at first was prosperous, and time went on rapidly. I felt my strength increase the longer I was at sea, and when we arrived off the southern coast of Florida, my feelings were like those of another man.
>
> It was toward the evening of the 14th day, two hours before sunset, that we espied a sail astern of us. As twilight came, it neared us with astonishing rapidity. Night closed, and all around was impenetrable darkness.... It was a fearful and appalling darkness, and in spite of my endeavors I could not compose myself. At the windlass on the forecastle three of the sailors, like myself, unable to sleep, had collected for conversation. On joining them, I found our fears were mutual. They all kept their eyes steadily fixed upon the unknown vessel, as if anticipating some dreadful event. They informed me that they had put their arms in order and were determined to stand or die.
>
> At this moment a flash of light, perhaps a musket burning priming, proceeded from the vessel in pursuit, and we saw distinctly that her deck was covered with men. My heart almost failed me. I had never been in battle, and I knew not what it was. Day at length dawned, and setting all her canvas, our pursuer gained alarmingly upon us. It was evident that she had followed us the whole night, being unwilling to attack us in the dark.
>
> In a few minutes she fired a swivel [mounted gun] and came along side. She was a pirate. Her boat was lowered, and about a dozen hideous looking objects jumped in, with a commander at their head. The boat pushed off, and was nearing us fast as we arranged ourselves for giving her a broadside. Our whole stock of arms consisted of six muskets and an old swivel used as a signal gun, belonging to the *Mary*, and a pair of pistols of my own, which I carried in my belt. The pirate boat's crew were armed with muskets, pistols, swords, cutlasses, and knives. When she came within her own length of us, we fired five of our muskets and the swivel into her. Her fire was scarcely half given, when she filled and went down with all her crew. At this success we were inclined to rejoice, but looking over at the pirate schooner, we observed her deck still swarming with the same description of horrid looking creatures.
>
> A second boat's crew pushed off, with their muskets pointed directly at us the whole time. When they came within the same distance as the other, we fired, but with little if any effect. The pirates immediately returned the fire, and with horrid cries jumped aboard of us.
>
> Two of our brave crew were lying dead upon the deck, and the rest of us expected nothing better. French, Spanish, and English were spoken indiscriminately, and all at once. The most horrid imprecations were uttered against us, and threats that fancy cannot imagine. A wretch whose black, shaggy whiskers covered nearly his whole face, whose eyes were only seen at intervals from beneath his bush eyebrows, and whose whole appearance was more that of a hell-hound than of a human being, approached me with a drawn cutlass in his hand. I drew one of my pistols and snapped it in his face, but it flashed in the pan, and before I could draw the other, the pirate, with a brutality that would have disgraced a cannibal, struck me over the face with his cutlass and knocked me down.... The blood ran in torrents from my forehead.
>
> In this situation the wretch seized me by the scalp, and thrusting his cutlass in my cravat, cut through it completely.... Without stopping to examine the cravat he put it in his pocket.... He pinioned my hands behind my back, led me to the gunwale of the vessel, and asked another of the gang, in French, whether he should throw me overboard.... [Instead of doing this,] he led me to the foremast, where he tied me with my face to the stern of the vessel....
>
> On looking around I found them all employed in plundering and ransacking everything we had. Over my left shoulder one of our sailors was strung up to the yardarm, and apparently in the last agonies of death, while before me our gallant captain was on his knees and begging for his life. The wretches were endeavoring to extort from him the secret of our money, but for a while he was firm and dauntless. Provoked at his obstinacy, they extended his arms and cut them off at the elbows. At this, human nature gave way, and the injured man confessed the spot where we had concealed our specie. In a few minutes it was aboard their own vessel....

Such accounts, of which the annals of the sea contain many, are not pleasant reading, but reflect the perils of ocean travel in the early years of our country. Pirates, based in Cuba and other Caribbean islands, roved for many years, despite numerous attempts to suppress them.

Regarding our unlucky traveler, in short order all

---

[1] In actuality, in addition to any salutary benefits it may have offered, the sea afforded the most practical method of travel between these two cities in this era before the railroad.

of the crew of the *Mary* and even the captain's Newfoundland dog were killed, and it was the passenger's turn next. Mercifully, a great blast of wind struck the ship at that time, and a storm rose without warning. The pirates abandoned their nearly lifeless victim lashed to the mast, scurried to their boat, and were soon aboard their ship. An hour or two later another ship passed, saw the distressed *Mary*, and rescued the passenger, who, as noted, lived to write about his harrowing experience.

Gibbs the Pirate

Hidden: 1830
Location: Near Long Island, New York
Treasure: Silver and gold coins

Aboard the *Vineyard*

Among the more tragic treasure tales of the sea is the misadventure of the brig *Vineyard*. Under Captain William Thornby, the ship left New Orleans on November 9, 1830, bound for Philadelphia.

After five days at sea, the young cook, Thomas J. Wansley, a native of Delaware, revealed to several crew members that $50,000 in silver and gold coins was aboard. Unbeknownst to most everyone, James D. Jeffers, who long since had assumed the alias Charles Gibbs, was also aboard. Gibbs was one of the most notorious pirates ever to sail the tropical seas. Obviously, mischief—or worse—was afoot!

But before this story, an account of Gibbs' life to that point:

Early Life at Sea

Charles Gibbs, born in Rhode Island in 1794, the son of a farmer, went to a fine school and was the apple of his father's eye. It was intended that he would follow the family trade in agriculture. However, he soon became a delinquent, and he and his father had a parting of the ways.

At the age of 15 he ran away from home and went to sea aboard the American warship *Hornet* under Captain James Lawrence. Apparently, he found life

Early nineteenth century woodcut of a battle with pirates.

aboard ship to his liking, and he performed well as a member of the crew, including during the vanquishing of the British ship *Peacock* in the beginning of the War of 1812. When Captain Lawrence assumed command of the *Chesapeake*, Gibbs transferred with him. Leaving Boston harbor on June 1, 1813, the *Chesapeake* encountered the British man-of-war *Shannon* off Boston Light. The American ship came in second best, and Gibbs and many of his crew mates were taken to Halifax, Nova Scotia, then to England, where they were tossed into Dartmoor Prison, where he remained until the cessation of hostilities.

Returning to the United States, Gibbs decided to rejoin his family at the Rhode Island farm. A few weeks spent in that activity convinced him for the last time that agriculture was not what he wanted. With a $1,000 stake from his father, the young man set off for Boston to enter the grocery business. Setting up in a sleazy part of town known as the early equivalent of the red light district, Gibbs obtained a liquor license and established a trading place that soon became a favorite hangout for the lower life forms there, including prostitutes who are said to have settled their bills in trade. The financial side of his business did poorly, and Gibbs sold out for $100 and decided to return to the sea.

His first stint was aboard the *John*, which took him to Buenos Aires, where he stayed ashore until his funds were exhausted. He then signed aboard a privateer, where he fomented discontent among the crew, stating they should have a larger share of the prizes they captured at sea. A mutiny followed, and Gibbs and his cohorts took over the vessel. At Florida the rest of the crew was put ashore, and the mutineers assumed sole occupancy of the ship.

Based in the West Indies, Gibbs and his crew of pirates would attack and take over a sailing ship, murder its crew, steal its cargo, then make a few changes to the captured vessel's appearance, run it to Havana—the most popular of the several Caribbean ports where

A 17-year-old captive Dutch girl pleads for her life with pirate Charles Gibbs, as illustrated in a nineteenth century account.

few questions were ever asked—and put it up for sale. Other ships were simply destroyed. As no captives were ever taken, no one lived to testify what happened. "Dead cats don't mew," another pirate once said. An estimated 500 crewmen and their passengers were killed in this way over the next several years during the plundering of about 30 to 40 vessels. In one lamentable instance an attractive 17-year-old Dutch girl was spared, kept on board for two months or so (one account says two years) to serve as Gibbs' companion, and then murdered when crew members became jealous of all the time Gibbs was spending with her.

Gibbs' Activities Revealed

Gibbs' activities were finally revealed when he and his crew captured the American ship *Caroline* while being watched by the crew of the British warship *Jarius.* The Britishers pursued the pirates into an inlet, where they were amazed to see 12 burned-out hulls of captured vessels. After an exchange of shots, Gibbs and his men fled into the jungle. Soon, he and his fellow pirates were back at the same game.

In October 1821, Charles Gibbs, who by that time commanded a fleet of four pirate ships and was laying waste to commerce off the coast of Florida, was caught in the act of plundering three commercial ships in Cuban waters. Commander Lawrence Kearney and the crew of the Navy brig *Enterprise* captured Gibbs, about 40 of his cohorts, and all four of his vessels. However, Gibbs escaped on shore. For the next decade he was a hunted man.[1]

Sometime in the early 1820s, he decided to give up his bloodthirsty career and return to the United States. With him was $30,000 he had taken from his bank account in Havana. A short time later he changed his destination and sailed to Liverpool, England, where he fell in love with a lady. She soon grew tired of his attention and spurned his further advances. Angered, Gibbs went back to America, and then sailed to Argentina, which had recently declared war with Brazil. Gibbs signed on as a crew member of a 34-gun Argentinean warship, the *Twenty-Fifth of May.* Serving with distinction, he was soon placed in charge of his own vessel, a privateer armed with two cannon and provided with a crew of 46.

After at least two successful sorties as a privateer, Gibbs was captured by Brazilian authorities and thrown into prison where he remained until the end of hostilities. Later, he went to New York City, secured passage aboard the *Sally Ann,* and went to the Mediterranean, hoping to engage in privateering during a war in progress between France and Algiers. Apparently, little in the way of piracy was accomplished, and Gibbs, now without funds, came back to the United States.

Back Aboard the *Vineyard*

The story returns to the *Vineyard* and its treasure of $54,000 in gold and silver coins headed by sea from New Orleans to Philadelphia.[2] On the night of November 23, 1830, Gibbs, Thomas J. Wansley, and two other conspirators, Henry Atwell and Edward Church,[3] killed Captain William Thornby and First Mate William Roberts, dumped their bodies into the sea, and took over the helm. After several rounds of drinks and other celebration, the "silver dollars" were divided among the pirates and three other crew members (John Brownrigg, Robert Dawes, and James Talbot) who had since joined in, although Dawes was primarily a bystander. All resolved—as per pirate tradition—to keep the entire matter a deep, dark secret.

The course of the ship was changed, and instead of

[1] In some accounts of Gibbs, the Britishers-pursuing-Gibbs and Commander Kearney's capture of Gibbs are merged into one incident.
[2] One account, that of Snow, says the coins were Spanish "dollars" consigned to Stephen Girard, Philadelphia banker.
[3] In one account as A. Church; Snow identifies John Brownrigg as John Brown.

Pirates climb aboard a victim ship preparatory to looting its cargo and, quite possibly, killing all those aboard (although crew members were sometimes given the chance to join the pirates' gang).

putting in at Philadelphia as scheduled, the *Vineyard* was directed toward Long Island, New York. In high wind, and about 10 to 20 miles (accounts vary) from the Southampton lighthouse, the crew scuttled the ship (or set it afire; accounts vary) and went with their treasure aboard small vessels, the jolly boat and the long boat (normally used for transfers to shore and to other ships). The smaller jolly boat was swamped on a sand bar two miles off shore, and Atwell, Church, and Talbot were drowned. An account continued:

> The long-boat was also in great danger, and was only saved from a like fate by throwing over several bags of specie. Nevertheless, the crew at last got on shore at Pelican Island,[1] where they buried their money, and found a sportsman who told them where they were. They then crossed over to Great Barn Island [believed to be Barren Island]....

After spending the night near the shore, Gibbs and his fellow conspirators were arrested by a search party, taken to New York City, brought to trial, and convicted. Gibbs confessed his life of crime (including details of the tragedy of the brig *Vineyard*), found religion, asked forgiveness by his victims and his Maker, wrote two letters to his former lady friend in Liverpool, and on Friday, April 22, 1831, went with Wansley to the gallows on Gibbet Island.[2] An account noted that "Wansley expired with only a few slight struggles. Gibbs died hard."[3] Both had few if any mourners.

Captain Gibert and His Pirates

By this time piracy was virtually gone from the waters near the United States, although there were a few isolated cases recorded later. On September 20, 1832, the brig *Mexican* was on her way from Salem, Massachusetts, to Rio de Janeiro with a cargo of $20,000 in silver (arranged in 10 boxes of $2,000 each). Captain Pedro Gibert and his fellow pirates from aboard the schooner *Panda* accosted her, stole the cargo, locked

[1] Part of what later became known as Coney Island, the seaside resort.

[2] Early name for what later became known as Ellis Island, the famous processing center for immigrants. The Gibbet Island name was derived from its use for hanging Anderson, a pirate, there in 1765.

[3] Sources (which differ in certain dates and details) include: R.M. Devens, *Our First Century,* Chapter 34; Frank Sherry, *Raiders and Rebels: The Golden Age of Piracy,* pp. 361-362; Edward Rowe Snow, *Pirates and Buccaneers of the Atlantic Coast,* 1944, pp. 273-287; Jeannette Edwards Rattray, *The Perils of the Port of New York,* 1973, pp. 89-93 (which gives details of the capture of Gibbs and his associates). Gibbs figured prominently in Charles Ellms, *The Pirates' Own Book, or Authentic Narratives of the Lives, Exploits and Executions of the Most Celebrated Sea Robbers,* 1837.

the crew in the forecastle, and set the ship afire. Luckily, the trapped crew was able to work free and put out the flames. Gibert and several of his cronies were apprehended at the Nazareth River in North Africa by British authorities in 1834, extradited to Boston, clapped into the Leverett Street Jail, tried, and hanged.[1]

Pirate Treasures

Legends abound concerning chests of doubloons and pieces of eight lost at sea or buried by Blackbeard, Jean Lafitte, and other old-time pirates. In practice, few such pirate chests have ever been found. Or, if they were, they have not been publicized.

There is, however, one very important exception:

In April 1717 the *Whydah,* commanded by the infamous pirate Samuel Bellamy, was headed for Green Island off the coast of Nova Scotia to be laid up for repairs.[2] The ship, with a crew of 200 and outfitted with 28 cannon, had terrorized the Atlantic coast from the Caribbean northward and Bellamy may have taken as many as 50 ships as prizes, often persuading their crew members to join in piracy. Bellamy's favorite targets were ships inbound to America from Europe, laden with commercial goods. Stories of Bellamy are found in just about every book about pirates ever to reach print.

Near Cape Cod the buccaneers captured a small ship, the *Mary Ann,* which to their great delight proved to be loaded with Madeira wine en route from Dublin to New York City. According to stories, seven of Bellamy's pirates were put aboard the *Mary Ann* to supervise her following the *Whydah* to her repair station. A captive from the former crew of the *Mary Ann* was kept aboard and agreed to steer the ship. As the two vessels were cruising before the wind on their way to Nova Scotia, the pirates tapped the stores of wine. In short order they were in a drunken stupor.

On April 26 a storm rose, and both ships were tossed violently in the waves. The captive at the helm feigned difficulties greater than were actually happening, and deliberately ran the ostensibly distressed *Mary Ann* on the shore of Nossett's Bay, Cape Cod. The pirate flagship *Whydah,* following close behind, ran on a shoal about a quarter mile off land. Bellamy was drowned in the surf, and most of the other seamen perished as well. From the two ships, only eight men survived, six of whom were adjudged to be pirates and were later observed by a "vast assembly of spectators" in Boston on November 15, 1717, as scaffolding was pulled away from beneath their feet, and they swung from the gallows.[3]

The *Whydah,* said to have great treasure aboard, slipped into the depths of the sea. For years thereafter it was recorded in nautical accounts as being one of the most potentially valuable of unlocated ships.

In the 1980s Barry Clifford, a Massachusetts businessman and treasure hunter, formed Maritime Explorations, Inc., to seek the wreck. Success attended his efforts, and by autumn 1985 he had recovered over 5,000 silver Spanish-American cob-style coins, some gold coins dated from 1632 to 1716, and the ship's bell bearing her name, conclusive proof of the wreck's identity.

The salvage of the *Whydah* represents a very unusual instance of the recovery of a pirate ship with its intact treasure—a field of which much as been written and dreamed of, but for which actual finds are virtually unknown.

Spanish Ships and Their Treasures

Recovered coins most often seen with a nautical connection are Spanish-American pieces brought up from shipwrecks. Sometimes these have been found one at a time, such as near Vero Beach, Florida, and Rehoboth Beach, Delaware, where many beachcombers and tourists have found stray pieces here and there,

[1] Douglas Botting, *The Pirates,* 1978, pp. 186-187; Edward Rowe Snow, *Pirates and Buccaneers of the Atlantic Coast,* 1944, pp. 152-166; Francis B.C. Bradlee, *Piracy in the West Indies and Its Suppression,* 1923, pp. 7-9. A first-hand account of the piracy of the *Mexican* by a crew member of the ravaged ship, John Buttis of Salem, appears in Ralph D. Paine, *Ships & Sailors of Old Salem,* 1923.

[2] An early account of Bellamy (from which many later authors seem to have drawn, without credit; of course) is found in Thomas Carey, *The History of Pirates Containing the Lives of Those Noted Pirate Captains,* compiled in 1825, published later including by Ezra Strong, Hartford, 1835 (of course, there is the possibility that Carey's account was not original, either), pp. 127-132. Also recommended: In his inimitable manner Edward Rowe Snow describes the activities of Samuel Bellamy and devotes Chapter 1 to him in *Pirates and Buccaneers of the Atlantic Coast,* 1944. Samuel Bellamy is the subject of Chapter VII in *The Pirates of the New England Coast 1630-1730,* by George Francis Dow and John Henry Edmonds, 1923. Bellamy's first name was not known to several other historians of piracy, who simply refer to him as "Bellamy" or in at least three books, as Charles Bellamy, this typically being in context with Bellamy referring to the captain of a seized ship as a "sneaking puppy," "hen-hearted numbskull," and other demeaning terms, in pirate lore. In past accounts the name of the *Whydah* has been spelled many ways including *Whidah, Whidaw,* and *Whido.* The earliest printed monograph on the subject is Cotton Mather's *A Brief Relation of Remarkables in the Shipwreck of Above One Hundred Pirates, Who Were Cast away in the Ship* Whido, *on the Coast of New-England, April 26, 1717.*

[3] Commentary from Cotton Mather's diary as quoted by Snow. The hanged pirates came from many different locations, reflective of the diversity of a crew of buccaneers: John Brown (Jamaica in the West Indies), Thomas Baker (Holland), Hendrick Quintor (Amsterdam, Holland), Simon Van Vorst (New York), John Sheean (Nantes, France), and Peter Hoof (Sweden).

presumably washed up from offshore wrecks. Other times they have been recovered in quantity, even by the thousands. Some of these may have come from pirate vessels or their prizes, but most probably came ashore from victims of the *weather* and did not involve cutthroat buccaneers. However, in at least one instance the coins aboard a ship were lost first to the weather, then recovered, only to be lost again, this time to a crew of pirates (Jennings and his crew).

Most romantic, most publicized, and most widely known to the public today are Spanish-American coins that have been salvaged from treasure ships sunken two centuries or earlier in American coastal waters near Florida. And, of these, the very most famous are the Spanish treasure fleet coins.

Each year or so a fleet of, typically, over a dozen ships would depart from Spain and sail to the New World, there to harvest the silver and gold that had been mined, stolen from natives, or otherwise acquired by Spanish agents in Central and South America during the past year. This treasure was often a combination of cast bars and struck coins.

On a few memorable occasions, several ships from Spanish treasure fleet, or even most of them, went to the bottom during hurricanes. At the time of loss, such coins were nearly all new and unused (Mint State), having gone directly from the mints to storage for export. However, salt water damaged nearly all silver coins in the years since their immersion in salt water, and today most are seen in poor condition, often heavily corroded. Gold coins fared better and typically have only slight etching, the equivalent of the earlier-mentioned "seawater Uncirculated" grade.

As an introduction to coins recovered off the coast of Florida the following account, which appeared in connection with a spectacular auction offering, may be of interest.

The Salvaged Treasure Fleet of 1715

Lost: 1715
Found: 1960s
Treasure: Spanish-American coins

Voyage to Spain

On a hot, quiet afternoon the Spanish general Don Juan Esteban de Ubilla rolled his weathered nautical charts into a tight bundle.[1] He could feel the sun of late July on his back as he gazed distrustfully at the hazy sky. Hurricane season was fast approaching, and he thought of the jingle popular in the West Indies which traditionally warned sea voyagers of the dangerous season ahead—a time of fierce storms which spelled death to ships and men alike (here anglicized):

> *June, too soon,*
> *July, stand by,*
> *August, come they must;*
> *September, remember;*
> *October, all over.*

It was Wednesday, July 24, 1715. The signal gun boomed from Esteban de Ubilla's flagship and the 11 treasure-laden galleons in his fleet began weighing anchor. They were about to set sail for the long, arduous voyage home to Spain.

The Spanish king each year sent two fleets to the New World to collect the royal share of all silver and gold minted in Spain's colonies, as well as precious commodities. One was the mainland fleet—the *Galleons de Tierra Firme*—and it sailed from Spain to New Granada (Colombia), where European goods were exchanged for such products from South America as emeralds, pearls harvested in those far-off ports, silver minted in Peru, and vast stores of gold coins and bullion.

The second fleet, known as the *Flota de Nueva Espana,* sailed from Spain to Vera Cruz on the Gulf of Mexico, where its ships were loaded with porcelain, Oriental silk, various deep dyes, and tons of silver which had been provisionally minted into crude coins of varied shapes. The Chinese silk and porcelain, both highly prized because they were rare in Europe at that time, were just ending a long journey on which they had crossed the Pacific to the west coast of Mexico, been borne by mule over the rough terrain of the interior, and stored at Vera Cruz for the annual trip across the Atlantic to Spain.

The two fleets would rendezvous in the harbor of Havana, Cuba, for the homeward trip. Traveling together, with the combined defenses of many heavy

[1] This account is from the Bowers and Ruddy Galleries auction catalogue of the 1715 Treasure Fleet Collection consigned to the firm by the Real Eight Co.—being the reference collection of that well-known group—and sold February 17-19, 1977.

guns, meant protection against pirates on the vast Atlantic.

"July, stand by; August, come they must," The ditty explained why the fleets spent the calm winter months attending to trade in the Caribbean, sailing by June for Spain—well ahead of the perilous time in the dead of summer when a suddenly brewed hurricane could devastate any vessel caught in the Straits of Florida.

But in this year, 1715, the two fleets under the direction of Spanish commercial magnate Antonio de Echeverz and General Esteban de Ubilla had not been able to set sail from Havana until the final dangerous days of July. The threat of hurricanes was real. The postponement had been unavoidable.

In addition to bureaucratic delays, a war in Europe disrupted communications and made routine schedules risky. It began when Spain's Carlos II (1665-1700) died without designating an heir other than the grandson of Louis XIV of France. In the War of the Spanish Succession which ensued, England in alliance with Holland and Austria attempted for years to reverse the trend toward Bourbon supremacy. This fierce war against Spain and France led the English and their allies to raid Spanish commercial fleets. Creating chaos in Spain's commerce was but a part of the allies' intent; the greater prize was the golden and silver plunder from those ships—the wealth of the New World which was behind Spain's military might.

An idea of the part played by Spain's treasure fleets in that nation's life may be gotten from the writing of one John Taylor, a captain's clerk on an English man-of-war. His contemporary account describes the Plate (or Silver) Fleet system:

> The King of Spain, whose dominions are now extended from the east to the west, whose kingdoms are full one third part of the known world, whose treasures in his western dominions are rich and durable mines of gold and silver...without bottom or a seeming end, from whence flows the wealth of Spain, by which the pomp, state, frontiers of that kingdom are maintained and defended, yearly sends his mighty ships of Spain into America, which moving road bring him home his annual treasure of gold and silver....

General Esteban de Ubilla's responsibility was immense. It would provide security for his homeland's economy during the coming year.

But it was nearly the time of the hurricanes. On board his 11 treasure ships was a king's fortune in gold doubloons, silver 8-real pieces, and bullion, not to mention the more fragile goods of commerce. The accompanying French ship *El Grifon* and his own cannon were some defense against enemy warships and buccaneers, but what defense could there be against torrential rains and a raging sea? Luck would have to be on the general's—and Spain's—side.

Devastation by Hurricane

By noon on Tuesday, July 30, 1715, six days after departing from Havana, the treasure fleet had progressed several hundred miles northward. Alarmingly, the winds had suddenly died, leaving the ships rolling in an eerie sea. The vessels were off the coast of Florida near the Sebastian Inlet, fifteen miles north of what is now Vero Beach. The atmosphere grew darker until by mid-afternoon the sky had turned an ominous gray and black; before night should have fallen, lanterns on the sterns of the ships flickered their golden embers into the dark expanse. The sea had begun to rage.

At 2:00 a.m. a high wind blew from the east-northeast and the hurricane struck! Tossed to and fro, the galleons threw seamen overboard amid tangled rigging, crushed masts, and decktop cargo. Mountainous waves drove some of the ships into the reefs while others simply sank, their hulls torn apart, their cargo spewed into the sea or lodged deep within the watery coffins they became.

When the storm subsided the next day, only the French escort ship was still afloat. Eleven treasure ships had disappeared along with more than a thousand men and millions of dollars' worth of silver and gold.

Early Attempts at Salvage

Within a week of that perilous night, news had reached Havana of the disaster. Attempting to divert what was to be a far-flung tragedy for the Spanish crown (and the ruination of merchants, shipowners, and creditors of the crown alike), the Spanish immediately began salvage efforts. Directed by Juan del Hoyo Solorzana, sergeant major at Havana, divers recovered several million dollars' worth of the sunken treasure from the galleons *Tierra Firme Almiranta,*[1] *Urca de Lima,* and *La Hollandesa*. But they were only three of the 11 treasure-laden ships.

Similar operations continued for several years, and over a period of time a small percentage of the precious cargo was recovered for its owners. Yet, most of the treasure still lay on the ocean floor, and in the decades following the disaster an undetermined amount was lost to illegal salvagers from all over the Caribbean. In 1718, for instance, Manuel Miralles and a Spanish squadron surprised and captured eight ren-

---

[1] Flagship of the Tierra Firme division of the fleet.

egade sloops in the act of looting the wrecks. Such bandits, usually working in groups, also hindered Spanish salvage activities by attacking camps along the seashore. An Englishman, Henry Jennings, commissioned by the British to suppress privateering in the Atlantic, reportedly turned to piracy himself and was one of those who attacked the main Spanish salvage camp. Jennings made off with cannon and several thousand pieces of gold and silver—including some 3,000 ounces of gold.

An account published only eight years after the event in *A General History of the Robberies and Murders of the Most Notorious Pyrates* describes Jennings' daring exploit of 1716:

> Several vessels from the Havana were at work, with diving engines [diving bells], to fish up the silver that was on board the galleons.
>
> The Spaniards had recovered some millions of pieces of eight and had carried it all to Havana, but they had at present about 350,000 pieces of eight in silver, then upon the spot, and were daily taking up more. In the meantime, two ships and three sloops, fitted out from Jamaica, Barbados, etc., under Captain Henry Jennings...found the Spaniards there, upon the wreck. The money before spoken of was left on shore...in a storehouse under the government of two commissaries and a guard of about 60 soldiers.
>
> The rovers came directly upon the place, bringing their little fleet to an anchor, and...landing 300 men, they attacked the guard who immediately ran away; and thus they seized the treasure which they carried off, making the best of their way to Jamaica.[1]

Yet the pirate Jennings missed far more than he recovered—for Hoya Solorzana had earlier sent at least millions of dollars' value in treasure to Havana.[2] And many millions remained buried in the sea.

By 1774 most of the stories of the great disaster which befell the 1715 Plate Fleet had been forgotten, though in that year the earliest British cartographer of Florida, Bernard Romans, visited the area and reported that the masts of the Spanish fleet were still visible above the water and that his crew "repeatedly found pistareens and double pistareens"[3] on the beach after a northeast wind.

In subsequent years the masts rotted away and what remained of the hulls disintegrated. The inability to see traces of the ships above the water line, the bad weather so frequent along the Florida coast, hostile Indians on the shore, and wars among the major European countries stopped further salvaging, for all practical purposes, for the next hundred years. Millions of dollars' worth of Spanish gold and silver awaited discovery by future treasure hunters.

Uncovered by Happenstance

We now find ourselves in the present century, more than 200 years after the Spanish misfortune. Kip Wagner, a house builder, went walking one day on the bluffs near Sebastian Inlet, north of Vero Beach on the Atlantic coast of Florida. The shore was familiar to Wagner, a tireless beachcomber, yet on this particular day he noticed a considerable change in its outline. One of the severe hurricanes of the 1950s had just wreaked considerable destruction on Florida as it passed up the coast—and here, on Wagner's favorite beach, the hurricane's waves had caused a massive displacement of sand, altering the shape of the shore.

Wagner began exploring with renewed interest. As he walked the length of the beach, kicking aside hunks of seaweed and other debris from the storm, he noticed something laying obliquely in the sand. Picking it up, he realized that it was a silver coin with a cross on one side and the royal coat of arms on the other. The date on this slug was 1715. He had found a legendary piece of eight—a treasure right out of a pirate's story!

Wagner was in the right place at the right time, and soon he had found another, then another, and still another silver coin. Within a short time others had been gathered from the sand. Wagner thought it curious that all were dated 1715 or shortly before. He was further intrigued when he heard through a friend of the Spanish disaster which had occurred in 1715 near Sebastian Inlet. The more he learned about it, the more he began to believe that he had discovered something of importance.

Thinking that he might have stumbled upon the key to the lost Spanish treasure fleet, Wagner went to the Archives of the Indies in Seville, Spain, and made photocopies of the documents and maps there. He then returned to Florida and for $15 purchased a surplus Army mine detector. Traversing the area along the shore where he had found the coins, he dug up many strange things—car springs, part of an old bed, tin cans, and what was left of an old coffee grinder made in the 1920s. But amid all this junk he also unearthed an old ship's spike and a clump of cannon-

---

[1] At the time, Jamaica was controlled by England, Cuba (Havana) by Spain.

[2] Jennings later obtained a pardon as part of a general amnesty granted by the king of England to buccaneers who were in Nassau at a particular time, and spent the rest of his life in retirement in Bermuda, perhaps comforted by a chest or two of Spanish-American coins.

[3] Pistareen = Spanish (not Spanish-American) 2 reals; double pistareen, a term not often used, designated a Spanish 4 reals coin. Probably, the coins found were 8-real silver pieces. Most early accounts are quite inaccurate from a numismatic viewpoint.

The 1715 Spanish Treasure Fleet

Real Eight divers inspect coins recovered from the 1715 Spanish treasure fleet.

Philip V (1700-1746). Undated 8 escudos, partial Mo, assayer XJ. (1700-1710).

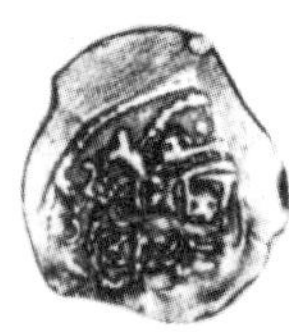

Philip V (1700-1746). [17]04 escudo, M[o], assayer X[J].

Philip V (1700-1746). 1710 escudo, Mo, assayer XJ.

Philip V (1700-1746). 1712 4 escudos, Mo, assayer XJ.

Philip V (1700-1746). 1712 escudo, Mo, assayer [J].

Philip V (1700-1746). [1713] Undated 4 escudos. Mo, assayer XJ.

Philip V (1700-1746). [16]54 Partially dated N.R. assayer R, 2 escudos from the Bogota Mint.

Philip V (1700-1746). [1913] Undated 2 escudos. M[o], assayer XJ.

Philip V (1700-1746). [17]10 partially dated SF 2 escudos from the Bogota Mint.

Philip V (1700-1746). 1714 8 escudos. Mo, assayer J.

Philip V (1700-1746). [1714] Undated Mo assayer [J].

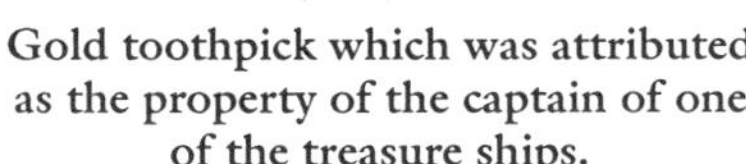

Gold toothpick which was attributed as the property of the captain of one of the treasure ships.

balls. It seemed that he had located the inland campsite, dense in the growth of prickly scrub high on the beach, where a few survivors of the Spanish treasure fleet and later salvagers had lived while recovering part of the drowned cargo.

It was obvious that the bulk of the wreckage, if indeed that was what he had found, must lay offshore. He hired a small plane to scan the shallows off the beach without having the slightest idea of what a sunken ship would look like. Would there be a decaying wooden hull with a broken mast and coins spilling from a strongbox? All he saw from the air was an oblong area in the lighter, sandy-colored bottom. He marked the spot and decided to dive on it as soon as possible.

The ship, or rather what remained of it, had nothing of a storybook appearance about it. The dark oblong shape seen from the air proved to be the ballast stones once carried in the ship's bottom.[1] These lay on the sea bottom just as they had been packed in the galleon's hold—smallest stones on the bottom, tightly lodged, with larger 50-pound stones on top. Around the border were 18 cannon, each encrusted with lime and marine life.

In the intervening centuries the galleon itself had made an excellent meal for generations of shipworms, or teredos. Its remains lay about a mile off shore in water just 15 to 20 feet deep. Ever-changing currents had carried off rotting fragments of the wreck many years before, and they were still distributing metallic chunks and coins, especially during a good blow. The treasure, Wagner thought, might be spread over acres of the ocean floor.

Real Eight Company Formed

A principal problem was how to move the immense quantities of sand which lay on the wreck site. After a few tentative dives, and little success, Kip Wagner formed the Real Eight Company, Inc., a group of eight divers and adventurers dedicated to the systematic uncovering of what they still only guessed was the wreckage of the Spanish Plate Fleet of 1715. The group's name was derived from the Spanish dollar-sized coin known as the eight real, or piece of eight, and was a play on words. Wagner and his company charted the area and drew precise plans before they began to salvage.

After making little progress with the conventional manner of dredging, Real Eight developed an efficient method of moving the tons of sand on and around the wreck. Instead of acting as a vacuum cleaner, Real Eight's dredger was a blower type of instrument which utilized the backwash from their diving boat's propeller. By means of this strong gust of undersea current, they could clear a depression 15 to 20 feet in diameter and five feet deep in the sand in less than five minutes.

Early in 1961, after two years of work, the divers found their first clumps of silver. Tons of sand had been shifted by the divers during good weather, only to be shifted back by the ocean during winter—sometimes, but not often, exposing new areas of the wreck. The job was tremendous, and when the silver was finally discovered it usually took the form of a blackened mass of as many as 2,000 silver coins adhering together.

What surprised the divers, after they had separated the coins by a harmless chemical process, was the diversity of the silver pieces. No two seemed alike, even though they bore the same date and general design. Investigation and the advice of numismatists told them that these pieces of eight had been minted by a very crude process: bars of silver were cast in long, flat strips, then pickled in a mild acid to remove the oxide coating and hammered to harden the metal; each bar was then cut by hand into small, odd-shaped pieces onto each piece of which were hammered dies bearing the royal coat of arms on one side and a religious symbol, the cross, on the other. These coins were of a temporary nature, too, as the Spanish king ordinarily ordered them melted and restruck into coin of the realm once they reached home. The English called these "chunk" coins—more familiarly, the aforementioned *cobs*—because of their irregular shape—a name which is still used.

Gold at Last!

The weather during those first venturesome years was not very kind to Wagner and his associates, nor was the underwater scene—for the men were bedeviled by storms, made anxious by sharks, and nibbled on by fish as they dug in the sands. But the lure of treasure persisted—and not long after the discovery of the first silver coins one diver brought up a handful of gold doubloons, each looking as if it had been

[1] Ballast stones were at once a necessity, nuisance, and nemesis of sailing ships. Needed to keep the ship in an upright position, the stones took the place of what could otherwise be valuable cargo. The stones proved to be a nemesis, as if a ship sprung a leak or foundered by the entry of water through open hatches, the weight of the ballast would take the ship to the bottom of the sea; without this load, wooden ships would have remained afloat. Sometimes ballast took other forms, as in one instance an iron coining press that was once used by Thomas Machin in his Newburgh, New York, private mint, but later, in the 1790s, carried as ballast aboard the sloop *Newburgh* (Isaac Belknap, captain; cf. Sylvester S. Crosby, ***Early Coins of America***, p. 191). It the steam-powered vessels of a later age, the engines served as ballast.

minted yesterday. They knew they had really found the lost treasure of 1715!

Large finds were few and far between, though. A constant clutter in the dredge soon added up to thousands of silver coins but only a few score of gold pieces. Two occasions were outstanding. The first occurred in the early 1960s when the water blower suddenly laid bare, as Wagner described it, "a carpet of more than 1,000 golden doubloons." Again in 1974 the divers began surfacing with handfuls of gold coins after an otherwise unproductive day—a long day of diving which eventually brought them more than a thousand gold doubloons.

These gold coins were all excellently preserved. Gold resists corrosion, and all of the doubloons recovered were nearly as fine as when they had been made—the only difference being some very light etching of the surfaces caused by more than two centuries of submersion in seawater. Only the silver cobs had to be treated to restore them to a desirable state—this by a careful chemical process which reconverts the sea-blackened surfaces to metallic silver. All of the silver coins whose surfaces were kept out of contact with the salt water (as when covered by other coins in a clump) came bright and virtually Mint State from the treasure wreck.

Along with the coins other interesting artifacts were discovered. Real Eight over a period of more than a decade brought to the surface muskets and pistol shot, pewter plates, iron and bronze fastenings, and even delicate porcelain fired in China more than 250 years ago—still intact! Fascinating, complexly crafted gold chains, rings, handmade silverware, crucifixes of precious metals, and a seven-pound gold ingot have also come to light. Yet it is the coins which remain perhaps the most fascinating—bearing an indelible date and the arms of Spain while coined of silver and gold minted in the New World. They are solid testaments to the discovery and exploration of a new land.

The coast of the United States is dotted with other sunken vessels, but probably none can surpass the romance or the original wealth of the Spanish treasure fleet lost at sea on that blustery night in 1715. How fortunate we are to be able to see and handle—perhaps even own—part of that fabulous wealth of early America intended for a king's treasury. If the ill-fated Spanish Plate Fleet had not sunk in that terrible storm 262 years ago, most of this native gold and silver would have been recoined in Spain. Only chance has saved it for us![1]

The Salvaged Treasure Fleet of 1733

Lost: 1733
Found: 1960s
Treasure: Spanish-American coins

Treasures from the Galleon *San José*

The stories surrounding the Spanish treasure fleets include many wondrous tales, not the least of which is the capture in autumn 1702 in the harbor of Vigo, Spain, of the fleet by English ships. The Britishers were so proud of their accomplishment that upon return to England they had silver and gold coins made from the metal they had swiped, such coins each bearing the boastful lettering VIGO above its date. However, that story has little to do with what later became the United States of America, and thus is not further described here.[2]

There is another treasure fleet which impacted (literally) on America and its history, the flotilla of the year 1733, worthy successor in treasure lore to the 1715 fleet.[3] Among these hapless vessels of the Spanish Main was a ship constructed in New England (of all places!) as the *Saint Joseph* circa 1727-1728. She was intended to be put in use in the lively commerce between the American colonies and England. However, she was soon sold to Spain. Her name was translated into Spanish, and she became the *San José*.

---

[1] Sources for the preceding 1977 account included: Kip Wagner, "Drowned Galleons Yield Spanish Gold," *National Geographic Magazine*, Vol. 127, No. 1 (January 1965), pages 1-37; and original reports and accounts of the salvage operations and discoveries supplied by the consignor, Real Eight Co., Inc., Cape Canaveral, Florida.

[2] Although the 1702 Vigo capture is discussed at length in C. Wyllys Betts, *American Colonial History Illustrated by Contemporary Medals*, 1894. Also see later footnote.

[3] Certain information is adapted from the present author's 1974 introduction to the catalogue featuring a consignment of recovered coins from the ship.

The Salvaged Treasure Fleet of 1733

Captain Tom Gurr looks over $25,000 worth of treasure trove from the galleon *San Jose*.

1733-Mo. F. Exceedingly rare Pillar dollar from the second year of issue of this type. One of the best preserved silver coins to be recovered from the *San Jose* treasure ship.

One of the 25 coral-encrusted cannons is brought onto the boat

In 1733 the ship was part of the annual flotilla that brought gold and silver to Spain from the New World. In a rerun of the 1715 disaster, off the coast of Florida—this time to the south in the region of the Florida Keys—the intense wind and high waves laid waste to the heavily laden ships, and many went to the bottom of the sea.

The Spanish dispatched a salvage crew to the site, and many coins and ingots were recovered. However, much treasure eluded their grasp. In time, the wreck was forgotten.

Captain Thomas Gurr

The oceans are the last great frontiers of the earth. The mysterious depths yield a wealth of information and sometimes even treasure to those adventurous enough to seek it. Captain Tom Gurr is one of those men with a well-developed sense of adventure.

While working as a flood control engineer in Miami, Tom Gurr's fascination with maritime history soon became more than a hobby to him. He began diving around old shipwrecks on weekends only, but the pull of the ocean and her hidden treasures finally overcame him. Quitting his job he moved with his family to the Florida Keys to be closer to good diving sites. Once there he formed the Marine Tech Salvage Co. With that event begins another story of a romantic Spanish treasure ship and the salvage operation which brought to the surface coins and other artifacts buried under the ocean floor for over 200 years.

Clues from an Old Map

On May 27, 1968, having studied carefully a copy of an old Spanish map and with the assistance of some secret electronic devices, Tom and fellow diver Rudy Palladino located the wreck of the *San José* in the water off Plantation Key. The large armed galleon had remained undiscovered, untouched since 1733! Palladino was the first overboard and went down to a depth of 35 feet. All he saw was sandy bottom and a few grassy patches. He quickly started fanning the sand away with his eager hands, and after two feet of digging came upon ballast stones—a sure sign of an old sunken ship!

Gurr and Palladino quickly gathered a crew. Using powerful vacuum cleaner-type suction pipes they began to remove the sand burying the old ship. It was this layer of sand which had actually saved the ancient galleon from complete destruction by the devouring teredo worms.

Smithsonian Assists

As the massive ribs and planking of the ship were exposed, the Smithsonian Institution was called in to help identify and preserve all of the artifacts the wreck was expected to yield. They sent Mendel Peterson, considered by many to be the nation's foremost authority on maritime history and shipwrecks. Peterson was a close friend of the aforementioned Edwin A. Link.

Peterson positively identified the wreck as the *San José*. Based on ancient documents located in the Archives of the Indies in Seville, Spain, he also determined that the ship, bound from Havana to Spain, was carrying one-half of the "Royal 5th" for that year. This was a 20% tax on all coins minted in the New World—a cache of gold and silver coins worth an estimated $2 million! In fact, the four galleons of the 1733 fleet were carrying the entire output of the New World mints for 1732, a transition period from the crudely made "cobs" to the famous "pillar dollars."

Coins and Artifacts

Found at the time were one copper coin, 242 silver coins, and a gold escudo, plus many artifacts. The next year, 1969, Gurr recovered 82 silver coins including a pillar 8-reals or "dollar" of 1732, a gold 2 escudos, and many more artifacts. In 1970, 12 silver coins were brought up.

The majority of the coins found on the *San José* were 4- and 8-real "cob" types of the genre made by taking a slice from a crude silver bar, clipping it by hand to the proper weight, and then stamping it by hand.

Certain transitional silver pieces found by Gurr are known as "recortados" and are especially prized as numismatic rarities. These coins, of the value of 4 and 8 reals, are squarish in shape like the older "cobs," but they show definite signs of having been made with the new screw-type presses early in 1733.

Most of the artifacts brought up from the *San José* were items of historic value. A partial inventory includes 25 cannons, three massive anchors, pistols, golden wedding bands, compasses, silver spurs, a pewter inkpot, gold religious medallions, a barber's pouch with razors and an ivory comb, clay pipes, an Oriental blown glass figurine, lovely blue and white K'ang-Hsi porcelain, a lead water pump dated 1728 (determined to be the oldest mechanical pump ever discovered), and finally, one of the most unique finds: a human skull believed to be the only one ever found on a treasure ship wreck in the Western Hemisphere!

The State of Florida Intervenes

After Thomas Gurr and his associates made some notable additional discoveries of treasure in 1972, among which were about 250 1732 pillar-type 8 reals, several clumps of oxidized silver coins, and more artifacts, Gurr became involved in a highly publicized squabble with the state of Florida concerning ownership. With a CBS television cameraman recording the incident, Gurr dramatically threw some recovered treasure back into the sea. In the halcyon days of treasure hunting in the 1950s and early 1960s, the state did not interfere with the pursuits of Alex McKee and others.

Later, without making any financial or other contributions, the state claimed generous shares of what was found, imposed many regulations, and in general created first-class headaches for anyone involved in undersea searches for anything of value. Many scuba divers, underwater archaeologists, and other highly qualified individuals with good motives, interested in treasure ship salvage, were viewed as criminals!

Gurr made some additional discoveries later, but as will be seen, the problems with Florida continued.

The State of Florida (Again)

In need of funds for legal expenses and to continue exploration, Captain Gurr consigned a group of recovered coins to an auction sale to be conducted by Bowers and Ruddy Galleries in February 1974. Interest ran high, and it was anticipated that many fine pieces would soon be owned by appreciative numismatists, and Captain Gurr's checking account would register a substantial balance.

However, that was not to happen.

The state of Florida placed an injunction on the sale, claiming the coins as its property. Gurr protested. It was agreed that the auctioneer would retain custody of the unsold pieces until the matter was settled. A long time afterward, Florida achieved legal ownership and acquired the pieces, much to the distress of just about everyone involved.

Capt. Gurr on Treasure Hunting

In an interview published as part of the auction catalogue, Captain Thomas Gurr shared some of his philosophies concerning the proper way to salvage treasure:

> One of the first priorities of a marine archaeologist is to preserve the historical aspects of finding an old wreck. Anyone with any feeling for the past must be aware of the terrific responsibility that underwater archaeologists carry. Nobody I know tears apart a wreck the old way.
>
> If you're under the impression that treasure diving is a lot of glamorous fun with little work, your view is a fantasy! Before a suitable wreck is found many fruitless hours are spent in the blazing sun covering miles of open ocean, eyes stinging from the salt water spray while intensely watching the needle of a magnetometer hoping to see it jump! The work of salvaging fragile artifacts as well as mapping their positions in the wreck for historical purposes is a long and tedious job. But the rewards of excavation and the excitement of the search far outweigh the hard work, danger, and insecurity of this type of career. When the going's tough, the one thing that spurs me on is the thought that I might have to take a regular job again!

Related Coastal Shipwrecks

Lost: Various times
Found: Various times
Treasure: Spanish-American and other coins

While a detailed worldwide listing of treasure ships containing recovered Spanish-American coins is not within the scope of this book, a listing of some of the more notable finds in American (mainly) and eastern Canadian coastal waters may be of interest, listed in order of the years in which the ships were sunk. These include specific ships from the 1715 and 1733 treasure fleets described above. Of possible interest may be a treasure ship of a different sort—if it even ever existed—that created a mystery for residents of Long Island, New York, in 1816:[1]

1554. Three Spanish treasure ships. Sunk off Padre Island, Texas. For many years coins have washed up on the shore. Additional pieces have been salvaged from the wreck sites including in a major effort in 1967 when treasure hunters from Indiana discovered a wreck about a half mile off the coast, recovered many silver coins (including 1-, 2-, and 4-real silver coins, undated, of Charles and Johanna) and artifacts. These were brought back to Indiana by the finders, trading as Platoro, Inc., only to precipitate a furor when the Texas Land Commission claimed ownership for that state. In American history this is an especially early wreck. The settlement of Jamestown, Virginia (1607) and the landing of the Pilgrims in Massachusetts (1620) were still generations away.

1554. Spanish galleon. Said to have been lost with much gold and silver aboard in the Atlantic off the coast of present-day Palm Beach.

---

[1] Information is from many sources, important among which is Thomas H. Sebring's numismatically authoritative *Treasure Tales,* 1986, of which Chapter IX is a listing titled "Salvaged Treasure Wrecks."

1586. ***San Juan.*** Said to have sunk, with two or three others, off the southeast coast of Florida. Much treasure was lost.

1622, September 6. ***Nuestra Señora del Atocha.*** Part of the Spanish treasure fleet consisting of six galleons, 17 cargo vessels, and five scouts. The *Atocha* was sunk, along with three other ships, southwest of Key West, Florida. The *Atocha* is said to have had over 250,000 silver coins and much other treasure aboard. The travails and final triumphs of the salvage of the *Atocha* by Mel Fisher, his family, and associates (Treasure Salvors Corporation), have been the subject of many articles and other publicity including in *National Geographic Magazine,* June 1976, and a book, *The Search for the Atocha,* by Eugene Lyon, 1979. The first significant coins were found in 1971, but discovery of the main part of the treasure did not occur until 1986.

1622, September 6. ***Nuestra Señora del Rosario.*** A traveling companion of the *Atocha,* this ship met the same fate.

1622, September 6. ***Santa Margarita.*** Part of the aforementioned Spanish treasure fleet. Salvaged in 1979 by Treasure Salvors, Inc. Many thousands of Spanish-American silver coins were found in the wreck of the *Santa Margarita* as well as numerous artifacts. Featured in *National Geographic Magazine,* February 1982. Many coins from the *Margarita, Atocha,* and another, unnamed ship probably also sunk in 1622 (the "Dry Tortugas Wreck" mentioned below) have come to the market in recent times.

1622, September 6: "Dry Tortugas Wreck." This unnamed ship, probably also sunk in 1622, was discovered and salvaged in the vicinity of the Dry Tortugas Islands southwest of Key West, Florida, in 1989-1991 by Seahawk Deep Ocean Technology. Called by salvors the "Dry Tortugas Wreck," the remains were located in 1,500 feet of water, necessitating recovery by the firm's ROV (Remote Operated Vehicle). Items found included over 1,200 coins, over 75 olive jars, many thousands of pearls, and dozens of gold bars. The silver coins seen by the author are extensively etched by salt water. Certain of these were placed into a museum. Beginning in 1996, a few came on the market.[1]

1628, late summer. Spanish galleons. Several treasure-laden vessels are said to have gone down in a storm off the Florida coast, off present-day Biscayne Bay.

1641, November 1-2. ***Concepcion.*** Part of the annual Spanish treasure fleet, this ship struck a reef off Hispaniola on November 1, 1641, sustained some damage, but was freed, only to be wrecked again on the reef the next day. Over 300 people died of the complement of 514 aboard. The rich wreck was lost until 1687-1688, when American captain William Phips (spelled Phipps in certain accounts), with the financial backing of the Duke of Albemarle, located 37,538 pounds in silver 8-real and related coins and 27,556 pounds of silver bullion, not to overlook 25 pounds of gold and various jewels. Later, Phips became governor of the Massachusetts Bay Colony.[2]

In 1968 noted French undersea explorer Jacques-Yves Cousteau sought to find the wreck, thought he had when certain artifacts (but not dated coins) were recovered, but soon learned via the 1756 date on a scale weight that the wreck was more than a century younger than the *Concepcion.* In 1977-1978 Burt Webber and his associates in Seaquest International relocated the *Concepcion* and found a king's ransom in treasure including over 60,000 silver coins, including some rarities from the Cartagena and Bogota mints.

1659 (circa). ***San Miguel el Arcangel*** (tentative attribution) wrecked close offshore at Jupiter Inlet, Florida. Various silver cobs have been salvaged.

1715, July 31. Spanish treasure fleet. This was a bad year for bullion and coin returns to Spain, and ships on the way there from Central America ran into hurricane that came up with ferocious intensity off the east coast of Florida.[3] By the time the winds and waves diminished, 11 or 12 ships were at the bottom of the ocean and with them an untold amount of silver and gold treasure. Many lives were lost. Some of the survivors reached the Spanish outpost of St. Augustine with their tales of woe.

Beginning in the late 1950s these ships were investigated seriously by Kip Wagner and, later, his Real Eight Company, described above, and finds of incredible historical and numismatic importance came to light. Eventually, over 10,000 gold cobs and over 100,000 cobs in silver were brought up from the sea bottom. Most coins were of the reign of Philip V and were struck at the Mexico City and Lima mints. At least six wreck sites have been found, and others await discovery.

In *The Practical Book of Cobs,* Daniel Frank Sedwick gives tentative identification of these six ships, in order from northernmost along the coast to southernmost:

Regla (a.k.a. ***Nuestra Señora de la Regla***). Off the coast of the strand ("outer coast") off Wabasso,[4] just south of Sebastian Inlet.

San Roman. Off the outer coast about half way between Wabasso and Vero Beach.

Carmen (a.k.a. ***Nuestra Señora del Carmen y San Antonio***). Off the outer coast opposite Vero Beach.

Rosario. Off the outer coast about half way between Vero Beach and Fort Pierce.

Urca de Lima. Off the outer coast just north of the inlet to the Intracoastal Waterway and Fort Pierce.

Nieves (a.k.a. ***Nuestra Señora de las Nieves y las Ánimas***). Off the outer coast a few miles south of the Fort Pierce inlet.

---

1 Cf. Daniel Frank Sedwick, Price List, Autumn 1996.

2 The *Concepcion* is listed here because of this American connection, although it was not wrecked in American coastal waters. Information is largely from Sebring, pp. 22-25, although this recovery is well known and is cited in most standard texts on treasure. Certain coins from the 1977-1978 wreck were offered at auction by Henry Christensen, Inc., in 1982. There have been a number of other salvages of Spanish treasure fleet wrecks in the Caribbean area (the *Maravillas,* found in the Bahamas, being an example) that are beyond the scope of the present text. Sir William Phipps (sic) is noted in C. Wyllys Betts, *American Colonial History Illustrated by Contemporary Medals,* 1894, pp. 34-36, where medals pertaining to this recovery are described. Of related interest is the commentary in Betts, pp. 11-15, concerning the capture by the Dutch on September 8, 1628, of the Spanish treasure fleet near Matanzas, a Cuban bay; pp. 44-50, the aforementioned capture by the British of the Spanish treasure fleet in the harbor of Vigo, Spain, on October 22, 1702; and p. 169, the capture by the British of three Spanish treasure ships off the coast of South America on July 10, 1745.

3 Among the many published accounts of this tragedy Robert F. Burgess, *Sinkings, Salvages, and Shipwrecks,* 1970, is one that gives numerous details.

4 Wabasso appears to be a reversal of the word Ossabaw (see Ossabaw Island, Georgia, in Chapter 22, also a potential treasure site).

1733, July 14-15. Spanish treasure fleet. History repeated itself, and a group of ships from the annual return of gold and silver to Spain encountered a hurricane near the northern stretch of the keys near the mainland of Florida (also see "The Salvaged Treasure Fleet of 1733" above). Twenty(!) were sunk. Wreck sites were investigated shortly after the disaster, and quantities of coins and ingots equivalent to 11,500,000 8-real pieces in value were recovered. In more recent times additional coins have been salvaged from various wrecks, an effort pioneered by Art McKee and joined in by many others including the aforementioned Thomas Gurr.[1] Often wrecks from this ill-fated fleet have been spotted in recent decades by looking for piles of ballast stones on the sea bottom, the wooden parts of the ship having deteriorated ages ago. From that point, poking around in the sand or blasting it away by the directed wash from a propeller has often brought to light various silver and gold coins, ingots, pieces of china, and numerous relics.

Among the ships in the 1733 hurricane, the *Aviso Delores, Gran Poder,* and *Murgia* were sunk, but refloated in the same year by Spanish salvage crews. The *El Africa* was buffeted about, but was able to anchor out of harm's way in about 200 feet of water. The list of ships that were not so lucky includes these:

Angustias (a.k.a. ***Nuestra Señora de las Angustias***). This wreck was found near Long Key by Jack Haskins and Richard MacAllaster, trading as the Peninsular Exploration and Salvage Co., in 1971.[2] The ship had been presumed to have been refloated and sent back to Spain, but Haskins found a clue in an old poem which stated that the keel of the ship had been broken, which, it seemed to Haskins, meant that the ship was never recovered, but still might be on the ocean floor. Additional information was obtained in the course of five trips to Spain to study charts and accounts preserved the Archives of the Indies in Seville. The wreck was located between Duck Key and Long Key, a stone's throw from the Overseas Highway to Key West. Exploration yielded many coins, the most important of which was a rare die-struck 1732 gold four escudos "royal" that was later auctioned for over $17,000.

Chavez. Wreck site discovered in the 1960s.

El Infante. This popular and easily accessible wreck site is in 30 feet of water on Little Conch Reef off Plantation Key. Art McKee, Tim Watkins, and many others have found various coins there.

El Populo. (a.k.a. **El Pingue, Nuestra Señora del Populo**). This wreck was discovered in September 1966 by the combined efforts of Lee Harding, Carl Fredericks, Carl Ward, and Bob McKay. What was left of her was spotted in 32 feet of water off Lower Matecumbe Key, and eventually yielded several cannon, many cannonballs, various artifacts (among which were an ivory lice comb and a pair of scissors), and, at first, a rare 1732 pillar-type 8-reals silver coin. Later, a few more coins were located. This ship was a scout or escort, not laden with treasure, and is said to have carried a cargo of tobacco. By keeping the location a secret, the salvors had two years to "work" the wreck. In September 1968 the site was discovered by others, and several cannon and other items found but not yet raised from the sea floor were spirited away by competitors. Such were the facts of life in treasure hunting in the 1960s.

El Terri. The wreck site is in 20 feet of water a mile offshore from Lower Matecumbe Key.

Herrera. This wreck is off Upper Matecumbe Key in 18 feet of water, in Hawks Channel two and a half miles south of Snake Creek Bridge. It has given up cannonballs, clay figurines, and other artifacts, but is not regarded as a source of numismatic treasure.

La Capitana. (a.k.a. ***La Capitana del Rul***). The wreck of this ship on Little Conch Reef off Plantation Key has been salvaged by Art McKee and others and has yielded many coins. In 1994, students in a 10-day diving school were scheduled to dive on the wreck. It was planned that exploration with the Fisher 1280-X electronic detector would be part of the program.[3]

San Fernando. Wreck site discovered in the 1960s.

San Ignacio. Widely scattered remains of this ship are at Coffin Patch in shallow water off Grassy Key.

San José (a.k.a. ***San José de las Animas***). An account of this New England-built Spanish ship and its discovery off Plantation Key in 1968 by Captain Thomas Gurr is given above.

San Pedro Lost off Lower Matecumbe key, this wreck has yielded many silver coins.

Sueco de Arizón (a.k.a. ***Nuestra Señora del Rosario, San Antonia, y San Vicente Ferrer***). Wreck site discovered in 1966 by Bob Weller, Brad Patten, and Pat Patterson, who styled themselves as "weekend divers." In short order enough silver coins to fill three five-gallon buckets were brought up!

Tres Puentes. The remains of this ship have been found in about 20 feet of water about three miles SSE of Snake Creek Bridge, and have disclosed numerous coins and other artifacts over the years.

1744, February 5. *Looe.* This British frigate with 44 guns, under Captain Ashby Utting, was wrecked on a small reef in 35 feet of water about five miles off of the Florida Keys about 25 miles southwest of Marathon, Florida.[4] In 1950, Dr. and Mrs. George Crile, Jr., explored the site and located some copper coins (among which was a Swedish half-ore of 1720) and various artifacts. Today, the site is known as Looe Reef. If additional coins have been recovered, the author has not read an account of them.

The *Looe* had been intended for coastal service to protect the British colonies of Georgia and South Carolina from possible invasion by the Spanish. Although the scenario changed many times over the years, at this particular point in history, England and Spain were adversaries, and France and England were friends.

On the 4th of February, 1744, crewmen aboard the *Looe* sighted a ship in the distance, gave chase, and upon contact

---

1 Sources are numerous and include Thomas H. Sebring, *Treasure Tales,* 1986; Bob Weller, *Famous Shipwrecks of the Florida Keys,* 1990; Daniel and Denise Berg, *Florida Shipwrecks,* 1991.

2 Daniel and Denise Berg, *Florida Shipwrecks,* 1991; no mention of numismatic items recovered.

3 *Fisher World Treasure News,* 1994.

4 Mendel Peterson, *History Under the Sea,* 1965, Chapter II, gives a detailed account of the exploration of this wreck. Peterson, a consummate undersea archaeologist who worked with and, to an extent, was sponsored by Edwin A. Link, was very concerned that during wreck site explorations those involved should record with cameras and ledgers the location of various artifacts, etc., to contribute to history and scholarship, and his book, published by the Smithsonian Institution, gives many suggestions in this regard. Peterson is also mentioned under the account of Thomas Gurr's discovery of the *San José.*

found it was a former British ship now flying a French flag. Around this time, a man aboard the strange ship was seen to throw an oilskin-covered packet of papers overboard, which upon retrieval had certain instructions in Spanish as well as French. Captain Utting felt that the ship was an impostor, was really Spanish, and took her as a prize for investigation, and headed toward Charleston, South Carolina. The captain consulted his charts, determined his position to be clear of any danger, set his course, and retired to his cabin. The helm was placed under the watch of James Bishop, sailing master, who at shortly past 1:15 in the morning of the 5th was startled to see breakers crashing over a reef dead ahead-this in an area that was supposed to be open sea!

The ship was blown onto the reef and was soon shipping water, which quickly reached a level of six to eight feet in her hold. The Spanish "French" ship she held as a prize was also impaled on the reef, and quickly sank. The remainder of the night was spent salvaging as much as possible from the *Looe,* which continued to break up. As luck would have it, a small Spanish sloop hove into view. Utting and some of his crew members, heavily armed, gave chase in a longboat, and captured the enemy vessel. The sloop returned to the wreck site, took aboard what could be easily handled, the smashed hulk of the *Looe* was set afire so as to render her useless to anyone else, and as the sloop pulled away from the reef, the remains of the stricken British gunboat exploded as the flames reached the store of gunpowder and munitions. The heavily overloaded captured sloop, Captain Utting directing, headed for Port Royal and landed there on February 13.

1759. *Tilbury.* The British warship *H.M.S. Tilbury* was lost off the coast. Coins from this wreck were salvaged by Pierre LeClerc and others. 430 silver and 16 gold coins were found, including pillar-type 8-reals of Ferdinand VI, struck at the Mexico City Mint.

1761. *La Auguste.* Lost off Breton Island, Canada. Of the 123 persons aboard, only seven survived. The wreck was salvaged in 1977 and was found to contain French écus of the 1726-1730 years and 8-reals from the Mexico City Mint, 1757 and 1758.

1766, September. *El Constante.* Part of a small fleet of six Spanish treasure ships sailing from Vera Cruz, Mexico, to Spain, she foundered and sank in the Gulf of Mexico off the coast of Louisiana. Her remains were discovered by chance by a shrimp trawler in 1979, after which state archaeologists from Louisiana supervised the salvage of about 30 pounds of silver and 40 pounds of gold treasure.

1785, September 2. *Faithful Steward.* This ship has been a mother lode to generations of treasure seekers who have gone to the shore at Rehoboth Beach, Delaware, after storms or high tides and have beachcombed for coins.[1] Often they have been rewarded by finding regal as well as counterfeit British and Irish copper coins from the eighteenth century, survivors from an estimated 350,000 pieces shipped from England to America aboard this ill-fated sailing vessel. A friend who summered in New Jersey brought me a handful of such beach-recovered coins in the 1950s, and I recall examining the oxidized, worn pieces, and contemplated their source. The pieces were mostly of a light brown to orange color, having been "cleaned" by action of the saltwater and sand. At the time there was little authoritative in print in the way of undersea treasure wrecks, although the *Faithful Steward* is identified as the ship of origin in Tom Penfield's 1952 treasure review and map published by Rand McNally. The great age of treasure ship discovery and publishing awaited its inception in the 1960s.

The vessel in question was en route from Londonderry, Ireland, to Philadelphia, with crew and passengers totaling 249, when she ran onto a shoal in stormy seas late at night while the second mate was the only officer on duty. At the time Captain McCasland and many of his crew were otherwise occupied—engaged in a drunken party. Finally, in a stupor the captain was taken to his bed.

In the darkness after the *Faithful Steward* ran aground just north of the Indian River outlet, those aboard decided to remain there, rather than try to go to an uncertain shore, although land was only about 100 yards distant. The ship was pounded by waves during the wee hours, and by morning only 68 people remained alive, those by clinging to pieces of the wreck or swimming to shore. As often happened in maritime disasters, the captain and 11 of his crew made it to safety, while nearly all of the women and children perished.

A survivor, James McEntire, later wrote that during the day after the wreck, the shore was crowded with local citizens, "not to aid in the cause or console the bereaved or administer to their wants,. No, but solely to plunder until they could plunder no more." The ghouls busied themselves "stripping the lifeless bodies of their clothing, snatching everything of apparent value, heaping the plunder on wagons and hauling it away." When a naked corpse was found, or an alive and still-clothed survivor, "many looked with eyes of disappointment...as there was no hope of gain."

1788. Spanish galleon. Said to have been lost with millions of dollars' worth of treasure off Pigeon Key, Florida.

1798, May 25. *DeBraak.* Built by the British to fill an order from France in the 1780s, the small 255-ton, one-masted, 84-foot merchant vessel was purchased by the Dutch after the French order was not honored. She was christened the *DeBraak,* a name she would retain for the rest of her sailing career. In the next decade the ship was captured by the British, who added a second mast and equipped her with guns. By 1798 she had sailed since June 1797 as a warship, the *H.M.S. DeBraak,* name unchanged from the original.[2]

On May 25, 1798, the ship, needing repairs, sailed into Delaware Bay off Cape Henlopen, where Captain James Drew figured she would stay for a time so that the necessary work could be done, after which the ship would return to England. Aboard were silver and gold coins captured from Spanish vessels in the Caribbean plus £80,000 in British gold that had been loaded aboard the ship in Jamaica for transport to England. Many Spanish sailors were kept aboard in chains as prisoners. Accompanying the *DeBraak* was the captured Spanish merchant ship, *Don Francisco Xavier,* on which

1 Certain information is adapted from Gary Gentile, *Shipwrecks of Delaware and Maryland,* 1990, pp. 76-78, among other sources. A detailed account of this wreck, together with much numismatic information relative to its importance, is found in Dr. John Kleeberg, "Shipwreck of the *Faithful Steward,*" proceedings of the Coinage of the Americas Conference, American Numismatic Society, October 28, 1995, pp. 55-77.

2 Sources include Thomas H. Sebring, *Treasure Tales,* 1986, pp. 101-104; Gary Gentile's *Shipwrecks of Delaware and Maryland,* 1990, pp. 54-73 (with a fascinating, detailed account of the modern recovery with many attendant controversies); original account in the *New York Gazette,* May 30, 1798 (cited by Gentile; not seen by the author).

the manacled unfortunates once sailed. Once in England, the officers and crew of the *DeBraak* would receive shares of the value of the commercial cargo and ship they had seized. Anticipation ran high.

Just as the ship was about to lower its anchor in Delaware Bay a mile offshore from a lighthouse, preparatory to the captain going ashore in a small boat to Lewes Town, a ferocious storm arose. The heavily-laden *DeBraak* was not able to maneuver and foundered in short order. To the bottom in several fathoms of water went Captain Drew, 37 crew members, and nearly all of the prisoners. Contemporary accounts made no mention of treasure being aboard. Portions of the masts and rigging remained above the water line, mute testimony to the disaster.

Salvage efforts commenced immediately, but not for treasure. That would come in time as stories arose about vast quantities of gold and silver aboard. One scribe after another embellished earlier writings, and in due course the *DeBraak* was believed to secrete a king's ransom in doubloons and pieces of eight!

Despite the relatively shallow water the supposed great treasure in the hold could not be accessed. One attempt involved using chains to raise the entire ship, but the hull proved to be too heavy. Over the years the richly laden treasure ship was not forgotten, and other salvors tried their hands, but none met with success. Various accounts continued to be advanced as to the extent and composition of the treasure aboard. Taking a contrary view, one claim—said to have been carefully researched in the British Admiralty—averred that there were no silver or gold coins at all, but only 200 tons of copper bars and quantities of cocoa beans aboard the captured, but not sunk Spanish ship, which is similar to an account printed in 1798 shortly after the ship's loss. Of course, just about every ship carried some gold and silver to pay the crew and take care of unexpected repairs, activities when calling at various ports, etc., but only a few carried cargoes that could be described as treasure.[1]

In the summer of 1984, Sub-Sal, Inc., a corporation based in Nevada, finally succeeded in bringing up some artifacts including cannon, bottles, and china. Divers located a quantity of diverse Spanish-American silver 8-real and gold 8-escudo pieces, British gold guineas, and other coins dated from 1792 to 1796. A ring with a personal inscription relating to Captain James Drew's brother John was found, firmly identifying the wreck as the long-sought British vessel. Difficulties with finances developed, and exploration of the wreck was transferred under a business arrangement to John Davidson, a real-estate developer from Lake Winnipesaukee, New Hampshire. Later, Sub-Sal went bankrupt, and another firm under Davidson named Drew Associates took charge. The new team made additional finds, these being mostly of a non-numismatic nature, although a hundred or so coins were found. One of the most interesting was a human corpse in a barrel now filled with silt, but apparently once filled with alcohol to preserve the remains of a man who had died at sea, but who was designated for a burial on land.

The treasure hunters despaired of finding much more by using divers, and decided the definitive recovery would be made by raising the wreck in its entirety. This was accomplished amid much publicity on August 12, 1986, when a sea crane lifted the hull onto a barge. By that time the wreck had turned over in its harness and had to be taken from the sea in an upside-down position, with tons of interior silt and artifacts falling back into the water.

In the absence of finding a vast quantity of gold and silver coins, the salvors determined that the great treasure, being very heavy, had separated from the hull many years earlier and still remained in the bottom of the bay. Despite intense exploration and rearranging of the sea bottom with a clamshell bucket scoop—amid bitter controversy as to whether the attempts were being done in a historically and archaeologically acceptable manner—a vast amount of treasure did not materialize. Somewhat fewer than 600 coins and many artifacts were recovered—not to be sneezed at, but not enough to satisfy the hopes of the salvors who, it was reported, had invested well over $3 million. Among the coins recovered were spade guineas (so-called from the spade-shaped shield on the reverse) of George III.

1816, autumn. "Money Ship." Stories related that this vessel, designated as the "Money Ship" as its real name has ever been learned, was of unusual build—perhaps like an old Spanish vessel.[2] After a fierce storm this stranger was seen off the coast of Southampton, Long Island, New York, apparently under full sail. The next day she was seen adrift and abandoned, and the day after that she ran onto a sandbar opposite Shinnecock Bay. Three locals—Mike Herman, Christopher Jagger, and Steven Sayre—were the first to reach the ship. Climbing aboard, they were surprised to see food on the tables, clothing scattered here and there, and furniture in disarray—as if, for some reason, the vessel had been abandoned suddenly, without advance notice or preparation. For future historians here was a ship in the category of the greatest sea mysteries, joining the crewless, passengerless, but cargo-intact *Mary Celeste*, for example.

She remained stranded on the sand. The master who attended to sea wrecks and salvage advertised her for sale. On the first day of the auction when the rigging and contents were sold, a bystander found a Spanish-American 8-real coin hidden in a block of wood. On the following day the hulk was sold *in situ*. A sale attendee found another silver 8 reals, this one in the sand.

A few weeks later, two whalers—Henry Green and Franklin Jagger—went aboard the wreck to look around, and one saw a silver dollar laying on the main cabin floor, washed by waves which at high tide came over that part of the ship. The next evening, when the tide was at low ebb, the two men returned, poked around, and espied a bright glimmer in a crack in the cabin ceiling. Prying off some boards, Green was inundated by a cascade of the silver dollars, seemingly a pleasant experience for just about anyone! He was startled and dropped his lantern. The coins rolled off the floor, over the side of the ship, and into the sea (apparently, each and every coin did this). The two scavengers kept their find quiet, returned later,

---

[1] Perhaps representing the other end of the potential desirability spectrum is the wreck of the *Nathan Esterbrook, Jr.*, which slipped under the waves off the coast of North Carolina, February 20, 1893, taking a load of bird dung (formally called *guano;* used for fertilizer) to Davy Jones' Locker. Nor should we overlook the account of the unfortunate three-masted schooner, *Alfred Brabrook*, out of Boothbay, Maine, which wrecked on the shore of Cape Hatteras on March 7, 1899, with a cargo of *ice* headed for the refrigerators of warm Charleston, South Carolina. (Both citations from David Stick, *Graveyard of the Atlantic,* 1951.)

[2] Adapted from *Ship Ashore!* By Jeannette Edwards Rattray, 1956.

and were able to recover some of the coins from the water plus others they were able to find still hidden on the ship.

During the winter of 1816-1817, the seas pounded the hull, and it broke up. For many years after that time, Spanish-American silver coins washed ashore. One farmer brought a team of horses and a plow to the beach and was able to turn up 60 pieces. In the late nineteenth century, William D. Halsey, a resident of Bridgehampton, recalled that "beach dollars" were found for a long time, and that he had two in his possession. On the beach at East Hampton, apparently in the 1890s, Mrs. Mary E. Bell found a 1774-dated "Spanish" coin. Another account said that a local man, who was known as "The Captain," surname not recalled by anyone, spent 10 years searching the beach and finally found a jar filled with "Spanish" gold coins. Theories were advanced that the Money Ship was a pirate vessel or perhaps even a slave ship that had strayed far off course from its intended route in the Caribbean.

Annals of meteorology record that 1816 was the "year without a summer." Apparently, the weather was hostile and stormy, and parts of New York and New England were startled by the appearance of snow in July and August. Perhaps this fits in with the "strayed far off course" theory.

Spanish Treasure Coins on the Market

As have many numismatists, I have handled many sea-salvaged coins over the years. As coin collectors know well, but as romanticists and, sometimes, treasure hunters, do not seem to realize, the ultimate value of a sea-recovered coin depends upon standard *numismatic* characteristics. Among these are date, mintmark, and assayer, type or variety; grade, quality of surface, and demand. In general, a heavily etched Spanish silver "dollar" that, in addition to its sea immersion for centuries has been poorly cleaned in recent times, is of little value to a collector. No number of accompanying certificates, display boxes, and photographs of treasure wrecks will turn a low-value coin into a high-value one. Stated another way, an ordinary silver 8-real coin in undamaged Very Fine grade, with an unknown history, is worth more than a corroded Very Fine coin attributed to a treasure wreck to 99% of the potential buyers. However, in a proper numismatic context, a pedigreed coin, sea etched or corroded, if described by an authoritative person, will draw interest from a numismatic clientele. Florida dealer Daniel Frank Sedwick noted that while many of the larger finds have been subjected to undue promotion and publicity, a number of scarcer, smaller finds have not, and there is a great deal of interest and appreciation for the latter.[1]

Further—and also surprising to the novice—a professional numismatist with a specialty in Spanish-American coins will be a better source of fine pieces for reasonable prices than will be most treasure-salvage companies or promotional offers. The late Henry Christensen, who specialized in Spanish-American coins, related many stories of investors in treasure hunting expeditions who received sea-salvaged silver coins as their "dividends" and thought them to be worth many hundreds of dollars or even far more, when on the numismatic market choicer and more desirable pieces could be bought retail for $50 to $100.

Equipped with detectors made by White's Electronics, Randy Smith, Ken White (president of the firm), and Keith Zorger recovered gold coins off the coast of Florida. Here they are shown with some of their prizes and the detectors used.

[1] Letter, October 1996.

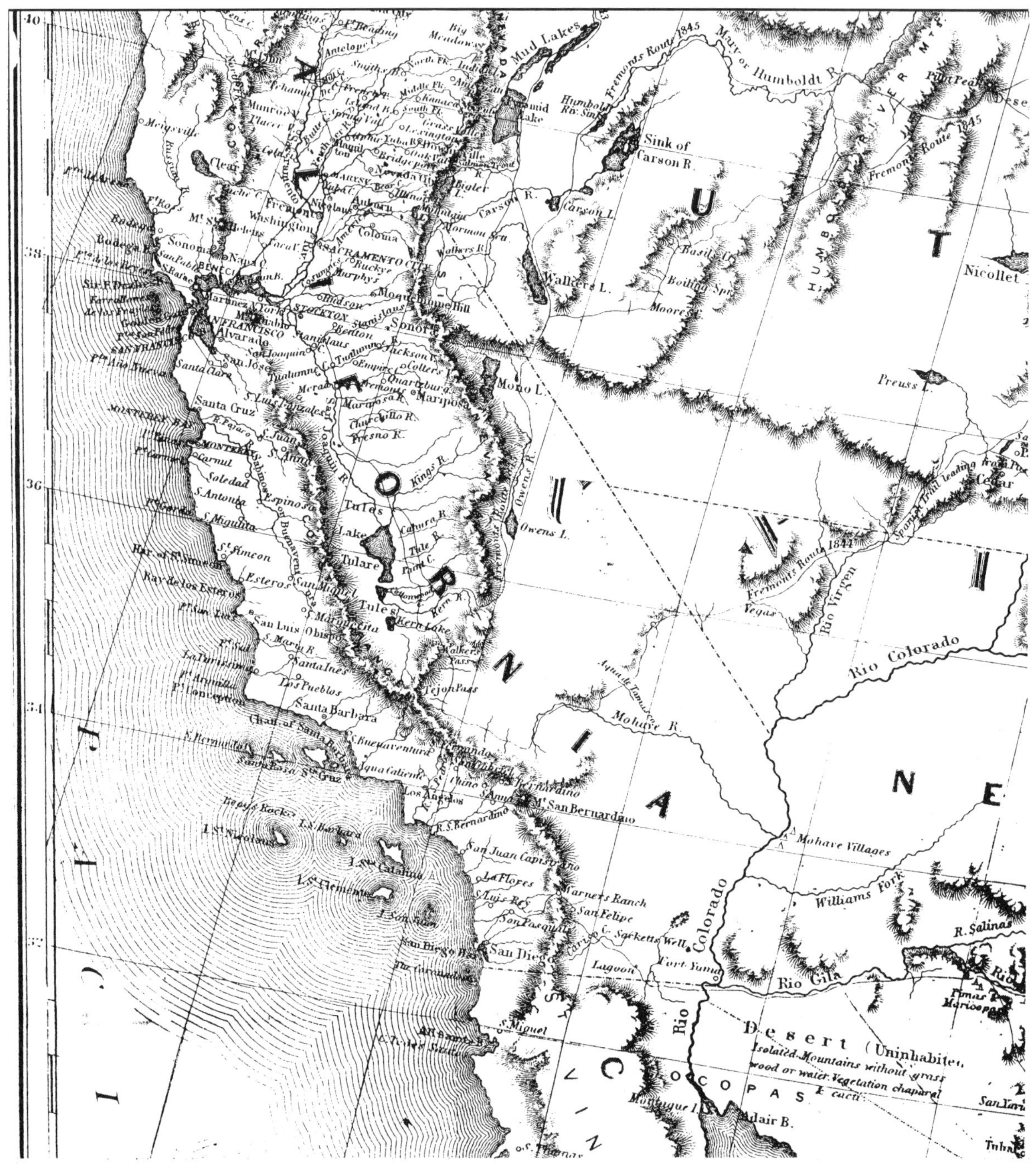

California and the Pacific Coast as shown on an 1855 map.

CHAPTER 11

Gold from the Briny Deep

Tales of Gold Rush Shipwrecks and Their Treasures

Gold in California!

Gold! The story begins in January 1848 when flakes of the yellow metal were discovered by John Marshall at Sutter's Mill on the American River in California. Thus was set in motion the great Gold Rush, which within the next several years would attract untold thousands of fortune seekers to the West and in the process build an empire, completing the United States map from the Atlantic to the Pacific.

The news spread slowly at first, and it was not until the following autumn that adventurers began to arrive in notable numbers in the formerly quiet port of San Francisco. This was a one-way traffic, and the crews of the ships as well as their argonaut passengers did not want to return to sea. Abandoned ships accumulated in the harbor with no one to man them on outbound voyages. One was brought close to shore and made into a hotel (called the Niantic).

Newspaper stories about gold and instant wealth became prevalent in the Atlantic states toward the end of the year. Fact was often difficult to separate from fiction as writers with little hard information on hand tried to outdo each other with wondrous tales of adventure and fortune. Eager readers became excited by the news of easy wealth to be obtained by a few days of digging in the West. Gold was there for the taking.

Yerba Buena Cove, San Francisco, as it appeared in the winter of 1849-1850. The bay was clogged with inbound ships deserted by gold seekers.

One story told of the Gold Bluffs, where nuggets littered the sandy beach just waiting to be picked up. A slightly more fanciful account told of a volcano spewing precious metal instead of the usual lava!

In December 1848 a shipment of gold was received at the Philadelphia Mint and subsequently coined into $2.50 gold coins, each with the distinguishing counterstamp "CAL." on the reverse to identify the origin of its metal. Sent from the United States representative in San Francisco, William L. Marcy, the small chest of precious metal officially confirmed the new Age of Gold, the new Golconda, the new El Dorado, as it came to be known.

After late 1848 and early 1849 it was a free-for-all in the eastern states as thousands dropped their saws, plows, fishing nets, and other implements of employment and commerce and headed west to make their fortunes.

Getting There

The overland trip by ox-drawn wagon took about five months in the early days of the Gold Rush. The actual time varied depending upon the route taken and the equipment possessed. Happy adventurers in high spirits formed wagon trains in Independence, Missouri, and a few other places, and singing *O Susanna* and other rollicking melodies, headed westward, with each night's stop being an occasion for festivities and celebration—at least at the start of the trip. The tragic fate of many in the Donner Party stranded on the way to California in the winter of 1846-1848 was known to easterners, but such misfortune would certainly not happen again. In reality, there were many hazards along the way including Indian attacks, outbreaks of cholera, lack of water, and extremes of temperature and weather. Many died. Their bodies were simply abandoned along the trail, along with dead and bloated cattle, or buried in shallow graves only to be dug up by coyotes. All too reminiscent of the Donner group, wagons broke down or there were no oxen remaining alive to pull them. Much valuable equipment had to be abandoned. Despite such travails—and the trip was not easy for anyone—many thousands did arrive at their destination.

Around Cape Horn by sailing ship from New York to San Francisco could take 150 days or even more, depending upon the vessel, the number of shore stops, and the weather. Few were interested in this arduous, largely unknown method of travel through unfamiliar seas. The overland route seemed to offer more security. Later, clipper ships with billowed sails and sleek hulls would cut the travel time to below 100 days, but these primarily carried bulky cargo, not passengers. By that time, the sea transfer route across Central America would be in place, as will be subsequently related.

In California

Upon arrival in California many Forty Niners found a combination of wealth and excitement in the gold fields in the foothills of the Sierras inland from San Francisco. However, even more came to the reality that gold hunting was hard work and settled into other pursuits including clerking, farming, lumbering, and other trades. Wages were higher than back home in Massachusetts, Illinois, or Pennsylvania, but living expenses were higher as well, and, usually, there was no net gain.

Eventually, gold mining became concentrated in the hands of large partnerships and corporations which dug deep tunnels into the earth or used high-pressure streams of water to blast away hillsides in search for nuggets and ore.

Very few people came to California from the East, went to the gold fields and found enough to make them wealthy, and then returned home to live a life of luxury. This was the dream of thousands, the reality of only a few.

Gold Coins Minted

Beginning in the heady days of 1849 several assayers, bankers, and entrepreneurs in San Francisco and nearby towns produced gold coins and hallmarked ingots to serve as exchange in an economy in which gold was plentiful, but coins were scarce. In 1850 additional privately-produced coins were made. In 1851 Augustus Humbert arrived by ship from New York City to become the government's agent under the title of United States Assayer of Gold, California, an arrangement which soon led to the establishment of the U.S. Assay Office of Gold.

In 1854 matters were made more formal with the opening of the San Francisco Mint in the facilities formerly occupied by the partnership of Curtis, Perry & Ward, private coiners of Moffat-imprint gold coins. By this time there had been many different kinds of gold coins in general circulation for several years. Included were federal issues as well as coins of Humbert, Miners Bank, Kellogg, Baldwin, Moffat, and Wass, Molitor & Co., among others. Most impressive were the large $50 gold "slugs" of octagonal shape minted in large quantities in 1851 and 1852.

In time, large amounts of gold coins and ingots were concentrated in commercial channels, primarily in San Francisco, from which port the "treasure" (as it was

An artist's conception of Sutter's Mill on the American River near the time of the gold discovery (actually slightly later, for no residences were on the opposite river bank in January 1848).

openly referred to in newspaper accounts and shipping notices, seemingly with little thought for security) was sent by sea to Nicaragua, Panama, Liverpool, and other destinations. Large amounts of gold were received at the Philadelphia and New Orleans mints, both of which experienced great difficulty in refining the metal so as to remove at least part of the large amount of unwanted silver that existed as an "impurity."

Coastal Steamships

On March 3, 1847, Congress passed an act calling for bids to transport the mail by one line of steamers in the Atlantic Ocean from New York City to the sleepy town of Chagres at New Granada (later called Panama) on the Isthmus of Panama, continuing by another line on the western side from Panama to Astoria, a fur-trading center in the Oregon Territory in the Pacific Northwest. At the time gold had not been discovered in quantity in California, and the San Francisco region was mainly agricultural in its emphasis. Sutter's Fort in Sacramento, which had furnished some relief to members of the Donner Party in the early months of 1847—nearly the same time as the congressional act, was a regional trading center and outpost for farming, lumber, and cattle enterprises.

The Atlantic steamships were to be of 1,500 tons burden, constructed strongly, and able to be purchased by the government, upon option if needed, and converted into war steamers. Their route was to be from New York to Panama twice a month, stopping at Havana.[1] Another planned steamship route from New York, also twice a month, touched at Charleston, terminated at New Orleans, and, "if practicable," called at Savannah and Havana. Port stops were needed not only to take on or unload passengers and freight, but to restock provisions and coal for fuel.

On the more lightly-traveled Pacific side just three vessels were needed, and of smaller size, two to be 1,000 tons or more and one of 600 tons. These were to go once a month from Panama to Astoria to take care of what commerce that could be arranged. Although there were exceptions, the ocean on the Pacific run tended to be calmer and without fierce squalls and devastating hurricanes, providing another reason why lighter ships could be employed.

Contracts Awarded, Ships Built

The Atlantic contract was given on April 20, 1847, to Albert G. Sloo, who transferred it on August 17 to George Law (whose name would be significant in a later account of sunken treasure), M.O. Roberts, and B.R. McIlvaine of New York. The government provided the substantial annual subsidy of $290,000 and mandated that the first two ships be completed by October 1848.

The Pacific Coast contract went to Arnold Harris, a speculator who assigned it to William H. Aspinwall. This arrangement provided for a 10-year subsidy of $199,000 per annum.

The Pacific Mail Steamship Company was incorporated on April 12, 1848, for $500,000. After it became generally known that gold had been discovered in quantity in California, the arrangement was modified whereby the route was to be from San Francisco to Panama, with any mail going farther north to Astoria or elsewhere to be carried separately by sailing vessels. After this time, San Francisco became the most important trading center on the West Coast. At the time Los Angeles was a sleepy little village of a few hundred inhabitants. It would not become important in the Gold Rush, and little attention was paid to it.

All vessels in Atlantic and Pacific coastwise service were of the sidewheel type powered by steam engines fired by coal (although wood could be used if absolutely necessary). For contingencies and to take advantage of prevailing winds, auxiliary sails were employed, typically supported by one large and two smaller wooden masts. The two large paddlewheels, one on each side, were made of wood and covered with a semi-circular wooden housing, often with ornate cut-out decorations or geometric designs, and bearing the ship's name. On some ships, a meter was connected to the drive shaft via reduction gears. In this way, it could be determined how many revolutions of the paddlewheels had occurred during a given voyage. Sometimes bets would be taken on the outcome.

Most of the ships were built in New York City, a center of the industry. The steamers, braced in some sections with iron and with hulls made of wood, proved to be well built as subsequently evidenced by their durability in service.[2]

Early Voyages to California

The first of the Pacific route mail-subsidy vessels, the *S.S. California,* 1,050 tons, left New York City on October 6, 1848, and within the next two months was followed by the *S.S. Oregon* and *S.S. Panama.* There being no excitement in the East about gold in California at the time—the only news reaching the East being regarded as rumors—only the crew members and no through passengers were aboard the *S.S. California.* This was a tranquil time with no hint aboard ship of the pandemonium that would soon characterize the sea lanes to San Francisco.

The *S.S. California,* its crew ignorant of the new El Dorado, went through the Straits of Magellan at the tip of South America, being only the third steam ves-

[1] In many early accounts, today's Havana was designated as Habana; Panama was often given an accent, as Panamá, on the last letter. By the 1840s, pirates no longer infested the harbor there.

[2] Within the next decade it was generally felt that the "iron screw propeller" type of drive on "screw steamers" (as they were called) was better than sidewheel paddles for ocean travel, but the mail lines continued using sidewheels.

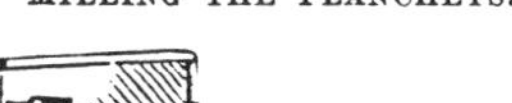

MILLING THE PLANCHETS.

RUNNING THE GOLD INTO INGOTS.

ADJUSTING ROOM.

Scenes of the San Francisco Mint as published in the *Hutchings' California Magazine*, October 1856.

Sailing ship on what appears to be a relatively calm day in the Strait of Magellan.

sel to ever do so (the first two were the 700-ton English West Coast Line steamers *Peru* and *Chili* years earlier in 1840). Of the only seven passengers who had booked fare at New York City, none was going as far as San Francisco. Not a single person had bought a through ticket. The Straits, the nemesis of many sailing vessels and the focal point of many frightening tales, took the *S.S. California* nearly 42 hours' time under steam, plus 108 hours at anchor in fog and high winds, to negotiate.

The *California* mail ship reached Callao, Peru, on December 29, 1848, where innocence ended. The thrilling news, "there's gold in California!" had reached this port, and on the docks a small crowd clamored for passage to the north. Seventy-two were provided with berths or staterooms. The next stop was at Panama on January 17, 1849, where 1,500 eager gold-seekers wanted to board, and some of them were entitled to do so from arrangements they had made earlier in New York, although in absence of any communication with the home office, the crew of the *California* had no inkling of the impending wave of humanity.

Upon arrival in Panama in January 1849 the *California* had comfortable accommodations for about 100 more passengers beyond those picked up in Callao, but after a great deal of argument and controversy, over 300 more people were accommodated from the milling crowd of gold seekers. The 72 Peruvian travelers who boarded at Callao were now bumped from their interior sleeping quarters and were forced to spend their remaining evenings on makeshift beds on the deck. Some of the new travelers paid as much as $1,000 for a steerage ticket, far more than a first-class fare and stateroom should have cost. Eager to get to the land of gold, travelers were all to happy to bed down on coils of rope if that is what it would take to secure passage, and some joined the Peruvians on deck.

Then followed a star-crossed voyage of four weeks northward from Panama. The first stop was at Acapulco, followed by a call at San Blas. About this time a stowaway was discovered and, worse, it was learned that he had been helped by one of the ship's firemen. The guilty crew member was put in irons, whereupon his fellow firemen stopped shoveling coal, and the ship stopped, dead in the water. After much acrimony, the *California* resumed its voyage, and at the next port, Mazatlan, crew members who had participated in the strike were involuntarily disembarked and placed in the hands of Mexican police. For the rest of the trip the remaining crew was sullen. Affairs went from bad to worse, and while off of Point Conception, the ship ran out of coal. Spare masts, wooden cabin trimmings, and other structural and ornamental items were sacrificed to the boilers. Then someone remembered that about a hundred bags of coal were stored as ballast in the bottom of the ship. This proved to be enough fuel to permit transit to Monterey, where enough firewood was obtained to complete the voyage. Passengers helped load the wood aboard.

Meanwhile, food was in short supply on shipboard as few healthy provisions had been available in Panama, and the extreme overcrowding made conditions unpleasant. However, despite these delays and discomforts, the *S.S. California* reached San Francisco on February 28, 1849, a truly memorable day in the history of the American West. Except for a boy who oiled the engines, the entire crew deserted the ship, and many headed for the gold fields.

Repairs had to be made to the *California* to replace the wooden components that had been burned as fuel. After some difficulty the crew roster was partially filled, and on May 15, 1849, the ship left for her first return trip to Panama with $300,000 worth of unrefined gold aboard.[1] By this time, private minters of coins had not yet started in business, with the possible exception of a small firm known as Norris, Gregg & Norris. This partnership was composed of plumbing supply outfitters who had come to Benicia City, California, from New York City and who are known to have struck off a few $5 gold pieces by the end of May.

Subsequently, mail steamers would typically drop anchor in San Francisco twice each month, the arrival being known as "Steamer Day," a time of celebration

[1] Wiltsee, p. 11, and other sources.

as letters, newspapers, and goods were received from the East. When an incoming mail boat was sighted from a hill in the city, a flag would be run up so that citizens could take immediate notice and throng to the docks to greet it.

By January 1849, the month that the *S.S. California* touched at Panama and continued its inaugural voyage to San Francisco, at least six sailing vessels and two steamers had recently landed gold hunters on the Atlantic side of the Isthmus of Panama, in addition to other ships that had arrived in the preceding nine weeks. The outpouring from these ships helped fill the aforementioned crowd of 1,500 who sought passage northward on the other side of the Isthmus.

At the time—and continuing for years afterward—the overland transit of the Isthmus was fraught with dangers of disease, especially cholera which killed more than a few adventurers. The travelers who had landed at the town of Chagres on the Atlantic side took a combination of pack animals and small boats to cross the about 50 miles of land to reach the Pacific-side jumping-off spot for the voyage continuing north to the land of golden opportunity. Local boat operators on the Chagres River that went part way across often quoted one price for service, then after the gold-seekers had gone a few miles, demanded additional money to go farther. Food and lodging were primitive, and the land part of the crossing was dense jungle. The transit at Panama was often a daunting experience.

Ships from eastern United States ports continued to pour passengers into Chagres, and before long the western or Pacific side of the narrow land strip was crowded with travelers who had crossed the 50 miles of land. The fortune hunters had great amounts of enthusiasm and often a comfortable amount of money, but no tickets or reservations for passage north to San Francisco. It was catch as catch can. Some were lucky. Some were not.

Pandemonium and a mad scramble for passage greeted both the *S.S. Oregon* on March 13 and the *S.S. Panama* in early May. Some would-be passengers had bought tickets from agents in eastern ports and others had acquired reservations in Panama. All tickets had been sold by greedy passenger agents who disregarded the limited space actually available.

In addition to the substantial vessels of the Pacific Mail Steamship Company, the owners of many private sailing ships—some of questionable seaworthiness—on the Pacific side seized the opportunity for revenue and helped alleviate the congestion. Some eager travelers even attempted to paddle north on their own by purchasing small boats and canoes, and met with various misfortunes.[1] Many voyagers had no clue as to how distant San Francisco was or the way to get there. A few hardy souls even attempted to walk northward along the Panama shore.

Steamship Trade Expands

Following the crowded conditions of the first couple of years, the mail steamers connecting from the East to California via Panama were able to handle all comers. After that time, what little passenger service there had been around Cape Horn diminished to virtually nothing except for longer-distance voyages to and from Liverpool and other European ports. The famous clipper ships of the era built by McKay and others were primarily cargo vessels, traveled faster than steamers on the same routes, but did not regularly carry significant numbers of passengers.

Departure of a steamship from San Francisco harbor in the 1850s.

Cornelius Vanderbilt, who had cut his teeth in the steamship trade with the *Lexington* on Long Island Sound in the 1830s, developed a competing steamer service connecting from the East to California, which flourished 1849-1851 and which used a combination land, lake, and river passage across Nicaragua. As this Central American country was farther north than Panama, the route could claim a savings of two days' time over what the mail steamers offered—quite important in the minds of many gold seekers who envisioned making their fortune almost immediately upon

[1] An interesting account of travel to California in 1849 (on the *S.S. Falcon* on the Atlantic side and the *S.S. Oregon* on the Pacific coast) is found in Bayard Taylor, *Eldorado, or Adventures in the Path of Empire, a Voyage to California Via Panama*, etc., 1850, chapters 1-5. For an account of the same journey in 1851 (on two small sailing vessels) see J.D. Borthwick, *Three Years in California*, 1857, corrected edition retitled *The Gold Hunters*, edited by Horace Kephart, 1917.

landing in California, and for whom every minute counted.[1]

The Nicaragua route was, indeed, hundreds of miles shorter than the Panama route, but the amenities seem to have been fewer, and most travelers went via Panama. The crossing at Nicaragua consisted of about 12 miles on land, a long distance on large Lake Nicaragua, and the balance of the journey by navigable rivers. As the land part of the trip was considerably less than the Panama option, there was less risk of disease and infection via the Nicaragua route.[2] During the decade of the 1850s Nicaragua underwent political contortions, including an invasion by an American soldier of fortune and his comrades—enough episodes to fill several books! In 1854 a New York firm acquired a franchise from Costa Rica for a crossing in that country, but it never proved worthwhile.[3]

In the 1850s the Pacific Mail Steamship Company vessels on the western run included the *California, Golden Age, Golden Gate* (later burned off the coast near Manzanillo, Mexico, July 27, 1862, with loss of an estimated 223 lives and $1,400,000 in treasure, the latter mostly recovered later),[4] *Panama, Sonora, John L. Stephens, Tennessee* (wrecked while lost in dense fog near the entrance to San Francisco harbor, March 6, 1853, without loss of life), the *Winfield Scott* (of which more will be said) and others.

Shipments of Gold

While many gold coins and ingots made in California were used in trade on the West Coast and for export payments, vast quantities were shipped to the East for deposit at the new (opened in 1854) New York Assay Office and the Philadelphia Mint.[5] In fact, so much gold came through the port of New York City that the legislative solons from that state petitioned Congress, unsuccessfully, to establish a mint there.

There were several ways to ship gold from San Francisco to the East Coast. One was the seldom-used (in an eastward direction) hazardous and difficult overland route by wagon and, continuing in the eastern area, by rail. Another route was around Cape Horn by ship (95 to 105 days by clipper; these outran steamships which took 150 or so days with many stops). The most popular by far, and the fastest passenger route, was via Panama, a passage of about 25 days depending upon the scheduling.

The Panama Connection

Under the last method, passengers and freight were transported by a Pacific Mail Steamship Company vessel or other steamer from San Francisco to Panama, a pleasant voyage of about 14 days. The typical ship of the line was steam-powered but employed auxiliary sails. On board were many amenities including fine food, gaming tables for those with a sporting turn of mind, and salons for relaxation including reading and music.

An advertisement for the July 20, 1857, departure from San Francisco of the Pacific Mail steamer *S.S. Golden Gate* proclaimed:[6]

> TO PANAMA, connecting via Panama Railroad with steamers of the U.S. Mail Steamship Company at ASPINWALL for New York and New Orleans direct.
>
> The only reliable and safe route. Departure from Vallejo Street Wharf. The favorite steamship GOLDEN GATE will leave Vallejo Street Wharf with the United States mails, passengers, and treasure,[7] for PANAMA, Saturday, July 20th, 1857, at 12 o'clock A.M. punctually.
>
> Passengers by the P.M.S.S. Co.'s line are landed, on their arrival at Panama, upon the wharf at the railroad terminus, by the company's steam ferry boat, and proceed immediately by RAILROAD ACROSS THE ISTHMUS.

---

[1] For a time a small steamer bearing the nameplate *Central America* was in service on Lake Nicaragua, but had no relation to a certain Atlantic Ocean steamship that would be given the same designation in 1857. This particular lake is one of the most scientifically interesting bodies of fresh water on earth (right along with lakes Baikal and Titicaca) and is home to tuna and sharks, normally only found in oceans. The author has encountered no reports of shark problems by gold seekers in the 1850s, however.

[2] Ernest A. Wiltsee, *Gold Rush Steamers of the Pacific,* 1938, pp. 52-53.

[3] Certain historical background adapted from Hubert Howe Bancroft, *History of California,* Vol. VI, pp. 126-142.

[4] A Currier & Ives print, small folio, is titled "Burning of the Steamship 'Golden Gate,' July 27, 1862" and has the subtitle: "On her voyage from San Francisco to Panama, having on board $1,400,000 in treasure, 242 passengers, and a crew of 96 persons of whom only about 100 are known to have been saved. Coffman, p. 262, comments that some salvage occurred, but little was recovered, and $2 million in gold was lost.

[5] The Assay Office at New York was established in 1854. A report tendered by the Director of the Mint on October 12, 1857, noted that as of that time the facility had separated and refined $52,191,443.33 worth of gold and silver bullion. Most of the gold came from San Francisco.

[6] Oscar Lewis, *Sea Routes to the Gold Fields,* advertisement reproduced opposite p. 240. Text lightly edited. Aspinwall, on the Atlantic side of the Isthmus of Panama, was a new city built on a filled-in swamp and was named on February 2, 1852, for William H. Aspinwall, founder and president of the Pacific Mail Steamship Company, which in 1847 obtained the contract for Pacific coast mail service. Earlier, the nearby port of Chagres was employed. (Today the town is known as Colon, Panama.) The first steamer of the Pacific line was the *California,* which entered service in 1848, followed by the *Oregon* and the *Panama.* As the Pacific Ocean was calmer than the Atlantic and the route to Panama from San Francisco was longer than the corresponding route in the Atlantic from Panama to New York, the Pacific steamers were generally larger and more elegantly appointed than their eastern counterparts.

[7] The transport of "treasure" was openly advertised and discussed in San Francisco newspapers for an extended period of years. While today this might seem to have been a breach of security, at the time it was viewed as a publicity benefit: any ship worthy of carrying gold treasure would surely be safe and pleasant for passengers, and its operators would be perceived as being financially sound.

Transfer of passengers to the Panama Railroad as shown in the late 1850s.

Trial striking on an 1849 U.S. copper cent of a token bearing on one side the inscription COLL [indistinct] BRANDON & CO./COLON (ASPINWALL)/2-1/2 Cts., and on the other side an engine, tender, and two cars of the Panama Railroad, with a palm tree in the background. Possibly issued circa 1863-1864. (2x enlargement)

San Pablo Station on the Panama Railroad route across the mountains from the Bay of Panama on the west side to Aspinwall on the east.

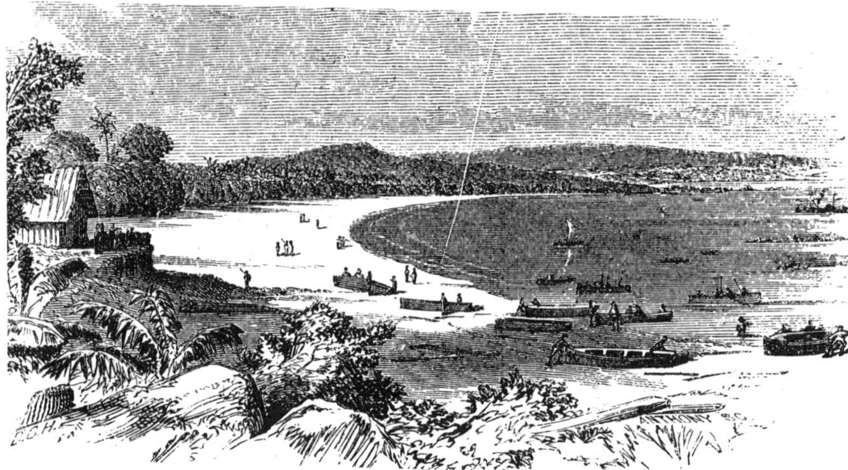

View of the Pacific terminus of the Panama Railroad. Steamers dropped anchor in Panama Bay, and passengers were taken by lighters to the nearby shore where they boarded rail cars.

Highest point on the Panama Railroad.

Gone were the days of uncertain travel across land at Panama, the terrors of the jungle, bargaining with rivermen, and other inconveniences. However, the threat of disease remained, but was minimized due to the shorter time needed to make the transit.

Panama Railroad Inaugurated

The Panama Railroad link, slightly over 47 miles long, was completed on January 27, 1855. Great celebration took place soon thereafter, to usher in a new era of travel convenience. Among those attending were 16 invited dignitaries who had come from New York City with 457 other passengers aboard the *S.S. George Law,* which arrived in port decorated with streamers and bunting.

Engines pulling strings of small cars shuttled passengers between ocean ports on each side of the Isthmus. The Panama Railroad line consisted of a single track with several turn-off or bypass areas to facilitate passing or stopping.

Prior to completion of the Panama Railroad, portions of the track were utilized, as noted in a May 16, 1854, advertisement by the Pacific Mail Steamship Co. in *The San Francisco Herald:*

> Safety and speed! No sickness! No river travel! Thirty-one miles by railroad.... The progress of the railroad, and consequent reduction in the distance for mule travel, render the transit of the Isthmus at present a mere pleasure trip of from six to eight hours.

Transfer of Golden Treasure

An account written a few years later told of the arrival by steamer after a voyage from San Francisco, the railroad experience, the transport of coins and bullion, and conditions in Panama:[1]

> The heavy eyes of the fourteenth morning [after departure from San Francisco] were wide open, when we approached Panama from the south. A long point of land compels vessels to go 100 miles below before entering the great bay, surrounded by wooded hills. On our left appeared Toboga with two English steamers, which ply down the coast of South America, lying before it. Winding among high mountain islands, which stud the bay, we came in view of New Panama, while the old city, destroyed by earthquakes and buccaneers, was pointed out six miles distant.[2] Three men-of-war—two English and one American—three ships of the mail line, and one steamer of the Panama Railway for plying up the coast, were lying in the harbor.
>
> At ten o'clock—precisely the minute appointed at the beginning of our long voyage two weeks before—the *Sacramento* made fast to a buoy; for shallow water and wicked reefs forbid first-class steamers to approach within two miles of the shore.[3] Three of us took passage in the captain's dispatch boat, protected by umbrellas from the broiling sun. We pulled two miles out of our course to avoid the sharp teeth of the long reef standing above water at that stage of tide. Here the Pacific rises and falls 30 feet; at Aspinwall, just across the narrow isthmus, the variation of the Atlantic is only as many inches....
>
> After our little boat was pulled up by the beach by coal-black natives, we landed among tumble-down buildings. Climbing rickety stairs and passing under a crazy arch, we were in the narrow streets of Panama, shaded by tall dwellings of adobe and stucco. The population is 6,000.
>
> As this was January first, a church holiday, the thoroughfares were thronged with gaily attired natives of every hue, from jet black to light buff. A few, boasting untainted Castilian blood, are as fair as the people of Louisiana and Mississippi; but chocolate is the prevailing tint of the mob. Interspersed were Frenchmen, Germans, Jews, English, and Americans, all in white linen from head to foot; and richly dressed Spanish ladies with dazzling eyes, and clear rich complexions tinctured with olive.
>
> Women of the poorer classes (these low latitudes where bountiful nature supplies absolute wants without labor, have no working classes) wore light linen gowns with immense frills about the neck, and exhibiting one entire shoulder and breast. The chariest maid of Panama is prodigal enough only when she unmasks her beauty, not merely to the moon, but to the blazing sun and entire populace. The whiteness of her drapery is in sharp contrast with her tawny skin. Some boys under 12 wear shirts, but most are entirely naked; while girls appear "in the elegant costume of the Greek slave." They form striking couples for promenade—young ladies arrayed only in straw hats, and juvenile gentlemen in the same attire with hats omitted. The youthful republicans of New Granada are incredibly callous to the prejudices of civilization, and flagrantly rebellious against "the Paris milliner who dresses the world from her imperious boudoir." If there be any Calvinism in dress, they are hopeless examples of total depravity.[4]

---

1 The quotation is from Albert D. Richardson, *Beyond the Mississippi,* 1867, which chronicled his adventures beginning in 1857; his steamer and railroad experience via Panama was in December 1865 and January 1866. Additional information is from John H. Morrison, *History of American Steam Navigation,* 1958, pp. 434-504 (contains much basic information, lists of mishaps, etc.).

2 Concerning pirates in Panama and elsewhere in Central America, Alex. Oliver Exquemelin (a.k.a. John Esquemeling), *The Buccaneers of America,* 1684, offers many interesting stories.

3 Other accounts indicate that anchorage varied from one and one-half to four miles from shore; quite probably, ships of shallow draft moored closer to shore.

4 In this era of Victorian manners, there was a double standard. Popular magazines and newspapers in the United States printed many tales of loose women and depraved men and sold many copies of their publications as a result; on the other hand, human sexual body parts were rarely if ever named nor were such explicit terms as "pregnant" often used (except in crime cases). More than just a few contemporary accounts of travel and experiences in California in the 1850s concluded with adverse comments concerning gambling, non-observance of Sunday as the Sabbath for Christians, intoxication, and prostitution. The activities of Mormons—in particular their practice of polygamy—were nearly universally condemned by the press in the East. It was very difficult for a writer from the East Coast to observe a different society (such as that of the Panamanians in their native land or of relocated Americans in the California gold camps or of Mormons in Salt Lake City) and write objectively about it. Every account of length seemed to require a moral point, as if readers would be disappointed without it.

The large, well stocked trading houses sell goods cheaper than New York; for Panama is a free port, a paradise for smokers who love genuine Havanas, and for homeward-bound Yankees, who purchase for wives, daughters, and sweethearts, exquisite gowns of Irish linen which are said to last a hundred years. Price, 30 cents per yard, specie.[1] Panama hats, which endure water and crushing like gutta percha, sell for from three to 15 dollars.

There is a large American hotel and a cathedral seemingly a thousand years old. Many buildings are shattered by earthquakes and war. The "old" city is reduced to a pile of ruins; and "New" Panama, apparently about the oldest town in the world, is tending in the same direction. Crumbling walls surrounding the city, adobe ruins within, even roofs of tall buildings and church towers, are profusely covered with growing vines and shrubs. Here nature accumulates while men decay; here vegetation triumphs over masonry.

The ancient cathedral facing the plaza is a quaint, irregular pile of stone and stucco, with half-a-dozen medieval Spanish bells in one of its towers, and crumbling walls covered with mosses and vines.... Now no religious services were held, as the republican leader of the late revolution had driven away all the priests. Ordinarily, a revolution in a Spanish-American town attracts little more attention than a thunder-shower in the United States....

Then seeing a little steamer filled with our passengers, like a hive black with bees, moving to the shore, we hastened down the hot, narrow, winding streets, to the railway station at the water's edge; and elbowed through the dense, panting crowd into the cars, which have cane seats, and wooden blinds instead of glass windows. The locomotive shrieked, and we moved out of the city, following endless curves, slowly winding around foot-hills and through jungles, toward the summit of that narrow neck of land which divides two unbounded seas.

The Panama Railway, begun in 1848, was completed in seven years, costing $160,000 per mile. Again and again its work was suspended, for the fever-breeding air poisoned all who breathed it. Natives, West Indians, Irish, French, Germans, Austrians, Coolies, and Chinese were successively employed as laborers, and to all it proved fatal. The 48 miles are ridged with graves.... Jamaican Negroes and whites from our northern states bore the climate best and finished the work. Think of men breathing fever, penetrating cane-brakes, wading swamps, fighting noxious insects, dodging boa-constrictors, cougars and crocodiles, and constantly braving death, for one or two dollars per day!

The road pays larger dividends than any other in the world.[2] It charges $25 in specie for a ride of 48 miles[3] and corresponding prices for freight. Seven-eighths of its passenger and two-fifths of its other receipts are from the California trade. This freight includes treasure. Estimating it by the ton much the larger portion[4] goes southward. The European and United States trade with the west coast of South America is very heavy. British mail steamers ply from Valparaiso to Panama: and on the east side another line connects Aspinwall with Liverpool....

Beside the track are the dwellings of native workmen and villagers—little steep-roofed cabins, thatched with tiles, grass or cane, with walls of sticks and plaster. They look dry and cool; but during the rainy season they must admit water like sieves, and their occupants become aquatic. The women were

View of the new town of Aspinwall on the Atlantic side of the Isthmus of Panama.

---

1 Payments in paper money not wanted.

2 And was listed on the New York Stock Exchange. In 1857, the year of the *Central America* incident, shares of the Panama Railroad sold in the 90s.

3 This was the rate in 1866 and probably for first class; in 1857 rates were considerably lower. In various accounts of steamer travel, railroad crossings, California gold field experiences, etc., various people would write about the same things, and often their recollections of prices, weights, and measures would differ.

4 Manufactured goods, foodstuffs, and other freight usually went around Cape Horn, as the extra time involved still yielded a saving over the off-loading at Panama and the rail transit method. Treasure, however, had time (interest) value and usually went via Panama if it was destined for New York.

Transferring gold coins from a steamship (in the background at the left) to a car on the Panama Railroad (right). This process took about two hours, during which time over a million dollars' worth of gold coins and bars were typically brought ashore.

celebrating the day in clean frocks and bits of finery. All wear Panama hats like the men. Prolific nature has blessed them with innumerable dusky babies. I have seen nothing like it save in Salt Lake streets and on Missouri prairies.[1]

Here is the richest, densest vegetation in the world—an impenetrable tangle of mangoes, plantains, palms, oranges, bananas, limes, India rubber trees, and thousands of shrubs and parasites new to northern eyes.... All is profusion, luxury, gorgeousness. Every prospect pleases, and only man is vile.

Eleven miles from Panama we crossed the summit, through a natural gap 300 feet above the ocean. From these mountains one can see both Atlantic and Pacific at once. For several miles we followed down the Chagres River, against whose muddy current natives used to pole up early California emigrants in canoes.

Aspinwall has an excellent harbor, enabling first class steamers to come to the wharf without ferriage. On the chief street is a long row of wooden buildings, with projecting roofs or sheds, used as trading houses and eating and drinking saloons. The motley population of less than one thousand is composed of natives, Jamaica Negroes, and Americans. Aspinwall owes its birth to the Panama Railroad, and

[1] This commentary is reflective of a common journalistic prejudice of the day. Those who bore more than just two or three children were often thought of as being of a lower class of humans than high-bred city folk. Most if not all people from the inland parts of Missouri were perceived as illiterate and ignorant of the proper ways of society. Mormons (in Salt Lake City) could do no good in the eyes of most writers from the East.

was surely born too soon—sent to this breathing world scarcely half made up. Surrounded and intersected by stagnant pools—water unfit for drinking or cooking without distillation; air close and malarious; and population by hybrid—it is the dreariest, wretchedest, most repulsive city of fact or fiction, not excepting Cairo, Illinois, in the days of Martin Chuzzlewit....[1]

An hour after us arrived a second train, bringing only the specie. Once admitted through the great gate and over the long wharf to the steamer *New York,* we could not leave the boat while the treasure was being transferred. Muscular, half-naked Negroes received from freight cars the bare bricks of silver, bars of gold sewn in canvas, and boxes of coin, each taking a ticket describing his parcel, to deliver with it on the ship. Bending and perspiring under these precious burdens, the tawny workmen marched in constant procession between rows of men who illuminated the wharf gangway and deck with lanterns. This novel spectacle lasted for two hours, convincing me that a million of dollars in bullion is a good deal of money, and would be awkward to carry around. Afterward, while the heavy freight was coming on board, and the Negroes pleasantly diverting themselves in smashing our trunks, we were permitted to go ashore to get limes for lemonades and claret punches, to soften the asperities of the trip.

The Atlantic Route

At Aspinwall a ship of the United States Mail Steamship Company or other line continued the route by sea to New York City with an intermediate stop for coaling, often at Havana, Cuba, but sometimes elsewhere.

An 1856 advertisement of the U.S. Mail Steamship Company noted that it operated "10 first-class steamers on the Atlantic," connecting with "the Pacific Mail Steamship Co.'s 16 first-class steamers plying between Panama and San Francisco." Each steamer was said to have "a surgeon at the service of the passengers." Railroad transit across Panama varied from $12 to $30, payable only in silver or gold coins, with the exact fare depending upon the amount of baggage.[2]

On the Pacific Coast the captains of steamers had to be careful to stay away from shore and island points so as to avoid rocks, many of which were submerged only slightly and did not appear on charts. The weather was generally peaceful and the water calm.

On the Atlantic leg the steamer captains' main concern was weather, for sometimes unpredictable storms of frightening intensity could arise from seemingly nowhere, especially in the late summer. This was the season when hurricanes would rise in the tropics, such as the one that caused passenger discomfort aboard the *S.S. George Law* in December 1853. However, such weather usually proved annoying for just a short time, after which the skies cleared.

Thus, the setting is in place for the story of various steamships laden with gold that plied the Pacific and Atlantic coasts in the heady times of the 1850s, continuing until the late 1860s when the transcontinental railroad became a reality.[3]

Most voyages were completed as scheduled, and the treasure and passengers aboard reached their destinations. There were, however, some notable exceptions.

Eternal Father, strong to save
Whose arm hath bound the restless wave,
Who bids the mighty ocean deep
Its own appointed limits keep:
O hear us when we cry to Thee
For those in peril on the sea.[4]

The Last Voyage of the *Winfield Scott*

Lost: December 2, 1853
Location: Anacapa Island, California
Found: 1965
Treasure: Miscellaneous gold coins

The Story of a Steamship

Among the vessels in service under the Pacific Mail Steamship Company flag was the 1,291-ton *S.S. Winfield Scott.* The ship had been named for Gen. Winfield Scott (born in 1786) who had distinguished himself in the Mexican War, in which service he marched from Vera Cruz to Mexico City and served as the governor of the city 1847-1848. In 1852 Scott was the Whig party candidate for president, but lost to Franklin Pierce. Some ranked him as the pre-eminent American military figure of the first half of the nineteenth century.

---

1 Title character of a novel written by Charles Dickens in 1843, drawing upon his largely unfavorable impressions of America gathered during a visit in 1842.

2 Oscar Lewis, *Sea Routes to the Gold Fields,* advertisement opposite p. 241.

3 The golden age of the mail steamers to and from Panama ended with the completion of the transcontinental railroad in 1869, by which New York City and San Francisco were linked by 3,377 miles of track, and the rail journey could be made in less than seven days (cf. R.M. Devens, *Our First Century,* Chapter 55).

4 *Navy Hymn;* words by William Whiting.

The *S.S. Winfield Scott* was built by Westervelt and McKay in New York and launched on October 27, 1850. She measured 225 feet long, had a draft of 14 feet, and was powered by two 370-horsepower side-lever steam engines fed by coal stored in bunkers capable of holding 300 tons.[1] The specifications called for a capacity of 165 passengers in first and second cabins and 150 in steerage. The dining salon, 96 feet in length, could seat over 100 at a time. To each side of the dining area were staterooms. For the relaxation of passengers a parlor at the stern, 80 feet long by 14 feet wide, was lined with sofas on the sides. Part of one end could be closed off by folding doors to allow privacy for ladies or families. Another parlor was in the fore part of the ship.[2]

Ship namesake Winfield Scott, American military hero of the War with Mexico.

The *S.S. Winfield Scott* arrived in San Francisco for the first time on April 28, 1852, having made the transit from Panama with 700 passengers in just 14 days. She bore the flag of the Independent Line for the remainder of the year, after which she was in service for the New York & San Francisco Steamship Company.[3] She departed San Francisco on May 6, 1852, with 580 passengers to Panama, and was back in California on June 16 with 600 passengers including 85 ladies.[4] In May 1853 the ship was purchased by the Pacific Mail Steamship Company.[5]

San Francisco to Panama

On December 1, 1853, the *S.S. Winfield Scott* weighed anchor in the harbor of San Francisco and headed toward Panama. Captain Simon F. Blunt was at the helm, the first ship he had ever commanded.[6] On board were about 400 passengers, the crew, sacks of mail, and over $875,000 in gold treasure (per the manifest) plus coins and various personal effects carried by the passengers. By this time, travel along the Pacific Coast was routine, there was no congestion at the docks, and the gold fever had largely subsided. Once an individual enterprise, gold hunting in California was now mainly the purview of large corporations which mined gold-bearing quartz and processed it in stamping mills or used large hydraulic "monitors" to blast away hillsides with streams of water under high pressure. "Forty Niners" had settled in and were typically engaged in trades other than gold prospecting.

On the trip to Panama the passengers aboard the *S.S. Winfield* Scott enjoyed many amenities including games and entertainment on board, walking on the deck and observing the distant coast provided there was no low fog (called "smoke" by sea travelers), and taking the opportunity to relax. Through a spyglass, sometimes glistening brown seals could be seen sunning or cavorting on rocks.

Meals were of excellent quality, with the meat coming from poultry, sheep, cows, and pigs kept alive in pens on board.[7] Sumptuous tables were set for first cabin passengers. Those in steerage often had to eat while standing at counters, but the food was good. Stocks of wine and other spirits were abundant and could be tapped at reasonable cost. First cabin accommodations provided travel at its finest—even better than the mail steamers on the Atlantic side of Panama, as the later generation of Pacific steamers built after the Gold Rush traffic became a reality tended to be of larger size and with more commodious parlors and public rooms. However, on both coasts, steerage accommodations could be primitive, cramped, and noisy.

[1] One account says 235 feet in length, draft of 20 feet; often ship specifications in contemporary as well as later publications are approximate.

[2] John Haskell Kemble, *The Panama Route, 1848-1869,* 1990 edition, p. 252.

[3] Wiltsee, p. 80; Kemble, p. 252.

[4] Wiltsee, p. 82.

[5] Kemble, p. 65.

[6] Blunt, who had graduated from the Naval Academy at Annapolis in 1849, was sent as his first assignment to participate in the Government Geodetic Survey of the Coast of Oregon and California.

[7] Livestock pens were used only on the Pacific coastal steamers; on the Atlantic side meat was packed in ice in New York City for trips in both

"Let her rip!"

On the next day, December 2, 1853, off the coast to the south of Santa Barbara, California, and about 30 miles distant from it, the *S.S. Winfield Scott* became lost in a dense fog.[1] Around 9:00 the first officer asked the captain's advice, and the latter, believing he was in open ocean, said, "Let her rip!" Fog was common in the area, especially at that time of year when the night air was cool.

At full speed she proceeded through the gloom, and shortly before midnight struck the rocks on the north side of Anacapa Island, carving two large holes in her bow. The two large sidewheel paddles were thrown into reverse, the damaged ship backed away only to hit other rocks and smash her rudder. Then "the boat drifted off a distance of about 300 yards, and went ashore bow on, striking upon a high bluff. She had already commenced filling, and soon after striking for the last time sunk up to her guards."[2]

In the wee hours of the morning of December 3rd the passengers and crew took provisions and bedding to a tiny uninhabited island about a mile west of the crash scene, where they spent the night in company with mail sacks and the gold treasure. The rescue operations were supervised by Captain Blunt and were not over until the crack of dawn. Meanwhile, the hull sank in deep water and was a total loss.

Most of the passengers' baggage and personal effects, among which were at least a few gold coins, were left behind in the wreck. The next morning the passengers and saved cargo were transferred to another, larger island nearby.

At eight in the morning of December 4, the *S.S. California,* A.V.H. LeRoy, captain, saw the smoke from a signal gun fired by the stranded voyagers (but did not hear the shot), and within the next two to three hours rescued the female passengers from the island and transferred the gold treasure and mail on board.[3] The *California* reached San Francisco on December 6 at 8:00 a.m. Passengers disembarking numbered 309 of which 77 were ladies.

The *S.S. Southerner* arrived at the *Winfield Scott* wreck scene at daybreak on December 10 and brought ashore ample provisions for the remaining survivors, who were waiting for the *S.S. Republic* which had been sent to take them aboard.[4] At five o'clock the same day, the *Republic* arrived on the scene. From that time until the morning of the 12th, rescue and additional salvage operations were conducted, after which the latter ship headed back to San Francisco amid high winds and heavy seas.

By all accounts, throughout the entire incident Captain Blunt did a superb job of assisting with the

Hydraulic mining in California. By means of high-pressure hoses, streams of water blasted away entire hills. Alluvial gold flakes and nuggets were recovered in the stream as it exited the site.

directions including the return from Panama. Meat was segregated by type, with beef in one group of barrels, chickens in another, pork in still another, etc.

1 Certain information adapted from an account, "Arrival of the California; Loss of the Winfield Scott; No Lives Lost; Safety of the Mails and Treasure," *Alta California,* December 7, 1853, p. 2. Purser Watkins of the stricken ship provided most of the details to the newspaper. The "Let her rip!" account appears in the Edward Bosqui narrative subsequently quoted and in other texts.

2 *Ibid.*

3 The *California* had departed from Panama on November 19, 1853, with 500 passengers and 254 mail bags, some of which had connected from New York on the *S.S. Illinois* and from New Orleans on the *S.S. United States.* On November 30, on the way to San Francisco, the California had passed "the boilers and other remains of steamer *Independence,* high and dry on the shore of [Santa] Margarita Island" (613-ton steamer owned by Cornelius Vanderbilt, wrecked on March 16 of the same year, 122 lives lost of 283 aboard).

4 The *Republic,* an 852-ton, 201-foot wooden sidewheel steamer, had been put in service in 1849 for the Baltimore Steam Packet Co. Like so many eastern steamers, in 1851 she was sold to western interests and entered the lucrative Pacific Coast run, mainly calling at ports along the *California* shore, her activity during the Winfield Scott wreck. Later she plied the San Francisco to Portland and Victoria route. In the 1860s her engine was taken out and put in the *Del Norte,* and later the hull was scrapped or simply rotted away (accounts differ). The 337-ton *Southerner* was launched as the *Aurora* in 1846, sold to the Navy in January 1847 and renamed the *Scorpion,* and rebuilt after October 1848 and renamed the *Isthmus,* and in 1854 renamed the *Southerner.* She is a different ship from that used in the New York City to Charleston run and damaged in the hurricane of September 1857 (as noted under the account of the *S.S. Central America*). The present steamer *Southerner* was employed on the San Francisco to San Diego run. After sailing from the port of Umpqua, Washington, in December 1854 she struck a sandbar at the mouth of the Columbia River, sprang a leak, and was lost; all passengers were saved, but the cargo went down with the ship (cf. Wiltsee, pp. 129, 131, 150-151; Kemble, p. 232, there as the *Isthmus*).

landing of the passengers, the removal of what cargo that could be taken ashore, and other matters.[1]

Recollections of a Passenger

Edward Bosqui, a passenger on the fateful voyage, later recalled the experience:[2]

I had now been absent from home three years. During that time I suffered extensively from home-sickness, which finally grew intolerable; and in December, 1853, I set out for Canada on the steamer *Winfield Scott,* Captain Simon Blunt, U.S. Navy, commanding. There were about 300 passengers. On board were quite a number of army officers, who had been ordered East from their stations in Oregon and other points in the Northwest. Among them were Captain Sully, Lieutenant Polk, nephew of ex-president Polk, and Captain Taylor, brother of ex-president Taylor. There were also many distinguished veterans of the Mexican War on board, and several of Colonel Frémont's guides and mountaineers who had accompanied him on his last expedition, with most of whom I was acquainted.

We sailed through the Golden Gate in high spirits, but on the evening of the second day out, in the latitude of Point Conception, the weather became cloudy and squally. At about nine o'clock in the evening the first officer of the ship crossed the threshold of the captain's cabin, where a group of army officers were telling adventures, and diverted the attention of the party, of which I was a member, by very abruptly addressing Captain Blunt with the words: "Captain, the weather is dirty and squally. Shall we keep her out?" The captain answered, "No; let her rip!" None of us paid much attention to the incident, and soon afterwards separated for the night.

At midnight I was suddenly awakened from a sound sleep by a terrible jar and crashing of timbers. Tumbling out of my berth, I was confronted by the horror-stricken visage of my toothless and baldheaded state-room companion, who had no time to secure his wig and false teeth and was groping about to find them. Leaving him paralyzed with fear, I hurried out on deck, where my attention was fixed on a wall of towering cliffs, the tops of which were hidden by the fog and darkness and appeared about to fall and crush us. All around was the loud booming of angry breakers surging about invisible rocks. Our predicament seemed awful in the extreme; some of the passengers appeared to be stunned, others were panic-stricken, while all were overpowered with a sense of utter helplessness. I joined a little group of army officers who stood on the after-deck of the sinking vessel very calmly looking around and contemplating the awful scene. Some of the passengers were running aimlessly to and fro; others were fighting for life-preservers.

As one of the life-boats was being lowered, a mad rush was made to get into it before it was clear of the deck. On this the captain drew his pistol and ordered the crowd, in a determined voice which sounded clear above the noise of the breakers, to clear the boat. His command was instantly heeded. Then he shouted, "Bring the women and children now; this boat is for them." Another rush was made to get into this boat, when the captain threatened to shoot the first man who boarded her. Soon afterwards the boat which left with the women and children returned, and the officer in charge reported that all were landed in a little cove nearby. There was no further confusion. Boat-load after boat-load left the side of the ship, until by daybreak all were disembarked without casualty and in the most orderly manner at the only point on the rocky islet of Anacapa where it was possible to gain a foothold. It was astonishing to see a few brave men reduce to perfect order and submission a crowd of panic-stricken human beings....

As already intimated, early in the evening a strong wind was blowing and a southwest storm was predicted; but at midnight, when the ship struck the rocks, a dead calm fell over the sea. This, together with the fact that the vessel had lodged on the rocks, accounted for our providential escape. At daylight it was found that although the bow of the vessel was lodged high up on the rocks, the upper deck at her stern was submerged below the water line and washed by the waves. Under her stern soundings were made of 22 fathoms, while at the bow were only three or four fathoms, showing that two-thirds of the vessel rested on a shelf of rock and that her stern overhung a precipice. All the passengers being safely landed, immediate steps were taken to get water and provisions ashore, and by night we were as well provided for as could be expected, and duly grateful that our lives had been spared.

Early in the morning after the wreck our attention was attracted by a small sailboat, which turned out to be that of an old otter hunter named Neideiver.[3] Being among the first to board the little craft, I secured from the old hunter all the lines and fish hooks he had; and later Captain Blunt readily complied with my request to let me have one of the ship's boats to go fishing off the island. I got three or four to accompany me, and in a very short time we caught a fine mess of fish. After this, relays of crews were engaged fishing from morning till night while we remained on the island.

The day after we landed we discovered on the island overlooking the wreck a considerable cave in the rocks, and in its comfortable shelter a party of congenial companions read, mused, and commented on our lonely condition from day to day, and scanned the horizon to discover a passing vessel....

On the morning of the second day a steamer was sighted on the horizon. As she neared the island we signaled to her, and soon ascertained that it was the steamer *California* on her way to San Francisco from Panama. She remained only long enough to communicate with Captain Blunt,[4] and has-

---

[1] Wiltsee, pp. 130-132, quoting accounts in the *Alta California,* December 7, 13, and 15, 1853. Wiltsee, p. 348, notes that the vessel hand-stamped its mail, this being marked "Steamer Winfield Scott." Capt. Blunt was dismissed by the Pacific Mail Steamship Company, although he was never formally censured. He was not able to find employment as a captain elsewhere. He died in 1854, some said of a broken heart, despite a comment in the *Alta California,* December 7, 1853, "We do not think that his well-established reputation as a careful and skillful navigator will suffer from this unfortunate loss."

[2] Excerpted and lightly edited from *Memoirs of Edward Bosqui,* Holmes Book Company, Oakland, California, 1952. Foreword by Harold C. Holmes and introduction by Henry R. Wagner.

[3] Sea otters were and still are common in the area, and feed upon abalones which they retrieve from the sea bottom. Their fur was a minor staple in California coastal commerce in the 1850s.

[4] The transfer of the *Winfield Scott's* women and children to the *California* at this time is omitted from Bosqui's account.

tened on her way to secure the necessary relief. Within seven days she returned to the island, when we embarked on her and continued on our voyage to Panama. Captain Blunt and the crew of the *Winfield Scott* remained at Anacapa for some time to secure all they could from the wreck.

Seven days after leaving the scene of our shipwreck we arrived at Acapulco. It was a very sudden and strange transition to pass from the restless ocean into the calm basin which forms the harbor of Acapulco, surrounded by granite cliffs frowning over the deep waters of the bay. The town is defended by the Old Spanish Fort Diego, on an eminence, looking quaint and grim, like all old fortifications. The town has always been an important place from the earliest date of its settlement by Cortez, being the port from which most of his expeditions of discovery were fitted out. It was likewise the great *entrepôt* of Spain's commerce with Mexico and the Indies. In fact, it is the only safe seaport Mexico possesses on the Pacific Coast. The Pacific Mail Steamship Company has a coal depot and a resident agent there, and all the steamers of the line stop on their way to and from San Francisco and Panama.

We remained at Acapulco only a few hours. Our chief amusement was in watching the naked natives dive for coins[1] the passengers threw overboard in the deep, clear waters of the bay, and admiring the picturesque surroundings of the old seaport.

A Newspaper Account

The *Panama Herald,* December 27, 1853, carried this report:

> Arrival of the *California* on Saturday afternoon:
>
> The anxiety for many days past prevalent about the overdue mail steamer from San Francisco, was dispatched by the arrival of the *California,* Capt. LeRoy, which came to anchor in our bay about 4 o'clock and brought the intelligence of the *Winfield Scott,* on the 2nd inst.; wrecked on the Island of Anacapa in the Santa Barbara channel.
>
> The following memorandum kindly furnished to us by Purser Davis [of the *California*] gives the particulars:
>
> P.M.S. steamer *California* from San Francisco, Dec. 7, arrived at Panama 24th, inst.; at 4 o'clock p.m. The 4th, on the upward trip, saw steamer *Winfield Scott* ashore at Anacapa Island, in the Santa Barbara Channel, about 25 miles from the mainland. Immediately ran in towards her, and finding nothing could be done to save the steamer, received on board the gold dust, (which had already been landed) and also ladies and children.
>
> She went ashore about midnight, Dec. 3d., in the midst of a dense fog and will prove a total loss. All the passengers were landed without confusion or accident, owing to the cool conduct of Capt. Blunt, aided by his officers and some more experienced among the passengers.
>
> Immediately after the *California* arrived at San Francisco with the intelligence, preparations were made for her to return to the wreck, and thence to Panama. She sailed from San Francisco at 4 p.m. Dec. 7, 29 hours from the date of arrival, and reached the island at daybreak on the 9th. Capt. LeRoy approached the shore as near as was prudent, and all the boats of each steamer were put into requisition for the conveyance of passengers, mails, baggage and express matter from shore. In seven hours this was effected, and the *California* sailed for Panama, perfectly prepared for sea in less than five days from the time she left the same spot on the upward trip. Passengers are in excellent health. Shipment of treasure: per *Winfield Scott* for England, $138,860.96.[2]

Diving on the Wreck

Over the years many divers visited the site including salvors Capt. Maginn and Col. George Baker who lifted a steam engine piston, a unopened chest (the contents of which were not disclosed by the finders), brass fittings, and other artifacts from the sea bottom in 1894. However, the author has located no accounts of coins being found. It is said that during World War II additional pieces of copper and brass were salvaged as scrap for the defense effort.

Years later in 1965, scuba diver Glenn E. Miller relocated the remains of the wreck, this time with numismatic success.[3] Miller operated the 62-foot charter boat *Emerald* out of Santa Barbara and often took divers on exploration trips to examine undersea life (including lobsters) and curiosa. On one such lobster-hunting sortie to Anacapa Island with 28 divers aboard, an undersea investigator reported seeing strewn pieces of iron, brass spikes, and other nautical items. Here, possibly, was a wreck to be explored! Miller donned his suit to see for himself. He was soon rewarded by the sight of the center part of an old paddlewheel sticking about 15 feet out of the bottom and remains of another about 40 feet away. In between were scraps of metal, perhaps from a long-forgotten sidewheel steamer, with the wooden parts long since rotted away.

Miller returned home and headed for the local library to see what he could learn. Before long, the story of the ill-fated *S.S. Winfield Scott* emerged as old clippings were read.

Soon thereafter, he enlisted Jim Gurdy, who had come to Santa Barbara from Sacramento and who had

---

1 The present author cannot help but wonder how many United States coins of various sorts still remain on the bottom of the Acapulco Bay.

2 Apparently a designated small portion destined for transshipment to Liverpool from the more than $875,000 in gold aboard on the original voyage of the *Winfield Scott.* During that time, much gold sent to New York City was en route to England (the world's premier financial center at the time); much other gold went to the Philadelphia Mint.

3 Information concerning the wreck exploration is adapted from: Glenn E. Miller, "Ghostly Gold," *Skin Diver,* March 1967. Dick Anderson, "There is Gold on the Winfield Scott," *Skin Diver,* September 1969, which also reprinted a news account from the *Panama Herald,* December 27, 1853; Anderson, "Yes, Virginia, There is a Winfield Scott Treasure," September 1972. Anderson, *Argosy Treasure Hunting,* 1977 Annual, "Gold from the Winfield Scott."

done gold diving on rivers in the northern part of the state. Gurdy, who was to receive 10% of anything valuable found, had a portable dredge for underwater work. Miller and Gurdy took the apparatus to the Anacapa Island wreck site and soon found pieces of lead and copper, spikes and nails, a well-preserved ceramic spittoon, and several gold nuggets.

On Memorial Day 1969, Miller and other divers including Paul Tizimoulis, publisher of *Skin Diver* magazine, and Jack McKenney, editor, went to the site. Dick Anderson, who later wrote several articles about the experience, including an account in the September 1969 issue of the *Skin Diver,* recalled:

> As soon as I hit water I began fanning the sand away from bedrock crevices. In less than five minutes I spotted what had to be a gold coin. It is hard to describe the thrill associated with such an event, but monetarily speaking it would be much like finding a hundred dollar bill in the middle of a field and knowing that there had to be a lot more of them around.
>
> I picked up the coin and looked at it. Even after 116 years of salty immersion the octagonal coin was in nearly perfect shape and the markings legible: "1 DOLLAR CALIFORNIA GOLD, 1853." Part of the coin still glistened with the original mint lustre. I swallowed hard and continued fanning. In just moments I had uncovered two more gold coins: an octagonal half dollar and a round gold dollar.

Among those who read Anderson's article was Don Robinson, a former director of the Channel Islands National Monument, who gently advised Anderson and others that unauthorized salvage operations could not be conducted on any undersea wrecks within a mile of Anacapa Island, but divers were free to explore and look to their hearts' content.

From 1965 onward, Glenn Miller worked on the sea bottom. He as well as Dick Anderson, Pete Greenwood (charter operator of the *Scuba Queen* out of San Pedro, the port of Los Angeles), and Mark Williams found many gold coins. Separately, Cliff Croft obtained several small denomination gold coins.[1] Presumably, these pieces were from "passenger gold"—coins carried by travelers and left behind during the disaster. The "treasure gold" was carried off the ship soon after it was wrecked and, apparently, was saved intact.

The following gold coins are among those known to have been found by divers beginning in 1965:[2]

SMALL DENOMINATION CALIFORNIA GOLD COINS:

25¢ octagonal: 1853 Small Liberty Head by Frontier & Diviercy,[3] 9 stars. Breen Gillio-101 (5 pieces)

25¢ round: Undated. Small Liberty Head by Frontier & Diviercy, 12 stars. BG-205.

25¢ round: Undated. Small Liberty Head by Frontier & Diviercy, 10 stars. BG-206.

25¢ round: 1853 Small Liberty Head by Frontier & Diviercy, 10 stars. BG-209. (2 pieces)

25¢ round: Undated. Small Liberty Head by A.L. Nouizillet,[4] 12 stars. BG-222 (State I).

25¢ round: Undated. Small Liberty Head, 12 stars. BG-222 (State II).

25¢ round: Undated. Small Liberty Head by A.L. Nouizillet, 12 stars. BG-223. (10 pieces)

50¢ octagonal: 1853 F.D. Liberty Head by Frontier & Diviercy, 13 Stars, eagle reverse (with rays behind the eagle, giving it at quick glance the appearance of a peacock, by which appellation it is sometimes known). BG-302. (3 pieces)

50¢ octagonal: 1853 BG number uncertain, 301 to 304. By Frontier & Diviercy.

50¢ octagonal: Date and variety unknown.

50¢ round: 1853 Variety unknown.

50¢ round: 1853 Liberty Head by Frontier & Diviercy, 13 stars. BG-401.

50¢ round: 1853 Liberty Head by Frontier & Diviercy on behalf of Gaime, Guillemot & Co.; with G.G. initials below portrait, 13 stars. BG-414.

50¢ round: 1853 Liberty Head by M. Deriberpe and signed D,[5] 11 stars. BG-421.

50¢ round: 1853 Liberty Head by A.L. Nouizillet, 13 stars. BG-428.

50¢ round: 1853 Liberty Head by A.L. Nouizillet, 13 stars. BG-430. (3 pieces)

---

[1] Jay Roe, letter, September 3, 1996, enclosing inventory of the Croft pieces, which Roe had obtained years earlier from Walter Breen.

[2] Numismatic information is from Robert D. Leonard, Jr., furnished to the author, August 1996; also furnished were copies of letters from Leonard to dealer Kenneth W. Lee, August 13, 1978, and Lee to Leonard, August 18, 1978, magazine articles, and research notes. Lee, of Glendale, California, studied small denomination California gold coins over a long period of years from the 1930s to the 1970s. Leonard, with Jay Roe, is currently (1996) working on a new reference book for that series. Attributions are to Lee numbers (Lee, *California Gold Dollars, Half Dollars, Quarter Dollars,* 1970) and to Breen-Gillio or BG numbers (Walter Breen and Ronald Gillio, *California Pioneer Fractional Gold,* 1983; originally created as a catalogue to the Lee estate, but this property was sold intact, and the work was subsequently published as a stand-alone reference).

[3] Frontier & Diviercy (Pierre Frontier, Eugène Diviercy), 81 Bush Street, San Francisco.

[4] Antoine Louis Nouizillet was located at 58 Kearny Street, San Francisco, circa 1852-1854 and was associated at times with M. Deriberpe and Isadore(?) Routhier.

[5] Deriberpe, an engraver, maintained premises at 58 Kearny Street, San Francisco, 1852-1853 and was associated at one time with Nouizillet.

50¢ round: Date and variety unknown.
$1 octagonal: 1853 Liberty Head, by M. Deriberpe and signed DERI. 8 stars. BG-514.
$1 octagonal: 1853 Liberty Head by Deriberpe, 8 stars. BG-519. (2 pieces)
$1 octagonal: 1853 Liberty Head by Deriberpe, 8 stars. BG-525.
$1 octagonal: 1853 Liberty Head by Deriberpe, 8 stars. BG-526. (2 pieces)
$1 octagonal: 1853 N. Liberty Head by A.L. Nouizillet, 13 stars. BG-530. (15 or 16 pieces)
$1 octagonal: 1853 Liberty Head by A.L. Nouizillet, 13 stars. BG-531. (2 pieces)

LARGE DENOMINATION CALIFORNIA GOLD COINS:
$5 Moffat & Co. 1849.
$5 Moffat & Co. 1850.
$10 Augustus Humbert 1852 (found by Pete Greenwood, 1965).

FEDERAL GOLD COINS:
$1 (gold dollars): 14 miscellaneous unattributed, some of which may have been California gold dollars, others federal.
$2.50 gold: 5 pieces. Varieties not known.
$5 gold: 3 pieces. Varieties not known.

OTHER ITEMS:
Peruvian silver (8 reals?), 1833, reported but not later numismatically verified (found by Pete Greenwood, 1965).[1]
Gold nuggets, at least seven, probably more.
Gold ring inscribed "H.G. Wadleigh from G.W. Stinson."

Many if not most of these coins were sold to Southern California dealer Kenneth W. Lee, who did not realize the historical interest they might have to later researchers, but simply acquired them as stock in trade. "I guess at the time it did not occur to me to keep details!" he later commented to numismatic researcher Robert D. Leonard, Jr.

While collectors have long known that small gold quarters, half dollars, and dollars had been minted in San Francisco by various private interests and had served to facilitate small transactions, it was less clear when these first became popular. The situation is complicated by the practice employed after the 1850s of back-dating certain dies so as to give the coins the aura of age and, thus, acceptability. Such small-denomination gold coins were never officially sanctioned and, in fact, were made illegal by federal statute in 1864.

The presence of these small gold pieces in the littered remains of the *Winfield Scott* verified that the varieties in question actually circulated in California during the time indicated. Early documentation of these small gold coins is hard to find in newspaper accounts or travelers' reminiscences. Probably, they were too familiar at the time to be chronicled in print.[2]

Gold from the *S.S. Yankee Blade*

Lost: October 1, 1854
Location: Near Port Arguello, California
Found: 1977 or earlier?
Treasure: Gold coins

An "Opposition" Steamer

The Independent Steamship Company's *S.S. Yankee Blade* was one of several steamers owned by that company and Cornelius Vanderbilt's Nicaragua Line that mounted competition to the longer-established Pacific Mail Steamship Company on the western run from San Francisco to Panama (or the crossing at Nicaragua).

In the heady days of the Gold Rush, passenger travel advertising had two emphases: fastest total speed (combined time for the Atlantic leg, land crossing, and Pacific leg) from East to West, and the lowest fare.

The 1,767-ton *Yankee Blade* was built at

The final moments of the *Yankee Blade*. (Artist's depiction by Sandy Martin)

[1] Described as a silver-dollar size coin from Peru; 8-reals coins were made in Peru over a long period of years; those dated 1833 are common in the context of that series.

[2] Further sources include: Walter Breen and Ronald J. Gillio, *California Pioneer Fractional Gold,* 1983, pp. 5-6, most of which information came from Robert D. Leonard. Frank Soulé, John H. Gihon, M.D., and James Nisbet, *The Annals of San Francisco,* 1855, p. 473. A modern description of the wreck site is found in Darren Douglas, *Guide to Shipwreck Diving, Southern California,* 1990, pp. 49-52. Sidewheel spokes and scattered parts of the ship can be seen. Visibility changes as sands cover and uncover the wreckage.

Williamsburg, New York, in 1853 by Perrine, Patterson & Stack, the same firm that had launched the *Brother Jonathan* (see later account) in 1850. She measured 274 feet long. Power was provided by a single coal-fired steam engine with a 6'4" cylinder with a stroke of 12 feet, built by the Allaire Iron Works.[1]

Her first voyage was under the Independent Opposition Line flag on the New York to Aspinwall run, leaving in December 1853 and arriving the next month. The "Opposition" name had been used in the seafaring passenger trade for many years and was typically employed by entrepreneurs who sailed at lower rates (as extensively advertised) and minimal amenities (not mentioned in publicity) against the longer-established and better-outfitted ships that held lucrative government or other contracts.

On her first voyage to the Pacific the *Yankee Blade* left New York City on February 2, 1854, doubled Cape Horn, and arrived in San Francisco on May 4, in service for the Independent Opposition Line and, soon thereafter, the somewhat similarly named Independent Steamship Company.[2]

Along the Pacific Coast

The first few months of the *Yankee Blade's* western service were rather uneventful. On September 1, 1854, she arrived in San Francisco from Panama, with six of her 500 passengers dead from cholera. However, this was not particularly unusual, as cholera, typically acquired in Panama during the land crossing, ravaged many steamers of the era and in some instances accounted for far higher mortalities. Accounts of incoming ships published in the *Alta California* and *San Francisco Herald* often gave death notices in the same accounts as cargo and passenger information.

On another trip, September 28, the *Yankee Blade* sailed for Panama with about 900 aboard, posting through rates (including the Atlantic connection by another steamer) to New York City of $175 first cabin, $150 second cabin, and $50 steerage.[3] The ship's large capacity for passengers made her difficult to fill, and the line sustained heavy losses. As a result, amenities for passengers were often found wanting, and passage aboard the *Yankee Blade* was anything but an exercise in luxurious travel. As in other areas of commercial endeavor and public service, highest price and lowest quality were not compatible.

A team of miners uses a "long tom" device to wash gold from a California stream bed, a method that was far more efficient than panning.

Reflective of the *Yankee Blade* and a related ship a ballad of the day, *The Humbug Line,* noted in part:[4]

> The greatest imposition that the public ever saw,
> Are the California steamships that run to Panama.
> They have opposition on the route, with cabins very nice,
> And advertise to take you for half the usual price;
> They get thousands from the mountains, and then deny their bills,
> So you have to pay their prices, or go back to the hills.
>
> You are driven round the steerage like a drove of hungry swine,
> And kicked ashore at Panama by the Independent Line;
> Your baggage is thrown overboard, the like you never saw,
> A trip or two will sicken you of going to Panama.

1 The name of the proprietor, James Allaire, is well-known today to collectors of Hard Times tokens issued in connection with the Howell Works in New Jersey.

2 Wiltsee, p. 252. Wiltsee is a valuable source for steamer data, but there are some unexplained inconsistencies including varying departure dates for identical voyages. The *Yankee Blade* is discussed in Don B. Marshall, *California Shipwrecks,* 1978, pp. 34-35. An illustration of the ill-fated ship, from the Bancroft Library, is reproduced on p. 41. A modern description of the wreck site is found in Darren Douglas, *Guide to Shipwreck Diving, Southern California,* 1990, pp. 24-27. Large sections of the steam engine cylinders can still be seen as can be parts of the paddlewheels, brass fittings, and other items.

3 Wiltsee, pp. 138-139.

4 Kemble, p. 68. Humbug was a popular term for deception or fraud. The ballad was published in the *Panama Weekly Herald,* October 17, 1853, this being shortly before the *S.S. Yankee Blade* entered service.

Chorus:
Then come along, come along, you that want to go,
The best accommodations, and the passage very low;
Our boats they are large enough, don't be afraid,
The *Golden Gate* is going down to beat the *Yankee Blade.*

Trying for a Speed Record

On September 30, 1854, with an estimated 812 passengers and 122 crew members aboard, Captain Henry T. Randall of the *S.S. Yankee Blade* tried to establish a speed record from San Francisco to Panama, as such an accomplishment could have excellent effect in advertising and perhaps focus favorable attention on the vessel.[1] The ship needed some good publicity.

Just outside of the harbor the *Yankee Blade* "stopped her engine, and allowing the *Sonora* to pass her, raised her flag as a challenge of speed, and then getting again headway, passed the *Sonora* at the bar. It was understood at San Francisco that a bet of $5,000 was pending on the race to Panama."[2] The two ships were rivals, not only from flying flags of different lines, but because there had been a recent commotion when the captain of the *Sonora* had seen a distress signal from the *Yankee Blade,* which was out of coal, but had not stopped to aid her. Instead, the *Sonora* reported the stranded ship when she made port. Just as public sentiment against the crew of the *Sonora* was running high, the *Yankee Blade* arrived under her own power after her crew and some volunteer passengers went ashore on Coiba Island and cut firewood.[3]

Now in the September race with the *Sonora,* the *Yankee Blade* was packed to nearly overflowing, as revenue was the main concern of her owners. One estimate, later discredited, held that there were over 1,200 aboard.[4] As was so often the case, an exact passenger count was not possible. While there was a list of those who had purchased their tickets by advance reservation, there were usually others who arrived at the docks at the last minute to buy passage and whose names were not recorded. This lack of passenger roster precision was true of virtually all vessels on both coasts.[5]

Supposed to be in Deep Water

Cutting close to the California coast, at about 3:30 in the afternoon of October 1, in thick fog the *Yankee Blade* struck a submerged reef off Port Arguello, although the captain thought she was in deep water about 20 miles from shore (but later suggested that a "powerful current" out of his control drew the boat onto the rocks). At the time the ship's paddlewheels were turning at the rate of 13 revolutions per minute.

The vessel was stranded at a rakish angle with the first 60 feet of her bow raised on the reef and her stern submerged in about 50 feet of water. Confusion reigned among officers and crew as they sought safety, apparently with little concern for the passengers. Waves breaking over the stern caused extensive damage and broke away some wooden sections.

About $152,000 in specie[6] consigned by the San Francisco banking house of Page, Bacon & Co. was stored in a vault at the bottom of the hull, which quickly flooded. Even upon first inspection the treasure was found already covered by five feet of rapidly rising water, making recovery impossible. Adams & Co. had consigned a bag to New Orleans via Panama, but it contained only papers. Fretz & Ralston, San Francisco agents for the *Yankee Blade,* advertised for shipments, but, apparently, had no specie or bullion aboard for their own or anyone else's account booked through them. It was common for agents to solicit shipments of treasure up to a few hours before a vessel's departure.

Passengers had varying amounts of personal effects and money.

Captain Randall's Actions

Soon after the crash Captain Randall took about 30 passengers on shore in a lifeboat, but elected to remain in safety there and not return to the wreck. His first officer did likewise, but as his lifeboat was nearing the shore it became wrecked and 17 of the 22 aboard were drowned.

---

[1] Sources include accounts in *Alta California,* October 10, 11, 16, 22, and December 1, 1854; also January 5, 7, 10, 14, 16, 18, 23, 26, and 27, and April 6, 1855. *New York Times,* November 10, 1854, and January 26, 1855. Copies furnished to the author by Dan Owens.

[2] *Alta California,* December 10, 1854. Soon thereafter the *Sonora* was to be the venue for an on-board theft of treasure in which it was reported that six $20 gold coins had been hidden by the boatswain, "$300 to $400 was found sewn up in one of the beds," etc., this being a part of 96 boxes of treasure containing $15,000 to $25,000 each, and two bags, one with $15,000 and the other containing "a few thousands" (latter account in *Alta California,* January 5, 1855).

[3] Erik Heyl, *Early American Steamers,* 1953, pp. 395, 463.

[4] *Ibid.* Another account, this one the statement of Captain Bell, passenger on the rescue ship *Goliah.*

[5] Further, the passenger lists that do exist are usually rife with misspellings and wrong information.

[6] Per some reports; specie (minted coins) was the normal form of shipment. For example, the *New York Times,* November 10, 1854, mentioned "the specie on board." However, "gold dust" is mentioned in several contemporary accounts.

Meanwhile, Randall's young son, Henry, Jr., was appointed to remain on board and supervise, but events quickly proved that he was incompetent to do so. By evening about 200 of the passengers and crew had been transferred to the beach where they stayed with the captain and first officer, while the remaining occupants waited for the morrow.

The wind rose in the night, and the wooden hull began to break up on the rocks. Absent the commanding officer and his assistant, confusion and panic reigned aboard the ship. Steerage passengers broke into the liquor lockers, and many became drunk. A rampage of shooting, looting, and terrorizing the first-cabin passengers ensued.

Details of the conduct aboard appeared in the *Alta California,* October 10:

> As soon as the ship struck, a gang of fiends armed themselves, broken open the bar, and then proceeded to cut and break open the trunks of passengers. The ship was entirely under their control, and passengers did not dare to go below for their baggage, which might in many instances have been saved. Knives and pistols were used, and passengers who dared to interfere to save their own property were summarily knocked down, and kicked, and threatened with being shot. Several pistols were fired, and it is said one or two passengers were killed. It is supposed by some that the compass had been tampered with, for the purpose of losing the ship, that these plunders might be committed.
>
> The passengers have lost their baggage, and nearly all of them their money. We think the loss of passengers, besides the treasure list, may be safely put down at half a million of dollars....
>
> When the steamer was threatening to go to pieces any minute, some of the gang of pirates on board got possession of the life preservers and demanded enormous prices of the passengers for them, in some cases taking gold watches for them. A Mr. Gaston informs us that he purchased one from the steward [J. Belknap] of the *Yankee Blade,* for which he paid him $40.[1] Such things as this speak little for human nature.

More of the same was printed in a subsequent account in the *New York Times:*[2]

> When the captain left the ship in the first boat, all on board was in confusion, and not five minutes had elapsed before the hell hounds were at their work. A band of robbers seemed organized at once, and began plundering the cabin. They were armed with revolvers and knives, and proceeded coolly to open carpet bags and trunks, which they ransacked with all possible dispatch, as it was necessary to hasten through their job in that portion of the boat where the water was rapidly coming in.
>
> In the steerage they had full control all night, and no one dared to enter or to interfere. At one time cries of murder were heard below, and a young man called for help to protect his friend, but none were willing to go down. One passenger subsequently exhibited a severe gash in the back of his head which was inflicted while they were taking his watch.
>
> Some passengers had to draw their pistols and present them in order to get the women and children on the boats the first day. The plunder party got possession of one of the boats, and money was exacted from several who got on board. A lot of men on shore of the same stripe would give up nothing that they had obtained without pay. They provided themselves with canvas and blankets, while the women were without covering or protection from the weather save a quantity of brush.

The purser, Samuel L. Vought, later recalled additional details of the panic:[3]

> Night coming on, and the fog, which had for a short time disappeared, again set in, the boats were stopped running, not being able to find the shore, and the terror of our situation began to stare us in the face....
>
> Confusion in the wildest sense prevailed, for there were those who had prepared to swim ashore, stiffened with the cold; those who had sought to drown their fear in the frequent libations of the ardent; while some, with calm resignation, had prepared themselves for the worst, and waited their fate in peace. Thus we passed the dismal night, made still more solemn by the church like tolling of the bell, which seemed to beck us on to our funeral.

Help Arrives

At 8:00 the next morning the small coastal steamer *S.S. Goliah,* under Captain Samuel Haley, came by and amid heavy seas succeeded with her lifeboats in putting about 600 passengers on board.[4] Supplies including clothing, food, and canvas were landed on the beach for the use of the 200 or so still stranded.

The *Goliah* took the survivors to Santa Barbara and San Pedro (port of Los Angeles) on the way to its final port of San Diego where the majority of the passengers were disembarked. The *Goliah* then returned to pick up those who had remained on the shore near the wreck. Unfortunately, in the meantime the beach had become a scene of self-inflicted disaster, as the ship's firemen and a few others—brandishing firearms—took most of the provisions for themselves and also relieved helpless passengers of their money and other valuable goods that had been brought ashore. A

[1] Equivalent at the time to a month's wages for a typical laborer on the East Coast.

[2] November 10, 1854. Accounts from several eyewitnesses were printed.

[3] *New York Times,* November 10, 1854, part of an extensive account in which Vought was careful not to criticize his captain, Henry T. Randall (that part of his story is not quoted here).

[4] The *Alta California,* October 10, 1854, quoted an account stating that 850 passengers from the Yankee Blade were taken aboard to add to the 135 already on the *Goliah.* The 145-foot wooden sidewheel steamer was built in 1848 as a tug, but was later sent to California to do service on the Sacramento River, there bearing the name *Defender.* In 1854 she was rebuilt and refitted and renamed *Goliah,* and used as a coastwise steamer. Her name is incorrectly spelled as *Goliath* in some accounts, a logical error. Years later she served as a tow boat in Puget Sound, and was dismantled in 1899.

rare exception to the behavior of the crew was Third Officer J.H. Kennard, who expressed concern for the welfare of the passengers and did as much as he could to help them.

Seventeen to 50 passengers, mostly women and children, lost their lives.[1] Some accounts suggested an even greater mortality. J.P. Pittman of Downieville, California, a passenger who assisted with the rescue of many women and children, averred that "at least 200 perished."[2]

The survivors included Frank Jones (said by some to have been "the cleverest gambler in San Francisco" and by others to have been a prominent New York socialite), Jones' black servant Charley, and Charles Reed, all three of whom would later figure in the memorable voyage of the *S.S. Central America* in September 1857.[3]

Aftermath

By the morning of October 3, 1854, the *Yankee Blade* had broken apart. In the immediate area nothing was to be seen afloat except the pilot house and part of the deck. The hull, ruptured by a break estimated to be a foot wide and 30 feet long, was on the ocean floor.

The conduct of Captain Henry T. Randall and his thieving, ghoulish crew in the *Yankee Blade* disaster was truly a sorry reflection upon human nature, and they were widely condemned in later accounts of the mishap. Some suggested that Randall and his cohorts had staged the wreck for their own personal profit.

However, others came to the aid of his reputation, such as evidenced by a published letter in the *Alta California,* October 11, from J.B. Goddard, a passenger who stated that "Capt. Randall did all that he could, or that could be expected of him or any man on the occasion, and the calamity is severe enough upon him without the addition of unfounded aspersions from men not accustomed to a ship and the emergencies of a wreck."[4]

Of course, it could be countered that, indeed, few passengers were accustomed to the emergencies of a wreck either. The main thesis of the captain's supporters was that he was busy on shore with the shuttling of passengers and could not be aboard the ship at the same time.

A lengthy exculpatory statement from Captain Randall appeared in the same issue of the *Alta California.* Randall stated that his actions represented the most prudent and practical course and elected not to mention the insurrection and looting aboard the ship in his absence. In later testimony he suggested that crooks who were aboard had placed iron near the compass to deflect its needle and purposely cause the ship to go off course. Rumor had it that a gang of San Francisco ruffians known as the Shoulder Strikers had acquired positions as crew and were responsible.

On October 15, survivors held a mass meeting in Portsmouth Square in San Francisco to address their concerns.[5] Resolutions passed included these:

> Resolved: That after a careful investigation and by an unbiased judgment, we have come to the firm conclusion that sheer negligence upon the part of the managers of the *Yankee Blade* in directing her course, and in running so near a coast well known to be dangerous, was the cause of the disastrous wreck.
>
> Resolved: That duty compels us to censure Capt. Randall, in so quickly deserting the wreck, and leaving the boat without a leading officer on board to quiet the passengers and prevent the plundering. Had the Captain remained on board, it is our candid opinion this could have been done.

Certain survivors were brought back to San Francisco by the *Brother Jonathan,* under Captain C.P. Seabury, and the crowd in Portsmouth Square proposed to present him with a gold watch "as a mark of esteem for the hospitable manner in which the destitute passengers were treated on board of his ship on the way from San Diego to this port."

On the darker side of events, the agents for the *Yankee Blade* "sent to the police office and requested the marshal to send down five or six police officers to prevent any outrage" at the mass meeting. A committee of five survivors was deputized to meet with the steamship agents, but an interview was denied.

All of the passengers had been on their way to Panama when the wreck occurred. There was general

---

[1] Kemble, pp. 144 (account from *San Francisco Prices Current and Shipping List,* October 14, 1854) and 252. Oscar Lewis, *Sea Routes to the Gold Fields,* pp. 239-240, 248-250 (among others). Wiltsee, pp. 144-147 (the quotation of a small part of Vought's extensive commentary is from this source; unlike most other observers, Vought did not criticize the captain—under whom he had served). Richard M. Benson, *Steamships and Motorships of the West Coast,* p. 80. William M. Lytle, *Merchant Steam Vessels of the United States 1807-1868,* p. 245. *Harper's New Monthly Magazine,* January 1855, p. 110; there the number of deaths was given as "about 30." Kemble, p. 144, states "some 30 lives were lost." Other estimates were as low as 15.

[2] *New York Times,* November 10, 1854. Another account in the same issue placed the number of passengers aboard at 812 plus a crew of 122, for a total of 934, of which "we are satisfied that not more than 50 perished."

[3] Normand E. Klare, *The Final Voyage of the Central America 1857,* pp. 54-55.

[4] *Alta California,* October 11, 1854 (letter was dated October 10).

[5] Reported in *Alta California,* October 16, 1854.

unhappiness expressed at the line's policy of bringing them back to their port of embarkation, rather than giving them accommodations to their intended destination of Panama. In San Francisco the line offered to refund *just 25%* of the ticket purchase price, "evidently taking refuge behind some clause that gave the purchasers passage on that particular steamer."[1]

The entire *Yankee Blade* affair remains one of the sorriest chapters in the annals of the American passenger steamship trade.

Divers on the Wreck

On October 22, 1854, the *Alta California* reported that the "body of a man, apparently 40 years of age, came ashore, badly cut about the head, and the pockets of his clothing rifled.... They thought that he had been murdered on board the steamer by some of the ruffian gang of whose horrible work much has been said." The same account noted that heavy waves were rolling over the shipwreck site, and that although a box of liquor and valise had been found by divers using underwater breathing apparatus, no trace of the treasure had been found. The empty wooden hull had separated from the heavy engine and had washed on shore.

Back in San Francisco, the much-condemned Captain Randall offered his services to assist in salvage efforts which, as events would prove, would further reflect his cupidity.

On December 1, 1854, the *Weekly Alta California* (an adjunct of the usual daily edition) reported the return of Capt. Fowler and his pilot boat, *Dancing Feather,* which with its crew of divers had spent about five weeks seeking the lost treasure under the watchful eye of Captain Randall. "It is reported that two boxes of specie have been recovered, the amount of which could not be ascertained." Among other artifacts seen but not brought to the surface was a brass cannon described as "a very valuable one, and it is said it was exhibited at the great exhibition [Crystal Palace, 1853] in New York, and cost originally $1,150."

Another account datelined January 7, 1855, noted that the *Dancing Feather,* now under Captain Hutchins, but with Randall still advising the recovery attempts, had recently returned from the wreck site, but that "the bad weather which prevailed most of the time prevented any successful operations, and no further amount of the sunken treasure had been recovered."

Other salvage efforts continued, as evidenced by an account in the *Alta California,* January 5, 1855, which reported that Samuel Wheland, Thomas Matthews, and Robert Wilson had been charged for "stealing gold dust from the wreck of the *Yankee Blade,* the property of Page, Bacon & Co.," which they had recovered clandestinely while ostensibly under the hire of official salvors, and had brought back to San Francisco aboard the *Pilgrim.*

Subsequent court reports concerning the alleged theft noted that Captain Randall "testified that at the wreck he saw some of the prisoners bring up two boxes, resembling treasure boxes. They might, however, have been decoy boxes, as the parties in search of the treasure were in the habit of deceiving and misleading each other."[2] Other discussions revealed that Page, Bacon & Co. had shipped $152,000 ($1,000 less than reported earlier), that passenger Mrs. E. Bloomingdale lost $10,000, and another traveler lost $6,000. Separately, Captain Randall was charged by other parties with "having plundered a box of treasure of about $17,000 in gold dust." The entire affair was beginning to sound rather farcical.

On January 14, the *Alta California* printed more on the wreck salvage attempts, quoting a Mr. Haven, president of the Steam Tug Company, who had been hired by the insurance underwriters to help recover the treasure. He reported that a visit to the location by his ship, the *Caroline,* which had left San Francisco on October 16, was unproductive. However, Haven recalled, "The *Dancing Feather* on her first trip brought up four boxes of treasure, about $69,300, roughly." Under contracts given by the insurers, salvage ships and their operators were to receive 60% of what they found.

Charges of theft against the salvors aboard the *Pilgrim* were dismissed shortly afterward. The rascally Captain Randall, who became deeply implicated in further testimony, settled claims against him by paying $6,000.

Efforts continued at the wreck, and in March 1855 the *Ada* was at the site but "did not procure anything," while the brig *Boston,* under Captain Hutchins and "with a diving machine on board," abandoned the *Yankee Blade* effort and sailed for Chile on March 11 "to search for copper lost in a vessel on that coast some time ago."

Later Salvage Efforts

For many decades thereafter the hull of the *Yankee*

[1] Wiltsee, p. 148.

[2] *Alta California,* January 10, 1855.

Blade remained in its watery grave off the coast of California in an area that spelled doom to many other ships, often under similar circumstances of becoming lost in low-lying fog. In 1948 the hull was located, but strong currents and unfavorable weather prevented any recovery.[1]

Artifacts from the steamer *S.S. Yankee Blade* were salvaged by divers in 1977, and about 300 specimens of 1854-S gold $20 coins are said to have been found (although the author has found no accounts of such coins in contemporary reports). As is often true of treasure salvage situations, little factual information found its way into print. It is known, however, that a generous supply of Uncirculated 1854-S double eagles came on the rare coin market about that time, and that these coins were uniform in appearance. All were sharply struck, had somewhat subdued lustre from microscopic etching by seawater (which attacks the copper element of the 90% gold—the 10% copper alloy of the pieces), and displayed a fine network of die cracks on the reverse.[2]

When these unusually fine 1854-S double eagles appeared in coin-collecting circles in the late 1970s, explanations as to their origin were not readily forthcoming. The only allegedly informed person the writer was able to locate at the time stated that these coins were found between the studs of a wall in an old building in San Francisco when it was torn down. However, that did not account for the obvious indication that these pieces had been immersed in seawater.

Walter Breen's Complete Encyclopedia of U.S. and Colonial Coins (p. 564) implies that a hoard of "at least 100 pieces" came to light in July 1977, but was different from another cache he mentioned, "Many more porous 'seawater Uncirculateds' came from a wreck (allegedly the *Yankee Blade*), some still encrusted." However, in absence of factual evidence to the contrary, the present writer believes that there was just one find, and that all coins show slight effects of seawater immersion.[3] Whether the *Yankee Blade* was the source is only guesswork.

Concerning quantities of the 1854-S $20 coins, David W. Akers added this information including another rumored source:[4]

> I know I have personally handled or seen 50 or more pieces from this hoard, and the surface texture varies widely. Some are, as you indicate, "lightly etched," but many others are very monochromatic with what I call heavily granulated surfaces. I have even seen a few that have very little trace of "seawater" etching yet obviously came from the same group.
>
> As for them coming from the *Yankee Blade,* I can't say. One of the rumors I heard persistently in the 1970s was that they were found at the bottom of a well in the San Francisco Bay area, the water brackish, which might account for the variations I've noted in surface texture.

The *S.S. Central America* Treasure

Lost: September 12, 1857
Location: Off the coast of North Carolina
Found: 1987
Treasure: Vast quantity of gold coins and bars

An Enjoyable Trip to Panama

In the annals of undersea treasure hunting for United States coins the saga of the *S.S. Central America* is an adventure to end all adventures.[5] Its final chapters are still being written in our own time.

In San Francisco on August 20, 1857, more than 400 people who had booked passage on the Pacific Mail Steamship Line's *S.S. Sonora* hastened aboard the vessel. The destination was Panama to be followed by

---

[1] Coffman, p. 260 (who called her a schooner and estimated her treasure to be worth from $4 million to $32 million).

[2] In the case of gold coins minted in California—and some others minted in other locations—silver existed as an "impurity" as part of the 10% copper alloy; silver, too, is readily attacked by salt water.

[3] Includes information from John J. Ford, Jr., 1993.

[4] Letter to the author, June 22, 1996. Notably, he reported seeing some 1854-S $20 coins with light etching and others with more extensive etching.

[5] An important source of historical information for the present account is Normand E. Klare, *The Final Voyage of the Central America 1857.* Passenger quotations are from citations in Judy Conrad, *Story of an American Tragedy: Survivors' Accounts of the Sinking of the Steamship Central America.* Ms. Conrad used contemporary newspaper and other accounts in a reconstructed time line to tell the story. Chapter 64, "Foundering of the Steamer Central America in a Gale Off Cape Hatteras—1857," in *Our First Century,* by R.M. Devens, 1876, gives a detailed account of the tragedy and cites several passenger experiences; this is an excellent overview. Walter Breen, "The S.S. Central America: Tragedy and Treasure," *The Numismatist,* July 1990, is perhaps the most comprehensive account to appear in a numismatic periodical and is particularly valuable for its numismatically authoritative descriptions of certain coins and ingots; also personal communications between Breen, who examined many of the coins, and the author.

Wells, Fargo & Co. (building at the right) as seen in this San Francisco street view from the mid-1850s.

a train trip across the Isthmus, then a connecting passage on another ship at Aspinwall for the Atlantic run. Accompanying the passengers were over 100 bags of mail and a cargo of gold valued at over $1.2 million consigned by nine major shippers including Wells, Fargo & Co. The ultimate destination of the travelers and cargo was New York City.

In addition to the manifest amount of over $1.2 million in gold, many passengers had their own treasures variously estimated to average from about $1,000 to $5,000 per person, perhaps, when added to the commercial cargo, bringing the total to well over $2 million.

The gold was in various forms including rectangular ingots and bars from various assayers, recently-struck $20 pieces from the San Francisco Mint, and an assortment of other coins ranging from British sovereigns to American issues to pieces struck in California by assayers and private minters. Some of the larger coins were $50 "slugs" of octagonal shape made by the U.S. Assay Office of Gold. The coins and bullion were destined for New York clearing houses and bankers, the New York Sub-Treasury, and the Philadelphia Mint, with a lesser value to be transshipped to the London market.

As nearly always, the Pacific trip was an enjoyable experience, what with finely appointed salons and other public areas, fresh meat from livestock on board, and other amenities. To be sure, there had been a few mishaps recorded in the annals of San Francisco to Panama voyages—with, perhaps, the wrecks of the *Winfield Scott* and the *Yankee Blade* being remembered by some who had read newspaper accounts a few years earlier. On the other hand, with thousands of ships engaged in commerce in and out of American ports, incidents were bound to happen. Not to worry. The *Sonora* had a fine record and had experienced no major problems since it entered the Pacific service in 1854.

With a brief stop at Manzanillo on the Mexican coast, and an overnight respite at Acapulco to take on coal for the boilers, the *Sonora* arrived at the Gulf of Panama on the evening of September 2. The trip had been uneventful, as expected, and, seemingly, all aboard had savored the experience.

Connections Across Land

Early the next morning the passengers were transferred by small boats to shore, after which they had a rail trip across nearly 48 miles of land. This took from three and a quarter hours for those who departed early, to nearly six hours for the last in line. Several transits were required to accommodate all of the travelers and cargo from the *Sonora*.

The Panama Railroad cars that traversed the track across the Isthmus to Aspinwall were hardly luxurious and were described as "toys" by one passenger. Along the way there were several concessions for food and drink set up by natives in tents, and those taking the ride could stop and be refreshed. No doubt, some of the September 1857 travelers did.

After arrival on the Atlantic side of the Isthmus at Aspinwall the travelers boarded at several hotels. Even though the village was relatively newly built, health and sanitation facilities were uncertain, and the passengers were advised to be careful of the quality of the food.

Ahead was the final leg of the trip to New York City, about 2,000 miles, and taking less time than the Pacific part of the journey.

Captain Herndon and His Ship

On Thursday afternoon, September 3, 1857, passengers continuing from California plus others picked up at Panama were greeted at the dock at Aspinwall by Capt. William Lewis Herndon as they boarded the *S.S. Central America* for the passage to New York.

Herndon, born in 1813, was a career Navy officer. Among his accomplishments was his service under Commodore Matthew Calbraith Perry[1] in the Mexican War and his 1847 command of a small steamer, the *Iris*. In 1851-1852 he was the first American to traverse the Amazon River from the ocean to its headwaters, a distance of about 4,100 miles. His published report on the exploration had been well received.

Once comfortably settled in their cabins and berths, the nearly 600 passengers and crew members aboard the *S.S. Central America* looked forward to their voyage, traveling at slightly over 12 miles per hour, with a scheduled stop in Havana.

Earlier Voyages of the Steamer

The 278-foot, 2,141-ton *S.S. Central America*, owned by the U.S. Mail Steamship Company and recently renamed from the *S.S. George Law*,[2] was a veteran on the Atlantic coast-wise route, having traversed it 43 times since her first departure from New York City to Aspinwall on October 20, 1853, and having carried one-third or more of the total value of California gold shipped to Eastern banks and government agencies during that period. Indeed, the *George Law* had been on hand to deliver passengers for the celebration that attended the opening of the Panama Railroad early 1855.

The *George Law* had been built in New York by William H. Webb and equipped with two oscillating steam engines made by the Morgan Iron Works. Launching took place on October 28, 1852, but it was nearly a year before she was fully outfitted and ready for her maiden voyage.

On a late autumn run from Panama to New York City in 1853 with 467 passengers and $877,000 worth of gold aboard, the *George Law* encountered a hurricane after departing Havana. However, apart from some discomfort, there were no problems. Upon arriving in New York on December 12, it was learned that damage had been extensive in Atlantic coastal areas and that those awaiting the ship had been apprehensive for her safety.[3]

Another trip of the *George Law*, this being the jaunt south from New York City to Panama, had been chronicled in 1855:[4]

> On the 5th of January [1855] the good steamer *George Law* left the wharf at New York, bearing, in addition to its usual miscellaneous crowd of California emigrants, the company of invited guests, and the United States minister to Granada.
>
> A "Notice to Passengers," conspicuously posted up—intimating that no deadly weapons were to be worn on board, and no fire-arms discharged, and that it was out of order for any person to make his appearance at the dinner table with his coat off—might have been a little startling to the nerves of a timorous or fastidious person; while the ostentatious display of "life preservers" hinted at the possibility of drowning too plainly to be altogether agreeable to one who was not insured against that mode of leaving the world, by a premonition that he was reserved for a certain other fashion of exit.
>
> Nobody, however, was shot, stabbed, or drowned, and the brave vessel, passing within sight of the green hills of Cuba and Hayti, and the Blue Mountains of Jamaica, dashed with never-resting wheels among the islands of the Caribbean Sea, and at length, on the 11th day, lay motionless as a captured whale, at the dock at Aspinwall, the Atlantic terminus of the Panama Railway.

With many amenities for passenger comfort, entertainment, and food, and with a light breeze caused by the ship's forward motion, the present trip in Septem-

---

[1] Perry had a strong numismatic interest; his holdings included Hard Times tokens, an original 1836 Gobrecht silver dollar, and various world coins.

[2] Law, an important member of the firm earlier in the decade, had since departed, and it was desired several years earlier to rename the ship. However, there was a law against this, and the renaming did not occur until 1857, after the law was changed. This was her second voyage under the *S.S. Central America* flag. Changing the name of a ship was bad luck, some said (also see the later account of the *Brother Jonathan* which at one time was called the *Commodore*).

[3] Heyl, 1953, pp. 171-172, gives an account of the history of the *George Law*.

[41] *Harper's New Monthly Magazine*, October 1855, "A Trip on the Panama Railroad," p. 616.

Medal issued in 1858 to observe the loss of the *S.S. Central America*. The obverse shows the ship sinking stern-first, while the reverse bears an inscription. Made for presentation to Captain William Lewis Herndon's widow, the medal was also placed on sale to the public. (Bowers and Merena, sale of the Witham and Sansoucy Collections, now in the Thomas Sebring Collection)

Hand-engraved silver medal depicting on the obverse the sinking *S.S. Central America*, and on the reverse this wording in engraved script: "Presented by the Central America Fund Committee to William Blommerth, in token of their appreciation of his humane and successful efforts toward saving the lives of these unfortunates cast adrift on the ocean by the foundering of the Steamer Central America. Sep. 12, 1857." (Alan V. Weinberg Collection)

ber 1857 was surely considered by many passengers to be the height of luxury in a tropical cruise. Many on board had taken this route before as had their families. Indeed, travel from California to Panama and onward to New York City had become routine. The "adventurous" days were over. As had been implied in the foregoing 1855 narrative and in other accounts of mail steamer travel, there seemed to be no real need for life preservers.

Fall from Grace

However, there was another view, not so glamorous. Perhaps the glory days of the *George Law*, now renamed the *Central America*, were past. Nearly a century later, historian Erik Heyl commented:[1]

> In July 1857 the name of the *George Law* was changed to *Central America*.... The steamer continued on the same run as heretofore, but the new management was more interested in profits than in providing safe and satisfactory service. The newspapers published ever increasing complaints about skimpy and spoiled food, overcrowding, filthy accommodations and insufficient and untrained crews. It was rumored that the *Central America* was not seaworthy, having been allowed to deteriorate through neglect and stinginess.

In checking contemporary as well as modern accounts concerning the accommodations on board any steamer of the 1850s, it is soon learned that 10 different passengers can describe the same vessel in 10 different ways. No doubt this was caused in part by the type of accommodations purchased. Someone with comfortable first-cabin accommodations and fine meals with the other first-class passengers might well write a more favorable account than someone traveling in steerage with an economy ticket. There is no doubt, however, that in the era of the *Central America*, ocean-going ships tended to deteriorate quickly, and after several years of service this particular vessel probably was in need of refurbishing. Indeed, later testimonies and an investigation would suggest this.

On to New York

The *S.S. Central America*, now on its 44th voyage, departed Aspinwall on September 3, 1857, in calm seas under bright blue skies interrupted by a few cumulus clouds. Every indication was a good omen for another smooth, pleasant trip to New York. For those in the best class of accommodations, this was travel at its finest. Others with lesser-priced tickets expected what they paid for, but in any event it was a nice time of year for an ocean voyage.

Few aboard the *S.S. Central America* in September 1857 knew or cared that travel in the Caribbean Sea and up the Atlantic Coast could be perilous in September. Hurricanes often struck without warning and with terrific force in the late summer season, such as in the largely forgotten disasters of years earlier in 1715 and 1733 when virtually entire fleets of Spanish ships carrying silver and gold treasure were sunk off the coast of Florida.[2]

No doubt some travelers on the *Central America* had read of more current happenings in such weather, such as delineated in the popular account, *A Second Visit to the United States*, 1849, by Sir Charles Lyell. In September 1845, Lyell was aboard the 1,200-ton Cunard Line steamer *Britannia* in the North Atlantic when she was caught in a hurricane. This ship, which came through the storm without permanent injury, was only about half the size of the *Central America*:[3]

> Another gale of still greater violence came up on the night of [September 14], when the ship was running at the rate of ten and one-half miles per hour. The wind had been from the northeast when, suddenly and in an instant, it blew from the northwest. I was in my berth below when this squall struck the vessel, and supposed that we had run upon some floating timber or an iceberg. We felt the ship heel as if falling over. The captain had time to get the sails hauled half up, all except the top-sail, which was torn to pieces.
>
> In a few minutes the wind had veered rapidly around the compass, a perfect hurricane for 23 hours; the spray being carried mast high so that there was a complete mingling of sea and sky. Among our passengers were some experienced American sea captains who had commanded sailing vessels of their own round Cape Horn, and, being now for the first time on a steamer at sea, were watching with professional interest the *Britannia's* behavior in the storm.
>
> They came to the conclusion that one of these steam vessels, well appointed, with a full crew, skilled officers, and good engineers, was safer than any sailing packet. The power of steam enables them always to make way, so as to steer and keep their head to the wind, on which safety depends.
>
> We were going at the time at the rate of ten and one-half miles per hours, and the paddle wheels were revolving fifteen and a half times per minute, but during the gale they made only six or seven revolutions, the engineer, to avoid too great a strain on the machinery, having then burned much less coal, and going no more than half speed.

Obviously, should a hurricane come up, great care was needed in the management of the engines and the steering of the ship. However, such matters were distant from the mind of those aboard the *S.S. Central America* 12 years after the *Britannia* voyage just de-

[1] *Early American Steamers*, p. 171.
[2] As described in Chapter 10.
[3] Lyell, Vol. I, pp. 14 ff., here paraphrased.

scribed. Besides, the *Britannia* was a small vessel in comparison to the *Central America.*

Previous passages of the *Central America* had been made without unfavorable incidents, save for a couple of groundings on reefs and the storm-tossed voyage of December 1853. Life preservers and lifeboats remained unused.

Most often, travel aboard the ship was smooth from beginning to end. In this era there was no way to reliably forecast tropical storms and hurricanes, and their origins and paths were not well known. In the unlikely event of a storm, the cabins, parlors, and other rooms on mail steamers provided comfort and many possibilities for entertainment and whiling away the hours until the clouds passed. Presumably, the crew was well trained to cope with any emergencies, should such should arise.

Not to worry. There was no sign of any storm, much less of a hurricane.

A Stop at Havana

On Monday afternoon, September 7, 1857, the *Central America* made the port of Havana. Coal was taken on and a few passengers ventured on shore, but not as many as usual, for yellow fever was rampant there. Cuban cigars were a favorite purchase at that harbor and were highly acclaimed for their quality. Captain Herndon was among those who enjoyed smoking them.

In Havana there were some slight changes in the passenger manifest, and on the continuing trip to New York City there were an estimated 492 passengers and 105 officers and crew members including some newly-boarded survivors from the recently wrecked bark *Vespasian* which had met its fate on Old Providence Island in the Bahamas. However, two intended passengers were disappointed. In Havana, J.C. Lenea had purchased passage on the *Central America,* but while he was arranging for his luggage to be brought from his rooms to the dock, the ship departed without him. Also left on shore was a Mr. Jacobs who had sought to buy a ticket, but who was told that all the berths were filled. Being delayed in Havana wasn't all that bad. There were many amusements in the city, cigars and other items to be purchased, and, if all else failed, one could curl up with something to read, perhaps Harriet Beecher Stowe's best-selling *Uncle Tom's Cabin* which since its appearance in 1852 had been all the rage. Stowe taught classes at Bowdoin College in Maine, the same institution of higher learning that offered a chair to poet Henry Wadsworth Longfellow, who years earlier had missed the boat—the steamer *Lexington.* Things like that happen.

At 9:25 a.m. on Tuesday, September 8, the fully-loaded *S.S. Central America* hoisted anchor in Havana and headed toward New York City via the Straits of Florida. The weather was pleasant and was made even more so by a light breeze from the ship's forward motion. Everything was set for the continuation of a really enjoyable voyage.

Strong Winds

At 5:30 a.m. on Wednesday, September 9, the ship's second officer noted that the ship had gone 286 nautical miles in the preceding 26 and one-half hours, and that there was a fresh breeze kicking up swells. Perhaps a storm was coming. In any event, there was no alarm. This was a large ship, well equipped, and with an experienced crew capable of handling any storm. Meanwhile, the ship plowed onward toward New York.

As the hours passed, the breeze intensified to a strong wind, finally reaching gale force. The *S.S. Central America* was tossed about in the waves, but continued on her course. The discomfort would soon be over, as storms usually passed quickly, although this one seemed a bit rougher than usual. In the meantime, card games, reading, and other amusements in the finely-appointed parlors were restricted. Many seasick passengers huddled in their cabins that afternoon, continuing into the night, waiting for the wind to subside and looking forward to a bright morning. Squalls and gales sometimes sprang up along the Florida coast and were usually just a passing inconvenience.

Passenger B.M. Lee later recalled: [1]

> I again went to bed, thinking that it would be over in the morning. Down below, at this time, nothing was to be heard but the crying of children and the moans of those suffering seasickness, and rising above all the sounds that proceeded from the inside of the vessel was the continued dashing and splashing of the waves against the sides of the ship, and the howling of the storm as the wind surged through the steamer's rigging. Amid all this I fell asleep.

Thursday, September 10

The expected calm did not come. By daybreak on Thursday, conditions had worsened, wind was screaming through tattered sails and rigging, passengers remained below deck, and the *S.S. Central America* was in the middle of a raging hurricane. Throughout the

[1] *New York Herald,* September 21, 1857; Conrad, p. 16.

day the fury of the storm and wind-whipped waves increased, but the ship remained watertight and the engines functioned properly. Onward to New York! Certainly, the storm would end soon.

Passenger Alonzo C. Monson recalled events similar to those of the night before:[1]

> During Thursday evening the evening games of cards and other pastimes for diversion and amusement usual in the cabin were dispensed with. The storm was the leading topic of conference. Some expressed their apprehension, particularly the ladies, as to the safety of the steamer. Most of the gentlemen, myself among others, did everything to prevent any alarm among the passengers.

Friday: The Fury of the Storm

Instead of subsiding as hoped, the fury of the storm continued to increase. High winds and waves wracked the ship, and it was all the captain could do to keep the bow headed into the waves. This was an important precaution to observe as, indeed, anyone who had read Lyell's account of the small steamer *Britannia,* knew well. Besides, it was simply good seamanship. And, didn't the *Central America,* well-financed and with great experience on the route, have the best crew that money could hire? So it was thought.

On Friday morning, September 11, the crew was still in control, but the steamer had begun to take on water through the drive shaft, some broken or open lights (windows to illuminate the below-deck areas), and elsewhere. The ship was tossing violently, making it virtually impossible to feed coal into the boilers.

Meanwhile the rising water reached steam pipes and became hot. Conditions in the engine room worsened. The crew down below either did their best, or they were woefully unconcerned and neglectful (depending upon which later accounts are read). In any event, water was sloshing around and the boilers and engines could not be tended properly. By any reckoning it was a tough situation.

At 11 a.m. Captain Herndon told the passengers that the ship was in danger and enlisted the aid of all men to bail water with a bucket brigade. At one point the ship listed sharply to the starboard (right side), and the captain ordered all passengers to go to the port side for balance.

Friday Afternoon

At 1:00 in the afternoon the main engines stopped, although an auxiliary steam engine operated a pump until the early evening when it also failed. From several accounts it seems that George E. Ashby, the chief engineer, made little serious attempt to keep the engines running. A cowardly man, he intimidated many others aboard, and placed his personal safety above all else. Passenger Thomas W. Badger, himself a captain and certainly in a position to be a qualified observer, recalled that Captain Herndon had called out, "For God's sake, Mr. Ashby, don't wait until the ship is full of water. Start the men to work bailing now."[2] Keeping the engines running so as to maintain control of the vessel was considered to be the first order of seamanship when running in high waves.

Again, the masterful control of the smaller *Britannia* in the 1845 Atlantic hurricane comes to mind.

By mid-afternoon, the lower deck and many cabins of the *S.S. Central America* were uninhabitable, food service had been suspended, and passengers scavenged to eat crackers and drink water or wine. A small spanker sail was rigged in an attempt to keep the ship headed into the wind, for if it was broadside to the waves it risked being swamped. However, it and all other canvas sails were soon ripped to shreds.

Saturday, September 12

After a tumultuous wind and wave-whipped night, the powerless *Central America* wallowed helplessly in a raging sea on Saturday morning. Decks were awash. This was disaster experienced first-hand, not an ordinary tropical storm, and passengers and crew alike feared for their lives.

Capt. Herndon ordered the American flag to be flown upside-down as a distress signal. The Atlantic coastal route was well-traveled, and surely it would be a short time until other ships came along.

Despite the leadership of Herndon, problems developed on board as some male passengers refused to work on the bailing brigade and quarreled with each other and the crew. Others, some of whom were men of leisure and knew little of physical labor, toiled ceaselessly. Ladies volunteered to help, but the men in a display of chivalry would not let them. However, the idea spurred the workers to renewed effort. Children frolicked one moment and cried the next. All were afraid.

Helpless in the Hands of Fate

Before 8:00 a.m. the ship listed sharply on its side, and many portholes, some broken, were now under water. Captain Herndon once again announced that if

[1] *New York Herald,* September 27, 1857; Conrad, p. 17.

[2] *New York Times,* September 23, 1857; Conrad p. 18.

The bailing brigade aboard the *Central America*, representing one artist's view of the event.

the ship could be kept afloat for a few more hours, surely help would come from other ships plying the same route. He reminded passengers that another steamship, the ill-fated *S.S. San Francisco,* had remained afloat for over 11 days after being disabled, and this in bitter cold weather. Perhaps Herndon did not mention that the passengers aboard that vessel suffered great privation and many died.[1]

Really rough weather arose at sea now and then, and in time the passengers of the *Central America* would be safe at home. Probably, any long-time sailor aboard could relate stories of high winds and waves experienced during his career.

Good news finally arrived. By 10:00 a.m. the hurricane showed signs of abating. The worst was over.

However, bad news took precedence. Seemingly, too much damage had already been done to save the ship.

Water continued to fill what air spaces remained in the cabins and compartments in the wooden hull, and it seemed inevitable that the *S.S. Central America* had but a short time left. Still, the bucket brigade struggled against the tide, and by the use of hoists and barrels recently emptied of ice-packed pork, the men remaining on the line were able to purge the ship of about 400 gallons per minute. Unfortunately, this was not enough to make a difference. Distress flares and rockets were launched.

Free Gold Coins!

At about 1:00 p.m. on Saturday afternoon, the sail of the brig *Marine* was seen on the horizon. This storm-damaged vessel, under the command of Captain Hiram Burt and 10 crew members, drew closer. Aboard the sinking *S.S. Central America* Captain

2 For a gripping account of the loss of the *S.S. San Francisco,* December 1853, see *Harper's New Monthly Magazine,* February 1854, pp. 404-407. Also Kemble, p. 245, and Heyl, 1953, pp. 379-380. The ship foundered from December 23, 1853, until January 5, 1854; over 500 were aboard of whom about 195 perished (when a section of cabins was washed off the after-deck) before the others were taken off the ship. J.F. Loubat, *The Medallic History of the United States of America, 1776-1876,* published in 1878, pp. 411-417, described a medal (by Anthony Paquet) authorized by Congress for award to rescuers and gave a lengthy account of the *S.S. San Francisco* disaster.

Herndon ordered women and children on deck, preparatory to boarding lifeboats. Ladies left behind unnecessary baggage. Some, "as if to illustrate how little value was the gold, brought out bags (not entrusted to the purser) and scattered it on the floor, asking all who wanted money to help themselves."[1] A few ladies picked up pieces, but none took more than two $20 coins.[2]

Meanwhile, a carpetbag filled with $16,500 in $20 gold pieces was too heavy to remove from a cabin, and Mrs. Jane Badger, who had packed it by emptying the coins from a trunk, left the golden array behind. Later, her husband, Capt. Thomas W. Badger,[3] dumped the glittering coins from the bag onto the floor of the captain's stateroom. Several other men spread their coins about, amounting to an estimated several hundred thousand dollars' worth.[4] Two ladies threw a further $10,000 worth of $20 gold pieces on the floor, but no one cared. Purses containing in some instances thousands of dollars in gold coins were left untouched on sofas.[5]

A later account summarized the golden scene:[6]

> According to the statements made by many of the survivors, there was seldom so large an amount of money owned by the passengers as was the case with those who came by the *Central America,* and the quantity of treasure on board was, consequently, far greater than the one and a half to two millions named on the freight list. Many, indeed, were persons of large means, and there were but few whose immediate wealth did not amount to hundreds, while numbers reckoned their gold by the thousands of dollars.
>
> The greater portion of the passengers were returned miners, some on their way to invest the capital they had realized, in hopes to live a life of greater ease as a result of their industry,[1] and others to get their families and once more go to the land of gold.
>
> But, as the storm continued to rage, less and less was thought of gold, and when, on Saturday, it became evident that they were likely at any moment to be buried beneath the waves, wealthy men divested themselves of their treasure belts and scattered the gold upon the cabin floors, telling those to take it who would, lest its weight about their persons—a few extra ounces or pounds—should carry them to their death. Full purses, containing in some instances thousands of dollars, lay around untouched. Carpetbags were opened, and the shining metal was poured out on the floor with the prodigality of death's despair. One of the passengers opened a bag and dashed about the cabin twenty thousand dollars in gold dust [*sic*], and told him who wanted to satisfy his greed for gold to take it. But it was passed by untouched, as the veriest dross.

Rescue Attempts

The first lifeboat leaving the *S.S. Central America* was smashed, and other difficulties were experienced as women and children climbed into the small boats. Some were lowered in hastily-fashioned rope loops or nooses in which they sat, but most jumped from the *Central America* into the boats below. Some missed the target and landed in the sea, and were fished out by those already in the little vessels.

In the coming hours the storm-damaged brig *Marine* took dozens aboard. Finally, men were allowed into the lifeboats, and a few went over to the *Marine* including some of the crew of the *S.S. Central America,* an action that caused many unfavorable comments in later investigations, as passengers expected that crew members would remain in the rescue boats to shuttle regular passengers to safety. They were wrong.

Meanwhile, many incidents continued aboard the stricken steamer including threats and fights among the remaining passengers, drunkenness of several, and numerous injuries from falling or being hit with storm-tossed wreckage. In nine shuttle trips 109 passengers were saved. The *Marine* eventually drifted several miles away and could no longer render aid.

The contemptible chief engineer, George E. Ashby, "turned out to be a thoroughgoing coward," according to historian Heyl. "He jumped into the last lifeboat as it was still loading, having only a half-dozen people in it, and by brandishing a huge knife prevented others from leaving the steamer and getting into the boat." The same writer laid the entire unfortunate incident at Ashby's feet.

Meanwhile, the Boston sailing ship *El Dorado* came close to the *Central America,* but it was too disabled by the storm to be able to help with rescue work, despite intentions of its captain to do so.

The *Central America* continued to fill with water. By now, all bailing efforts had ceased, and most of the ship was inundated. Pounding waves broke up

---

[1] Account in *Frank Leslie's Illustrated Newspaper,* October 3, 1857.

[2] Klare, p. 200.

[3] Of the bark *Jane A. Falkenberg* out of San Francisco.

[4] Interview with Jane Badger, *New York Times,* September 24, 1857; Conrad, pp. 28, 41. Klare, p. 199 (there Badger's gold is valued at $17,000 to $20,000).

[5] Klare, p. 200.

[6] R.M. Devens, *Our First Century,* pp. 642-643. $20,000 worth of gold *dust* is mentioned and may be the same anecdote as $17,500 to $20,000 in *coin* mentioned in other accounts; scarcely two retellings of the *Central America* disaster were alike in all details.

[7] This scenario seems highly dramatized. By September 1857 there were relatively few miners with enough cash reserves to return to the East and live lives of luxury. Other accounts do not support the stories of earning permanent wealth in the gold fields. However, the *Central America* did, indeed, have its share of wealthy non-miners aboard and, perhaps, a few miners, too.

cabin walls and floors and tore away sails, spars, and equipment. Some of the men ripped planks and railings off the ship to make crude rafts, while others found single boards. At about 7:50 in the evening, Captain Herndon ordered rockets to be fired downward to signal that the ship was sinking, meanwhile bravely trying to reassure the 438 men remaining on board that other rescue vessels were bound to come along.

The Last Moments of the *Central America*

A few minutes past 8:00 a tremendous wave hit the *S.S. Central America*. She shuddered, timbers broke, and with hundreds of men huddled at the front of the ship and Captain Herndon on the starboard paddlebox, she slipped at a sharp angle beneath the waves. Many including Herndon went down with the ship, while others clung to wreckage or bobbed about in hollow tin or cork-filled life preservers. As passengers were drowning or clinging to flotsam, George Ashby and certain of his fellow crewmen were being comforted aboard the *Marine*.

James Birch, president of the California Stage Company, went down with the steamer, taking with him $70,000 in gold.[1] Two brothers from Missouri, John and Anson Horne, had $4,000 to $6,000 in gold in a valise, brought it on deck, took seats on either side of their treasure, clasped hands, and went down with the ship.[2] Luckier was Stephen C. Caldwell, a steerage passenger from New York, who "had 20 pounds of gold dust and assorted coins in a belt about his waist; he kept himself afloat upon a cabin door which he secured shortly after the ship sank."[3]

Soon thereafter the *Central America* came to rest in the darkness 8,000 feet below the surface, about 160 miles offshore of Charleston, South Carolina. Passenger gold was scattered here and there around the ship's hulk and the surrounding sea bottom. In the hold, still stored in the wooden boxes that had been carried along the Pacific Coast by the *Sonora,* followed by a trip on the Panama Railroad, the treasure of gold coins and ingots remained intact.

Later Rescues

Several dozen adrift passengers and crew members were rescued the next day by the Norwegian bark *Ellen* under Captain Anders Johnsen.

Three more castaways from the *S.S. Central America* drifted at sea for many days and endured hardships, but were picked up on September 21 by the British brig *Mary.* One of these survivors was Alexander Grant, who three times earlier had been involved in maritime disasters: as a boy he was aboard a steamer out of Fall River, Massachusetts, that was wrecked in the Bay of Fundy, and he barely escaped with his life; later he was fireman on the *Arctic* steamship of the Collins line and was rescued after clinging to a piece of timber; and still later he was a fireman on the *S.S. Crescent City* when she went ashore in the Bahamas.[4]

Among the rescued was John Lorimer Graham, Jr., a numismatist of some renown. Several years later in 1860, no doubt with mixed emotions, he purchased at auction a silver impression of a medal observing the loss of the *S.S. Central America.* By 1867 it was stated that Graham's cabinet, "in intrinsic worth alone, is one of the most valuable in the country."[5]

At final reckoning of the *S.S. Central America* disaster, about 435 souls were lost. Only 162 were saved.[6]

From a nineteenth-century engraving titled "Victims of the Central America."

---

[1] Klare, p. 199.

[2] Klare, p. 200. Perhaps reminiscent of the humorous rejoinder relating to accumulated worldly treasures, "If I can't take it with me, I'm not going."

[3] Klare, p. 116, noted that Caldwell had mined the gold himself in California; this was equal in value to about 15 years' wages for a working man at the time. Account of William Chase, *Detroit Free Press,* September 23, 1857; Conrad, p. 46. Caldwell was picked up by the *Ellen.*

[4] "Alexander Grant, the Man Who Couldn't Be Drowned," *Harper's Weekly,* October 17, 1857. Also R.M. Devens, *Our First Century,* pp. 640-641.

[5] *American Journal of Numismatics,* May 1867, p. 9. Most modern (1980s and 1990s) accounts of the *Central America* have overlooked this numismatist. However, he is mentioned (but not with a numismatic connection) by Normand E. Klare, pp. 213-214, as being a "political and personal friend" of President James Buchanan. Although no account is given of Graham's experience aboard the ship, it is stated that on October 19, 1857, Graham petitioned President Buchanan to give an award to Captain Hiram Burt of the brig *Marine,* who assisted in the rescue of passengers.

[6] Passenger lists were not complete, and accounts vary. The numbers quoted here are from Klare, p. 247.

News as it Breaks...

The *Brooklyn Daily Eagle,* informed its readers of developments as they were learned. Reprinted here, they give a first-hand view of the event:[1]

September 18, 1857:

LOSS OF THE *CENTRAL AMERICA*
ONLY SIXTY LIVES SAVED!

The most appalling event we have been called upon to record since the loss of the ill-fated *Arctic,* is the total loss of the steamship *Central America,* with nearly all that were on board. The following dispatch from Charleston embodies all the information as yet received:

Charleston, Thursday, Sept. 17.

The steamship *Thomas Swann,*[2] from New York, has arrived at this port, and reports having spoken,[3] on the 15th inst., about 15 miles north of Cape Hatteras, the Norwegian Bark *Eloise* [actually *Ellen*], which had on board 40 of the passengers of the steamship *Central America.* The passengers state that the *Central America* foundered on the 12th inst., and that only 60 out of over 500 passengers were saved. Nothing is mentioned concerning the specie she had on board.

No mention is made of the remaining 20 of the saved who were not on board the *Eloise.* As near as can be ascertained at present, the total number of lost and saved is as follows:

Number of passengers	525
Number of officers and crew	101
Total on board	625
Number saved	60
Total lost	506

She carried treasure to the amount of a million six hundred thousand dollars, and a valuable cargo and mails from the Pacific. On the evening of the 9th the heavy gale, which has proved so destructive on our Southern coasts, set in from the northwest, and it came to its height on Saturday, 12th inst., when it blew a perfect hurricane. And it was in this awful tempest that the *Central America* foundered, carrying down with her 500 souls.

The *Central America* (*nee* George Law), was considered as one of the staunchest of vessels, an excellent sea-boat, and her owners had full confidence in her ability to weather the gale through which the other steamers passed in safety. She was built in 1853, by William H. Webb, for the United States Mail Steamship Company. She was constructed of the best materials, and all her planking was billeted edgewise through and through. Only three months ago she was taken on the drydock and thoroughly overhauled and partly recoppered;[4] the main portion of it still being in good order.

THE STORM: The storm is described as one of the most terrible ever experienced along the Southern coast, and the damage to shipping has been very great. The steamer *Norfolk,* running between Philadelphia and Richmond, Va., was wrecked, but fortunately all her passengers and crew were saved. The following account of the wreck is given by a passenger.[5]

The steamship *Norfolk,* Capt. J.R. Kelly, which left Philadelphia on Saturday last, at 9 o'clock A.M., for Norfolk and Richmond, with 26 passengers, and a crew composed of 21 persons, and laden with a valuable cargo of merchandise, encountered a heavy gale from E.S.E. on Sunday evening, which continued to increase in violence during the night. Between 10 o'clock P.M., and 4 A.M., she sprung a leak, carried away jib, spanker, and fore spencer, and to lighten her, a large portion of cargo was thrown overboard. Her head was then turned toward the beach, with the view of running her on, to save the lives of those on board. However, the rudder broke off, and she was left a helpless wreck in a violent gale and heavy sea. At daylight on Monday she broke into pieces, then about 10 miles south of Chincoteague [in Maryland], the passengers and crew barely having time to take to the boats, saving nothing but what clothes they had on before she went down, and was lost entirely from view.

Further Accounts This Morning
More of the Passengers Saved.

A telegraph dispatch from Norfolk, Va. this morning says: Twenty-six females were saved from the *Central America,* by a brig which had arrived at the Hampton Roads.

Another dispatch says 50 passengers were taken off the wreck by a Moravian bark reported off the Hampton Roads.

All the officers of the *Central America* perished except Mr. Frazier [*sic;* actually James M. Frazer, second officer], the chief engineer.

Engineer [George E.] Ashby abandoned the vessel in a boat.

The above vague announcements are all the additional information received this morning, but they are readily believed as they not only bring the cheering news that at least 80 lives have been saved, but lead us to hope that a greater number of the passengers may have been picked up by other vessels. The excitement in New York is intense.

It was announced in Wall Street, this morning that the underwriters would pay the insurance on the treasure on board the *Central America* on demand, on presenting the legal proofs without waiting the time allowed by the policies.

---

1 Articles furnished by Wayne Homren. Author's modern emendations are in brackets and footnotes.

2 The *Thomas Swann,* 462 tons, was built in Philadelphia in 1853. She remained in service for over 10 years, until stranded on January 16, 1864, at Cape Henry, Virginia.

3 To speak a ship: a nautical phrase referring to the communication by a voice horn of a crew member of one ship across a short distance of water to the crew member of another. The typical speaking was meant to determine the name of the ship and her registry (if this was not obvious from signs and pennants), her destination, and, perhaps, to exchange news, the latter if the ships were meeting while coming from opposite directions. When one ship spoke another, the event was entered in the logs of both.

4 Hulls of wooden ships were sheathed in copper to impede growth of barnacles and to prevent infestation by teredos (shipworms).

5 The reference is to the *Norfolk,* a 494-ton, 196-foot wooden steamer launched as the *Penobscot* in 1843 for the Boston to Bangor passenger and freight run. The 21 crew members and 26 passengers all escaped in lifeboats and were picked up by other ships. The location of her beaching was given in later accounts as Hog Island, Virginia.

[By Telegraph]

Forty-five More Saved.
SAVANNAH, Sept. 18:

The bark *Saxony* arrived here this morning with five of the passengers of the *Central America*. She reports the total loss of the vessel, treasure and mails, and about 500 of the passengers and crew. She reports that 40 women and children were saved by the brig *Marine* of Boston. The sea was very heavy. Forty-nine other passengers of the *Central America* were picked up by the [*Ellen,* and five were transferred to the *Saxony*]. [Aboard the *Saxony*] were H.H. Childs, of the firm Childs & Dougherty, of New York; Jabez Howes, of the firm of George and Howes & Co., of San Francisco; George W. Lock,[1] of Maine and Adolph Fredericks of San Francisco.

September 19, 1857:

THE *CENTRAL AMERICA*
VESSELS SAILING UNDER FALSE COLORS

When the recent calamity on the ocean, burst upon the public, everybody wanted to know what vessel the *Central America* was. Nobody suspected that it was the old *George Law* under a new name.

It is quite a common practice, when a steamer is considered worn out and unseaworthy, and even when formally and legally condemned, to touch them off with a little paint and emblazon a new name over the wheel house, when the vessel is launched as an entirely new craft. Numerous tow boats in the river may be seen with one name on the stern and another on the wheel-house. We may mention the case of a boat now traversing the North River as the *Broadway,* which was first known as the *George Washington,* then as the *Metropolitan* and now sails under her third metamorphosis.

The general principles of action among the owners is to run them under one disguise or another until they go to pieces or are blown up; and each of them generally sacrifices the last cargo of passengers and freight. Such a practice is reprehensible, and who will doubt it? In tow boats and large river craft, what shall be said of it when practiced in the case of ocean steamers, bearing hundreds of devoted passengers? When the public have seen the name of one steamer long enough before them to know that she is old and tattered, it is the grossest deception to withdraw her and bring her forward as a new vessel under another name, and when so much property and human life is at stake the culpability is atrocious. There ought to be a law constituting it felony to assume and name for a vessel except under which she is originally launched.[1]

October 6, 1857:

Central America Wreck
THREE MORE PASSENGERS RESCUED

The Bremen bark *Laura,* from Bremen arrived New York this morning. She reports that at 2 P.M. on the 20th Sept., latitude 40, longitude. 54, she spoke the British brig *Mary* from Cardenas for Queenstown, and took from her J. Tice, 2nd Engineer, and Alexander Grant, fireman, and S.W. Davison [actually George W. Dawson], a passenger, whom the brig has rescued from the wreck of the steamship *Central America.*

Mr. Tice, 2nd Engineer of the *Central America* makes the following statement:

"From the time of the wreck I drifted SEVENTY-TWO hours on a plank. I succeeded in getting into a boat on the fourth morning after the wreck, and on the fifth picked up also Grant, fireman, who had been for five days on a part of the hurricane deck, from which he swam to my boat. We pulled to the hurricane deck and rescued G.W. Davison, passenger. Twelve men had once been on that part of the wreck. Of them George Buddington, John and Patrick Baule, coal passers, Eves, fireman, and six coal passers whose names are not known, died there.[3] David Grant and myself were without food or water eight days, the sea all the time making a breach over us. Two days after the steamer went down we saw several passengers on pieces of the wreck but could not assist them."

Mr. Tice saw Captain Herndon just before the ship went down. Davison and Grant are sick and badly bruised.

Accounts Continue

For many weeks accounts of the disaster were carried in newspapers as passengers were rescued and brought to various ports. Considerable blame was placed upon the engine-room crew, and it was asserted that had they been properly attentive to their duties, the ship would have maintained power, continued its forward progress with its bow headed into the waves rather than wallowing in troughs, and the disaster would not have happened. A few other accounts suggested that the ship's owners were derelict in their management of the line. Several articles in *Harper's Weekly* in September and October related that the vessel was in very poor condition and suggested that the owners should go on trial for murder. Others raised a similar cry.

Little attention was paid to other ships damaged in the same storm, as there had been no loss of life. The aforementioned *Norfolk* was wrecked. The 1,751-ton steamer *Empire City,* which had left Havana for New York City an hour after the *Central America* did on the morning of Tuesday, September 8, was caught in the same hurricane and off Cape Hatteras lost all her sails and her starboard paddlewheel box, and sustained

[1] Names given as Henry Childs, Adolph Frederick, Jabez Howes, Samuel Look, and Billings Ridley in Klare, p. 137. Similar names were in an account in the *Eastern Argus,* Portland, Maine, September 21, 1857 (quoted by Conrad, p. 53).

[2] Notwithstanding the intent of the author of this piece to prove his point, the owners of the former *George Law* had desired to change the name of the ship earlier, for its namesake was no longer connected with the steamship line. As mentioned in an earlier note, they were prevented from doing this until 1857. While the *Central America* may have appeared as a "new" ship to some, and while its accommodations may have been criticized by some passengers, the name change does not seem to have been done with the intent to deceive.

[3] Klare, pp. 256-257, identifies Buddington as the third assistant engineer. Among the coal passers in Klare's crew list there are none with the surnames of Baule, although Arnold Bell and Richard Bell are listed. Among the firemen there is no one named Eves or with a surname even slightly resembling this.

much flooding from broken light ports and other openings. She ran out of coal, but to keep running the crew ripped trim and other parts from the ship and threw the wood into the boilers. On the 15th the badly damaged *Empire City* came into Norfolk. After receiving repairs enough to permit the voyage to resume, she continued to New York City on September 18, on the way encountering the Norwegian bark *Ellen* and transferring many *Central America* survivors to the ship. The *Empire City* arrived in New York on the 20th.[1]

The *Southerner*, a 785-ton steamer completed in September 1846, entered the Atlantic Coast service, with her first trip departing on September 12 from New York City to Charleston. For many years she plied the same course with great success. Notice was made of her being damaged in the September 1857 hurricane, but few details appeared in the popular press.[2]

Investigation of the Disaster

The New York Times, December 1, 1857, commented upon the findings of the Committee of Inquiry investigating the disaster:[3]

> It cannot and should not be concealed that the testimony before the Committee goes to show that the *Central America* was not sound and equipped as she ought to have been, that her crew was not sufficiently numerous, that she was without a carpenter or suitable carpenters' tools, and what seems to the Committee a most serious defect, being common, it is feared, in many of our passenger steamers, there is a want of proper organization in regard to the relative authority and duties of the officers and crew of the vessel; each department appearing to be independent of the others, instead of being strictly subordinate and responsible to the Captain...and this independence of action was the more observable in the department of the engineer.

Steamship historian Erik Heyl easily concluded: "The entire blame for the disaster was laid on the management of the U.S. Mail Steamship Co., as was graphically shown in ballads sung at that time."

Despite the inadequacies of the ship and the negligence of its owners, Captain Herndon earned uniformly high marks for his bravery and conduct, despite the poor conduct of his crew, especially engineer Ashby. Unlike the captains of many other vessels involved in maritime disasters, Herndon did, indeed, go down with this ship—making the ultimate sacrifice in the finest tradition of the sea.

William Ede Reminisces

In 1896, William Ede, a survivor of the wreck, remembered the days of years before in a lengthy commentary, a small part of which is given here:[4]

> We had some good weather from Aspinwall to Cuba, but it began to be nasty as soon as we left Cuba. It began to blow pretty hard on the first day, but on the second the vessel was thrown upon her beam ends and began to leak most terribly. I had $1,500 in gold with me and was on my way back from California to Wisconsin to be married, so you see I was naturally displeased with the situation.... The storm, which began on the 8th of September, never abated its fury until the vessel went down on the 12th....
>
> [After an arduous experience in which I nearly lost my life] I was the first one of 49 men saved by [Captain Johnson of the *Ellen*]. We were given safe passage and landed at Norfolk, Va., where we were treated with the utmost hospitality. We were not allowed to spend a dollar for anything. We were feted and feasted, and I was taken clear to my home in Wisconsin without paying out a dollar for anything. The $1,500 I had when I started went down with the vessel.
>
> Captain Johnson was rewarded for his humanity by a popular subscription of $16,000. The United States government repaired his vessel at a cost of $10,000, for she had been buffeted by the same storm that had wrecked us, and President Buchanan gave him a gold chronometer....
>
> The people of San Francisco took no stock in the steamship company's report of the seaworthiness of the lost steamship, for on the 2d of November, 1857, they met in mass meeting and adopted resolutions condemnatory of the "heartless cupidity of the steamship company" in permitting an unseaworthy vessel to carry so many passengers upon so dangerous a voyage....
>
> The Central America Fund Committee caused silver medals to be created—with both the obverse (depicting the scene of the disaster, with the *Central America's* stern underwater) and reverse engraved, rather than die-struck. Examples were awarded to people who assisted with the rescue of passengers.

The Panic of 1857

The loss of human life was tragic, but did the sinking of the *S.S. Central America* play a pivotal role in American economics as well?

---

[1] A detailed account of the *Empire City* is found in Cedric Ridgely-Nevitt, *American Steamships on the Atlantic*, 1981, pp. 121-124 (history) and 125 (photograph). Damage from the hurricane necessitated her being out of service until early January, 1858, after which she resumed the New York City to New Orleans (via Havana) route. She continued in use in various capacities until 1869. Heyl, 1953, pp. 141-142 gives specifications and much other information, but not about the 1857 storm. She was scrapped circa 1870.

[2] Ridgely-Nevitt, p. 124 (passing mention of storm damage). Heyl, 1953, p. 403 (specifications and history). The *Southerner* was scrapped in the summer of 1858. This ship is no relation to the steamer *Southerner* which figures in the account of the loss of the *S.S. Winfield Scott.*

[3] Quoted by Conrad, p. 66.

[4] *San Francisco Chronicle*, February 23, 1896, which gave a retrospective of the disaster and printed interviews and recollections of four survivors who were known to live in San Francisco as of that date; copy supplied by Alan Victor Weinberg, owner of one of the engraved silver medals discussed.

Scene on Wall Street, New York City.

In the winter and spring of 1857 there had been great speculation in railroad stocks and in land. Banks and insurance companies made many risky investments. In June and July it was recognized that severe problems lay ahead, and in August the failure of a leading insurance company set in motion a chain of unfortunate financial events. In September several dozen banks failed in New York, Pennsylvania, and other eastern areas, which led to the suspension of specie payments by many eastern banks in October, a situation that was not remedied until December.

Throughout the summer of 1857 there had been many rumors of financial instability arising from earlier speculations. Inflation was rampant, and most American citizens felt that these were, indeed, good times. Record amounts of consumer goods and other cargoes were imported from Europe, the Orient, and elsewhere. This overseas purchases required payment in gold, but there was no problem. After all, so much gold had been found in California (and also in Australia) that silver was becoming "scarce" by comparison.

Freshly-minted gold coins, usually $20 pieces as these were most convenient to handle, flowed out at a record rate from the port of New York City to pay for incoming goods. In Washington, D.C., the secretary of the Treasury expressed alarm that a gold coin shortage might be in the offing. It was popularly thought that the periodic arrival in New York City of treasure-laden ships from Panama pumped vitality into the eastern markets with "new money" to help alleviate the situation, although few took the time to look at the actual numbers involved. This item in *Harper's Weekly,* June 20, 1857, is representative of that outlook:

> The country is prosperous, no doubt, but we are going ahead so fast, and living so absolutely from hand to mouth, that the first hitch in the machinery may upset the whole concern. The loss of a single specie-steamer from California would break no one can tell how many mercantile houses in New York, Philadelphia, and Boston.

An article in the August 22, 1857, number of the same magazine stated that there was a trade imbalance of about $100,000,000 in American trade. Further:

> How is this to be paid? It can only be paid in specie.... We shall probably receive, during the remaining five months of the year, sixteen or seventeen millions—at the outside—from California. Any arithmetician can calculate what proportion this will bear to the amount that we shall have to send abroad.

The General Sherman Connection
or
Was the Sinking of the *Central America* Responsible for the Burning of Atlanta?

It is not widely known that General William Tecumseh Sherman, famous for his Civil War exploits, at first pursued a career in banking.

Perhaps he should have stayed with banking.

But, he didn't.

In early 1857 Sherman was in San Francisco heading up a bank there, a branch of a St. Louis firm under the direction of James H. Lucas, a midwesterner said to be worth several million dollars. There were many problems with the economy of the city on the Golden Gate. Debt collections were difficult, real estate sold slowly if at all, and there was a general gloom in the business community. The branch that Sherman headed could not sustain itself. Thus, on May 1st he waved goodbye to friends, packed up his family, boarded the *S.S. Sonora* for Panama, to cross the Isthmus and head for New York City.

Arriving there, apparently with very few assets, he kept his oar in the financial water through associations with the Metropolitan Bank, the Bank of America, and the private firm of Schuchardt & Gebhard. However, all was not well. In his memoirs, General Sherman related:[1]

> Everything went swimmingly until the 21st of August, when all Wall Street was thrown into a spasm by the failure of the Ohio Life & Trust Company, and the panic so resembled that in San Francisco, that, having nothing seem-

[1] *Memoirs of General William T. Sherman,* D. Appleton & Co., New York, 1887, Vol. I, pp. 162-164.

> ingly at stake, I felt amused. But it soon became a serious matter even to me. Western stocks and securities tumbled to such a figure, that all Western banks that had held such securities, and had procured advances thereon, were compelled to pay up or substitute increased collateral.... In September the panic extended so as to threaten the safety of even some of the New York banks not connected with the West, and the alarm became general, and at last universal.
>
> In the very midst of this panic came the news that the steamer *Central America,* formerly the *George Law,* with 600 passengers and about $1,600,000 in treasure, coming from Aspinwall, had foundered at sea off the coast of Georgia, and that about 60 of the passengers had been providentially picked up by a Swedish bark, and brought into Savannah. The absolute loss of this treasure went to swell the confusion and panic of the day.

As it developed, the Lucas' banking house in St. Louis soon closed out its accounts although without apparent serious injury to its founder, who later died years later with an estate valued at eight million dollars. The firm dispatched Sherman to the West Coast to help collect some overdue money. On January 5, 1858, he boarded the steamer *Moses Taylor* for Aspinwall,[1] connecting to the *Golden Gate* (Capt. Whiting) on the western slope on January 15, then to San Francisco, arriving on January 28. There his efforts to collect some notes due Lucas met with varying degrees of success. Debtors were very innovative and elusive, including one man who feigned insanity when Sherman showed up at this doorstep. The returned Easterner quickly found that economic conditions in the West were unfavorable and that "property continued to be almost unsalable, and prices were less than half of what they had been in 1853-1854."

Sherman remained in San Francisco until July 3, when he departed on the *S.S. Golden Gate* and, in due course, returned to his family homestead in Lancaster, Ohio. What next? In his words:

> I was then perfectly unhampered, but the serious and greater question remained, what was I to do to support my family, consisting of a wife and four children, all accustomed to more than the average comforts of life?

A question arises—like the shoe that was lost for want of a nail, the horse that was lost for want of a shoe, etc.: If the *Central America* had remained afloat, would Sherman's banking company have done likewise, and would he have remained in the banking profession? If so, in the spring of 1861 he would not have joined the Union Army. If he had been busy cashing checks and collecting overdue accounts at his desk in 1864, he would not have pillaged the state of Georgia and the city of Atlanta in a dazzling (or despicable) march. And, what would Margaret Mitchell have done for a theme when she decided to write a novel about the Civil War?

History can sometimes turn on a single event.[2]

The *Central America* in Perspective

In mid-September 1857, when the sinking of the *S.S. Central America* was announced in the New York papers, there seemed to be more concern in the popular press about the loss of the gold aboard than there was about the fate of the passengers. While the somewhat less than $1 million in official shipments of gold coins and ingots aboard the *S.S. Central America* and intended for payment to New York City concerns may have helped financial conditions slightly had they arrived, the overall effect could not have been large, notwithstanding the opposite view taken in some dramatic commentaries by modern historians.[3]

It is also to be remembered that the insurance companies rushed forward with statements that claims would be paid immediately upon proof, without the usual delay, as in this previously quoted statement of September 18, 1857, immediately after news of the disaster reached New York City:

> It was announced in Wall Street, this morning that the underwriters would pay the insurance on the treasure on board the *Central America* on demand, on presenting the legal proofs without waiting the time allowed by the policies.

Historical Notes

Among accounts of the *S.S. George Law* and its reincarnation as the renamed *S.S. Central America,* few

---

[1] This ship, under Capt. McGowan, was nicknamed the *Rolling Moses,* supposedly for her instability in high waves.

[2] The recitation of this string of events is intended to be somewhat whimsical (of course, the reality of the march through Georgia was anything but).

[3] *E.g.,* Breen's breathless prose in *The Numismatist,* July 1990: "Wall Street had gone into crisis in August, but the worst effects were delayed because banks and other creditors were expecting gold to arrive from California in September (including the three tons from the *Central America*). Without it, they could neither meet payrolls nor pay debts. In a terrifying domino effect, banks failed, factories and stores closed. People were unemployed, homeless and starving all over the East Coast, and soon also in England and on the Continent. Beyond doubt, this shipwreck was partly responsible for one of the worst financial panics in American history." It is worth noting that Hubert Howe Bancroft, *History of California,* Vol. VII, p. 118, gives these figures: In 1856 records showed that $51,000,000 worth of gold was exported from San Francisco. From this amount it was estimated that $40,000,000 worth of gold was shipped to New York City, $8,700,000 to England, $1,500,000 to China, and $800,000 elsewhere including Panama, Pacific islands, South America, East Indies, and Australia. However, Bancroft suggests that the true export figure may have been closer to $56,000,000. Probably about $40,000,000 officially and perhaps 10% more than that unofficially, or about $45,000,000 went to New York in 1857. Of this amount it is seen that the *S.S. Central America* in September 1857 had but a tiny fraction, perhaps slightly more than 2% (or if gold in the hands of passengers is considered—really irrelevant, however—then the figure may have been 4% to 5%).

remembered an earlier tragedy involving the vessel's passengers, but not the steamer. Over a year before the ship's fatal voyage, on May 5, 1856, at the end of a 15-day trip from New York City, the vessel disembarked over 1,100 passengers at Aspinwall. Early in the morning of the next day, two trains of nine cars each were filled with passengers and followed another train with mail and baggage. The locomotive of the freight train jumped the rail and blocked the track. The two passenger trains came upon the scene, and the cars of these two trains were coupled to one of the engines, permitting the other engine to help clear the track. The engine hauling 18 cars headed back to Aspinwall. One car became uncoupled, left the rails, and was followed downhill at breakneck speed by eight more cars. In the wreck nearly 100 people were killed.[1]

In time, the September 1857 lost treasure ship and its passengers were largely forgotten. Indeed, even authoritative almanacs and anthologies of disasters and shipwrecks often omitted mention of it despite its being one of the greatest of all American maritime disasters up to that point. Perhaps the news of the slavery question and the ensuing Civil War obscured many memories. Consequently, few aficionados of the "trivia" games and quizzes so popular a century later would have heard of the ill-fated *Central America,* although the story of the *Titanic* disaster was known even to grade-school children.[2]

Finding the Wreck

The scene changes to decades later in the 1980s:

Thomas G. Thompson of the Battelle Memorial Institute, Columbus, Ohio, was a student of shipwrecks, and in 1980 he began directing his efforts toward the long-forgotten *S.S. Central America.* In 1985 a group of entrepreneurs and investors headed by Thompson and two associates, Robert Evans and Barry Schatz, formed the Columbus-America Discovery Group in Ohio. A ship, the *Arctic Discoverer,* was outfitted with electronic gear and other devices for exploration, old charts and accounts were studied, and a search commenced. The *Nemo,* a remote-controlled mini-submarine, was constructed and was equipped with sophisticated instrumentation, lights, cameras, and a grappling device. Of particular note was a mechanism which could dispense a chemical substance at the undersea wreck site. This liquid could surround coins and other objects, harden, and then be retrieved as a solid mass without harming the items encased. Later, the hardened casing could be dissolved, and any encased treasures would be intact.

In September 1986 success was theirs, and a hulk believed to be the *S.S. Central America* was discovered in her watery grave. On July 8, 1987, a lump of anthracite coal from the vessel was brought to the surface and airlifted to Norfolk, Virginia, where it served as sufficient evidence to permit Judge Richard B. Kellam to declare that Thompson's group had, indeed, found a potentially valuable ship and were entitled to legal protection from other would-be salvagers.

In time her identity was confirmed by the recovery of the ship's bell which was marked "MORGAN IRON WORKS NEW YORK 1853" by the ship's manufacturer. Much of the wood part of the steamer had rotted away and the metal components had rusted. However, a video camera image revealed that one of the large side paddle-wheel covers was largely intact. A subsequent dive of the *Nemo* proved to be wondrous: visible through the cameras was a veritable sea-bottom carpet of glittering $20 and $50 gold pieces and other coins! Keeping the coins company were starfish and other deep-sea fauna.

Soon thereafter, an intense publicity campaign was mounted, and glowing accounts of the find were carried in newspapers and magazines and on national television. Estimates of the worth of the treasure trove typically ranged up to $1 billion or even much more, obviously a rich reward for the stockholders and investors in the venture. Walter Breen was tapped to write an article about the treasure for publication in *The Numismatist,* the promotional talents of Los Angeles sports tycoon Bruce McNall (who had launched his career by making a fortune in numismatics) were enlisted,[3] and James Lamb of the Coin Department of Christie's art auction house greeted reporters and television crews. John J. Ford, Jr., was signed as numismatic advisor based upon his knowledge of Western gold coins and bars. Financing of the venture included $12.7 million from private investors later followed by about $3 million from Bruce McNall and a secured line of credit of about $20 million from Christie's.

---

[1] *Alta California,* May 23, 1856; quoted by Wiltsee, p. 199. In 1856 the ship was known as the *George Law.*

[2] History can be selective. Likewise, few know today about the horrendous loss of 1,547 lives in the explosion of the sidewheel steamer *Sultana* on the Mississippi River above Memphis on the night of April 27, 1865; there were 1,886 recently mustered-out Union soldiers plus several hundred others aboard a ship licensed to carry 376 people including the crew (cf. *Way's Packet Directory,* p. 436).

[3] McNall owned Numismatic Fine Arts, a 51% interest in the Superior Galleries coin dealership and auction business, and was the main stockholder of the Los Angeles Kings hockey team, whose star player Wayne Gretzky was a close personal friend (and who at one time bought a set of six pattern 1873 trade dollars at a Superior auction).

The *Arctic Discoverer*, used by the Columbus-America Discovery group to locate the wreck of the *Central America.*

Contemporary accounts and illustrations relating to the *Central America* disaster, found in *Frank Leslie's Illustrated Newspaper.*

However, no specific distribution plans were announced. Numismatists, historians, romanticists, and others awaited news of how the coins, ingots, and other items would be sold or otherwise made available. Alas, that was not to happen, at least not for a while. Multiple claims including from interests representing over two dozen old-time insurance companies and others, some of whom claimed to have pinpointed the location of the wreck earlier, or to have held ownership title, were filed against the Columbus-America Discovery Group. For years afterward the matter dragged through the courts in Norfolk, Virginia, where the *Arctic Discoverer* was based. Hassles increased and legal bills mounted.

The December 2, 1996, issue of *Coin World*, reported the court's decision regarding the *Central America* treasure:

> U.S. District Judge J. Calvitt Clarke in Norfolk, Va., issued the ordering giving "in excess of 92.4%" of the treasure to the Columbus-based group, according to a spokeswoman for Columbus-America.
>
> The remaining percentage will be distributed among insurance companies that paid off claims after the *S.S. Central America* sank in a hurricane in 1857.

While waiting for the decision "Tommy" Thompson, Bob Evans, and their associates have created museum and educational exhibits, have worked with more than 50 scientists concerning marine species at the wreck site, and have been involved in other aspects of research. Judy Conrad of the firm compiled a fascinating anthology of news accounts and passenger recollections, *Story of An American Tragedy: Survivors' Accounts of the Sinking of the Steamship Central America.*

It is said that the water at the 8,000 foot level is about 37° Fahrenheit. This coldness plus the great pressure combined to preserve the gold coins in far above average condition, free of the "seawater etching" so often seen on salvaged pieces, according to reports.

The Golden Treasures

Although no detailed inventory of the coins has yet reached print, it is understood that the most plentiful find consisted of thousands of 1857-S $20 pieces in Mint State. In fact, of the first 500 coins found, 387 were 1856-S and 1857-S double eagles.[1] A subsequent find of more 1857-S $20 pieces included coins arranged in piles or "towers" of stacked coins (one containing 300 pieces), just as they were packed in wooden crates in 1857, but with the wood long since rotted

John J. Ford, Jr., James Lamb, and Bob Evans (standing) examining gold coins and ingots from the *Central America*. (Photograph courtesy of John J. Ford, Jr., and Christie's, November 1989)

away.[2] Additional $20 pieces of 1854-S, 1855-S, and 1856-S in various grades were aboard as were a smaller number of Mint State 1857-S $2.50, $5, and $10 pieces, and worn earlier issues among which were half eagles of 1834 (no motto), 1842-D Small Date, 1844-D, 1849-C, and 1850-D.

Many gold bars were found, aggregating 6,000 ounces or more, with stamps attributable to five different California assayers and the San Francisco Mint. About 60% were marked by Kellogg & Humbert or the United States Assay Office of Gold.

A sample listing of assay firms and ingot weights, finenesses (percentage of gold metal), and bullion values at the time the bars were made includes the following:

> **Blake & Co.** (Sacramento, California): 4.95 ounces. .795 fine. $81.34. (equivalent to $20.67 per ounce of pure gold, but possibly including an allowance for the natural alloy of silver)[3]
>
> Blake & Co.: 16.75 ounces. .722 fine. $249.99. ($20.67/ounce of gold)
>
> **Harris, Marchand & Co.** (Harvey Harris and D Marchand; offices in Sacramento and Marysville): 13.52 ounces. .807 fine. $225.54. ($20.67/ounce of gold)
>
> Harris, Marchand & Co.: 22.52 ounces. .878 fine. $408.78. ($20.67/ounce of gold)
>
> Harris, Marchand & Co.: 295.20 ounces. .877 fine. $5,351.73. ($20.67/ounce of gold)

[1] *Numismatic News*, October 3, 1989, p. 2, quoting James Lamb.

[2] In the first quarter of 1856 there is an expense item in the records of the San Francisco Mint (source: contemporary report preserved in the Bowers and Merena archives), to Gardner Elliott, "making twelve coin boxes," for $46.25 the lot. "The price for coin boxes appears high, but they are made of the best materials, dovetailed and bound, with handles, etc." Such were undoubtedly used for export such as for freshly-minted coins aboard the *S.S. Central America*.

[3] This particular ingot was featured on the front pages of *Numismatic News*, January 30, 1990, and *Coin World*, January 31, 1990.

Henry Hentsch (San Francisco): 12.52 ounces. .973 fine. $251.82. ($20.67/ounce of gold)

Justh & Hunter (San Francisco and Marysville): 22.83 ounces. .883 fine. $416.72. ($20.67/ounce of gold)
Justh & Hunter: 16.83 ounces. .864 fine. $300.59. ($20.67/ounce of gold)
Justh & Hunter: $102.40.[1]
Justh & Hunter: 754 ounces.

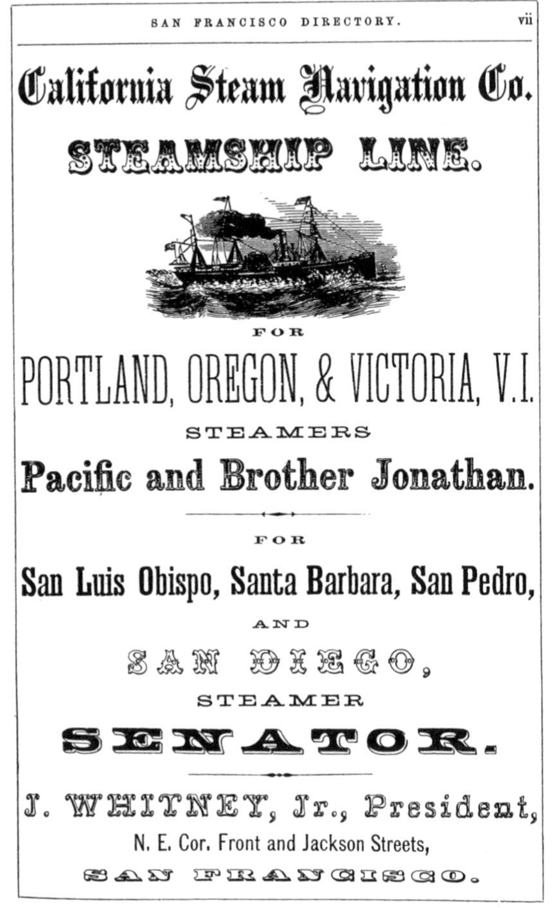

Advertisement for the steamers *Pacific* and *Brother Jonathan* run on the route from San Francisco north by the California Steam Navigation Company. (From *The San Francisco Directory for the year commencing 1864*, published by H.G. Langley, San Francisco)

Kellogg & Humbert (John Glover Kellogg and Augustus Humbert; San Francisco): 23.34 ounces. .898 fine. $433.26. ($20.67/ounce of gold)
Kellogg & Humbert: 36.68 ounces. .864 fine. $690.84. ($21.80/ounce of gold)[2]
Kellogg & Humbert: 208.10 ounces. .874 fine. $3,759.78. ($20.67/ounce of gold)

San Francisco Mint gold bar: 62 pounds.

In addition there were various privately minted $5, $10, $20, and $50 pieces circa the early and mid-1850s. These included two 1851 Baldwin & Co. $10 pieces; an 1852 Augustus Humbert $10; a dozen or more U.S. Assay Office of Gold octagonal $50s; several 1853 U.S. Assay Office of Gold $10 pieces (of .884 and .900 THOUS. varieties); a Wass, Molitor & Co. round $50, several scarce $10 of the same firm (an 1852 Wide Date $10, and *three* of the erstwhile rarities 1855 $10 with "Head of 1852"), and others.

Given the care that the Columbus-America Discovery Group is expending, in time the *S.S. Central America* find will probably be the best reported of all undersea treasures.[3]

The *Brother Jonathan*

Lost: July 30, 1865
Location: Near Crescent City, California
Found: 1916 or later
Treasure: Gold bars

The Ship's Early Days

The *Brother Jonathan*[4] was one of dozens of vessels engaging in the Pacific Coast trade. Launched at the shipyard of Perrine, Patterson & Stack, Williamsburg, New York, on November 2, 1850, the 1,181-ton ship was made of locust, white oak, live oak, and cedar and cost about $190,000. Her measurements were 220 feet 11 inches long by 36 feet wide with a draft of 13 feet

[1] Illustrated on the cover of *The Numismatist*, July 1990.
[2] The figure of $21.80 per ounce is too high and probably represents either a miscalculation of the assayer (such errors were frequent on bar stampings according to the assayer at the Philadelphia Mint, which received many such bars) or a modern error in reading or transcription.
[3] "Insurers to Share Shipwreck's Gold," *New York Times*, August 28, 1992; value of "up to $1 billion" stated. *Guide Book of United States Coins*, 1996 edition, pp. 287-288 (brief description of numismatic items; sample listing of bars). Also various articles by Gerald Tebben in the *Columbus Dispatch* and by different authors in *Numismatic News* and *Coin World*. The town of Herndon, Virginia, is named for the ship's captain. A recent popular account of the *Central America* wreck is found in Nigel Pickford, *The Atlas of Ship Wrecks & Treasures*, 1994, pp. 94-95.
[4] Brother Jonathan was a popular term for America as part of the "family" of lands in the British empire, an early-day counterpart of Uncle Sam (England was sometimes known as John Bull). A clever Yankee in a play (America's first stage comedy), *The Contrast*, by Royall Tyler, produced in 1787, was named Brother Jonathan. In 1842 the *Brother Jonathan*, published in New York, became America's first illustrated weekly paper. The name was often used in cartoons and elsewhere to denote a shrewd or clever young boy or an American citizen contemplating some new turn of politics or invention. Russell Rulau, *Standard Catalog of United States Tokens 1700-1900*, p. 219, describes a token listed as NY-492, attributed to the year 1858, struck in silver, 31mm: "John Bull and Brother Jonathan exchanging lightning bolts across the sea. At left HOW ARE YOU JONATHAN. At right PURTY WELL OLD FELLER / HOW'S YOURSELF." The reverse bears the advertisement of George H. Lovett, medal and diesinker at 131 Fulton Street, New York.

Above: The *Brother Jonathan* under steam and sail (as shown by an artist and illustrated in *Marine History of the North West*, by Lewis and Dryden, 1859). The artist was not familiar with science or meteorology, for he has the sails bellowing to the left while the smoke from the stack is drifting off to the right! (Similar errors have been made many times before, including certain ships illustrated on United States pattern coins of 1875.) (Courtesy of Oregon Historical Society, Portland, Oregon, negative 6807)

Right: Gold ingot of the San Francisco Mint. Believed to have been salvaged from the *Brother Jonathan*. (Henry H. Clifford Collection, 1982, Lot 178)

10 inches. Power was provided by a vertical steam engine made by the Morgan Iron Works. Accommodations including 24 staterooms were provided for about 365 passengers. The staterooms offered extra amenities for those wishing to pay a higher fare, but most voyagers were content with simple berths.[1]

The vessel started operations early in 1851 on the New York to Panama route, carrying cargo and gold seekers. Owner Edward Mills offered discount rates and attracted a poorer class of passengers. During this year she was involved in two separate disputes when passengers who had bought through-trip tickets from New York to San Francisco were landed at Panama, but could not complete their connections on the western leg. The first incident was precipitated when the steamer *Union* with 236 passengers and $270,000 in gold was wrecked early in the morning of July 5, 1851, when her helmsman, who with the rest of the crew was drunk from their Fourth of July celebration, fell asleep. The second problem was similar and occurred when the steamer *Monumental City* failed to arrive on schedule to complete the Pacific leg. In both instances the relatively penurious passengers that had bought cheap tickets through Mills' agency in New York City became stranded when the higher-priced Pacific Mail Steamship Co. would not honor their tickets unless they paid a large surcharge.

In an article, "Brother Jonathan: Pioneer Steamship of the Pacific Coast," Alfred L. Lomax described the ship early in its career *before* it entered service on the West Coast:

> People liked the *Brother Jonathan*. According to one who had booked return passage, the ship presented so impressive an appearance when it was fully illuminated at night with its glittering, reflecting ornaments that it vied with the drawing-room of an imperial palace. Oilcloth of a bright and variegated pattern covered the floor. Crimson cushioned settees and chairs provided comfortable reading and writing facilities. The cuisine must have been excellent as meat was served regularly from freshly killed cattle, swine, sheep and poultry which the vessel carried and kept on ice....

Vanderbilt as Owner

This schedule, apparently including very attractive accommodations for those aboard, continued until March 1852 when Commodore Cornelius Vanderbilt acquired the ship from Mills, reconfigured it to accommodate 750 passengers, and put it on the San Francisco to San Juan del Sud (port at Nicaragua) route. After being refitted the *Brother Jonathan* was equipped with three masts and a 400 horsepower steam engine.

Vanderbilt (1794-1877) was known for his filthy ships, spartan accommodations, and disregard for passengers' interest or safety. Emphasis was solely on profits to be made. In one particularly memorable eight-month period in the 1850s, three of his steamers were wrecked. Many complaints about his poor service reached print. Historian John Haskell Kemble commented:[2]

> Vanderbilt's ships maintained a reputation which was hardly enviable. They were described in the press of both coasts as "floating pig sties," not half manned and badly provisioned, and their owner was characterized as the "Nero of the sea."

Erik Heyl, another historian of renown, echoed the sentiments:[3]

> Some exceedingly bitter denunciations of Vanderbilt and the filthy conditions of his steamers, the poor and often spoiled food, and the ignorance and insolence of his captains and crews were published in the San Francisco daily newspapers. It was alleged that some of the Vanderbilt captains had never had any high-seas experience, but had been ferry-boat captains before being put in charge of the Pacific steamers.

After operating the *S.S. Brother Jonathan* for slightly more than half a year, Vanderbilt transferred the title to it and his other ships to his Accessory Transit Company, operators of the Nicaragua Steamship Company. Under this flag Vanderbilt maintained control of it for the next several years.[4] Among her activities during this period she assisted in 1854 with the passage back to San Francisco of the passengers of the ill-fated *Yankee Blade,* whose story was recounted earlier.

A typical notice by an express agent soliciting cargo for the *Brother Jonathan* appeared in *The San Francisco Herald,* May 16, 1854:

> WELLS, FARGO & Co.'s
> Express Notice
> For the Steamers of May 16th
>
> Our regular express for the Atlantic states and Europe will be dispatched on Tuesday, May 16th, at NOON by the steamers
>
> GOLDEN GATE
> J.T. Watkins, Esq., Commander
> BROTHER JONATHAN
> C.P. Seabury, Commander
>
> In charge of a special messenger on each steamer. Treasure received for shipment (and insured) until 9 o'clock a.m.

---

[1] Concerning the weight of the ship, William M. Lytle, *Merchant Steam Vessels of the United States 1807-1868,* states 1,359 tons. Erik Heyl, *Early American Steamers,* 1953, pp. 63-64, gives an excellent account of the *Brother Jonathan.*

[2] *The Panama Route, 1848-1869,* p. 96, for this specific quotation attributed to the *San Francisco Alta California,* July 14, 1860; numerous other comments in the same vein are given elsewhere in the text.

[3] *Early American Steamers,* 1952, p. 407, in an account of the negligent breakdown at sea of Vanderbilt's steamer Samuel S. Lewis.

[4] Heyl, p. 64.

of Tuesday, May 16th, and small packages and parcels until within one hour of the time of sailing.

Under Commodore Vanderbilt's ownership the vessel operated through 1856 when the government of Nicaragua revoked the charter of the Accessory Transit Company.[1]

In 1857 the ship was sold to John T. Wright of the Merchants Accommodation Line, who changed her name to the *Commodore,* a rather curious turn of events inasmuch as Commodore Vanderbilt's company had just stopped operating her. The *Commodore* ran from San Francisco to Seattle and also called on Vancouver and Portland. The British Columbia gold fever (see below) was rampant, and the *Commodore* and her sister ship, the *Pacific,* profited immensely from the related cargoes.

On one trip in the summer of 1858 the *Commodore* ran into heavy weather two days out of San Francisco on the way north, and with several feet of water flooding her holds, returned to port. Disgruntled passengers forced the line to pay refunds of about $12,000.[2]

In 1861 she became the property of the California Steam Navigation Company and underwent repairs at North's Shipyard in San Francisco to strengthen her superstructure. The old dining room was eliminated in favor of a new one measuring 120 feet long on the upper deck. One deck was eliminated, resulting in two instead of three. In December 1861, sporting its old name of *Brother Jonathan,* the ship was advertised as being ready:

> The new [*sic*] and splendid steamship *Brother Jonathan* built expressly for this route and with unequaled accommodations for passengers and freight, Samuel J. Dowel, commander, will leave Pacific Street Wharf for the above ports [Portland and Victoria] on Thursday, December 19, 1861....

North from San Francisco

Her most eventful voyage—the one that was to be her last—commenced on July 28, 1865.[3] Overloaded with freight far beyond her 900-ton capacity, and riding low in the water, the *Brother Jonathan* left San Francisco headed north toward its intended destination of Vancouver Island. Captain Samuel J. DeWolf had strongly protested the overloading, but was told that if he complained further, there were many other ship captains who would like to have his job at the helm.

The passengers numbered nearly 180, or a fraction of the capacity of close to 700. Among them were Mrs. J.C. Keenan, a popular proprietor of a San Francisco brothel, and seven girls in her employ, all heading north to seek new customers and opportunities.[4] General George Wright with his wife was on the way to assume his new post at Fort Vancouver under the Department of Columbia. Victor Smith, who had recently survived the wreck of the *Golden Rule* on Roncador Reef, Ecuador, was aboard, as was Anson C. Henry, governor of the Washington Territory. Fifty-four crew members were aboard. Among the cargo were two camels and a pair of horses, the latter the personal steeds of Gen. Wright.

No sooner had she gone through the Golden Gate marking the entrance to San Francisco Bay than she ran into a fierce gale. High winds continued through July 30, as the *Brother Jonathan* passed Crescent City on the coast of Northern California.

Shortly after 1:45 on the afternoon of the 30th, under clear skies in a sea whipped by the still heavy winds, she is said to have run onto rocks hidden beneath the surface off St. George's Point.[5] The concussion ripped a great hole in front of the engine room, causing the foremast to topple across the deck. Three cannon shots were fired, alerting citizens on the nearby shore, which soon became crowded with spectators.

In a scene which has been variously described from calm to confused, six small boats (four Franklin Patent Metallic Lifeboats and two surf boats) were put into the water. Five were immediately swamped, and only one, a surf boat commanded by James Patterson (the third mate) and carrying three children, five women, and 10 crewmen, was able to reach shore, representing the only survivors from the 232 people comprising the crew and passengers.[6]

---

[1] Later, Vanderbilt increased his fortune and became a major force in the operations of the New York Central Railroad. His heirs spent money lavishly on personal pleasures including building The Breakers, renowned as the most lavish "cottage" at the seashore in Newport, Rhode Island, and luxurious yachts.

[2] Jim Gibbs, *Disaster Log of Ships: A Pictorial Account of Shipwrecks, California to Alaska,* 1971, pp. 20-29, is the source for certain information including the refund demand.

[3] An excellent account and a passenger list of the *Brother Jonathan* are found in Marshall, 1978, pp. 157-167. Harry Rieseberg and A.A. Mikalow, *Fell's Guide to Sunken Treasure Ships of the World,* .1965 pp. 138-139, "The Deep-Fathomed Tomb of the *Brother Jonathan,*" includes useful information.

[4] Marshall, p. 159. In keeping with popular parlance, certain later accounts referred to the ladies as "soiled doves" and "fallen angels."

[5] A.k.a. St. George Point. A crag known as Jonathan's Rock is said to have administered the fatal hull puncture.

[6] William M. Lytle, *Merchant Steam Vessels of the United States 1807-1868,* gives the deaths as 171. Marshall, p. 157, quotes a contemporary account stating that one lifeboat was successfully launched, two were swamped, and three remained on board. Later stories varied.

About 45 minutes after the impact the *Brother Jonathan* was at the bottom of the sea.

The quartermaster, who was one of the survivors, later told his tale:[1]

> I took the helm at twelve o'clock. A northwest gale was blowing and we were four miles above Point St. George. The sea was running mountain-high and the ship was not making headway. The captain thought it best to turn back to Crescent City and wait until the storm had ceased. He ordered the helm hard to port. I obeyed and it steadied her. I kept on due east. This was about 12:45. When we made Seal Rock the captain said "Southeast by south." It was clear where we were, but foggy and smoky inshore.
>
> We ran until 1:50 when she struck with great force, knocking the passengers down and starting the deck planks. The captain stopped and backed her, but we could not move the vessel an inch. She rolled about five minutes, then gave a tremendous thump and part of the keel came alongside. By that time the wind and sea had slewed her around until her head came out of the sea and worked off a little. Then the foremast went through the bottom until the yard rested on the deck. Captain DeWolf ordered everyone to look to his own safety and said that he would do the best for all.

On that fateful day Albert D. Richardson was returning from Victoria, British Columbia, to San Francisco, a 740-mile voyage costing $45 for a ticket on a coastwise steamer.[2] His ship expected to rendezvous at sea with the *Brother Jonathan* and receive from it the current San Francisco newspapers. Richardson later recalled:

> [As our southbound ship] threaded St. George's Reef—a series of dangerous rocks near the land; some rising two or three hundred feet, others entirely under water—we hoped to meet the *Brother Jonathan,* with papers from San Francisco only 24 hours old. The swell was very high, and our captain's face wrinkled with anxiety until the perilous point was passed. Meanwhile we were discussing the chances for life one would have, shipwrecked in that heavy sea.
>
> We missed the *Brother Jonathan,* but two hours after we passed the reef she reached it, struck a rock, and in 45 minutes went to the bottom Of her passengers and crew only 16 were saved. One hundred and fifty, with their human hopes and fears, their loves and longings and ambitions, were engulfed in that repository which keeps all its treasures and all its secrets till the sea shall give up its dead....
>
> Marine disasters are far more frequent and appalling on our coasts than in any other quarter of the globe.... Our whole system of travel by river and sea is shamefully hazardous. Our best ocean steamers are without boats enough to hold all their passengers, even in smooth waters. And when an inspection is to take place, owners and officers often know it in season to borrow hose, boats, and other needful articles of outfit. The slaughter will never cease till proprietors and managers are held to strict responsibility. Convict and punish them for homicide whenever it occurs through their penuriousness, heedlessness, or neglect of precautions which law and humanity require.

At the time the *Brother Jonathan* disaster represented the greatest loss of life of any shipwreck on the Pacific Coast of the United States. For days afterward bodies, some wearing ineffective life jackets, floated ashore up and down the shoreline.[3] Ghouls cut off of the fingers of many of the corpses that floated up on the beach, so that their rings could be recovered. Local authorities blamed these amputations on Indians in the area, but it was later disclosed that white citizens of the town had done it.[4] Many of the bodies were buried in the Brother Jonathan Cemetery, a part of the Masonic cemetery established in Crescent City about 10 years before the wreck.[5]

Readers of newspaper accounts found it curious and a sad reflection on human nature that 10 male *crew* members survived, but not a single adult male *passenger* was saved. Perhaps reflecting the late lamented *Yankee Blade,* it was—once again—seemingly a case of "crew first, passengers last," although there were many excuses given.

Fort Vancouver would be without its new general, the Territory of Washington was now governor-less, the northern region would have to get along without a bevy of seven ladies of the night and their employer, and hundreds of other hopes, dreams, and schedules would have to be rearranged. Perhaps the only person to plan far ahead was James Nisbet, of the *San Francisco Bulletin,* who sat on deck and wrote his will when the possibility of drowning became obvious. One dead camel later washed ashore as did one horse carcass and the body of Nisbet with his will intact and readable in an inside pocket. Most of the passengers and nearly all of the cargo were never accounted for.

Captain DeWolf's wife was among the ladies who lived. Later, she stated that the ship did not strike a rock of any kind, but, instead, had a hole torn in her bottom when a huge, heavy cast-iron ore crusher broke loose in the hold.[6]

Relationship to British Columbia

In his *History of British Columbia* volume in his nineteenth-century "bookshelf" of texts about west-

---

[1] Citation furnished by John J. Ford, Jr.

[2] Richardson, *Beyond the Mississippi,* 1867, pp. 418-419.

[3] Life jackets of the era were of two main types: with hollow tin compartments which were subject to leaking if damaged, and cork-filled.

[4] *The Guide,* April 12, 1965, "Brother Jonathan Was Great Maritime Tragedy," by Wallace E. Martin.

[5] In 1955 the Del Norte County Historical Society registered the cemetery as a State Historical Landmark.

[6] Marshall, p. 161. The same writer discounted Captain DeWolf's supposed last words, "Tell them if they hadn't overloaded me, this would not have happened!" It seems improbable that a cargo shift caused the wreck, in view of the quartermaster's testimony (earlier quoted here) that the *Brother Jonathan* was, for a time after its impact, firmly stuck on a reef.

ern North America, historian Hubert H. Bancroft mentioned this wreck in connection with the gold discoveries made in the 1850s in British Columbia near the Fraser River. By this time the California Gold Rush was history, and many adventurers were seeking new opportunities:

> California was now rapidly losing population. Men of all classes abandoned their occupations in the interior and followed the crowd to San Francisco. Money was borrowed at exorbitant rates of interest to be advanced on goods for British Columbia. [In view of the situation, the newspapers of San Francisco painted a bad picture of the conditions near the Fraser River, seeking to "stem the current" of northbound travelers.]
>
> The whole of California in April 1858 was in a ferment. Business in the interior was deranged, and in many places broken up. Hundreds too impatient to wait for the steamers mounted to horses and hastened overland, especially from the northern counties of California, making the distance in 18 days. While towns in the interior were being deserted, San Francisco derived the benefit of the influx and of the outfitting of the miners, and the shippers rejoiced at the prospects of the Fraser trade. Shrewd storekeepers in the mountain counties hurried down to establish themselves in San Francisco.
>
> During April and May, the rumors of more or less fabulous gold discoveries in the north continued to circulate throughout California and in the Oregon and Washington territories. Vessels left San Francisco carrying three times the number allowed by law. John Nugent, a special agent of the United States, estimated that in May, June, and July 1858, 23,000 persons went from San Francisco by sea, and about 8,000 more overland—safely 30,000 or 33,000 in all in the course of the season—and that out of these there returned before January 1859 all but 3,000. None were too poor and none too rich to go. Young and old and even the decrepit. Some out of restlessness or curiosity; others for profit or prey."

Bancroft quoted the account of one Lundin Brown, who noted that "never in the history of migrations of men has there been such a rush, so sudden and so vast." The historian continued and mentioned the *Commodore,* the name which the erstwhile *Brother Jonathan* had assumed by that time:

> It was reported that the first major load of emigrants, consisting of 450 adventurers, left San Francisco on the steamer *Commodore* on April 20, 1858. From then through the beginning of the second week in June, 2,500 miners had departed by sea, while it was estimated that 5,000 more were at Puget Sound further north and on their way to the Fraser River. The steamboat owners perhaps profited most from the migration and helped promulgate and expand the many tales of treasures to be found.
>
> Although many newcomers to British Columbia were rewarded with success, as in California the golden dreams of most evaporated into the mist. It was later stated that the most important effect of the gold excitement was to lay the foundation for permanent settlements in British Columbia and to bring to the area many energetic individuals who later turned their attention to other enterprises....
>
> The foundering of the [now-renamed] steamer *Brother Jonathan* off Crescent City...with the loss of many of her passengers, was a shock which gave the final impress to the idea that the rush had continued too long. The immigration suddenly stopped; and more: in a few months the adventurers were nearly all back again in "God's country," as they called the sunnier regions of the south, full of bitter denunciations of the route, the country, the resources, yet knowing no more, after the return, of the extent and wealth of the mines than they knew before leaving in quest of them. It was argued that the deposits on the lower Fraser River must be small, and if the head-waters contained greater wealth, the remoteness, Indian difficulties, want of supplies, and the short duration of the mining season, would forever make them inferior to California as a mining resort.

The same account quoted population figures for the Fraser River district as 17,000 in 1858 (the peak), 8,000 in 1859, 7,000 in 1860, and only 5,000 in 1861. The estimates of gold production for 1858 were relatively modest and ranged from $500,000 to $2,120,000, tiny fractions of the California counterpart years earlier.

A Golden Cargo

It is believed that on that fateful day in 1865 when the *Brother Jonathan* impacted a rock off the coast of Crescent City, her cargo was valued at $300,000 to $500,000, including machinery for a woolen mill, mining apparatus (with the allegedly fatal ore crusher) for the Owyhee district in eastern Oregon and Idaho, 346 barrels of whiskey, and $200,000 in payroll for United States troops at Fort Vancouver, Washington. One account stated that the payroll was in federal "greenback" notes, part of a shipment totaling $250,000 in such currency.[1] It is also thought that the Wells Fargo agent on board, Joseph Lord, had with him about $250,000, and that close to $100,000-or even far more, depending upon the account—in jewelry and cash was in Purser John S. Benton's safe. William Logan, Indian agent for Uncle Sam, was on the voyage, carrying with him $105,000 in gold in compensation payments, it was said. Possibly, this was part of the purser's holdings. In time, accounts of the coins and cash aboard the ill-fated ship achieved large proportions.

[1] Dudley L. McClure, "$250,000 Face Value Now Worth Millions: Shipwreck Deposited Legal Tender Notes with Davy Jones, Recovery Still Possible?" *Numismatic News,* April 17, 1976. This writer suggested: "Probably because the *Brother Jonathan* losses in paper currency seemed to lack impact, the dollar totals consistently reached the public prints in terms of gold and silver coins." The same account mentioned "a few ingots which somehow were recovered, possibly having come ashore in trunks, boxes, crates, and other such flotsam from the wreck."

About the Ingots

The 1855 *Mint Report,* dated January 31, 1856, included the suggestion by Director James Ross Snowden that large bars of gold were the most economical way to process this metal for export and for trade. In fact, it might be wise to eliminate all gold coins above the $5 denomination and use gold bars instead, he commented. While this did not happen, it seems apparent from Mint records that the various Treasury facilities turned out a large number of gold (and some silver) bars in the years ahead.

Snowden's comments are given in part:

> Before the act of Congress authorizing the issuing of gold in stamped bars, there was, it is true, a necessity for the issue of large coins, as well as to meet the demands for shipment to Europe as, in some measure, to relieve the pressure upon the Mint. There was no kind of propriety in going through the manipulations and bearing the expense of making small gold coins to be directly melted down in foreign mints or refineries. But since the important change in our mint laws, a distinction has been made to meet the demands of trade, by which gold intended for exportation is cast into fine bars, whilst that which is needed for home currency is converted into coin.
>
> If we look to the example of the wealthiest and most civilized nations of the globe we shall find that their largest gold coin, to speak in a general way, does not exceed our half eagle in size.... It would no longer be an embarrassment to the principal mint [Philadelphia], nor to the branches, except perhaps the branch at San Francisco (and to that institution these views are not intended particularly to apply), to coin all the gold that is likely to be offered in pieces of $5 or less....
>
> The manufacture of fine bars at the Assay Office in New York, and the coinage of the branch mint at San Francisco, have so divided the work upon gold bullion as to remove all apprehension of difficulty or delay.... It is not by any means assumed that the coinage of the eagle and double eagle should be discontinued. On the contrary, they will be indispensable at San Francisco; and they may, in some emergencies, be required at Philadelphia and at New Orleans. But, as a general rule, adapted to the principal mint and to the branches in the Atlantic States,[1] it is believed that the time has come to return to the smaller denominations of gold coin, issuing almost the whole in pieces not larger than the half eagle....

No doubt, comments such as the preceding presaged the increased usage of gold bars in international trade and commerce including, perhaps, the gold bars aboard the *Brother Jonathan.*

Salvage Attempts

As is the rule, not the exception, with sunken treasures, little factual information has reached print concerning salvage of the *Brother Jonathan.*

One of the earliest efforts was that of the steam tug *Mary Ann,* which left San Francisco on August 20, 1865, and sought the site, but without success.

Many parts and artifacts from the ship washed ashore during the weeks after the disaster. The ship's wheel was recovered, and for many years it was displayed over the bar in Scovill's tavern in Crescent City.

A Crescent City sailmaker and a local old-timer named Captain Gee investigated the lost ship in 1890, but, apparently, achieved little success.[2]

In 1894 some fanfare was given to an adventurer claiming to be the Champion Deep Sea Diver, who said he found the *Brother Jonathan* resting in good condition on the sea bed, walked her deck, and planned to raise her and put her back into service. Nothing tangible materialized.

The Lund-Freese-Francisco explorers of 1916 seem not to have been chronicled in detail in any standard reference, nor were other efforts of the early twentieth century, including one in the 1930s. Along the way it is believed that some San Francisco Mint gold bars were raised.

Mention is made of Frank L. Mooreman, a West Coast capitalist, who in 1927 was a partner with the United States government in exploration of the wreck. Uncle Sam was interested in Civil War military pay records which might be found, thus helping clear certain pension claims. Mooreman was interested in the gold. Apparently, dissension arose among those involved. What gold or other treasure was recovered was not documented.[3]

Gold Bars on the Market

The sale presentation of the Henry Clifford Collection, catalogued by the author and Dr. George Fuld (with many contributions from John J. Ford, Jr.) in 1982, included the following description for Lot 178:

> $500 U.S. Mint San Francisco gold ingot, dated 1865, weight 24.24 ounces, believed to have been carried as cargo by the *Brother Jonathan,* a side-wheel steamer which was wrecked in the same year.
>
> This immense gold ingot bears the prepared circular stamp of the United States Mint, San Francisco, 1865. The fineness is 998 thousandths, nearly pure gold; the weight is 24.24 ounces, the serial number is 2180, and the valuation

[1] The reference here must be to the mints in Dahlonega (Georgia) and Charlotte (North Carolina), but these mints had never produced any coins above the $5 denomination.

[2] B.A. Tompkins, *Treasure*, pp. 164-165.

[3] Tompkins, pp. 164-165.

The transcontinental railroad, the nemesis of the San Francisco to Panama to New York treasure transport by sea, was completed at Promontory Point, Utah, in 1869, as depicted in the ceremony shown above.

is $500. The number 14 appears at the left and right ends of the bar, and on each of the two trimmed corners are to be found letters, E on one and M on the other. The serial number 2180 is repeated on the back.[1]

While most San Francisco Mint gold and silver bars are of odd denominations, depending upon the weight of the piece (which cannot be ascertained in advance when the ingot is being poured), in this instance an effort was made to produce a bar valued at an even amount, $500. This was done by making the bar slightly heavier than required, then filing the corners until the desired weight was obtained. So that the filed corners would not viewed as detracting from the weight stamped on the bar, the letters E and M were affixed indicating that this was done at the Mint.

The condition is nearly as issued, with slightly matte surfaces due to action of salt water on the metal.

This ingot is one of 11 of varying values obtained in 1970. All have serial numbers, running consecutively from 2178 to 2188. John J. Ford, Jr., has advised the cataloguer (QDB) that in addition to No. 2180 (offered here) an example (2184) was sold by NASCA, April 30, 1980; and pieces bearing numbers 2178, 2181, 2182, 2183, and 2185, formerly on display by The Bank of California in San Francisco, have been divided between the bank and Ford, several having been returned to the Ford Collection, joining the three that the New York collector-dealer initially retained. Ingot No. 2186 was sold as Lot 184 in Stack's Gibson Sale, November 11, 1974, and realized $19,000. It had a stamped value of $308.73....

While the exact history of these gold bars is not known, the preceding description suggests that they may have been carried aboard the *S.S. Brother Jonathan*. John J. Ford, Jr., theorizes that they could have been brought up from near the wreck by the Lund-Freese-Francisco expedition circa 1916 or by another group which explored the area 20 years or so later, in the 1930s. Examples of these bars came on to the numismatic market beginning in 1970.

Ford, checking the records kept by the San Francisco Mint,[2] concluded that these bars were made in late spring of 1865, although the data are not complete in this regard.

While there is only limited documentary evidence specifically linking this and the bars to the *Brother*

---

[1] This ingot is also illustrated in Don P. Marshall, *California Shipwrecks*, 1978, p. 165; photograph supplied by Henry Clifford. Marshall stated that such ingots were *not* part of the treasure stored in the strongroom or the Doblier safe aboard. Presumably, they were "passenger gold."

[2] *Assayer's Register 1854-1865.*

Jonathan, the man from whom they were acquired had them in his family for many years and attributed them to that source.

In the April 1980 NASCA offering of one of these bars as Lot 2422, this comment was included:

> A group of 11 of these were recovered, sequentially numbered, from a point between the wreck and the shore, and had probably been in one of the lifeboats which capsized (presumably along with the owner of the bars).

Modern Exploration

In 1993 Donald Knight and his partners in an outfit named Deep Sea Research, Inc., obtained rights from the ship's insurers and claimed to have relocated the wreck in about 180 feet of water four miles from shore and about two miles from where it is supposed to have struck a rock. In the absence of reliable records on the cargo, the potential recovery was stated to be worth in the $25,000,000 to $50,000,000 range today.[1] A claim of ownership by the State of California was denied in court.

The hull was reported as being essentially intact. Six items were recovered by Knight including a plate, medicine bottle, and wine bottle, the total value of which certainly did not challenge the $25,000,000 to $50,000,000 estimate of the treasure waiting to be found. No word yet of gold coins or ingots.

Extensive plans were discussed including the possible building of a Brother Jonathan Museum in nearby Crescent City. Donald Shomette, marine author and historian, was quoted by the *Los Angeles Times* as saying, "The real profit for treasure hunters comes from raising money from investors."

Treasure Ship Postscript

Searching for information about treasure ships is, of course, a very enjoyable pursuit. As the footnotes in this chapter indicate, the sources were extensive and varied. It becomes the task of the historian—me and anyone else writing on such a subject—to sift the wheat from the chaff. And, chaff there is aplenty.

Only by reading many contemporary accounts and weighing the information against what modern scholars have concluded, can even a semi-factual account be created. I say semi-factual, as much of the truth is forever lost, and even the best of accounts, early and late, sometimes differ in important details.

To share some of the "chaff" that one can find in newspapers, books, and elsewhere I reprint accounts of two individuals discussed earlier in this chapter. The first is of Commodore Cornelius Vanderbilt, whose steamers in real life left a poor record of filth, wrecks (in one particularly unfortunate streak, three of his ships were wrecked in an eight-month period), and other problems. The second is of Captain Randall, of the *Yankee Blade,* who in real life was a living exponent of "me first, passengers second" philosophy and, moreover, stole some of the treasure he was paid to recover. A sorry pair, these two men.

Contrast actuality with these nineteenth-century accounts:

Vanderbilt's Flawless Record

This account is excerpted from James D. McCabe, Jr.'s 1871 book, *Great Fortunes and How They Were Made,* which bears the subtitle, *Struggles and Triumphs of our Self-Made Men.*

> [In 1829 at the age of 35, Vanderbilt] resolved to build a steamer of his own, and had saved thirty thousand dollars.... He built a small steamer, called the *Caroline,* which he commanded himself. In a few years he was the owner of several other small steamers plying between New York and the neighboring towns. He made slow progress at first, for he had strong opposition to overcome....
>
> He made his way gradually in the business, until he rose to the head of the steamboat interests in the United States. He has owned or been interested in 100 steam vessels, and has been instrumental in a greater degree than any other man in bringing down the tariff of steamboat fares.
>
> He never builds a vessel without giving his personal superintendence to every detail, so that all his various craft have been models of their kind. He selects his officers with the greatest care, pays them liberal salaries, and as long as they do their duty, sustains them against all outside interference or intrigue. In this way he inspires them with zeal, and the result is that he has never lost a vessel by fire, explosion, or wreck.

Capt. Randall's Sterling Character

This obituary appeared in *The New York Times,* July 9, 1874:

> Captain Henry Randall, well known as a steamship commander, died at his residence at East 23rd Street yesterday morning, aged 72 years. His birthplace was Berlin, Rensselaer County, New York, and he was for several years commander of the steamboat *Empire* on Lake Erie.
>
> After removing to this city, in 1850, he was appointed to

[1] Richard C. Paddock, "Treasure or Time Capsule?" *Los Angeles Times,* March 17, 1996; "Court Rules Salvage Firm Holds Rights to Wrecked Ship," *Los Angeles Times,* July 18, 1996. No information was given as to how the $25,000,000 to $50,000,000 estimate was derived (nor are clues for readers typically given in other accounts of treasure valuation).

> the command of the steamer *Yankee Blade,* in Mills' Independent Line. He had also been captain of the steamship *Northerner,* one of the first steam vessels sent from this port to the land of gold.
>
> After spending several years on the Pacific Coast he returned to New York.... Captain Randall was a man of most exemplary character, had great energy combined with keen business qualifications, remarkable industry, and patient application. He leaves a large circle of warm friends to lament his death.

Another tidbit, this from William S. Lindsay's four-volume study today considered to be a standard reference in its field, *History of Merchant Shipping and Ancient Commerce,* 1879, Vol. IV, p. 162, in which Captain Randall's skill at the helm of the *Yankee Blade* is showcased, but a little incident seems to have been overlooked:

> [Captain Randall] commanded the *Yankee Blade,* a vessel of still larger dimensions, with a draft of 11 feet of water on her voyage from New York to California round Cape Horn, encountering, successfully, a gale in which many vessels foundered; afterwards, he continued to ply with her for some years on the station between San Francisco and Panama.

A selection of California gold bars. (Photograph courtesy of John J. Ford, Jr.)

CHAPTER 12

Gold Bars from Way Out West

Introduction

Gold and silver bars (a.k.a. ingots) were produced over a long period of time in the second half of the nineteenth and first third of the twentieth centuries in the American West. Smelters and assayers cast metal into molds and invariably marked the resulting ingots. Large ingots or "pigs" were usually rough-surfaced and were intended to form a convenient way to transport metal from the mine smelter.

Ingots were not only manufactured for transport, but for use in commerce, banking, and as a medium for bulk transactions and foreign exchange. They were marked not only with serial numbers, but with the fineness of gold (expressed as a part of 1,000, such as .950, which was equal to 950/1000th or 95% pure gold). Such bars were assayed before marking, bore the imprint of the assayer who issued them, and also denoted the weight, and sometimes the value in dollars at the rate of $20.67 per ounce. Ingots of reliable firms were readily accepted in trade at the value marked, less a tiny charge for handling.

Due to their high intrinsic value, most bars were melted soon after they were made. However, due to various circumstances some were buried or otherwise stored and forgotten. Although such ingots and bars were common in their time and were, in fact, received in bulk in the East (cf. the preceding *S.S. Central America* account), virtually no numismatic notice was taken of them for many years. Quite probably, Jacob R. Eckfeldt and William E. DuBois, who built the Mint Collection at the middle of the nineteenth century and also took note of various private California gold items that interested them, considered assay bars to be simply items of commerce. On the other hand, they considered certain $16 bars of Moffat, bars of Kohler, and some others to have been used in day to day commerce. In any event, it is obvious that large numbers of gold bars from the West passed under their collective noses, and no numismatic accounting was made of them.

Moreover, years later in the early twentieth century, no interest was evinced in them either, and even gold bars stamped with imprints of the San Francisco Mint, the Denver Mint, and various U.S. Assay Offices were not included in studies by Edgar H. Adams, in the many notices of territorial gold coins in various catalogues by B. Max Mehl (which were attractive, but which contained little new information not in Edgar H. Adams' works), and the works of others.[1]

Beginning in the 1950s, John J. Ford, Jr., mounted an intensive advertising campaign to locate such pieces in the Western mining states, often enlisting his friend Paul Franklin to act as an intermediary and do the footwork. Brochures were printed, advertisements were run, notices were inserted in mailings, spreads were printed in New Netherlands Coin Company catalogues, and other efforts were mounted. Over a period of time this unprecedented publicity created a great deal of interest and resulted in dozens of gold bars coming to light.

Elsewhere in numismatics, publicity has also done

[1] Although Mehl handled many important numismatic cabinets containing specialized series—the Slack, and other collections of territorial gold, the Dr. French collection of large cents, and the Dunham collection of encased postage stamps are but several of many examples that could be cited—Mehl did not insert meaningful scholarship in to any of these offerings. As Mehl himself would have been the first to admit, his role was that of a numismatic merchant, auctioneer, and publicist—a role he enjoyed immensely. Historical and technical numismatic matters were left to others. Over the years, considering them to be curiosities, the Fort Worth dealer retained a number of assay ingots acquired as part of collections. He sold his holding of these at the 1949 A.N.A. convention.

INFORMATION CONCERNING

GOLD, ELECTRUM, SILVER BARS & INGOTS

OF NUMISMATIC INTEREST

WANTED!

From 1849 to about 1906, various individual Assayers, Private, State and even Federal Assay Offices, Bankers and Mining Companies, manufactured and issued bars and ingots. Composed of Gold, Silver, or a combination of both as a natural alloy (Electrum), these pieces originated in the territories and states of CALIFORNIA, ARIZONA, NEVADA, UTAH, NEW MEXICO AND COLORADO. Some have even been found from OREGON, WASHINGTON and IDAHO; others, from MONTANA and SOUTH DAKOTA, are said to have been made. In addition to these western bars and ingots, similar items were made about the country at the various U. S. Government Assay Offices, along with issues of Alaskan-Canadian manufacture (from the period of the Klondyke gold rush, 1897-99).

Sometimes crudely cast, often carefully finished, these precious metal bars and ingots were invariably stamped with the name of the issuer, sometimes with the place and date of manufacture. Almost all have the composition and fineness, the weight, and the value in Dollars and Cents also stamped upon them. Rarely, some are found with a stamp from a die, resembling a coin in appearance.

In the early days, Gold, Electrum and Silver bars and ingots were freely used as money, and are found with "even amount" denominations, such as Ten, Fifteen, Sixteen, Eighteen, Twenty, Twenty-Five, Fifty, One Hundred and Two Hundred Dollars. If dated, and from either California (1849 to 1856) or Colorado (1859 to 1862), issues of this type can be of great importance to a collector. However, the great proportion of these pieces, are found stamped with highly odd amounts ($2.66, $8.76, $13.55, $31.60, $54.50 and so forth), representing their exact value at the time. Almost all of them are the results of conversion, by an Assayer, of raw dust or metal brought to him, assayed and put into identifiable form.

Tremendous numbers of these bars and ingots were issued by a great many individuals and firms. Only in recent years, have collectors and numismatists began the study of them. While made in very high quantities, a large number of these pioneer bars and ingots were melted, either at the U. S. Mint in San Francisco, or as they were brought back east. Those that were saved or retained, were kept as souvenirs or mementos, and are generally the very small pieces, although a few medium size ones have been discovered. Obviously, the really large ingots and bars (often made to discourage stage robbers and highwaymen), were worth considerably more as they found their way towards civilization, and few people could afford to hold onto any of them for sentimental or historical reasons.

While not rare in the literal sense of the word, the various bars and ingots made are now hard to find. Almost all are held by people as family curiosities, and must be searched out. Although only a limited number of collectors of coins and western material are interested in these pieces, those that are do pay substantial premiums (over the present day intrinsic or metal value) for them.

The value of a given bar or ingot is based upon how much is stamped upon it, when and by whom it was made, and its general appearance. The size of a piece means little or nothing. While a small gold ingot, marked Ten Dollars, and issued in 1852 could be worth ten to thirty times its present day bullion content of about $16-17.50, a large gold piece might only command double the metal content. Electrum bars and ingots are of somewhat lesser importance than gold ones, and silver ones bring from $15 to $100 each, the latter figure only in rare instances.

Of equal importance to the actual bars and ingots themselves, is the historical data and background concerning them. Letters, correspondence, drafts, checks, broadsides, directories, and even contemporary newspaper accounts, relating to any individual or company that made bars or ingots is of interest and collector's value. Also collected are gold coins made in the west, patterns and trials in any metal for them, unofficial coin dies and hand presses, paper money privately made in any western state before 1890, the letter and numeral punches used for making bars and ingots, bar and ingot moulds and almost anything else concerning western coins, bars and ingots, 1849-1906.

On this and the following page are reproduced the two pages of a prospectus sent out in quantity by John J. Ford, Jr., circa 1957, soliciting information and numismatic items relating to western mining.

Valuable, privately struck fifty dollar piece.

California State Assay Office bar, issued in 1850. U. S. Assay Offices made similar pieces, particularly "The United States Assay Office of Gold," San Francisco.

Small, unidentifiable gold bar, made early in the Gold Rush, to satisfy a strong demand for convenient mediums of exchange. Of interest, but most collectors prefer bars and ingots bearing the maker's name and location.

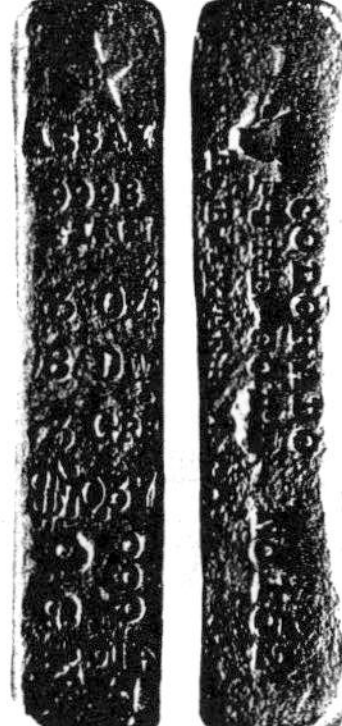

Unusually pure, long bar, made by Bates, Baxter & Co., about 1865, Mountain City, (Central City Dist.), Colorado Territory.

The fractional note at right was printed in Albany, N. Y., and was intended for use, 1851-52, in San Francisco. Several firms made and issued their own paper money in the West, 1850-1897. Bank, Express and Mining Company drafts and checks are also of interest to collectors. While hardly as valuable price-wise as are many bars and ingots, such paper script is of great historical importance. Still, this money you can't spend is often worth more than the regular kind.

Gold ingot for $272.23, made in New Mexico Terr., 1870-75.

At right, an electrum or mixed metal assay ingot, issued at famous Virginia City, Nevada, by L. Kuh, a Chinese assayer, in the hey-day of the great Comstock Lode.

Silver bars are often found. This one, dated 1880, came from the Silver King mine. A great difficulty is locating data concerning these pieces.

WRITE TO

JOHN J. FORD, Jr.

COMPILER, THE SPECIALIZED CATALOGUE OF U. S. GOLD COINS, BARS AND INGOTS.

176 HENDRICKSON AVENUE

ROCKVILLE CENTRE, L. I., NEW YORK

MEMBER AMERICAN NUMISMATIC SOCIETY — FELLOW OF ROYAL NUMISMATIC SOCIETY, LIFE MEMBER, NO. 250, AMERICAN NUMISMATIC ASSN. — SOCIEDAD IBERO-AMERICANA DE ESTUDIOS NUMISMATICOS, — ACTIVE MEMBER, CALIFORNIA HISTORICAL SOCIETY

Send detailed description or careful pencil rubbing of any bars or ingots located; other material describe very carefully.

ALL CORRESPONDENCE ANSWERED. INFORMATION EXCHANGED, APPRAISALS GIVEN IN CONFIDENCE.

wonders. For example, in the October 1930 number of *The Numismatist*, a letter was published from E.T. Wallis of Los Angeles, in which he reported the discovery of an 1817/4 overdate half dollar, a variety hitherto unknown to even the most dedicated specialists in the series, despite study and the publication of reference works on half dollars by such numismatic luminaries as John W. Haseltine (1881) and M.L. Beistle (1929). Since that time, six other specimens of the 1817/4 have been found![1] Today there are seven known. Similarly, today in the 1990s there are many dozens of Hard Times tokens of the 1832-1844 era that have been described by Russ Rulau and others, but were not known at the turn of the century to the pre-eminent scholar in that field, Lyman H. Low.

Over a period of years several caches of gold and silver bars were found in the West. Separately, there have been many new startling and impressive finds of gold and silver ingots among Spanish-American treasure ship wrecks and, of course, the spectacular group brought up from the *S.S. Central America*.

Certain other bars from the American West are described below.[2]

Thorne Mining & Refining Co. of Arizona

Hidden or lost: Late 1880s onward
Found: Circa 1952
Treasure: Silver and gold ingots

John J. Ford, Jr., gave a first-hand account of this find:[3]

> The first major hoard of assayers' ingots that I and/or New Netherlands Coin Company handled took place in the summer of 1953. My records indicate that there were 87 ingots in total in the Thorne Hoard. These were apparently found in 1952 or early 1953 in a safe in Prescott, Arizona. That's about all I know of their origin.
>
> Daniel Conner Thorne was the proprietor of the Thorne Mining & Refining Company located about 165 miles east of Prescott in the Arizona Territory. According to census and other records, Thorne was born in New York state in 1830 or 1831. His age at his last birthday prior to the June 1870 census was listed as 39. At that time he gave his occupation as a speculator. In the 1880 census he was a saloonkeeper. Thorne was unable to write, according to the census. His wife Marion died in March 1880 due to complications of childbirth.
>
> In the winter of 1876-1877 Thorne, Prescott merchant C.P. Hegg, E.J. Cook, John Corning and John Moore (who at one time was a county sheriff) staked three claims known as the Tip Top, Tip Top South, and Joker on an old Indian trail that ran from near the present village of Black Canyon and Humbug Creek. After working their mine and sending the ore to San Francisco, it was purchased for $60,000 by San Francisco investors. This profitable experience must have given a Thorne taste for mining which led to his later having his own firm.
>
> The mine that was to later bear Daniel Conner Thorne's surname had been discovered by others about 1880, who began development of the ore, but fell on lean days and sold out. The buyer, Thorne, owned a gambling hall and saloon in Prescott. He had better luck than the previous owners of the mine, and extracted about $300,000 worth of silver, but this was not enough to keep his creditors from the door. Charles M. Clark, president of the Arizona Pioneers Association and a writer on mining history, was a subsequent owner. The Thorne name was retained. Over a period of time, silver ore from the Thorne Mine was processed by the Selby Smelting Works in San Francisco, the firm that undoubtedly made the Thorne-imprint ingots.
>
> All of the known authentic specimens of the Thorne Mining and Refining Company ingots were discovered in one hoard in 1952-1953. The New Netherlands Coin Company, Inc., of New York, of which I was then a principal,

Ingots of silver and gold await transport near a western mine.

[1] Sheridan Downey (half dollar specialist), letter, February 22, 1996, enclosing a schedule of these, in connection with the author's research for the 1997 sale of the Louis E. Eliasberg, Sr., Collection specimen of the overdate.

[2] In addition the interested reader is referred to the Henry H. Clifford Collection sale, Bowers and Ruddy Galleries, 1982, the most diverse offering of ingots and bars from the American West ever to cross the auction block. Earlier extensive offerings include the Gibson Sale (Stack's, November 1974) and the NASCA sale of April 1980. Historical data for all of these events was provided by John J. Ford, Jr., accounting for a certain similarity of the information contained in each.

[3] Edited by Q. David Bowers from a transcript of a recorded interview of John J. Ford, Jr., Phoenix, Arizona, by Michael Hodder, August 20, 1996. Ford noted that certain information was from "Workings of Prehistoric Mines," Charles M. Clark, *Arizona Mining Journal*, Volume 9, No. 2, June 15, 1925, p. 26.

purchased the entire lot excepting a few silver pieces retained as souvenirs by the various other parties involved.

There were two gold ingots in the group:

One of the gold bars was the same shape and style as the majority of the silver ingots, but the lower obverse seven-line stamp was placed vertically rather than horizontally. This piece bore the serial number 948, denomination $65.25 and a weight of 3.3 ounces. In individual letter punches it had been stamped ECHO MINE NO. 48 3 OZS 6 DWT 1 GR. This relatively large gold ingot showed a fineness of 999.8.

The other gold ingot was more of a square in shape. The obverse bore the regular Thorne die stamp with scales. The reverse had a five-line die stamp different from that found upon the other gold and most of the silver Thorne ingots. The serial number was 15, denomination $16.37, and the weight given as pennyweight 17, grains 17. The fineness of gold was .895, of silver .104.

Both of these gold ingots were sold by Charles Wormser and me to the late Don Keefer of Chicago in late 1953 or early 1954. Keefer died in the summer of 1954, and the New Netherlands Coin Company repurchased the two gold bars from his estate, selling them to the late Morton Stack on November 15, 1954. From Stack's they passed to the Josiah Lilly Collection in Indianapolis, and are now on display in the Smithsonian Institution.

There were a large number of Thorne silver ingots. I made a complete listing of all these that we had, by serial number, value and weight. The following numbers were in the original group: 23, 24, 97, 177, 191, 196, 198, 199, 201, 210, 212, 214, 217-220 inclusive, 222-247 inclusive,[1] 251-255 inclusive, 259, 261-274 inclusive, and 276-299 inclusive. I not only have the data heretofore referred to, but I have listings as to whom these various items were originally sold to, subsequent owners, auction records, and so forth.

There's an interesting story about silver ingot No. 231, stamped with a value of $3.96, marked with a weight of 3.07 ounces. This piece was originally sold through New Netherlands to a small New York dealer who in turn sold it to the principals of another local firm. These particular gentlemen had great faith in the biblical tale of the loaves and fishes. I say that because the new owners of the Thorne silver ingot serial No. 231 came up with the idea of having copies cast by a jewelry manufacturer, thus vastly increasing their stock.

In late 1953 the market was quietly flooded with $3.96-value Thorne ingots each with serial No. 231, a rather comical situation upon reflection, except that it was taken seriously at the time. The following year, the unsuspecting Charles Green in Chicago was offering one as Lot 2016 in his mail bid sale of July 31, while its twin was being offered in New York City! According to my records, the genuine, original No. 231 weighed 1,473.6 grains. The first fake submitted to me for checking weighed only 1,136 grains, and others seen later were of still different weights. The fakes I made notes of in 1953-1954 all had an artificial blue-gray patination. Later, other fakes were made bearing different imprints. In July 1972 the late Virgil Hancock, who took the lead in having the American Numismatic Association combat fakes, compiled a list of such copies.

The following Thorne silver bars, all .9998 fine, were illustrated and offered in the Henry H. Clifford Collection sale, 1982, and are listed to give representative stampings found on such pieces:

> Lot 183, serial no. 177, 3.98 oz., $5.13 stamped value • Lot 184, no. 210, 4.05 oz., $5.22 • Lot 185, no. 234, 1.86 oz., $3.68 • Lot 186, no. 242, 3.11 oz., $4.00.

The Eagle Mining Company

Hidden or lost: 1880s
Found: 1960s
Treasure: Gold and silver ingots

Gold and silver bars marked EAGLE MINING CO. have come to light on several occasions since the early 1950s.[2] Trouble is that the Eagle name is somewhat generic—hardly unique—and the ingots are not definitively marked as to their geographical origin.

Among the possibilities for authorship of the bars is the Eagle Gold Mining Company located at the mouth of Gamble Gulch in Gilpin County, Colorado, which is said to have been unprofitably operated in the 1860s, then reopened with better financial results in the 1870s. However, the absence of the word "Gold" in the company name on the bars does not reinforce such an argument. Concerning this outfit, *The Mines of Colorado,* 1867, contains this entry:

> They have a first-class 50-stamp mill at the mouth of Gamble Gulch. The building is 75 x 90 feet, contains the batteries, plates, 60-horse engine, and boilers, and that is all. It was run through June 1865, but without paying result. It was shut up and is likely to remain so until further developments in the art of treating Colorado ores. The company has a boarding house, barn, and other necessary buildings near their mill on South Boulder.

The Eagle mining claim, also in Gilpin County, but

---

[1] Nos. 243 and 247 later appeared in NASCA's sale of April 1980, lots 1449 and 2450.

[2] Adapted by the author from a transcript of a recorded interview of John J. Ford, Jr., Phoenix, Arizona, by Michael Hodder, August 20, 1996. Certain information is from the commentary preceding Lot 2438 of NASCA's April 1980 sale provided by Ford.

A mine, smelter, and attendant operations in a gulch in the Rocky Mountains.

at Lake Gulch in the Lake Mine District, is another possibility.

Alternatively, the bars could have been made elsewhere from Gilpin County gold shipped to a refiner, or could have been made by or for the account of any one of various Eagle mines and prospects in the West.

Today it seems that 10 dated and four undated Eagle Mining Company *gold* ingots are known, three of which are marked "CO" for Colorado. Of the dated pieces, one is marked 1875, three 1877, five 1878, and one 1879. A gun dealer from New England turned up two of these in central Colorado in 1965, one of which later appeared in Stack's 1974 Gibson Sale. An 1878-dated rectangular bar, No. 25, 5.79 ounces, stamped value $118.70, was Lot 2438 in NASCA's April 1980 auction, and was followed in the same offering by Lot 2439, a round "button" of gold, also dated 1878, No. 71, 2.91 ounces, stamped $54.25.[1]

Complicating matters further is an advertisement printed in the *Numismatic Scrapbook Magazine,* June 30, 1954, in which R. Green, the Chicago dealer, offered a $50 gold ingot attributed to the Eagle Mining Company of Eagle City, Arizona, and bearing a stamp indicating its origin in the Arizona Territory. Green, who apparently had access to some historical information, further said this company used gold from other mines in the Cienega Mining District about 60 miles above Park and five or six miles below the mouth of the Bell Williams Fork in Yuma County, Arizona.[2]

About two dozen silver ingots with the Eagle Mining Company imprint are known and may have first come on the market from a small group unearthed in Arizona in the 1950s. A representative example, No. 365, undated, 7.36 ounces of .999 fine silver, $9.42, was offered as Lot 2440 in the aforementioned NASCA auction.

John J. Ford, Jr., has suggested that one or more employees of the Eagle Mining Co. in Colorado moved to Yuma County in Arizona Territory and created further ingots there.

Surprise at an Arizona Ranch

Hidden: 19th century
Found: 1957 onward
Treasure: U.S. Assay Office of Gold items

In autumn 1952, John J. Ford, Jr., made the acquaintance of Paul Franklin of Massapequa Park, New York, a town on Long Island not far from Ford's residence in Rockville Centre. Ford had an abiding interest in coins, ingots, and memorabilia of western assay offices, private mints, and other enterprises of the nineteenth century gold and silver finds.

Ford learned that Franklin had similar interests and had made earlier trips to the West, where he had purchased two mixed-metal (gold and silver) assay bars. Such items, although not unknown, were fairly elusive in numismatic circles. Ford reasoned that with Franklin's help a publicity campaign in the American Southwest might bring to light additional specimens. Ford later related:

> Soon [Paul Franklin] had a network of people, including the field employees of a local telephone company, looking for privately-made gold coins and assay bars of gold or silver or the mixed metal combination of both. These people scoured banks and assay offices, jewelry shops, and antique stores, not only in ghost towns but in cities the size of El Paso and Phoenix. Franklin joined the Arizona Small Mine Owners Association and advertised in the various mining trade papers and journals.
>
> In time I prepared an elaborate circular that explained what numismatic bars and ingots were and which illustrated pioneer gold coins, western paper currency, and assay bars. Thousands of these were printed bearing Paul Franklin's name and address and distributed by him throughout the western states. People having items of possible importance were asked to tell Franklin what they had, or, preferably, to send him a pencil rubbing. If an item was of interest to me, I advised him what it was worth and he either sent the money to a friend or an agent so that the piece could be picked up, or else he flew west on a weekend or over a holiday and purchased directly....
>
> We had a good thing going. Franklin found the material and I researched and sold it. Occasionally, something was of particular personal interest and I kept it. Franklin also retained a few pieces.... Our working arrangement was simple. Our arrangements were made early during our joint operations and under it Franklin was not to tell me where he obtained his material although he was to give me original source names wherever possible for my records. On the other hand, I was not to reveal to him the names of my customers with whom I was dealing.
>
> My confidence in Paul Franklin was well founded as, for example, in 1956 he located an unpublished ingot of F.D. Kohler, issued at the State Assay Office in Sacramento, and because he paid a nominal price for the piece he gave it to me at his cost plus expenses, since he questioned its authenticity. It was only after the late F.C.C. Boyd insisted that it was genuine, that he would accept from me a generous profit for finding the ingot.... Since a great many of the items he unearthed were unknown or not previously published, it was my responsibility to find out exactly what they were, and why and when they were made. In instance after instance,

[1] Cross-referencing auction and other appearances of Eagle Mining Co. and other Western bars is beyond the scope of the present book. However, the auction catalogues cited in this chapter will provide an excellent beginning for anyone interested.

[2] Thomas Edwin Farish, *History of Arizona,* 1915, Vol. II, p. 71, writes of an Eagle Mine tapping a vein of silver ore to the east of the Mowry Mine, in the Santa Cruz Sierra mountain district.

Franklin argued with me, always taking the conservative position....

Early in 1957 Paul Franklin stumbled upon what turned out to be his greatest and most prolific find. This consisted of a hoard of coins and related pieces from the United States Assay Office of Gold, situated in San Francisco, and operative in 1852-1853. His initial contact was a teller in a Phoenix, Arizona, area bank, but eventually he did business with the bank president. In time, he met the owner and source of these items, an elderly gentleman, who in the 1950s supposedly resided on an Arizona ranch.

Included in the hoard were seven perfect prooflike $20 gold pieces of conventional design, that Paul Franklin obtained directly from the owner [K.M.L. of Ajo, Arizona] on a trip to Phoenix, February 19-23, 1958. These coins, together with three other impaired impressions, were wrapped in three or four old, yellowed linen handkerchiefs. Eight of the pieces had the weight marked in grains on the handkerchiefs in lead pencil, one or more of the coins also had the alloys inscribed in similar fashion on at least one handkerchief. Franklin could not obtain the handkerchiefs, nor could he copy the information marked on them, since the owner was afraid that his family would somehow find out that he was selling coins and realizing funds from them.

In spite of the old man's fears and general reluctance to give out information, Franklin managed to make a note that one of the seven perfect prooflike pieces contained .020 part copper, a fact he conveyed to me when he delivered the lot, together with the information that he was convinced that most or all of the seven perfect specimens, and probably some of the impaired ones, represented experimental alloy strikings.

Franklin had obtained a few United States Assay Office of Gold items prior to his first 1958 trip, and on subsequent visits to the Phoenix area picked up others. On a trip west by car during the summer of 1958 he purchased the only steel die in the hoard, paying the bank president $50 on August 14, 1958, on behalf of the owner. This die was obtained only upon my strong insistence, as were some of the lead trials, because of their great historical value. It was delivered to me by Franklin at the ANA convention held in the Los Angeles Statler Hotel, August 13-16, 1958. I only paid him his purchase price for it, because he had picked it up for me as a personal favor and because the die was very badly rusted and corroded, being hardly identifiable.[1]

All of the United States Assay Office of Gold items obtained from time to time, and classified as trial coin ingots, experimental pieces, trial coins, assay bars, proofing pieces, and such, were purchased for my benefit. This material continued to be available, on a rapidly diminishing basis, for several years after 1958. I obtained at least one proofing piece as late as 1962, and I know that Franklin sold another he had just obtained to a California dealer in September 1965. Franklin was given the information several times that nothing more was available, but he was also told upon numerous occasions that many items had been distributed over the years to various members of the owner's family. Apparently a casual effort was made from time to time to recover these, as they could be found, in order to sell them to us....

John J. Ford, Jr., went on to relate that while many pieces were sold to him personally and to New Netherlands Coin Co., additional specimens were placed privately by Paul Franklin.

Over a period of time certain of these finds appeared on the auction market including in Stack's sale of the Gibson Collection, 1974, and the Bowers and Ruddy Galleries sale of the Henry Clifford Collection, 1982. Certain examples are included in the Josiah K. Lilly Collection at the Smithsonian Institution.[2]

River Bank Yields Gold Bars

Hidden or lost: 1870s
Found: June 1965
Treasure: Knight & Co. gold bars

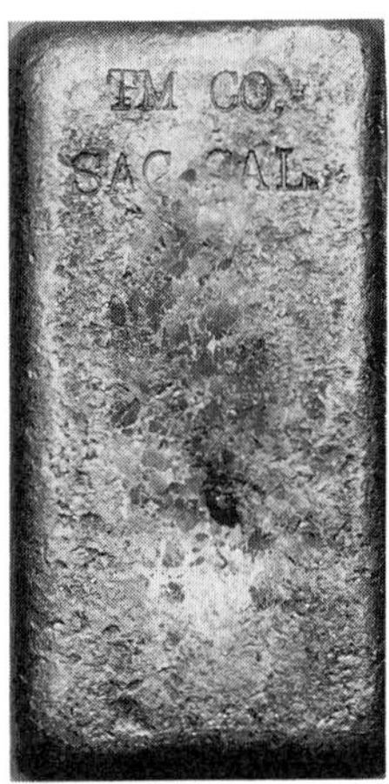

The Henry Clifford Collection sale, 1982, included many "treasure" items from the American West, including these two:

Lot 55: Knight & Company, Assayers, Marysville, California. $232.23 gold ingot. 11.44 ounces. Actual weight 5,494.5 grains. Extremely Fine or better. Virtually as issued.

One of a group of 15 ingots of varying weights found by Carlton Wells of Oakland, California, in June 1965, on the

[1] This particular die, of unpublished design, and the only known impression from it, were later displayed at the Bank of California's Museum of Money of the American West, San Francisco.

[2] Information in this section is primarily from comments made by John J. Ford, Jr., and reprinted in the Bowers and Ruddy Galleries sale of the Henry Clifford Collection, 1982, and, to a lesser extent, an interview between the author (QDB) and Ford on June 24, 1996. In August 1967, John J. Ford, Jr. prepared a written 100+ page commentary which was used in an arbitration situation concerning an 1853 United States Assay Office of Gold $20 piece; certain information is from that source as well, courtesy of Mr. Ford. Additional information and illustrations will be found in the Clifford catalogue and in *Walter Breen's Complete Encyclopedia of U.S. and Colonial Coins* (see pp. 616 of the latter book, "Controversial Coin Ingots").

bank of the Sacramento River. Serial numbers range from 1782 to 1796. Quite possibly these were seized years ago in a stagecoach or other robbery and were secreted by desperadoes who never returned to claim them. A similar piece, serial no. 1782, appeared in the April 1980 NASCA sale as Lot 2027.

In the form of a bar, there is the serial number 1794, the inscription KNIGHT & CO., an Internal Revenue stamp, and further inscriptions noting the weight to be 11.44 ounces and the fineness to be 982. The value $232.23 is given below. The stamp "SMV" indicates "standard mint value." The edges of the bar are plain. The back is stamped with the inscription "TM CO. SAC. CAL." for the Tecumseh Mining Co. in Sacramento.

Lot 56: Knight & Company.... $182.10 gold ingot. 9.51 ounces. This ingot, bearing the earlier serial number 1722, differs slightly in style from that offered in the preceding lot. The "TM CO, SAC. CAL." inscription appears on the front, in addition to the inscriptions referring to Knight & Company, the serial number (1722), and other information. On one edge of the bar is stamped G $181.26, and on the other edge is stamped S $.84, indicating the respective values of gold and silver. The back of the bar contains a faintly impressed Internal Revenue stamp. Extremely Fine or better condition.

The Knight assay office was located at 32 D Street in Marysville, the seat of Yuba County, in the Mother Lode district of California. The firm was in business by the early 1860s, according to directory listings, and remained active through at least the early 1870s. A quarter-page advertisement for Knight & Co. appeared in the 1867 edition of the *Pacific Coast Business Directory*, p. 65.[1] Most probably the office was a small one and served regional mines and miners. The latest listing encountered is in the *San Francisco Semi-Annual Trades Guide and Pacific Coast Directory* issued by D.M. Bishop & Co., San Francisco, July 1874.

Front Street, Sacramento, in the Gold Rush era.

Knight may have been located earlier in Sacramento or had a branch there at one time. In the John J. Ford, Jr., Collection is a $31.58 gold ingot with a very low fineness of .593, marked with Sacramento as the point of origin.

The Marysville ingots discovered by Carlton Wells are believed by John J. Ford, Jr., to have been made by Knight for the Tecumseh Mining Co. of Sacramento, and buried along a stagecoach route, probably loot taken from a robbery. As each bar bears a U.S. Internal Revenue bullion tax stamp imprint, they would have been made after the June 30, 1864, passage of the act authorizing same. One of the Knight & Co. ingots, No. 1795, is on display at the Smithsonian Institution.

John J. Ford, Jr., told the story of their discovery:[2]

> It was related to me via Paul Franklin how Carlton Wells and his friends found these ingots. They were on a hunting trip or a walking expedition on a particular bank on one side of the Sacramento River, when they saw something shining on the opposite bank. They thought it was a reflection because it was late in the afternoon and the sun was going down, but the problem was, the more they walked the reflection stayed on the river bank.
>
> They kept going until they found a place where they could cross, after which they worked their way back. It was almost dark when they returned to where they had seen the reflection. Practically in the water, and certain to be covered if the river rose even a little bit, was what was left of an old wooden box or chest containing 24 [*sic;* an earlier account says 15] gold ingots. The puzzle of the reflection was solved and the hikers picked up the ingots. The trip was a great success.

"AF" (American Flag Mine?) Ingots

Hidden or lost: 1870s
Found: 1970
Treasure: 14 gold bars

A hoard of crudely made gold ingots, each stamped "AF," was found in the West in September 1970 by Paul Franklin, acting as agent for John J. Ford, Jr.[3] Apparently, a cache of 14 ingots had been unearthed in the eastern part of California by a treasure seeker equipped with an electronic metal locator. Ten of the bars were melted for their bullion value before Franklin learned of them. The remaining four were later as-

1 Published by H.G. Langley, San Francisco. As is the case with virtually all directories, listings were not necessarily current.
2 Adapted by the author from a transcript of a recorded interview of John J. Ford, Jr., Phoenix, Arizona, by Michael Hodder, August 20, 1996. Also see the NASCA sale of April 1980, Lots 2425-2427, Knight ingots with serial numbers 1720, 1724, and 1782 respectively.
3 Adapted by the author from a transcript of a recorded interview of John J. Ford, Jr., Phoenix, Arizona, by Michael Hodder, August 20, 1996.

signed (by Ford) provisional numbers 11 through 14.

The poured ingots were simply made, bore minimal markings, and were intended for convenience in shipping (Ford calls them "transport ingots"). These differ from carefully-made ingots (such as those from the San Francisco Mint) which are marked with serial numbers, weight, fineness, authorship, and, often, value, and which were generally intended for use for banking purposes and large commercial transactions.

The "AF" markings led Ford to suggest that the gold bars may have been made from metal taken from the American Flag Mine in the Ely District of Lincoln County, Nevada. The purchased ingots were numbered 11 through 14 and are further described below.

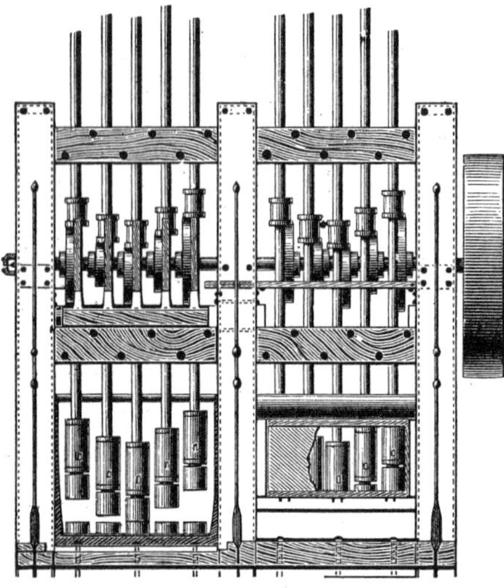
TEN-STAMP QUARTZ MILL.

A 10-stamp quartz mill of the general type widely used in the American West.

According to historical accounts the American Flag Mine operated circa 1872-1876 and was equipped with a 20-stamp quartz mill. Such an apparatus consisted of heavy iron castings arranged on a long steel rod so that at any given time some stamps were at the bottom of their cycle pulverizing quartz or other stone, others were being raised from that position, others were at the high point of their travel, others were beginning to descend, etc.—a complex version of the camshaft used to raise and lower merry-go-round animals in a circus ride. The entire affair was powered by a steam engine or water mill. Shipments of bulk bullion gold were sent from the American Flag Mine to San Francisco to be assayed and converted into coins.[1]

The attribution to the American Flag Mine is conjectural, and it is possible that the origin was elsewhere. For the present, the stated information seems likely.

When the Franklin-Ford consortium purchased them, the price was based upon their weight and fineness. Ingot No. 11 was taken to Jacob's Assay Office, 10th Avenue, Tucson, Arizona, on September 8, 1970, and was found to be .950 fine (95% pure gold). At the time gold was worth $35 per ounce.

The four ingots were later distributed as follows:

No. 11: 53.85 ounces; placed on loan from Ford in the display of the Bank of California National Association, San Francisco, in February 1971 and remained on display there until 1975-1976. Ford later recalled: "At the moment I can't recollect if it was returned to me when my agreement with the bank terminated. I may still have an American Flag ingot and I may not." This is the bar that was assayed as .950 fine.

No. 12: 17.24 ounces; sold to Robert F. Batchelder, Ambler, PA, in September 1970, the month Ford acquired the cache.[2]

No. 13: 55.25 ounces; also sold to Batchelder. The pair brought $3,000.

No. 14: 24.41 ounces; sold by Ford to Henry H. Clifford for $980.

Gould & Curry Silver Mining Co.

Hidden or lost: Circa 1860s
Found: 1972
Treasure: Silver-gold bars

The Gould & Curry Silver Mining Co. was organized June 25, 1860, in Virginia City, Utah Territory.[3] A few years later the district became the state of Nevada. When pioneer prospector Albert Gould sold for less than $450 his half interest in the undeveloped Gould & Curry mine he rode into town drunk and boasted of having duped the naive Californian buyer.

---

[1] That the American Flag Mine was so equipped and engaged in these procedures is noted in several sources (supplied by John J. Ford, Jr.) including the *Biennial Report of the State Mineralogist of the State of Nevada* for the years 1873 and 1874, pp. 65-66; *5th Annual Report* of R.W. Raymond, Washington, 1873, pp. 176-179; and *The History of Nevada,* Thompson & West, 1881, pp. 484-485.

[2] Robert Batchelder, at one time a prominent figure in professional numismatics, shifted his emphasis to dealing in old autographs and manuscripts where he became well known and highly respected.

[3] Adapted by Q. David Bowers from a transcript of a recorded interview of John J. Ford, Jr., Phoenix, Arizona, by Michael Hodder, August 20, 1996.

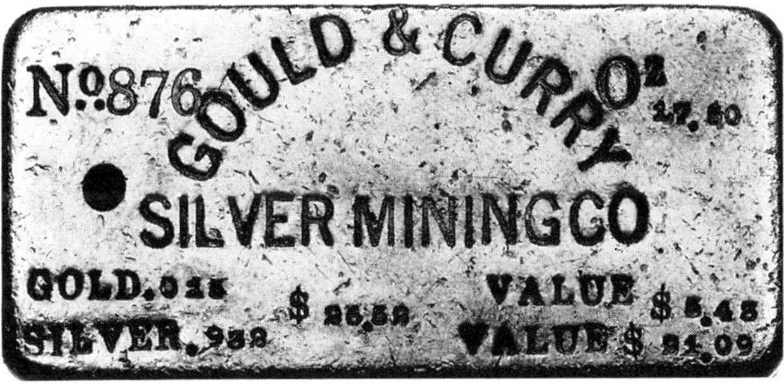

However, his claim eventually yielded $15,000,000, the buyers achieved great wealth, and Gould went in the opposite direction, ending his days operating a peanut stand in Reno.

Among the incorporators and trustees of the Gould & Curry Co. after its purchase from Curry and Gould were Lloyd Tevis, John O. Earl, Alpheus Bell, Thomas Bell, and a couple other gentlemen including George Hearst, the father of William Randolph Hearst of Hearst newspaper empire fame.[1] In time the Gould & Curry mines became the largest producer of silver (primarily) and gold in the area. In the early years of the firm the ore from its underground workings assayed at $70 per ton, but as the best veins were exploited, the quality of subsequent finds diminished. The glory years of the mine were 1863 and 1864 during which time stockholders received dividends totaling $2,908,000. The facilities were described by historian Eliot Lord as being lavish and extravagant in their appearance, but[2]

> in accord with the prodigal temper of the time, and partly exaggerated, it may be, in order to assure the minds of shareholders of the unprecedented value of their stock and to dazzle and impress possible investors, for a plausible outward show of prosperity is worth as much to a mine as to an insurance office. Marble fronts, plate glass windows, glittering signs, and obese porters have a recognized value above their intrinsic cost.... It is certain that terraces and fountains and painted mills, and costly pigs and high mettled horses could be made to serve a similar purpose.
>
> It is probable, however, that in the particular instance of the Gould & Curry mill the expenditures were the natural expression of the liberal nature and fancy of the superintendent, and not a deliberate advertisement to enhance the value of the stock of the company.

Apparently, the fact that the ore processing mill had the foregoing accouterments and even a pool with a gilded water nymph and a fountain in the shape of a swan did not set well with that particular writer. However, such "extravagance" often had another purpose apart from pleasing superintendents and impressing stockholders. The Gold Coin Club erected in the 1890s a few steps from the entrance of the Gold Coin Mine in Victor, Colorado, is another example of furnishing memorable, comfortable surroundings in the evening for men who often were far from home, and spent their days working in dark, poorly-illuminated, and unsafe underground workings.

Besides, it had not been very many months since Virginia City was an exceedingly rustic sort of place, as in this description of the town in 1860, also by Elliot Lord:[3]

> Words can scarcely picture the chaotic confusion in which the camp was plunged by the arrival of these motley swarms [of miners and assorted ne'er-do-wells coming across the border from California]. Wretched huts of canvas, wood, and cobblestones covered the slope, forming a shapeless city traversed by three main lanes styled streets by courtesy. A restless crowd blocked these narrow passages, flowing in and out of their bordering saloons and gambling houses. The cheerless hovels were deserted for these lighted rooms, the real homes of the citizens.
>
> Little stacks of gold and silver fringed the monte tables and glittered beneath the swinging lamps. A ceaseless din of boisterous talk, oaths, and laughter spread from the open doors into the streets. The rattle of dice, coins, balls, and spinning markers, the flapping of greasy cards and the chorus of calls and interjections went on day and night, while clouds of tobacco smoke filled the air and blackened the roof timbers, modifying the stench rising from the stained and greasy floors, soiled clothes, and hot flesh of the unwashed company.

Perhaps for a swan or gilded water nymph to grace the landscape a few years later was not completely out of order.

The success of the Gould & Curry in the early 1860s was largely responsible for agitation that led to the

---

1 Additional information can be found in *The Gould & Curry Bonanza, W.C. Ralston and the Founding of the Bank of California.*

2 Eliot Lord, *Comstock Mining and Miners,* 1883, pp. 126-127; certain other figures are from the same source.

3 *Ibid.,* p. 73, quoting from accounts in San Francisco and Sacramento newspapers.

construction and opening (1870) of the Carson City Mint. Abraham Curry was its first superintendent. This had its shortcomings, as some of his competitors in Nevada shunned the new mint and preferred to send their bullion to San Francisco for converting into coins.

In 1972 when searching for American numismatic items in the mining districts of the West, Paul Franklin located a man who had eight ingots issued by Gould & Curry. These were unparted or mixed-metal bars, were numbered 871, 875, 876, 877, 878, 882, 883, and 885, and ranged in weight from 15.43 ounces to 19.92 ounces. Drilled test marks on the ingots indicated that they had been assayed after their manufacture.

As an example, ingot No. 877 had these inscriptions:

> No. 877 / GOULD & CURRY SILVER MINING CO / Oz 15.03 / GOLD .019 1/2 VALUE $6.06 / . $23.84 [representing the entire value of the bar] / SILVER .914 VALUE $17.78.

The story was that the precious ingots had been found buried in five or six inches of soil under the floor of a bar that had flourished in Virginia City in the 1860s. The finder sold them to a dealer in antique firearms who sold them to Franklin who sold them to Ford.

Of the Gould & Curry ingots acquired by Ford, No. 877 was later sold to Henry H. Clifford (Lot 229 in the Clifford sale). Nos. 878 to 883 went on display at the Bank of California in San Francisco. No. 871 was sold to territorial gold coinage specialist Jack Klausen, and No. 875 went into the cabinet of Jon Hanson. Ford retained three ingots in his own collection.

Star Mining Co.

Hidden or lost: 1880s
Found: July 1968
Treasure: 52 or more gold bars

John J. Ford, Jr., recalled that 52 or more ingots relating to the Star Mining Company were found with the aid of a metal detector.[1] As Ford did not obtain the bars directly, the account concerning their location is sketchy. The F.G. Hoard and Star ingots are said to have turned up in July 1966 and were handled by Paul Franklin, who before leaving on an extended trip to Europe sold them to a dealer in old guns, who then sold them to Ford, the latter being the prime market for them. Ford acquired them over a two-year period 1969-1970. Sizes and shapes ranged from small, square ingots to a mammoth ingot weighing over 20 ounces with many variations as to fineness and imprint styles.

Meanwhile, the gun dealer consigned some to Glendining & Co., the London auction house. Ford was the successful bidder on some of these and brought them back to the United States after obtaining the then-necessary import permits through Leland Howard, director of Domestic Gold and Silver Operations for the government. In those days, gold ingots could not be bought or sold without special permits unless they had previously recognized numismatic value (as, for example, $16 Moffat & Co. San Francisco ingots).

The Star Mine was operated from the 1870s until 1895 by a William Jones of Rose Creek, Sonora (Tuolumne County), California. The mine can be seen on contemporary maps of the area. The bars included some marked "[star emblem] Mining Company," and others marked "[star emblem] G. Mining Co.," the former dated 1880, the latter 1877. As indicated, the "Star" is in the form of an icon or emblem, an impressed five-pointed star punch; the word is not spelled out.

Pieces consigned to Glendining & Co. were catalogued for their sale of November 13-14, 1969.

These numbered ingots were included in the Glendining sale and other appearances:

> **No. 42,** marked CAL. [five-pointed star emblem] MINING Co., a mixed ingot of .678 fine gold and .288 fine silver, weight 7.27 ounces (NASCA's April 1980 sale, Lot 2434) • **No. 43.** .678 gold, .288 silver, 6.42 oz. • **No. 45,** 6.51 oz. (Auction '79, Lot 1482) • **No. 48,** 7.34 oz. • **No. 49,** 7.01 oz. (NASCA's April 1980 sale, Lot 2435) • **No.**

[1] Adapted by Q. David Bowers from a transcript of a recorded interview of John J. Ford, Jr., Phoenix, Arizona, by Michael Hodder, August 20, 1996.

58, 2.94 oz. • **No. 59,** 3.73 oz. • **No. 60,** 2.98 oz. • **No. 63,** 3.03 oz. • **No. 64,** 4.25 oz., dated 1880 (appeared in Superior Galleries 1975 ANA Convention Sale, Lot 1720) • **No. 66,** 3.78 oz. • **No. 67,** 3.90 oz. "No." stamp double-punched (Auction '79, Lot 1483) • **No. 68,** 3.60 oz. • **No. 69,** 3.76 oz., dated 1880 (NASCA's April 1980 sale, Lot 2433) • **No. 232,** 5.28 oz., .994 fine gold • **No. 234,** 3.23 oz., .994 fine gold • **No. 235,** 4.15 oz., .994 fine gold, dated 1880 (NASCA's April 1980 sale, Lot 2432) • **No. 236,** 3.75 oz., .994 fine gold • **No. 237,** 4.35 oz., .994 fine gold, dated 1880 • **No. 238,** 2.96 oz., .994 fine gold • **No. 376,** 10.97 oz., .990 fine gold • **No. 377,** 8.82 oz., .990 fine gold, dated 1880 (NASCA's April 1980 sale, Lot 2431) • **No. 380,** 6.11 oz., .995 fine gold • **No. 429,** 4.55 oz., .995 fine gold **No. 521,** 5.43 oz., .995 fine gold (Henry H. Clifford Collection sale, 1982, Lot 111; earlier in the Glendining & Co. sale of November 1969, then to NASCA, April 1980, Lot 2436, to John J. Ford, Jr.) • **No. 523,** 5.48 oz., .995 fine gold • **No. 525,** 4.53 oz., .995 fine gold • **No. 526,** 4.41 oz., .995 fine gold.

Felix Grundy Hoard, Assayer, Hoard

Hidden or lost: 1860s or early 1870s
Found: July 1968
Treasure: Gold bars

It is certainly unusual that someone with the surname of Hoard would figure in an account of a hoard, but that is the case in this instance![1]

Felix Grundy Hoard, whose first two names were from Felix Grundy (for a short time an attorney general in the Martin Van Buren administration),[2] did business as an assayer in Fiddletown,[3] Amador County, California, per a listing in the 1867 edition of the *Pacific Coast Business Directory.* His trade must have undergone a change, for the 1871-1873 edition of the same guide lists him as a stock and money broker with no mention of assaying. The point may have been moot to readers of the *Directory,* for Hoard passed away on March 3, 1871.

The Hoard Hoard (the author could not resist calling it that) of gold bars came to light in California about July 1968, the same time as the Star Mining Co. ingots emerged. The pieces, about 15 to 20 gold bars totally, were located by Paul Franklin and sold to John J. Ford, Jr. As has been the case with most hoards of silver or gold bars, the pieces bore serial numbers that are consecutive or nearly so.

Mining for gold in a stream bed in the foothills of the Sierra Nevadas in California.

Lot 24 in the Henry Clifford Collection sale, 1982, consisted of ingot No. 2179, weight 9.43 ounces, fineness .999, or nearly pure gold. A prepared counterstamp on the obverse identified it as the product of F.G. HOARD / ASSAYER / AMADOR / CO. / CAL. Other punches defined the weight and other characteristics, as noted. On the reverse the punch USM (for United States Mint) was impressed to indicate that the F.G. Hoard bar was accepted there.

John J. Ford, Jr., has supplied these notes (here edited and in some instances expanded) concerning specifically numbered F.G. Hoard ingots:

---

1 *Ibid.*

2 Felix Grundy was a congressman from Tennessee 1811-1815, senator from the same state 1829-1838, attorney general for Buchanan 1838, and senator again 1839-1840.

3 Name assigned in 1849 by the founders of the town, who were from Missouri. It is said that fiddlers entertained miners at work, but a visitor to the village in 1850 could find not a single fiddle or fiddler. In 1878 the picturesque name was changed to Oleta. (Certain information is from the Bowers and Ruddy sale of the Henry H. Clifford Collection, 1982, Lot 24.)

No. 2173: Weight 9.34 ounces, .999 fine. Total weight is equal to 4,488.20 grains. This and all following ingots have USM stamped on the reverse • **No. 2174,** 8.87 ounces (henceforth, abbreviated oz.), .999 fine • **No. 2175,** 8.80 oz., .999 fine • **No. 2176,** 9.96 oz., .998 fine (Superior Galleries ANA Convention Sale, 1975, Lot 1719) • **No. 2177,** 10.25 oz. (auctioned by NASCA in April 1980, Lot 2429) • **No. 2178,** 10.88 oz. (appeared in Auction '79, Lot 1740) • No. 2179, 9.43 oz., .999 fine (Henry H. Clifford Collection sale, 1982, Lot 24; the ingot had been obtained by Clifford from Superior Galleries in 1971) • **No. 2183** Stamped 9.22 oz., .999 fine • **No. 2185,** 9.29 oz., .999 fine • **No. 2186,** 10.80 oz., .999 fine (appeared in Stack's Lighthouse Sale, June 1978, Lot 693) • **No. 2187,** 9.73 oz., .999 fine (auctioned by NASCA in April 1980, Lot 2430) • **No. 2188,** 9.82 oz., .999 fine • **No. 2189,** 10.38 oz., .999 fine • **No. 2191,** 8.95 oz., .999 fine • **No. 2192,** 9.74 oz., .999 fine • **No. 2194,** 8.17 oz., .999 fine • **No. 2195,** 10.35 oz., .999 fine (appeared in Auction '79, Lot 1481) • **No. 2196,** 9.70 oz., .999 fine • **No. 2197,** 10.58 oz., .999 fine • **No. 2198,** 8.77 oz., .998 fine • **No. 2199,** 8.78 oz., .998 fine • **No. 2200,** 10.72 oz., .999 fine • **No. 2203,** 10.53 oz., .997 fine • **No. 2205,** 9.08 oz., .999 fine (Henry H. Clifford Collection sale, 1982, Lot 24; "Obtained from R&B Coin Co., the firm of John Rowe and Mike Brownlee, Dallas, in 1969; earlier from John Miller, California gun collector who also supplied a Star Mining Co. ingot") • **No. 2206,** 7.75 oz., .999 fine • **No. 2207,** 8.10 oz., .999 fine • **No. 2235,** 6.16 oz., .999 fine.

The Future

The past several decades have yielded discoveries of gold and silver bars hitherto unknown and, in many instances, unsuspected to numismatists. What with the large and impressive pieces from the Spanish treasure wrecks off the coast of Florida (discussed in Chapter 10), the pieces that Paul Franklin found in the West, and the incredible pieces from the *S.S. Central America* (Chapter 11) for starters, the stage is certainly set for the advancement of a new field of numismatic study. At the same time, I hope that there will be an increased awareness of the place that banking and commerce have played in the distribution of such bars as well as coins themselves.

No doubt with the increased sophistication of electronic metal detectors and undersea exploration in particular, and the expanded awareness of silver and gold bars in general, many more important discoveries are yet to be made.

CHAPTER 13

Treasures of the Civil War

The Confederate States of America 1861-1865 had its own paper money, bonds, and—almost—coins. Today all CSA financial items are highly collectible. The following accounts center upon treasures and caches of such pieces.

Spent in a Tavern

Hidden: 1861
Found: 1873
Treasure: Confederate cents

Captain Haseltine

In 1908 old-time dealer John W. Haseltine addressed American Numismatic Association members in convention that year in Philadelphia.[1] It was a fine gathering of those interested in coins, and among those attending the conclave were Mr. and Mrs. Henry Chapman, who acted as hosts; Samuel W. Brown, who worked at the nearby Philadelphia Mint and who in 1913 would become interested in Liberty Head nickels and, perhaps, cause a few to be struck; and—important to the present narrative—Capt. John W. Haseltine.[2]

Haseltine became interested in coins in the 1860s. By 1869 he was associated in the numismatic profession in Philadelphia with Ebenezer Locke Mason, one of the more intellectually curious and literate dealers of his era. In the 1870s Haseltine hung out his own banner. Among his employees were the enthusiastic young brothers S. Hudson and Henry Chapman who, as is well known, went into business for themselves in June 1878 and went on to achieve their own measure of renown.

The 1870s and 1880s were heady times on the Philadelphia numismatic scene—an era pitting the

[1] Sources include Haseltine's account in *The Numismatist* and various narratives re: the 1908 ANA convention published in the autumn of that year; Garrett Collection sale, 1980, Bowers and Ruddy, lots 1995-1996; P. Scott Rubin, "An Even Closer Look at the Confederate Cent," ***Rare Coin Review*** No. 112, 1996; Breen, ***Encyclopedia***, 1988, pp. 666-667 (who cited Haseltine's January 1874 sale but did not quote it directly); P. Scott Rubin, "Check Contemporary Sources," ***The Asylum***, Fall 1994 (centered on the description of Lot 665 in Haseltine's 1874 sale).

[2] Life dates: September 6, 1838-February 28, 1925. In the Civil War he was in action on the Union side and saw action in several theatres including Bull Run and Gettysburg.

United States Mint on one side against the broad community of rare coin dealers and collectors on the other. Dr. Henry Linderman, an insider at the Mint and one-time director, enjoyed making "special pieces" for his own cabinet and, presumably, for occasional sale and trade. Others within Mint walls had their own agendas that included producing "rare" pattern coins, hitherto unknown die combinations, restrikes of earlier rarities of various sorts—the list goes on. Among the more notable productions were "restrikes" of Proof silver dollars bearing the dates 1801, 1802, and 1803, but apparently struck on trade dollar planchets (420 grains) sometime circa 1873-1875.

Many dealers—the roster includes W. Elliot Woodward and S.K. Harzfeld as two of its more vocal members—railed against the production of such special coins. It was very frustrating for them to know that beautiful and rare pattern coins (in particular) and other delicacies were being made, but there was no way that the average person could purchase them, except through certain sources, most particularly Capt. Haseltine, who sold much, but said little.

Haseltine produced many auction catalogues and price lists from the 1870s through the mid-1880s. Best remembered today is his November 1881 catalogue, known for many years thereafter as *Haseltine's Type Table,* which for the first time in a single publication gave die characteristics of early-date quarter dollars, half dollars, and silver dollars. This remained the standard reference for decades.

For reasons that are not apparent today, in the mid-1880s Capt. John W. Haseltine packed his magnifying glass and coins away and turned to other pursuits. For about a decade he was a securities broker and also worked with his brother's art gallery. He returned to rare coins in the mid-1890s, and for the second leg of his career was content to engage in private transactions, although he did find time in 1898 to turn out an auction catalogue for the T.F. Nealis Collection.

By the time of the 1908 ANA convention, Haseltine was known as the "Numismatic Refrigerator," as from time to time he disclosed his ownership of important rarities that were seldom seen, or in a few instances—such as the 1884-1885 trade dollars and the 1877 pattern gold $50 pieces—were not known to exist. Certain of these items were acquired from his father-in-law William K. Idler (1808-1901) who had connections at the Mint. More about these rarities will be found in Chapter 18.

In a Tavern

To the assembled conventioneers in 1908 Haseltine told stories of the days of long ago, including how he discovered a hitherto unknown rarity. It seems, per the account, that one day in 1873 a man wandered into a tavern in Philadelphia and tendered a handful of coins in payment for what was served. In those days the coins in circulation mainly consisted of copper-nickel and bronze Indian cents, but—wait a minute!—here, indeed, was something unusual. Bearing the date 1861 one of the little copper-nickel cents did not have an Indian portrait on it at all, but showed the head of some sort of a goddess. This lightly-worn curiosity was taken by the barkeep to John W. Haseltine, who looked at it and recognized the diecutting style of Robert Lovett, Jr. The same goddess had been used on various tokens of the early 1860s that numismatists knew well and were known to be Lovett's work. The little cent spent at the tavern was different in that it bore the inscription CONFEDERATE STATES OF AMERICA / 1 CENT.

Engraver Lovett was still working in Philadelphia, and Haseltine visited him to learn the story first hand. Lovett revealed that in 1861 he had been contacted by local jewelers Bailey & Co. (later known as Bailey, Banks & Biddle), who in turn had been asked by a representative of the Confederate States of America to investigate having dies made for a CSA one-cent piece. Apparently, die-cutting talent was hard to find in the Confederacy. The trade was concentrated in the North in such cities as Philadelphia, New York, and Cincinnati. Lovett was well known to the Bailey firm and had done contract work for them from time to time.[1]

To create a one-cent piece for the Confederacy, the engraver used his standard "goddess" punch that had been employed on various tokens as a obverse motif. In fact, this must have been his favorite motif, as indicated by its earlier use as the obverse of an advertising token for himself, dated 1860. For the reverse of the Confederate coin a wreath was made to display products of the South including a bale of cotton, the latter bearing the tiny initial L for the engraver. Appropriate lettering was added to both dies.

Fearing the Union authorities would look askance

[1] Among his various earlier medallic productions, Lovett had designed the 1860 Washington Light Infantry / Captain Simonton medal. Simonton later became a Confederate officer and in 1861 was commissioned to stop the resupply of Fort Sumter. Thus, chances are excellent that anyone in a position to have ordered coinage dies for the Confederate States of America would have known of Lovett's earlier work in this regard.

at his work for the enemy, Lovett had second thoughts about the matter and concealed the dies and 12 coins he had made as samples. No one was told about the creation of the coins, and no one suspected their existence.

By the time of Haseltine's visit to Lovett in 1873 the fear had passed, and the engraver told of the piece he spent by accident in a Philadelphia bar, and showed the dealer 10 or 11 (Haseltine's recollections varied) still on hand, all arranged in a neat little row in a wooden drawer. Haseltine bought the remaining pieces and the pair of dies. In 1874, with J. Colvin Randall, he had Philadelphia diesinker and medalist Peter L. Krider make restrikes. These were struck in bronze (55 pieces), silver (12), and gold (several, perhaps as many as seven). The die is said to have broken on the 55th bronze impression, ending the project. No restrikes had been made in copper-nickel, thus preserving the integrity of the originals.[1]

However....

The preceding story, a la Haseltine's 1908 recollections, constituted the history of these pieces and was widely cited by authors, cataloguers, and others over a long period of years. However, there were some suspicions that the story was inaccurate or incomplete. A warning flag was raised by Walter Breen in his 1988 *Encyclopedia:*

> Less is known about the Confederate pattern cent of 1861, and that little is derived from Capt. John W. Haseltine, whose memory at best was unreliable, and whose honesty has been justly questioned.

At the 1992 convention of the American Numismatic Association, held that year in Orlando, Florida, numismatic historian and bibliophile P. Scott Rubin mounted an exhibit which included a copy of John W. Haseltine's January 13-15, 1874, auction catalogue. Lot 665 offered one of the original copper-nickel 1861 Confederate cents which was described as:

> CONFEDERATE CENT, 1861, head of Liberty; inscription, 'Confederate States of America'; rev., '1 Cent' in two lines, surrounded by a wreath of ears of corn and wheat, with a cotton bale at the bottom; nickel; Very Fine; excessively rare.
>
> The dies for the above piece were made by Mr. Lovett, of Philadelphia, in 1861. Mr. Lovett says that they were ordered in 1861, for the South, and that the dies were delivered. Previous to delivering the dies, he struck 12 pieces, but showed them to no one and kept the matter quiet, fearing that he might be arrested if it were known. It was not until about six months since Mr. Lovett parted with all he had (either 10 or 12) to Dr. E. Maris, of Philadelphia, from whom this one was obtained.
>
> Although it is evident that the Southern Confederacy did not adopt this piece, still it will always be considered interesting and valuable as the only coinage designed for the Southern Confederacy, and will no doubt bring a high price. I have been some been somewhat particular in giving the facts about this piece, as there are persons who always sneer at and doubt anything new and interesting that is discovered by other than themselves.[2]

The preceding erroneously indicates that Lovett delivered the dies to the Confederacy, which he did not. The story of the discovery of the first coin centering about Lovett spending one in a bar was not included in Haseltine's 1874 commentary, which today must be considered more reliable than his 1908 recollections. Whether Edward Maris, M.D. (March 15,1832-June 13, 1900), a collector in the private sector, bought the original cache *en bloc* from Lovett, or through the intermediation of Haseltine, is not known.[3]

One of the original 1861 Confederate cents was in Harlan P. Smith's 1886 sale of the Maris Collection and another was in the Chapman brothers' 1900 auction of other pieces from the Maris Collection, indicating that at least two were retained by Maris for years afterward.

Today, the 10, 11, or 12 original 1861 copper-nickel Confederate States of America one-cent pieces are in various private collections and are highly prized. The 1874 restrikes by Krider are also avidly sought by numismatists, and the 1961 copy pieces by Robert Bashlow (see footnote) likewise have a following.

---

1 Years later the cracked, rusted dies went to Judson Brenner, later to John J. Ford, Jr., to Q. David Bowers, to Robert Bashlow, circa 1961. Bashlow sought to make additional restrikes from the damaged dies, but learned they were too fragile for that purpose. He enlisted the Philadelphia diesinking firm of August Frank to make copy or transfer dies, and from these new dies had "restrike" cents made in bronze, silver, etc., and trials and impressions on ingots, spoons, and other matrices. These 1961 Bashlow "restrikes" show heavy evidence of die corrosion and irregularities and are different in appearance from Krider's 1874 restrikes. Moreover, they are considerably thicker than the 1874 restrikes. Mintage figures for the Bashlow issues are given in Breen, *Encyclopedia,* 1988, p. 667.

2 Apparently, there had been some suspicion that these Confederate cents had been made up long after 1861, as a numismatic delicacy, by employing Lovett's well-known portrait punch and adding new lettering.

3 Maris was one of the most avid numismatists of his era. Today he is remembered for his 1869 monograph, *Varieties of the Copper Issues of the United States Mint in the Year 1794,* which described the dies of cents of that year and assigned fanciful names to them, based upon terminology from medical and classical history sources, examples being *Patagonian Head* and *Venus Marina.* In 1881 his large-folio study, *A Historical Sketch of the Coins of New Jersey,* reached print and gave illustrations and details of New Jersey copper coins of the 1786-1788 years; today, these copper issues are catalogued by Maris' numbers. Maris' own cabinet of New Jersey coppers was sold to T. Harrison Garrett of Baltimore, Maryland.

Found in Tennessee

Put away: Early 1860s
Found: 1875
Treasure: Confederate paper money

The *Nashville Banner,* day date not known, printed this account, subsequently reprinted in the *American Journal of Numismatics,* 1875, p. 7, titled "A Bushel of 'Confed' Changes Hands":

> John Gill, of San Francisco, yesterday purchased from Mr. Wm. Duncan, of this city, $750,000 in Confederate money and $50,000 worth of Confederate bonds, paying $50 in gold for them. The money and bonds were purchased by Wm. Duncan at the sale of the assets of the Tennessee Bank, lately. Mr. Gill has five thousand specimens of Confederate issue and scrip. He left last night for Atlanta, where he will doubtless find millions more of the same sort.

Oops! Into the Trash!

Put away: 1864
Found: Circa 1962
Treasure: Confederate $5 and $10 notes

Circa 1962 a banker walked into the premises of Spink & Son, Ltd., rare coin dealers on King Street, St. James, London. With him were several bundles of Confederate States of America $5 and $10 notes issued in 1864 and shipped to England at that time, possibly in payment for goods.[1] The notes had been found sealed in an old vault. Apparently, there were tens of thousands of each denomination. As it happened, Douglas G. Liddell, manager of Spink's numismatic department, was not in his office that day, and it fell to a newly hired young man to wait upon the banker. "Confederate notes are worthless, and we are not interested in buying them," the employee stated.

The man left a couple packs of these "worthless" notes behind, with his business card, in the hope that Spink's might want some at another time. A month or two later the writer was in London, was poking around the various cabinets at Spink's, and met the employee in question. He paused for a moment, then remembered that he had a few hundred of these Confederate notes that the banker had left behind during his recent visit. I recognized them as being of numismatic worth, and wanted to buy them, which I did for sixpence each, and then asked if there were more. The seller looked up the telephone number of the banker, made a call, and learned that the entire hoard, apparently consisting of tens of thousands of notes, had been pitched in the trash a few days earlier!

Treasure Lost, Found, and Lost Again

Hidden: 1861
Found: December 5, 1962
Treasure: Liberty Seated silver coins

The Unfortunate Mr. Tilley

This is the story of a treasure that at one time created a mini-Klondike rush for treasure on a Missouri farm, but of which the details have since become obscured.[2] While, apparently, someone who recognized New Orleans-struck coins was on hand at the time, his or her identity has also become lost. The treasure itself is a will-o'-the-wisp, almost, but not quite.

This is the story not of Confederate States of America coins, but of a sympathizer to the great Lost Cause:

It is said that Wilson Tilley, a well-to-do Missouri farmer, had accumulated a private reserve of gold and silver coins. With the onset of the Civil War in 1861, he buried them on his property, as having obvious wealth could have been dangerous at the time. Al-

---

1 Or for some other reason not presently known. Before many months had passed on the calendar in 1864, the financial reputation of the Confederacy reached a low level, and its paper was poorly regarded.

2 Adapted from "Civil War Treasure," by Leo Mullen, *St. Louis Post-Dispatch,* April 15, 1984; clipping furnished by Kenneth V. Voss.

What might have been: Impression of the pattern reverse die made for the 1861 Confederate States of America half dollar. Although four pieces were made as patterns, no coinage for general circulation ever materialized. (Enlarged photograph; the coin is the size of a United States half dollar)

though no accounting was kept, it is believed that the face value amounted to about $2,400, a sizable amount in that era.

On September 10, 1861, Tilley was murdered by raiders and his home was burned to the ground. His children fled into the woods to escape danger. His wife Elizabeth was away on a visit to nearby Waynesville. Elizabeth returned to bury her husband on the property. Eventually, a new house was built on the site.

A later generation of Tilleys would believe that while Elizabeth may have dug up several hundred dollars' worth of these coins to finance the rebuilding of her home, the larger part remained hidden. Perhaps even she did not know where it was.

A Remarkable Find

A century after the Civil War, on December 5, 1962, a crew was bulldozing land in a farm field to build new barracks buildings for Fort Leonard Wood, south of Waynesville. Contractor James Mace was at the controls when his blade caught on two home-made maple boxes, each about the size of a cigar box and each somewhat deteriorated. Contemporary accounts had it that one box burst open and spilled its contents, revealing a vast array of old silver coins!

Mace and his co-workers converged on the broken boxes and grabbed what they could. Word spread, as treasure tales have a way of doing, and by nightfall a swarm of treasure hunters with metal detectors turned the site into a free-for-all. Hundreds of additional silver coins were found, mostly of the half dollar denomination, apparently these from the first box.

The second box was found to be chock full of half dimes and quarter dollars, most or all from the New Orleans Mint. The pieces were reported to be of the Liberty Seated design and bear dates from 1840 to 1861. The next day many soldiers from Fort Leonard Wood descended upon the area and with detectors and shovels found a few more coins plus some nails and other items, including relics from Tilley's burned-out homestead.

Over 20 years later in 1984, Kim Combs, curator of the small museum at Fort Leonard Wood, learned of the tale, and he sought to wrap facts around the fuzzy story. Information about farmer Tilley and his murder could not be found, and although a Springfield (Missouri) minister recalled that the second, intact box was confiscated in its entirety by the authorities at Fort Leonard Wood in 1962, no evidence could be found to substantiate this. The same Springfield man reported that each box had $1,000 face value in silver. If so, each box would have had to have been larger than the "cigar box" size earlier described.

Tilley Legends

It was learned that Tilley had been engaged in the horse and mule trade and, like many in the border state of Missouri, had sided with the Confederacy. Sentiment for the South ran high in the area, and a Confederate flag was put up on the county courthouse lawn. Waynesville historian Theodore Wolff commented that local citizens were urged to take the banner down, but did not do so until Union General John C. Frémont moved in close to the town and sent cavalry to enforce his presence. Local history has it that the horsemen were forgotten by Frémont, and remained in the area to live off the land. Known as "bushwhackers," these renegade ex-soldiers pillaged and murdered at will. If someone was believed to have wealth, they became a target for plunder or worse.

Legends about Tilley's specific situation proved plentiful, facts elusive. Some said he was killed for being a Confederate sympathizer, others that he was murdered for his wealth. One account has it that he was shot and then hoisted up into a tree. Another has him hanged, and his body dropped on a road to serve as a warning to others with a rebel leaning. Still another story avers that he was shot and castrated.

Historian Wolff has written that on the same day of Tilley's death, bushwhackers hanged a Mr. Burchard in Waynesville, who refused to say where his money was hidden. The home of Lottie Christenson, an abutter to the Tilley farm, was looted and burned. About a year later, in a shooting match between Union troops and insurgents, a wounded man named Oscar Blount was taken prisoner. Labeled a bushwhacker, he confessed to being a party in the Waynesville rampage that resulted in Tilley's murder.

Treasure Legends

The coin treasure of Wilson Tilley was found in 1962, but in time it, too, became a legend. Neither local historians nor regional numismatists seem to know where the pieces went, even though there must have been many thousands of specimens. Some have suggested that the treasure itself is a legend.

Most probably, at least some coins were found—perhaps even quite a few. If the face value was, indeed, $2,000 and was composed of quarters, half dollars, and other, smaller silver coins, this would indicate that somewhere over 5,000 pieces were found. Where did they all go? Can anyone identify even a single piece directly attributable to this remarkable find?

Perhaps the coins exist here and there in collections, whose owners have no clue as to their tragic pedigree.

Related to the Civil War?

Hidden: 1861
Found: 1969
Treasure: Gold and silver coins

In 1969 a small but numismatically exciting hoard was found near Prairie Town, Illinois.[1] The cache, which came to light when the basement in a farmhouse was being excavated, amounted to about $600 in face value. The man who found the pieces offered the hoard intact to collector Kenneth V. Voss in the early 1970s for $7,500, but Voss declined. A few years later one of his friends and fellow workers bought the lot for about $12,500.

Silver coins in the hoard were dated from 1851 to 1861, while gold coins bore dates from 1834 to 1861. This would seem to place 1861 as the likely time the pieces were hidden. It was suggested at the time of the find that the coins may have been secreted by a traveling peddler who was active in the area. Perhaps the owner went off to the Civil War and never returned.

The hoard included these (partial inventory):[2]

Quarters and half dollars combined: 93 pieces.
$2.50 gold: 9 pieces.
$5 gold: 40 pieces including 1838-C and 1839-D.
$10 gold: 7 pieces including 1856, 1856-S, 1858-S, and 1860 (2).
$20 gold: 12 pieces.

At least five choice 1861 $20 pieces were in the group, one gem example of which was sold for at least $11,000 in 1979 at the American Numismatic Association Convention in St. Louis. The silver coins, although showing little actual wear, were in most instances damaged from moisture during the century they were buried.

Mississippi Plantation Hoard

Hidden: 1860s
Found: By 1973
Treasure: Gold coins

The time was 1863, and the place was Mississippi. General Ulysses S. Grant and his Union Army were advancing toward Vicksburg in what would prove to be a pivotal encounter of the Civil War. Fearing the worst, a plantation owner is said to have buried three caches: two of gold coins and one of jewels, silver plate, and other family treasures.

The worst happened. The owner was killed and the plantation mansion was burned to the ground. Over a century later in 1973, treasure hunters found one of the gold coin deposits, which upon inspection was found to contain examples of the following coins:

$5 gold: 1834 Classic Head, 1835, 1844-O (2 pieces), 1846-C, 1849-C, 1860-C.
$10 gold: 1843-O, 1847-O, 1853, 1854-O, 1855, and 1858-O.
$20 gold: 1859-O.

The finders elected to keep several of the pieces (not the most numismatically valuable), and the rest were consigned to the saleroom. At the American Auction Association event in February 1974, the coins were described as follows and realized the prices indicated:

Lot 1. 1835 $5. The "Classic Head" type as struck from 1834 to 1838. VF. $200.
Lot 2. 1844-O $5. Brilliant Uncirculated, some usual bagmarks. $700.
Lot 3. 1844-O $5. Another of this issue. AU. $375.
Lot 4. 1846-C $5. Very scarce issue; only 12,995 were minted. Attractive VF-EF. $300.
Lot 5. 1849-C $5. Just 64,823 pieces were minted of this scarce Charlotte issue. Attractive EF-AU grade—really outstanding condition for this variety. $500.
Lot 6. 1860-C $5. One of only 14,813 half eagles struck at Charlotte, North Carolina this year. Extremely Fine, with some suggestions of prooflike surface on the obverse. An extraordinarily excellent specimen of this rare issue. $550.
Lot 7. 1847-O $10. AU, with nearly a full quotient of original mint lustre. Quite probably a coin which never saw

[1] Information from Kenneth V. Voss, letter, August 1996.
[2] Inventory and certain other information is from Bennie Hutchins, interview with Rosalie Minnerly, September 12, 1996.

much actual circulation but which was stored with other $10 gold pieces in a bag. Only 12,000 1847-O eagles were minted. We estimate that fewer than two to three dozen survive today in a condition equal to the present example. $975.

Lot 8. 1854-O $10. Large date variety (cf. p. 145 of *Scott's Comprehensive Catalogue of U.S. Coins)* with huge numerals as more properly intended for the $20 gold issues. Beautiful EF-AU condition. One of the finest known examples. Scott notes that this variety is unknown in Uncirculated grade. $675.

Lot 9. 1859-O $20. A magnificent Brilliant Uncirculated specimen with usual bagmarks. Suggestions of prooflike surface in fields. This coin, retaining nearly 100% original mint lustre, was probably in bank-to-bank "circulation" for three or four years before it was buried in 1863. Only 9,100 1859-O double eagles were made. For years this has been considered as one of the rarest issues, and specimens in any grade are hard to locate. The "name" gold sales of the past nearly all had specimens in lesser condition than the presently-offered coin. The Dunham and Wolfson Extremely Fine coins and the Gilhousen Very Fine coin are examples. The value of the 1859-O double eagle we offer is difficult to estimate. As one of the very finest of its kind, or perhaps even *the finest*, it will be a "treasure" for its new owner in more ways than one. $7,250 [a high price which stunned everyone in the audience; this was in the era before the price rises of the late 1970s and late 1980s; all the coins would be worth much more today].

The other two caches buried on the plantation in 1863 remain undiscovered treasures.[1]

A Treasure Trove of C.S.A. Bonds

Stored: 1860s-1880s
Found: By 1987
Treasure: Thousands of bonds

Financing the Confederacy

Certainly one of the most interesting and impressive hoards of any that have been found in recent decades is the cache of Confederate States of America bonds that came to light in London in the 1980s.[2]

First, some background:

To finance its military campaign against the Union, the Congress of the Confederate States of America authorized the issuance of bonds under acts from February 28, 1861, to June 14, 1864. Most often these were in the form of bearer or non-registered bonds, with interest coupons attached, the coupons to be redeemed every six months. Interest ranged from 4% to 8% depending upon the series and time of issue. The principal amount was generally stated as being payable six months after a peace treaty was signed, the implication being that the Confederate States of America would triumph over the United States of America (Union). The typical bond had a central illustration (engraved vignette) depicting a scene relating to the American South or to the Confederacy, a recitation of the terms of the loan, and hand-inked serial number and signatures.

The first bonds totaled $15,000,000 in face amount, matured in 10 years, carried an 8% interest rate, and were backed by revenues from an export tax on cotton.

Sales of the bonds were made wherever possible including to banks, businesses, and individuals in the South and to overseas investors. Many of the latter were in England, where in the early years of the conflict there were some strong sentiments and business reasons for supporting the Confederacy, especially in view of American cotton being an exceedingly important raw material for the numerous textile mills in the British Isles. England was willing to trade actively with the Confederacy and even build ships for it (*e.g.*, the *Alabama*), but did not extend diplomatic recognition. In late 1862 and early 1863, French banker Emile Erlanger, stirred up interest in raising European money for Confederate "cotton loans," but France did not recognize the Confederacy either.

Through sales efforts in England, France, and elsewhere, millions of dollars' worth of Confederate bonds were sold, until Confederate military reverses in 1863 forewarned that such investments might be even riskier than earlier supposed. After early 1864, Europe was no longer a viable source for funding. Meanwhile, at home the paper money in the South became increasingly worthless as new issues with no solid backing were floated.

Confederate Bonds

On April 3, 1865, Richmond fell to the Union forces, and on April 9, General Robert E. Lee surren-

[1] Information from an American Auction Association sale (Q. David Bowers and James F. Ruddy), February 7, 1974, lots 1-9.

[2] Certain information, particularly about the distribution of the hoard, is from Michael W. Sherman (letter, August 28, 1996; Sherman handled the bidding for Heritage), Heritage Rare Coin Galleries; thanks also to David Lindvall for facilitating the author's inquiries.

The fall of Richmond as shown in a nineteenth-century engraving.

dered his army to Union General Ulysses S. Grant, thus ending the four-year Civil War. Although Confederate financial obligations had sunk to very low value in the preceding months, now they were absolutely worthless. In the following months and years the Union made no effort to indemnify the holders of paper money or bonds.

As it has been said many times, hope springs eternal, and in situations involving money this is especially true. British investors appealed for relief to Secretary of State William Seward, stating that they had always appreciated the United States of America, even during the Civil War; that as the principal of the Confederate bonds was payable six months after a peace declaration, British financial interests were subtle forces in bringing about a peace, etc. Despite such entreaties, the United States evinced no interest or intention of redeeming even one cent worth of bonds. As if to secure the position, the 14th Amendment to the United States Constitution, ratified in 1868, made it illegal for any state or the federal government to "assume or pay any debt or obligation incurred in aid of insurrection or rebellion against the United States." Moreover, there was much strong feeling against England's perceived complicity in the whole matter, particularly with regard to the *Alabama* privateer outfitted in the British Isles, which sailed against and captured or destroyed 69 Union vessels.

Will the U.S. Honor the Bonds?

As an interesting footnote to history, the closely fought Samuel J. Tilden-Rutherford B. Hayes presidential contest fought in 1876 raised hopes in England that the Republican Party—which had been in power during and since the Civil War—would be ousted from control, and that the Democratic Party would come into power and be favorably inclined toward some sort of a settlement on the old obligations of the Confederacy, or that the Southern states on their own would do so.

In London a trade arose in the old C.S.A. bonds, bid and ask prices were posted, and at one point they traded at about 2% of their face value. Stories were bandied about that the Bank of England held millions of dollars in gold that had been deposited by the Confederacy before 1865. The implication was that if the United States government would redeem the old Confederate bonds, the Bank of England would turn loose the stored gold. The Republicans won the election, and hopes of redemption were dashed until 1884, when Democrat Grover Cleveland was chosen as president. Hopes were renewed. However, Cleveland showed no interest in the British claims, and by that time Judah P. Benjamin, former secretary of state for the Confederacy, had long since denied that any such gold deposits were ever made in the Bank of England.

Legacy of the Confederacy

Decades later a truly remarkable treasure was revealed.

Long-forgotten bonds stored for over a century in England were described as follows in a one-lot catalogue bearing a sale time of 4:00 p.m., Tuesday afternoon, November 24, 1987. The seller was Sotheby's in London.

> **Bearer Bonds of the Confederate States of America:**
> The Property of United Kingdom Trustees
>
> **Lot 1: A Major and Extremely Extensive Archive of Unredeemed Bearer Bonds Issued by the Confederate States of America between 1861 and 1864,** comprising over 75,000 individual certificates for numerous Loans authorized by Acts of the Confederate Congress, all with their original integrally-printed coupons for interest payments intact as appropriate; the great majority carefully rolled into bundles (and therefore requiring flattening for individual examination or display), protected by brown paper wrappers dated *circa* 1883 and all now housed in 30 card packing cases, *with excellent representation of scarce or rare as well as common types, a small proportion impaired by water staining, corrosion, or other damage but otherwise generally very well-preserved, a highly interesting and probably uniquely large group. (over* 75,000 items)
>
> Offered as a single lot, this exceptional holding represents the entire surviving portfolio of Confederate Bonds controlled by United Kingdom Trustees since the 1880s. The original objective of the Trustees, to obtain a degree of compensation in respect of the outstanding Southern States Debt following the American Civil War, has long since been abandoned.
>
> Estimate: £180,000-220,000

Furious Bidding

Excitement prevailed on the American side of the Atlantic as word of this vast holding spread around the numismatic community. While certain such bonds were rather plentiful in collecting circles, to find even a few hundred all at once would have been interesting. The chance to bid on tens of thousands in one fell swoop was simply amazing!

Various dealers planned their strategies. At Bowers and Merena Galleries in New Hampshire, Ray Merena and the author figured that at several hundred thousand dollars the group would be a great buy. With this in mind we were on the other end of an open telephone line to Sotheby's at the appointed date and hour. Others were in the fray as well.

Bidding was spirited, and it soon became evident that the estimate was going to be left far behind. After several tense minutes, the lot went to buyers in America. Michael W. Sherman, who was the successful bidder on behalf of Heritage Rare Coin Galleries, later commented:

> The cost of the lot was split evenly between Heritage and John Saunders (London Coin Galleries of Mission Viejo, CA). Estimated at £180,000-£220,000, the lot was hammered at £320,000. With buyer's charge, VAT [Value Added Tax] and a bidder's fee, the total cost of the lot to the purchasers was £357,300, or about $655,000 at the time.
>
> The lot consisted of about 86,500 bonds, and comprised much of the European holdings of CSA bonds which had been "consolidated" by a group of trustees in the early 1880s. Virtually every type listed in Grover Criswell's reference on the series was present, with only three or four exceptions.
>
> Most of the rarer bonds were immediately consigned to NASCA and these were sold in four or five sales over the next three years. The balance of the hoard was advertised in various Civil War publications and in a color brochure mailed by Heritage. We sold the last of the bonds in June 1996.
>
> On an anecdotal note, the bonds had been rolled for storage, and every bond needed to be "hand ironed" before it could be sold. We paid Heritage employees 10¢ per bond for their ironing efforts. The large number of bonds in the hoard also enabled me to do some research regarding signature combinations and "changeover" points for various signers. Further, questions were answered concerning various paper varieties and the Trans-Mississippi series.

Confederate Gold Coin Holdings

Although the aforementioned cache of United States gold coins said to have been deposited in the Bank of England by the southerners may have been illusory, there exist some other accounts of transactions in such pieces. The Confederate States of America paid for many of its obligations in earlier-dated United States gold coins in an era in which its paper obligations were depreciating in value. Historian Douglas B. Ball has written:[1]

> The government did not negotiate a foreign loan until early 1863, thus the only way the Confederate government could cover its overdrafts in Europe was by shipping coin or selling it for the foreign exchange of those banks that would not take bonds or Treasury notes.
>
> Coin, made up in packages of $25,000 to $100,000, was shipped in the fall of 1862. Such shipments were revived in late 1863 and continued until early 1864 when Wilmington was captured. From the Treasury's incomplete correspondence, it would appear that in 1864 alone, $1.7 million in gold coin was shipped, of which about $1.5 million reached Europe, $127,750 was captured, and $50,000 was rescued by the purser of the wrecked *Lynx* and safely brought back to Wilmington. [The purser was given $500 in gold as commendation for his act.]
>
> From these facts we may estimate that $2 million in coin was sent abroad.

However, despite rumors to the contrary, no deposits of Confederate gold coins ever came to light in later years in England or elsewhere.

1 *Financial Failure and Confederate Defeat,* University of Illinois Press, 1991, p. 129.

The Confederate Raider *Alabama*

The 252-foot, 1,736-ton steamer *Ariel*, whose first owner in 1854-1855 was Cornelius Vanderbilt, saw service under charter to the federal government during the Civil War, a duty punctuated by commercial trips on the New York to Aspinwall route during the same era. On December 7, 1862, while off the coast of Cuba on the way to Panama, she was stopped by the 1,040-ton Confederate raider *Alabama*. Captain Raphael Semmes decided to spare the *Ariel*, but to disarm 120 marines who were aboard and take what money he could find. While busy with the *Ariel*, the *Alabama* missed capturing the *Champion* which was traveling the same route, but northbound, with $1,350,000 in specie aboard. This is one treasure that the Confederacy didn't get—what might have been, but wasn't.

The saga of the *C.S.S. Alabama* is one of the most exciting and controversial in the annals of the Civil War. Built by Laird & Sons at Birkenhead on the Mersey River near Liverpool, England, as the *290*, the steamship had a wooden hull with a coppered bottom and was driven by a screw propeller. In an era of transition between sail and steam, she was also rigged as a bark. The *290* was launched on the Mersey in late July, 1862, and took a large party of ladies and gentlemen aboard to celebrate her maiden voyage. After suitable festivities, the guests were sent back on another ship, and instead of coming back to port as had been announced, the *290* under Captain Bullock and a crew of 93, most of whom had seen service as gunners in the British Naval Reserve, headed to a distant and somewhat mysterious rendezvous. The skipper learned that the United States gunboat *Tuscarora* was in St. George's Channel, and elected to take another route. However, if the *290* had been challenged, Captain Bullock was well equipped with "English papers and other presumptive proofs of her neutrality."

Eight days later the ship reached Tarissa Island, one of the Azores belonging to Portugal. Captain Bullock told the local authorities that the steam engines had broken down, and the *290* would be anchored until repairs could be made. The crew was indeed busy, but not with the engines, which were in perfect working order. Instead, they readied the *290* to receive guns and other armament.

Meanwhile, a large sailing ship left the Thames River in England and headed to Demerara and the West Indies, but really with a sinister purpose in mind that involved an entirely different destination. On board packed in crates were armaments and other military supplies. Once in the West Indies, the bark turned east across the Atlantic toward the Azores to meet with the *290*. Arriving at Terissa, the second vessel drew close to the *290*, and the transfer of munitions commenced. Portuguese officials were quite confused with the activities of these foreign ships and, after inquiry, were told that the bark had sprung a leak, and the *290* crew was helping to fix it.

Soon thereafter, when most of the guns and other armament had been installed on the *290*, another ship hove into view: the *Bahama* with Captain Raphael Semmes, a former United States Navy officer, aboard and officers and crew of about 20 from the Confederate States of America privateer *Sumter*. Aboard the *Bahama* were more weapons and ammunition to be mounted on the *290*. At this time the Portuguese officials lost patience with what seemed to be illogical excuses and bewildering actions, and insisted that all three ships leave Terissa immediately. This was done, and some miles away the trio rendezvoused in international waters and completed their business. Captain Semmes, crew members from the *Sumter*, and a contingent of British seamen now constituted the complement of the *290*.

Next, the true purpose was revealed. With a due show of ceremony, Captain Semmes emerged from his cabin and opened a document from President Jefferson Davis of the Confederate States of America, personally directing Semmes to take command of the "British" ship *290*, henceforth to be known as the *Alabama*, to raise the Confederate flag, and to "sink, burn and destroy everything which flies the ensign of the so-called United States of America." A rousing speech was given to the crewmen, who shouted and applauded the new venture and praised the Confederate States of America. Onward and upward!

Soon thereafter, an American whaling ship was met, captured, and burned, to become the first of dozens of victims of Semmes and his crew of privateers. Or, was this a Confederate warship? No one was quite sure.

Reminiscent of the lawless pirates of the preceding century, the crew of the *Alabama* would sail under the British flag (per some accounts), capture a Union vessel, then raise the Confederate flag in triumph. In England, many observers of the American conflict thought this was jolly good sport. Semmes became a military hero in the South.

In June 1864 the *Alabama* was in the neutral port of Cherbourg, France. At the same time the American gunboat *Kearsarge*, under Captain John A. Winslow, was in Flushing, Holland, on the same coast. Winslow was notified by telegram from Mr. Dayton, American ambassador to France, that the *Alabama* was at Cherbourg. Around the same time, Captain Semmes and the crew of the *Alabama* learned of the location of the *Kearsarge*. Through the diplomatic service Captain Semmes challenged the *Kearsarge,* stating that he would like to measure the strength of the *Alabama* against her, and would do so if the *Kearsarge* would remain outside of the port of Cherbourg. Such an encounter would not long detain the *Kearsarge,* Semmes boldly suggested.

The challenge was accepted, and for five days the *Kearsarge* was posted in the sea off the coast of France awaiting her adversary, who was in Cherbourg preparing for the swift kill. Finally, at about 10:30 in the morning of June 24, 1864, the *Alabama,* with a French ironclad steamer nearby to watch the action, came out of the port.

It is not every day that one can see two warships locked in mortal combat, and the opportunity was not lost. The French coast was lined with thousands of spectators. Additional visitors came from England and remained on ships nearby to watch the action, such as Captain Couronne and the yacht *Deerhound,* whose contingent included boat's owner, Mr. Lancaster, a member of the Royal Yacht Club, who had brought his wife and children along to watch the excitement. A rousing good party, this! The *Alabama,* never vanquished, was a heavy odds-on favorite, and it would be just a short time until the schoolchildren and other sightseers would have a first-hand lesson in history as the *Kearsarge* was blown to pieces.

The *Kearsarge* was several miles off the French coast when the *Alabama* was first spotted. Seeking to prevent the Confederate ship from running to shore in case of damage, and also to have the encounter in international waters so as to avoid any diplomatic problems, the *Kearsarge* went still farther offshore, to about seven miles from the coast. The *Kearsarge* was not going to give up without a fight. Captain Winslow had no intention of being added to the raider's long list of conquests.

Both ships bristled with armament. The *Alabama* had one seven-inch Blakely rifle, one eight-inch smooth bore 68-pound cannon, and six 32-pounders, quite enough to lay any adversary to waste, as had been proven time and again. The *Kearsarge* was outfitted with two 11-inch smooth-bore cannon, one 32-pound rifle, and four 32-pound cannon (Dahlgren howitzers). The officers and crew of the Confederate ship totaled about 150 men, versus 162 for the Union vessel.

At 10 minutes before 11 a.m., the *Kearsarge* turned about to approach the *Alabama.* At a distance of about three-quarters of a mile, the *Alabama* fired a broadside with her starboard cannon. It would be only a matter of minutes until the entire matter was dispensed

The Confederate raider *Alabama* (foreground) succumbs to the fire of the Union gunship *Kearsarge* in a naval challenge off the coast of Cherbourg, France.

with, and the *Alabama* could continue on to other, more important business.

The *Kearsarge* remained silent for the moment, but drew nearer to its adversary, then fired six guns at the *Alabama.* Both ships kept their starboard batteries active while circling each other—seven times by actual count—for slightly over an hour at distances ranging from about 1,500 to 3,000 feet. This, indeed, was a contest! The spectators, of course, were delighted. The *Kearsarge* should have been on the bottom by now, but the action continued. How exciting!

The *Alabama* fired at an increasingly rapid and intense pace, but with less aim and focus. Most projectiles splashed harmlessly into the sea. Meanwhile the *Kearsarge* was more deliberate and endeavored to fire heavy cannon at her adversary's water line and lighter guns at the upper deck.

Volleys continued. Then, obviously damaged, the *Alabama* hoisted a white flag of surrender and headed out of international water and directed her course for the French shore. The contest was over. In time, the *Alabama* would be repaired, probably after being towed to Liverpool, and would fight again. There was rejoicing aboard the *Kearsarge.* The challenge had been met and won!

But wait!

A couple of minutes later the *Alabama* unexpectedly opened fire again. The surprised *Kearsarge* gunners responded with a fusillade of shots across the bow of her rival. The fight was not over!

But it was.

Soon thereafter, the crew of the *Kearsarge* saw boats lowered from the *Alabama.* One of the lifeboats came alongside and stated that the ship had indeed surrendered, *really* this time. Within 20 minutes the once-proud *Alabama,* terror of the seas, went stern-first to the sea bottom. The time was 24 minutes past noon.

Captain Semmes threw his sword into the water, then jumped in. In quick time the British yacht *Deerhound* rescued him and 13 other officers. Meanwhile, others of the *Alabama* crew were picked up by the *Kearsarge* and nearby vessels. In all, 119 Confederate sailors were saved and about 30 were killed aboard ship or drowned. Three aboard the *Kearsarge* were wounded.

Semmes was taken to "neutral" England, where he was invited to a banquet to be tendered in his honor(!), but declined, probably wisely. In the ensuing weeks and months Semmes was reviled in the Northern press, as he had been for some time.

It was later estimated that the *Alabama* had fired about 370 shells of which 13 or 14 hit the hull of the *Kearsarge.* The Union ship fired less than half as many, or about 173 shells, of which a particularly lethal one killed or wounded 18 men aboard the *Alabama* and at the same time disabled one of its guns.

Semmes later complained that the naval engagement was unfair as the *Kearsarge* had been covered with iron plate hidden beneath planks on the side. Not quite. The *Kearsarge,* to protect its powder magazine, draped two layers of chain over the side. Besides, who was Captain Semmes to complain about fairness on the high seas?

After the end of the Civil War, Captain Semmes was pardoned, then later brought up on charges stemming from his past naval activities. Unlike General Robert E. Lee who was treated with respect, Semmes was *persona non grata* to those in the government (*i.e.,* the victorious Union forces and their political heirs), and circumstances were made difficult for him for much of his remaining life. The "Alabama claims" by aggrieved parties who lost merchandise or vessels because of the Rebel raider dragged through the courts for a long time thereafter and, in the year 1871 in particular, were widely reported in the popular press.

That little love was lost for Semmes is evidenced by many later accounts, including this one printed 12 years after the naval encounter:[1]

> Had justice, reason, and law [prevailed during the Civil War] the commerce of the United States would not have been swept from the ocean by a few predatory cruisers like the *Sumter,* the *Florida,* the *Georgia,* and chief of all, the *Alabama,* the latter commanded by Captain Raphael Semmes, formerly an officer of the United States Navy, and a man of acknowledged professional abilities. No feature in the devastations which accompanied that sanguinary conflict appears now, at this remote view of the period when it occurred, more causeless and deplorable than this indiscriminate destruction of merchant shipping, the hapless crews of which were composed largely of natives of other countries, and therefore in no wise involved in or responsible for the war.

Certain artifacts of the *Alabama* were later salvaged from the sea off the coast of France and put on display in a British pub. The ship's bell was consigned to a Harmer Rooke (New York City) auction in the early 1990s, but was withdrawn (as learned by the author when trying to place a bid). Although it has been suggested that gold coins and other "treasure of the Confederacy" went down with the *Alabama,* this is not confirmed by any contemporary reports encountered by the writer. In fact, it is believed that Captain Semmes offloaded any valuable items he had at Cherbourg to prevent their possible loss in the naval encounter. Of course, he had not expected to lose.

[1] R.M. Devens, *Our First Century,* 1876. Chapter XCIX is devoted in its entirety to the *Alabama-Kearsarge* contest. This formed the basis for much of the account given here.

An Earlier Incident Involving Semmes

J.F. Loubat, in *The Medallic History of the United States of America,* 1776-1876, pp. 300-303, reproduces a letter from Lieutenant R. Semmes, then of the U.S. frigate *Raritan,* December 10, 1846, addressed to Commodore M.C. Perry, "second in command, Home Squadron."

Semmes, noted that under his command the brig *Somers* had been lost off the shore of Verde Island, after the ship had spent 45 days maintaining the blockade of the Mexican port of Vera Cruz. The *Somers,* lightly loaded with less ballast than normal and virtually no supplies or cargo, could not be controlled in a fierce squall that arose, and soon foundered with the loss of more than half of her crew.

On March 7, 1847, the Senate voted that medals be prepared and presented to the officers and men attached to the several ships that rescued survivors from the *Somers,* these being *Endymion, Alarm,* and *Daring* (under the British flag), *Mercure* and *Pylade* (French), and *Louisa Fernandez* (Spanish).The dies for the medal were cut by Charles Cushing Wright (1796-1854), the most acclaimed medalist of the 1820-1854 era.[1]

The Sabine Pass Medal

Hidden or lost: Late 19th century
Found: 1994
Treasure: Rare Civil War Medal

(Photo courtesy of Michael Hodder, from John J. Ford, Jr.)

In 1994, Bert Green, of Texas, was exploring with his Fisher 1265-X metal detector.[2] On one particular day he was in Bryan, Texas, near the site of an old railroad spur that had been used by both Union and Confederate forces during the war between the states. Here, indeed, was the possibility of finding something interesting! Hopes were raised further by Green's earlier success at the same place, when he found some Civil War military artifacts.

It was a lucky day, and in due course an old Mexican "silver dollar" was found. However, this was no ordinary Mexican 8-real coin. Rather, it was one that now had the form of a rare medal, one that had been ground down and used for engraving to create a highly prized numismatic piece.

The medal and several similar pieces—fewer than 10 are known—are at once rustic and historic. The obverse bears the inscription "D.G." above a Maltese cross. The reverse displays the wording, "Sabine Pass / September 8th / 1863." At the top of the medal is a small attached loop for suspension.

The "D.G." notation refers to the Davis Guards who participated on the Confederate side of the military encounter that took place on the date indicated. This Confederate battle award, hand engraved and not struck, comes as close as one can to a "medal." Although the Confederate States of America recognized its heroes and, in fact, in 1862 had prepared a "Roll of Honor" for illustrious service as of that date, no die-struck medals were ever made for the South, one reason being the lack of diecutters and private minting facilities in that territory.

The Davis Guards medal was commissioned by citizens of Houston, Texas, upon the first anniversary of the 1863 skirmish. Charles Gottchalk engraved the medals by hand, after which examples were presented to members of the Guards, whether or not they had taken part in the battle. A banquet was also tendered in their honor, and the Congress of the Confederate States of America passed a resolution to pay tribute to the event.

At first, Bert Green did not realize that he had a valuable piece. However, in due course he was shown a description of a similar example in the Ford Family Trust holdings that had been catalogued for Stack's by Michael Hodder, and realized his was identical, and quite possibly worth thousands of dollars!

Fisher Research Laboratory, the maker of the electronic detector used for the find, became interested and made it possible for Bert Green to go to Arizona and have the medal checked by John J. Ford, Jr., rec-

[1] The medal is described under varieties NA-24 and NA-25 by R.W. Julian, *Medals of the United States Mint: The First Century, 1792-1892,* 1977, pp. 170-171. Also see Bowers and Merena, Dreyfuss Collection Sale, 1986, Lots 5340, 5341.

[2] Certain information appeared earlier in Michael Hodder's cataloguing of this particular find for Stack's sale of September 1995, Lot 82. While this entry would certainly be appropriate for inclusion in the single-item finds that form the majority of the entries in Chapter 21, it seems more relevant to include it here with related Confederate items.

ognized as expert in this field and as the one-time owner of the recently auctioned specimen catalogued by Hodder.

Good luck! It was indeed genuine, and soon thereafter Fisher showcased the find in its monthly magazine, *Western & Eastern Treasures,* issue of March 1995, as one of the 10 best finds of the year. It was also featured in the 1996-1997 edition of *Fisher World Treasure News.*

Subsequently the Green find was catalogued by Michael Hodder as well, and was featured in Stack's sale of November 1995. As part of the description, Hodder noted (here adapted):

In terms of its military outcome, its effect upon the war, the Confederate triumph at the Battle of the Sabine Pass was but a small affair by Civil War standards. In terms of public opinion, however, the Confederate victory was a great morale builder. It is said that 42 Confederate light artillery troops repelled a Yankee contingent of 15,000 men under General Franklin, who had arrived on 27 ships from New Orleans.

Southern newspapers carried dispatches and copper plate engravings of the battle for the next several weeks. Northern newspapers were harsh in their criticism of the Union's action in the confrontation and later pointed out that more than one third of all Union losses for the entire year of 1863 had occurred at Sabine, Texas!

News of the Sabine Pass defeat of the Northern forces, followed shortly by dreadful reports from Chickamauga, Georgia, boosted gold prices by 5% domestically, and in London the value of Confederate bonds rose 2% to 3%.

The World's Columbian Exposition, held in Chicago in 1893, furnished the occasion for America's first commemorative silver coins—half dollars dated 1892 and 1893. Shown here is the exhibit mounted at the Exposition by the United States Mint. Suspended from the ceiling in a bunting-draped frame is Peter, stuffed, who was at one time the Mint's mascot and flew in and out of the building; he is believed to be pictured on the Gobrecht silver dollars of 1836-1839 and the Flying Eagle cents of 1856-1858. In glass-fronted cases in the foreground are rare coins brought from the Mint Cabinet (formed in June 1838), a display of United States, world, and ancient specimens.

CHAPTER 14

Hoards of Commemoratives

Silver Commemoratives

Unsold or saved: various times before 1960
Found: various times
Treasure: Commemorative coins

Although the 1848 gold $2.50 coin with CAL. counterstamped on the reverse is rightfully a commemorative, the first United States commemorative coin offered in quantity to all comers was the 1892 Columbian half dollar issued for the World's Columbian Exposition held in Chicago a year late in 1893.[1] From that time until 1954, many different designs and varieties of half dollars were produced. Today, collectors seek 48 different basic motifs for a type set, or, more expansively, a complete set of 142 types, dates, and mintmarks. In addition, there were two other silver commemoratives: the 1893 Isabella quarter dollar and the 1900 Lafayette silver dollar.

In general, silver commemoratives of the 1892-1954 era were produced to be sold at a premium for fairs and expositions (such as the 1893 Columbian, 1915 Panama-Pacific, and 1926 Sesquicentennial, among others); anniversaries of towns, counties, and states (such as 1927 Vermont Sesquicentennial, 1934 Maryland Tercentenary [300th anniversary], 1936 York County [Maine] Tercentenary, etc.); or recognition of historical figures (1922 Grant Centennial, 1934-1938 Boone Bicentennial, 1946-1951 Booker T. Washington, etc.); or recognition of historical events (1920-1921 Pilgrim Tercentenary, 1924 Huguenot-Walloon Tercentenary, 1926-1939 Oregon Trail Memorial, etc.).

Many issues, including some of the preceding, were produced by individuals or profit-oriented groups to exploit the collectors' market, with no nationally meaningful anniversary or other occasion to be commemorated. Perhaps most egregious in this regard is the 1936 P-D-S Cincinnati set of three half dollars planned, ordered from the Treasury Department, and entirely sold by Thomas G. Melish; these were strictly for his private profit, although the coins bore reference to the 50th anniversary of that city as "A MUSICAL CENTER OF AMERICA."[2]

In a typical distribution situation, quantities of coins were ordered from the Philadelphia (usually), Denver, and/or San Francisco mints and shipped to the issuing entities. These coins were placed on sale at a premium. Unsold coins were usually returned to the Treasury Department and melted, although in a few instances remainders were placed into circulation. In some instances—discussed below—groups and quantities were retained by the original distributor, sold in bulk to coin dealers, or otherwise retained in hoards after the main distribution had been completed.

---

[1] In conjunction with this chapter a perusal of the commemorative listings in *A Guide Book of United States Coins,* or another standard source, will give information about mintages, designs, and reasons for issue. For expanded information and technical details, Bowers, *Commemorative Coins of the United States: A Complete Encyclopedia,* may be useful.

[2] However, no historian has ever been able to locate anything significant or innovative musically that occurred in Cincinnati 50 years earlier in 1886.

Today in the 1990s, virtually all hoards have been dispersed. A few still linger, most notably a group of 500 1946-dated Iowa Centennial half dollars held by that state and intended for distribution in the year 2046.

Not discussed here are hoards of modern commemorative coins from 1982 to date, some quantities of which remain in groups in numismatic hands.

Silver commemorative coins of the classic 1892-1954 era are listed in the approximate chronological order of production and distribution.

1892-1893 Columbian half dollars: Vast quantities of these were placed into circulation for face value, and examples did not command a significant premium on the collectors' market until decades later. The writer knows of no original (non-numismatic) hoards of Mint State coins. However, later collectors and dealers sometimes accumulated quantities, such as a group of over 600 pieces assembled by a eastern stamp dealer in the 1980s in anticipation of a value increase in 1992 when the 500th anniversary of Columbus' landing was to be observed.[1]

Every so often small groups or hoards of worn coins will come on the market, typically consisting of a few dozen or more pieces. These represent coins taken out of circulation years ago when they were viewed as novelties by bank tellers and others who handled quantities of money.

1893 Isabella quarter dollars: Writing in *The Numismatist* in May 1923 dealer Thomas L. Elder commented: "I bought 1,000 Isabella quarter dollars from the Exposition Committee once for 40¢ each, and many others at 45¢."

Texas dealer B. Max Mehl wrote the following about Isabella quarters in his 1937 monograph, *The Commemorative Coins of the United States:* "A great percentage of this number was purchased by a prominent member of the Board of Lady Managers and were afterwards released as the demand required. I well remember that these coins were obtained from the late Mr. Stevens of Chicago at 50¢ or 60¢ each in lots of 100 or more until about 10 or 12 years ago."[2]

The "prominent member" was Mrs. Potter Palmer, wife of the owner of Chicago's famous Palmer House watering hole, and the quantity of Isabella quarters she sequestered was about 10,000, an incredible number.

Possibly as many as 15,000 Isabella quarters were sold at the Exposition and by mail to collectors and dealers in 1893, a minuscule quantity compared to the Columbian half dollar coins distributed. The biggest buyer is believed to have been the Scott Stamp & Coin Company, which purchased several thousand Isabella quarters late in the year 1893. Today in the 1990s no intact hoards are reliably reported.

1900 Lafayette silver dollars: Relatively few of these were sold to coin collectors, and not much excitement appeared in print concerning them. By a year or two later examples were available on the market for less than the $2 issue price.

Reporting in *The Numismatist,* January 1903, on a meeting of the Providence (Rhode Island) Curio & Numismatic Association, George C. Arnold noted: "Another member stated that early in November when over to New York, he had purchased four Lafayette dollars for $1.10 each, and these you remember were issued at $2.00 each, the total issue being only 50,000." Arnold went on to relate: "Some 1,800 were left in the hands of the committee, 10,000 being returned from France" (where the statue depicted on the reverse of the coin was erected; these coins were among those intended to be sold at the 1900 Paris International Exhibition).

Chicago numismatist Virgil M. Brand acquired a cloth bag filled with 1,000 pieces.[3] This was sold after 1926 when his estate was dispersed.

Over a period of time approximately 36,000 Lafayette dollars were distributed. It is believed that some of the pieces were released into circulation at face value, and it is a certainty that many who acquired them at a $2 premium subsequently tired of the novelty and simply spent the pieces, for today it is not unusual to see examples in grades such as Extremely Fine and AU.

The unsold remainder, amounting to 14,000 coins, went to the Treasury Building in Washington, D.C., where, unknown to collectors, the pieces were stored in cloth bags of 1,000 each in the same vault used to store large bundles of currency (including $5,000 and $10,000 notes).[4] In the meantime Lafayette dollars had become desirable numismatic items. In 1945 the Treasury Department converted the pieces to silver bullion, not realizing that the coins could have been

---

[1] Comment from David Lindvall, who examined the hoard, to the writer; coins were mostly in varying levels of Mint State.

[2] S.C. Stevens was well-known on the Chicago numismatic scene for many years and was an advertiser in *The Numismatist.*

[3] Information from David E. Tripp, letter, September 13, 1996.

[4] However, circa 1903 at least 10 bags of Lafayette dollars were photographed in this vault, and the image was subsequently reproduced on several widely-distributed postcards including the one published herewith.

Photograph of a vault in the Treasury Department Building, Washington, D.C., circa 1903, showing hundreds of 1,000-coin bags of silver dollars. The bags by themselves near the center, on the floor, are each marked LAFAYETTE and contained Lafayette commemorative dollars!

sold at 10 times face value or more. Aubrey and Adeline Bebee, dealers who specialized in commemoratives, learned of the cache from government records, but, upon contacting the Treasury Department, found that their inquiry did not come in time to save their destruction. Today in the 1990s no hoards are known.

1915-S Panama-Pacific International Exposition half dollars: None (no significant later hoards known; unsold pieces were melted).

1918 Lincoln-Illinois Centennial half dollars: A Springfield, Illinois, bank retained about 30,000 pieces until the "Bank Holiday" of March 1933, after which most went to dealers for a slight premium over face value, and a small number may have been released into circulation.

Apparently there was a shortage of regular half dollars in the Midwest around this time.[1] M.E. Taylor, cashier of the Iowa State Bank in Iowa City, Iowa, related that in 1918 and the first part of 1919 he had not been able to obtain any half dollar coins, despite repeated requests to the Federal Reserve Bank in Chicago. Finally, in 1919 he got a $1,000 bag, opened up these and found they were 1918 Illinois commemoratives. The bank tried to use these, but none of its customers wanted the strange-looking pieces. Taylor picked out 100 pieces and put them in the bank vault, then shipped the remainder back to Chicago. Years later he showed the 100 Illinois commemoratives to numismatist Dean Oakes, who found that they were heavily bagmarked with much evidence of shipping and handling, and concluded that the Federal Reserve had tried to dispose of them elsewhere before sending them to Iowa City. Taylor also had a 1910 Proof $10 gold piece that someone had brought to the Iowa State Bank in the early 1930s to cash in, but he had exchanged his own funds for it—which, in view of the later value of a Matte Proof $10 of this date, proved to be a good move.

Large quantities of Lincoln-Illinois commemorative halves remained on the market until early 1936, at which time the numismatic demand for commemoratives of all kinds was such that the surplus was readily absorbed by the market. In the 1980s several hundred coins were offered in nu-

[1] M.E. Taylor as told to Dean Oakes; related to the author by Oakes on August 12, 1996.

mismatic channels, but the writer does not know if these were undistributed originals or a later made-up numismatic holding.

1920 Maine Centennial half dollars: Just 50,000 Maine Centennial half dollars were struck (half of the original authorization) plus 28 pieces for the Assay Commission. Offered at $1 each, sales of the half dollars were fairly brisk, and 30,000 or more were disbursed soon after receipt. The others were kept by the office of the state treasurer and were parceled out through much of the year 1921, although quantities remained on hand for years afterward. However, most if not all were distributed by the end of the 1930s.

1920-1921 Pilgrim Tercentenary half dollars: A large hoard of thousands of 1920 Pilgrim half dollars, all in original Mint cloth shipping bags, was sold by Paramount International Coin Corporation circa 1967-1968.[1] The market was not particularly strong at the time, and most of the coins were sold for about $8 each. Today they are widely dispersed and are valued much higher.

1921 Alabama Centennial half dollars: No significant hoards have been reported.

1921 Missouri Centennial half dollars: No significant hoards have been reported.

1922 Grant Memorial half dollars: No significant hoards have been reported, although there were scattered quantities in the market through at least the mid-1920s.

1923-S Monroe Doctrine Centennial half dollars: While it is certain that thousands of pieces were sold at a premium for $1 each, by and large the sales effort was a failure, and soon thereafter "nearly all went into circulation at face value,"[2] a situation which certainly gained no friends among those who had paid $1 apiece.

Fred Woodson, a California banker who was also an active coin collector during the 1930s, recalled that such pieces were common in pocket change and were frequently received at tellers' windows. He amassed a small hoard of pieces in this manner. Graded by the author in the late 1970s the coins were found to be mostly in the AU-55 to MS-60 category.

1924 Huguenot-Walloon half dollars: Of the 142,080 Huguenot-Walloon half dollars struck at the Philadelphia Mint in February and April 1924, it is believed that 87,000 were sold for $1 each to the public, primarily through the Fifth National Bank of New York and by bulk sales to certain groups. A quantity of 55,000 pieces went back to the Treasury Department, which is said to have placed the coins into circulation. However, it seems unusual that relatively few worn pieces exist today.

1925-S California Diamond Jubilee half dollars: In 1991 dealer Dwight Manley reported that he had been advised that a Southern California man owned a small hoard of about 400 pieces which had remained intact since the year of mintage. This same individual also had hoards of other coins, including 1935-S and 1936-D San Diego half dollars.[3]

1925 Fort Vancouver Centennial half dollars: In 1982 a hoard of several hundred pieces surfaced. My firm purchased 257 of these and was told that this was a substantial majority of those found. As is usually the case when treasure troves turn up precise information was lacking, but I was eventually led to believe that no more than 500 totally came to light. One account had it that they had been the property of a historical society and museum, while another stated that they were owned by a local citizen who inadvertently turned them into a bank for face value!

In 1980, before this hoard came on the market, commemorative historian Anthony Swiatek estimated that fewer than 300 choice Mint State coins survived. Today, no hoards are known to exist.[4]

1925 Lexington-Concord Sesquicentennial half dollars: No hoards have been reported. However, many eventually found their way into general circulation, most probably from citizens who had bought them as souvenirs and later tired of the novelty.

1925 Stone Mountain Memorial half dollars: A number of hoards and groups were set aside at the time of issue, and occasionally these come on the market. At one time financier Bernard Baruch was said to have owned over 100,000 pieces. A number of Baruch's coins were sold circa 1956-1958 for $3.25 each for the benefit of the United Daughters of the Confederacy through the Citizens & Southern National Bank of Atlanta, and others have been marketed since that time.[5]

1926-1939 Oregon Trail half dollars: Wayte Raymond, who had distributed many of these coins at the time of their

1 Recollection of Raymond N. Merena to author; Merena was general manager of Paramount when these coins were sold.
2 *Coinage of Commemorative 50-Cent Pieces,* p. 29; Government Printing Office, 1936.
3 Conversation with the author, January 8, 1991.
4 Fort Vancouver (the fort, not the commemorative coins) is mentioned in Chapter 11 as part of the account concerning the loss of the *S.S. Brother Jonathan.*
5 The monograph, *The Selling of the Stone Mountain Half Dollar,* by William D. Hyder and R.W. Colbert, gives more information on this and numerous other aspects of the distribution.

mintage, had on hand for years thereafter a tremendous supply of 1933-D, 1934-D, and other Oregon commemoratives.

John J. Ford, Jr. remembers buying them from Raymond in the early 1950s for $2 apiece by the roll.[1] Ford continued: "He had even larger quantities of 1936-S. He had them all over the place. I think that Wayte took a position on these and actually owned the coins he was selling because otherwise he wouldn't have had them after they took the official distributorship away from him. Many of these were in bank-wrapped rolls of 20 coins each, with the paper rolled up tightly at each end so as to expose the center of each of the end coins. The end coins always had minute marks on them, which we didn't pay much attention to because they were badly tarnished on the ends anyhow and you couldn't easily see the marks. The machine that rolled them made marks at the end. I always remember I used to kid him that the coins at the end should be a little cheaper. I don't remember the prices, but vaguely they were two bucks apiece, some of them were two and a half, and we used to sell them by the roll.... Wayte Raymond sold me up to his death [in 1956] large numbers of Oregon Trail commemoratives, and after that his widow Olga had large numbers of commemoratives. I think she still had issues up to and including the 1936-S."[2]

1926 Sesquicentennial of American Independence half dollars: No hoards reported.

1927 Vermont Sesquicentennial half dollars: No hoards reported.

1928 Hawaiian Sesquicentennial half dollars: In 1928 a commemorative half dollar was issued to observe the 150th anniversary of the "discovery" of the Hawaiian Islands by Capt. James Cook. Designs were prepared by artist Juliette Frazer and numismatist Bruce Cartwright, Jr. (whose immense collection has been quite neglected by later historians of our hobby), both of Hawaii, and were translated into models by sculptor-engraver Chester Beach. At the Philadelphia Mint 10,000 pieces were struck for distribution, plus eight coins for the Assay Commission.

Sales to the public were effected through the Bank of Hawaii, Ltd., in Honolulu. The issue price was set at $2 per coin. Action was brisk, and thousands of half dollars went to residents of Hawaii and additional thousands to collectors on the mainland. Almost immediately, the coins were sold out, and the market price advanced as specimens were later traded.

A quantity of these, variously estimated as being from 500 to 1,500 pieces, was said to have been purchased by investors and kept off the market. Possibly some coins remain intact today in the 1990s.

An unrelated hoard traces its origin to a gesture of appreciation to his employees by the president of the Bank of Hawaii. He put one of the commemorative coins on display and invited staff members to buy one wholesale for about $1 or $1.50 (recollections differ). The displayed coin was swiped. The bank president became angry about this and locked up the remaining pieces, 137 in all, and they remained untouched in a vault for over a half century thereafter.

In 1985 the Bank of Hawaii brought the hoard back into daylight, consigned them to auction, and on January 23, 1986, the coins were sold to a new generation of numismatists. Today, a Mint State 1928 Hawaiian retains its status as the most desired single "type" or design in the entire commemorative half dollar series.[3]

1934-1938 Boone Bicentennial half dollars: In the 1930s Howard E. MacIntosh, owner of Tatham Stamp & Coin Company, purchased many hundreds—if not thousands—of Boone coins and sets of various issues. At the time of MacIntosh's death in 1958 many hundreds of pieces remained. These were later sold by New Netherlands Coin Co. Concerning these, John J. Ford, Jr., recalled: "Among the hoard of commemoratives I remember the 1935 Boone sets with 'Small 1934,' which they only made 2,000 sets of, and MacIntosh had 180 to 200 sets."[4] Maurice Rosen recalled that when he worked at First Coinvestors, Inc., in the early 1970s the firm purchased "two superb Mint State roll sets each of the 1937-P-D-S and 1938 P-D-S Boones; these were acquired from John J. Ford, Jr. [New Netherlands Coin Co.], I believe during 1972-1973. There were other deals

[1] Interview with the author, February 20, 1991.

[2] Olga Raymond lived in an apartment overlooking the East River in Manhattan. The author (QDB) recalls visiting her one day circa 1965 to discuss coins, after which she telephoned New York City toy store F.A.O. Schwarz and had two large stuffed toy rabbits delivered to my sons Wynn and Lee; we were staying at the Plaza Hotel for a few days.

[3] Bowers and Merena sale of the Bank of Hawaii Hoard, 1986. Although there are two other commemorative half dollars—the 1935 Hudson and 1935 Old Spanish Trail—with similar mintages of 10,000 pieces, each of these two was sold primarily to dealers and collectors, with very few going to the general public. Thus, unlike the case of the 1928 Hawaiian halves, most of the other two varieties were safely preserved.

[4] Recollection of John J. Ford, Jr., to the author, February 20, 1991.

including a few rolls each of Clevelands, Elgins, Long Islands, and Roanokes."[1]

1934 Maryland Tercentenary half dollars: No hoards reported.

1934-1938 Texas Centennial half dollars: Most were distributed or melted. B. Max Mehl bought at least 1,000 by 1936,[2] but these were probably all sold to his mailing list (Mehling list as he called it) customers.

1935-1939 Arkansas Centennial half dollars: No hoards reported.

1935 Connecticut Tercentenary half dollars: No hoards reported.

1935 Hudson half dollars: None in later years, although in 1935 virtually the entire mintage was sold intact to two dealers in a transaction that took the numismatic community by surprise. These two professionals later reaped handsome profits by selling them for several dollars apiece.

1935 Old Spanish Trail half dollars: These were distributed by promoter L.W. Hoffecker of El Paso, Texas, who issued many pronouncements about how fair he was being in the sale of the pieces, how they were soon sold out, etc., etc.[3]

However, much of what Hoffecker said and wrote was false. In a letter to Abe Kosoff, Numismatic Gallery, Beverly Hills, California, February 10, 1953, Hoffecker revealed, probably unintentionally, that he indeed had a quantity of Old Spanish Trail half dollars on hand: "Received your letter of the 9th and say we have a very limited number of the Old Spanish Trail coins, and many collectors seem to like to buy from the designer of the coin, and we have no trouble selling 2 or 3 coins at $15 each every week." This was equal to a quantity of 100 to 150 coins sold per year.

In a letter to B. Max Mehl, dated February 27, 1954, Mrs. L.W. Hoffecker stated: "In reference to the Old Spanish Trail half dollars, we only had 12 of these coins and Mr. Hoffecker decided to keep them for his grandchildren and great grandchildren, as the coins will mean more to them than the money would mean to him." At the time Hoffecker was very ill and under a doctor's care.

When coins from L.W. Hoffecker's estate were sold by Superior Galleries, February 1987, the following commentary appeared on p. 372 of the catalogue (emphasis ours): "The following group of SIXTY-THREE Old Spanish Trail half dollars...comes from the estate of L.W. Hoffecker...."

In the late 1970s the estate of Rev. Edward M. Catich, a Catholic priest who taught (but did not have his own parish) and was a coin dealer on the side, was appraised by Dean Oakes. Found were 400 Uncirculated 1935 Old Spanish Trail half dollars, which were subsequently sold for a million dollars at the height of the 1979-1980 coin investment boom.[4]

1935-1936 San Diego half dollars: Although thousands of these coins were sold at the California-Pacific International Exposition and to the distributor's mail-order clients in the 1930s, quantities remained for years afterward.

Anthony Swiatek and Walter Breen, writing in 1980, related that a large hoard of 31,050 pieces of the 1935-S issue, a staggering quantity amounting to a significant percentage of the net coinage after melting, was retained by an official associated with the Exposition and was dispersed after 1966. In the market of the 1970s and 1980s quantities of this particular coin changed hands from time to time.

Dwight Manley advised the author that beginning in the early 1980s a Southern California individual, whose grandfather had been associated with the Exposition and who had obtained them for face value, dispersed over 5,000 1935-S San Diego half dollars from a holding estimated at 10,000 and also sold his complete holding of 5,000 to 6,000 1936-D pieces.[5] The owner of the half dollars had retained them for many years and in the early 1980s had given some as Christmas presents to employees. The employees took them to San Diego area coin shops and sold the coins at prices from $20 to $100 or more. Eventually the owner learned of Dwight Manley, and most, if not all, later transactions were handled through him. Many thousands of coins from the hoard were sent to the Professional Coin Grading Service, and most were assigned grades in the MS-64 and MS-65 categories.

1936 Albany Charter half dollars: In October 1936 the full authorized coinage of 25,000 pieces, plus 13 extra examples for the Assay Commission, was effected at the Philadelphia Mint. The Albany Dongan Charter Coin Committee offered them for sale at $2 each. By this point in autumn 1936 interest in commemoratives had dwindled sharply, and despite a lot of advertising puffery and hyperbole on the part of the issuing committee, quantities amounting to thousands of pieces remained unsold. The committee continued offering Albany half dollars for six more years.

At one time Abe Kosoff was given the opportunity to purchase the entire remaining stock for just $50 above face value for the lot but could find no takers! In 1943 some 7,342 unsold, unwanted coins were sent to the Philadelphia Mint and melted. However, quantities still remained on hand. Les Zeller advised the author that circa 1954 it became known that the State Bank of Albany had between 1,600 and 2,400 undistributed pieces in its vaults and was willing to sell them for the issue price of $2 each. Jacob Cheris, Charles French, Dr. Kenneth Sartoris, and other local dealers and collectors quickly purchased the entire supply.

---

1 Letter, March 28, 1991.

2 *Coinage of Commemorative 50-Cent Pieces,* Government Printing Office, 1936.

3 Details and specific references appear in Bowers, *Commemorative Coins of the United States: A Complete Encyclopedia,* pp. 301-311.

4 Dean Oakes, interview, August 12, 1996. Father Catich, who always wore a black cleric collar, was a familiar figure at coin conventions in the 1950s, often in the company of his friend and fellow Iowan, Loyd Gettys.

5 Telephone conversation with the author, January 8, 1991.

1936 Bridgeport Centennial half dollars: It was announced in *The Numismatist* in February 1938 that the unsold Bridgeport half dollars had been acquired by the Community Chest and Council, Inc. of Bridgeport, which was going to offer them for sale. A quantity estimated to be on the order of several thousand pieces still remained unsold, and was eventually wholesaled for a small premium above face value through dealers.

Years later, Toivo Johnson, dealer in commemoratives who was a prolific advertiser in the *Numismatic Scrapbook* and who did business by mail from East Holden, Maine, acquired a large quantity, perhaps up to 2,000 pieces or so. I bought rolls of these pieces from Johnson in the 1950s and recall that substantial quantities were available to anyone desiring to purchase them. During that decade it was common practice to see rolls of Bridgeport and also Robinson-Arkansas and Cleveland half dollars change hands at conventions; these were the three issues in particular from the 1930s that existed in quantity in numismatic circles then. The residue of the Toivo Johnson coins was later sold to Joe Flynn, Jr., of Kansas City, and to First Coinvestors, Inc., of New York.

Maurice Rosen reported that when he worked at First Coinvestors circa 1972, "We dispersed 1,400 specimens of the Bridgeport half dollar. The coins were acquired from Toivo Johnson. Our cost was $25 each. These were 'original rolls,' assuming they were packaged that way in 1936, and based on today's grading would probably be at least MS-64."[1]

Walter Breen once referred to P.T. Barnum, whose visage graces the obverse of this coin, "the patron saint of coin collectors." Barnum had a coin collection himself, in connection with his American Museum (lower New York City) and other attractions, but the writer has never seen a numismatic description of what was on display. One collection was mentioned as follows by veteran dealer Augustus B. Sage in 1867:[2] "About seven years ago the old Museum (Barnum's) contained a very fair cabinet; a miscellaneous collection it is true, but scattered here and there in the cases were some very rare specimens of our earlier coinage. At the time of the 'clock excitement,' I believe, the rarer specimens were purchased at 'one dollar each all round' by a prominent collector of New Jersey. There can be no question, I take it, that the exhibition of the cases of coins in Barnum's at the time I have referred to, was an incentive for a great number of present collectors to turn their attention to the subject; and the public exhibition of such frames in all museums tends greatly to stimulate the study."

This sale of the coins to a New Jersey collector circa 1860 was for the best, for Sage no doubt knew—but forgot to say—that the American Museum was gutted by fire in 1865, on July 13 to be exact. Far better it is for the coins to be hidden in a New Jersey collection than to be molten blobs in the cellar of the burned-out museum. On the other hand, perhaps Sage had a poor memory, for the "clock excitement" to which he referred was the failure of the Jerome Clock Company and the great financial difficulty Barnum, as cosigner of the company's notes, had in 1856.

Interior of Barnum's Museum (later known as Wood's Museum), New York City. P.T. Barnum, the most famous figure in Bridgeport, Connecticut's history, furnished the subject for the city's 1936 commemorative half dollar.

1936 Cincinnati half dollars: None are reported from hoards after the distributor and his friends sold those they had held back; this was within a short time following the original issuance.

1936 Cleveland-Great Lakes half dollars: Enough 1936-dated Cleveland Centennial half dollars were minted that anyone desiring an example could have as many as he or she wanted. For years thereafter thousands of pieces remained unsold. Many of these went to dealers Abe Kosoff and Sol Kaplan, both close friends of distributor Thomas G. Melish (who also distributed the Cincinnati half dollars). In an effort to stimulate interest in Cleveland half dollars and to increase the value of those already in his possession, Sol Kaplan ran numerous advertisements seeking to buy additional pieces. As late as the 1950s it was not unusual for rolls (20 coins per roll) to be offered at coin conventions.

1936 Columbia Sesquicentennial half dollars: No hoards reported.

1936 Delaware Tercentenary half dollars: All but 4,022 were sold of the 25,000 struck for distribution. The undistributed coins were returned to the Mint to be melted. As was the case with several other 1936 issues, large quantities of this issue were common in numismatic circles for the next decade or two.

[1] Letter, March 28, 1991. Also, Anthony Swiatek, "Barnum Appears on Bridgeport Obverse," *Coin World,* May 29, 1991, p. 96.
[2] Cf. *American Journal of Numismatics,* May 1867.

Head of the "Pioneer Scout" as depicted on the 1936 Elgin half dollar, as photographed in 1996 in the studio used by the late Trygve Rovelstad, who created the design for the coin. (Courtesy of Gloria Rovelstad).

1936 Elgin Centennial half dollars: Most pieces were sold in or near the year indicated, with the balance returned to the Philadelphia Mint to be melted. The distributor, L.W. Hoffecker, kept about 250 coins which he parceled out over a long period of time. A few hundred others were owned at one time by Howard E. MacIntosh of Tatham Stamp & Co. Gloria Rovelstad, widow of the engraver, retained a few pieces years thereafter, some of which were sold to numismatists in the 1980s and 1990s (including to the author). The 1936 Elgin half dollar continues to make the news, and in 1996 a float depicting the design was a highlight of a parade in that Illinois city. Interestingly, the Pioneer Memorial, for which certain funds were designated in 1936, still has not been built, but not for lack of trying. More money needs to be raised.

1936 Gettysburg half dollars: No hoards reported.

1936 Long Island Tercentenary half dollars: In an interview with the author, John J. Ford, Jr. told of a hoard which surfaced in the 1950s:[1]

"Of my experiences with commemoratives one of the most memorable occurred sometime in 1953 or 1954. I was at the [New Netherlands Coin Co.] office one day and was feeling a bit ill, when I received a telephone call from a guy who inquired, 'Is this the Scott Stamp & Coin Company?' I said 'Yes,' because I didn't feel up to explaining to him that the office was no longer Scott's, but was now New Netherlands' and that my name wasn't Scott.

"He said, 'I have a half dollar here, and it's a funny half dollar as it's got two men's heads on the front.' I thought at the time that this could have been one of any number of commemorative half dollars. I then asked, 'What does it have on the back?' He said there was a ship. Immediately I knew that it was probably a 1936 Long Island Tercentenary half dollar. I went on to say that if it was in brand-new condition, absolutely brand new, I probably could pay two dollars for it.

"It was his turn, and he said, 'How many would you buy for that price? Would you buy 100?' I said, 'Well, if I am going to pay two dollars apiece I want to buy all you've got. How many do you have?' He said, very hesitantly, 'One thousand." And then I said, 'Who are you?' At this point he was only a voice on the other end of the telephone line. "He said, 'I'm the cash teller at the Williamsburg Savings Bank in Brooklyn. We were checking out the cash, and I found these bags that say 'Long Island Tercentenary Commission,' and they have these half dollars in them.' So, I said, 'Well, how many are in a bag?' And he said, 'Five hundred dollars' worth.' I said, 'That's 1,000 pieces. I will give you 2,000 bucks in cash for the bag.' The guy—in those days bank tellers were making $50 or $60 a week—nearly flipped. So he said, 'Where are you located?' I said, 'Fifth Avenue at West 47th Street, One West 47th.' Then he said, 'I'll take a cab and I'll be over there in an hour.'

"I went to cash a $2,000 check at the Chase Bank around the corner and was waiting for this guy. He was about 25 years old, and he was huffing and puffing carrying this 30 pound bag, or whatever it weighed, in the elevator and into the office. It had a metal seal on it which had been opened, apparently by him, to see what these things looked like. He was still huffing and puffing—I guess he was so excited the adrenaline was flowing. In my haste I just took a scissors and cut the top off the bag and looked in—and they were all brilliant white Uncirculated Long Islands. I gave him the $2,000 cash. I carried them into our back office, and Charles

[1] February 20, 1991.

Wormser and I put them in envelopes and sold them for four bucks apiece to anybody that wanted them. I remember Werner Amelingmeier[1] bought about 200 or 300. About 15 years later I bought them back from Amelingmeier for $18 each and sold them to Stanley Apfelbaum, who was just launching his company, First Coinvestors. Apfelbaum marked them up to about $40 and sold them to investors.

"Anyway, several weeks after my deal with the bank teller we still had about half of the bag of Long Island coins left, and my partner, Charles, was getting nervous, like he often did, and was wondering what we were going to do with the rest of them. Just about this time, the bank teller called again and said he had found another bag. Charles said to me, 'Don't pay him as much. Pay him a dollar and a half.' I told Charles that I couldn't pay him less, so I paid him two bucks per coin. New Netherlands Coin Co. had Long Island half dollars in quantity for years after that. We bought at least two bags from the guy, possibly three."

1936 Lynchburg Sesquicentennial half dollars: No hoards reported.

1936 Norfolk Bicentennial half dollars: Although many unsold pieces were returned to the Mint and melted, at least several thousand were wholesaled to dealers. Bulk quantities remained in numismatic circles for years afterward.

1936 Rhode Island Tercentenary half dollars: Well-known dealer Horace M. Grant was in the middle of the distribution of this issue, which was fraught with phony news releases, made-up stories of the pieces being sold out within *six hours* of being put on sale, etc. In later years at least two large groups of hundreds or more sets (each set had three coins, one each of the Philadelphia, Denver, and San Francisco varieties) came to light.

After the death in 1958 of Howard E. MacIntosh, John J. Ford, Jr., handled many of his coins, and later commented: "MacIntosh had immense quantities of commemorative half dollars, which he had bought from the issuing commissions. How he did it, I don't know, but he had the coins. I do know that he was very thick with Horace Grant in Providence, Rhode Island, and that MacIntosh had a hell of a lot of Rhode Island halves."[2]

The Amon G. Carter, Jr. estate (of Fort Worth, Texas), dispersed by John N. Rowe III in the 1980s, contained hundreds of Rhode Island coins which had been held since the 1930s.

1936 Robinson-Arkansas half dollars: In *The Numismatist* in February 1939, Stack's of New York City—the original distributor of the issue—placed an advertisement offering for sale to the highest bidder unsold 500 Robinson-Arkansas half dollars (and also 500 sets of 1935 Texas commemorative half dollars). Bids were to be received on or before February 15, 1939. This represented only a small portion of the unsold Robinson-Arkansas pieces.

Finally, the remainder of coins, said to have amounted to 8,000 pieces, was wholesaled to Abe Kosoff, who maintained a coin business in the same city. Other large lots were sold to still other dealers. There were large quantities of unsold Robinson-Arkansas half dollars in dealers' hands as late as the 1950s. The present writer recalls buying bulk groups of them from the Hollinbeck-Kagin Coin Company (of Des Moines; see below) and Toivo Johnson (of Maine). An original mint bag of 1,000 coins was reported to exist in Arkansas in 1991.

Arthur M. Kagin related this:[3]

"In about December of 1945, shortly after being discharged from the Army, I was visiting in New York. Joe Stack offered me 4,000 Robinson Arkansas half dollars at 85¢ each, which I bought. He had paid 65¢ each for them. Stack's was the distributor for the Arkansas issues. If the commission returned the unsold coins to the mint for melting they would have received only the face value for them. By selling the unsold remainder to Stack's at 65¢ each they were still ahead at 15¢ each. I believe there were about 9,000 unsold of the original 25,265 struck.

"At that time there appeared to be a market for about 10,000 commemoratives of limited nationwide interest such as Spanish Trail, Hudson, etc. For more general interest coins the market appeared to be around 15,000. Therefore, commemorative half dollar issues of 20,000 to 25,000 usually had unsold remainders which were later sold at discounts rather than returning them to the mint for melting. I recall Joe Barnet (I believe he was in Brooklyn) having various commemoratives available to dealers at somewhat less than the official issue price. In 1946 we sold the Robinsons at $1 to $1.25 each. By the time they had advanced to $1.50 the market softened for commemoratives. About 10 years ago we finally sold the remaining specimens of the original 4,000 at about $50 each."

1936-S San Francisco-Oakland Bay Bridge half dollars: As recently as the 1960s it was not unusual to see small quantities of these offered on the collectors' market. By now most such groups probably have been dispersed.

1936 Wisconsin Territorial Centennial half dollars: Remainder coins were still being sold by the state in the 1950s. By now all coins are believed to be in numismatic hands.

1936 York County Tercentenary half dollars: These were distributed by numismatist Walter P. Nichols, who endeavored to secure a wide market for them and to be honest in his news releases. After the initial burst of enthusiasm about 6,000 remained unsold and continued to be distributed through the 1950s, well after Nichols' death (August 8, 1941).

Historian Arlie Slabaugh relates the Association sold pieces in the 1950s for $15.50 per group of 10, at which

[1] John's personal friend, an automobile dealer on Long Island who had an investment interest in coins.

[2] Interview with the author, February 20, 1991.

[3] Letter, August 24, 1996.

time the remainders were quickly liquidated. When the writer's firm auctioned coins from the Nichols estate in 1984, a few York County half dollars were included, so technically it can be said that complete distribution was not concluded until that late time.

1937 Antietam half dollars: By any account the Antietam half dollar effort was a failure, for of the 50,000 coins produced for general sale, 32,000 were eventually returned to the Treasury Department for melting. By this time the heady market for new issues, which had characterized the numismatic scene in 1935 and 1936, had collapsed. No significant holdings ever appeared later, indicating that there were no dealers or hoarders brave enough to stock up on them.

Anyone wanting to have some fun with figures and statistics needs but contemplate the past market for commemorative half dollars. Demand for these has waxed and waned on any number of occasions. When the market is "hot" there are not enough coins to go around, everyone madly scrambles to buy them, and prices soar. When the market is quiet, prices drop, and the coins can't be given away (figuratively speaking). Of course, during such market slumps is precisely when wise investors should be buying!

1937 Roanoke half dollars: In January 1937, 25,015 Roanoke half dollars were struck at Philadelphia, followed by 25,015 more at the same mint in June. These coins were released too late to catch even a vestige of the wave of enthusiasm that characterized much of the market the year before, and only 29,000 were ever sold, many of these not until several years after the original offering. 21,000 coins went back to the Philadelphia Mint to be melted. Although small numbers from a few dozen or so upward were stocked by dealers at the time (such as Howard E. MacIntosh), it is believed that there were no significant hoards.

1938 New Rochelle half dollars: In April 1937 the Philadelphia Mint struck 25,015 1938-dated New Rochelle commemorative half dollars, which were turned over to the First National Bank of New Rochelle, for the government felt that issuing such pieces through the Westchester County Coin Club (which had conceived the idea) would set an unfavorable precedent. However, in retrospect it is hard to see how this could have been worse than selling 1935 Old Spanish Trail and 1936 Elgin coins to coin dealer L.W. Hoffecker or shipping the entire production of 1936 Cincinnati halves to numismatist Thomas G. Melish.

While citizens of New Rochelle undoubtedly purchased numerous examples, the main market consisted of collectors and dealers. When all was said and done, 9,749 remainder coins were melted. Just prior to this some members of the Westchester Coin Club purchased hundreds of unsold coins for face value.

George M. Cohan immortalized the town (and mortified many of its citizens with his lyrics) in his 1905 song, *Forty-Five Minutes from Broadway.* New Rochelle was, in the early twentieth century, *the* place to have a suburban residence within easy commuting distance of New York City.

1946 Iowa Centennial half dollars: In November 1946, 100,057 coins were struck and shipped to the Iowa Centennial Committee in Des Moines in the same state. No new commemorative designs had been produced since the 1938 New Rochelle, and no continued strikings of earlier designs had been made since the straggling 1939 Arkansas and Oregon Trail Memorial P-D-S sets had been finally laid to rest. In 1946 the coin market was strong, and older commemoratives sold well. The new Iowa pieces found a ready sale at $2.50 each to residents of Iowa and $3 to buyers located elsewhere; 5,000 examples being reserved for out-of-state purchasers. The effort was a great success, and the available pieces were sold out by March 1947, by which time the price had been raised to $3 to all comers.

However, 1,000 coins were set aside for future distribution, 500 for the 150th anniversary of statehood in 1996 and an additional 500 for the Bicentennial celebration in the year 2046. In 1992, a few years ahead of time, the state began marketing its 1996-earmarked reserve, but as the state's minimum bid price of $500 plus $10 handling was several times what coin dealers were selling them for, interest among numismatists was sluggish.[1] By that time the unsold pieces were stored in a vault in the Norwest Bank, 666 Walnut Street, Des Moines. As of press time for this book, unsold remainders are still on hand from the 1996 allotment, and 500 further pieces remain in the wings for distribution in 2046.

1946-1951 Booker T. Washington half dollars: From 1946 to 1951, several million of these commemoratives were struck. Quantities varied widely, from a high of 1,000,546 1946 Philadelphia Mint coins to only 6,004 each for the 1949 and 1950 P-D-S sets. While many coins were sold to numismatists and some went to the general public, it is believed that most were melted.

These coins never achieved popularity with collectors, despite the relatively low net (after melting) mintages of certain P-D-S sets. The vast quantity of 1,581,631 unsold pieces was melted, but, as no specific inventory was kept of certain dates and mints, the net number distributed cannot be determined with certainty.

In the 1960s Stephen J. Ruddel, an Arlington, Virginia, rare coin dealer, obtained thousands of hitherto undistributed sets and made a strong effort to popularize and distribute them to a new generation of numismatists, and undoubtedly many were sold this way. Undaunted by lack of sales success, the same originators of the Booker T. Washington half dollars caused more pieces to be struck, the new Carver-Washington pieces issued from 1951 through 1954.

---

1 "Iowa Prepares for Auction of 1946 Statehood Half Dollars," *Coin World,* March 2, 1992, p. 55. Argie Manolis, "Price for '46 Iowa Commems Too High?" *Coin World,* July 27, 1992, p. 32. One commemorative expert stated that at $510 the coins were "definitely worth the price," while another was quoted as saying the price was outrageous. The coins ranged in grade from MS-63 to MS-65 or so.

Burnside Bridge across Antietam Creek, as photographed in September 1862. This structure was the center of some of the most intense fighting of the Civil War. In 1937 it was depicted on a silver commemorative half dollar.

1951-1954 Carver-Washington half dollars: In addition to the metal available from melting down earlier-dated Booker T. Washington half dollars, an unused authorization remained for earlier pieces that had not been struck, and this could be applied to the new Carver-Washington issues as well, giving a maximum authorization of 3,415,631 pieces. Coins were produced in P-D-S sets of three, plus additional strikings of several issues—1952 Philadelphia, 1953-S, and 1954-S—intended for wide distribution (including through banks). The effort was a failure, and many pieces were dumped at or close to face value. In the meantime the collectors' market absorbed several thousand or more P-D-S sets, but most sets remained unsold. Eventually 1,091,198 Carver-Washington coins were returned for melting.

Years later John J. Ford, Jr., of New Netherlands Coin Co., recalled:[1] "In the early 1950s we did business with the Chase Bank before it became the Chase Manhattan Bank. We had a very fine relationship, and Charles Wormser was a close friend of Vernon Brown, curator of the Chase Money Museum. Any coin deals that came to the bank Vernon Brown would refer to us. Around 1955 they had large quantities of Booker T. Washington and Washington-Carver half dollars of certain dates and mints. These were available at face value, but nobody wanted them. The bank had trouble getting rid of them to anyone. With some effort I was able to market these. You couldn't sell the P-D-S sets, but there was a limited market for rolls and quantities of particular issues, like the large-mintage 1950-S, 1951, 1952, 1953-S, and 1954-S. We would get these in large quantities for the face value of 50 cents apiece, and then I would pay some guy a $10 or $15 tip for bringing them over to New Netherlands. They were leftovers, remainders, what have you. The issuing commission was very poorly operated from what I understood at the time. We would take these things and I would sell them to guys who were looking for coins as an investment for sixty-five cents apiece or something. I think I sold Aubrey Bebee a large number of them. I know Aubrey always liked deals where he could get a big quantity of something. This situation lasted two or three years. I remember taking them to conventions, but nobody wanted them.... In fact, I probably even spent some for lunch a couple of times to get rid of them."

Gold Commemoratives

Put away: before 1930
Found: various times
Treasure: Gold coins

The first United States commemorative gold coins offered in quantity as souvenirs and sold at a premium were the 1903-dated Louisiana Purchase Exposition gold dollars in two styles: one bearing the portrait of Thomas Jefferson and the other of William McKinley. From that time until 1926, nine varieties of gold dollars, two of the $2.50 denomination, and two $50 varieties were struck in this metal.[2]

The high face value of gold coins militated against dealers or collectors saving pieces in quantity. Nearly all unsold pieces were returned to the Treasury Department and melted, with a few exceptions as noted below.[3]

Coins are listed in chronological order of production and distribution:

1903 Louisiana Purchase Exposition gold $1, Jefferson portrait: Large sales were anticipated, and 125,000 were struck for this purpose, with the promoter being numismatist Farran Zerbe.[4] Sales fell far below expectations. Circa 1914 some 215,000 coins—a mixture of both portrait types, Jefferson and McKinley—were converted back into bullion by the Treasury Department. In the meantime vast unsold quantities were available for a decade after the original issue. Today, Jefferson pieces are somewhat more often seen than are McKinley coins, indicating that fewer were melted.

1903 Louisiana Purchase Exposition gold $1, McKinley portrait: Large sales were anticipated, and 125,000 were struck for this purpose, the same number as for the McKinley portrait pieces. Circa 1914, most were melted. Meanwhile, quantities were available on the numismatic market until that time.

1904-1905 Lewis and Clark Centennial gold $1: Of the 25,028 pieces struck bearing the date 1904, 10,025 were sold, and 15,003 were melted down at the San Francisco Mint. About the same number were sold of the issue dated

[1] Interview with the author, February 20, 1991.

[2] The 1848 gold $2.50 with CAL. counterstamped on the reverse was produced at the Mint using metal recently received from California and is truly the first American commemorative. However, these were not sold at a premium to the general public.

[3] For complete information on the designers, issuing commissions, methods of distribution, prices over the years, and other aspects of silver and gold commemoratives, the writer's *Commemorative Coins of the United States: A Complete Encyclopedia*, 1991, gives much information for the specialist, as does *The Encyclopedia of United States Silver & Gold Commemorative Coins*, 1981, by Anthony Swiatek and Walter Breen. *The Commemorative Trail*, edited by Helen Carmody and published by the Society for U.S. Commemorative Coins, provides a continuing source for research findings, collecting ideas, and other topics of interest.

[4] The highest award bestowed by the American Numismatic Association is the Farran Zerbe Award, and perhaps as one of the honorees the author

1905 out of 25,000 made. No hoards are known to have survived to later years.

1915-S Panama-Pacific gold $1: 25,034 Panama-Pacific International Exposition gold dollars were struck, the extra 34 being reserved for assay. Sales were through agent Farran Zerbe. Sales of the gold dollars at the Exposition were satisfactory, more or less, and it is believed that thousands were sold. However, in the autumn of 1916, when sales efforts terminated, 10,000 remaining coins were shipped to the Treasury for melting, although Zerbe retained an ample quantity of additional unsold pieces. The net number of Panama-Pacific commemorative gold dollars eventually distributed totaled 15,000.

Examples of the 1915-S Panama-Pacific gold dollar remained plentiful on the numismatic market for decades thereafter with B. Max Mehl in particular having a sizable holding. Some of Mehl's coins were later sold in the 1950s to Sol Kaplan, a Cincinnati dealer, through the efforts of Abe Kosoff, who obtained them from Mehl. It is believed that by now in the 1990s all hoards have been dispersed.

1915-S Panama-Pacific gold $2.50: In June 1915 the San Francisco Mint produced 10,017 Panama-Pacific commemorative quarter eagles. After November 1916, 3,251 Panama-Pacific quarter eagles were returned to the Treasury Department for melting (17 assay coins had been melted earlier), leaving a net distribution figure of 6,749 pieces including many which Farran Zerbe kept at face value for future sales. However, any that Zerbe retained are believed to have been sold within the next decade or so.

1915-S Panama-Pacific gold $50, octagonal shape: 1,509 octagonal $50 pieces and 1,510 round versions were subsequently minted. Sales were not up to expectations, and after November 1916 a large remaining quantity went to the melting pot, leaving a net issuance of 645 pieces. Additionally, the majority of the round $50 were reduced to bullion, leaving a net issuance of just 483 pieces, a number which was to remain the lowest distribution quantity figure for any United States commemorative coin. No hoards of either variety remained for later distribution.

1915-S Panama-Pacific gold $50, round shape: No hoards reported.

1916-1917 McKinley gold $1: In August and October 1916, 20,026 McKinley commemorative gold dollars were struck at the Philadelphia Mint. In February 1917 a further 10,014 McKinley gold dollars of the same design—these dated 1917—were struck at the same facility. Of the 30,000 1916- and 1917-dated McKinley gold dollars produced for distribution, about 20,000 were sold, mostly bearing the date 1916.

About 10,000 were returned to the Mint for melting. Half or more of the melted coins are believed to have been dated 1917, thus constituting much of the mintage of the latter date. Apparently, the general public bought very few 1917 coins at the time of their initial offering. It is believed that Fort Worth, Texas, dealer B. Max Mehl bought about 7,000 of the 1916 coins and 3,000 or so of the 1917. Mehl sold them to his mail-order clients for many years thereafter. A few other dealers may have purchased lesser quantities from the unsold remainder.

1922 Grant Memorial gold $1: These were made in two varieties. In March 1922 the Philadelphia Mint struck 5,000 gold dollars with a small incuse star in the right field, and 5,016 without this feature. Few details are known about the sales of the gold dollars, except that B. Max Mehl eventually came into possession of thousands of coins, paying little over face value for them. In the opinion of the present writer, only a few were sold to the general public, and not many were sold to numismatists at the time of issue. Most were wholesaled to dealers, who parceled them out for a long period of time thereafter.

1926 Sesquicentennial gold $2.50: 200,226 Sesquicentennial quarter eagles were struck at the Philadelphia Mint, the odd 226 being for assay purposes. The Sesquicentennial Exposition itself proved to be a financial failure. Later 154,207 quarter eagles (or more than three quarters of the entire mintage) went to the melting pot, thus drawing the curtain on the last of the early United States commemorative gold coins. No significant hoards or groups are believed to have been saved apart from the one mentioned below.

The Parke-Bernet sale of June 9, 1976, Lots 49 through 72, featured 71 examples of the 1926 Sesquicentennial gold quarter eagle including a bank-wrapped roll containing 46 pieces that had been found in a safe deposit box.[1]

---

should not comment further. However, Zerbe in his era seems to have exploited the ANA for all it was worth, and today a survey of historical records would not seem to place him among even the top 10 who have been ANA benefactors in deeds or money. Worthy of the mantle would be Dr. George F. Heath, founder of *The Numismatist* and an organizer of the ANA, who devoted much of his life and money to the Association.

1 Information from the cataloguer, David E. Tripp, letter, September 13, 1996.

CHAPTER 15

The Great Treasury Hoard

Stored: 19th century onward
Found: various times, notably 1962-1964
Treasure: Bags of silver dollars

The greatest of all American coin hoards traces its roots to the Bland-Allison Act of February 28, 1878. At the time silver prices were depressed on the international market, and hard times were being felt in Nevada, Colorado, and other domestic areas of production.

In a classic case of a political boondoggle, western mining interests influenced congressmen to have Uncle Sam support the silver market. Beginning in 1878, the Treasury Department was forced to buy tens of millions of ounces of silver each year and to coin it into dollar coins that were neither wanted nor needed for commerce. While I am against boondoggles as much as anyone (outside of elected office in Washington) is, if there have to be such things, then this certainly is or, rather, was a good one!

In 1878 the Philadelphia, Carson City, and San Francisco mints began turning out Morgan-design silver "cartwheels" in unprecedented quantities, joined by the production facilities of the New Orleans Mint in 1879. From then until 1904, and again in the year 1921, hundreds of millions of Morgan dollars were struck. Most were put up in cloth bags of 1,000 coins and stored in vaults in the Treasury Department (Washington, D.C.), the various mints, and even post offices. In fact, the government ran out of space, and in one heroic instance Uncle Sam built a vault—looking quite like a Greek temple—in the open courtyard of the Philadelphia Mint and stuffed it with shiny new dollars.

In 1918 the Pittman Act mandated the melting of many of the long-stored dollars, and 270,232,722 were converted to bullion. In true government fashion, a few years later in 1921 over 85 million *more* Morgan dollars were minted, most of which again went directly into storage. Peace design silver dollars were minted from 1921 to 1935 and, again, were mostly stored by the Treasury.

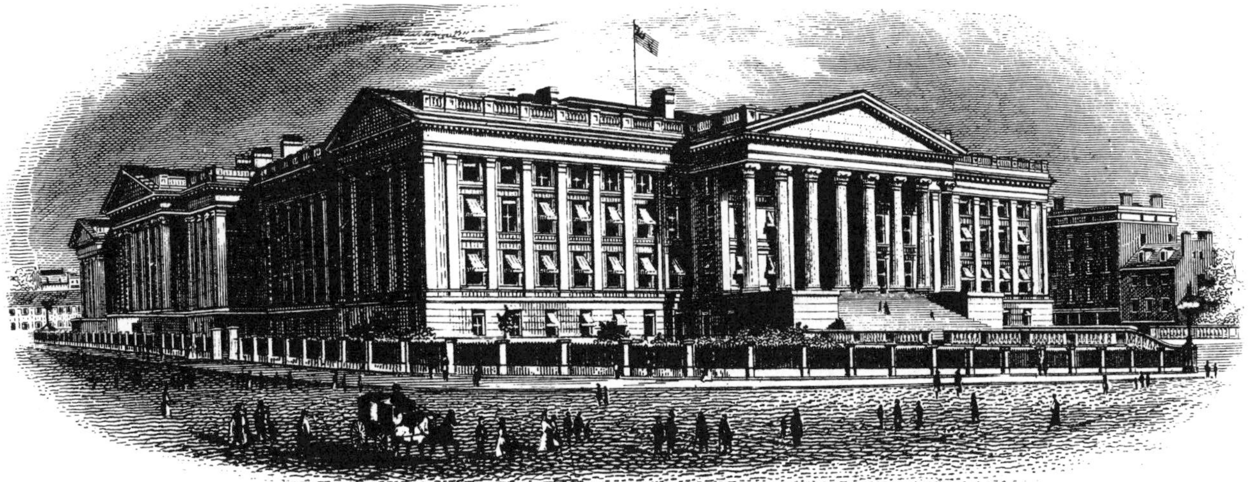

The Treasury Building in Washington, D.C., on Pennsylvania Avenue next to the White House, was the storage depot for many years for rare Carson City Morgan silver dollars and other numismatic treasures.

Meanwhile, over a period of years the Treasury Department would release bags of earlier Morgan and the later Peace dollars, especially in December during the Christmas season when there was a call for silver dollars as gifts. Occasionally a bag of previously "rare" coins would be released, such as several different Carson City dollar dates in the 1880s that were released in the 1930s, much to the delight of numismatists. At one time the 1889-S Morgan dollar was considered to be a prime rarity—indeed perhaps the rarest mintmarked issue in the series—but bags were released, and it became easily available.

By 1962 the Morgan dollar market was a side branch of numismatics—hardly in the limelight, but not in the shadows either. More popular were series such as Lincoln cents and Buffalo nickels. In the prime reference on values, the *Guide Book of United States Coins,* the great rarity among silver dollars was the 1903-O, which catalogued $1,500 in Uncirculated grade, or more than any other variety. Even if you had $1,500 to spend in 1962, such coins were not to be found. It was believed that only a few Uncirculated pieces existed.

Then, from deep in a vault in the Philadelphia Mint that had been sealed in 1929, in November 1962 came a few 1,000-coin bags, then more, filled to the brim with sparkling, brilliant 1903-O dollars! Accompanying them were two other highly prized rarities, dollars of 1898-O and 1904-O. The "silver rush" was on, a stampede ensued, and within the next two years—until March 1964—the Treasury vaults were emptied of hundreds of millions of silver dollars. In the process, the numismatic hobby underwent vast changes.

Along the way, Uncirculated bags were found of many dates, and groups and quantities of others. While perhaps only a few dozen Mint State 1893-S dollars were located, there were over a million of 1881-S and some other dates! The only issues that did *not* turn up in quantity were 1895 and 1895-O. In addition, some bags of circulated mixed dates of Liberty Seated silver dollars 1840-1873 were found as were 1,000 or more heavily bagmarked Mint State specimens of 1859-O and slightly more of 1860-O.

Thus was laid the foundation of what today is the most popular of all early coin specialties: Morgan silver dollar collecting. Books have been written about Morgan dollars, dealers have treated them as a prime focus, and even entire conventions have been built around them. To a lesser extent, Peace silver dollars have been in the limelight as well.[1]

The Treasury hoard in turn spawned many subhoards or secondary hoards, one of which is discussed in a section below under the title "The Redfield Hoard" (1976).

Although reading about old-time hoards is fascinating, it is to be remembered that many of the 1,000-coin bags referred to were simply "spent" in an era in which numismatic interest was just a fraction of what it became after 1962. This is particularly true of Peace silver dollars, which attracted very few buyers. Thus, a coin that existed in bag quantities in the 1940s can be quite elusive on the market today.

Here is a summary of Liberty Seated silver dollars (1840-1873), Morgan silver dollars (1878-1921) and Peace silver dollars (1921-1935) together with information about Treasury (mainly) and other hoards of each.[2]

LIBERTY SEATED SILVER DOLLARS

1840-1873 Liberty Seated dollars: Somewhat over 10,000 circulated Liberty Seated dollars came to light during the Treasury release of 1962-1964, these being found late in 1962 and early 1963, in Federal Reserve banks in the Midwest. I had the pleasure of buying a quantity of unsorted pieces at the time. As they were taken out of bags I arranged them in piles like poker chips.

Among early Liberty Seated dollars of the without-motto type (1840-1865) the most plentiful date was 1847. Among dollars of the 1866-1873 years the most often seen was 1871. The typical coin graded VF or EF and had light gray toning. I recall no Mint State coins at all, nor any extremely worn ones. There were no great rarities such as 1851 or 1852, but there were a number of scarcer dates such as 1844, 1848, and 1870-CC.

1859-O Liberty Seated dollars (mintage 360,000). Somewhat over 1,000 1859-O Liberty Seated dollars were found during the early days of the 1962-1964 Treasury release of silver dollars. Virtually all were heavily bagmarked or abraded.

---

1 In the present writer's two-volume set, *Silver Dollars and Trade Dollars of the United States: A Complete Encyclopedia,* many pages are devoted to the Treasury hoards of silver dollars together with comments concerning the number released of each date and mintmark.

2 In my two-volume study, *Silver Dollars and Trade Dollars of the United States: A Complete Encyclopedia,* I discuss each of these Treasury releases in detail and give recollections of many of the people who were involved in the distributions and finds. Certain of the figures given here are adapted from that text.

1860-O Liberty Seated dollars (mintage 515,000). Up to several thousand came to light during the 1962-1964 Treasury release of silver dollars. Nearly all were very heavily bagmarked. A lesser quantity of 1859-O dollars was found at the same time.

1871 Liberty Seated dollars (business strike mintage 1,073,800). Walter Breen has stated that at least 2,000 Uncirculated pieces were released in 1962-1963,[1] but no independent confirmation of such a quantity has been possible, and it seems highly unlikely. Only a few Mint State coins have come on the market.

1872 Liberty Seated dollars (business strike mintage 1,105,000). Walter Breen has stated that at least 1,000 Uncirculated pieces were released in 1962-1963,[2] but no such quantity can be verified. After the Treasury Department releases of that era, rumors were a dime a dozen. In the 1980s and 1990s, while researching information for the book, *United States Silver Dollars and Trade Dollars: A Complete Encyclopedia,* I conducted numerous inquiries, interviewed many people, and had many consultants (including Walter Breen), but quantities of Mint State 1871 and 1872 dollars remained only a rumor. So far as is known, the only quantities of Liberty Seated dollars in Mint State found at the time were 1859-O and 1860-O, described above.

MORGAN SILVER DOLLARS

1878 8 Tail Feathers Morgan $1 (business strike mintage estimated as 699,300+):[3] Morgan dollars with 8 tail feathers were released in quantity in 1878 and in the immediately following years, and never were rare. In 1953, a number of bags came on the market, probably from storage at the Philadelphia Mint. The number must have been few; at least, not many went into the hands of dealers.

From that point through the early 1960s, additional bags were released. Many came out in Las Vegas in the early 1960s; Philadelphia dealer Harry J. Forman bought several bags at the time. Forman and his business partner Ruth Bauer were prominent in the unfolding saga of silver dollar releases, and the Forman name recurs in many accounts. While Treasury hoard coins distributed over a period of time provided the supply of pieces we now enjoy, I am not aware of any mint-sealed bags currently in existence.

1878 7/8 Tail Feathers $1, a.k.a. Doubled Tail Feathers (business strike mintage estimated as 544,000+): So far as I know, 1878 7/8 TF dollars were primarily issued mixed with the new 7 TF dollars and, to a lesser extent, with the older 8 TF pieces. As this variety was neither widely known nor widely collected until the 1960s (although scattered listings appeared in the 1950s), there is no numismatic documentation of Treasury releases.

In the early 1960s, when bags of 1878 7 TF dollars were issued, some of these contained 7/8 TF coins. In April 1964 Florida dealer Charles ("Shotgun") Slade suggested that the 1878 7/8 TF was four to five times scarcer than the 1878 8 TF, based upon his knowledge of coins recently released by the Treasury.

1878 7 Tail Feathers $1 (business strike mintage of the variety with parallel top arrow feather, a.k.a. Second Reverse, flat breast to eagle, is estimated as 7,200,000). Variety with slanting top arrow feather, a.k.a. Third Reverse, convex breast to eagle, is estimated as 2,000,000). The 7 TF coins were not divided into Second and Third Reverse types until relatively recently. Thus, in numismatic literature there is no record of when one reverse or the other was released in quantity.

It is known that the 7 TF dollar in general was distributed by the Treasury Department over a long period of time, from the year of striking onward. It has always been considered common. A group of bags came out of the Treasury in 1953, and for a while they were especially plentiful in dealers' hands. Additional quantities of bags were paid out during the 1962-1964 Treasury release, especially during 1963, but no account was kept of them. In comparison to certain other issues, the quantities that came out in the early 1960s was small. Today, mint-sealed bags may not survive or are very rare.

1878-CC $1 (business strike mintage 2,212,000): In the late 1930s, when quantities of CC coins were paid out by the Cash Room at the Treasury Building in Washington, D.C., very few 1878-CC dollars were among them. The Cash Room looms large in the present account of silver dollar hoards, and what an exciting place it must have been, being adjacent to vaults where silver dollars had been stored since the nineteenth century, augmented by later arrivals including a massive shipment from Carson City in 1911. Some 1900 Lafayette dollars were stored there as well (see earlier account of commemorative coins).

The scarcity of Mint State 1878-CC dollars in the marketplace continued until late 1946 or early 1947, when several bags came out of Washington, and a few others may have been paid out from storage at the San Francisco Mint. In addition to the Treasury Building in Washington, the San Francisco Mint became a storage depot for CC dollars after the Carson City Mint ceased operations.

In 1950, large numbers of 1878-CC Morgan dollars came out of Treasury vaults, and the coins fell in value as they became one of the most plentiful varieties. In the early 1950s, many more were paid out by the Treasury, and bags were handled by dealers on both coasts. Quite a few ended up in the hands of casino owners in Nevada.

Dealer Steve Ruddel stated that about 50 bags (50,000 coins) were released from the Treasury Building in 1955, and that this was the start of large-scale dispersals from that location.[4] By 1954, the 1878-CC was probably the most

1 Breen, *Encyclopedia,* 1988, p. 342.
2 *Ibid.*
3 All mintage figures for business strike 1878 dollars given in this text are estimates, despite their precise-appearing aspects.
4 Advertisement in *The Numismatist,* January 1964.

common Uncirculated dollar variety of this mint in dealers' hands. Around that time, Treasury dispersals trickled down to a virtual halt. Perhaps additional bags were deeper in the vaults and thus inaccessible. Whatever the reason, when quantities of other CC dollars started coming out in large numbers in 1955, the 1878-CC was not well represented among them. However, there were some scattered exceptions, such as the 1958 release of 1878-CC bags in Montana.

Probably, well over 100,000 coins were paid out by the Treasury from the early 1950s until toward the middle of that decade. I bought a bag of these in 1956 from Rev. Edward W.W. Lewis, a Congregational Church minister in Willimantic, Connecticut, who dabbled in coin dealing. Around the same time, Harry J. Forman bought three bags in Las Vegas. Since the 1950s and early 1960s, more examples of certain other dates, namely 1882-CC, 1883-CC, and 1884-CC, have come on the market, and the 1878-CC has been scarce by comparison.

Held back from the Treasury release of 1962-1964 were 60,993 1878-CC dollars that were dispersed by the General Services Administration in 1972-1974. The G.S.A. hoard figures given in the following text for 1878-CC through 1893-CC do not include 84,165 cull coins and mixed circulated pieces, as well as 311 Carson City pieces of various dates which the General Services Administration did not consider to be salable.[1] All told, probably about 150,000 to 250,000 1878-CC dollars in Mint State were released in the 1950s, early 1960s, and the G.S.A. hoard.

1878-S $1 (business strike mintage 9,774,000): It is believed that as of June 30, 1913, the majority of the original mintage of 1878-S (probably five to six million coins out of a total of 9,774,000), and nearly all of the original mintages of 1879-S, 1880-S, 1881-S, and 1882-S were stored at the San Francisco Mint, to be paid out over a period of decades thereafter.

Especially large quantities were released in the early 1950s—so many that 1878-S was one of the most often seen Mint State Morgan dollars for years afterward. Many bags were also distributed later in the 1950s and especially during the 1962-1964 dispersal. In *The Forecaster*, September 15, 1971, John Kamin gave his opinion that about 7% of the original mintage of 1878-S was released circa 1962-1964, a figure equal to about 600,000 coins. Harry J. Forman bought 10 bags from Phil Carlino; they probably came to Las Vegas by truck directly from the San Francisco Mint or the San Francisco Federal Reserve Bank (to which depot many silver dollars were transferred in the late 1930s, when the old San Francisco Mint operations were transferred to a new facility on Duboce St.).

This date was said to represent the fourth largest single holding of Morgan silver dollars in the LaVere Redfield hoard.[2] One estimate placed the Redfield quantity at 5,000 coins and noted that the coins were in lower Mint State grade ranges. By 1982, Wayne Miller considered the 1878-S to be the least available of the early San Francisco Mint Morgan dollar issues 1878-1882 in Mint State. However, earlier this was not the case, and he recalled a January 1964 advertisement to buy all Uncirculated silver dollars with the exceptions of the following, which at the time were considered to be the most common: 1878-S Morgan, 1921 Morgan, 1922 Peace, and 1923 Peace.

1879 $1 (business strike mintage 14,806,000): As is the case with most other Philadelphia Mint coins in Mint State—and this commentary can be applied to virtually all other dates 1878-1904—the availability of specimens in early years is difficult to ascertain, as most collectors preferred Proofs, and Uncirculated coins, rare or not, were generally ignored.[3] However, enough Mint State coins appeared on the market that it is evident that the 1879 Philadelphia Mint issue has been common virtually from the year of mintage.

Bags came on the market in the late 1940s from storage at the Philadelphia Mint and possibly from Federal Reserve vaults. By 1950-1951 Mint State 1879 dollars were commonly available in quantity. The 1879 dollars remained plentiful during the decade of the 1950s, and in the Middle Atlantic states were a common sight in banks, where, as before, little numismatic attention was paid to them. By the time that the 1962-1964 Treasury dispersal took place, most were gone.

Wayne Miller noted in his *Morgan and Peace Dollar Textbook* that this issue was extensively promoted on the coin market in the late 1970s and early 1980s by "a few wealthy investors.... One person has accumulated several bags of this date.... This is another example of the ease in which a thin market like silver dollars can be manipulated."

1879-CC $1 (business strike mintage 756,000): Years after the closing of the Carson City Mint, quantities of 1879-CC dollars were shipped in two directions for storage: westward to vaults in the San Francisco Mint, and eastward to Washington, D.C. In 1942-1943, several bags of 1879-CC dollars were paid out at face value in San Francisco. The Cash Room in the Treasury Building in Washington distributed at least several thousand Uncirculated 1879-CC dollars in the early and mid-1950s, but by 1955-1956, the lar-

1 Excellent details concerning the G.S.A. sales are to be found in the Van Allen-Mallis book, *Comprehensive Catalog and Encyclopedia of Morgan & Peace Dollars,* third edition.

2 Information concerning the Redfield hoard of dollars is largely conjectural, as no specific figures were ever released. Sources for information in the present text include the writings of John Highfill, Wayne Miller, and Les Fox; expanded information is found in Bowers, *Silver Dollars and Trade Dollars of the United States: A Complete Encyclopedia.* Also see the subsequent entry in the present chapter, "The Redfield Hoard" (1976), for expanded commentary.

3 Although Proofs were preferred over business strikes, the total number of numismatists seriously interested in collecting Proofs was very small. Many Proofs were spent.

gesse stopped. Sometime around this period, Harry J. Forman bought 500 coins from a bag of 1,000 pieces owned by J. Grove Loser, of Steelton, Pennsylvania, who, like Philadelphia dealer Charlie Dochkus, had a special "in" at the Cash Room.[1]

The Treasury kept back slightly over 4,000 coins, which may have been deep in a vault in the 1950s and thus not known to the numismatically-wise people in the Cash Room. As part of the General Services Administration sales in 1972-1974, some 4,123 1879-CC dollars were sold, representing coins found in the Treasury Building in Washington. Of these about 600 (Walter H. Breen is more conservative and estimates just 300) were of the Large CC over Small CC (popularly, the "Capped CC") variety. Most were what would be graded today as MS-60 to MS-62.

The Redfield hoard, first marketed in 1976, was said by some to have had 400 to 500 pieces of the Large CC over Small CC, nearly all of which were in lower grades and heavily bagmarked. However, in connection with the present book, David W. Akers, the manager of Paramount at one time and the buyer from A-Mark of *all* the 1879-CC dollars in the Redfield hoard, stated, "The total was less than 100 pieces."[2]

According to California dealer John Skubis, the Treasury unintentionally sold another bag to someone in "Montana or in Seattle." These coins came from storage in the San Francisco Mint.

1879-O $1 (business strike mintage 2,887,000): I have no specific record of early Treasury releases, but quantities must have filtered onto the market over a long period of time. By the late 1940s and early 1950s, 1879-O Morgan dollars were considered to be on the scarce side and were not among issues *recently* released in mint-sealed bags.

This scarcity changed in 1957 when an estimated five to 10 bags came out and went into the hands of dealers. In the September 1957 issue of *The Numismatist,* Harry J. Forman advertised that he had 1879-O dollars in quantity. In March 1958, Dan's (Dan Morafka) was retailing 20-coin rolls at $37 each, which was equivalent to $1.85 per coin.

Multiple bags of 1,000 Uncirculated coins came to light in October 1962 and with other New Orleans dollars were among the first of the Treasury releases that led to the depletion of the government supply of dollars. Releases of 1879-O continued well into the summer of 1963. However, the total quantity eventually released did not even remotely compare to such plentiful issues as 1883-O, 1884-O, 1885-O, 1898-O, 1903-O, and 1904-O. For some reason, 1879-O dollars did not get into the numismatic mainstream of bulk investment and dealer sales. Perhaps most went to banks in remote areas. In time, the 1879-O once again became scarce in quantity lots.

Around 1975, Harry J. Forman bought a bag of 1879-O dollars from the estate of Paul Dinerman, of Philadelphia.[3] Earlier, this had come from the 1962-1964 Treasury release. Some Uncirculated 1879-O coins were found mixed in with other contemporary issues.

Apropos of this, John V. Kamin, publisher of *The Forecaster,* wrote the following:[4] "I had the chance to go through many bags of O-Mint silver dollars with mint seals from the New Orleans Mint or the Federal Reserve, bags sealed up in 1880, 1881, 1882. Estimated over 90% of the contents of these bags was 1881-O, 1882-O silver dollars, with the rest evenly split between 1880-O and 1879-O [also see commentary under 1887-O for a related situation]. I've always assumed that the storage vault was flooded; that the original bags rotted. And, since manual counting of coins was the way it was done in those days, the coins were later quickly counted and scooped into new cloth bags, without regard to date in the early 1880s. Just a few mint bags consisting solely of 1879-O silver dollars came out, and those had different seals on them. They were all Uncirculated, not mixed dates, all the same coins in the bag. Those coins were of a much higher quality. They weren't water-marked, and commanded a premium, up to triple face value at a time when most Morgans couldn't even bring 50% over face value. They were obviously Uncirculated, compared to those mixed O-Mint bags that were probably roughly scooped, handled, and maybe even shoveled more than once."

In addition to Mint State hoards, bags turned up of lightly worn dollars of 1879-O, 1880-O, 1881-O, and 1882-O. Wayne Miller commented concerning this: "For reasons which have never been explained, these dollars were then gathered up after they had been lightly circulated, brought back to the Mint, and resealed into Mint bags. Mint sealed bags of these dates often contain over 90% lightly circulated pieces, including a few dollars from the Philadelphia, San Francisco, and Carson City mints, which happened to be circulating in the New Orleans area at the time of recall."[5]

1879-S $1 (business strike mintage 9,110,000): It is believed that as of June 30, 1913, most of the original mintage of 1879-S was stored at the San Francisco Mint, to be paid out over a period of decades thereafter.

Vast quantities were released by the San Francisco Mint in the twentieth century, particularly in 1942 (when many dozens, possibly hundreds, of bags were distributed) and the 1950s. The Treasury Department released many additional bags in the 1962-1964 era. In *The Forecaster,* September 15, 1971,

John Kamin ventured the suggestion that about 10% of the original mintage of 1879-S was released circa 1962-1964, a figure equal to about a million pieces. Year in and year out, over a long period of time, the 1879-S has been readily available in quantity. Nearly all of these bags contained coins of the Third Reverse type, some Redfield hoard coins being a notable (and rare) exception.

1880 $1 (business strike mintage 12,600,000): Bags of 1880 dollars probably came on the market over a long period of time, but I have been able to find no documentation of mass releases prior to the 1940s—although they may have occurred. As noted, Philadelphia Mint business strikes were not particularly sought after by specialists, as there were enough Proofs around to satisfy the demand. Morgan silver dollars were hardly in the mainstream of numismatic interest in the early twentieth century.

---

[1] Interview with Harry J. Forman, September 9, 1992.

[2] Letter, July 7, 1996. Other citations by David W. Akers concerning silver dollars in this book supersede figures and estimates in earlier books, including Bowers, *Silver Dollars and Trade Dollars of the United States: A Complete Encyclopedia.*

[3] Conversation with the author, August 11, 1992.

[4] Letter, October 29, 1992.

[5] *The Morgan and Peace Dollar Textbook,* p. 85,

In the early 1940s, bags came on the market from storage in Philadelphia Mint vaults. Dollars of this date remained plentiful throughout the 1950s, with a particularly large release occurring in 1955. In the 1950s, Mint State coins were commonly found in bags of mixed dollars, and, occasionally, a full bag of just this one date would turn up. It was probably the case that most original bags paid out in the 1950s slipped into circulation, and by the early 1960 were "sliders."[1] In terms of mint-sealed bags still around today, few remain.

1880-CC $1 (business strike mintage 591,000 business strikes; net 495,000 after melting): Several bags of Uncirculated 1880-CC dollars were paid out from the Cash Room in the Treasury Building, Washington, D.C., in 1938. Apparently, the Cash Room payouts of this variety trickled to an end sometime in the late 1930s or early 1940s, and after that time the 1880-CC once again became scarce on the market.

History repeated itself, and what occurred in 1938 happened again in 1955. Out of the vault in the Treasury Building in Washington, D.C. came many mint-sealed bags, which went into the hands of dealers with the right connections. Dealer Steve Ruddel stated that, for starters, about 50 bags (50,000 coins) were released from the Treasury Building in that year.[2] About 1957, Harry J. Forman bought several bags from Charles J. Dochkus, who obtained them from the Cash Room. J. Grove Loser was properly fixed with Washington friends, and quite a few bags reached the market through his coin dealership. Quantities remained plentiful until 1959-1960, after which the supply dried up. After that point, quantities were rarely offered.

Circa 1962-1964, when the Treasury began releasing dollars in quantity, many more 1880-CC dollars came to light, and some bags were paid out. In March 1964, the government took stock of the Treasury Building drain and called a halt, deciding to hold back 131,529 1880-CC coins, which were sold by the General Services Administration beginning in 1972. The G.S.A. sale coins included the 1880/79-CC overdates, a.k.a. Second Reverse coins; in total, these probably represented about 20% of the 1880-CC dollars released.

1880-O $1 (business strike mintage 5,305,000): Little record exists of releases or dealer offerings of quantities of 1880-O dollars. Circa 1946 a few bags were released, and for several years single coins were more plentiful in dealers' stocks than they had been earlier in the decade. Around 1956-1957, additional quantities came out from Treasury holdings. Again, the supply diminished, and 1880-O dollars became scarce in quantity in the early 1960s.

Then came the Treasury release of New Orleans dollars beginning in October 1962 and continuing at least through July 1963. At least a few bags were released during this time, but I have located no specific documentation as to quantities, which must have been small.

According to Wayne Miller, in *The Morgan and Peace Dollar Textbook,* a bag or more of 1880-O dollars came on the market in 1974. In 1977, the Superior Stamp & Coin Company handled the R.D. Donovan hoard of silver dollars, which is said to have contained a bag or more of this issue. Some mint-sealed bags of *slightly circulated* 1880-O dollars were also released (see comment under 1879-O above). The 1880-O is one of those Morgan dollar issues which does not immediately come to mind when scarce varieties are reviewed, but upon examination it is found that there aren't many around.

1880-S $1 (business strike mintage 8,900,000): It is believed that as of June 30, 1913, most of the original mintage of 1880-S was stored at the San Francisco Mint, to be paid out over a period of decades thereafter. Dollars of this date were available in quantities at face value from that location through the mid-1950s. In addition, numerous 1,000-coin bags were released by the Treasury in 1962-1964.

In *The Forecaster,* September 15, 1971, John Kamin estimated that about 20% of the mintage of 1880-S was released circa 1962-1964, a figure equivalent to about 1,600,000 coins. Many were released in 1963. The Redfield hoard contained dozens of bags, grading mostly MS-61 to MS-64, with just a few higher, according to John Highfill. The 1880-S is said to have represented the second largest single holding of Morgan dollars in the Redfield property. Bag quantities of 1880-S dollars were also in the Continental-Illinois Bank hoard.[3] On August 21, 1967, when trading in 1,000-coin bags of silver dollars commenced on the New York Mercantile Exchange, a bag of 1880-S dollars was displayed to watching commodities traders and brokers by coin dealer Charles Ross. The 1880-S dollars were said to be representative of a common date, such as those that would be traded.

1881 $1 (business strike mintage 9,163,000): In the early 1950s, the 1881 Philadelphia Mint Morgan dollar was very common in Uncirculated grade in Eastern banks and elsewhere, indicating that many must have been released before that time, in addition to large quantities dispersed in the late 1950s and early 1960s. Quite a few bags came out in 1955, after which time they were plentiful in dealers' hands for a while.

In general, large numbers of Uncirculated dollars of Philadelphia Mint dates 1878-1887 were seen in quantity in the early 1950s. In later times the situation changed. Today, few if any original mint-sealed bags are known to remain. However, single specimens remain plentiful.

1881-CC $1 (business strike mintage 296,000): At the time of mintage, probably fewer than 50,000 1881-CC dollars were released. As the years went on, the issue was recognized as a scarcity, although occasionally a few Uncirculated coins would come to light.

In 1938-1939, the Cash Room at the Treasury Building in Washington, D.C. parceled out a few Uncirculated coins, but not enough to seriously affect the market. Coins of this date became increasingly scarce as numismatic demand for

---

[1] The term *slider* was popularly used to refer to a high-level About Uncirculated coin with notable friction on the surface; *commercial Uncirculated* was another phrase for high-grade AU. After the ANA Grading System began to be employed in a large way in the 1980s, such terms were largely forgotten.

[2] Advertisement in *The Numismatist,* January 1964.

[3] As reported by Clark A. Samuelson and Leon E. Hendrickson in "The Continental-Illinois Bank Deal," part of John Highfill's *The Comprehensive U.S. Silver Dollar Encyclopedia.* These bank hoard coins were mostly from earlier Treasury bulk releases from the 1950s through and including the large dispersals of 1962-1964. Chicago dealer Edward Milas figured prominently in the dispersal of the Continental-Illinois coins.

Morgan dollars grew stronger. In 1954, the Cash Room paid out several bags of 1881-CC dollars. Washington professional numismatist Steve Ruddel stated that about 50 bags (50,000 coins) were released from the Treasury Building in 1955, and that this was just the beginning of a new wave of releases.[1]

In the meantime, the San Francisco Mint shipped bags of 1881-CC dollars to Nevada casinos, where they were recognized as being desirable; many were resold to dealers. It was popular for casino operators in the downtown area of Las Vegas to squirrel away at face value "interesting" bags of Morgan dollars as part of their cash reserves.[2]

By and large the quantities held in the private sector were soon dispersed—a bag here, a few rolls there, and a few coins somewhere else. By the early 1960s, the 1881-CC was relatively scarce once again. However, the Treasury Building in Washington still had more, and an additional 147,485 Uncirculated pieces remained in March 1964. These were sold through the General Services Administration beginning in the early 1970s and ending in 1980.

Leroy C. Van Allen and A. George Mallis estimated that about 40% of the total consisted of VAM-2 (Breen-5564). Probably, about 200,000 of the original mintage of 296,000 1881-CC dollars still survive in Mint State. To my knowledge, mint-sealed bags have long since been dispersed. Today, even rolls are seldom seen in dealer-to-dealer transactions. However, individual coins are relatively plentiful. There is an especially romantic connotation to Carson City silver dollars of all dates, as these have a rich "Wild West" history and these are the only CC-mintmark coins generally available in Mint State. Because of this, all other things being equal, there has always been an extra demand for Carson City Morgan dollars.

1881-O $1 (business strike mintage 5,708,000): Throughout the 1950s, a small but steady stream of Uncirculated 1881-O dollars trickled into the market. Occasionally, a bag would surface and be broken up and absorbed into dealer stocks. Beginning in October 1962, many additional bags of 1881-O dollars were released by the Treasury Department, a dispersal which continued through at least the summer of 1963. Up to that point, 1881-O dollars were somewhat scarce, although hardly rare, in Mint State preservation. Some mint-sealed bags of *slightly circulated* 1881-O dollars were also released (see comment under 1879-O above).

1881-S $1 (business strike mintage 12,760,000): It is believed that as of June 30, 1913, most of the original mintage of 1881-S was stored at the San Francisco Mint, to be paid out over a period of decades thereafter. In 1938, many bags were released. During the 1950s, additional large quantities were paid out from storage in the minting facility. Enough remained in government hands that many more millions of 1881-S dollars were released by the Treasury Department in the early 1960s, especially in 1963.

In *The Forecaster,* September 15, 1971, John Kamin gave his opinion that about 50% of the original mintage of 1881-S was released circa 1962-1964, a figure equivalent to over 6,000,000 coins. Many thousands of 1881-S dollars were squirreled away by LaVere Redfield, whose estate is said to have had more 1881-S dollars than coins of any other date. Large quantities also went into the vaults of the Continental-Illinois Bank, to be discovered by Chicago dealer Ed Milas, who was in the right place at the right time when the financial institution ran into trouble and had to liquidate its 1,500,000 silver dollars, many of which were of the 1881-S issue.

According to John J. Ford, Jr., Philadelphia dealer Harry J. Forman brought to New Netherlands Coin Co. 126 bags (126,000 coins) of this date alone among many others in the early 1960s. Many coins were prooflike gems and many were DMPL. (John J. Ford, Jr., in an interview on May 12, 1992, recalled that he handled 140 bags totally of 1881-S dollars).

Today in the 1990s the 1881-S dollar stands as the single most available Morgan silver dollar in gem Mint State preservation. Thus, it is an excellent "introductory coin" for anyone with a beginning interest in the series. However, the buyer is apt to be spoiled by the 1881-S, for the typical coin is very well struck and extremely attractive, not at all representative of many other issues in the series (for example, most New Orleans Mint coins are lightly struck).

1882 $1 (business strike mintage 11,100,000): Mint State coins have been common for many years, even before the Treasury release of 1962-1964. Many of this date were stored at the Philadelphia Mint and also by the Federal Reserve System. However, by now it is probably the case that most original mint-sealed bags have been broken open and dispersed.

1882-CC $1 (business strike mintage 1,133,000): The Cash Room in the Treasury Building in Washington had a huge quantity of 1882-CC dollars. These were released sparingly over a period of time. In 1938-1939, larger quantities became available at face value. During the 1940s few 1882-CC dollars were released by the Treasury, and the price in the numismatic market crept up.

In 1955 bags came out from two storage areas: the San Francisco Mint and the Treasury Building in Washington. Dealer Steve Ruddel stated that about 50 bags (50,000 coins) were released from the Treasury Building in 1955, and that many more came out later.[3]

The 1962-1964 Treasury releases apparently included some bags of 1882-CC, but probably not many. When the government shut the floodgates of dollar distribution in 1964, 605,029 Uncirculated 1882-CC dollars remained on hand, or well over half the original mintage! These were subsequently sold through a series of auctions staged by the General Services Administration. Today, Morgan dollars of 1882-CC, 1883-CC, and 1884-CC are the most often seen in G.S.A.-sealed black plastic holders.

1882-O $1 (business strike mintage 6,090,000): During the 1950s every now and then a mint-sealed bag of 1882-O dollars would come on the market through some lucky finder, who picked it up at a bank. Although this date was not in the common category at the time, it was not rare either.

[1] Advertisement in *The Numismatist,* January 1964.

[2] The writer recalls that Amon G. Carter, Jr., of Fort Worth, Texas, was the numismatic advisor to two downtown casinos, both of which had quantities of Carson City dollars.

[3] Advertisement in *The Numismatist,* January 1964.

Beginning in October 1962, the floodgates opened, and hundreds of thousands of 1882-O dollars poured out into the market, and were distributed in the Midwest and East. When the dust settled early in 1963, a few months later, the 1882-O was solidly entrenched as one of the most common issues in the series. Distribution of 1882-O continued throughout much of 1963, until at least the autumn. Some mint-sealed bags of *slightly circulated* 1882-O dollars were also released (see comment under 1879-O above).

1882-O/S $1 (business strike mintage is unknown; probably hundreds of thousands): Released as a small part of Treasury dispersals of 1882-O. No specific hoards reported.

1882-S $1 (business strike mintage 9,250,000): It is believed that as of June 30, 1913, most of the original mintage of 1882-S was stored at the San Francisco Mint, to be paid out over a period of decades thereafter. Later, some of these were transferred to the Treasury Building in Washington, D.C. However, enough coins dribbled onto the market over a period of years that 1882-S was never considered to be a rarity in Mint State.

During the 1926 convention of the American Numismatic Association in Washington, D.C., numerous attendees were delighted to obtain at face value Uncirculated 1882-S dollars which were being paid out at the Cash Room of the Treasury Building in the same city. What a treat!

Although the San Francisco Mint usually served as the storage depot for its own coins, portions of the mintage of several issues—including 1882-S and 1904-S—were shipped to vaults in Washington. For many years, through at least the early 1950s, 1882-S dollars were available at face value from the San Francisco Mint. Further, probably well over a million were released by the Treasury Department in 1962-1964, especially in 1963.

In *The Forecaster*, September 15, 1971, John Kamin suggested that about 10% of the original mintage of 1882-S was released circa 1962-1964, a figure equal to about a million coins. Dollars of 1882-S were among the most abundant varieties in the Redfield and Continental-Illinois Bank hoards.

1883 $1 (business strike mintage 12,290,000): The 1883 Morgan dollar was one of the most common dates seen in bank bags in the early 1950s. Large quantities were released in the early 1960s as well. 12,000 to 15,000 1883 dollars, including many high-grade examples, were in the Continental-Illinois Bank hoard.

1883-CC $1 (business strike mintage 1,204,000): For much of the present century a vast reserve of 1883-CC dollars was stored in the Treasury Building in Washington, D.C. From this source, examples trickled out over a period of years, with a significant release occurring in 1938-1939.

Many bags were given out at face value in the 1950s, when dealers such as Charles J. Dochkus sought to buy them, but demand was such that the market could only absorb limited quantities. Dealer Steve Ruddel stated that about 50 bags (50,000 coins) were released from the Treasury Building in 1955, and that at least that many were released of all other CC Mint Morgan dollars except 1879-CC, 1889-CC, and 1893-CC.[1] By the late 1950s, the Treasury stopped paying them out.

After the initial Treasury silver dollar releases of the early 1960s, which included very few 1883-CC dollars, a quantity amounting to 755,518 coins, or over 62% of the original mintage, was held back. These were subsequently marketed through the General Services Administration from 1972 to 1980.

1883-O $1 (business strike mintage 8,725,000): The 1883-O, minted in large quantities, was never rare in Mint State on the numismatic market. This date was released in bags of 1,000 coins as long ago as 1938 from the Treasury Building in Washington, D.C., which, earlier, had paid out small quantities of this date. Dealer John Zug was among those who obtained these for face value in the early 1930s.

Bags were distributed at later intervals as well, including a major release in 1952, followed by occasional bags until about 1957. From a sealed vault in the Philadelphia Mint many more bags were released beginning in October 1962, and continuing well into 1963. Some of the latter found their way to the Continental-Illinois Bank and were sold on the coin market about 15 years later. As a result, today the 1883-O is very common in Mint State. The 1883-O, 1884-O, and 1885-O constitute the bulk of approximately 10 million coins released from a long-sealed vault in the Philadelphia Mint, beginning in October 1962. My estimate is that the breakdown of these three dates is about as follows: 1883-O: 1,500,000 to 2,500,000 coins; 1884-O: 2,500,000 to 4,000,000 coins; and 1885-O: 2,000,000 to 3,500,000 coins. Of course, these coins are in addition to hoard coins released from other vaults earlier.

While many 1883-O dollars were saved by the public, investors, and collectors, other coins—possibly amounting to millions of pieces totally—went into circulation. Many of these were melted in the late 1970s and early 1980s during a sharp increase in silver bullion prices, which on January 21, 1980, hit $52.35 per ounce. This rise in silver was due in large part by one the Hunt brothers, in Texas, endeavoring to corner the market. For much of 1979 and early 1980, common-date silver dollars found a more ready market to be melted down for bullion than they did as collectors' items on the numismatic market. The same was true of many other Mint State silver coin issues, notably rolls of Washington quarters from the 1940s onward and Franklin half dollars of the 1948-1963 era.

1883-S $1 (business strike mintage 6,250,000): The 1883-S dollar in Mint State is one of the more curious Morgan dollars from a rarity and price history viewpoint. Decades ago it was considered to be a common San Francisco issue. From the nineteenth century onward, specimens were readily available. Single coins, rolls, and bags dribbled out from storage in the San Francisco Mint for many years.

In 1950, a few bags were released. In the 1950s John Skubis had at least one bag of 1883-S, possibly more. Bags were broken up, and virtually every dealer in Morgan dollars had a good supply, often roll quantities, during that decade.

By the mid-1960s, most quantities of 1883-S dollars in dealers' stocks had been distributed, but singles abounded on the market. One by one, most singles found homes, and

---

[1] *Ibid.*

by the late 1960s and continuing through the 1970s, many collectors in the market, and many dealers as well—most of whom had not been active until after the 1962-1964 Treasury releases—came to view the 1883-S as rare. However, silver dollar hoarder LaVere Redfield had a full bag of 1,000 coins plus two additional specimens.[1] These coins were retailed by Paramount after the Redfield coins were auctioned in 1976. Today, most of the Redfield coins would grade in the MS-60 to MS-63 range.

Now in the 1990s, the 1883-S is considered to be among the more elusive San Francisco issues. Without doubt, and having no close challengers, the 1883-S is far rarer in Mint State than any other S-Mint Morgan dollar from 1878 to 1883.

1884 $1 (business strike mintage 14,070,000): 1884 Morgan dollars have been common for decades. The Treasury releases each year in the 1940s and 1950s, particularly at Christmas time when the holiday demand called for silver dollars for use as gifts, often contained bags of this and other Philadelphia Mint dates from 1878 through 1887. A particularly large release occurred in December 1954.

The great Treasury release of 1962-1964, extending to March 1964, saw additional quantities of the 1884 (and many other) Philadelphia Mint dollars brought out from storage in government vaults. However, the number of bags of 1884 dollars released was small in comparison to certain New Orleans and San Francisco issues. Apparently, most 1884 dollars were distributed in the 1950s, and by the mid-1960s they were somewhat scarce in a comparative sense.

Sometime in the 1960s, 12 to 15 bags of 1884 dollars were stashed away in the reserves of the Continental-Illinois Bank, to come to light about 15 years later. Today in the early 1990s, single Mint State coins are encountered with regularity, but I believe that most bags have been broken up. In 1982, Wayne Miller wrote of several wealthy investors hoarding this date, with one acquiring several bags. I do not know if these bags are still intact.

1884-CC $1 (business strike mintage 1,136,000): The 1884-CC Morgan dollar is one of the most remarkable coins in the annals of silver dollar history. The original production amounted to 1,136,000 pieces. Of that number, 962,638, amounting to 84.7% of the original mintage, were still in the hands of the Treasury Department after March 1964, when a halt was called to the great Treasury release that began in October 1962, and were sold in the later G.S.A. sales.

Earlier, in 1938, bags of this date were also released, and during the 1950s the Cash Room at the Treasury Department paid out a further steady stream of 1,000-coin bags. Dealer Steve Ruddel stated that about 50 bags (50,000 coins) were released from the Treasury Building in 1955.[2]

The total number of Uncirculated 1884-CC dollars in existence is not known with precision, but it is undoubtedly over a million. No wonder that *circulated* coins are rare!

1884-O $1 (business strike mintage 9,730,000): Mint-sealed bags of 1884-O Morgan dollars were released in 1933-1934, 1938, and again in the 1950s, from storage in the Treasury Building in Washington, D.C. These dispersals were insignificant compared to the veritable deluge of 1884-O dollars that spewed forth from storage in the Philadelphia Mint beginning in October 1962. Some from the latter distribution later showed up in the memorable hoard owned by the Continental-Illinois Bank.

David Sundman with a group of Carson City silver dollars and a cloth bag that originally was filled with 1,000 of these coins.

The 1883-O, 1884-O, and 1885-O constitute the bulk of approximately 10 million coins released from a long-sealed vault in the Philadelphia Mint, beginning in October 1962. While many went into the hands of investors, hoarders, and collectors, others—possibly amounting to millions of pieces totally—went into circulation. Many of these were melted in the late 1970s during the run-up in silver bullion prices.

1884-S $1 (business strike mintage 3,200,000): In 1926 many were released to banks from storage at the San Francisco Mint. Limited numbers of this issue dribbled out from storage in the Treasury Building in Washington, D.C. as early as the early 1930s, and continuing through at least the very early 1950s; if any full bags were paid out during this span, I have not learned of the situation.

In the 1950s, a few bags came out from storage at the same facility. In 1957-1958, and possibly for a year or two later, additional quantities were paid out by this source. Although I have found no records of mint-sealed bags of 1884-S dollars changing hands, as late as 1964 rolls of 20 Uncirculated coins were being advertised. By that time, Treasury holdings had been long since exhausted. It has been years since I have seen an Uncirculated roll. I am aware of no current hoards.

1885 $1 (business strike mintage 17,785,000): Large quantities of 1885 Morgan dollars were released by the Treasury Department from the 1930s through the 1950s, particularly in 1954, followed by many more bags in the early 1960s. As a result, to the past two generations of numismatists the 1885 has been a very common date. In fact, of the

1 David W. Akers, letter, July 7, 1996; this information is new to the silver dollar field and supersedes earlier estimates.

2 Advertisement in *The Numismatist,* January 1964.

early Morgan dollars of the 1878-1904 period, the 1885 is one of the most often seen and is outranked in availability only by the dates 1886 and 1887. Most quantities of 1885 dollars were released in the 1950s, with fewer in the 1960s. Bags of 1885 dollars are not common today. Most have been broken up.

1885-CC $1 (business strike mintage 228,000): Uncirculated 1885-CC dollars were considered to be very rare, the *creme de la creme* of the series, until the 1930s, when John Zug (of Bowie, Maryland) and a few others obtained small quantities from the Cash Room at the Treasury Building in Washington.

In 1941-1942, several bags were released, after which the supply seemed to dry up. In 1955, multiple bags came out of hiding in the Treasury Building, and 1885-CC dollars became common on the market, a situation that remained until 1957-1958. In 1958, multiple bags were released in Montana; these were probably from storage at the San Francisco Mint or one of the Federal Reserve facilities.

Additional quantities, probably modest in total, of Uncirculated 1885-CC were turned loose during the Treasury dispersals of 1962-1964, at the end of which 148,285 were held back for later sale by the General Services Administration. These were offered in the 1972-1974 mail bid sales. All but 31,569 sold, and those went in the final 1980 sale. Earlier conventional wisdom had it that the Redfield hoard may have contained as many as 1,000 coins, but in connection with the present book, David W. Akers, former manager of Paramount (the firm that bought certain hoard coins from A-Mark), stated that there were far fewer than that.[1]

1885-O $1 (business strike mintage 9,185,000): Following the closing of the New Orleans Mint, quantities of 1885-O dollars were shipped to the Treasury Building in Washington, D.C. and the Philadelphia Mint for long-term storage. From the Washington vault 1885-O dollars were paid out beginning by the early 1930s, and in multiple-bag quantities in 1938, 1953, 1954, and 1957.

In October 1962, continuing into early 1963, vast quantities, probably amounting to millions of coins, were released from storage at the Philadelphia Mint. While many went into the hands of investors, hoarders, and collectors, others—possibly amounting to millions of pieces totally—went into circulation. Many of these were melted in the late 1970s during the run-up in silver bullion prices, a fate that befell many Treasury hoard dollars that were not considered to be rare at the time. Many Uncirculated 1885-O dollars were in the Continental-Illinois Bank hoard and had come from the Philadelphia release of circa 1962.

1885-S $1 (business strike mintage 1,497,000): Quantities of 1885-S dollars were stored at the San Francisco Mint during the early part of the present century, but few people knew it. Soon after World War II the San Francisco Mint paid out a lot of early Morgan dollars, 1885-S among them.

Awareness of the availability of dollars at the San Francisco Mint spread, and West Coast dealers tapped this source from time to time. By 1955, the 1885-S was sufficiently common in numismatic circles that bags had little premium value. The supply of 1885-S dollars was steady for the next two or three years.

During the great Treasury release of 1962-1964, especially in the year 1963, a number of bags of 1885-S dollars were paid out, but I have no specific record of them. Steve Ruddel noted that 1885-S was among the hoard coins coming out in the early 1960s, but did not mention the quantities involved.[2] I suspect that most later quantity offerings—which seem to have been rolls rather than bags—were mainly left over from San Francisco Mint payouts of the mid-1950s. While the 1885-S remained plentiful, it was scarce in relation to some of the Morgan dollar varieties that had flooded the market from the 1962-1964 release.

Writing in *The Morgan and Peace Dollar Textbook* in 1982, Wayne Miller stated this: "The 1885-S is still available in large quantities." However, he told of two groups of 15 rolls each, or 600 coins—hardly a "large quantity" in comparison to such issues as 1879-S, 1880-S, 1881-S, etc., which commonly traded in bags. Miller also gave details of a 1978 hoard of 35 to 40 rolls (700 to 800 coins), virtually all of which were of mediocre quality. "Not one coin could be called a gem."

1886 $1 (business strike mintage 19,963,000): Quantities of 1886 dollars were released by the Treasury over a long period of years, with large numbers coming out in 1951, 1952, and, especially, December 1954. In the 1950s, anyone finding a $1,000 bag of 1886 dollars would "throw it back" to the bank, like a fisherman tossing back an undersized trout. Bags of these and most other early Philadelphia Mint Morgan dollars were not wanted, even for face value. If a buyer could be found—and I remember the situation well—a good wholesale price would be $1,100.

In 1962-1964 more bags were set free by the Treasury, some of which ended up in the coffers of the Continental-Illinois Bank.

Due to melting in the late 1970s, Mint State coins are less plentiful today than hoard releases might indicate.

1886-O $1 (business strike mintage 10,710,000): Among Morgan dollars, the 1886-O is somewhat of an anomaly. The mintage figure of 10,710,000 business strikes is overwhelming and even puts in the shade such common coins as the 1883-O, 1884-O, and 1885-O. By all rights, like these other coins, a million or more 1886-O dollars should have come to light in the great Treasury release of 1962-1964, and today a beautiful MS-65 1886-O should be in every collection. It didn't happen.

What *did* happen isn't known, at least not with certainty. At or near the time of striking in the nineteenth century, probably a few million coins, say 2,000,000 to 4,000,000, were placed into circulation and saw commercial use. Probably, millions of other coins, perhaps as many as 6,000,000 to 8,000,000 pieces, went to the melting pot under the terms of the 1918 Pittman Act.

Whatever happened, apparently no more than a few bags dribbled onto the market in the 1940s and 1950s. In the Treasury release of 1962-1964 probably a few bags came out, but I have obtained no specific record of them. Harry J. Forman recalled that he never had an intact bag of 1886-O dollars, but he did find several hundred "minimum Uncirculated" coins in a bag containing various dates.

1886-S $1 (business strike mintage 750,000): Apparently, very few were released into circulation near the time

[1] Letter, July 7, 1996.

[2] Advertisement in *The Numismatist,* January 1964.

of striking. It is believed that hundreds of thousands were melted under the 1918 Pittman Act provisions, although it is not possible to verify this today. In the mid-1920s, additional coins were released into circulation from storage at the San Francisco Mint. Beginning about 1942 and lasting until the late 1950s, bags were available at face value, with few takers. John Skubis, for one, recalls turning such bags back for face value. Although there was a decent market for singles and a slight market for rolls, few investors wanted bags. Those who might have—such as Nevada casino operators—could get them at face value without going through a coin dealer.

In addition to the coins paid out by the San Francisco Mint, scattered bags were released by banks in the West, including some in Montana in 1956. The 1962-1964 Treasury release included some 1886-S dollars, but probably not many.

It was said that the Redfield estate hoard had 3,000 or more coins (three or more bags) grading MS-60 to MS-63 by later standards, and this is probably the main source for pieces seen on the market today. However, in a recent commentary for this book, David W. Akers stated that there were 10 to 12 bags (10,000 to 12,000 coins) with "quite a few gem MS-64 and MS-65 coins."[1]

1887/6 $1 (business strike mintage unknown; part of 1887 mintage): No specific hoards have been recorded of the 1887/6 variety, except as a part of Treasury releases of 1887, the latter being a common date.

1887 $1 (business strike mintage 20,290,000): The 1887 dollar was plentiful years ago, and additional Treasury releases from coins stored at the Philadelphia Mint took place in 1938, the 1940s, the 1950s (particularly in December 1954), and the early 1960s. One lot of 100 bags existed as late as 1978.

The Continental-Illinois Bank hoard, which was estimated to contain as many as 1,000 original bags of brilliant Uncirculated dollars plus an estimated 500 bags of circulated coins (1,500,000 coins totally), included quantities of Mint State 1887 Morgans. The 1887 may be, as Wayne Miller has written, the most plentiful Morgan dollar in terms of 1,000-coin bags still in existence.

1887/6-O $1 (business strike mintage unknown; part of 1887-O): A group of 400 was sold at the 1977 ANA convention and, possibly, was part of the 1962-1964 Treasury distribution of 1887-O dollars. This variety was not well known until recent times, and no track was kept of it in the earlier days.

1887-O $1 (business strike mintage 11,550,000): On the coin market the 1887-O Morgan dollar seems to have always been available in Mint State, possibly from a supply augmented by occasional releases of mint-sealed bags, which are known to have occurred in 1938, 1953, 1957, and probably a few other years as well.

In the 1962 emptying of the hoard of 10 million New Orleans coins from a sealed vault in Philadelphia, many 1887-Os turned up, but it was not one of the more plentiful dates. Bags from Treasury holdings were released by the government as late as March 1964, and were among the last issues paid out.

Reminiscing in *The Comprehensive Silver Dollar Encyclopedia,* Dean Tavenner said that he obtained one bag of prooflike 1887-O dollars with bagmarks in April 1964 just at the time his bank in Deer Lodge, Montana, was running out of silver dollars at face value. He also noted that EF and AU 1887-O dollars, as well as New Orleans dollars of certain other dates, were released in quantity in mint-sewn bags. (See related note under 1879-O.) Quite probably, releases of 1887-O over the years included some of the 1887/6-O overdate.

1887-S $1 (business strike mintage 1,771,000): Apparently, many 1887-S dollars were put into circulation in the late nineteenth century, after which undistributed quantities remained in storage at the San Francisco Mint. I have located no record of any quantity of these dollars being released during the early twentieth century.

Beginning in late 1941 or early 1942, mint-sealed bags of 1,000 coins each were paid out at face value. From that point until the early 1950s, bags continued to be available at face value from the Mint. Within the next three or four years, quantities began to be scarce, and no longer were bags of 1887-S dollars obtainable easily from the Mint. It could have been that an occasional bag or two came to light later, for roll quantities remained plentiful until the end of the decade.

After the late 1950s the supply of 1887-S in quantity seems to have dried up. There is no record of the issue being included in the massive Treasury releases of 1962-1964, although it is possible some may have been. LaVere Redfield obtained an estimated five to 10 bags of this date, probably from Nevada casinos or from California dealers who had acquired them in the 1950s. Upon dispersal of the Redfield estate, these coins were found to be of "high quality" (per Wayne Miller's comment in his *Morgan and Peace Dollar Textbook*). The Redfield coins are believed to have been sold to a wide number of buyers. Today, rolls of 1887-S are seldom seen.

1888 $1 (business strike mintage 19,183,000): As is the case with a number of other Philadelphia Mint issues, the 1888 was not considered to be a common coin in Mint State until the 1950s. Apparently, quantities were released into circulation at or near the time of mintage, and these quickly became worn. After that, many went into storage, while probably millions of others were undoubtedly melted under the 1918 Pittman Act.

In the mid-1950s, 1888 dollars were released in quantity—probably by the millions. Few were saved by collectors, investors, or dealers. Most eventually ended up in mixed bags of Morgan dollars. The quantities were so vast that even though most bags were broken up, individual coins remained very common. During the great Treasury release of 1962-1964, many more 1888 dollars were paid out. In fact, bags of 1888 dollars were still being shipped by the Federal Reserve in March 1964, the last month that silver dollars were available in quantity at face value from the government.

1888-O $1 (business strike mintage 12,150,000): Like many of its sister New Orleans issues, the 1888-O dollars dribbled out of government storage and into the coin market in small quantities in 1946 and during the 1950s, especially from about 1955 to 1957-1958. Some of these came

[1] Letter, July 7, 1996.

from the Treasury Building in Washington, D.C., where they had been stored since the New Orleans Mint ceased operations.

In 1962-1964, many more 1888-O dollars were released from a long-stored cache in a sealed vault at the Philadelphia Mint. This additional quantity may have amounted to over 100,000 coins, with some suggesting many hundreds of thousands, if not a million or more. Many of these were released in Montana. As an example of the quantities of 1888-O dollars on the market for a decade afterward, Wayne Miller told of buying nine original mint sealed bags of 1888-O dollars in 1971 and examining 16 additional bags in the same six week period, amounting to a total of 25,000 coins.

Concerning quantities of 1888-O dollars, John V. Kamin wrote as follows:[1] "I disagree with Wayne Miller on how many bags of these came out. I was searching for quantity lots of 1888-O all during the 1960s, and only encountered a couple of bags. I don't know of any that came out after early 1964. 1888-O was always considered a premium date of silver dollars, as evidenced by the 1963 *Guide Book,* where it is listed at $6.50 in BU condition, while most other 'common date' silver dollars are listed at much lower prices, including some scarcer dates. I will be most pleased if 1888-O is considered a common date by Wayne Miller, and other dealers, for many more years, giving my friends a chance to buy up any bags that come on the market. I think 1888-O is at least 300 times scarcer than bags of 1883-O, 1884-O, 1885-O, and similar 'common date' bags!"

Comments such as the preceding indicate that opinions about hoard quantities sometimes differ widely. As it is, I consider myself fortunate that I was present and participated in the silver dollar releases from the mid-1950s onward and later interviewed some of the largest "players" in the market.

1888-S $1 (business strike mintage 657,000): The market and hoard history of the 1888-S bears a close resemblance to its cousin, the 1887-S. On the numismatic market the 1888-S was considered to be quite scarce in Mint State until bags were released in 1942 from storage in the San Francisco Mint. From then until the mid-1950s, quantities could be obtained for face value from that source.

In 1956 bags were released in Montana. However, dealer and collector interest was limited, and investor interest was nil. Most that were paid out went to Nevada casinos or to banks, where they were put into circulation and quickly descended the grading ladder to AU or lower levels. After the mid-1950s, the supply seems to have dried up.

The massive Treasury releases of 1962-1964 added few if any quantities to the supply of Mint State coins in numismatic and investment circles, although this is contrary to conventional wisdom that many bags came out at that time. The Redfield hoard (1976) is said to have had five to 10 bags, including thousands of prooflike coins. Today, the 1888-S is moderately scarce in quantity, although singles are easy enough to find.

1889 $1 (business strike mintage 21,726,000): The story of the 1889 dollar echoes that of 1888 and certain other Philadelphia Mint issues of the 1880s. Many were placed into circulation in or near the time of mintage, after which quantities were relegated to storage. It is likely that millions were melted under the 1918 Pittman Act. Occasional mint-sealed bags were paid out over a period of years—not enough that Mint State coins became common, but a sufficient quantity that 1889-dated dollars never became expensive either. A few bags were released in the postwar market of the late 1940s.

Beginning about December 1954, large numbers of bags containing millions of coins were dispersed through banks, mainly in the East. Collectors, dealers, and what few investors there were, looked at the gargantuan mintage figure and ignored the coins. As a result, most ended up in mixed bags of dollars, where they were among the most common dates. Additional quantities continued to be paid out for a long time, including during the 1962-1964 Treasury releases. Doubtless, many of these went to bullion melting pots in the heady silver bullion market of the late 1970s.

1889-CC $1 (business strike mintage 350,000): When Carson City silver dollars were being paid out from the Cash Room at the Treasury Department in Washington, many thousands of all issues 1878-1893 were distributed, *except* 1889-CC. Apparently, only a few single coins and rolls were given out, some of them as early as 1933-1934. By the 1950s, possibly only a few hundred coins remained on hand at the Cash Room. I have found no record of bags being distributed from Washington during that decade or any time later.

It is probably the case that more 1889-CC dollars were stored at the San Francisco Mint and/or in Federal Reserve stocks in the West than at the Treasury Building. In 1925 and 1926, quantities of 1889-CCs were paid out at face value from storage at the San Francisco Mint. Bags that came to light in the 1950s were all from the San Francisco Mint vaults, so far as I know. In the 1950s a bag of 1,000 pieces was released in Montana, followed by another in the early 1960s. Apparently, the first bag contained many heavily marked coins of a quality that today would be called AU-55 or 58. In addition, at least two intact bags were in existence in 1976 (one of these is from the Ben Stack group mentioned below). Probably, these have not been distributed.

Harry Warner of Mill Valley, California, told Walter Breen that he once owned a bag of 1,000 coins. Ben Stack told Harry J. Forman that he bought two bags by advertising in 1954 in the *Las Vegas Sun,* and another was acquired in this way or by buying it separately.[2] One of these bags went to Irving Davidoff, owner of the Klondyke Coin Exchange in New York City; another was dispersed by the roll; the third was still owned by Ben Stack as of February 1976, for he offered it to me at that time.

Only one solitary *coin* was left in the Treasury when the government decided to hold back CC dollars after payouts were halted in March 1964! Today in the 1990s the 1889-CC is recognized as a prime rarity, and individual Mint State coins are few and far between on the open market.

1889-O $1 (business strike mintage 11,875,000): Bags of 1889-O dollars were released over a period of time in later years, beginning at least as early as 1938 and continuing in small numbers to the mid-1950s. These pieces, coming from vaults in the Treasury Building in Washington, D.C., attracted little attention.

The 1962-1964 Treasury release of specimens stored in a sealed vault in the Philadelphia Mint included 1889-O

[1] Letter, October 29, 1992.

[2] Benjamin J. Stack (1925-1984) operated the Imperial Coin Company in Las Vegas at the time.

dollars, but it was not one of the more plentiful dates. Harry J. Forman had at least one Treasury bag in 1962. Reminiscing in *The Comprehensive Silver Dollar Encyclopedia,* Dean Tavenner said that he obtained one bag of 1888-O dollars in April 1964 just at the time his bank in Deer Lodge, Montana, was running out of silver dollars to pass out at face value. John Highfill reported having bags of this date and finding that 80% to 90% of the coins were flatly struck. Maurice Rosen reported handling bags of this coin, mostly consisting of MS-60 to MS-62 coins, lightly struck. A bag of 1,000 pieces came on the market from Pennsylvania in 1979. John Love once had a bag of 1889-O dollars, mostly prooflike, in the same decade.

1889-S $1 (business strike mintage 700,000): Until at least the mid-1920s, the 1889-S was considered to be the rarest of all Morgan dollars, outranking such issues as the 1889-CC, 1892-S, 1893-S, and 1895. Most old-time collections lacked an example in any grade. At the time of minting, nearly all 1889-S dollars went into storage, mostly at the San Francisco Mint. Finally, a few bags broke on the market in 1937, and many in the early 1940s, after which the 1889-S became common. During the early 1950s, quantities were available for face value at the San Francisco Mint. The sum of these releases is not known, but I imagine that somewhere on the order of 50,000 to 100,000 coins went into the hands of dealers, investors, collectors, casino owners, and others who saved them.

Today in the 1990s, the 1889-S, with its relatively low mintage, is one of the scarcer San Francisco Morgan dollars in Mint State, although it is hardly rare. The Redfield hoard (1976) is said to have contained several thousand Mint State coins, most of which were heavily bagmarked.

1890 $1 (business strike mintage 16,802,000): Uncirculated 1890 dollars were available on the numismatic market virtually from the time of striking. Quantities of the date were dumped on the market in 1941-1942, the mid-1950s, and after that time, continuing through the great Treasury release of 1962-1964. As was the case with its Philadelphia Mint brethren from the years of the 1880s, the 1890 was ignored by just about everyone. When it came to stashing away a few rolls or bags for investment, most hoarders seemed to prefer coins with mintmarks. In any event, most Mint State coins distributed in the 1950s found their way into bags of mixed dollars.

The bag quantities released by the Treasury in the 1950s and 1960s mostly consisted of lower Mint State grade coins. Wayne Miller reported that many of these were coated with a dark, greasy substance that did not hurt the coins, but which had to be carefully removed with a solvent. I personally do not recall seeing cosmoline—or whatever it was—on quantities of 1890 dollars in Eastern banks, but enough greasy coins must have existed at one time that notice was taken of them by others.

1890-CC $1 (business strike mintage 2,309,041): After the Carson City Mint closed down its coinage facilities, quantities of undistributed dollars remained there. Later, many bags were shipped to the San Francisco Mint and to the Treasury Building in Washington, D.C., for storage.

In 1942-1943 many bags of 1890-CC dollars were paid out at face value by the San Francisco Mint. Probably two or three bags went to dealers and collectors at the time, and the rest went into circulation in the West, particularly in Nevada. The Treasury Building, directly across the street (to the left) from the White House, was the repository for millions of Carson City dollars in the early twentieth century. In the early 1930s, several bags of these came out, and from these, hundreds of coins were snapped up by dealers and collectors. In 1941-1942, additional bags were released, after which the payouts slowed for the rest of the decade.

In the early and mid-1950s many bags of Uncirculated 1890-CC dollars were released at face value to dealers with connections; a familiar story by now. Steve Ruddel, who was one of the most active dealers in Morgan dollars in quantity, stated that about 50 bags (50,000 coins) were released from the Treasury Building in 1955, and this was only part of the story.[1] Some of these were also given out in the 1950s from storage in the San Francisco Mint—in effect, a distribution on both coasts. By 1956-1957 they were becoming scarce, but Harry J. Forman handled at least 10 bags during this time. The Treasury stock dwindled, and in the late 1950s an order was given to stop paying them out.

During the 1962-1964 Treasury release of dollars, it is unlikely that many 1890-CCs were involved. In 1964 the Treasury took stock of its remaining holdings, by which time only 3,949 1890-CC dollars remained. These were sold in the 1970s by the General Services Administration. The Redfield hoard is said to have contained about two bags, including many mirrorlike coins.

1890-O $1 (business strike mintage 10,701,000): Probably at least 500,000 of these, if not far more, were held by the Treasury (and stored in Philadelphia) until the 1960s, and released during the 1962-1964 era. Earlier, 1890-O dollars had been paid out over a long period of decades including an especially large release occurring in 1953-1954.

1890-S $1 (business strike mintage 8,230,373): Quantities of 1890-S dollars were placed into circulation at or near the time of mintage. Many others were stored in the San Francisco Mint, from which location several million or more probably were melted under the terms of the 1918 Pittman Act. In addition, over a long period of years, occasional bags were released. As a result, the 1890-S is one of the San Francisco Mint issues that has never been rare in Mint State—quite a contrast to its 1889-S sibling.

In the 1940s and 1950s, many bags were paid out from the San Francisco Mint; so many, in fact, that this date became extremely common. Not having a low mintage figure to bolster their appeal, most coins slipped into circulation, where they quickly became AU and then EF. Still, many thousands remained in the hands of collectors, dealers, investors, and other buyers. The Redfield hoard (1976) contained 26 bags,[2] mostly MS-60 to 62 in grade, probably obtained from storage at the San Francisco Mint.

1891 $1 (business strike mintage 8,693,556): The Federal Reserve released many bags of these in 1954-1955 and again in the late 1950s and very early 1960s (before the massive releases of 1962-1964). There were so many that

[1] Advertisement in *The Numismatist,* January 1964.

[2] David W. Akers, letter, July 7, 1996; this information is new to the silver dollar field and supersedes earlier estimates.

Harry J. Forman reported that virtually every bank in Philadelphia was loaded with them, and that they were by far the most common dollar date available.

The 1891 dollar was not represented in quantity among the dollars released in 1962-1964. By that time, most had been dispersed. Many had acquired light wear and had slipped into the "slider" category. By the mid-1960s the supply had been absorbed by the public and by investors, and the 1891 was no longer considered to be among the more common dates.

1891-CC $1 (business strike mintage 1,618,000): In the early twentieth century, large quantities of Carson City dollars of the 1891 date were shipped to the San Francisco Mint for storage. In 1925-1926, in the early 1940s, and particularly in 1942, many bags of these were paid out at face value, so many in the 1940s that silver dollar dealer specialists such as Norman Shultz stopped buying them. By late 1942, the 1891-CC dollar was by far the commonest Carson City issue in collectors' and dealers' hands in Mint State. These continued to be paid out at face value to dealers and others in the 1950s, and also shipped to Nevada for use as casino coins. Harry J. Forman bought at least 10 bags from John Skubis and Arnold Rosing; these originally came from San Francisco Mint storage.

Early in the present century, additional quantities of this issue were also shipped to the Treasury Building in Washington, D.C., for storage. In the 1950s, bags of 1891-CC dollars were released from the Cash Room at the Treasury Building. The quantities are not known, but dozens of bags were involved. Dealer Steve Ruddel stated that about 50 bags (50,000 coins) were released from the Treasury Building in 1955 alone.[1] Dean Tavenner recalled that one bag was released in Deer Lodge, Montana, circa 1958-1959. By that time, no more were being released from Treasury stocks.

So far as I know, few if any came out in the 1962-1964 Treasury release. However, some were still on hand at the Treasury Building in Washington. 5,687 leftover coins from this source were sold by the G.S.A. in the 1970s, with an additional 19 pieces later sold in the "mixed lot" offering. The Redfield estate (1976) was estimated to have contained three to five bags of Mint State coins, most of which were heavily bagmarked. These probably came out of the San Francisco Mint, to Nevada casinos in the 1950s. Today, few quantity lots of 1891-CC dollars survive.

1891-O $1 (business strike mintage 7,954,529): The 1891-O has received little publicity over the years. Part of this is because the typical coin is poorly struck and aesthetically unappealing. Mint State coins have always been available on the market, and at low prices, probably indicating that occasional bags were released over a long span of time.

A significant dispersal occurred circa 1946-1947, after which roll quantities were held by various dealer specialists. The supply then tightened. Around 1955-1956, some bags were paid out of the Cash Room at the Treasury Department in Washington, and for a time the 1891-O was plentiful, but not common. The supply seems to have dried up, to the point at which Uncirculated specimens were scarce by October 1962, when O-Mint coins were released in quantity from storage at the Philadelphia Mint. Harry J. Forman, for one, handled many bags of 1891-O dollars in the early 1960s. Still, the issue was not common in the sense that 1883-O, 1884-O, and 1885-O dollars were.

From the viewpoint of numismatic legislative history the 1891-O dollar occupies a special niche in the annals of the denomination (for reasons that the reader may want to investigate).

1891-S $1 (business strike mintage 5,296,000): Quantities of Uncirculated 1891-S dollars were stored at the San Francisco Mint after striking, and remained there for many years. Bags were released from time to time—not many, but enough to keep the market price in the "common date" category. In 1941-1942 a major payout occurred, and from that time through the next 10 years, 1891-S dollars were plentiful, especially in West Coast bank vaults and in the stocks of dealers there. The supply seems to have diminished during the early 1950s, and by later in the decade bag quantities were no longer seen and roll holdings were sparse.

It said that the 1962-1964 Treasury dispersals included a few 1891-S dollars, but I have no record that any significant quantity came out. Probably, most had been paid out before that time. The Redfield estate (1976) is said to have contained about 5,000 pieces, which Wayne Miller described as being well struck and lustrous, but "with plentiful abrasions."

1892 $1 (business strike mintage 1,036,000): Large quantities of Mint State 1892 dollars were released by the Treasury in the late 1950s and early 1960s, before which time they were rare. By the late 1950s, they were very common. Harry J. Forman reported that Uncirculated 1892 dollars were second only to 1891 dollars from the standpoint of availability through Philadelphia banks at the time. However, by the time that the Treasury began emptying its vaults in earnest, circa 1962-1964, most 1892 dollars had already been paid out. The date was not well represented among later Treasury hoard coins. It has been suggested that the Redfield hoard had a partial bag of coins, and these mostly graded MS-60 to MS-62.

1892-CC $1 (business strike mintage 1,352,000): When the Carson City Mint closed down, quantities of 1892-CC dollars were shipped for storage to the San Francisco Mint and, to a lesser extent, to the Treasury Building in Washington, D.C. From the San Francisco Mint, quantities were paid out over a period of years, including 1925-1926, but particularly in the late 1940s and early 1950s. Some bags, but probably not many, were dispersed from the Cash Room at the Treasury Department in Washington during the same time frame, up through 1950-1953. Then came a quantity dispersal. Dealer Steve Ruddel stated that about 50 bags (50,000 coins) of 1892-CC dollars were released from the Treasury Building in 1955 alone.[2]

Few if any 1892-CCs were part of the Treasury release of 1962-1964. When the government took stock of the situation in March 1964 and stopped paying out Morgan and Peace dollars of any and all dates, just a single Uncirculated 1892-CC dollar remained! The news of the non-availability of the 1892-CC in the surviving Treasury cache caused a run-up in prices in the 1960s and 1970s.

---

[1] Advertisement in *The Numismatist,* January 1964.

[2] *Ibid.*

The Redfield hoard, bought by A-Mark in 1976, contained 1,700 Uncirculated specimens, a group acquired in the same year by Paramount International Coin Corporation, Englewood, Ohio.[1]

Wayne Miller in his *Morgan and Peace Dollar Textbook,* 1982, reported that as of that time, "large quantities of this date still exist in BU condition." Probably, most such holdings have been dispersed by now.

1892-O $1 (business strike mintage 2,744,000): The 1892-O dollar has always been available in Mint State on the coin market. Generous quantities were released at and immediately following the time of mintage. A few bags were released in the 1950s from storage in the Treasury Building in Washington, D.C. However, the great deluge of this issue came during the unsealing in October 1962 of a vault in the Philadelphia Mint holding about 10 million Uncirculated New Orleans dollars. After that time, Harry J. Forman handled at least 20 bags and reported that the issue was very common in bag quantities. The Redfield estate (1976) is said to have had two to four bags, with the coins heavily damaged by a counting machine used during the pre-auction appraisal. In 1977 a bag from another source, said to have contained numerous gems, was dispersed. In the 1980s, Bowers and Merena Galleries handled a bag of 1892-O dollars from a Pennsylvania estate. Most coins in the latter group were in the range of about MS-62 to MS-63.

1892-S $1 (business strike mintage 1,200,000): San Francisco Mint dispersals from storage in the 1940s and 1950s apparently yielded no bags of this date, nor were any among the untold millions of Morgan dollars paid out by the Treasury during the 1962-1964 emptying of government vaults. However, it is known that at least one bag of 1892-S dollars was paid out by the San Francisco Mint decades earlier in 1925-1926. Few coins reached numismatic circles, as there was little collecting interest in Morgan dollar mintmarks at the time. Perhaps, some of the AU coins now known came from that release. which went into circulation. Today no quantity holdings are known.

1893 $1 (business strike mintage 378,000): Many bags of 1893 dollars were released by the Treasury in the mid-1950s and very early 1960s. John J. Ford, Jr., handled at least one bag in 1952, dribbling out the contents for years. Circa 1959, John Love reported handling one bag. At least one bag was sold by LaVere Redfield prior to his death, and multiple bags were bought by Superior Stamp & Coin Co. from Redfield's widow prior to the sale at auction of Redfield silver dollars in January 1976, by which time the holding had been reduced to two to four bags. Few bags were in the 1962-1964 Treasury release.

1893-CC $1 (business strike mintage 677,000): Mint bags of 1893-CC dollars came on the market as early as 1920 at face value through the Cash Room at the Treasury in Washington and, in particular, from storage at the San Francisco Mint. However, the quantity was small in comparison to certain other Carson City dates, particularly those of the early and mid-1880s. The supply seems to have been exhausted by the late 1950s, and there are no records of any quantities being paid out after that time. However, during the 1950s the 1893-CC was sufficiently plentiful that Harry J. Forman handled at least 10 bags (10,000 coins), and other quantities were bought and sold by other dollar specialists. Just one solitary coin turned up in the General Services Administration's holding held back in March 1964.

The Redfield estate contained a single bag of 1,000 coins, most of which were damaged when they were run through a mechanical counting machine.[2] These probably came from storage at the San Francisco Mint and were probably paid out in the 1950s. For example, in 1955 a bag of 1,000 was released through a bank in Great Falls, Montana.

In the modern market, groups of 1893-CC dollars are seldom seen. Most 1893-CC dollars are very extensively bagmarked (they share "honors" with 1895-S in this regard).

1893-O $1 (business strike mintage 300,000): A few bags of 1893-O dollars were paid out at face value from the Cash Room of the Treasury Building from about 1948 to 1955. These may have been released a few coins at a time, rather than in intact 1,000-coin bags. These furnished the source for dealers' stocks. About 1958-1959 it was realized that even rolls were scarce. I have no record of bags of 1893-O being included in the 1962-1964 Treasury releases.

1893-S $1 (business strike mintage 100,000): I have located no record of any 1,000-coin bags being released in the past half century. However, 20 examples of 1893-S are said to have been found mixed in with a bag of Uncirculated 1894-S dollars which came to light in Great Falls, Montana in the early 1950s (reported by Wayne Miller). These were sold into the market over a period of years, and all were gone by the mid-1970s. Harry Warner told Walter Breen that he knew of a mint bag of 1,000 1893-S dollars, but this has not been seen, and I know nothing about it. In the early 1970s, dealer Aaron Stollman told Maurice Rosen that he had handled a brilliant Uncirculated roll of 1893-S.[3] Today the 1893-S is a landmark rarity in Mint State.

1 David W. Akers, letter, July 7, 1996; this information is new to the silver dollar field.
2 *Ibid.;* this information is new to the silver dollar field and supersedes earlier estimates.
3 Undated commentary from Maurice Rosen, received by the author November 2, 1992.

1894 $1 (business strike mintage 110,000): Several 1,000-coin bags of Uncirculated 1894 dollars were released in the 1950s and early 1960s. A bag from Great Falls, Montana, was sold by John B. Love around 1961. In the early 1960s, a bag containing a mixture of Uncirculated 1893 and 1894 dollars was located in San Francisco. This date was not represented in significant quantities in the Treasury release of 1962-1964, so far as I know.

1894-O $1 (business strike mintage 1,723,000): A few bags of Uncirculated 1894-O dollars came on the market in the East during the early 1950s. In 1962-1964, other 1894-Os came out during the dispersal of O-Mint dollars from storage in a sealed vault at the Philadelphia Mint, but probably not more than a few thousand coins. Steve Ruddel told Wayne Miller that he declined to buy a bag of Uncirculated 1894-O dollars (and also a bag of 1896-O dollars) for $3 per coin, for "at that time no one knew what was going to be available next." Harry J. Forman handled one bag of this date. Wayne Miller wrote that in the 1970s, groups of 20 to 100 coins (one to five rolls) were common.

1894-S $1 (business strike mintage 1,260,000): Bags of 1894-S dollars were distributed in San Francisco in the 1950s. Several bags were released in Deer Lodge, Montana, in the early 1950s, one of which contained 20 1893-S dollars mixed in with 980 1894-S pieces. John Skubis reported buying a bag of 1894-S dollars for face value from the San Francisco Mint in the 1950s.

Apparently, most quantities of 1894-S dollars were released well in advance of the Treasury dispersal of 1962-1964. This is one date that did not get a "play" during the fast and furious trading times of the early 1960s. Probably for this reason, the Redfield estate had none. In 1982 Wayne Miller wrote that many hoards containing up to 100 coins had appeared on the market in recent years. By now in the 1990s, most if not all such quantities have been widely dispersed. Indeed, few caches remained intact after the great investment bull market of the late 1970s.

1895 $1 (business strike mintage 12,000): It is not known for sure if any business strikes were made. Mint records indicate 12,000, but these may have represented coins dated 1894. The writer has never seen a Mint State 1895, and perhaps none exist. No hoards are rumored or known, although the search for such has been the Holy Grail of Morgan dollar specialists for decades. In 1895 Proofs were minted to the extent of 880 pieces, and these represent the sole supply.

1895-O $1 (business strike mintage 450,000): Around the 1950s a small number of Mint State coins were released from storage in the Treasury Building in Washington, D.C. Probably from a few dozen to a couple of hundred went into the hands of dealers and collectors and have largely "disappeared into the woodwork" since that time. Market information is difficult to obtain today, for listings of "Uncirculated" coins years ago were apt to represent what we would call AU today. Harry J. Forman, who has handled as many O-Mint dollars as anyone, never heard of a quantity of true Mint State 1895-O dollars. Apparently, no 1895-O dollars were represented in the Treasury release of 1962-1964. The true rarity of high-level Mint State 1895-O dollars was not appreciated until the present decade of the 1990s. From a "sleeper rarity" viewpoint the 1895-O dollar deserves some sort of award!

1895-S $1 (business strike mintage 400,000): Examples of 1895-S filtered out of the San Francisco Mint over a long period of years in the normal course of business. A few bags of 1895-S dollars were released by the San Francisco Mint in 1942, much to the delight of the few Bay Area numismatists who might have been interested at the time. From then through the very early 1950s more bags were paid out., but then the distribution stopped. By 1953-1955, 1895-S dollars were considered to be rare. John Skubis recalled that K.O. Cunningham, of Nevada, offered a bag for sale at this time, but John did not buy it for he was fearful that a lot more would be released at face value. Indeed, some additional coins were released, but most went to casinos or the public—rather than to dealers.

The Redfield estate had a mint bag of 1,000 coins,[1] nearly all of which coins were bagmarked, and many of which were said to have been damaged by a coin counting machine.

Mint State 1895-S dollars are known for their extensive bagmarks; a characteristic also common among 1893-CC dollars.

1896 $1 (business strike mintage 9,976,000): Vast quantities of Uncirculated 1896 dollars were released in the mid-1950s and early 1960s, making this one of the most plentiful of all Philadelphia Mint dollars and one of the most frequently seen Morgan dollars dated in the 1890s. I imagine that half a million or more Mint State coins exist, and the number may be well over a million. John B. Love handled 16 or 17 bags from the Redfield estate, selling many of these to John Kamin of *The Forecaster* newsletter. However, the Redfield coins were just a drop in the ocean in relation to the total number of Uncirculated coins in existence.

Among rare coin dealers there is an awareness that if it is a Morgan dollar and if it is dated in the 1890s, chances are good that it may be rare. However, there are a few exceptions, the most obvious of which is the 1896—which is among the most common of all Morgan dollars. Other contenders for being seen frequently are 1897, 1898-O, and 1899-O.

1896-O $1 (business strike mintage 4,900,000): In 1953, New York dealer Philip Maul broke up one bag, possibly two. A few more bags came out in 1956. Little attention seems to have been paid to this date. It was considered neither rare nor common. Striking was not of the best, and for this reason 1896-O dollars were not especially sought.

In the early 1960s, some additional bags came out, probably from storage in the Philadelphia Mint. John B. Love recalled buying a bag of coins in Billings, Montana, a quantity consisting of weakly struck pieces without a prooflike coin in the lot. Steve Ruddel, Washington, D.C. dealer in quantities of dollars in the early 1960s, told of turning down a bag at a low price, as he did not know if this was just the tip of the iceberg; for all he (or anyone else) knew, hundreds of bags might have been forthcoming (as in the case with 1898-O and other issues).

A bag of 1896-O dollars was reportedly stolen from LaVere Redfield in 1963 as part of a burglary involving about 100,000 coins (Miller, p. 6).

[1] David W. Akers, letter, July 7, 1996; this information is new to the silver dollar field and supersedes earlier estimates.

A few other bags of 1896-O dollars turned up in the early 1960s, but the number could not have been large. Harry J. Forman, an astute observer of the Morgan dollar scene, stated that he had neither heard of nor handled a bag of this issue. Survivors in Mint State are nearly all in lower ranges such as MS-60 and MS-61.

1896-S $1 (business strike mintage 5,000,000): Bags of 1896-S Uncirculated dollars were paid out from the San Francisco Mint during the very early 1950s, when scant attention was paid to them as they had little value at the time. A few years later, John Skubis and Arnold Rosing jointly bought a bag which turned up at a bank in Oakland, California. Perhaps another bag or two came out as well during that era. The issue seems to have been plentiful enough as singles in the 1950s and 1960s, but rare in quantity, although it should be noted that Harry J. Forman advertised a 20-coin roll in May 1965.

At least several hundred coins, probably from a California or Nevada dealer source, found their way to the holdings of Reno investor LaVere Redfield and were later included in his estate. Reportedly, most of the Redfield coins would grade from MS-60 to 63 if evaluated today. Wayne Miller reported that roll quantities of 1896-S dollars appeared on the market in the early 1970s, but by the early 1980s they were largely dispersed.

1897 $1 (business strike mintage 2,822,000): Once considered rare, Morgan dollars of 1897 were later released in large quantities, and by the 1950s mint bags were common in Eastern banks. By that time, they had no premium value, so no attention was paid to them. Among dollars of the 1890s, they are second only to the common 1896 in terms of availability today.

The Treasury release of 1962-1964 brought forth other bags, probably by the hundreds or more. Bags were released in Montana early in 1963 and in California and Nevada shortly thereafter. Later, in the mid-1970s, an estimated 16 to 18 bags were in the Redfield estate and were sold through John B. Love, reportedly many to John Kamin, publisher of *The Forecaster* newsletter.

In 1982, Wayne Miller wrote: "This date is a favorite of promoters because it is readily available and has a deceptively low mintage." A lot of water has gone under the numismatic bridge since 1982, and what was common then is less so now; at least, what was concentrated in just a few places then is apt to be widely dispersed now. I recall that in the 1950s I could have bought a truckload of Mint State 1897 Morgan dollars (or any one of several other dates) for face value. Now, even a single bag of this common date would be worthy of notice if it came on the market.

1897-O $1 (business strike mintage 4,004,000): A few bags of 1897-O dollars came on the market in the East in the greater area comprising New Jersey, eastern Pennsylvania, and southern New York, in the late 1940s and again in the early 1950s. These were from storage in the Treasury Building in Washington, D.C. There was little investor interest at the time.

It has been said that a few bags of 1897-O dollars were part of the Treasury release of 1962-1964, from storage in a sealed vault at the Philadelphia Mint, but I have found no specific record of them. Harry J. Forman, who never handled a bag of 1897-O dollars, reported that New York dealer Joel Coen is said to have had 10 rolls (200 coins), perhaps from the 1962-1964 distribution. Other 1897-O dollars turned up in quantity through the branch of the Federal Reserve Bank in Helena, Montana, but these were lightly circulated coins mixed in with "slider" 1894-O, 1895-O, and 1896-O pieces. A bag of 1897-O dollars was reportedly stolen from LaVere Redfield in 1963 (Miller, p. 6). The 1897-O issue is not one to have attracted much attention for the typical piece is lightly struck and unattractive.

1897-S $1 (business strike mintage 5,825,000): The 1897-S was issued in bag quantities from the San Francisco Mint in the mid-1920s, 1950s, and early 1960s and was not worth a significant premium at the time, nor was it ever considered to be a scarce date. Many from the distributions of the 1950s and 1960s went to the gaming tables in Reno and Las Vegas. Some found their way to investors and hoarders, including LaVere Redfield, who reportedly had as many as 20 bags. Quantities persisted on the coin market for much of the 1970s, but by now in the 1990s groups are seldom seen. The ability of Americans to absorb quantities of Morgan dollars is remarkable, and throughout the Morgan series many issues that were once plentiful would be difficult to find in one place today, even a holding of a dozen or two pieces.

1898 $1 (business strike mintage 5,884,000): The 1898 was released in large quantities by the Treasury Department through the Federal Reserve and by the mid-1950s Mint State coins were very common in Eastern banks. However, before that time Uncirculated coins were scarce, or even rare. Additional large quantities were released in the late 1950s and early 1960s. By the mid-1970s, most such quantities had been widely dispersed, with the result that the Redfield estate holding, estimated to have been about 16 to 18 bags, was a novelty at the time. Most of these Redfield coins went to John Kamin, publisher of *The Forecaster* newsletter.

1898-O $1 (business strike mintage 4,440,000): If you had been a collector of Uncirculated Morgan dollars in September 1962, high on your want list would have been the 1898-O, along with the 1903-O, and 1904-O. These three were the most formidable rarities among Mint State New Orleans dollars, and even the most in-depth dealer's stock was not likely to have an example of any one of the three! If you could have found one, it would have set you back $300 to $400 or more. The current *Guide Book* listed the value at $300, or double the price of the 1889-CC. A bag of 1,000 coins, if such existed, would have had a theoretical market value of over $300,000!

None were to be had, although a few bags had come out of storage in the Treasury Building in Washington, D.C. in the 1940s and early 1950s and, except for a few hundred pieces that went into dealers' stocks, the coins had slipped into circulation.

But, not to worry. In October 1962, the rarity status of the 1898-O and certain other key issues changed, and with it changed the face of American numismatics. From deep within the vaults of the Philadelphia Mint, where millions of New Orleans dollars had been stored since they were moved there in 1929, came a cascade of bright, sparkling 1898-O dollars, along with 1903-O, 1904-O, and other dates. Distributed through the Federal Reserve System, some of these 1898-O dollars were released in Michigan; perhaps the first ones were. Before long, they were coming out in many places. How the mighty had fallen, and within a few months a bag of 1,000 1898-O dollars was worth not $300,000, but in the $1,200 range!

How many bags of 1898-O dollars were released? The answer is not known, but it was at least many hundreds, if not a thousand or more—the latter amounting to 1,000,000 or more coins. All of a sudden, the public became fascinated with Morgan silver dollars. Collectors who had ignored the series earlier, became interested. The number of available Morgan dollars multiplied many times over, but the number of collectors interested also multiplied. The rest is history. For closely related commentary, see 1903-O and 1904-O listings.

1898-S $1 (business strike mintage 4,102,000): The Treasury Department released numerous bags of 1898-S dollars in the mid-1920s and again in the 1940s and 1950s, primarily from storage in the San Francisco Mint. They had little value as collectors' items in the 1920s, and very little in the 1940s and early 1950s either, and were widely dispersed, including to visitors to Nevada casinos. By the time of the 1962-1964 Treasury dispersal, most 1898-S dollars were gone.

The Redfield estate auctioned in 1976 contained "several thousand prooflike Uncirculated coins, some of which were very nice."[1]

1899 $1 (business strike mintage 330,000): From the early 1950s through the very early 1960s, numerous bags came to light. Harry J. Forman reported handling about 10 bags, mostly obtained from Las Vegas (an unusual source for Philadelphia dollars; most coins surfacing there were from the San Francisco or, less often, Carson City Mint). Probably, somewhere between 50,000 and 100,000 Mint State coins were released at the time.

The Treasury dispersal of 1962-1964 saw more 1899 dollars brought out into the open from long-term storage. Bags were released in Montana early in 1963 and in California and Nevada shortly thereafter. Today, 1899 dollars are usually seen one coin at a time.

1899-O $1 (business strike mintage 12,290,000): Beginning in 1947-1948 and continuing through the early 1950s, several bags of 1899-O dollars were released in the East from storage in the Treasury Building in Washington, D.C., and were distributed among banks. A few dealers took advantage of the opportunity to stock up on a bag or two or a few rolls. Prior to this time, the 1899-O was a rarity in Mint State, although few collectors or dealers realized this.

However, it was not until October 1962 that large quantities of bags of this issue became available. The occasion was the well-known release of long-hidden New Orleans Mint dollars from a sealed vault in the Philadelphia Mint. In the great Treasury release of 1962-1964, 1899-O coins were among the first silver dollars in quantity to see the light of day.

1899-S $1 (business strike mintage 2,562,000): A steady stream of Uncirculated 1899-S dollars—singly, in groups, and by the bag—was paid out by the San Francisco Mint during the period from 1942 through the mid-1950s. By the time of the great Treasury release of 1962-1964, only a few bags were left.

Conventional wisdom has it that the Redfield hoard had a bag of high quality coins (per Wayne Miller) or less than a full bag, in MS-60 to 63 (per John Highfill), probably from the San Francisco Mint in the 1950s via casino shipments to Nevada. However, a contribution to the present book from David W. Akers clarifies the situation: "Redfield had several thousand coins, some of which were very nice, as Wayne Miller says."[2]

1900 $1 (business strike mintage 8,830,000): Bags of 1,000 dollars were released on the East Coast in the 1950s, and the issue came to be recognized as a common date. By the time of the massive Treasury release of 1962-1964, extending to March 1964, most had been paid out; few bags were distributed at this time. In terms of Treasury dispersals and of surviving coins, certain parallels can be drawn between Philadelphia Mint 1900 dollars and those dated 1896.

1900-O $1 (business strike mintage 12,590,000): After the New Orleans Mint was closed, many bags of 1900-O dollars were shipped to the Treasury Building in Washington, D.C. and in 1929 to the Philadelphia Mint for storage. Bags of 1900-O dollars dribbled out from the Treasury Building holding by the early 1930s, continuing through at least the early 1950s.

Unlike the 1898-O, 1903-O, and 1904-O, all of which were deemed to be great rarities in Uncirculated grade, the 1889-O, 1890-O, 1894-O, 1896-O, 1897-O, 1899-O, 1900-O, and 1901-O were on the market in bag and roll quantities in the early part of the 1950s. For example, Philip Maul, a Hudson, New York dealer, advertised rolls of these particular issues in *The Numismatist* in September 1953. In the September 1957 issue of *The Numismatist,* Harry J. Forman advertised that he had Uncirculated specimens of the following New Orleans issues available in quantity: 1879-O, 1881-O, 1882-O, 1883-O, 1884-O, 1885-O, 1887-O, 1888-O, and 1901-O.

In October 1962, the 1900-O was front row center in the great dispersal of New Orleans dollars from long-term storage at the Philadelphia Mint. Hundreds of thousands were released. Wayne Miller wrote in 1982 that in roll quantities, 1900-O was believed to be scarcer than 1898-O, 1899-O, 1902-O, and 1904-O, and ran a close contest with 1901-O. Even so, today in the 1990s there are plenty to go around.

---

[1] *Ibid.*

[2] Letter, July 7, 1996. David W. Akers was general manager of Paramount International Coin Corporation, who bought these coins from A-Mark, successful bidder for the Redfield estate dollars.

1900-O/CC $1 (business strike mintage unknown; a small part of 1900-O): Bags of 1900-O dollars had O/CC coins mixed in. In the mid-1980s, Bowers and Merena Galleries handled a quantity of unsorted Mint State 1900-O dollars from a Montana holding, and about a third to a quarter were 1900-O/CC. However, I believe that this was an unusual situation, and that the total population of 1900-O/CC dollars is only a tiny fraction of that of 1900-O.

In 1992, Dwight Manley, then associated with Spectrum Numismatics, obtained and began the dispersal of a full original bag of 1900-O/CC dollars from a Chicago source. The distribution of grades (PCGS certification) was as follows: MS-67: 1 coin, MS-66: 10, MS-65: 150, MS-64: 260, MS-63: 340, and MS-60 through 62 (not certified): 239.[1]

1900-S $1 (business strike mintage 3,540,000): Vast quantities of 1900-S dollars were stored at the San Francisco Mint. These were paid out over a period of years in the late 1930s, 1940s, and 1950s. Many went to Nevada casinos in the latter decade. In the 1962-1964 period, many additional bags were released. By the time that the government stocks were exhausted 1900-S was a plentiful coin in the hands of investors, dealers, and the public.

1901 $1 (business strike mintage 6,962,000): So far as is known, this date was not represented in any Treasury releases of the 1940s, 1950s, or the remarkable early 1960s. Today, Mint State coins are scarce and anything truly MS-63 or finer is a great rarity. On the other hand, well-worn pieces are extremely common.

1901-O $1 (business strike mintage 13,320,000): The story is a familiar one. After the New Orleans Mint ceased business, quantities of silver dollars were shipped to Washington, D.C. and Philadelphia for storage. From vaults in the Treasury Building in Washington, D.C., Uncirculated 1901-O dollars dribbled out onto the market from the early 1930s onward. Prior to that time, the 1901-O in Uncirculated grade was a major rarity, although in the absence of research on the subject few numismatists realized this.

In 1953, a major release occurred, followed by distributions through the mid-1950s. Obtaining coins indirectly from this source, Philip Maul advertised rolls in *The Numismatist* in September 1953. In the September 1957 issue of *The Numismatist,* Harry J. Forman advertised that he had Uncirculated specimens of 1901-O available in quantity. In general, anyone who stocked Uncirculated dollars was apt to have a supply of this date.

Any quantities released in the 1950s paled into insignificance in October 1962, when a long-sealed vault in the Philadelphia Mint was opened, and countless thousands of sparkling, new 1901-O dollars were released.

1901-S $1 (business strike mintage 2,284,000): 1901-S dollars were paid out by the San Francisco Mint over a long period of years, beginning at least by 1925. In addition, bags of this issue were stored in the Treasury Building in Washington, D.C. and were released from time to time, as early as the 1930s. Quantities remained in dealers' hands as recently as the 1950s. In later years, the 1901-S became harder to find.

Quantities released in 1962-1964 were probably small. John B. Love noted in ***The Comprehensive U.S. Silver Dollar Encyclopedia*** that two bags of these were found in Idaho in the early 1960s and were bought by Bill Holdman in Great Falls, Montana.

1902 $1 (business strike mintage 7,994,000): Like a number of other Philadelphia Mint Morgan dollars, the 1902 in Mint State was elusive before the 1930s. Circa 1947-1948, the Treasury paid out bags of 1902 dollars, but still they remained somewhat scarce. In the early 1950s, additional quantities were paid out, and in the closing years of the decade, many bags came to light. Today, probably well over 100,000 Mint State coins exist, but these are usually seen just a few coins at a time or as singles.

1902-O $1 (business strike mintage 8,636,000): Although 1902-O dollars seeped out over a period of years from storage in the Treasury Building in Washington, D.C., especially in the late 1950s and very early 1960s (before autumn 1962), the date was not considered common until a vast torrent of hundreds of thousands emerged from a sealed vault in the Philadelphia Mint in October 1962 and ensuing months. Earlier, the 1902-O was considered to be a rarity in Mint State, and for a period of years it was priced higher than, for example, the 1884-S.

1902-S $1 (business strike mintage 1,530,000): Large quantities of 1902-S dollars were paid out from storage at the San Francisco Mint over a long period of years, with substantial releases occurring in the late 1920s, 1940s, and early 1950s, plus at other intervals.

Conventional wisdom has it that the Redfield estate (1976) had up to a bag of 1902-S dollars, most being either of MS-60 to MS-63 grade (per John Highfill) or of high quality (per Wayne Miller). However, in a recent contribution to this book, David W. Akers, who handled the coins at the time, stated that there were "several thousand pieces, but not many of high quality."[2]

1903 $1 (business strike mintage 4,652,000): Mint State specimens of 1903 remained elusive until 1955, when many bags were paid out in the East. In the 1960s, a dealer in Salinas, California made a specialty of 1903 Philadelphia Mint Morgan dollars and at one time accumulated a cache amounting to over 50 bags (50,000 coins).[3] The Redfield estate (1976) is said to have had less than a bag of coins, grading MS-60 to 63.

1903-O $1 (business strike mintage 4,450,000): In terms

[1] Dwight Manley, letter, October 28, 1992.
[2] Letter, July 7, 1996.
[3] Recollection of Steve Markoff; telephone conversation with the author, April 15, 1992.

of historical significance relative to Treasury hoards and its impact on the numismatic hobby, 1903-O is THE Morgan dollar of all time. In fact, in all of American numismatics there is probably no other single coin that led the way for a sweeping changes as did the 1903-O. (If there is a runner-up it is the 1950-D Jefferson nickel.)

For decades the 1903-O was considered to be the rarest and most desirable of all Morgan dollar varieties. Even major collections were apt to lack a specimen in Mint State, and it was believed that fewer than a half dozen existed. When B. Max Mehl sold the William Forrester Dunham Collection in 1941, the Uncirculated 1903-O was featured as an important rarity.

In what may be the most single watershed hoard release in the history of American numismatics, and an event which forever changed collecting preferences, dozens of 1,000-coin bags of 1903-O dollars were released in autumn 1962 and early 1963. Exactly how many coins were involved is not known, and guesses have ranged from 60,000 or so to over 1,000,000. Wayne Miller's estimate is 60,000 to 100,000. Probably, the truth lies somewhere between 60,000 and several hundred thousand. I suggest 200,000 to 350,000.

As the 1903-O is rare in worn grades, probably most of the 4,450,000 coins originally minted were melted under the Pittman Act of 1918. Reminiscing in *The Comprehensive Silver Dollar Encyclopedia,* Dean Tavenner said that in Helena, Montana a banker had 1903-O dollars available in quantity by February 1963. Writing in *The Numismatist* in January 1964, Steve Ruddel told of an unspecified Kansas City dealer who "panicked...when he got a bag of '03-Os. He soon flooded his local market and got $3 or $4 each. At the same time I had a standing offer of $15,000 a bag and couldn't buy any."

I was first told about the release of 1903-O (and 1898-O and 1904-O) dollars by Harry J. Forman, who telephoned dealers and collectors around the country in autumn 1962 to alert them to the situation and also to warn them against deception. It seems that a few clever insiders obtained coins of these three formerly-rare dates, and hurried to dealers' stores to sell them for cash—at prices based upon the old catalogue listings. One such insider flew to London, where he endeavored to steal a march on B.A. Seaby, Ltd., A.H. Baldwin & Sons, and Spink & Son, Ltd., the three leading British rare coin dealers at the time.

After the news broke, I was offered a few bags for $17,000 each in late 1962 or early 1963 by a Detroit source, but I declined, as I was fearful that about four million more coins would be coming out of the Treasury; I was wrong on the four million, but time would have vindicated a purchase at $17,000 per bag.

Today, the 1903-O remains as one of the most legendary coins in American numismatics, but one that can be purchased for a very reasonable price. Because of the 1903-O dollar release and its consequences the Morgan dollar series, formerly the specialty of relatively few numismatists, became the most popular early collecting series. In time, books were written about Morgan dollars, conventions were held to focus on this specialty, and at least two societies were formed for those interested in these dollars.

1903-S $1 (business strike mintage 1,241,000): Quantities of 1903-S dollars were stored at the San Francisco Mint and paid out in small numbers over a long period of years until November 1953, when several bags were released, followed by other dispersals during the next several years. At one time John Skubis owned a bag of this date. By the late 1950s, apparently most were gone from government storage. The issue was not represented to any extent in the 1962-1964 Treasury release.

1904 $1 (business strike mintage 2,788,000): Quantities of 1904 dollars dribbled onto the market in the 1941-1942 years, in the 1950s, and again in the early 1960s, but, apparently, there was no ***major*** release at any specific time. Quantity offerings by dealers were few and far between. A very mediocre bag of 1904 dollars entered the market early in 1979; Wayne Miller examined nearly 300 pieces from the lot, but found no gems.

1904-O $1 (business strike mintage 3,720,000): In October 1962, vast quantities—well over 1,000,000 coins—of 1904-O dollars were released from long-term storage at the Philadelphia Mint. Previously, the 1904-O in Mint State had been considered one of the prime rarities in the Morgan series along with 1898-O and, especially, 1903-O. Additional bags of 1904-O dollars were released from storage in the Treasury Building in Washington, D.C., from which location some coins had dribbled out in small numbers since the 1930s. Today, there are more 1904-O Mint State dollars in existence than there are of any other New Orleans dollar after 1885-O.

1904-S $1 (business strike mintage 2,304,000): Although the San Francisco Mint served as a storage depot for its own coins, many bags of Uncirculated 1904-S dollars were shipped to the Treasury Building in Washington, D.C., and from time to time in the 1930s and 1940s an occasional bag would be paid out from there.

In 1941-1942 there was a particularly large release, which would serve to augment dealers' stocks for a long time. Although in later times the 1904-S would be recognized as one of the rarer issues, a perusal of advertisements of the 1950s will reveal that most dealers had a supply of Mint State 1904-S dollars. However, John Skubis, who was one of the most active dealers in bulk S-Mint dollars in the 1950s, recalled that the only S-Mint Morgan dollars he did ***not*** handle by the bagful were 1892-S, 1893-S, and 1904-S. One or more bags of 1904-S dollars came out through Los Angeles banks in the early 1950s. Bebee's, then located in Omaha (having recently moved from Chicago), bought some from this hoard.

I have found no accounts of any being in the 1962-1964 Treasury release. None were in the Redfield estate (1976).

1921 Morgan $1 (business strike mintage 44,690,000): Many bags of coins were released over a long period of time. Eventually, they became so common that dealers' buying prices for Uncirculated bags and rolls of Morgan dollars often said "except 1921." As a result, most bags were broken up. Today, relatively few original mint-sealed bags exist. However, individual coins from these bags are exceedingly common. All 1921 Morgan dollars—Philadelphia, Denver, and San Francisco—are from dies in shallow relief and tend to show friction and bagmarks after even slight jostling in mint bags. Aesthetic appeal is usually not a consideration among Morgan dollars of this date. Because of this, when quantities were released most went into circulation. In Nevada casinos in the very early 1960s, this and the Denver version were the most seen dollar varieties on roulette and other gaming tables.

In 1979 and 1980 the price of silver rose to unprecedented heights on the bullion market, challenging the $50 per ounce price at one time. During this era untold millions of silver dollars and other silver-content coins went to the melting pot, for their melt-down value was more than their numismatic value. Besides, there was not much of a market for anything other then gem Uncirculated 1921 dollars. Huge quantities of bank-wrapped Uncirculated dimes, quarters, and half dollars from the 1940s onward were melted, as were even greater quantities of worn pieces. In the process many common silver dollars such as the 1921 Morgan, while they did not become rare or even scarce, certainly became less plentiful than they once were.

1921-D $1 (business strike mintage 20,345,000): Vast quantities of Mint State 1921-D dollars were released in the 1950s and early 1960s. The issue was considered common, and most dealers did not desire to buy them. Today, original mint-sealed bags are few and far between, and the coins themselves are fairly hard to find in quantities of even a few dozen at a time. Far fewer Mint State 1921-D dollars exist than do 1921 Philadelphia or San Francisco issues.

1921-S $1 (business strike mintage 21,695,000): Dollars of this date and mint were scarce during the 1920s, for relatively few were released. This changed when quantities were paid out from storage at the San Francisco Mint at intervals from the 1930s through the 1950s. 1921-S dollars were little esteemed in their time, thus few original mint-sealed bags were saved. Not even casino operators and other silver dollar hoarders liked the 1921 Morgan from any of the three mints or wanted to save them.

Today, while individual coins are exceedingly common, bags of 1921-S are few and far between. The Redfield estate (1976) apparently had a partial bag. *The Numismatist,* December 1939, told of a recent release of 1921-S Morgan dollars. In comparison to surviving 1921 Philadelphia Mint coins, 1921-S dollars are far more elusive than the respective mintage differences (approximately 2:1) would indicate.

PEACE SILVER DOLLARS

1921 Peace $1 (business strike mintage 1,006,473): I have never heard of even one original mint bag of 1,000 1921 Peace dollars coming on the market, and during extensive research I never came across a quantity offering of any kind. This makes the 1921 Peace dollar unique in this regard among coins of this design, for all other Peace dollar varieties 1921-1935 were available at one time or another in multiple-roll and bag quantities several years or more after they were minted.

When I asked Philadelphia dealer Harry J. Forman (who has handled as many dollar bags during his numismatic career as anyone), he knew of no original bags either. Indeed, I have never even seen an original Uncirculated roll of 20 coins! On the other hand, dealer Maurice Rosen reported that around 1979-1980 he bought a roll of Uncirculated pieces from Don Apte, and that: "if my recollection is accurate, they would make today's MS-64 and 65 grades. All were frosty white with above average surface characteristics for the issue."[1] However, a roll of 20 pieces is hardly a large quantity.

1922 $1 (business strike mintage 51,737,000): Mint-sealed bags of 1,000 Mint State 1922 Peace dollars seem to have been released over a long period of time, with the result that this date has never been rare. Often, Eastern dealers searching for rare dates would find to their annoyance that shipments to their banks from the Federal Reserve would consist of $1,000 bags of this date.

Particularly large quantities were released through banks in 1949 and 1950, but there was little call for them from numismatists. Bags were still readily available in 1953 and 1954. Most often, such bags remained in bank vaults unwanted. Bags remained available through the rest of the decade and were still being distributed by the Treasury as late as March 1964. In later years, bags traded frequently. In 1982, Wayne Miller wrote that in one recent year he and his partner sold 40 bags (40,000 coins).

1922-D $1 (business strike mintage 15,063,000): Bags of 1922-D dollars were available on the market in the 1940s and very early 1950s. No one paid much attention to this date, and most languished in bank vaults or were paid out for use in circulation (in the West) or in gambling casinos. Bags of 1,000 Uncirculated coins were still readily available in 1953 and 1954.

In the late 1980s and early 1990s a hoard of 50 bags (50,000 coins) began to be marketed. Dwight Manley examined them and found that the average bag of 1,000 coins contained Mint State examples approximately as follows: MS-66: 5 coins; MS-65: 70; MS-64: 200; MS-63: 225; MS-60 to MS-62: 500.[2]

John Highfill's *Encyclopedia,* 1992, p. 1145, notes that "Uncirculateds are often heavily bagmarked, well struck bags are available," which I take to mean that Uncirculated coins, when seen, are often with heavy bagmarks, and that bags of coins (with heavy bagmarks on the coins?) are in existence and contain coins that are well struck.

1922-S $1 (business strike mintage 17,475,000): In 1941, 1922-S and 1926-S dollars were released in quantity through the San Francisco Mint, where they had been stored for many years. Several bags or more came on the market, but the demand for Peace dollars was not very great. Although more could have been obtained from the Mint had dealers desired them, probably no more than two or three thousand went into numismatic channels at the time. Quite a few went to Reno, which had an active casino industry (the growth of Las Vegas was yet to come, and Meyer Lansky,

[1] Letter, September 8, 1992.
[2] Letter, July 6, 1992.

"Bugsy" Siegel, and other developers of gambling spas had probably not yet set foot on the place).

In the spring and summer of 1942, many bags ($1,000 face value) of 1922-S, 1923-S, 1925-S, 1926-S, and 1927-S dollars were paid out by the San Francisco Mint and mostly went to banks and into general circulation in some areas of the West, where they became worn. Had the release occurred a quarter century later, all of these S-Mint Peace dollars would be exceedingly common today.

More bags of 1922-S came on the market in 1949 and 1950. Bags of this issue were still readily available in 1953 and 1954. In 1955 and 1956, the San Francisco Mint paid out many more bags of 1922-S, 1923-S, and 1926-S dollars. However, the end was getting near, and soon the Mint would be out of them.

Bags of 1922-S dollars were in the Redfield hoard (1976), and, according to John Highfill, represented the largest single holding of Peace dollars in this famous group. A number of Redfield bags, mostly containing weakly-struck MS-60 to MS-63 coins, were marketed through Paramount International Coin Corporation of Englewood, Ohio.

1923 $1 (business strike mintage 30,800,000): Bags of 1923 Peace dollars descended upon the channels of commerce in the mid-1940s. Bags remained common in bank holdings until the early 1960s and were paid out by the Treasury until the early months of 1964. After that, they remained common in the hands of investors (in particular) and dealers. In all grades from well-worn to high-grade Mint State, the 1923 may account for 5% to 10% of the silver dollars in existence today, Wayne Miller suggested in his 1982 text.

1923-D $1 (business strike mintage 6,811,000): In an article in *The Numismatist*, July 1925, collector E.S. Thresher stated that six years earlier he had embarked on a search to find each and every date of coin variety believed to be available in circulation. In the Peace dollar series, still a relatively new specialty when he wrote his letter (1925), he had located every issue from 1921 through 1925 except for 1923-D, 1925-D, and 1925-S, the latter two not having been released yet. From this it is apparent that the 1923-D was rare in its own time, and may not have been released in 1923 or 1924, through early 1925 (for the article to have appeared in the July 1925 issue, it was probably received in April or May).

Many bags were paid out by the Treasury Department from the late 1930s through at least the 1950s, after which time the government stock of mint-sealed bags of this issue was largely depleted.

1923-S $1 (business strike mintage 19,020,000): The 1923-S dollar was readily available throughout the 1930s. In the spring and summer of 1942, many 1,000-coin bags were paid out by the San Francisco Mint. In 1949 and 1950, many more bags of 1923-S dollars came on the market and were obtainable through banks in the San Francisco and Oakland area. By 1953-1954 there were still quantities of bags available for anyone desiring them. Many went to casinos in Las Vegas and Reno, and a few to silver dollar hoarders.

Many more bags came out in 1955-1956, and it is said that more came to light during the Treasury release of 1962-1964. This may be where LaVere Redfield obtained his. His estate is said to have had quite a few bags; these graded MS-60 to 63 and were weakly struck, noted John Highfill in his *Comprehensive U.S. Silver Dollar Encyclopedia.*

1924 $1 (business strike mintage 11,811,000): Many 1,000-coin mint-sealed bags of this date came out in 1949 and 1950 in addition to bags released before that time. In 1953-1954 there were large quantities of bags in Eastern banks, but there was little dealer interest in buying them, even for face value. These stocks remained in bank vaults through the rest of the decade. However, in comparison to certain other Peace dollars, apparently bags of 1924 were elusive by the time that the 1960s rolled around.

John Highfill in his 1992 *Encyclopedia* noted that 12 bags were handled by John Love in the late 1960s and two by Highfill in June 1980. Wayne Miller saw fewer than five other original bags of 1924 dollars in the 15 years before 1980. Fully BU rolls of 1924 dollars should be purchased whenever found, Miller concluded.

John Kamin, publisher of *The Forecaster* newsletter, recalled the following:[1] "I had often been of the opinion that 1924 and 1925 Philadelphia Mint dollars were about equal in rarity, that is substantially more common than the scarcer dates such as 1927-S, 1928, and 1934-S, but about 100 times scarcer than the super-common 1922 and 1923 Peace dollars, and 1921 Morgan dollars. But then, around 1969, I bumped into a hoard containing nearly 100 bags of 1924 Peace dollars, with no other dates in the group, from the Tennessee area. *Forecaster* clients bought nearly half that group, the best condition ones we could find, and the rest were sold elsewhere."

1924-S $1 (business strike mintage 1,728,000): Unlike 1922-S, 1923-S, and 1926-S, of which many bags came on the market from the San Francisco Mint in the 1940s and 1950s, quantities of 1924-S seem to have been paid out only occasionally. This particular issue was and is notorious for its being extensively bagmarked, a situation which facilitated its being ignored by numismatists.[2]

A few 1,000-coin bags were released in the late 1950s and were quickly absorbed at prices of about double face value, a high premium at the time. The Redfield estate is said to have had a few hundred individual Uncirculated coins, but no bags.

1925 $1 (business strike mintage 10,198,000): In 1940,

[1] Letter, September 8, 1992.

[2] As a rule of thumb, Philadelphia Mint Peace dollars of all dates are seen less extensively bagmarked than mintmarked varieties. This is a combination of their being handled less often in banks and in the Treasury Department, and their generally plentiful quantities which permitted a lot of picking and choosing by numismatists. Branch mint dollars 1922-1925, 1927-S, and 1928-S are usually extensively bagmarked. Branch mint dollars of 1926, 1927-D, and the issues of 1934 and 1935 are much less so.

the 1925 Peace dollar was considered to be the rarest Philadelphia Mint issue in Mint State, but by 1945 it had dropped slightly in rank to second rarest (after the 1923). In numerous offerings early in that decade it was priced higher than the 1934-S. However, by late 1940s, enough had been released from Treasury vaults that the 1925 Peace dollar was demoted to the status of a plentiful issue. Walter H. Breen in his *Encyclopedia* stated that many of the 1925 dollars paid out in the 1940s were heavily bagmarked. Apparently, most of these newly-issued coins disappeared into collections and into the "woodwork," so that by the early 1950s, the 1925 was back on the scarce list again.

Catalogue values remained high until hundreds of bags were released in 1954-1955, after which the date became very common. I remember selling a large quantity obtained for face value at a Pennsylvania bank to Charles E. Green, of Chicago, who traded under his wife's name of R. Green. By the mid to late 1950s, the 1925 Peace dollar was so common that specimens were a nuisance for dealers searching for rare dates. I recall that at the time they were a drug on the market, along with 1922, 1923, and, to an extent, 1924 (the 1924, common elsewhere, seemed to be somewhat more elusive in Pennsylvania, where I searched through dollars).

However, by the early 1960s, most must have been distributed, for Wayne Miller in 1982 wrote that in his experience, bags of 1925 dollars were elusive. Perhaps he was referring to the West, where, apparently, few bags of Philadelphia Mint Peace dollars were paid out.

1925-S $1 (business strike mintage 1,610,000): In 1938 and again in the spring and summer of 1942 many bags of 1925-S Peace dollars were paid out by the San Francisco Mint. The issue became common in dealers' stocks. However, the numismatic market for Peace dollars was limited—as it would continue to be for many years,[1] and I imagine that following the 1942 release no more than two or three thousand Uncirculated pieces were sold to collectors during the ensuing 12-month period.

In 1949 and 1950, many more bags of 1925-S dollars came out through San Francisco, Oakland, and other California banks. There was little interest in them at the time, however. Some additional bags were paid out in the late 1950s. This last quantity was not large, but at least 10 to 20 went into the hands of dealers. These may have included the five bags that were later owned by LaVere Redfield, of Reno. John Highfill reported that Redfield sold a full or partial bag to Dean Jones in 1974, and four other bags, all with weakly struck coins, were auctioned by the Probate Court as part of the Redfield estate in January 1976.

1926 $1 (business strike mintage 1,939,000): In November 1941 in an advertisement in *The Numismatist,* the Hollinbeck Stamp & Coin Stores referred to the 1926 Peace dollar as the scarcest coin in the series. The honor for the scarcest issue changed from time to time, as hoards were dispersed. Later, the 1926 became common.

In 1944, bags were released. Several authorities—John Highfill, Walter Breen, and Wayne Miller among them—reported that most of these were extensively bagmarked. In 1953 and 1954, a large number of bags came out through Eastern banks, but they were generally ignored. It was felt that 1926 dollars would be forever common. However, these bags were soon dispersed, and as the decade wore on, not many others came to light, although a few are said to have emerged in 1962-1964.

1926-D $1 (business strike mintage 2,348,700): While large releases of S-Mint bags of Peace dollars were well documented, and while similar releases of Philadelphia coins were also publicized, relatively little was said about Denver issues. During the course of research for my *Encyclopedia* on silver dollars I did not find a single verified instance of a bag of 1926-D dollars being released before 1950, and yet many must have been. It is my guess that most slipped quietly into the channels of commerce before that time.

A bag or two came out in the Midwest around 1953-1954 and were quickly absorbed. It has been suggested that a few bags came out in the Treasury release of 1962-1964. In 1982, Wayne Miller wrote that rolls were plentiful, and doubtless they were at the time.

1926-S $1 (business strike mintage 6,980,000): In 1941 quantities of 1922-S and 1926-S dollars were released through the San Francisco Mint, where they had been stored for 15 years. Several bags or more came on the market, but the demand for Peace dollars was not very great. Although more could have been obtained from the Mint had dealers desired them, probably no more that two or three thousand coins went into numismatic channels at the time, and even this estimate may be overly generous. As was true of 1922-S dollars, quite a few of both dates went to casinos in Reno, Nevada.

More bags came out in the spring and summer of 1942. Quantities remained unsold in dealers' stocks, and for a long time the 1926-S was considered to be very common. Still more bags were released in 1949 and 1950, mainly through banks in the San Francisco and Oakland area. Additional bags of 1926-S dollars were released from storage in the San Francisco Mint in the 1950s, particularly from 1953 through 1956.

What numismatic market there was, consisted of sales through such dealers as Norman Shultz and Bebee's, who mainly retailed single pieces to customers. Dealers were reluctant to buy bags, as they could not be sold for more than face value. There were relatively few silver dollar dealer specialists until during and after the great Treasury releases of the early 1960s. Some 1926-S bags were included in the 1962-1964 Treasury dispersal.

By the early 1970s, most 1926-S dollars floating on the market had found homes, and the issue was not often seen in quantity. In 1982, Wayne Miller wrote that the issue was rarer than 1926-D until the Redfield coins came on the market. The Redfield hoard (1976) contained several or more bags, probably obtained from Nevada casinos in the late

[1] Although Morgan silver dollars (1878-1921) often appeared attractive after having been jostled about in mint bags for many years, this was not true of Peace dollars. Often a very small amount of handling resulted in the coins becoming unsightly, with heavy marks particularly on the obverse portrait and surrounding field. Add to that the planchet abrasions often seen (particularly on San Francisco and Denver coins of the early 1920s) on the higher parts of the eagle, and the result was an overall "scruffy" appearance. While hoards of Peace dollars released in the 1940s and 1950s are historically interesting to read about, probably most such coins went back into circulation (in the West) or became part of mixed-date bags and holdings (in the East). Although no records survive, of the many thousands of 1925-S dollars paid out in 1942, probably no more than a thousand or two ever reached numismatists who preserved them.

1950s and early 1960s. John Highfill has written that the 1926-S was the third most plentiful Redfield hoard Peace dollar issue, and that many were damaged by the mechanical counting machine used by the firm hired to inventory the group. All of the Redfield 1926-S dollars went to numismatists and investors.

1927 $1 (business strike mintage 848,000): The low-mintage 1927 is a coin that has slipped through the cracks so far as news of bag releases is concerned. Little about this date appeared in print years ago. On the other hand, the historical record shows that its cousin, the 1927-S Peace dollar, was once plentiful in bag and roll quantities, from releases directly from storage in the San Francisco Mint. Today, the 1927 Philadelphia issue ranks as one of the scarcer Peace dollar issues in higher levels of Mint State, although it never has been in the numismatic limelight.

1927-D $1 (business strike mintage 1,268,900): In the late 1930s, the 1927-D dollar was considered to be one of the scarcer dates in the Peace dollar series. However, in keeping with most other dates, it was not necessarily expensive. Then, in late 1939 several bags broke in the Midwest. Soon this supply dwindled, and once again the 1927-D gained the status of being an elusive issue.

The Treasury releases of 1962-1964 came and went, and few if any quantities of 1927-D Peace dollars were released. In 1982, Wayne Miller noted that scarcely any rolls had appeared on the market during his career, and that Mint State 1927-Ds were rarities.

Surprises can and do happen. If in early 1992 you had asked a specialist about hoards of 1927-D Peace dollars, you would have been told that roll quantities (20 coins) remained rare, and offerings were few and far between. As for bag quantities, forget it. That changed on June 23, 1992, when Sotheby's auctioned two and a half original bags of 1927-D dollars, a hoard amounting to 2,500 coins, in groups which added up to about $400,000 when the auctioneer cried "Sold!" for the final lot. The story went that these were given by an ancestor of the consignor to his wife as a 25th anniversary present in 1927. Two thousand coins were in two original Denver Mint cloth bags bearing serial numbers 5758 and 5799. The remaining 500 coins were in a Bank of Denver bag. These 2,500 coins were a 25th anniversary present from a man to his wife, "a nice touch," commented David E. Tripp, who catalogued the pieces.[1]

Dwight Manley examined the group at Sotheby's prior to the sale and estimated the grades to be as follows: MS-65: 50 coins; MS-64: 300; MS-63: 550; MS-61 and MS-62: 700; MS-60: 900.[2]

Apart from this hoard (and this is a big "apart"!), few groups of 1927-D dollars have come on the market in *recent* times. These 1927-D dollars were absorbed into the market during the next several years. In the long-term view of things it is significant to note that in early 1992, prior to knowledge of this hoard, John Highfill wrote in his *Encyclopedia* that: "No original rolls are known."

1927-S $1 (business strike mintage 866,000): On the coin market in 1935 and 1936, a 1927-S dollar in Uncirculated grade was just another common issue. However, most became scattered, and for a time in 1938 they were scarce in numismatic hands. However, around that time a few bags were released from the San Francisco Mint, again to become widely distributed.

In the summer of 1942, more bags came out, and the price slipped, but just slightly. Probably not more than a couple thousand additional specimens emerged from storage at that time. The 1927-S Peace dollar remained basically scarce on the numismatic market, but hundreds of thousands were in storage at the San Francisco Mint and would remain so until the 1950s. Whenever a group of bags came on the market, the price would fall. The low-mintage 1927-S dollars were scarce in Uncirculated preservation, but specialists in Peace dollars were even scarcer.

In 1949 and 1950, many bags of 1927-S dollars came on the market through the San Francisco Mint, which paid them out to banks in the area. There continued to be relatively little numismatic interest in them at the time. In 1953 and 1954 another group of bags came out in the San Francisco area, and this time dealers took the opportunity to stock up on what they could use, but not too many, for it was realized that the vault at the San Francisco Mint could be tapped if any more were needed. Before anyone was truly aware of it, the supply had become dispersed—into circulation, over the California border to the casinos in Nevada, and to other places.

By 1960, the 1927-S dollar was somewhat scarce and any number of dealers would have given an eyetooth to turn the calendar back to the days when bags were going begging. Soon, bags of these and other S-Mint Peace dollars became the stuff of which legends are made. After the Treasury release of 1962-1964, many new dealers and investment analysts came into the dollar market. Few of them ever knew about the "good old days" of the 1940s and early 1950s when virtually every S-Mint Morgan and Peace dollar variety ever made could be obtained at face value from San Francisco Mint storage. In fact, there was very little in print anywhere about the historical distribution of either Morgan or Peace dollars. The information explosion in the dollar series did not happen until the 1960s.

By the early 1970s, the 1927-S dollar was decidedly elusive, and few dealers had a decent supply. Then came the distribution of the Redfield coins beginning in 1976, and a for a time the 1927-S was plentiful once again. Several or more bags are said to have been in this famous Reno hoard. Wayne Miller said that the Redfield coins were of generally high quality, while John Highfill took a different stance and stated that many were in lower grades such as MS-60 to 63 and were damaged by the mechanical counting machine used in the appraisal process. Apparently, many coins were somewhat prooflike on the obverse, due to minute striae from die polishing. I didn't see the Redfield 1927-S dollars, thus I have no further comment on them.

1928 $1 (business strike mintage 360,649): I have never seen, nor have I a firm record of an original mint-sealed bag being preserved. However, rolls come on the market occasionally. Tradition has it that some bags came out in Ohio and Pennsylvania in the 1950s and were used to pay

---

[1] Letter, August 1996.

[2] Letter, July 6, 1992.

millworkers. Quantity lots must have escaped the active coin dealers at the time. Walter H. Breen told me that Cleveland and Pittsburgh were dispersal points.

In the 1950s, high-grade 1928 Peace dollars were common and were found in mixed bags of dollars. Most of these ranged from AU grade to what we might designate as MS-63 today. Dollars of this date have a distinctive beveled rim, making them easily detectable in a bag, even if the date is hidden under another coin.

1928-S $1 (business strike mintage 1,632,000): Many bags of 1928-S dollars came on the market in the late 1930s and early 1940s. More bags were released in 1949 and 1950 when the San Francisco Mint distributed them through banks in its area and by direct shipment to Nevada casinos. There was little numismatic interest in them, however, as Peace dollars were not a popular series and, in any event, the market was in a slump.[1]

John Highfill wrote that possibly four to six bags were in the Redfield hoard (1976), and that most had deep scratches from a mechanical counting machine employed while they were being inventoried.

1934 $1 (business strike mintage 954,057): Bags of 1934 dollars were paid out through Eastern banks from the 1930s onward. Little documentation of 1,000-coin bags exists, and I do not know if any original mint-sealed bags survived.

This is one issue which for many years seemed to be "common" and "ordinary" per conventional wisdom, but anyone checking closely would find that few if any quantities were to be had.

1934-D $1 (business strike mintage 1,569,500): In 1982, Wayne Miller wrote this: "All of the available evidence suggests that the 1934-D is the only Peace dollar which was never released in bag quantities during the silver dollar rush of the early 1960s or from the Redfield hoard." (This implies that all other Peace dollars were released in bag quantities in 1962-1964, but I doubt this; for starters, I have never heard of a bag of 1921 Peace dollars.) Occasionally, a roll of 20 pieces will turn up. Some pieces are extensively bagmarked, especially on the face and cheek of Miss Liberty. Sometimes, coins will be marked on the portrait and on the eagle but have virtually flawless fields, leading to the thought that some of these may have been on the original planchet before striking.[2]

1934-S $1 (business strike mintage 1,011,000): As Treasury holdings of San Francisco Mint dollars were distributed from the San Francisco Mint, various Federal Reserve banks, and elsewhere in the 1950s, the rarity of various silver dollar issues sorted itself out.

In the 1950s, the 1934-S dollar was considered scarce, but not rare. A San Francisco dealer told me that he personally saw over one million coins still stored at the local mint, which made a good story, and one that impressed me at the time. The same dealer was interviewed by me later and did not remember having seen such a hoard; thus, it falls into the category of an entertaining numismatic tale. I estimate that perhaps a bag or two or three (1,000 to 3,000 coins) saw distribution from the San Francisco Mint in the late 1940s through the mid-1950s. Probably, many thousands more were released from the mid-1930s through the mid-1940s.

By the early 1960s, Uncirculated specimens of the 1934-S had been largely absent from dealers' stocks for nearly 15 years. Often, listings of Mint State Peace dollars would commence with 1921 and end with 1935-S, and give prices for each issue, except for 1934-S which would be marked "Wanted."

The 1934-S was not realized for its rarity until the 1950s, although prices had risen beginning in the late 1940s. A hoard of several hundred pieces turned up in San Francisco in the early 1960s (per Wayne Miller and others) and was distributed over a long period of time. At the January 1978 Florida United Numismatists Convention, a group of 35 pieces was broken up; by that time, such a holding was considered unusual.

1935 $1 (business strike mintage 1,576,000): I am not aware of any extant mint-sealed bags. Rolls sometimes come on the market. David W. Akers recalled buying a group of 200 superb gem coins from Rarcoa in the late 1970s.[3] To an extent the remarks under 1934 (Philadelphia) are pertinent to this issue as well.

1935-S $1 (business strike mintage 1,964,000): Many bags of 1935-S dollars were released by the San Francisco Mint to banks in its immediate area in 1949 and 1950. Most of these coins showed only light traces of handling and were what would be called gems a generation later. Unfortunately, there was relatively little numismatic interest in them, and while Norman Shultz and several other dealers of the time bought a total of a bag or two, most were ignored and eventually slipped into circulation.

I recall being offered a bag of them around 1955 and declining to buy at $1,200. I couldn't figure out what to do with more than a few dozen pieces (what a mistake!).

Wayne Miller wrote that a hoard of this date came on the market in San Francisco in the 1960s and was dispersed over a period of time. The Redfield estate (1976) had a number of bags, but most of the coins were poorly struck. I did not know Redfield personally, but from all of the comments about his coins in John Highfill's book, it seems that he was anything but a connoisseur.

---

[1] The rare coin market rose steadily from 1943 until 1948, after which it stumbled and fell. The years 1949 and 1950 were very slow. Revival began in 1951, and in 1952 the New Netherlands Coin Co. section of the ANA Convention sale may have furnished the spark of enthusiasm that signaled a strong growth in numismatic interest.

[2] Such "planchet abrasions" (a term developed at ANACS in the late 1970s, per Thomas K. DeLorey, letter, September 29, 1996) have been generally ignored in coin grading literature. Within popular twentieth-century series, planchet abrasions are most often seen on the high parts of the skirt on the obverse of the Liberty Walking half dollar and on the high parts of the eagle on the reverse of the Peace dollar.

[3] Letter, July 7, 1996.

The Redfield Hoard

Hidden: 1950s-1970s
Dispersed: 1976
Treasure: Silver dollars

Many stories could be written about sub-hoards based upon the great Treasury release of silver dollars 1962-1964 and of Treasury dollar dispersals of earlier times. Many investors, dealers, collectors, and others purchased bags of 1,000 coins and put them away. In many instances, these "new hoards" came on the market later and achieved fame in their own right. Some of these are mentioned earlier in the present chapter. However, it may be appropriate here to expand upon the best known of these secondary hoards, the now legendary LaVere Redfield estate coins.

Born in Utah in 1897, Redfield did odd jobs in his teens and twenties. While clerking in a department store in Idaho at age 24 he married a co-worker, Nell, who was four years his senior. At a later time the couple moved to Los Angeles, where Redfield became a securities broker and displayed a sufficiently good knack for trading that by the late 1930s he was a millionaire. Some of his profits were invested in real estate including a 51,000-acre spread near Reno, Nevada, the city to which he later moved.

He and his wife distrusted banks and apparently kept large amounts of cash in his simply furnished 15-room house. On at least two occasions he brought grocery bags full of currency to land auctions to pay for purchases. He had numerous run-ins with the Internal Revenue Service, one of which landed him in jail in 1960.

LaVere Redfield enjoyed playing blackjack at the local gaming tables (often with lady companions), drank only in moderation, and did not smoke. At the local library he often watched travel films. He and Nell were generous to those in need, including strangers, and often disbursed money without asking for repayment.

Redfield liked "hard assets," and in his home he accumulated hundreds of bags of coins from Lincoln cents to half dollars. However, silver dollars were his passion, and although he had a passing numismatic knowledge, he preferred quantity to quality. As it turned out, he got some of both. From casinos, banks, and friends in Reno and elsewhere he bought 1,000-coin bags of dollars, particularly Morgan dollars of the San Francisco Mint. Other bags contained worn, mixed dollars mostly of common dates.

In 1952 a burglary of his home was reputed to have yielded $1.5 million in booty (one or two of his gambling lady friends are said to have set it up), and a 1963 burglary saw the loss of 100,000 silver dollars.

On September 6, 1974, LaVere Redfield died. In due course his will was probated, but not without many claims and counterclaims. Eventually—and to make a very long story very short—an auction was held of his silver dollars, with Bowers and Ruddy Galleries (in a consortium with Joel Rettew and David Hall) bidding up to $7,200,000, after which A-Mark bid $7,300,000 and won.

Contents of the Redfield silver dollar hoard were never made public, but it was said that the deal included over 407,000 Morgan and Peace silver dollars, of which 351,259 were Uncirculated. John Highfill stated in his *Comprehensive U.S. Silver Dollar Encyclopedia* that the Redfield estate silver dollars included the dollars described below.

Morgan dollars in quantity, in descending order from the largest quantity: 1881-S (largest number of any one issue in the hoard), 1880-S, 1879-S, 1878-S, 1882-S, 1896, 1898, 1897, 1897-S, 1890-S.

This next group, in date order, appeared in the Redfield hoard in quantities from nearly 10 bags down to fractions of a bag each: 1883-S, 1886-S, 1887-S, 1888-S, 1889 (just a few, apparently), 1889-S, 1890,

1890-CC, 1891 (just a few), 1891-S, 1892-CC, 1893-CC, 1896-S, 1898-S, 1899-S, 1900-S, 1902-S, 1903, and 1921-S (just a few).

John Highfill gave a separate list of these Morgan dollar issues, each of which was in very small quantities, 1885-CC, 1891-CC, 1892, 1893, 1895-S, and 1879-CC (the smallest quantity of all).

The Peace dollar holdings in large quantity in the Redfield estate were as follows: 1922-S (most plentiful of all), 1923-S, 1926-S, and 1935-S.

Then came smaller quantities of these Peace dollars: 1928-S, 1927-S, 1925-S, and 1924-S (fewest of any Peace dollar issue).

By the present era, the 1990s, most if not all of the Redfield silver dollars have been dispersed, and many have been resold multiple times.

CHAPTER 16

U.S. Gold in Foreign Banks

Exported: 1933 and earlier
Discovered by numismatists: 1950s
Treasure: Gold coins

Beginning in the 1940s there was a great flurry of interest in collecting United States gold coins by date and mintmark varieties, a specialty that had been largely ignored earlier (except for the smaller denominations). Writing in 1893 in his *Treatise on Mint Marks,* Augustus G. Heaton stated that he knew of *no one* in the numismatic community that collected mintmark issues of $5, $10, or $20 pieces.

Later, in 1909, when Edgar H. Adams published his *Official Premium List of U.S. and Territorial Gold Coins* not much interest in large denominations was shown either.

Virgil Brand, millionaire Chicago brewer who began collecting in the 1880s and by the time of his death in 1926 owned over 300,000 coins, had many large-denomination gold coins by mintmark varieties, but as the numismatic market for them was nil, his heirs, brothers Armin and Horace, simply turned most of them in at banks for face value. Ditto for much the paper money he had acquired.

In the 1940s the auction catalogues of several firms—notably B. Max Mehl, Numismatic Gallery (Abe Kosoff and Abner Kreisberg), and Stack's—showcased several collections featuring large-denomination gold coins by dates and mints. This fueled interest, as did the search for rare specimens by Louis E. Eliasberg, Sr., Jacob Shapiro (a.k.a. Jake Bell), and, several other collectors.

Especially in the limelight in the numismatic market of the 1940s were rare varieties of Saint-Gaudens $20 pieces such as 1924-D and S, 1925-D and S, 1926-D and S, 1927-D and S, and all issues after 1928. Most prized of all was the 1926-D double eagle, which was viewed as one of the greatest of all American rarities. Second on the "most wanted" list was the 1924-S, and some considered it to be number one. Curiously, the 1927-D, considered today in the 1990s to be the rarest issue of the 1920s, received very little attention back then.

In his catalogue of the sale of the Adolphe Menjou Collection in 1950, Abe Kosoff stated that the 1924-S was "the rarest of all double eagles; perhaps there are less than five extant." This would have put it on about par with the famous 1913 Liberty Head nickel and the 1885 trade dollar, of which just five were (and still are) known of each.

In 1955 the dam broke, and the "Bank of France" yielded dozens upon dozens of previously rare varieties after someone furnished lists of desired dates and mints to bankers there. From various banks in Paris, long-stored gold coins were examined, and over a period of time the 1926-D descended from being the *creme de la creme* coin of the $20 series to being simply "scarce" or "rare." In time, probably 100 to 200 came to light from French banks and other locations. Ditto for the 1924-S, 1926-S, and certain other issues.[1]

[1] "Rare Double Eagles Discovered in Europe," *Numismatic Scrapbook Magazine,* September 1955, p. 1354. "An enterprising dealer furnished the

This set off a treasure hunt in other overseas banks. Switzerland proved to be a particularly rich source as millions of United States gold coins—primarily of the $5, $10, and, especially, $20 denominations—were stored there. Such coins had been received in various transactions, but particularly as exchange payments during the general era 1880-1932, and had remained there. There were many earlier shipments of American gold coins to Europe as well, and a perusal of specie exports reveals large amounts on almost a continuous basis in the early nineteenth century.

During the late nineteenth and early twentieth centuries Swiss and other foreign banks were not the slightest bit interested in holding United States paper money, and when President Franklin D. Roosevelt called in gold coins in 1933-1934, Swiss and other banks held on to their gold reserves more tightly than ever.

By the late 1950s several Swiss banks, primarily based in Zürich, had established numismatic departments. The writer visited several such banks for the first time in the early 1960s. Typically, purchases of gold coins were conducted by a bank officer taking a prospective buyer to a private room and discussing the customer's wants. At one prominent bank in Zürich I asked what the price would be for a large quantity of unsorted Saint-Gaudens $20 coins in Uncirculated grade. The banker told me that he could quote a figure then and there for 100,000 pieces, but if I wanted more than that he would have to excuse himself for a moment and check with others. I could not afford any such number, despite their current market price of about $40 each (the coins had a melt-down value of about $35, and during the 1950s the bulk price on the numismatic market had been as low as $36-$37). The banker was aware of rare dates and owned a copy of the *Guide Book of U.S. Coins,* the standard price guide at the time. He separately sold me a few dozen scarce issues for a higher premium.

In New York City the Lentex Corporation, primarily a dealer in platinum, imported vast quantities of United States double eagles from Europe. Those of numismatic significance were bought and marketed by New Netherlands Coin Company (who had first peek at each shipment) and others.

Along the way quite a few $2.50 quarter eagle coins came to light in Europe, among which were attractive Uncirculated specimens of the Liberty Head or Coronet design dates from the 1880s to 1907, with most being in the early twentieth century. Some of the latter were beautiful, frosty gems. However, quarter eagles were in the distinct minority in comparison to the large denominations.

European banks occasionally furnished gold dollars and $3 pieces, typically worn issues. I am not aware of any cache of a particular date, not even one with dates in the 1880s (the range in which most high-level Mint State pieces in existence today are dated).

In Englewood, near Dayton, Ohio, working from a pine-paneled office in the basement of his home, erstwhile jeweler-turned-numismatist James F. Kelly was active in the importation of gold coins and always had a large selection of the highly-prized Carson City $20 pieces. Usually, when an ordinary Liberty Head $20 sold for $40 to $50, a "CC" issue would sell for $60 to $80. Kelly's typical pieces were in grades of Very Fine and Extremely Fine punctuated by an occasional AU and an even more occasional Uncirculated coin. When asked, Kelly stated that his source was a supplier in Argentina or, on other occasions, Venezuela.

Gold-buying activity in the United States engendered more activity, and before long there was a great nationwide interest in squirreling away gold coins, especially $20 pieces, as a hedge against inflation and as security in the event that the American monetary system collapsed. Eventually, this became the "hard money" or "tangible asset" sector of the investment community. I recall that one of our numismatic customers in Los Angeles started Monex in the 1970s and went on to offer financing for bulk coins and bullion, and did *hundreds of millions* of dollars in business. Other big players beginning around that time included A-Mark, MTB (Manfra, Tordella & Brookes), Mocatta Metals, and the Republic Bank (New York).

In Europe the public interest in hoarding gold coins had a longer standing, what with the unfortunate experiences of two world wars and untold political and economic turmoil. By the 1960s bullion exchanges or sales counters were familiar sights in many banks and currency exchanges throughout Europe. Such smaller displays were in the nature of boutiques, were not staffed by anyone with numismatic knowledge, and offered examples of popular gold coins from England, France, and Germany mainly, but others as well including restrikes from the Austrian Mint. Usually some American gold coins were on display as were some gold coins of Mexico, particularly the large 50-pesos denomination, typically bearing the date 1947.

It was my experience in the 1960s and 1970s that

Bank of France with a list of rare dates.... That is why a 1926-S sold in the convention auction for less than $700 as compared to its former $2,000 price tag."

such boutiques, if they had anything rare in the United States series, usually had counterfeits. This was particularly true of $1 and $3 gold pieces, for which fakes abounded for many different dates. These phony $1 and $3 pieces were occasionally seen in the stocks of numismatically knowledgeable Swiss banks as well. I recall helpfully pointing out a rather obvious counterfeit $3 on display in Zürich and receiving a reply to this effect: "Well, I guess you won't want to buy this one." The coin remained on display.

In the years since that time, continuing to the present day, the importation of United States gold coins from overseas sources has remained a big business. Several American citizens live full-time in Europe and act as suppliers and pickers for stateside firms. In the 1990s France has been an important supplier of scarce issues and may have surpassed Switzerland in this regard.

To prevent price drops and to avoid scaring buyers, very little information is ever given in print as to what specific coins are imported, especially if there is a cache or quantity of a given date. However, after a time the existence of such coins is revealed by their plenitude on the market and their increased listings in the population reports issued by commercial grading services such as ANACS, the Numismatic Guaranty Corporation of America, and the Professional Coin Grading Service.

As a general rule of thumb, overseas hoards have included these items:

Gold dollars: Relatively few *authentic* examples have turned up overseas in modern times. Most of the genuine examples seen are in circulated grades and dated in the 1850s. Counterfeits abound, but are rarely imported by numismatists as buyers on this side of the Atlantic are too knowledgeable. However, a significant quantity of these are brought in by tourists, and today just about any gold specialist sees with some frequency these modern counterfeits.

The American Numismatic Association Authentication Bureau (ANAAB), under the talented direction of J.P. Martin, 818 North Cascade Avenue, Colorado Springs, CO, will for a fee determine the authenticity (or lack thereof) of any coin; the commercial grading services such as ANACS, NGC, and PCGS have a sharp eye for fakes and guarantee that any coin they certify will be genuine (coins that are questionable will be returned to the submitter). The best protection in any event is to buy scarce and rare gold coins from an established professional numismatist with an office in the United States, who guarantees the material sold, and/or to buy ANACS, NGC, or PCGS certified pieces.

$2.50 gold: Fairly scarce as a denomination in foreign hoards, but thousands have been imported. Those dated from 1834 to about 1880 are nearly always in circulated grades. Most early pieces are of the Liberty Head style, but some Classic Heads are mixed among them. Occasionally a Charlotte or Dahlonega coin will be found.

In general, availability is in proportion to original mintages, except that earlier dates are scarcer than later ones (there is seemingly a straight-line diminution in this regard; this is true of all pre-1880 denominations). Those from about 1880 to 1907—the later part of the Liberty Head era—are typically Mint State, especially if dated in the twentieth century, and sometimes include frosty gems. Indian Head $2.50 pieces 1908-1929 are a mixed bag and are typically EF or AU, although some Mint State coins have been found. The design of the Indian Head quarter eagles is such that the flat field, normally the area in lowest relief on a coin, is on these pieces the highest part (except for mintmarked issues, for which the raised mintmark is higher yet). Thus, even with a minimal amount of contact, such pieces show abrasions.

$3 gold: Same comment as for gold $1. Lots of fakes are on the overseas market, where they appeal to bargain-seekers. Reality occurs when the coins are brought back home to the United States and shown to a reputable rare coin dealer or grading service. Notwithstanding this comment, a few authentic $3 coins have turned up over the years.

$5 gold: Classic Head issues 1834-1838 are scarce but available and are typically VF or EF. Liberty Head issues of the 1839-1880 years nearly always show evidence of circulation, with the branch mint coins being especially so. From about 1880 to 1908, Liberty Head coins are a mixture of VF, EF, and Mint State grades.

Except for certain twentieth-century dates, gems are elusive in foreign bank hoards and in many instances are very rare. Indian Head $5 pieces 1908-1929 are virtually all of the 1908-1916 years, typically in VF, EF, or AU grades. Mint State coins are elusive, and gems are very rare, as this design was easily damaged during storage of coins in bags (for reasons cited above under Indian Head $2.50).

$10 gold: Liberty Head issues dated from 1838 to 1907 are plentiful, especially those dated toward the end of the range. Eagles before about 1880 are nearly always circulated and in grades of VF, EF, or AU. From about 1880 to 1907 the register is mixed and includes many EF and AU coins. Mint State pieces dated before 1900 are usually heavily bagmarked, although highly lustrous.

Among early twentieth-century issues gems can be found of certain dates, and prodigious quantities have turned up of 1901-S. However, most of these have been sold into the general investment (not numismatic) market, thus there is hardly a glut. If anything, a gem coin of a common issue is available for a reasonable price, making it easy to get a nice one for a type set.

Among Saint-Gaudens $10 pieces of the 1907-1933 era, the Indian design, many coins have turned up, including numerous choice examples dated 1926 and 1932. Earlier issues range from VF to Mint State; if the latter, usually low-end. A peculiarity of the Indian design is that the cheek of Miss Liberty is apt to acquire many contact marks and friction while the fields remain frosty. As such, grading practices are apt to vary widely, and one person's About Uncirculated can be another's Mint State.

Greg Roberts, of Spectrum Numismatics, who has handled as many $10 in quantity in recent years as has anyone, recently commented that the typical Mint State $10 of this design is apt to be closer to MS-60 in grade than to MS-65.[1]

A representative find of Saint-Gaudens Indian $10 coins is mentioned in this 1996 catalogue description by David W. Akers:[2] "1911-S Indian $10, PCGS Mint State-65: A gorgeous, original coin with full mint frost, excellent lustre, and superb color, a modulated medium orange and greenish gold. Almost no marks of any kind occurring since striking, but there is a die imperfection in the lower left obverse field that is nearly always seen on this date, and often on the 1913-S. Undoubtedly one of the finest examples from a mini-hoard (less than 100 pieces) that came out of Europe in the late 1970s. Prior to the appearance of this group, the 1911 S was all but unknown in Mint State, much less in gem condition."

$20 gold: This is the workhorse denomination in the United States gold series, and vast quantities were shipped overseas. It was easier for a bank or national treasury to handle and account for a single $20 than two $10 coins, four $5 coins, or eight $2.50 pieces. Thus, the $20 became the denomination of choice for international trade.

Today, Liberty Head coins from overseas sources, dated from 1850 through about 1880, are typically VF, EF, or AU. For certain issues of the 1860s and 1870s Mint State pieces occur, but they are nearly always very heavily bagmarked, even cut or scratched, typically looking as if they have been "through the mill."

For a long time the 1876-CC $20 was considered to be very rare in Mint State, and I can recall having seen only a scattered few. That changed in 1993 when many dozens—quite possibly over 100 pieces—came to light. I remember attending a convention, and while reviewing a dealer's stock, having another dealer quickly show me two Uncirculated 1876-CC double eagles. How unusual, for the 1876-CC was a rarity! However, I was busy with the other dealer at the time, and I told the owner of the $20 pieces to come back in an hour or two. Meanwhile, I soon found in the dealer's stock I was examining at the time about 20 more Uncirculated 1876-CC $20s! Nearly all of these were bright in surface appearance but were extensively

[1] Conversation, September 26, 1996.

[2] From the "Chicago '96" sale, a joint public auction by Rarcoa (Ed Milas) and David W. Akers, page, 72, Lot 449.

bagmarked, a typical grade being MS-60.[1]

Liberty Head dates of the 1880s and 1890s exist in the same grades, although Mint State pieces are more numerous, typically grading MS-60 to about MS-63. Often a variety can be common in MS-63 grade but a great rarity if MS-65. At the same time there seems to have been a "grade inflation" or loosening of interpretations among graders, and what is called MS-60 today might have been called an AU coin a decade or so ago (my opinion here).

Among Liberty Head $20 pieces of the early twentieth century several issues are scarce due to their low mintages. 1901-S, 1904, and 1904-S are common as gems, have mostly been sold outside of the numismatic market, and furnish the opportunity for relatively inexpensive "type" coins. Saint-Gaudens $20 pieces 1907-1932 are typically Mint State at the levels of MS-60 to MS-63, although the Philadelphia Mint dates of the mid-1920s average higher and are often seen MS-63 to MS-65. What's rare and what's not can be determined by checking grading service population reports and popular price guides; the market tends to adjust itself nicely and correctly over a period of time.

Numismatists can be very thankful for the overseas bank hoards. In the United States the government called in all large-denomination ($5, $10, and $20) coins beginning in 1933-1934. Under penalty of law, banks and citizens were forced to empty their vaults, safe deposit boxes, and in-home savings (numismatists were exempt). Hundreds of millions of dollars' worth of gold coins from dollars to commemorative $50 pieces went to the melting pot. Were it not for the overseas hoards, there would be very few gold coins for American numismatists to collect today.

Double Eagle Rumors and Facts

During the past 15 years there have been many stories and comments concerning $20 gold double eagles emerging from one or more caches found in Guatemala or other Central American countries. As an example, ***Walter Breen's Complete Encyclopedia of U.S. and Colonial Coins,*** 1988, noted the following (to which modern comments by gold coin authority David W. Akers have been added):[2]

1908-S: The report of a bag of 1,000 found in Central America has not yet been verified. (David W. Akers: Not true; no such bag was found.)

1910-S: A bag of 1,000 was discovered about 1983 in Central America. (David W. Akers: There were many more than just 1,000 pieces.)

1913-S: The report of a bag of 1,000 from Central America remains unconfirmed. (David W. Akers: No such bag was found.)

1915-S: A bag of 1,000 was recovered in Central America, 1983.

1916-S: Uncs. are mostly from a hoard of at least 3,000 discovered in 1983 [location not stated].

1922-S: At least 7,000 Uncs. turned up in summer 1983. (David W. Akers: Only a few hundred coins were found, some of which were of high quality.)

1926-S: The report of a bag of 1,000 Uncs. from Central America remains unconfirmed. (David W. Akers: No such bag was found.)

Quite possibly related to the preceding is this further commentary from David W. Akers:[3]

[With reference to $20 gold coins from Guatemala or another country in Central America] I have knowledge of the pieces dispersed by MTB [Manfra, Tordella & Brookes] in the early 1980s.

It is my understanding that there were approximately 47,000 $20 coins in the deal, many of them worn, but the majority Uncirculated. The following dates, some previously all but unobtainable, were present in quantity in the deal in choice to gem Mint State: 1908-D No Motto, 1908-D with Motto, 1909-D, 1909-S, 1910-S, 1911-S, 1914-S, 1915-S,

[1] For the 1876-CC also see Douglas Winter and Michael Fuljenz, "Type Two Double Eagles 1866-1876," *Coin Dealer Newsletter Monthly Supplement,* September 13, 1996.

[2] Letter, July 7, 1996.

[3] Letter, June 22, 1996.

1916-S, and 1922-S.

Among Liberty Head $20s were large quantities of 1901-S, 1902-S, 1905-S, 1907-S and 1907-D, all in nice Uncirculated, many MS-63 or better.

I do not know the exact quantities present of all these dates, but there were several thousand each of 1910-S, 1911-S, 1914-S, 1915-S, and 1916-S. The 1916-S were particularly nice, many grading MS-65 or MS-66. I personally sold 500 1911-S $20 to one customer of mine who still has them. For the heck of it, we certified one roll (20 pieces) at random. None graded below MS-63, most were MS-64 and five were MS-65.

I sold many other rolls of individual dates including dozens of choice Mint State 1909-D and 1922-S. Of the latter, at least 200 Choice Mint State pieces were in the hoard, most with moderate to heavy copper spots.

Today in the mid-1990s, the 1908-S, 1913-S, and 1926-S quantities mentioned by Walter Breen are believed to have been without foundation,[1] and each of these varieties is quite rare in Mint State.

In June 1989, Heritage Numismatic Auctions of Dallas, Texas, held a sale at the Dallas Market Hall and, among many items, offered "the El Salvador hoard of 1909-S double eagles."[2]

---

[1] Observation of the author; also David W. Akers, letter, July 7, 1996.

[2] "Heritage Schedules Sale for June 15-18 in Dallas," *Coin World,* June 7, 1989, p. 20.

CHAPTER 17

Paper Hoards

Paper money hoards are scarcer than those containing coins, most probably because the archetype hoarder liked "hard money," especially if made of gold or silver. However, over the years a number of important caches of paper notes have been found, several of which are delineated here.

Bureau of Engraving and Printing, Washington, D.C., in the late nineteenth century.

The Davenport Bank Hoard

Put away: 1860s and later
Disclosed: 1950s-1994
Treasure: Currency and coins

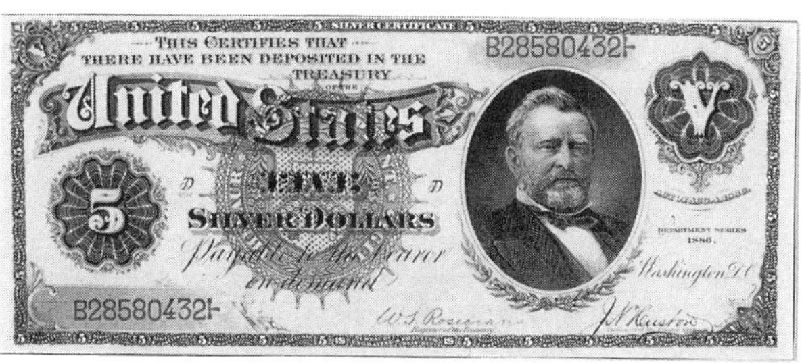

The Davenport Bank Hoard began to be dispersed in the 1950s, but there were enough items remaining on hand that in 1994 about $600,000 worth of rare numismatic items were sold to two buyers. Dean Oakes, who seems to have had an inside track on quite a few caches and treasures in the Midwest, appraised the remaining coins and bills in 1990 and assisted with the 1994 sale.[1]

The story goes back well over a century, to the 1860s when the First National Bank of Davenport, Iowa, organized on June 22, 1863, Charter No. 15, was the very first National Bank in America to open its doors, not by intention but by mistake. Authorities in Washington, D.C., had instructed banks under the new charter system to start business on a given Monday, but someone misunderstood the directions. Apparently the notice arrived on Saturday, and the bank threw open its doors on that very day, beating everyone else by 48 hours!

The First National Bank issued National currency with its own imprint. Many thousands of dollars' worth

[1] Adapted from an interview by the author with Dean Oakes in Denver, CO, August 12, 1996.

of these notes, from the early First Charter bills of the 1860s, continuing through later issues, were stored as "vault cash" by the bank. Denominations ranged from $1 to $100.[1]

The hoard was generally unknown in numismatic circles until 1957, when Dean Oakes was shown a First Charter "Lazy Two" $2 note of the bank by Phil Sorensen, of Mechanicsville, Iowa, who said that the bank in Davenport still had a lot of these and other early notes and that, in fact, he had seen "a little pile" of Lazy Two notes a few years earlier.

In the same decade, numismatists Ted Hammer and Loyd B. Gettys, both of Iowa, had access to the bank hoard, and on behalf of the institution offered many notes for sale, among which was an example of the $100 "Watermelon" Coin Note of 1890, one of the great classics in American currency.

After the 1950s, the remaining items in the bank were more or less forgotten. About 1980 Dean Oakes, remembering his conversation with Phil Sorenson of years earlier, decided to check on the hoard. At the time the Davenport Bank & Trust Company, successor to the First National Bank of Davenport, was under the presidency of V.O. Figgie, who had held the post since 1942 (and would continue to do so until 1992; he died in 1995). Seeking to establish a connection with the Davenport institution, Oakes and his business partner at the time, John Hickman, went to their local bank in Iowa City to see if anyone could help. He learned that Figgie was a very conservative man who with family members in his bank kept his own counsel and privacy and usually would not give information to outsiders. However, an officer in Iowa City knew someone in the Trust Department in the Davenport bank, and a door was opened.

A day later John Hickman and Dean Oakes made arrangements to visit Davenport. Opening the vault was like seeing the inside of Fort Knox, Dean Oakes later recalled. Among the treasures were $2 red-seal notes from 1928 to 1953 with a face value of $18,000; an original bag of $20 face value of 1883 without-CENTS Liberty Head nickels, some 400 coins in all, that had been put in the vault in 1883; $100 face value in 1946 Iowa silver commemorative half dollars; 50 $500 bills; 50 $1000 bills with consecutive serial numbers; one $5000 bill; a type set of First Charter notes (Gettys and Hammer had disposed of the main cache of these in the 1950s, it was learned); a group of red-seal $100 notes on the First National Bank of Davenport; about $300 to $400 worth of gold coins that had been turned into the bank during the 1930s and 1940s and kept there; about 15 $1,000 bags of silver dollars (common issues such as 1882-O, 1887, and 1921 Morgan); 30 bags of common silver coins put away in the early 1960s; and rolls of 1948 Franklin half dollars.

Additional items among the paper money holdings included 1,000 notes in 10 bundles with bank straps on them dated 1868 and 1871, of the $5 Legal Tender notes of 1862, 1863, and 1869, these representing 10% of the $50,000 the old First National Bank was required to keep on hand to satisfy the requirements of its charter. The notes were well used, but yielded a few examples of the Friedberg-61, a variety considered to be rare.[2] Silver Certificates of 1880 and 1891 through the $100 value were also well represented, plus Legal Tender notes of all series through the $100 and $500 Series of 1880. National Bank notes were there from all over the country and included two sheets of small-size Nationals, one from Texas and the other from Wisconsin. Several serial number 1 notes from the First National Bank of Davenport were on hand as were several other #1 notes from other Iowa banks. What a treasure trove!

The hoard that got away: Large bundles of old United States currency notes being cut in half by two attendants at the Treasury Department, circa 1903. Such notes were considered to be too stained or tattered for further use.

[1] Details of the bank's evolution and mergers over the years and quantities of notes issued may be found in John Hickman and Dean Oakes, *Standard Catalogue of National Bank Notes,* p. 283.

[2] Per Robert Friedberg, *United States Paper Money,* various editions from the 1950s onward.

In 1990 when the Davenport Bank & Trust Company sold out to the Norwest Bank chain, Dean Oakes appraised the holding. In 1994 he assisted with the sale of the items to two buyers, one for the coins and the other for the paper money.

The Oat Bin Hoard

Hidden: 19th century
Found: By 1966
Treasure: Rare currency

$1,000 note from the "Oat Bin" hoard. Notes of this denomination are exceedingly rare. This certainly is one of the foremost prizes in the field of American currency. (Courtesy of Dean Oakes)

In the annals of hoards of scarce, rare, and interesting United States paper money the so-called Oat Bin Hoard ranks as one of the more significant finds.[1]

In 1966 Dr. Howard Carter of Leawood, Kansas, purchased a fabulous cache of paper money comprising over $28,000 face value that had been "brought to the Midwest from Virginia shortly after the War Between the States; they were later found in an oat bin that had not been emptied for many years."[2] Other notes were probably acquired in the Midwest at a later date. One of the foremost treasures in the cache was a $1,000 Legal Tender note of the early 1860s.

Carter owned a bank in Kingswood, Missouri, and through its connections put out inquiries seeking old currency. From time to time he was rewarded by success, but never so much as when he learned of an estate that had a wondrous quantity of paper money found in the southern part of the state. A premium of some type was paid above face value, and the estate representatives and Carter were both satisfied.

Seeking to sell the notes to collectors, Carter took them to the American Numismatic Association Convention held that year in Bal Harbour, Florida. However, by the time that several days had passed at the show, only a few had been sold, despite his having printed a list that included a Dakota Territory note.

Dean Oakes, one of America's leading dealers in currency and owner of A&A Coins, Inc., in partnership with his fellow Iowan, Don Jensen, went to Dr. Carter's hotel room, viewed a sampling of the notes, and a week later went to Leawood, Kansas, and bought the entire deal. Oakes and Jensen went as partners in the National Bank notes in the group, and Oakes on his own bought the "type" currency. The Nationals were mostly from Booneville, Missouri, and several Kansas towns including St. Marys, Wamego, and Topeka.

In 1968 Dean Oakes and Don Jensen brought a display of 50 of the choicest Oat Bin Hoard notes, mostly First Charter National issues, to the Professional Numismatists Guild show in Chicago, where they were stolen. Oakes and Jensen ran advertisements in the coin papers to seek information. With the assistance of Chicago dealer Dennis Forgue, a listing of the missing notes and serial numbers was compiled.

In due course, two notes—a rare Texas First Charter $20 and a rare Selma, Alabama, $100 note—turned up in the hands of a small-town dealer in Wisconsin, not far from the Illinois border. The new "owner" of the pieces offered them for sale. Don Jensen notified the Federal Bureau of Investigation and with an FBI agent arranged a "buy." Don pretended to have his cousin with him, who came along, the story being that he wanted to buy an old car in the same town. Don and his "cousin" met with the holder of the notes, inspected them, and suggested that the $2,000 asking price was too high, and countered with $1,800 in the form of several cashiers' checks. This offer was accepted. Minutes later, as the seller of the stolen notes went out the back door to his car, FBI agents grabbed him, confiscated the checks and also, for evidence, the two notes. Later, the notes were returned by the FBI to the rightful owners.

Fast forward to spring 1979, eleven years after the theft. Forty-eight notes were still missing. As luck would have it, two men walked into Rarcoa, the Chicago dealership owned by Ed Milas, where Dennis Forgue was employed at the time. Forgue, quite familiar with the missing items and who had helped make up a list of them earlier, feigned interest in acquiring the notes, and set up an appointment three days later

---

[1] Adapted from an interview by the author with Dean Oakes in Denver, CO, August 12, 1996.

[2] Information is also from "Storied 'Oat Bin' Nationals Go To Auction," *Bank Note Reporter,* November 1979, p. 1. Citation furnished by David Harper.

A selection of notes from the fabulous "Oat Bin" hoard. Backs are facing up. (Courtesy of Dean Oakes)

to buy them. At the scheduled hour the men reappeared and were greeted by the police.

The men had various alibis and excuses, but could not prove they held title to the notes. The stolen notes were confiscated by the police and returned to Oakes and Jensen. Unfortunately, the statute of limitations on the theft was 10 years, and now it was in the eleventh year after the crime, so no prosecution could be made. Dennis Forgue received the Professional Numismatist Guild's Sol Kaplan Award for his work in the recovery.

The notes were subsequently offered in an auction by Hickman & Oakes (John Hickman and Dean Oakes) on November 24, 1979, and by now are widely dispersed.

The Ella Overby Hoard

Put away: Early 20th century
Found: 1960s
Treasure: Rare currency

In addition to the fabled Oat Bin Hoard, professional currency dealer Dean Oakes figured in other caches of paper money over the years, of which the Ella Overby Hoard is one of the most interesting.[1]

This remarkable holding of old-time bills had been the property of one Ella Overby of Starbuck, a small village in Minnesota. Sometime around 1910 her husband, who worked for the railroad, passed away at an early age. For many years afterward Mrs. Overby, who apparently had other income as well, received a pension from the railroad line.

Each month when her check would arrive she would take it to the local bank, cash it into bills, and put the currency in an envelope. She lived very frugally and thus did not have to draw upon the cash that continued to accumulate in the envelopes. For meat she bought wieners one at a time at the local market. Her spartan style of life continued until she died in the early 1960s.

The executor of her estate advertised that the hoard of notes would be sold as a single lot, and Mort Melamed of Minneapolis learned of it in this manner. In due course Melamed was the high bidder among several dealers who inspected the holding. His personal interest was National Bank notes from Minnesota highlighted by the amazing quantity of 130 or more from the hitherto "rare" town of Starbuck. The firm of Hickman & Waters bought the other National Bank notes, while Dean Oakes bought the "type" notes, among which were about 75 of the Chief Onepapa $5 silver certificates in high grades including some with consecutive numbers, a couple hundred large-size $1 notes with Washington's portrait, and many others, the entire estate comprising about $130,000 face value. Many small-size notes of 1929 and later, Federal Reserve notes, and other items with little or no numismatic value were cashed in for face.

A Jar Stuffed With Money

Hidden or lost: By the early 1930s
Found: May 31, 1971
Treasure: Gold Certificates

On May 31, 1971, R.W. Kirkland of Carrollton, Texas, was operating a backhoe as part of a storm sewer

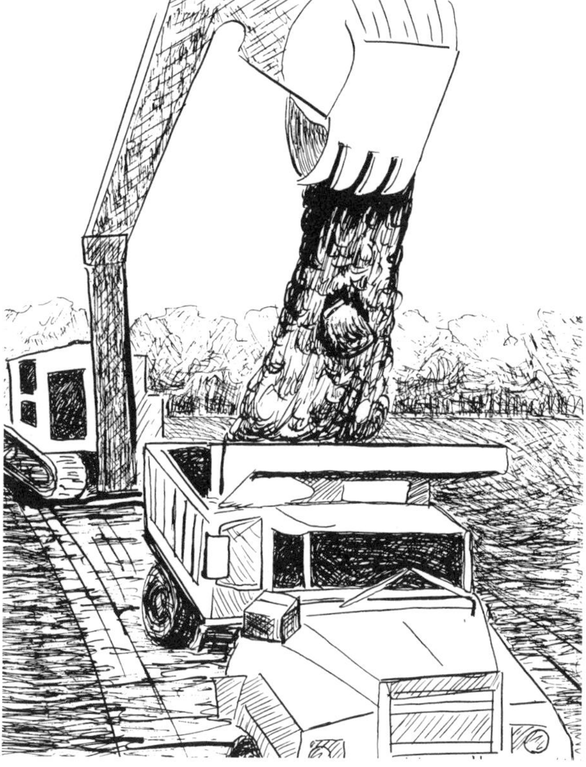

[1] Adapted from an interview by the author with Dean Oakes in Denver, CO, August 12, 1996, plus other information sent by mail on October 8, 1996.

Ladies at the Bureau of Engraving and Printing sort through piles of currency. What a great hoard this would make! On the left the attendant is viewing a sheet of four $100 notes, while on the table in the foreground is a sheet of four Chief Onepapa $5 bills.

construction project. Assisting were C.D. Doolittle and L.C. Stanciel. As a bucket load of earth was dumped, a jar tumbled out. Upon inspection it was found to contain a staggering $47,400 face value in Gold Certificates! Such certificates were issued during the late nineteenth and early twentieth century by the United States Treasury Department and were payable in gold coins upon demand.

Obviously a man of very high personal standards, the first thing Kirkland did was to call the local sheriff's office. The sheriff himself appeared and took possession of the treasure trove. Word of the find spread, and "claims were filed immediately" by five people including present and past owners of the land.

After due consideration, District Court Judge Spencer Carver of Dallas ruled on December 29, 1971, that the finders were keepers, with the largest share going to Kirkland. Virtue, indeed, had its reward.[1]

Famous for Meteorites and, Now, Bank Notes

Hidden or lost: Early 20th century
Found: 1970s
Treasure: Rare currency

In the annals of meteorite collecting and research, Estherville, Iowa, is one of the most famous locations in America. Late in the afternoon of May 10, 1879, about 5:00 clock, the sky over this rural farming town was illuminated by a brilliant fireball, which exploded and showered the area with meteoric fragments. Eventually, over 700 pounds of stony-iron meteorites were recovered, with the largest weighing 427 pounds followed by another that checked in at 151 pounds. Any reference book on American meteorites by necessity includes information on the fabulous Estherville fall. Indeed, it is a focal point in the history of that scientific specialty.

In the 1970s Estherville became even better known to a certain class of collectors: numismatists.[2] It was realized that years earlier the only two banks in Emmet County, Iowa, had each issued National Bank notes, one bank in Armstrong and the other in Estherville. As collectors are wont to do, Bill Higgins of the Higgins Museum in Okoboji, Iowa, sought to own and display one or more notes from each of the banks in Iowa that had issued currency with their own imprint.[3]

The trouble was that while Estherville meteorite specimens appeared on the market from time to time and were well-known in just about any representative museum or private collection of such visitors from outer space, currency collectors had no such luck. The First National Bank of Estherville (organized on January 23, 1892, with a capital of $50,000) had issued notes of only two denominations, $50 and $100, and not a single one was known to exist! Typically, if a bank issued notes, they were of the $5, $10, or $20 denominations. Only a very few institutions had higher values, and these banks were apt to be in large cities. For a small town in the hinterlands of Iowa to have issued $50 and $100 and no lesser values was virtually unbelievable.

Being of an innovative turn of mind, John Hickman, curator of the Higgins Museum, came up with the idea of broadcasting on a nearby station in Spencer, Iowa, a reward offer of $50 to any listener who might provide information leading to the purchase of one of these Estherville bills. A farmer who had been plowing his field all morning came into his house for lunch, heard the reward, and asked his daughter to telephone the Higgins Museum to say she knew of *one* such note.

Curator Hickman, who was also well known as a currency collector and dealer, was asked to go to Estherville and check the note, which he did. At the bank he met the old farmer, Fred Clayton, and his

[1] "Judge Awards Hoard of Gold Certificates to Workers," *Coin World,* January 12, 1972, p. 15.

[2] Adapted from an interview by the author with Dean Oakes in Denver, CO, August 12, 1996; additional commentaries and notes submitted by Dean Oakes, October 8, 1996. Town name misspelled "Esterville" in some printed accounts.

[3] In a newsletter dated September 1996, currency dealer Lyn F. Knight noted that the Higgins Museum in Okoboji, Iowa, is a "Mecca" today for collectors of National Bank notes. In the collection there are over 2,400 such notes from various cities and towns and about 20,000 photographic postcards. The holdings represent the combined work of the late Bill Higgins and his associate, the late John Hickman. A research library may be used by visiting scholars.

daughter, was cautiously shown a $50 1882 greenback National Bank note from Estherville, and, after first paying the $50 reward, was allowed to purchase the note itself for an additional amount.

Then he was asked if he would buy more than one note, and, if so, would additional $50 rewards be paid for others. In due course Hickman parted with two more rewards and purchased another $50 note and a $100 note! At that time, the farmer asked:

> Do you buy other old money? We have other large-size old bills. My wife used to sell eggs and kept the money at home. When the banks closed in the 1930s we lived off her egg money. We still have a small box full of this kind of cash. I took them to the bank, but they told me that they will only accept the small notes now, and that the large ones are not worth anything.

The old farmer kept his large-size notes and was delighted to learn from Hickman that they, indeed, had value, even more than the denominations printed on them. After he died his family found the cache, which amounted to about $2,000 to $3,000 face value among which were Gold Certificates, three beautiful $20 "Technicolor" notes, 20 to 25 of the $5 Chief Onepapa notes, and some cut sheets. Each of the National Bank notes had been folded twice, yielding three vertical creases apiece. The notes from the farmer's estate, some gold coins, and other miscellaneous items were made up into four or five lots and offered for sealed bids by the estate executor. Don Mark bought the group and sold the "type" notes, including the $5 Onepapa bills, to Dean Oakes, but kept for himself the National Bank notes among which were about 30 $10s and $20s from Terril, Iowa.

The Wood River Currency Hoard

Hidden or lost: Early 20th century
Found: 1974
Treasure: Rare currency

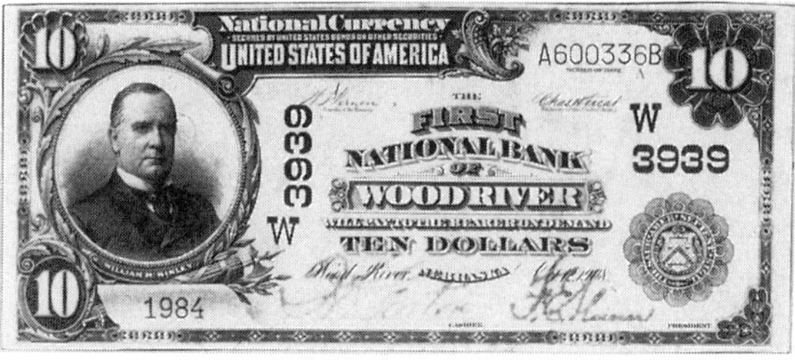

The Wood River Hoard came to light under circumstances that were never revealed. Dean Oakes and John Hickman, professional dealers in rare paper money, later purchased the group from a Nebraska dealer, Marvin Luke, and concluded that it had been hidden in the early part of the century.[1]

The notes appeared to have been tightly rolled up and stored in dry circumstances—not buried in the earth—perhaps in one or more cans, as some showed slight evidence of rust stains or, in some instances, larger areas of discoloration. The notes were on the Wood River National Bank in Nebraska and were of the 1902-1908 dated plain back Third Charter series.

Inspection and counting of the 236 notes acquired by Dean Oakes revealed that for every $20 bill there were three of the $10 denomination. This and serial number evidence suggested that they had been printed in the usual format of the time, in sheets of four notes, $10-$10-$10-$20, then cut apart and stored. These were later marketed to collectors including by listing the notes in Hickman & Oakes' 60th Price List, 1974, the last issued by that firm.

The Secret of a Picture Frame

Hidden or lost: By the early 20th century
Found: By 1994
Treasure: Rare currency

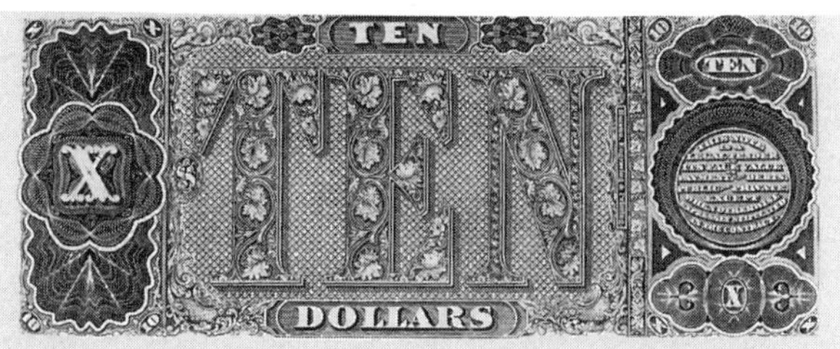

One can never tell what might be hidden behind an old picture or print mounted years ago in a frame.[2] There are stories of rare Currier & Ives prints coming

[1] Adapted from an interview by the author with Dean Oakes in Denver, CO, August 12, 1996.

[2] Adapted from an interview by the author with Don Jensen in Denver, CO, August 12, 1996. Also Jensen, letter, October 15, 1996.

to light this way, having been bought casually for next to nothing.

For Iowa numismatist Don Jensen, such a circumstance was even more important than a beautiful old print, even better than a Currier & Ives print of a Mississippi River steamship race or the *Old Homestead in Winter.*

On a memorable occasion, the significance of which was not realized until later, an Omaha dealer in antiques attended an auction and bought a framed picture, apparently of no particular importance. Probably, it sold for practically nothing and seemed to be a bargain. No doubt, someone could use the frame for a modern piece of art or old family photograph. There was always a ready market for such things, provided they were cheap.

Upon going home and taking the unwanted image from its wooden frame, the new owner of the frame was delighted to find 130 (wow!) old paper currency notes hidden beneath the picture. The paper money was recognized as being of value. The notes were sold to a fellow in Iowa who in turn told Jensen about them. One particularly important example was a rare $10 brown-back issue from Keokuk, Iowa. Another was a $20 red-seal note from the rare location of Juneau, Alaska, being the only such note known from that state!

Other notes were from such locations as Smith Centre, Kansas; Pawnee, Oklahoma; Pender, Nebraska; Stockton, Kansas; and Mounds, Oklahoma-to give just a short list.

This picture-frame hoard was large in scope and with excellent numismatic content—certainly a winning combination.

Don Jensen also told of another picture frame with a secret content: $20 gold coins! No details were made known to him, however. One suspects that this one must have been suspiciously heavy!

Catalogue and Book Hoards

Put away: 19th and 20th centuries
Found: Recent decades
Treasure: Desirable books and catalogues

Significance of Hoards

Hoards are the stuff of which numismatic dreams are made. Not only does this apply to coins and paper money, but caches of out-of-print numismatic books, auction catalogues, and price lists can have great fi-

Cover of one of four sale catalogues prepared 1994-1995 for the auction of the Armand Champa Library, the largest collection of American numismatic books and catalogues ever to cross the auction block.

nancial value as well as commanding historical interest. The Numismatic Bibliomania Society serves as a focus for interested collectors of old numismatic literature and publishes a journal *The Asylum*. Collectors of books and periodicals seem to enjoy a special camaraderie, but they can be as competitive as anyone when it comes to seeking a rarity. A community of numismatic booksellers stands ready to assist with "want lists" and purchases.

Among the items most desired by numismatic book collectors are these in the American series:

Auction catalogues, Nineteenth century: Catalogues by such luminaries as Edward Cogan, Lyman Low, New York Coin & Stamp Co., W.E. Woodward, John W. Haseltine, the Chapman brothers, and others can have significant value, especially if they are of a "name" collection containing many scarce and rare coins, or are of a specialty (large cents, Indian peace medals, colonials, tokens, etc.). If a catalogue is hardbound and contains photographic plates, all the better. Also adding value is a list of the prices realized at the sale, or, even better, a catalogue marked up with the prices obtained and the names of the buyers. In addition to the foregoing, complete or nearly complete sets and runs of the catalogues of a given dealer are always in demand. Also important are auction catalogues—no matter what they contain—of the very early years in American numismatics, 1860 and earlier.

Auction catalogues, 20th century: Catalogues of

the present century are more desired for their content and the scarcities and rarities showcased, than for the scarcity of the publications themselves. Thus, a fairly common B. Max Mehl catalogue of the 1941 Dunham Sale is in greater demand than a very rare catalogue of an auction held by French's at a particular time in the 1950s. Beginning with John J. Ford, Jr.'s in-depth, historically informative cataloguing (on behalf of New Netherlands Coin Co.) of the United States coin portion of the 1952 American Numismatic Association Convention sale, the bar was raised on the state of the art. From that time forward, a new level of catalogues transmitting valuable information appeared. It is probably accurate to say that a collection of auction catalogues of the second half of the twentieth century contains many multiples of the information found in catalogues from 1901 to 1950. Catalogues of the past several decades are, for the most part, very inexpensive and are easy to find.

Reference books: First editions and early printings of standard reference books on popular American series are in demand as collectibles. Crosby on colonial coins (1875), Browning on quarter dollars (1925), and Bolender on silver dollars (1950) are but three of many that could be mentioned. Price guides such as the *Standard Catalogue of U.S. Coins* (Raymond) and *A Guide Book of U.S. Coins* (Yeoman-Bressett) are often collected by editions, with earlier numbers or autographed copies having special value.

Periodicals: *The Numismatist* (first published in 1888, still published monthly today as the official organ of the American Numismatic Association), the *American Journal of Numismatics* (first published in 1866 and continued until about 1920, when it lapsed from quarterly appearance to a series of erratically produced monographs; issues from 1866-1920 are especially collectible), and dealer magazines issued in the nineteenth century by Mason, Scott, Frossard, and others are in demand, as are certain dealer magazines of the present century. Modern periodicals such as *Coin World, COINage, Coins, Numismatic News, Numismatic Scrapbook Magazine,* among others, have much worthwhile information, but are not widely collected in serial form—perhaps because they are too recent to be perceived as valuable. For the reader seeking knowledge, these offer many opportunities.

Price lists: Fixed-price listings issued by dealers can be of importance and value if they showcase an important specialized collection.

Ephemera: Various "go-with" items can often have value. Examples include old-time photographs taken at conventions and other gatherings of collectors, novelties and souvenirs bearing dealer imprints, etc.

The Celebrated Wylie Hoard

In the field of numismatic literature, one of the most celebrated hoards is that assembled by Alexander Parker Wylie. The recollection is of John W. Adams and the scenario is set in 1976.[1]

In the autumn of that year, Adams, a Boston numismatic scholar whose library is of incredible proportions and who wrote two definitive books on early American coin auction catalogues, was contacted by a friend who had some information to share.

A Wheaton, Illinois, real estate agent and raiser of buffalo for their meat, Richard Piper by name, had come into possession of a vast quantity of old auction catalogues. These were said to have been the property of Alexander Parker Wylie and had become the property of two of his spinster descendants.

Adams went to Illinois, met Piper and his wife, had dinner, and then began sorting the "grand total of 4,944 catalogues plus perhaps a dozen periodicals and/or books" into piles. The treasure trove was found to contain the following:

> 77 W. Elliot Woodward catalogues, pre-1867, of which four were large-format editions. Woodward catalogues are especially highly prized for their information content.
>
> 774 later Woodward catalogues including, remarkably, 118 with photographic plates—the latter being rare and highly prized.
>
> 279 Lyman H. Low catalogues, most of them with prices realized.
>
> 270 Édouard Frossard catalogues including 16 with plates.
>
> 449 various catalogues dated before 1876.
>
> 5 Harlan P. Smith catalogues of the Dr. Edward Maris Collection, one of which was plated.
>
> 10 J.W. Scott catalogues of which all had photographic plates.
>
> 216 Thomas L. Elder catalogues.
>
> 232 J.W. Haseltine catalogues.
>
> 294 Ebenezer Mason catalogues.
>
> 320 Edward Cogan catalogues.
>
> 179 Chapman brothers' small-format catalogues and 12 large format editions.
>
> And much more.

Of the 4,944 catalogues, more than 4,000 were duplicates including 50 or more copies of some catalogues. John Adams made an offer for the lot, which

[1] *The Asylum,* journal of the American Bibliomania Society, Winter 1993, pp. 3-5. Also, Frank and Laurese Katen sale nos. 44, 45, 46, 48, and 51. John Adams' collection of United States large cents dated 1794 appeared in a fixed-price catalogue issued by Bowers and Merena Galleries, 1984. His two reference books, ***United States Numismatic Literature,*** Vols. I and II, were published by George Kolbe, and stand as reference works on American auction catalogues from the 1860s to about 1950.

was not accepted. The owner subsequently consigned them to Frank and Laurese Katen, who offered them at auction in a series of sales beginning on March 19, 1977. In time, the Wylie hoard was distributed to many eager collectors of numismatic literature.

Varia

Many other hoards of numismatic literature could be recalled. A few:

In the 1950s Aubrey and Adeline Bebee came across a cache of hundreds of W.C. Prime's 1861 book, *Coins, Medals and Seals.* Some had to be rebound, but the contents of each copy were largely intact. These were sold over a long period of years to clients of their firm.

The Federal Reserve Bank of Philadelphia determined to simplify its library and deaccessioned just about anything it felt was not of current interest. In the author's library at present is a bound set of *Niles' Register,* complete through the year 1836, formerly the reference set of Nicholas Biddle and the Bank of the United States. Hundreds of counterfeit detectors describing early bank notes were disposed of at the same time, also the one-time property of this historical bank.

In the 1980s the American Antiquarian Society, a Massachusetts organization with an incredible library of historical publications, decided to define its prime literary interest as being items published in 1876 or before. Many valuable publications of later years were wholesaled to book dealers. Included were many banking journals, financial texts, and other items of interest to numismatists.

The Library of Congress, Washington, D.C., has deaccessioned many items over the years, sometimes simply by throwing them away. An official explained to the author that this was often simpler than advertising for bids, showing the unwanted books to prospective buyers, etc. Among the treasures disposed of in one way or another in the past several decades have been a large library of letter copies of Mint-related correspondence of the mid-nineteenth century, the very first copy (numbered as such and inscribed by the author, Richard S. Yeoman) of the first edition of *A Guide Book of United States Coins,* duplicates of annual *Mint Reports,* and much more. Most of these eventually reached the hands of appreciative numismatists. Mention should also be made of an unfortunate situation: during her tenure as director of the Mint in the 1970s, Ms. Stella Hackel ordered the destruction of thousands of Mint documents of the nineteenth and twentieth centuries, in an economy move, prompting noted researcher R.W. Julian to remark that this event was one of the darkest days the hobby has ever known.

In 1931 Charles C. Rood, in his *1st Catalog of Numismatic Literature,* commented: "It took nearly 2,000 odd numbers of *The Numismatist* for me to build one complete file, with the result that I now have the largest stock of back numbers available, and this is an example of the 'fun' I have had."[1]

In its basement at its headquarters at 155th Street and Broadway, New York City, the American Numismatic Society had for many years a vast holding of duplicates of its *American Numismatic Journal* dated from 1866 until well into the present century. In the 1950s, and perhaps even later, the duplicate copies were made available in loose copies combined by years, and in brown paper packages. Any desired year was available for just a few dollars, except that certain popular monographs of the early twentieth century were no longer available, these being the Adams works on territorial gold, Adams and Woodin on patterns, and Miller and Ryder's *State Coinage of New England.* It is said that later the entire remaining batch was acquired by a Midwest collector of numismatic literature who in due course became a benefactor to the Society.

In Los Angeles in the 1960s a hoard of nearly 50 original copies of J.F. Loubat's magnum opus, *The Medallic History of the United States of America, 1776-1876,* published in 1878, was sold to a dealer. The butterscotch covers were a bit tattered, but the contents were mint.

Many other stories could be related.

A Typical Bank Story

Original notes printed: Late 1830s
Found: Later years
Treasure: Broken bank notes

Background

In the first part of the nineteenth century many private banks issued their own currency notes. Typically, a group of local citizens including businessmen would form a company—the John Doe Bank for purposes of illustration, get a state charter, and acquire capital. The catch was that a bank could be capitalized

[1] Citation furnished by John W. Adams, who noted that Rood's "1st Catalog" was probably his only and last catalogue.

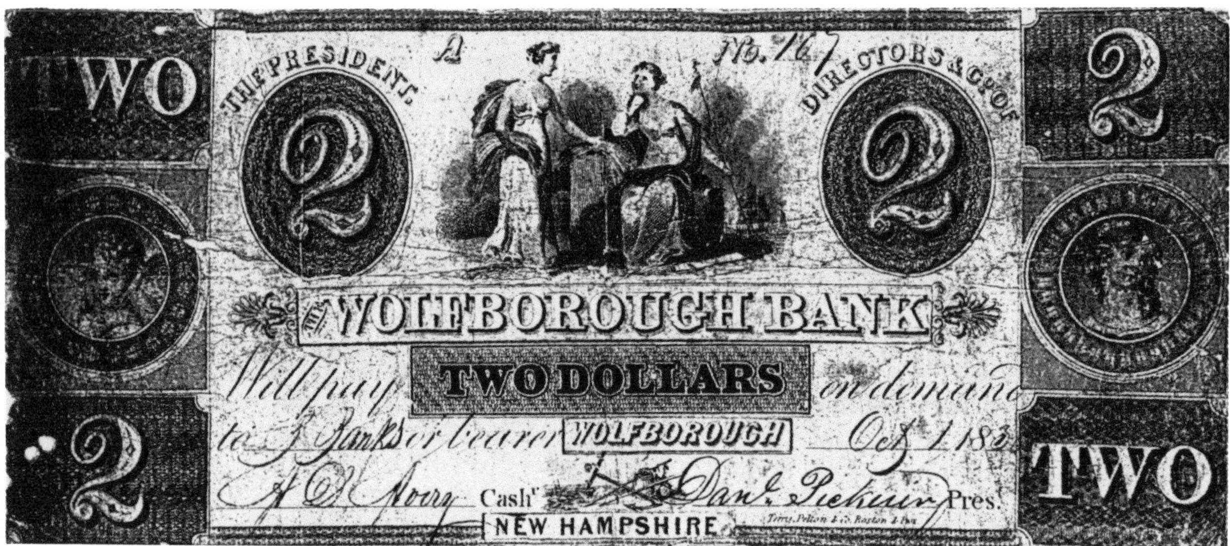

Bank notes bearing the imprint of Wolfeborough, New Hampshire, in the early nineteenth century. (Courtesy of Warren Henderson)

for, say, $50,000, but the founders would contribute very little actual money. Rather, promissory notes, stock certificates, and other assets—often worthless or of highly uncertain value—were pledged. It was not unusual for a bank capitalized at $50,000 to have less than $10,000, or even less than $5,000, in actual paid-in cash capital!

The next step was to contact one of the bank-note engraving companies in Philadelphia, New York, or Boston, and to order currency bearing the bank's imprint. The most popular denominations were $1, $2, $3, $5, and $10, but sometimes higher values were printed as well.

Returning to legitimate banks, but with uncertain capital strength, their notes would be placed into local circulation, where they would trade among merchants and townspeople, typically at par or face value. Anyone wanting to redeem a note for coins had but to bring it to the bank to do so. A perusal of nineteenth-century bank records by the author suggests that a typical bank with $50,000 in notes outstanding might have anywhere from $1,000 to $10,000 in coins in its safe, this being the only hard backing. This arrangement worked well as long as most notes stayed "out there" in commercial channels and were not cashed in. However, if a rumor of insolvency arose there would be a "run" on the bank, and those holding currency would be lucky to get pennies on the dollar. Most likely, they received nothing.

Of course, this ended the *local* credit of the bank in question, and those in the immediate area would not touch one of the paper bills with the proverbial 10-foot pole. However, at a distance of several hundred or more miles, a merchant or tradesman might have no way of knowing that a $5 note on the John Doe Bank was worthless. Seeking to make a sale, the merchant might take it at a discount, say in trade for $3 or $4 worth of goods. If he were alert he might subscribe to one of several newspapers called "counterfeit detectors," which might say, for example, that notes of the John Doe Bank were worthless or, perhaps, sold at a 50% discount, in which latter instance he would allow just $2.50 for a $5 note, and would then seek to pass the bill on to someone else as quickly as possible, reminiscent of Aaron White's admonition, "Never keep a paper dollar in your pocket till tomorrow."

Thus, authentic notes that once may have had some value, but which in the meantime had become totally worthless notes sometimes surfaced at remote locations and were used in scams.

Moreover, the engraving firms that made bank-note printing plates made no attempt to check the character or integrity of applicants. Some notes were fantasies—made for banks that never existed! In such a fraud, imaginative crooks would set up fake banks or issue new, fake notes using an old bank name. This seems to have been particularly prevalent in the state of Michigan, where "wildcat" banks, as they were called, were endemic.

Reflective of private banks of the 1830s, 1840s, and 1850s, in the twentieth century, dozens of caches of unsigned, undistributed notes were brought to the numismatic market and were widely dispersed. Most were from banks that once existed, but others are relics of deceptive schemes. None had any residual value as currency. However, it is poignant to observe that *any* $1, $2, $3, or $5 note—fraudulent or otherwise—today has a numismatic or collecting value greater than its face value! Interesting.

A Bank in New Hampshire

The following history is a true one, that of the Wolfborough (*sic*) Bank of Wolfeboro, New Hampshire.[1] Hundreds of similar accounts could be researched and published for as many different banks:

To begin with, there was, indeed, a Wolfborough Bank, and it prepared for and then was really in business from 1834 to the early 1840s, but was most active in late 1837, in 1838, and the first part of 1839.

On July 5, 1834, the Wolfborough Bank was founded with capital stock of $100,000, with a 20-year state charter. Most investors lived in New York City and Dover, New Hampshire. Only one Wolfeboro person owned multiple shares of stock, although prominent local citizens were tapped as founders of the bank, probably after being told by outsiders that they would profit immensely in due course. Such a bank was a fine addition to a busy town that had no financial institution up to that time. Doubtless, it would be a boon to its citizens.

Most bank stock shares were given out in exchange for well over $100,000 worth of documents, notes, and bonds left as security. It is thus seen that this bank

[1] The text is adapted from a study done by the author (QDB) for *The History of Wolfeboro, NH, 1770-1994,* published by the Wolfeboro Historical Society, 1996. The Wolfborough Bank ostensible issued the following denominations of notes in the 1830s as evidenced by extant notes today, although some may be counterfeit: $1, $1.25, $1.50, $1.75, $2, $3, $5, $10. The $1.25, $1.50, and $1.75 notes are rare, and the author knows of no extant specimen of the $10. The present commentary represents one of the most detailed commentaries of a bank of the 1830s ever given in a numismatic publication. The Wolfborough Bank name omitted the "e" in the town name. In the twentieth century the town is known as Wolfeboro, with the earlier "ugh" suffix omitted.

was in the early days a "good" bank. If anyone checked, the books showed that the $100,000 capital was even over-secured, but not in specie (coins). Truly, this was for all intents and purposes a bank with much more financial strength than required.

Adding to the cachet of this financial institution was the illustrious roster of incorporators, including many of the town's leading citizens: Samuel Avery, Adam Brown, William H. Copp, Samuel Fox, James Hersey, Samuel Leavitt, Henry Parker, Joseph L. Peavey, Daniel Pickering, Aaron Roberts, Henry B. Rust, and Thomas Rust.[1] Directors were Nathaniel Rogers, Samuel Avery, Joseph Hanson, John P. Hale, Daniel Pickering, John Williams, Thomas E. Sawyer. Daniel Pickering was president; Thomas E. Sawyer, cashier. Subsequently, Augustine D. Avery became cashier, and later Thomas Rust served in that post. All were highly respected and had excellent personal credit. However, these same people for the most part were conspicuously absent from the roster of people who put up money and actually invested in the bank. Most probably, being an incorporator was flattering to those involved. Of course, for those behind the bank—specifically the New York interests—this amounted to a free stamp of approval!

Out-of-town stockholders owned the vast majority of the stock:

Samuel D. Dakin, New York City, 600 shares valued at $60,000
Cyrus Moore, 100 shares, $10,000
John Williams, 100 shares, $10,000

Stockholders living in Wolfeboro owned only a small percentage, and nearly all of that was owned by just one person. Thus, this was more of a "New York City bank" than a "Wolfeboro bank." The local shareholders:

Daniel Pickering, 196 shares, $19,600
Nathaniel Rogers, 1 share, $100
Thomas E. Sawyer (the bank's cashier), 1 share, $100
Samuel Avery, 1 share, $100
Joseph Hanson, 1 share, $100

In 1836 the construction of a two-story brick headquarters commenced. Apparently, erection and finishing of the structure dragged on and was still in progress in summer 1838.[2] This edifice was purchased by the bank for $125 in the same year. Other real estate was acquired as well.

The Panic of 1837 swept through the United States in the spring and caused the failure of nearly a thousand banks. However, the Wolfborough Bank was a newcomer, not yet financially operational, and it escaped obvious problems—at least for the time being. The official organization of the bank was completed on October 11, 1837, and it became a going concern on or after November 10. This was not a particularly auspicious time in American financial history.

On November 11, 1837, an iron safe was purchased for $97.80. Shortly after that time the first notes—amounting to 1,200 $3 bills and 1,200 $2 bills—were placed into circulation, followed soon thereafter by 2,204 $2 and 2,204 $3 notes. Probably, these were received in uncut sheets of four notes per sheet, the supplier being Terry, Pelton & Co., bank-note engravers.

Daniel Pickering, the local stockholder with the largest holding in the bank, reassured anyone who asked that the bank was indeed a safe place to keep money and with which to transact business.[3]

An Examination of the Bank

However, questions arose concerning the Wolfborough Bank, and in June 1838 the state sent an examiner to review the situation. His report dated June 20 of that year gives an insight as to its condition:

Concord, June 20th, 1838
To His Excellency Isaac Hill,—

Pursuant to your instructions of the 16th instant, I attended at Wolfeborough on the 18th instant, for the purpose of making an examination of the standing and condition of the Wolfborough Bank, and of proposing certain interrogatories, as directed by the House of Representatives, in their resolution of the 16th instant. The officers of the Bank very readily submitted their books and papers for examination, and answered on oath the interrogatories above alluded to, and such others as were proposed to them,—and I now have the honor to submit to your Excellency the result of that examination.

The Wolfborough Bank was incorporated July 5, 1834, and the corporation was organized Oct. 11, 1837. The capital stock was fixed at $100,000, and was divided into 1,000 shares—and it was voted that ten per cent. of the capital should be paid in by Nov. 10th, 1837. No other assessment appears to have been made.

On the 28th day of October, the Directors voted that the President and Cashier be a committee to receive payment of the stock, and make such discounts as they may deem proper. On the 2d day of November, pursuant to a previous understanding, but without any particular vote appearing, the full amount of the capital stock was paid in, in

[1] *Laws of New Hampshire,* Vol. 10, p. 585.

[2] In the 1990s this building still stands on South Main Street in Wolfeboro and is known as the Scott House.

[3] Born in Greenland, N.H., in 1796 and educated at Phillips Exeter Academy, Pickering set up his first business, a store, in Wolfeboro about 1815. Later, he operated a brickyard and put up a three-story commercial block. His town businesses grew to include real estate trading, shoe manufacturing, and the operation of a woolen and satin mill. He died on February 14, 1856, by which time he had ownership interests in the largest local hotel (the Pavilion) and a steamship, *Lady of the Lake.*

Bank Bills, mostly of the Boston Banks—no specie was paid—and the same day the same money was loaned to the stockholders, each receiving back as a loan the money paid in by him. Some portion of these loans were made on the note of the stockholder alone, and for the residue an endorser was required.

The stock was pledged for the whole amount of the notes, whether endorsed or not. These debts remain essentially now as then, excepting a few changes produced by a transfer of stock; and the amount of notes secured only by about the same, as is now shown by the subsequent statement. At a subsequent meeting, the Directors approved of these proceedings by vote.

On the 14th day of December 1837, the Wolfborough Bank deposited in its own bills $20,000 in the Manufacturers' Bank at Belleville, New Jersey; and received from that Bank a certificate of deposit for that sum to be drawn, payable in New York City, and only as might become necessary for the redemption of the bills of the Wolfborough Bank at its counter, or in Boston—said drafts to be sold in Boston or other Eastern cities at the best premium, and the premium or exchange to be divided between the said Banks—the accounts to be settled every three months, and the rate of interest to be allowed was left for future adjustment. Four thousand dollars of that amount has been drawn by an arrangement between the said Banks, and was received in gold, and now forms a part of the specie in the Bank.[1] The remaining $16,000 is the sum named as in deposit, and referred to in the interrogatories proposed by the Hon. House of Representatives.

Of the shares, 259 are owned by various individuals in this State; 100 by an individual in Boston, Mass.; and 641 by an individual in the city of New York.

This bank has put in circulation $38,135, of which the sum of $9,660 was in bills of the denominations of five and ten dollars, and the remainder of twos and threes. Of this sum, $20,000 was deposited, as before stated, in the Bank of New Jersey, for the purpose of being put in circulation. The sum of $14,000 was placed in the hands of the New York stockholder, he having been appointed an agent to loan or exchange said bills, and having given a bond with sureties to account for the same, and for all interest received. $3,000 in addition were exchanged for New England bills with the same stockholder. On the 3d of November, $1,075 were exchanged in Boston for specie with one of the stockholders; and the balance of $60 has been put in circulation here. The officers of the Bank are unable to tell how much of said money has been loaned or exchanged by their said agents or depositaries.

The assets of the Bank are now kept in an iron safe at Wolfeborough, where the corporation is erecting buildings designed for a Bank, and a dwelling for the Cashier, which, with the out-houses when completed, it is estimated will cost over $3,000.

The President of the Bank stated, in explanation of the manner in which the bills of the Bank had been put in circulation, that in Nov. last he endeavored to make an arrangement with the Suffolk Bank in Boston for the redemption of their bills,—but the officers of that Bank declined, under existing circumstances, to open any new account with any Bank.[2] It was also said, that the Bank could not conveniently transact much business till the completion of their banking house.

The owners of stock in the vicinity of the Bank were said to be ready to pay the assessment of ten per cent—but it was not wanted, and had not been called for. Of their bills $212 only have been redeemed, and $100 of that re-issued. Redemptions have been made in other bills. Specie, it is said, has not been required but once, and for a small sum, and was not refused.[3]

The Bank has not assented to the Act regulating Banks and Banking, passed July, 1837, not having been organized till after the time limited for the acceptance of that Act had expired. No dividend has been made. No one dollar, or fractional bills have been issued; and no disposition has been made of their specie, except some small exchanges in the vicinity, as a matter of convenience to individuals. The $4,000 in gold was received a short time before making their return in May. My examination presents the following as the condition of the Wolfborough Bank, June 18, 1838, and confirmed by the statements under oath of the President and Cashier:

Means—	
Debts of all kinds, including interest on stock notes:	$119,861.61
Personal property:	97.80
Specie:	5,010.60
Foreign [other banks'] bills:	431.00
Funds in Manufacturers' Bank, New Jersey:	16,000.00
Real Estate:	475.00
TOTAL:	$141,876.01

Liabilities—	
Paper money in circulation	$ 38,023.00
Capital	100,000.00
TOTAL:	138,023.00
Showing a balance in favor of the Bank of	3,853.01
GRAND TOTAL:	$141,876.01

Debts due from other than stockholders:	$143.00
Debts due from stockholders on notes and obligations other than stock notes:	14,954.93
Debts due from directors on stock notes with endorsers:	6,331.76
Debts due from directors on stock notes alone:	6,890.05
Debts due from stockholders other than directors on stock notes with endorsers:	38,346.10
Debts due from same on stock notes alone :	53,195.77
Total amount of debts:	$119,861.61

The officers of the Bank did not seem willing to admit any of their debts to be bad.

---

1 Essentially worthless paper money had been transformed into gold coins by an arrangement with a bank far removed from New Hampshire. Ancient alchemists would have been proud!

2 The Suffolk Bank acted as a clearing house for the paper money issues of many regional banks.

3 In other words, the bank had been successful in keeping its paper money in circulation, and to this point only one person had requested gold or silver coins in exchange. Other redemptions were made the easy way: simply by paying out paper money of other banks. (Very little factual information of this nature has ever appeared in print in numismatic publications, and it is hoped that this delineation of the affairs of a typical bank will be of interest to those with a combined interest in history and collecting.)

$15,900 of stock is owned by individuals in the vicinity of the Bank, and their stock notes may probably be collected. Of other stockholders living at a distance, it is not easy to speak with exact justice. But of stock so held, I am inclined to think $20,000 is at least doubtful. One owner of $10,000 stock has an endorser said to be wholly irresponsible.

The residue of said stock, amounting to $64,100, is held by the individual in the city of New York before referred to: his endorser also lives in New York. The same stockholder is further indebted to the Bank, as appears above, in the sum of $14,000, for which the Bank has his obligation with two sureties, one of whom is his endorser on his stock notes. The same stockholder is also interested in the Manufacturers' Bank at Belleville, New Jersey. The officers of the Bank state that they have made inquiries, and believe that the claims against this individual are good and available. I have omitted any further particularity as to the stockholders, or their ability, because I have understood that, if further information should be required, it can easily be furnished here.

There has been paid in of the ten per cent. assessment but $830, unless the transactions of the 2d of Nov. be regarded as a payment of the capital.

All which is respectfully submitted.

LEONARD WILCOX,
Bank Commissioner.

Continuing Activities

On October 1, 1838, the bank issued 400 sheets of $5 bills, for a total of $2,000. This was followed by 38 sheets of $5 notes on October 16 and 562 sheets of the same denomination on October 22. On November 12 another 200 sheets of $5 bills went into circulation.

What may have been the first release of $1 notes consisted of 200 sheets (four notes to a sheet) on December 20, at the same time 200 sheets of $3 bills were paid out. On December 24, 1838, 1,000 single notes of $1 bills were distributed.

On January 9, 1839, 1,200 sheets each of $1 and $3 bills were issued. On March 2, 600 sheets each of the same two denominations were circulated. The last may have been the final notes officially released by the bank.

By 1839 the bank was of questionable solvency, but many new paper money bills were issued. By the end of the year the bank was essentially defunct, and its notes were worthless. Notwithstanding this, the bank paid Samuel D. Dakin par value of $100 each for 397 shares on October 10, 1840. As the bank had virtually no assets, perhaps unissued paper money was exchanged.

The Fraud

Now comes the fantasy part:

After the Wolfborough Bank's failure, the investors' notes and other securities held in escrow for payment of capital stock were turned to in order to make currency holders whole and to permit redemption of paper money at par. However, that was not to be. A state investigation found that "bonds and notes, which, to the amount of $141,066.03, remained unpaid in June 1840, and have proved almost entirely worthless."[1]

Meanwhile, large amounts of the bank's paper money remained in the hands of people outside of New Hampshire, especially the stockholders in New York City. Certain of this currency was placed into circulation in areas in which its worthless character would not be recognized, and the notes traded at a discount from face value. Still, getting $4 in goods in exchange for a $10 note was an easy if illegal road to profit. In 1840, the state of New Hampshire alleged that fraud had taken place.

In 1842, Thomas Rust, of Wolfeboro, a well-known and highly respected citizen, was appointed cashier to manage what was left of the bank's assets and reported that this amounted to about $150, but that about $13,000 worth of the bank's notes were still in circulation! The latest-dated transaction on the bank's books was a real estate sale in March 1844 to J. Thompson for $1,000.[2] By this time the institution had been out of business for about four years.

In 1849, certain stockholders in New York City attempted to reorganize the bank, but with no intention of actually engaging in legitimate banking. It was hoped to fraudulently float a new issue of paper money.[3] Apparently, new notes of various denominations were printed!

The attorney general of New Hampshire was instructed to proceed against the action. It was related that:

> Various attempts have been made by persons from abroad [outside of the state] to reorganize the bank and procure a new issue of its bills—that William Ingalls and Asa Hinckley of New York, are now engaged in such an attempt, having visited, and proposing again to visit Wolfborough for that purpose—that at Ingalls' request, at a meeting convened and attended by him, a board of directors was chosen, consisting of John H. Wiggins, Esq., of Dover, president; John Peavey, Samuel Bean, A.L. Hersey, Nathan Bailey, George W. Libbey, and Henry Sayward.
>
> Hersey alone was the holder of any stock. The residue held no stock whatever and yet assumed to elect one of their

[1] Most technical information concerning this bank is from New Hampshire state records, including the June 15, 1849 *Report of the Committee on Banks Relating to the Wolfborough Bank.* Certain records of the bank are preserved today by the Wolfeboro Historical Society.

[2] The bank's ledgers are preserved today by the Wolfeboro Historical Society.

[3] *Report of the Committee on Banks,* June 15, 1849. New Hampshire State Archives.

number president of an institution with which they had no connection, upon a mere assurance from Ingalls that he would convey to them a share of stock each, which, however, has not been done. Mr. Rust further deposed that he had reason to believe that Hinckley and Ingalls had procured new bills of the Wolfborough Bank to be engraved and printed. From another reliable source, I had evidence that the said Wiggins had signed certain of these bills as president, but had declared his intention to keep possession of them until they might properly be issued.

It appeared that Mr. Rust retained the key of the outer door of the bank, but that he had delivered the key of the vault to Mr. Wiggins. For this reason he was unable to submit the books and papers of the bank for examination. An attempt having thus been improperly made to re-organize a bank entirely insolvent, liable for large debts, as well as wholly without means of payment; directors having been chosen, and a majority of them acted in the choice of officers, without even the color of authority derivable from an ownership of its worthless stock; said directors having through their president received the custody of the vault and the large amount of old redeemed bills lodged therein; new bills having been procured for circulation, and partially prepared for circulation, under color of the charter of the bank, by persons who had no legal authority whatever to act under it, I thought proper to make, and did make a communication to the *New York Tribune* and another daily paper in New York City, cautioning the public against receiving the bills of the Wolfborough Bank, stating there was reason to apprehend that a movement was in progress for a new emission of them, and explaining briefly the totally insolvent condition of the bank.

I also took measures to procure more accurate information in reference to the amount of bills engraved, and made an arrangement with Henry F. French, Esq., one of the bank commissioners, to call upon Mr. Wiggins and propound to him certain interrogatories.

In answer to these interrogatories, he stated on oath that on the 6th day of March last he was elected president of the Wolfborough Bank; that he has twice since met the directors at informal meetings, the last of which was on the 26th of April last; that he has also signed new bills of the bank to the amount of $7,000, of the denomination of one, two and three dollars, but that said bills are now in the Dover Bank for safe keeping, subject to his order. Since the first meeting of the directors he has had the key of the vault, in which were sundry bills of former issues, amounting, as he was informed by Mr. Avery, former cashier, and Mr. Asa Hinckley, who had counted them, to $71,680.

When he first arrived at Wolfborough after his election as president, Asa Hinckley, who had been elected but not qualified, as cashier, had the keys of the bank. He knows merely that since he has taken the keys, none of those bills have been taken away. In addition to the above there were in the bank vault at the time he took the custody of it, $11,000 of bills never issued, but signed by Avery as cashier and Pickering as president. They still remain there.

He saw in the vault, at the time of the last meeting, various bundles of old bills, which he believes contain the sum of $71,680, though he did not count them. He knows of no means whatever which the bank has to redeem any bills it has issued or may issue. He holds no certificate of stock and does not claim to be the owner of any. Ingalls resides in the city of New York, he says, and claims to represent other persons there who owned stock in the old bank, or are the holders of its old and worthless bills.

When he consented to act as president, Ingalls assured him that the stock was to be paid in and every thing be done in a fair manner, and that he should have $250 per annum and expenses for his services and not be required to go to Wolfborough more than once or twice a month. In conclusion, he says, that he "desires to be relieved from the custody of the property and bills of the bank in such a way as will be safe to the community," and that "there is but one mind among the directors, and that is that nothing wrong shall be done."

It was further alleged that 4,000 $1 bills, 2,000 $2 bills, 6,000 $3 bills, 1,500 $5 bills, and 5,000 $10 bills had been printed to the order of Asa Hinckley, subscribing himself as "Cashier of the Wolfborough Bank."

The state bank investigator noted that local Wolfeboro citizens who were involved may have been imprudent, but, apparently, were innocent of duplicity.

More of the Same

However, the story did not end there. Long after the Wolfborough Bank closed its doors, some unscrupulous individuals issued a series of paper money dated April 1, 1853, and bearing signatures which were similar to, but different from well-known Wolfeboro citizens. Thus, Abel Haley appeared on notes as "Able Hadley," and John M. Brackett's name was signed as "John M. Brock." Doubtless, this helped avoid charges of forgery.

The Capers of Bill Dow

Capt. George P. Burnham, *Memoirs of the United States Secret Service,* provided biographies of notorious bank robbers, counterfeiters, and other quarry of that agency.[1] In the late 1830s, one William Dow, an ambitious "sharp-eyed, handsome boy of 16 or 17" was eager to earn money. In Concord, New Hampshire, he tended stables, worked at a restaurant, and did other odd jobs to support his interests including horses (of the riding, not racing, kind).

At the restaurant it was common to receive in trade various private bank bills of questionable authenticity. Rather than make a fuss about them, the restaurant owner considered them to be "as good money as any," and passed them along to his customers, while young Bill Dow watched.

And thus the boy's eyes were first opened to the chances before him. If these bogus rags could thus readily be passed

---

1 Pages 90-100. Book published by Laban Heath, 30 Hanover Street, Boston, 1872. Heath is familiar to numismatists as the publisher of various "infallible counterfeit detectors."

> in that establishment, he mentally argued that there was a bigger field of operations to be easily found, if one but took a little time to prospect for it!
>
> And, as the young man thought this affair over at his leisure, he concluded he would not purchase the horse he coveted, at the earliest convenient moment, and then turn his attention to something promising larger pecuniary results than were attainable in the meagerly rewarded service of a drudge in an eating saloon.
>
> He had previously formed an acquaintance with a New York horse-man, who came to the saloon in Concord frequently, and he had seen him and others "shoving the queer" [passing counterfeits] there so often, that he fancied it wasn't a difficult process....

Bill Dow went to New York City, and on 24th Street bought a fine horse, and on Houston Street made an alliance to acquire liberal supply of fake notes. Through Mike O'Brien he made the acquaintance of notorious crook "Dock" Young, who later was sentenced to state prison in Maine for robbing a U.S. mail coach in that state. From O'Brien, Young, and others, he learned the tricks of the counterfeiting trade while passing countless notes.

Dow determined that being a dealer in, rather than a passer of, counterfeit notes would be even more profitable than spending the notes one or two at a time. He bought groups of $5,000 to $10,000 in phony bills of private and state banks, parceled them out to pushers, and then returned to his suppliers for more.

Meanwhile, he became an expert safecracker, indeed, one of the best in the business. In a typical heist he would break into a bank, plunder its paper money supply, and then negotiate with "easy" police or detectives, who would arrange for the victimized bank to buy back its own notes at a discount.

Moving back to New Hampshire for a foray among banks there, Bill Dow, who by now looked and dressed the part of a gentleman, cracked the Concord Bank for $300,000 in its notes.

Important to the present narrative:

> He had made a pile of money, and he went to Mike O'Brien's place at High Bridge, N.Y., to rusticate a while. But soon he moved off again, quietly, and undertook the cracking of the bank at Wolfeboro', N.H.

Eventually, Dow's life of crime came to an end when Secret Service detective William W. Kennock, whose alias was "Jim Drake," became a drinking buddy, but, unnoticed by Dow, "only pretended to imbibe." The pair became fast friends, and Jim Drake was apprised of Dow's upcoming burglaries. After gathering all the evidence needed, the detective "put the collar upon Dow at Hooksett, N.H."

Bill Dow became a cooperative prisoner, provided the Secret Service with valuable information on counterfeiting dens in New York City, pleaded guilty to some counts and *nolo contendere* to others, and was sentenced to two years at the Massachusetts State Prison in Charlestown.

How the preceding may have fit into the history of the Bank of Wolfborough is not known, but Dow may have been the source for some of the undistributed notes of the defunct bank that were later put into circulation.

Collecting Commentary

Today in the 1990s, all notes of the Wolfborough Bank—rare originals issued 1837-1839 as well as the more often seen fantasy notes of later dates—are highly collectible. In addition, there were many counterfeits made of this bank's notes, these being circulated by persons who had no connection—early and legitimate or later and fraudulent—with the bank. Some of these fake notes were crudely printed and bear such misspellings as Wolf'sboro and Wolfboro.

Notes of "broken" or "wildcat" banks of the 1830s through the 1850s are one of the few American numismatic series in which spurious and unissued notes are avidly collected. As noted, smaller denominations bring as much if not more than the face value of the once-worthless noted. Unusual denominations such as $1.25, $1.75, or $4 bring much more. Interestingly, $3 notes were common among original issues of the era and were, in fact, one of the most popular denominations.[1]

Another interesting numismatic aspect is that worn "used" (signed in ink) notes are usually worth more than "mint" or unused notes from a given bank.

Every once in a while a "hoard" of unsigned, undistributed bank notes from this era will surface, as with thousands of four-subject sheets of the Canal Bank of New Orleans, or the Jamaica River Bank in Vermont, or another of many different long-forgotten institutions. These sheets, often called "remainders," were available in quantity in numismatic circles until just a few years ago. Somewhat scarcer are hoards of signed notes that were redeemed in the last century by the issuing bank or by another institution (such as the Suffolk Bank of Boston); these are often punch- or slit-canceled.

---

[1] The American Numismatic Association, Colorado Springs, has a large reference collection of $3 notes from hundreds of banks, the gift of the author.

Uncut sheets of obsolete currency of various banks, circa 1830s-1850s. Such notes, never used, are referred to as "remainders" by numismatists today.

CHAPTER 18

Secrets of the Philadelphia Mint

The Philadelphia Mint, which since 1792 has been in four locations within that city, has yielded many numismatic treasures over the years. As many of these delicacies have been wrapped in red tape and bureaucracy, the complete truth will never be known concerning their origin. However, based upon numismatic observation, Mint correspondence, and a knowledge of the characters involved, some strong theories have been brought forward.

For good measure this chapter also includes accounts of hoards found in the U.S. Assay Office (New York City) and of a mint sold at auction in England.

Dies Found in the Old Mint

Deaccessioned: 19th century
Acquired by numismatists: 19th century
Treasure: Coinage dies

The Mickley Confiscation

Today numismatists are familiar with several different varieties of "restrikes" of nineteenth-century coins made up from old dies, often mismatched (with obverses mated to incorrect reverses). Quite probably some of them had their genesis from the caches of dies described below.

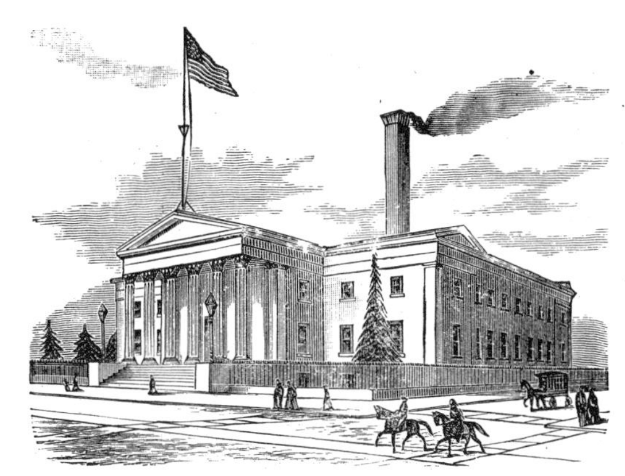

The Philadelphia Mint as it appeared in the second half of the nineteenth century. A vast hoard of pattern coins was accumulated therein and not made known to numismatists until years later in 1909.

The following appeared in the January 1879 issue of the *American Journal of Numismatics:*

> EDITORIAL
>
> The statement that the dies, hubs, &c. of U.S. coins, advertised for sale with the Mickley Collection, were seized by the United States authorities, has given rise to a great deal of comment. We have received from a gentleman in Philadelphia the following account of the affair:
>
> A few days previous to the sale, the United States authorities claimed the above, viz.: Some 20 obverse and reverse dies of the U.S. coinage, mostly in a damaged and corroded condition, the same having been condemned by the Mint authorities above "half a century ago," and as tradition says was the custom in those days, "sold for old iron." Since then we have grown more *artful*, and it has been deemed politic under existing laws, that the whole multitude of dated dies should be annually destroyed in the presence of three

designated officers of the Mint.

In the above described lots in the catalogue, there was not a complete *pair* of obverse and reverse dies. Even the obverse die of the half cent of 1811 was muled with the reverse die of a different year. We cannot conceive by what authority the government, after making sale of its "refuse material," could seize upon the same property without tendering some compensation. There is scarcely a numismatist in the United States, but who is aware of the existence and whereabouts of similar dies, and who is also aware of the many "re-strikes,"—*known to be such,*—being made from the dies, say of the 1804 cent, the 1811 half-cent, and of the 1823 cent, *outside* of the Mint.

Philadelphia, December, 1878.
R. Coulton Davis.

From what we have seen in the public prints in reference to this matter, we infer that the government authorities were somewhat hasty in their action, and claimed the property without first satisfying themselves as to the ownership. No one would for a moment suspect Mr. Mickley of any wrongdoing in the matter. The affair was settled, we believe, by a payment to the family of the estimated value of the dies, which were then presented to the Mint, and subsequently destroyed.

Charles Warner Remembers

This related article is from *The Numismatist,* December 1910:

COIN DIES ABANDONED IN THE OLD U.S. MINT

Reminiscences of Charles K. Warner

Various publications in recent months regarding the first United States Mint and the many discussions of the use and misuse of coin dies in early Mint days have been subjects of extraordinary interest to Charles K. Warner, the veteran medallist of Philadelphia.

In comparison with the recent destruction of all coinage dies excepting those in actual use, and the now prescribed rigid regulations as to the care and destruction of dies,[1] the following communication to *The Numismatist* from Mr. Warner makes interesting reading at this time:

"I have at times in the past promised to write you something regarding my boyhood days around the old Mint building, which still stands on the east side of Seventh Street and which was pictured and featured in the January and February *Numismatist* of this year.

"My father, the late John S. Warner, who from 1823 to 1868 was the oldest established medallist in the United States, was well acquainted with a certain William Sellers who for many years conducted the business of a silversmith in the old Mint building. He occupied the entire first floor and a greater part of the basement.

"In the latter part of 1857 Mr. Sellers gave to my father a large number of old coin dies which were a part of a great lot of both obverse and reverse dies for all the silver and copper denominations that Sellers found in the old building when he first occupied it years before. It was stated at that time that these were found among general rubbish when the basement was cleaned. Most of the dies were considerably rusted, chipped on the edges, or cracked across the face. My father having no use for the old dies gave them to a particular friend of his, the then Chief Coiner of the Mint, which was then located in Chestnut street near Broad.

"As a lad I frequently visited the old Mint building on errands to Mr. Sellers for my father and often played about the building with a son of Sellers, who was about my age. I well remember the old vault. I could have easily explored the vault, and no doubt could have found many things which, if preserved, would be of great interest today, but lad that I was, I had no interest in such things."

Lots of Stories

Other stories, theories, and reminiscences about old dies from the first Mint abound, often differing widely from each other. Walter Breen related that certain dies had been sold as scrap metal as early as 1833:[2]

The 1823 [large cent] was long believed scarce enough in upper grades that when Joseph J. Mickley found the broken original obverse die among batches of scrap metal sold by the Mint (1833), he and his friends eventually decided to make restrikes, using an 1813 reverse from a similar source. These dies suffered still more extensive breaks, but continued to be used at intervals for decades, at least until a later owner defaced them....

Further from Breen:[3]

1804 restrike [cent]. Copper. Struck about 1858 by parties unknown (Mickley? Dickeson?) from rusted dies retrieved from scrap metal sold by the Mint in 1833. Obverse altered from 1803 Sheldon-261, reverse of 1820. Both dies hand-strengthened.

Similarly from Breen, but ascribed to an 1816 Mint disposal of dies:[4]

The 1811 [half cent] restrike was struck outside the Mint about 1859 from genuine dies (the regular 1811 Close Date obverse with the 1802 reverse), which the teen-aged Joseph J. Mickley had retrieved in 1816 among rusted and broken dies sold by Mint personnel as scrap metal.

For many years the coin dealer Capt. John W. Haseltine used to claim that only six were struck; the correct number seems to be 12, of which 11 are traced.

Steigerwalt's Opinion

The following is from the January 1907 issue of *Coins, Paper Money, Etc., For Sale,* issued by Lancaster,

[1] The Mint deviated from this policy numerous times in this era and in later years as well.
[2] Breen, *Encyclopedia,* 1988, p. 202. This may have arisen from the earlier quoted account by R. Coulton Davis that certain dies had been sold as scrap iron by the Mint over 50 years before the Mickley Collection sale (which was held by John W. Haseltine on January 31, 1879).
[3] *Ibid.,* p. 198.
[4] *Ibid.,* p. 170.

Pennsylvania, dealer Charles Steigerwalt. Today in the 1990s, the so-called "restrikes" are eminently collectible as such, but Steigerwalt was no fan of them:

A certain kind of 1804 and 1823 cents have appeared in sale catalogues for years as "Mint Restrikes." The recent cataloguers may be excused on the plea of ignorance, but when these rank counterfeits are sold by those who have been doing so for years, it is time collectors knew their true character.

While at a recent sale, the lacking information regarding the 1823 was given by an aged collector,[1] who told how, years ago, he had found the dies in New York, probably sold with old iron from the Mint, brought them to Philadelphia, had a collar made, which was lacking, and the coins struck by a man named Miller on 7th Street, that city.

Later, the dies came into possession of a then leading dealer there and, when his store was sold out in 1885, the writer finding them among a lot of old dies purchased, they were at once destroyed so effectually that no more will ever come from that source.[2] These coins never saw the Mint, and are counterfeits pure and simple.

It was supposed the 1804 came from the same source as the 1823, but the originator of those disclaimed any knowledge of the 1804. An effort was made in a recent salę catalogue to throw an air of mystery around this 1804. That is simply ridiculous. The obverse has been identified as an 1803, but as that date was too common, a crude 4 was cut over the 3 and a reverse of the same period after the fraction was omitted, probably of about 1816 or later, was used in striking these abominations. By whom struck is unknown, but it was at a period long after, when the dies were rusty, and certainly not in the Mint.

Other Dies, Other Times

Dies from various Mint disposals reached the private sector on numerous other occasions.[3] In the nineteenth century many superannuated dies were used to create "restrikes," usually in different metals from the originals or with mismatched obverses and reverses. The list of such productions is a long one. Many pieces are described in Andrew W. Pollock's *United States Pattern Coins and Related Issues* and earlier texts on the pattern series. Examples range from an 1806 half dollar obverse die struck in white metal, combined with a postal embossed stamp die for the reverse, probably made in the nineteenth century, to impressions made in 1962 from the rusted reverse die of an 1814 dime with legend incorrectly spaced so as to read STATESOFAMERICA. These latter pieces were made to the extent of 536 pieces in Edinburgh, Scotland, to the order of Robert Bashlow and were typically combined with a modern obverse die lettered GOD PRESERVE PHILADELPHIA AND THE LORDS PROPRIETERS.[4]

In the American Numismatic Society's collection today are such productions as an 1818 cent Newcomb-9, 1805 25¢ Browning-2, 1806 50¢ Overton-102, 1806 O-123/4, and an 1803 $10 (not a die variety known to exist in original gold striking form).[5]

Two Tons of Three-Cent Pieces

Circulated: 1850s-1862
Found: 1882

Coins by the Wagon Load

As certain denominations and coinage formats became obsolete they were called in by the Treasury Department. Many accounts of such redemptions were printed over the years including this one in the October 1882 *American Journal of Numismatics,* reprinted from the *Boston Herald:*

[1] Certainly this circa 1907 meeting with the finder of the dies could not have been with J.J. Mickley (born in 1799, died in 1878, and by 1907 long since deceased), who Breen stated was the finder of the dies and the person responsible for first making restrikes from them. He could have been a later restriker who used the same die pair, but the Steigerwalt account implies that the 1907 interviewee was the sole person responsible. A fine biography of Steigerwalt is found in John W. Adams, *United States Numismatic Literature,* Vol. I, pp. 105-106.

[2] Not true. The author was offered this pair of dies in the 1950s by a New York specialist in large cents, toyed with the idea of acquiring them, but in the absence of any official (Treasury Department) guidance on the matter of privately possessing rusted and cracked (reverse) dies, declined. The dies would have been perfectly serviceable for making additional restrikes.

[3] Including in relatively recent times. After 1968, when the San Francisco Mint began striking Proof coins for collectors, used dies were extensively (but not completely) defaced and sold as surplus and found their way into the hands of dealers; a short time thereafter the dies were advertised in numismatic publications. A few years ago Bowers and Merena offered at auction the canceled Liberty Seated silver dollar reverse die, with CC mintmark, used to strike dollars in 1870. Other examples of canceled dies in numismatic channels could be cited.

[4] See Breen, *Encyclopedia,* 1988, p. 303, for further information including the seizure of these pieces by the Secret Service. The deliberate "PROPRIETERS" misspelling is in imitation of a 1694-dated copper coin bearing legends relating to the Carolinas. Bashlow, who lived near Washington Square, New York City, was one of the more innovative rare coin dealers and made restrikes of several other issues, most notably the 1861 Confederate States of America cent (from copy dies by August Frank, of Philadelphia). Circa 1958-1960 he imported vast quantities of obsolete bronze British farthings, conder tokens, and other British issues to America and sold them here. He died in the late 1970s in a hotel fire in Zaragoza, Spain.

[5] As studied by Michael Hodder.

The first Philadelphia Mint began business in 1792 and continued in use until the early 1830s. Years later it was employed for many other purposes, as in this illustration, circa 1903, in which it housed an umbrella factory and a cigar dispensary.

The United States Mint in Philadelphia has lately received over two tons of three-cent silver coins [minted from 1851 to 1873, but mostly 1851-1862], which by act of Congress have been abolished from the national coinage. This is said to be, however, only about one-fifth of the quantity of these small coins which are to be brought from the various Sub-Treasuries in the country, there having already been redeemed more than ten tons.

The three-cent pieces now in the Mint would fill three large wagons. They are to be recoined into dimes, as the three-cent nickel pieces [first coined in 1865] are to take the place of the old silver three-cent coins. The Treasury Department is redeeming the small coins as fast as possible, and in a few years they will entirely disappear, and only the nickels will be in circulation. The coins have lost a very considerable percent of their intrinsic value by usage, in some cases amounting to as much as 25%. In fact, they were rapidly wearing out. This is one reason why they were abolished and the harder and more convenient nickel substituted.

Finds at the 1792 Mint Site

Lost: 1792-1830s
Found: 1907-1911

In the early years of the present century, Philadelphia electrical contractor Frank H. Stewart purchased the original 1792 Mint buildings that had been used for coinage until a new Mint structure was occupied in 1833. Between that time and Stewart's purchase the old premises had housed a variety of private businesses. In 1907 he began to clear the area to make way for new construction by razing one of the smaller buildings.

In 1911 Stewart attempted to have the City of Philadelphia and other groups preserve the main building, suggesting that it be relocated to Fairmount Park (obviously an exceedingly expensive undertaking), but no interest was forthcoming from any officials or civic organizations. Accordingly, in the same year the front or main building was razed. During the process Stewart acquired several numismatic artifacts which were later presented to an exhibit at Congress Hall at 6th and Chestnut streets in the same city.

In 1924 Stewart wrote a fine book about the Mint, its history, and his experiences while demolishing it. He related that the following coins and related items had been found (partial listing):[1]

Draped Bust half cent, circa 1800-1808, date not readable (some of these pieces were probably loose change lost by employees and visitors, not undistributed coins).

1825 half cent, corroded.

(1792 silver-center cent): two blank planchets for these coins; this find was learned of by J.C. Mitchelson, numismatist of Tariffville, Connecticut, who came to Philadelphia in an effort to persuade Stewart to part with them.[2]

1816 copper cent.

1826 copper cent, corroded.

1832 copper cent. Worn, perhaps VF-30 grade.

1834 copper cent. Worn, perhaps VF-20 grade.

1795 half dime, pattern struck in copper, "damaged."

Half dollar planchet, no further description.

Half dollar coinage die showing the "eagle side." Sent to the Secret Service in Washington; later disposition not known.

Early silver dollar, date not stated, edge lettered ONE HUNDRED FOR A DOLLAR.

1804 $5, pattern struck in copper.

Various blank planchets and planchet cutter scrap.[3]

From Within the Mint

Minted: 19th century
Disclosed: 1909

In Philadelphia in 1908-1909 important numismatic personalities included John W. Haseltine and Stephen K. Nagy. Born in 1838, Haseltine became interested in coin collecting by the 1860s and in 1869 worked with dealer Ebenezer Mason before starting his own business. As noted in Chapter 13 under the discussion of the 1861 Confederate States of America one-cent piece, it seems evident that Haseltine had

[1] Stewart, *History of the First U.S. Mint.*

[2] Today, Mitchelson's collection is preserved by the Connecticut State Library, Hartford. See Chapter 19.

[3] Such scrap was known as *scissel,* a term not generally used today.

Interior sketch of the Philadelphia Mint in the 1860s.

Selection of various pattern silver dollars and trade dollars of the 1870s and early 1880s. Similar coins may have been included in the exchange by which William H. Woodin acquired in 1909 a hoard of patterns that had been stored at the Mint for several decades.

very close connections to certain individuals at the Mint, probably in the Medal Department, who produced patterns, restrikes, and Proofs. It was Haseltine who acted as the funnel to distribute Proof "restrikes" of 1801, 1802, and 1803 silver dollars and Class III 1804 dollars in the early 1870s.

By the early 1900s he was considered an old-timer in the trade and was nicknamed "The Numismatic Refrigerator" for his "rarities on ice," from which he withdrew morsels for sale from time to time. At the 1908 American Numismatic Association convention in Philadelphia Haseltine regaled listeners with tales, somewhat embellished, of the olden days in the coin trade. By this time he was associated in business with Stephen K. Nagy of the same city.

Haseltine continued to surprise numismatists with a stream of Proofs, patterns, and other rarities, some of which were not previously known to exist, such as the silver Proof trade dollars of 1884 (10 minted) and 1885 (five minted) which he made known to the collecting community in 1907-1908. These glittering Proofs were said to have come from the estate of his father-in-law, William Idler (1808-1901), who was engaged in the coin trade as early as circa 1859. Idler, too, had close connections to the Mint and was known as a distributor of 1804 dollars and other rarities.

In the period 1908-1909 a prime customer of Haseltine and Nagy was William H. Woodin (1868-1934), a manufacturer of railroad and other heavy equipment and who at one time served as the chairman of the American Car & Foundry Company.

Woodin was one of the first American numismatists to take a serious interest in collecting gold coins by date and mintmark, and at one time he owned the unique 1870-S $3 gold piece. In 1908 Haseltine acquired from somewhere or other—either from his own stock or from the current holdings at the Mint—two coins, the existence of which were not known earlier, sort of a replay of his recent disclosure of the rare 1884 and 1885 trade dollars. This time the coins were one each of two different varieties of 1877 "half union" $50 coins struck in gold. These were offered to Woodin and purchased by him forthwith. The price paid by Woodin was $10,000 each, far and away a record for any United States coin up to that time. A feature story about these treasures was published in *The Numismatist*.

An unexpected furor arose, and it was said by some that the pair of $50 gold patterns never should have left the Mint, implying that they may have done so *recently*. Otherwise, bygones were bygones, and there was no commotion at all about rarities that had slipped away from the Mint in earlier years to enrich certain employees within the halls of that venerable coinage institution—the Second United States Mint (which operated from 1833 until new premises were occupied in 1901).

To quiet the matter, Haseltine and Nagy re-acquired the pieces from Woodin and presented them to the Mint Cabinet, where they were duly put on display (today they are in the National Numismatic Collection at the Smithsonian Institution, Washington, D.C.). In exchange, the Mint searched its vaults and came up with several *crates* of old pattern coins, some of which dated back to the Gobrecht era.[1] These were given to Woodin, who with the era's pre-eminent numismatic scholar, Edgar H. Adams, used the coins for the basis of a book on the series. Published by the American Numismatic Society in 1913, it bore the title *United States Pattern, Trial and Experimental Pieces.*

No inventory of the 1909 Mint hoard of patterns was ever published, but from later evidence it was deduced that even a partial list would have included thousands of specimens among which were many previously unlisted pieces. Emphasis seems to have been on coins dated in the 1870s and early 1880s. All of a sudden, dozens or more specimens of certain beautiful designs by engravers James B. Longacre, William Barber, and George T. Morgan were revealed.

Quite possibly the most recently dated coins in the 1908-1909 cache were several hundred duplicates of

[1] Sources include contemporary articles in *The Numismatist* and conversations between the author (QDB) and Stephen K. Nagy, circa 1957; also information from Robert K. Botsford to the author in the 1950s.

the cent and five-cent shield-design patterns dated 1896. Most of the coins remained in Woodin's possession for many years.

Toward the end of his life Woodin served as President Franklin D. Roosevelt's first secretary of the Treasury, March 5, 1933, to December 31 of the same year, when he resigned in poor health, having been ill for most of his term to that point. Meantime, Henry Morgenthau, Jr., had served as acting secretary for much of the time. Under Woodin's watch (with Morgenthau as surrogate) there were vast changes in Treasury procedures involving gold coins and bullion. It is also worth noting that in 1933 the United States coinage included $20 gold coins that would later become quite prized and also somewhat controversial.[1] Woodin passed away on May 4, 1934. His pattern coins came on the market privately during the 1930s and 1940s—with a few stragglers in the 1950s[2]—and by now are widely dispersed in many different collections.

In the 1950s, Robert K. Botsford of Nescopeck, Pennsylvania, numismatist and numismatic philosopher (his advertisements from decades ago make interesting reading today), sold the author a hoard of many dozens of 1896 pattern cents and nickels in the 1950s. These long-forgotten leftovers came from the estate of Woodin, who had maintained a residence in nearby Berwick, Pennsylvania.

A Distinguished Guest at the Mint

Acquired: 1795
Disclosed: 1964
Treasure: High-grade early U.S. coins

An Englishman Visits the Mint

This is not the story of a secret of the Philadelphia Mint or a "find" there, but of a long-ago visit to that institution, then in the early years of its existence:

In October 1795, Sir Rowland Winn, an English traveler from a distinguished family, visited America and was an honored guest at the Philadelphia Mint. While there he was given selected specially-struck presentation coins on hand from the previous year, 1794, and new high-quality examples of the current 1795 coinage were made especially for him.

Although a number of very choice American coins survive from the 1790s, the visit of Sir Rowland Winn is the only instance of a specifically-identified numismatist being given the red carpet treatment at America's minting institution. Equally significant, the coins descended in a single family and exist today, each accompanied by this remarkable direct-from-the-Mint pedigree. Or so the story went.

Years Later

Reality: On October 13, 1964, the venerable London firm of Christie, Manson & Woods had an auction of coins from the Lord St. Oswald Collection. Emphasis was on ancient coins and other classic issues. However, along with the cabinet of fine numismatic material the consignor furnished a small pasteboard box containing miscellaneous and seemingly unimportant "loose change" that, presumably, an ancestor or someone else had probably brought from America in 1795 and which had been more or less forgotten since then.

A.H. Baldwin & Sons, Ltd., of London catalogued the pieces. It was soon recognized that such "loose change" items as Uncirculated 1794 large cents, two Uncirculated 1794 silver dollars, and other American coins primarily dated 1794 and 1795 were quite special. And, indeed they were.

The sale was not widely publicized in the United States, and some dealers on this side of the Atlantic thought perhaps some really good buys would be made. Professionals from America including Lester Merkin, Norman Stack, and James F. Ruddy were present on sale day, as were some collectors including silver dollar specialist A.J. Ostheimer III. It was evident at the outset that there would be some strong

---

[1] Of the 445,500 pieces struck of the 1933 $20, 100,000 were minted in March 1933, 200,000 in April, and 145,500 in May. On April 3, 1933, Franklin Roosevelt dictated that all gold coins be delivered to the secretary of the Treasury by May 1, 1933. Exactly why hundreds of thousand of pieces were subsequently minted in April and May that year only a student of government logic can answer. In any event, years after the fact the government took the position that all 1933 $20 pieces in the hands of collectors could not be legally held. Woodin, a very qualified numismatist and specialist in gold coins, had made no such declaration in 1933, nor did Morgenthau, and, in fact, 1933 $20 pieces were openly bought and sold for the next decade. It was not until 1944 that Uncle Sam went on a witch hunt for the pieces. On April 23, 1996, the author appeared on NBC television's *Today Show* (host, Bryant Gumbel) to present the numismatic side of the controversy and to give an opinion that the government was incorrect in its actions. Recently, the government had seized a 1933 $20 that was earlier in the King Farouk Collection and which had passed into the hands of a London dealer.

[2] Also see "A Cache of Patterns" (1950s) in the present work.

Placing coins in wooden kegs at the Philadelphia Mint at the turn of the twentieth century. Doubtless, every once in a while a few cloth bags from such a keg were left unopened at the destination—typically a bank or large commercial firm.

Striking coins at the Philadelphia Mint circa 1903.

competition! When all was said and done, this group of American coins far overshadowed the ancient and other coins in the Lord St. Oswald consignment, and created a sensation. This handful of "loose change" with a face value of under $10 brought a whopping $72,000!

Each of the 1794 dollars fetched $11,200 to buyers from the United States. The first was knocked down to Ostheimer. The second was awarded to A.H. Baldwin & Sons, Ltd., on behalf of Ambassador and Mrs. R. Henry Norweb. As to which was the better coin has been a toss-up in discussions since.[1]

Theories

After a time, theories began to develop, and before long Walter Breen firmly stated that the coins were "obtained by Sir Rowland Winn, about October 1795 on his visit to the Philadelphia Mint." Subsequently, numismatists were informed by Breen and others that Winn not only visited the Mint, but that he was rewarded by receiving "presentation pieces," certainly a rare honor.[2] Breen even described how a certain 1795-dated dollar had been made as a presentation piece—on a burnished planchet, struck from polished dies (possibly struck twice to assure extra sharpness), etc. This made a nice story, but one not supported by any facts that could be readily ascertained by reading Breen's or anyone else's commentary.

Obviously, this story of an accomplished numismatist being an honored guest at the Mint in 1795 furnished the possibility for further information to be gained, especially as it was the only known instance of such a visit by a knowledgeable collector during the 1790s.

Who Was Lord St. Oswald?

Enter Michael Hodder, research associate of the present book, who in 1993 and 1994 enlisted the assistance of Jack Collins and wrote an essay, "Who Was Major the Lord St. Oswald?" which in due course appeared in *The Asylum,* Fall 1994.[3]

First, by reviewing the 1964 catalogue issued by Christie's, Hodder noted that nothing was said there about anyone visiting the Mint or even going to the United States, nor were there any claims about presentation or other special coins. All that was stated was that the coins were included in a catalogue that featured a consignment from the St. Oswald family, currently living in Wakefield, Yorkshire, and nothing more.

From that point, Michael Hodder learned that Major the Lord St. Oswald (Major Sir Rowland Denys Guy Winn, M.C., the Fourth Baron St. Oswald), was *born in 1916* and died in 1984, and was not a coin collector. The nice story of Sir Rowland Winn visiting the Mint in *1795* began to unravel.

In 1993, Jack Collins had written to the Winn family in England seeking to learn more.[4] Derek Edward Anthony Winn, Fifth Baron St. Oswald, replied that he had no knowledge of which of his ancestors might have gone to America. The Sixth *Baronet* St. Oswald (1775-1805) was living in 1795, but "was never in good health and consequently would not have traveled much," Collins' correspondent advised. After his death, unmarried, at age 30, the direct male line died out, and the title seems to have lapsed, to be revived years later in 1885 and elevated at that time to a full barony.

There was, however, a member of the Winn family who did collect coins, Hodder subsequently learned. He was Charles Winn, born in 1796 and died in 1884. He never ascended to the baronetcy. Charles was an enthusiastic collector of books, pictures, and coins, most of the latter being ancient Greek and Roman issues. As Charles Winn had not been born by the time of the 1795 visit to the Mint, he was also eliminated as a possibility.

Michael Hodder had no choice but to conclude that no member of the St. Oswald family ever obtained coins directly from the Philadelphia Mint in 1795. There is a possibility that Charles Winn purchased them elsewhere in the 1820s when he was a collector, but there is no direct evidence of this, either. Further, there is no evidence that the pieces were "presentation coins" of any kind. In fact, those who examined the pieces at lot viewing for the 1964 sale did not consider them such, and such pieces as the pair of 1794 dollars have adjustment file marks, hardly a characteristic of a presentation coin.[5]

---

1 Personal recollections of the author; comments furnished by James F. Ruddy. Both James F. Ruddy and the author were in London at the time and we both viewed the lots; Jim Ruddy attended the sale which was held at Christie's auction rooms close by Spink & Son, Ltd.

2 Breen, *Encyclopedia,* 1988, p. 423, among other listings. Robert P. Hilt II, *Die Varieties of Early United States Coins,* 1980, stated that certain of the coins were "presentation pieces," and similar comments have reached print elsewhere including in auction catalogues by writers who relied upon Breen's statements.

3 Journal of the American Bibliomania Society, the leading organization of numismatic book collectors.

4 Jack Collins had nearly completed a manuscript on the 1794 silver dollar—giving provenances of all known specimens—and had sought to learn more about the origin of the two Lord St. Oswald specimens.

5 During lot viewing the coins were appreciated for their high quality (mostly AU and Uncirculated) by the intending American buyers, but the writer (QDB) recalls no one saying at the time that they looked like presentation or "special" coins. The prevailing sentiment in 1964 was that someone who

In Hodder's words, "all we know for sure is that the coins were in the St. Oswald family collection and were consigned for sale in 1964."

Thus, the cycle is complete: from casual information as printed in the 1964 catalogue, to exciting and unprecedented "facts" of a special Mint visit by an honored guest in 1795 and "presentation coins" given to him, and now back to casual information.

What goes around comes around.

Uncle Sam's Hoard of *Foreign* Gold

Items assembled: 1940s
Disposed of: 1979-1980
Treasure: Survival and evasion kits for airmen

This is the story of a very unusual hoard, not of United States coins and not from the Philadelphia Mint, but of foreign gold coins kept by the government in another official Treasury Department facility.

During World War II American pilots and crews in P-38s, B-17s, B-29s, and other craft flew many hazardous missions, always with the risk of being shot down over alien or enemy territory.[1] To help survivors elude capture and buy goods from local citizens, Uncle Sam created thousands of "survival and evasion kits." These were produced in two main variations, the "Atlantic kit" for use in Europe and the "Southeast Asia" kit for use in that area.

Each Atlantic kit, made of a waterproof hard rubber case, included five gold coins and three gold rings. Typical coins ranged in grades numismatists today would call AU to Mint State. One such set, sold at auction in 1966, was found to contain these gold coins in addition to the rings: France. 1914 20 francs • Great Britain. 1908 half sovereign • Great Britain. 1909 half sovereign • South Africa. 1927-S A sovereign • Switzerland. 1914-B 10 francs.

A typical Southeast Asia kit contained two gold rings, four connected gold chain links, a heart-shaped gold pendant, and a Milus (brand) calendar watch with band, but no coins.

After World War II ended, thousands of these kits remained and were sent to storage in New York City in the U.S. Assay Office there. Years later, on August 1, 1979, many sets were put up for sale in Battle Creek, Michigan, by the Defense Property Disposal Service.

On February 12, 1980, a second sale was held, this time through the Service's Columbus, Ohio, branch offering a hoard of 2,962 kits including 2,536 of the "Atlantic" (a.k.a. "European") style and 429 of the "Southeast Asia" type. Prices bid for the Atlantic kits ranged from $528 to $726 each. On that day the opening price of gold quoted by bullion dealers Handy & Harman, New York, was $694.50 per troy ounce, a high figure (by comparison to earlier and later gold levels) that accounted for prices far above what the kits originally cost to assemble. Each kit contained nearly a full ounce of gold (the 2,962 kits had a total of 2,742 ounces). For once, Uncle Sam was quite smart and sold out in a bull market! The Atlantic versions went to 625 successful bidders, while the less numerous "Southeast Asia" kits were bought by 168 bidders.

The remaining 1,896 Atlantic and 277 Southeast Asia kits were offered at auction in Columbus on March 27, 1980, with the ante upped considerably to a minimum required bid of $931.39 for the Atlantic and $970.95 for the Southeast Asia kit. Uncle Sam was a winner again, and gained even more this time around. The average bid for an Atlantic kit was $1,071.57 and for an Asian kit, $1,113.56. The highest bid for an Atlantic kit was $4,000 and for an Southeast kit, $2,026. About 200 kits remained unsold.

The Soho Mint Auction (England, 1850)

Items made: 18th and early 19th centuries
Disposed of: April 29, 1850
Treasure: Included items related to American coinage

Importance of the Soho Mint

In connection with the present chapter on the Philadelphia Mint it may be of interest to give some remarks concerning a "hoard" of dies at a foreign mint

was not a numismatist brought some pocket change to England from America in 1795, and the coins had been kept together since that time. The assortment of coins was random, with some duplication and with obvious gaps—hardly what a numismatist would have sought or requested if given carte blanche as a guest at the Mint. Walter Breen was not present at lot viewing or the sale itself.

[1] Sources include: Bowers and Merena, Burhop and Davis Collections sale, 1996, Lots 2429-2432 (kits); articles in *Coin World,* February 27, 1980; May 7, 1980; conversation by author with Jonathan Kern, 1995. Thanks also to Lawrence Irish.

THE SOHO MINT, NEAR BIRMINGHAM.

A CATALOGUE

OF

THE VALUABLE MACHINERY AND PLANT

OF

THE SOHO MINT,

long celebrated and in high repute with the Government of Great Britain, as also with Foreign powers in Europe, Asia and America, the East India Company, and with mercantile and other firms of eminence in all parts of the world.

THE MACHINERY

may be pronounced as the most perfect of its kind in existence, having been constructed entirely under the personal superintendence of the late proprietor, whose genius and great mechanical skill are too well-known to render further allusion necessary; it includes

FOUR COINING PRESSES,

highly finished and worked by Pneumatic Apparatus. Each Press is constructed in a massive iron frame, with 5¼-inch screw, working in a heavy metal nut; the dies are placed in a steel collar, which rises as the blank is struck, thereby preserving a square edge to the Coin. It is fed by a self-acting layer on, so formed as to reject an imperfect or improper Blank, and requiring merely the attention of a child in order to the efficient operation of the Machine. The speed varies from 60 to 80 blows per minute, according to the size of the Coin.

SIX CUTTING OUT PRESSES,

worked by the Steam Engine with pneumatic balance pumps; they are highly finished and erected in a circular iron frame, with fly-wheel and gearing, and capable of cutting 300,000 Blanks per day.

THREE MILLING MACHINES;

2 Shaking Machines, with Drying Stoves; Washing and Pickling Cisterns; Annealing Furnaces and Muffles;

A POWERFUL MEDAL OR MULTIPLYING PRESS,

to work by hand, with 5¼-inch screw, and metal nut, in massive iron frame; several smaller Punching Presses;

A 10 HORSE POWER CONDENSING STEAM ENGINE;

2 Steam Boilers; 2 Timber Beam Condensing Steam Engines, *one of which will be considered highly interesting from the fact of its being the first erected by James Watt*; 3 powerful Vacuum Pumps; 700 feet Iron Shafting; 100 pair Plummer Blocks and Brasses; self-acting Screw-Cutting Lathe; 1 self-acting Turning Lathe; 8 Engine and Foot-turning Lathes; Drilling Machines; an assortment of Taps and Dies, Stocks and Steel Tools; 50 dozen Files;

EIGHT PLATE AND BAR ROLLING MILLS,

the Rolls by "Wilkes;" Driving Pinions and Apparatus; the iron frame work for a Water Wheel; 100 Spur, Rigger and Pinion Wheels; Cutting Shears; Tilt or Stamping Hammer; Smiths' Forges, Bellows and Tools; Box, Beam and other Scales; 2 tons Weights; Crab Crane; Machine Crane and Jib; Grindstones and Frames;

AN ASSORTMENT OF EXPENSIVE PATTERNS,

including those of the Royal Mint and the East India Company's Mints at Bombay and Calcutta, also of the various Machines at the Soho Mint;

12 TONS OF THE FINEST DIE STEEL,

made expressly for the late Mr. Boulton, under his personal directions, and acknowledged to be the best Die Steel in the Kingdom; 2 tons Shear and Scrap Steel; 7 tons of best Die Iron; 6 cwt. forged Dies and Collars;

5 TONS OF COPPER AND LEAD,

in sheets and Scrap, Cisterns, Pipes, &c.; Swedish Copper for Alloy; 50 Brass Cocks;

THE EXTREMELY VALUABLE COLLECTION OF DIES

for the Coins and Medals, well-known as the Soho Collection, most beautifully executed, principally by the celebrated Kuchler, and by Droz and Philipp, also the Dies for many rare Coins, hitherto considered as almost unique, including a Dollar George III., 1798, a Britanniarum Penny, many specimens of proposed Coins, of various dates, and of the French Republic, 1790 to 1792, a pattern Half-penny George III. by Droz, and Provincial Tokens; also

A CABINET OF COINS AND MEDALS,

embracing 4 sets of the Soho Collection, and many others extremely rare.

THE OFFICE FITTINGS AND FURNITURE,

including 3 Iron Strong-room Doors, an Iron Safe, Wainscot Presses, Desks, Copying Machines, Office Stove, and a large variety of miscellaneous property.

Which will be Sold by Auction, by Messrs.

FULLER AND HORSEY,

On MONDAY, APRIL 29, 1850, and following days, at 11 o'Clock,

AT THE WORKS, NEAR BIRMINGHAM. IN LOTS. BY DIRECTION OF THE EXECUTORS OF THE LATE M. R. BOULTON, ESQ.

The Machinery may be seen in motion, and the other effects Viewed, on Thursday, Friday, and Saturday prior to the Sale. Catalogues, without which no person can be admitted, may be obtained at One Shilling each, of Messrs. FULLER & HORSEY, Billiter Street, London.

Front cover of the Soho Mint auction catalogue of 1850 (Birmingham Reference Library; illustrated in James O. Sweeny, *A Numismatic History of the Birmingham Mint*)

some of whose products related to the United States of America.[1]

The Soho Mint was established in Birmingham, England, in the nineteenth century by Boulton & Watt, the partnership of Matthew Boulton and James Watt. Both men became very well known in the field of mechanics, with Watt's steam engines featuring many improvements and inventions. At the time Birmingham was a hotbed of token manufacturing, and over a dozen firms kept busy turning out products. The large, sprawling, three-story Soho Manufactory was a center for technical improvements and innovations, and many consumer goods were made there, particularly items of a mechanical nature.

Perhaps significant to the present subject of numismatics, James Watt is quoted as having said, "Without a hobby-horse, what is life?"[2]

In the 1790s the Soho Mint was equipped with steam-operated presses with various automatic controls that permitted many sophisticated innovations for the time, including high-speed production and the imprinting of ornamented edges as part of the striking process. At the time the Philadelphia Mint was in the Dark Ages by comparison, with work being done by horsepower (literally) and manpower.

In 1792 Matthew Boulton described the facility, his Hôtel de Monnaie, as his employee Pierre Droz and French clients called it:[3]

> The Mint consists of eight large coining machines, which are sufficiently strong to coin the largest money in current use, or even medals; and each machine is capable of being adjusted in a few minutes, so as to strike any number of pieces of money from 50 to 120 per minute, in proportion to their diameter and degree of relief; and each piece being struck in a steel collar, the whole number are perfectly round and of equal diameter.
>
> Each machine requires the attendance of one boy of only 12 years of age and he has no labor to perform. He can stop the press one instant, and set it going the next. The whole of the eight presses are capable of coining, at the same time, eight different sizes of money, such as English crowns, [French] 6-livre pieces, 24-sous pieces, 12 sous, or the very smallest money that is used in France.
>
> The number of blows at each press is proportioned to the size of the pieces, say from 50 to 120 blows per minute, and if greater speed is needed, he has smaller machines that will strike 200 per minute....
>
> Mr. Boulton's new machinery works with less friction, less wear, less noise, than any apparatus ever before invented; for it is capable of striking at the rate of 26,000 [French] écus or English crowns, or 50,000 of half their diameter, in one hour, and of working night and day without fatigue to the boys, provided two sets of them work alternately for 10 hours each.

Such British coins as the 1797 broad-rim "cartwheel" copper farthings, halfpence, pence, and twopence were struck at the Soho Mint and were sensational in their time. Contract coinage was performed by Boulton and Watt for interests such as the East India Company and France, and entire mint facilities and machinery were, in time, erected by the firm in foreign countries through commissions from Denmark, India (Calcutta and Bombay mints), Mexico, Russia, and Spain, among others. The Soho Mint for a long time supplied copper planchets to the Philadelphia Mint for the coinage of one-cent pieces, but never erected coining presses there (had this been done, the history of American coinage as we know it would be vastly different!).

During the period of the 1790s and early 1800s the Soho Mint produced a number of items relating to the American series. Among these were Conrad

---

[1] Dr. Richard Doty, formerly of the American Numismatic Association and now with the Smithsonian Institution, has done extensive research on the Soho Mint and plans to publish information concerning it, in addition to his paper, "Coinage for the Confederation: Two Near Misses for Matthew Boulton," American Numismatic Society, Coinage of the Americas Conference, 1995.

[2] Samuel Smiles, *Lives of Boulton and Watt,* 1865, p. 490.

[3] *Ibid.*, pp. 396-397. Smiles also related that Boulton and Watt had much difficulty with Pierre Droz, who in France had devised a segmented collar of six parts by which lettering or other devices could be easily applied to the edge of a coin. However, when Droz was hired by Boulton and Watt, he was found to be "of a very troublesome disposition." Further, "Several of his contrivances, being found not to answer, were obliged to be better contrived or completely changed by Mr. Boulton and his assistants" (Smiles, p. 390).

Küchler's 1796 Myddelton tokens, the same artist's beautiful Washington Seasons medals (in three designs, ordered and used by the government as Indian peace medals including for distribution on Lewis and Clark's 1804-1806 expedition), and the 1783 Washington Draped Bust tokens and, perhaps, others as well.

A Memorable Auction

As the nineteenth century progressed, the Soho Mint fell upon difficult economic times. In 1850 an auction was held of its effects, the announcement for which noted that the mint's reference collection of coins and medals, tons of old dies, and many other items would be sold.

The auction presentation noted (in part):

> THE EXTREMELY VALUABLE COLLECTION OF DIES for the coins and medals, well-known as the Soho Collection, most beautifully executed, principally by the celebrated Küchler, and by Droz and Philpp, also the dies for many rare coins, hitherto considered as almost unique, including a dollar of George III, 1798, a Britanniarum penny, many specimens of proposed coins, of various dates, and of the French Republic, 1790 to 1792, a pattern halfpenny George III by Droz, and provincial tokens, also
>
> A CABINET OF COINS AND MEDALS embracing four sets of the Soho Collection and many others extremely rare.

As it turned out, most of the presses and other coining equipment items were purchased by Ralph Heaton, of Birmingham, who had been involved in the private minting of tokens for many years. In the second half of the nineteenth century the Heaton Mint, as it became called, produced coins on contract for many countries of the world, including Canada.

Relevant to the continuing United States connection with the tradition of the now-defunct Soho Mint, certain of the dies went to W.J. Taylor, of 33 Little Queen Street, Holborn (later, 70 Red Lion Street), London.[1] Among these were obverse and reverse dies of the 1783-dated Washington Draped Bust "cent." Taylor produced restrikes of these in copper (mainly), silver (perhaps a few dozen), and gold (just a few coins). In addition, the reverse of this token was muled with an irrelevant die dated 1851, picturing a kangaroo, and pertaining to Melbourne, Australia (this piece is little known to American specialists). W.S. Lincoln, also of London, is said to have made restrikes in the 1860s. Today, the 1783-dated Washington pieces are listed in the *Guidebook of United States Coins* and other reference books. A recent account by George Fuld, "Coinage Featuring George Washington," proceedings of the Coinage of the Americas Conference, October 28, 1995, is the most definitive.[2]

By the 1860s the site of the Soho Mint was a marshy fen, all traces of the building having been since removed.

---

1 Whose restrikes of the 1806 and 1807 tokens of the Bahamas are mentioned in Chapter 10.

2 Published in 1996 by the American Numismatic Society, New York. Dr. Fuld's connections with the Washington series extends back to the 1940s. In the interim numerous articles have been published and many discoveries have been made by him.

CHAPTER 19

Dealer and Collector Hoards

The Hoarders Among Us: Introduction

Hoards traceable to dealers and collectors—in other words, those with numismatic knowledge—form a special segment of the present narrative. Such hoards have the common thread that the pieces were set aside for numismatic purposes. Most coins in such hoards or accumulations were bought from other dealers and collectors and were already known to the numismatic community. Thus, these holdings differ from the "find" type of hoard.

These hoards, many of which are well known and others of which are delineated here for the first time, are caches made by numismatists who were not content with owning just one example of a given item. The greatest of all numismatic hoarders was Virgil M. Brand, but he had quite a bit of company. In other instances, the hoards were the result of dealers accumulating inventory in a special area of interest.

Before 1950

Investment in coins had been a part of the hobby for many years, in fact as far back as the 1870s and 1880s in which era one dealer attempted to "corner" Proof sets of the year 1858, as an example. Various appealing coins—including leftover, unsold current minor Proofs from the Mint—were often squirreled away as store stock. The market was generally rising, and in this era—as also in the years to come—dealers often found that it was more profitable to hold a coin in inventory than to sell it. This year's fully-priced coin was apt to be tomorrow's wholesale bargain.

In the early twentieth century various dealers set aside "new" coins as they were produced, again usually of minor denominations, especially the cent and nickel five-cent piece. To have saved quarter dollars or half dollars in quantity would have tied up too much precious capital, a commodity never in long supply among the majority of professional numismatists. In time such dealers as John Boss, F.C.C. Boyd, B. Max Mehl, David U. Proskey, William Pukall, and John Zug had in their safes and vaults many bank-wrapped rolls of such items.

The 1930s represented a watershed era for numismatics. Despite the national Depression on the economic scene, coin collectors were marching to the beat of a different drummer. The catalysts—and there were several—included many exciting and interesting innovations. Among these were the appeal of the low-mintage 1931-S Lincoln cent (the first cent in a generation to have a mintage below the million mark), the introduction by Wayte Raymond of the *Standard Catalogue of United States Coins,* the 1935-1936 commemorative boom, the introduction of easy-to-use and fun-to-fill coin albums by M.L. Beistle and Wayte Raymond, the related mass production of "penny boards" by Whitman Publishing Company—the list goes on. These were happy, exciting times. Coin values rose tremendously. The cat was out of the bag: coins were one of the best investments ever, it was said, and beginning about 1934, many people started putting away current rolls of Uncirculated coins from cents to half dollars. (Silver dollars were virtually ignored and might as well have been struck on a different planet.)

The pace would continue, despite a crash in mid-1936 of the overblown market for commemorative half dollars. In the same year, Proof sets were sold to collectors for the first time since 1916. The *Numismatic Scrapbook,* launched by Lee F. Hewitt in 1935, became popular and served as a forum for buying and selling coins. During World War II, cash was plentiful, but consumer goods were rare. Thus, a lot of money was put into coins, perhaps starting in a big way with Abe Kosoff's September 1943 sale of the Michael F. Higgy Collection, which saw coins sell for two, three, five, or more multiples of the latest catalogue prices. Common-date gold coins became exceptionally popular, and for the first time there developed a widespread interest in the large and heavy $20 double eagles, each of which contained nearly an ounce of gold. Displaced citizens of European countries had long sought financial comfort in gold, and now the sentiment extended to our own shores. Common-date $20 pieces, previously with a market value of under $40, jumped to $50, $60, or even more. Richard S. Yeoman's *Guide Book of U.S. Coins* made its debut in 1946, adding fuel to the market fire.

All the while, hoards small and large were being assembled by collectors, dealers, and investors who continued to put away bank-wrapped rolls of current coinage.

The 1950s

In the decade or so prior to 1960, coin collecting was mostly a leisurely pursuit, notwithstanding lots of exciting market news and a dazzling run-up in prices. Information was obtained monthly through *The Numismatic Scrapbook* and *The Numismatist* magazines, and out in Iola, Wisconsin, Chet Krause published his newspaper-format *Numismatic News* beginning in 1952. Pricing information was primarily gathered from the *Guide Book of United States Coins,* by Richard S. Yeoman, which was published annually.

In the 1950s bank-wrapped rolls continued to be popular items to buy and put away in quantities. Proof sets, which were made again in 1950, following suspension after 1942 due to the pressing needs of World War II, attracted a wide following and had a remarkable way of escalating in price. The 1950-D nickel, of which more will be said subsequently, was a brilliant beacon to anyone interested in buying coins that—as certain as sunset follows sunrise—would go up in price. However, investment was secondary to most numismatists and the formation of a collection by date and mintmark sequence was primary.

The 1960s Onward

In 1960 there were several changes. The 1960 Small Date Lincoln cent was produced at Philadelphia and immediately became valuable. Several bags containing $50 face value (5,000 pieces) of this variety were obtained by various people from banks and sold immediately at sharp advances, some for $10,000 to $12,000. This was exciting news, and stories were carried in newspapers nationwide, in *Time* magazine, and on television. In Syracuse, New York, dealer Jonah Shapiro made a market in these, and his telephone kept ringing off the hook. In Philadelphia, Harry J. Forman and his associate Ruth Bauer also had their hands full with 1960 Small Date cents.

In Sidney, Ohio, newspaper publisher J. Oliver Amos decided to issue a weekly newspaper about a hobby or sport, and after some consultation with his staff narrowed the field down to potential categories beginning with the letters A, B, and C; specifically, antiques, bowling, or coins. The last-named was picked, and *Coin World* was launched under the editorship of D. Wayne Johnson. Englewood, Ohio, dealer James Kelly was tapped to write a new feature, "Trends," which on a weekly basis gave coin values, a hitherto untried concept. Within a short time *Coin World* had tens of thousands on its subscription list, and within a year or so it would cross the 100,000 mark, an all-time high which to this day has not been re-attained.

From 1960 through 1964, *investment* was the key word. The market rose rapidly, and in a cause-and-effect relationship, thousands of people entered the hobby to make a profit, and did so. *The Coin Dealer Newsletter* was launched, Teletype networks linked dealers all over America, jet airplane travel made it possible to have breakfast in New York City and lunch in Los Angeles, and many other changes occurred as well. The darling of the investors was the marvelous low-mintage 1950-D nickel, which rose from $10 to $15 per roll (of 40 coins) in the mid-1950s to over $1,200 at one point in 1964. In the latter year the market softened, and in 1965 it foundered. The 1950-D nickel did the impossible: it fell from grace. Ditto for quite a few other "winners." Recovery of the coin market (but not the 1950-D nickel price) took place a few years later, and there were other investment peaks in 1979-1980 and again in 1989.

The Current Era

Today in the 1990s the market is very cosmopolitan. On one side there are more dedicated scholars than ever before, and more interest in numismatic specialties. Publications such as the *Colonial Newsletter, Colonial Coin Collectors Club Newsletter, The Asylum* (published by the Numismatic Bibliomania Society, a group of collectors of printed material), *Penny-Wise* (about copper cents and other issues), *Longacre's Journal* (Flying Eagle and Indian cents), *John Reich Journal* (early silver coins), *Gobrecht Journal* (Liberty Seated silver coins), *Token and Medal Society Journal,* and *Paper Money* provide technical information and historical notes to specialists in various series. Perhaps with *Walter Breen's Complete Encyclopedia of U.S. and Colonial Coins* (Doubleday, 1988) as a focal point, those entering the hobby can learn more worthwhile information today, and with much less effort, than could their predecessors a generation or two ago.

At the same time, the wider popular market for coins is catered to by general interest periodicals including *Coin World, COINage, Coins* magazine, *Numismatic News,* and *The Numismatist,* as well as *The Coin Dealer Newsletter* and a few other pricing sources.

The market constituting sales to coin buyers range from numismatically-oriented and very knowledgeable dealers with clienteles of serious collectors to investment-oriented sellers who offer investment-oriented coins to the public by telephone, television, and mass mailings.

All of the preceding elements give a rich diversity to the coin market as we know it today.

With these comments as a preface, it is appropriate to comment on various hoards, groups, accumulations, and other holdings of coins that have been set aside by numismatically knowledgeable people over a long span of years. No such enumeration will ever be complete, as virtually every dealer who ever sold a coin also set aside a few "extras" now and then, and collectors often acquired duplicates for investment or trading purposes.

Some of the dealer and collector hoards worthy of mention—ranging from well known to obscure—are given below in approximate chronological order. By including all in the same section, they can be compared to each other, as many dealer hoards are related:

Quite a Few Proof Sets

Acquired: Late 1870s and early 1880s
Dispersed: 1886
Numismatic hoard: Proof coins

In his October 1886 sale of the J. Colvin Randall Collection, W. Elliot Woodward offered quantities of Proof sets of the 1878-1882 era. Undoubtedly, these had been bought at the Mint by Randall, a Philadelphia dealer. It was the custom of the Mint to sell for face value any undistributed remainders. Those not placed with dealers were simply spent. The Woodward-Randall offering included the following:[1]

1878 three-piece Proof sets [Indian cent, nickel three-cent piece, Shield nickel], 10 sets.

1879 three-piece Proof sets, 82 sets.

1880 three-piece Proof sets, 76 sets.

1880 Proof sets [content not specified, but probably complete from the cent to the trade dollar], 35 sets.

1880 Proof trade dollars, 64 coins.

1882 Proof sets [content not specified], 32 sets.

Virgil M. Brand

Acquired: 1880s to 1926
Dispersed: after 1926
Numismatic hoard: Just about everything

A wealthy Chicago brewer, Brand began collecting coins in the 1880s and continued until his death in 1926.[2] Along the way he acquired over 300,000 coins of all descriptions. He was a hoarder *par excellence,* and his holdings included six 1884 trade dollars (only 10 were minted), one or more wooden barrels filled with Uncirculated Civil War tokens, gold coins by the thousands, and more.

His coins were dispersed for decades thereafter by his heirs—his brothers Armin and Horace—and their descendants. These provided a nice "working stock" for many coin dealers in the 1930s, 1940s, and 1950s, New Netherlands Coin Co. among them.

Major auction sales featuring some of Brand's

[1] Citation suggested by Bob Vail.

[2] A book could be written about Brand, and has, by me: *Virgil Brand, the Man and His Era: Profile of a Numismatist,* 1983. Thus, the account of his fascinating activities is only given in abbreviated form in the present work.

United States rarities were held in 1983-1984 by Bowers and Merena via the Jane Brand Allen family and the Morgan Guaranty Trust Co., New York, for which David E. Tripp acted as numismatic advisor.

David U. Proskey

Acquired: 1880s to 1928
Dispersed: after 1928
Numismatic hoard: U.S. minor coins

Entering the coin business in 1873, David Ulysses Proskey worked with several partners and firms over a long period of time and remained active until his death in 1928. One account stated that "he had a habit of going to the Mint early each January and buying up the stock of unsold Proof coins."[1] He seems to have concentrated upon minor Proof coins, those of the cent, nickel three-cent, and nickel five-cent denominations. Probably, he ignored Proof gold.

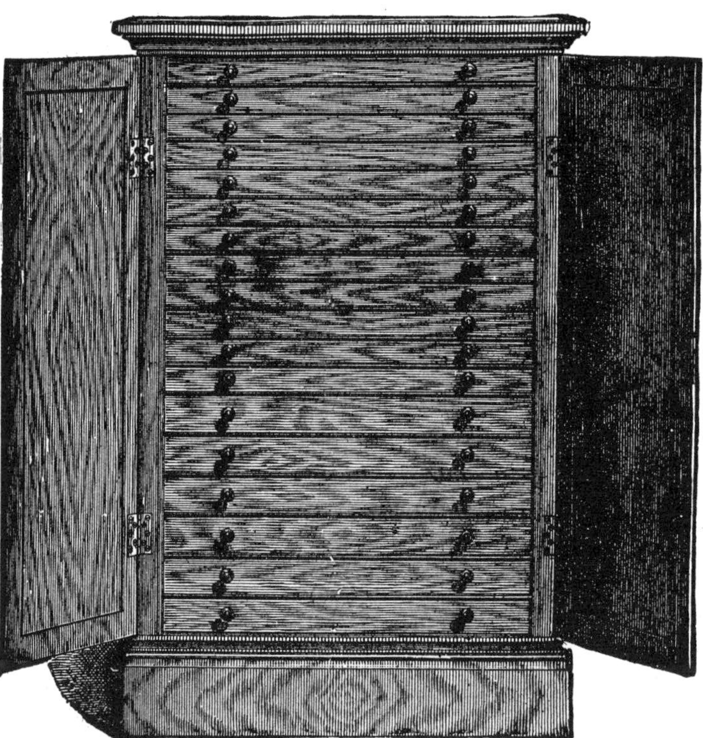

Wooden cabinet for storing a coin collection or inventory as used by numismatists in the 1880s and 1890s.

Probably most of his purchases occurred in the 1880s in an era in which minor Proofs were made in record quantities. In addition, Proskey acquired various coins in quantity from other sources. By the 1920s he had a vast holding of rolls and early Proof coins, many of which are said to have passed to F.C.C. Boyd, who in turn sold many to Howard E. MacIntosh of the Tatham Stamp & Coin Co., Springfield, Massachusetts.[2]

George W. Rice's Passion

Acquired: 1890s to 1906
Dispersed: after 1906, especially 1911
Numismatic hoard: 1856 Flying Eagle cents

In the 1890s and early 1900s, George W. Rice, of Detroit, took a fancy to the rare 1856 Flying Eagle cent and ultimately amassed a hoard of 756 pieces. Many of these were sold in 1911 and went into another hoard, that of John Beck, Pittsburgh industrialist (see listing below).

Of all nineteenth-century American rarities, the 1856 Flying Eagle cent is one of the most famous. In 1856 the Mint struck somewhat less than 1,000 of these as patterns for wide distribution to newspaper editors, congressmen, and others to acquaint them with the lighter-weight, smaller replacement for the time-honored "large" copper cent. Made of a new copper-nickel alloy, the new cents weighed 72 grains.

The obverse was designed by James B. Longacre, who copied Christian Gobrecht's flying eagle motif used on the illustrious silver dollars of 1836. The reverse was Longacre's own "agricultural" wreath, earlier used on the gold $1 and $3 pieces of 1854, and consisting of corn, cotton, and tobacco leaves.

---

[1] Pete Smith, *American Numismatic Biographies,* 1992, p. 189.

[2] A January 26, 1937, financial report on MacIntosh (copy furnished by David Sundman) noted that he was 26 years old at the time, married, and began dealing in stamps in 1927, later adding "numismatology." His mother, Caroline H. MacIntosh was a partner. Further, "The business occupies a 20 by 35 ft. space in a frame building located on a corner in a thickly populated residential district of the middle class. Management rests with the owners, and 6 to 10 are employed." MacIntosh's obituary, by Elston G. Bradfield, appeared in *The Numismatist,* October 1958, p. 1180, and noted in part: "MacIntosh, 47, took his own life by firing a 32-caliber bullet through his head in the basement of his home.... Recently he had worked about two hours daily following illness and an operation. He conducted a real estate business and a coin company...."

These pattern cents captured the fancy of collectors, and a great demand arose for them. At the same time, Mint Director James Ross Snowden (who served 1853-1861) sought to acquire Washington tokens and medals for the Mint Cabinet, in preparation for a special ceremony dedicating the Washington display, to take place on February 22 (Washington's birthday), 1860. Snowden announced that restrikes of certain pattern cents would be available to interested collectors. Later, a criticism of such restriking arose among dealers (in particular) and collectors, and the activity went "underground." Restrikes of 1856 Flying Eagle cents continued to be made through at least the early 1860s and perhaps later. All told, an estimated 2,500 or so 1856 Flying Eagle cents were made, considering originals and restrikes combined.

All through the late nineteenth century the 1856 Flying Eagle cent was an object of desire for just about every amateur collector. While the other two issues of Flying Eagle cents (1857 and 1858) were inexpensive and easily obtained, and while all Indian cents from 1859 onward presented no problem either, the centerpiece, the rarity of the collection was the 1856. By the 1890s, examples were selling for several dollars apiece.

While the Rice and Beck hoards were the most famous holdings, there were several smaller accumulations formed over the years. Just about everyone *enjoyed* owning an 1856 Flying Eagle cent. Perhaps reflective of this sentiment, dealer Abe Kosoff stated in the 1960s that it was good luck to have an 1856 Flying Eagle cent as Lot No. 1 in an auction sale, and from time to time his catalogues had such a feature.

A.M. Smith

Acquired: 1870s-1890s
Dispersed: 1935
Numismatic hoard: Proof sets, etc.

Anders Madsen Schmidt, who was born in Denmark on February 4, 1841, came to America at an early age, and changed his name to Andrew Mason Smith.[1] Today, he is best remembered as A.M. Smith, rare coin dealer.

However, before becoming a professional numismatist he did many other things including sailing aboard merchant ships, selling chickens in New Orleans, and serving in the Civil War with the 13th Indiana Regiment. (If anything, the backgrounds of many professional numismatists have been diverse!) In 1872 he married Botilla Elberg, a fellow Dane whom he met when he was working on the transcontinental railroad. The couple had six children.

In 1872 A.M. Smith became a wine dealer in Salt Lake City (which must have yielded sparse trade due to the Mormons' abstinence from alcohol) but by the middle of the decade he pulled up stakes and relocated to Philadelphia. He must have learned numismatics rapidly and well, for by 1879 he is said to have issued his first price list, and in 1880 he published a quarterly numismatic newsletter. By the mid-1880s a guide he had written about the Philadelphia Mint had gone through several editions.

Once a wine dealer always a wine dealer it may be. In any event, in 1886 he moved to Minneapolis, where he became a saloonkeeper and dealer in spirits until about 1905. However, he kept his hand in the coin trade—at least casually—and ordered Proof coins from the Mint for several years thereafter. His death occurred in 1915.

About 20 years later his widow Botilla had a Minneapolis bank consign her late husband's coin stock to dealer M.H. Bolender. In June 1935 Bolender published an announcement for his sale of June 29:

> The [A.M. Smith] collection contains over 3,000 large cents worth up to $100 each; over 2,000 half cents worth up to $50 each, over 1,500 U.S. Proof sets. It is a well-balanced collection, with something in every series.
>
> It was shipped to me by express in five boxes weighing

Salt Lake City in the 1870s.

[2] Information from Pete Smith, letter, September 8, 1996; also Pete Smith, *American Numismatic Biographies,* p. 217. *The Numismatist,* June 1935, p. 398, Bolender sale announcement.

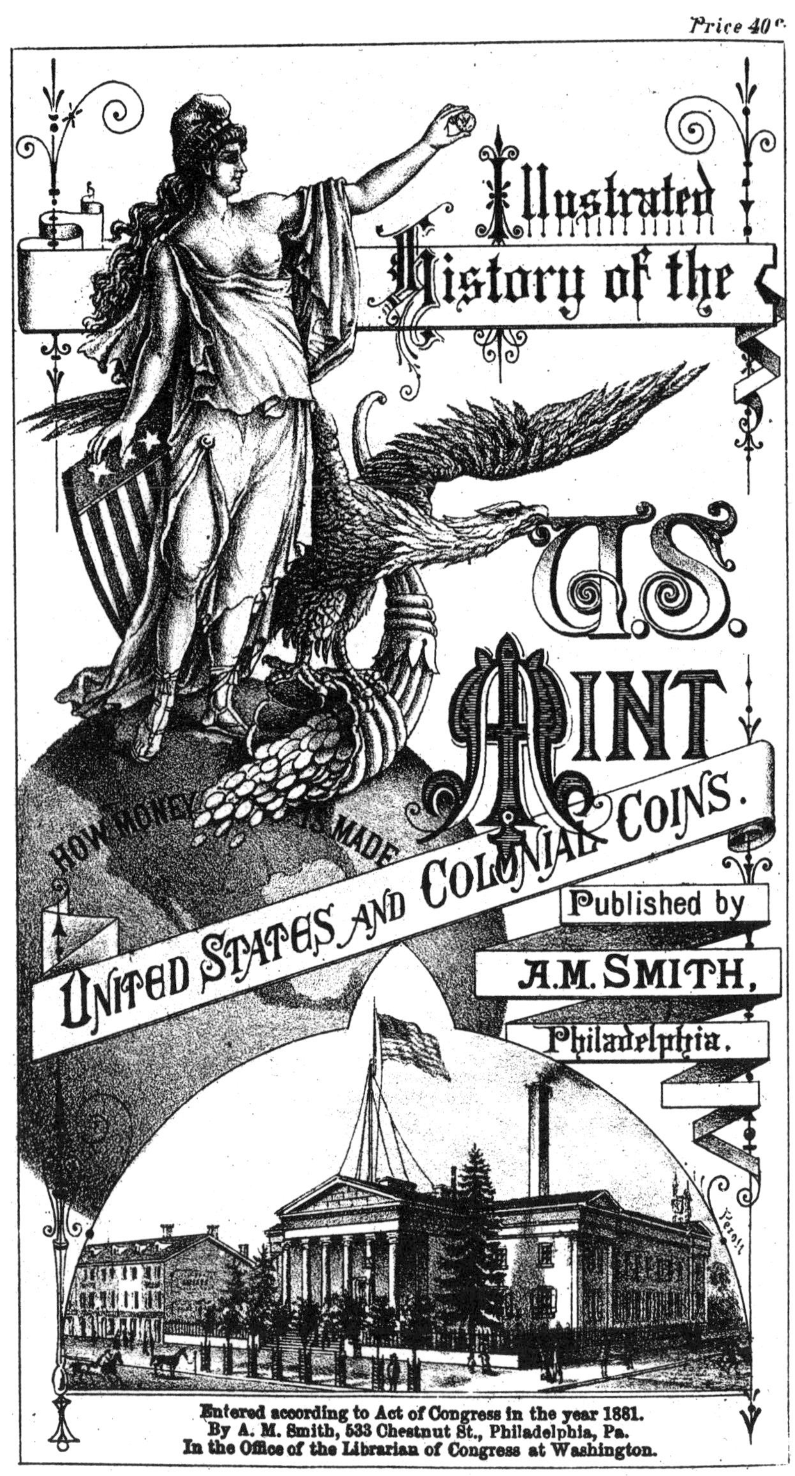

A.M. Smith published several editions to his guide to the Philadelphia Mint, the title page of one is shown here.

nearly 500 pounds. Over 15,000 coins in the collection. It required two weeks for Mr. Bolender and a capable assistant, and two stenographers, to appraise them.

Smith's 1,500 Proof sets from the nineteenth century (which certainly rank him as among the most prominent of dealer hoarders) and other properties were offered in Bolender's sales numbered 98, 99, and 100, all three of which included Proof sets dated 1878 through 1889 and 1893. Included in one sale was the unique 1884 Proof set struck in copper and including the 1884 trade dollar in that metal. This would suggest that Smith had close ties to the Mint at one time, as, indeed, would be suggested by his publishing multiple editions of his guide to that institution.

John Andrew Beck

Acquired: 1880s to 1924
Dispersed: 1970s
Numismatic hoard: 1856 Flying Eagle cents, $50 gold, etc.

John A. Beck, a collector of many items and owner of one of the world's greatest displays of rare and unusual smoking pipes and a world-class holding of Indian relics, hoarded 1856 Flying Eagle cents and ultimately amassed a hoard of 531 pieces, some of them from the Rice Collection. Beck, a Pittsburgh industrialist, also liked $50 gold "slugs" and bought dozens. Ditto for certain other types of coins.

Beck's gold coins and other important pieces were sold at auction by Quality Sales (Abe Kosoff and Jerry Cohen) in the 1970s, but most of the 1856 Flying Eagle cents were marketed privately at the same time.

Beck was born in Chestnut Ridge, Pennsylvania, on January 5, 1859. He followed the family trade and operated salt wells in the western part of Pennsylvania, later going into grocery sales via horse and wagon, and still later into the oil business. At the age of 10 he began collecting coins, a hobby he was to pursue for the rest of his life, until his death on January 27, 1924.

Certain of his non-numismatic collections went to the Carnegie Museum, Pittsburgh.

William L. Pukall

Acquired: Circa 1914-1950
Dispersed: after 1950
Numismatic hoard: U.S. minor coins

A New Jersey dealer, Pukall began buying Uncirculated coins directly from the Philadelphia, Denver, and San Francisco mints about 1914, and continued to do so for many years later (by which time the Treasury Department in Washington handled sales from the three mints). He seems to have concentrated on Lincoln cents and Buffalo nickels, but he acquired other coins as well, among which were commemorative half dollars from various issuing commissions.

At one unknown point he acquired many Proof Indian and early Lincoln cents, nickel three-cent pieces, and Shield, Liberty, and early Buffalo nickels, all wrapped in thin paper tissue as put up by the Mint at the time of issue. Possibly, these came through David U. Proskey, Henry Chapman, John Zug, or John Boss, all of whom had quantities in the 1920s. In any event, Pukall still had many of these coins in the 1950s, by which time there was a ready sale and most remainders were sold. Also set aside were large quantities of small-denomination foreign coins.[1]

[1] Personal experience of the author with William Pukall.

John Zug

Acquired: 1910s-1940s
Dispersed: 1910s-1940s
Numismatic hoard: U.S. minor coins

John Zug, born in Washington, D.C., on May 1, 1869, became interested in coins by the turn of the century. Like many collectors, he was fond of putting away quantities of lower denomination pieces. Circa 1918 he is said to have disposed of 25,000 1909-S V.D.B. cents for one and three-quarters cent each. He had purchased these at face value from the Mint in August 1909, according to an account.[1]

By 1920, then living in Bowie, Maryland, Zug was in the mail-order rare coin business. He continued to buy quantities of coins as they were issued, and at the same time would parcel some of them out to his customers. Thus, his "numismatic hoard" was more of a large working inventory, a movable hoard, so to speak.

In time he became well liked and well known. For over 25 years he ran full-page advertisements on the inside back cover of *The Numismatist.* Zug did not leave behind a corpus of coin books, auction catalogues, or philosophical articles (as did Thomas L. Elder, for one), thus he is little remembered today. However, he was very highly esteemed in his lifetime, and any comprehensive account of the rare coin business in the first half of the present century must necessarily include him. John Zug died on October 23, 1949. Among the last letters he wrote was one to Louis E. Eliasberg, Sr., of Baltimore, congratulating him on completing his collection of United States gold coins by date and mintmark.

Col. Edward H.R. Green

Acquired: 1920s to 1936
Dispersed: Late 1930s and early 1940s
Numismatic hoard: U.S. gold, rarities, currency, etc.

In the annals of American coin hoarders Green's name is in the first chapter, right along with Virgil M. Brand. However, while Brand was a consummate numismatist and devoted much if not most of his life to the hobby, Green had many other interests to divide his attention.

Born to eccentric millionairess Hetty Green (nicknamed "The Witch of Wall Street"), Green became heir to her fortune and enjoyed life as a roué and hoarder. On July 10, 1917, he married one of his favorite "ladies of the night," Mabel E. Harlow. Green collected and hoarded with a passion and acquired boats, real estate, a railroad, stamps (he once owned all 100 of the 1918 24¢ "Jenny" airmail inverts), and, especially, coins.

At the time of his death in 1936 it took eight armored cars to move his collectibles, the numismatic part of which was estimated to be worth $5 million.[2] Among his coins were all five of the five known 1913 Liberty Head nickels (these were later sold through B.G. Johnson of the St. Louis Stamp & Coin Co. to Eric P. Newman, and by the end of the 1940s were dispersed in the market), a reported seven specimens of the famous 1838-O half dollar, hundreds of $5 gold coins (his favorite gold denomination; some of these were sold through Stack's in the early 1940s), "many" 1796 dimes including numerous choice examples,[3] 200 or more Uncirculated 1796 quarter dollars,[4] and a vast holding of early large-size American currency notes including great rarities. Unfortunately, Green stored his paper money in cellulose nitrate envelopes which caused the notes to break apart into bits and crumbs.

Today in the 1990s the Green name is not as remembered as it should be, perhaps because his collection was not memorialized by catalogues.

Frederick C.C. Boyd

Acquired: 1910s-1930s
Dispersed: 1940s-1950s
Numismatic hoard: U.S. minor coins, rarities

New Jersey businessman F.C.C. Boyd (he headed a

---

1 Breen, *Encyclopedia,* 1988, p. 228; citation from Dr. George Fuld's comment in Kagin's Van Cleave Collection sale, 1986, under Lot 5012. The present writer has found no other mention of this remarkable group.

2 Pete Smith, *American Numismatic Biographies,* 1992, p. 105. F.C.C. Boyd was an appraiser of the coin part of the estate and evaluated the Green holdings in 1937 and 1938 (cf. *The Numismatist,* Boyd obituary, October 1958, p. 1180).

3 Breen, *Encyclopedia,* 1988, p. 299.

4 *Ibid.,* p. 337: "When Col. Green inherited his mother's millions, he became a collector of (among other things) railroad cars, pornographic films;

company that operated newsstands and kiosks in railroad stations) is remembered as one of the all-time great figures in twentieth century American numismatics.

With an office in New York, he purchased quantities of Proof coins from David U. Proskey and later from his estate. Many bank-wrapped rolls of coins—especially small denominations—were acquired at the same time. Boyd was a major advertiser in *The Numismatist* during this era, although he is best remembered as the owner of what was billed as "The World's Greatest Collection" when it was sold at auction by the Numismatic Gallery in 1945-1946. Other sections of United States coins in Boyd's collection were purchased *en bloc* by Numismatic Gallery, and were sold to King Farouk in Cairo, Egypt. Certain ex Proskey hoard coins were sold by Boyd to Howard E. MacIntosh of Tatham Stamp & Coin Co.

In the later years of his life he sold many of his non-federal coins such as tokens and medals to John J. Ford, Jr., of whom he was a close friend.

Wayte Raymond

Acquired: 1920s to 1940s
Dispersed: 1930s and later
Numismatic hoard: Rolls of minor coins, commemoratives, etc.

Born in 1886 in Connecticut, Raymond became interested in coins as a teenager, and by 1908 was issuing lists of coins for sale. Meanwhile, he put food on the table from his salary as a bank teller. In the annals of what might have been, but wasn't, in American numismatics, a partnership was envisioned with Texas dealer B. Max Mehl, but did not materialize. Had it done so, the history of the rare coin trade in America may have been quite different from what we know today.

Raymond formed an arrangement with Elmer Sears and conducted 43 auction sales from 1912 to 1918. In the 1920s he had his own business and among other things handled the $100,000 purchase through art dealer Knoedler & Co. of the James W. Ellsworth Collection, with financing provided by John Work Garrett, who was given first choice of the rarities. Along the way Raymond acquired large quantities of nineteenth-century and early twentieth-century bank-wrapped rolls and Proof coins, some of which were, apparently, acquired from old-time dealer David Proskey.

During the 1930s and 1940s he ran the numismatic department of the Scott Stamp & Coin Company. In the former decade he launched the expanded version of the *Standard Catalogue of United States Coins and Currency,* 1934, the first regularly-issued price guide to the American series. This work was the standard text until it was supplanted by the *Guide Book* in 1946 and eventually replaced by it. The last edition appeared in 1957, a year after Raymond's death, and was edited by his protégé, John J. Ford, Jr.

Raymond's line of "National" cardboard album pages, made by M.L. Beistle in Shippensburg, Pennsylvania, made its debut in the 1930s and revolutionized the coin hobby. Now for the first time collecting coins was like filling in a crossword puzzle: empty spaces beckoned and made it instantly obvious which coins were still needed. John J. Ford, Jr., related that this enabled Raymond to find an eager market for the untold thousands of dates and mintmarks he had accumulated earlier.[1] Earlier, collectors usually stored coins in 2x2" paper envelopes or in cabinet drawers.

In the 1950s Raymond underwrote the expenses of young Walter Breen in his research in the National Archives, which led to the discovery of much information not previously known to the numismatic community. Upon his death, Raymond was mourned as one of the best-liked and most influential persons the hobby has ever called its own.

---

and among his immense numismatic holdings was a hoard of over 200 Uncirculated 1796 quarter dollars, of which at least 100 were more or less prooflike—their fields more mirrorlike than on the others. Abe Kosoff and André DeCoppet dispersed many of these to date and type collectors during the 1940s." It is believed that Kosoff acquired the Green coins through Philadelphia dealer James G. Macallister; accounts vary. Separately, John J. Ford, Jr., conversation, June 27, 1996, stated that in the 1940s he had inspected the quarters when they were part of the Green estate, but that Macallister had bought them.

[1] Conversation with the author.

Ella Wright Sells Some Delicacies

Acquired: Late 19th and early 20th centuries
Dispersed: after 1935
Numismatic hoard: Dealer stock

After the death of Philadelphia dealer Henry Chapman (1859-1935) his inventory was liquidated over a long period of time by his secretary, Ella Wright. At the 1937 American Numismatic Association convention held in that city, dealers converged upon the erstwhile Chapman office and bought many standard dates and mintmarks of United States coins, generally ignoring a vast stock of important tokens and medals.

In 1942 John J. Ford, Jr. (born 1924) was in the earlier years of his illustrious numismatic career, which he had begun by collecting Lincoln cents as a preteenager in 1935.

Every few weeks in the early 1940s, Ford took the train from New York City, where he was working with Stack's at the time, to Philadelphia to visit various dealers and buy coins. During this time and in the course of several visits Ella Wright reached into some long-hidden reserve stock and sold him a large group of prooflike gem 1857 Liberty Seated quarter dollars, perhaps 50 to 100 in all; many prooflike gem 1858 Large Letters Flying Eagle cents; and several or more Proof 1921 Morgan dollars, the latter from a stock of a dozen or so that Ella Wright said Chief Engraver George T. Morgan "made specially for Mr. Chapman." Ella Wright always called Henry Chapman *Mister* Chapman. Proof Morgan dollars were not in demand by collectors at the time, thus Ford bought only a few.[1]

Leftover Chapman inventory coins and other properties went to many diverse locations in the 1940s and 1950s including to Edmund A. Rice (of Cranbury, New Jersey) and David M. Bullowa (Philadelphia professional numismatist).

Charles and Ruth Green

Acquired: 1940s and 1950s
Dispersed: Late 1950s onward
Numismatic hoard: Proof 1886 quarters

The Chicago dealer husband and wife team of Charles and Ruth Green liked the 1886 Proof quarter dollar, of which only 886 were minted, and determined to buy as many as possible. By the late 1950s they had acquired several hundred.

As is the case with all of the brief biographical notes of dealers given in this chapter, much more could be written about the Greens—perhaps a project for another time, another place.

Don Corrado Romano's Favorites

Acquired: 1950s and 1960s
Dispersed: unknown
Numismatic hoard: 1795 halves, 1878 trade dollars

In Boston, Don Corrado Romano operated the Worthy Coin Company, an issuer of yellow-covered premium catalogues giving prices paid to the public for selected rare coins. As an amusement, he took a liking to half dollars dated 1795 and Proof trade dollars of 1878, these being his two favorite issues. Over

1 Recollection of John J. Ford, Jr., conversation, June 27, 1996. For more information about Morgan's special, but confidential, services to favored numismatists see the 1921 Proof Morgan and 1922 Peace dollars offered in the Norweb Collection catalogue, November 1988, lots 3922, 3932, and 3922.

a period of time he hoarded many. The writer visited him in Boston in the 1950s and saw a few dozen of each, but these did not represent his entire holdings.

A.J. Mitula: The Nickel Man

Acquired: 1950-1951
Dispersed: 1950s-1960s
Numismatic hoard: 1950-D nickels

In 1950 the Denver Mint struck only 2,630,030 Jefferson nickels, the lowest mintage in the Jefferson series before or since. News of this attractively low figure was published in the *Numismatic Scrapbook,* and from almost the beginning there was strong collecting and hoarding interest. Eventually, the 1950-D led the investment market from about 1951 until 1964-1965. There were several players including a Milwaukee dealer with 8,000 rolls (40 coins per roll or 320,000 total pieces).[1]

However the biggest player was Houston, Texas, dealer A.J. Mitula, who apparently acquired over a million pieces at or close to face value (plus some tips to bank employees). Mitula sold coins to eager investors via advertisements in the *Numismatic Scrapbook* and was also a wholesale supplier to dealers. Profits were sufficient to pay for his "1950-D Nickel House" summer home on Route 24 in Cascade, Colorado, on the highway into the mountains to the west of Colorado Springs. In the 1970s and 1980s, while an instructor of the "All About Coins" course at the American Numismatic Association Summer Seminar in Colorado Springs, I would spend a day taking my students to Cripple Creek, high on the western slope of Pikes Peak. Always accompanying me in the front of the bus were Bill Henderson and Col. Adna Wilde, both of whom lived in Colorado Springs and did many fine things by sharing their talents with the ANA. Bill Henderson would always take the microphone as we headed up Ute Pass to Cascade, and tell all of us about the days of Mitula and his 1950-D nickels.

Concerning the number of 1950-D nickels saved in Mint State at or near the time of issue, estimates have varied widely. Thomas K. DeLorey, whose credentials in numismatic research plus a generous measure of common sense add up to a lot of ability, suggests that no more than a million were held back by investors and dealers.[2]

Max Mizel's Half Dollars

Acquired: 1950s
Dispersed: Unknown
Numismatic hoard: 1878 Proof coins

New York coin dealer Max Mizel took a fancy to Proof half dollars and trade dollars minted in 1878 and acquired dozens of them over a period of time. No other dates of this series interested him. It was 1878 and 1878 alone.

MacIntosh Has Much, Loses All

Acquired: 1930s to 1958
Dispersed: After 1958
Numismatic hoard: Quantities of coins

In Springfield, Massachusetts, Howard E. MacIntosh operated the Tatham Stamp & Coin Co. The firm dealt mainly with the general public and sold starter kits, packets, and groups of coins which were sent on approval to those requesting them. In the course of business he was an eager buyer whenever quantities of United States coins became available, as these could be advertised in his newspaper-style catalogues and other listings, and he would have the ability to fill multiple orders.

---

1 Breen, *Encyclopedia,* 1988, p. 264.
2 Letter, September 29, 1996.

At one time in the 1950s the writer purchased about 300 scarce 1879 Liberty Seated dimes from MacIntosh, each coin being a prooflike gem. In August 1958 I received a telephone call from Howard E. MacIntosh, who asked me if for about $200,000 I would like to buy his entire rare coin inventory, which he assured me was worth over a million dollars. He needed cash for a real estate development deal, he said, and would sacrifice his coin stock. I was skeptical that a coin dealer would offer such a discount for worthwhile material and did not investigate the matter further. On September 5, 1958, he became despondent and took his own life with a handgun.

It turned out that his coin inventory included many bank-wrapped rolls of Indian cents, early mintmark issues of Lincoln cents (including 1909-S V.D.B), nineteenth-century Proof coins, large quantities of 1936 P-D-S Rhode Island commemorative half dollars, certain Boone commemoratives of the 1930s by the dozens and hundreds (perhaps he had made a deal with the distributor, Frank Dunn, in that era), and much more, many pieces of which came from F.C.C. Boyd. The MacIntosh coins were later mainly sold through New Netherlands Coin Company.

Yes, the total amounted to well over a million dollars.

The Missing Numismatist

Acquired: 1961 and earlier
Dispersed: 1966 and later
Numismatic hoard:
Quantities of coins and notes

In 1966, under court order, a safe deposit box belonging to Charles Coble, of Wichita, Kansas, was opened. Coble, who lived in a shack and who was remembered by neighbors for his picking up old bottles, had disappeared in 1961. Later, the "shantytown," where he had lived, was bulldozed by the Urban Renewal Agency in an effort to "eliminate blighted areas."

Not much could be learned about Coble, and no local coin collectors or dealers could recall him when asked at a later date. However, his safe deposit box

> was brim full of coins and bank notes. On the table before the group was spread a pirate's delight hoard: gold coins that glowed under the overhead light, bank notes crisp and notes greatly worn, a pile of silver dollars. The more than 90 notes looked to viewers like a small fortune. More than a third of them were obsolete bank notes including three Republic of Texas notes, a $500 and two $50 bills.... The hoard contained a set of the $1 Legal Tender bills of 1869-1917 missing only the scarce 1874.... In the box were 59 silver dollars from 1797 down to 1928.

Many of the pieces were numismatically identified and were in 2x2" paper coin envelopes marked with sale prices. Years later an announcement was made that the coins were to be auctioned on January 14, 1978.[1]

Cornering the 1881 Gold $1 Market

Acquired: 1950s-1972
Dispersed: 1973
Numismatic hoard: 1881 gold $1

David W. Akers reported this cache:[2]

> In 1973 Paramount International Coin Corporation handled an interesting group, the Leon Lindheim hoard of 1881 "Proof" gold dollars. Lindheim, a well-known Cleveland collector and numismatic writer (with a regular column in the Cleveland *Plain Dealer*), set out to acquire as many specimens as he could from the reported 87-piece Proof mintage for this date, and over a period of many years he purchased many "Proofs." As it turned out, only eight coins were actually Proofs, the rest being business strikes. Some were fully prooflike business strikes, but many others were only partially prooflike or were frosty!

---

[1] Ted Hammer, "Hoard Defies Searchers," *Coin World,* November 30, 1977, and "Unclaimed Hoard Scheduled to Wichita Auction Block," December 7, 1977.
[2] Letter, July 7, 1996.

A "Church Collection"

Acquired: 1960s or earlier
Dispersed: 1987
Numismatic hoard: Various U.S. coins

In March 1987, John Rodrigues was exploring the banks of Guadelupe Creek in San Jose, California. He came upon a small pocket in the earth, and with the help of his family and the Treasure Hunters Society of Santa Clara Valley, he found a number of numismatically interesting coins including an 1872 Indian cent and a 1921-D dime. These and others, plus church-related items such as metal crosses and communion medals, appeared to have been subjected to intense heat and may have come from a 1966 burglary of the nearby Holy Family Church.

An article in *Coin World* mused: [1]

> But 1872 cents and 1921-D dimes are unusual coins to show up in church collection plates. It is also said that the church later burned down, and what remained was just pushed into the creek. This could explain the fused coins, perhaps. Or was some past priest a numismatist, who had left his collection in the church, undiscovered until this time?

Hoarding Panama-Pacific $50 Gold Coins

Acquired: 1970s-1980s
Dispersed: unknown
Numismatic hoard: 1915-S Pan-Pacific $50

Coin World, July 16, 1980,[2] reported that seven years earlier a small group of investors led by Chicago insurance executive Arthur L. Weiner sought to invest $250,000 in rare coins. "The intent going in to this was to buy the coin we felt had the greatest upside appreciation with minimal downside risks, and we came to the conclusion that the U.S. $50 gold piece was *the* coin. And, we haven't changed our minds."

Based upon current market prices, a *Coin World* writer estimated that the investors held between 19

and 26 of the coins, although the owners weren't talking numbers. Mr. Weiner made this further comment: "We went into it for materialistic reasons and not aesthetic reasons, and that's what upsets some of your friends like Dave Bowers, who believes the coin is probably one of the most aesthetic things man has ever created. I don't think so."

Long Forgotten "Goodies"

Set aside: 19th century
Brought to market: 1991
Treasure: Liberty Seated silver coins

Half dollar bedecked cover of Christie's catalogue for the September 1991 sale of 1860-O half dollars. (Courtesy of James Lamb, Christie's)

---

1 "Man Finds Old Coin Hoard in Creek Bed," *Coin World,* July 26, 1978, p. 10.
2 "Large Hoard of Pan-Pacs Overhangs Market."

Friday the 13th can be a lucky day for coin collectors.

On Friday, September 13, 1991, at Christie's auction rooms in New York City a consignment of coins from the estate of Mrs. Sumner A. Parker crossed the auction block. Assets from the Parker family home known as The Cloisters, in Brooklandville, near Baltimore, Maryland, had been given to found the Cloisters Children's Museum of Baltimore.

Now in 1991, coins and other items gathered by an numismatically inclined ancestor of Mrs. Parker, name not given, were offered for sale. The term "Baltimore Hoard" was used in the catalogue. Collectors were delighted to be able to compete for many high quality nineteenth- and twentieth-century specimens, among which were these quantity groups:

1879 nickel three-cent pieces. Mint State (6 pieces).
1880 nickel three-cent pieces. Mint State (12 pieces).
1881 nickel three-cent pieces. Mint State (10 pieces).
1862 half dimes. Mint State (7 pieces).
1888 Liberty Head nickels. Mint State (5 pieces).
1919 Buffalo nickels. Mint State (20 pieces).
1882 Liberty Seated dimes. Mint State (4 pieces).
1875-S Twenty-cent pieces. Mint State (12 pieces).
1918-S Standing Liberty quarters. Mint State (12 pieces).
1860-O Liberty Seated half dollars. Mint State (15 pieces).
Sheets of $5 Federal Reserve Bank Notes from Atlanta, variety known as Friedberg-789, each sheet containing four notes (5 sheets).

New York Subway Hoard

Acquired: 1940s-1950s
Dispersed: 1991-1996
Numismatic hoard: Various U.S. coins

(Photo courtesy of Stephanie Bean, Littleton Coin Co.)

Making Change in the Subway

In 1942 at the Philadelphia Mint a working die was begun with a 1941 master die and completed with a 1942 maser die, thus creating a working die that had the previous figure 1 visible under the final 2. This became known as the 1942/1 overdate.

In early 1943 it was found that many of these coins had been released in the New York City area. Token sellers operating kiosks in the subway system began to scan their change, and over a period of time several thousand 1942/1 overdates were found and sold into the numismatic market, where they eventually became worth several dollars or more apiece.

This spurred a certain token seller named Morris Moscow, a clerk on the D Train, to learn more about coins. Soon, he was seeking other scarce coins including 1916-D Mercury dimes and 1914-D Lincoln cents, a rewarding pursuit that continued for much of the next 20 years. Many of his finds were marketed through his brother-in-law, George Shaw, a Brooklyn rare coin dealer who advertised in the *Numismatic Scrapbook Magazine.*[1] Numerous pieces remained unsold after Shaw's death, and from 1991 through 1996 were acquired *en bloc* in a series of transactions by the Littleton Coin Co. amounting to about $250,000. Morris Moscow lived until 1993.

Highlights of the hoard included:

Forty-four 1914-D Lincoln cents, 160 1912-S Liberty Head nickels, 29 1918/7-D Buffalo nickels, 241 1916-D Mercury dimes, 600 1921 dimes, 450 1921-D dimes, 166 1942/1 overdate dimes, 29 1896-S Barber quarter dollars, 8 1901-S quarters, 20 1913-S quarters, 19 1916 Standing Liberty quarters, 3 1918/7-S quarters, and these Barber half dollars: 14 1892-O, 8 1892-S, 6 1893-S, 17 1896-S, 16 1897-O, 10 1897-S, 22 1898-O, 16 1901-S, 29 1913, 25 1914, and 36 1915.[2]

Other Littleton Finds

The Subway Hoard was the latest in a string of interesting "finds" acquired over the years by Littleton Coin Co.[3] In the mid-1980s the firm acquired from a dealer 90 unsearched bags of worn Liberty Head nickels (minted for circulation from 1883 to 1912), which amounted to exactly 360,000 coins! The intermediary in the transaction related that for many years the nickels had been stored in a barn under a pile of hay. The same person is said to have another 100 bags of

[1] His first offering of 1942/1 dimes appeared in the February 1945 issue.

[2] David Sundman, Littleton Coin Co., conversation, July 11, 1996, and letter, July 22, 1996. Certain of these coins were offered in the *Littleton Showcase,* July-August 1996, p. 1. James Reardon, Littleton's chief buyer, acted in the transaction. The quantities of coins given as "highlights" do not necessarily reflect the quantities or proportions of the coins found by Mr. Moscow, as many pieces had been sold by Mr. Shaw over the years. An article on Morris Moscow, "Cache-ing in on T.A.," by Gersh Kuntzman, appeared in the *New York Post,* August 14, 1996.

[3] David Sundman, letter, October 18, 1996.

Liberty Head nickels and over 100 bags of Indian cents! David Sundman, president of Littleton Coin, stated that his staff found about 25 specimens of the rare 1885 Liberty Head nickel when they sorted through the trove, and other scarce and rare issues were found as well.

Elsewhere on the Numismatic Scene

In the 1950s Cleveland dealer Michael Kolman, Jr., took a fancy to worn 20-cent pieces, which were selling for about $5 to $15 each, depending upon the grade. He amassed many hundreds of them, perhaps even more, while his colleagues looked on with amusement. Kolman had the last laugh, however, for in the 1960s there arose a great interest in collecting nineteenth-century coins by design types—when new albums were marketed by the Coin and Currency Institute and by Whitman Publishing Co.—and the value of his worn 20-cent pieces multiplied several times over! This account may be related to one told by David Sundman, who heard from a West Coast dealer (the "grapevine" is very active in numismatics!) that in the 1960s another dealer had accumulated "nearly a bag" of worn 20-cent pieces.

Then there is the story of more than 1,000 pieces of old currency in $500 and $1,000 U.S. bills that came on the market in the early 1990s. And, while we're at it, what happened to the seven $10,000 bills that Amon Carter, Jr., sometimes carried in his suit coat pocket as conversation pieces? This reminds me of the $1 million in $10,000 bills on display at Binion's Horseshoe Club in Las Vegas.

Doubtless, any old-time dealer or collector could add to the preceding list of hoards within the numismatic hobby, as the list is endless.

A Wise Museum Curator

Acquired: 1920s
Dispersed: 1995
Numismatic hoard: Scarce coins of the 1920s

In the 1890s and early part of the present century Joseph C. Mitchelson, of Tariffville, Connecticut, was a coin collector and dealer.[1] Actually, he seems to have been a collector first, and while he was buying coins he needed, if he saw some interesting duplicates or pieces that his friends wanted, he would buy these as well.

Born on May 22, 1856, in Tariffville, he entered the family tobacco business after completing his education. At the time, the Connecticut River Valley was a leading producer of tobacco, and Mitchelson was a wholesaler of that then-popular substance. Seeking markets and visiting clients, he traveled widely, including frequent trips to the Midwest and West. For a time he was located in Kansas and had branch outlets in Kansas City and San Francisco. In 1900 he returned permanently to Tariffville and conducted his business from that location, which included the family farm comprising more than 1,000 acres in nearby Simsbury.[2]

He acquired many coins as duplicates or selling stock. Among his numismatic clients was John M. Clapp, oil man and banker from Pennsylvania. The Clapp Collection, which had been augmented by later purchases by his son, John H. Clapp, was sold via Stack's to Louis E. Eliasberg, Sr., in 1942 for $100,000—a very impressive sum for the time, and one rivaled only by the J.W. Ellsworth Collection sold for the same amount in 1921 through art dealers Knoedler & Co. to Wayte Raymond and John Work Garrett.

Mitchelson passed to his reward on September 25, 1911, and his collection was bequeathed to the State of Connecticut. Before long his collection, valued at $70,000, was on display in specially constructed vaults in the Connecticut State Library in Hartford. Visitors were dazzled at the display which included sets of gold Proof coins from the second half of the nineteenth century, colonial rarities, early silver dollars, Fractional Currency, and other treasures. Provision was made for the collection to be supervised by the state librarian, who was, by legislative authorization, "to continue the Joseph C. Mitchelson Collection of coins, tokens, and medals by adding each year a Proof specimen, or if not so coined, an Uncirculated specimen of each variety of coin minted in the several mints of the United States."

As it turned out, in the mid-1920s the curator not only bought one each of certain coins, but acquired

1 Information is from Joseph C. Mitchelson's obituary in *The Numismatist,* October 1911, and personal visits to the Connecticut State Library and visits with curators Kathleen Plourde, David White, and Dean Nelson. David Corrigan of the Library also assisted during a visit.

2 Simsbury has its own numismatic connection as a source of copper for the Higley threepence coinage of 1737-1739.

numerous duplicates as well. Prominent among these purchases were two examples of the later-to-be-rare 1927-D $20 gold piece; roll quantities of 1924-D and 1925-D Buffalo nickels and Mercury dimes; a roll of 1924-D Standing Liberty quarters; and many other delicacies.

Over a period of time leading rare coin dealers and auctioneers beat a path to the steps of the Connecticut State Library, seeking to handle the Mitchelson coins as well as later acquisitions. In 1994-1995, the Library decided to deaccession certain coins acquired after Mitchelson's gift. Included were many sparkling gems from the 1920s among which were the aforementioned nickels, dimes, quarters, and one of the 1927-D $20 pieces. The nod was given to Heritage Numismatic Auctions, which featured them in a sale held on June 1-3, 1996, with the Long Beach Coin & Stamp Exposition in California. Great collector and dealer interest was shown, and intense bidding activity resulted. The wisdom of an earlier curator who in the 1920s had spent a few extra dollars for duplicates now came home in spades!

CHAPTER 20

Other Hoards and Accumulations

Hoarded: Various times
Dispersed: Various times
Numismatic items: Miscellaneous

Below are many brief descriptions—arranged in order by denomination and date—of hoards and numismatic accumulations not discussed elsewhere in the text. Emphasis is on scarcer issues and earlier dates. After the early 1930s every issue of coin from the Lincoln cent to the Liberty Walking half dollar was saved in roll (sometimes bag) quantities by investors and dealers. Thus, these later issues are not treated, for there would be no end to the accounts.

Over the years a number of collectors and dealers have endeavored to hoard one variety or another in a favorite series. As numismatic accumulations are different in concept than hoards and do not represent newly-found items coming onto the market, these have the notation "(numismatic accumulation)" after each.[1]

1856 Flying Eagle cents: This pattern cent has been the object of desire of several hoarders including the aforementioned (see earlier entries) Messrs. George W. Rice and John A. Beck.

R.B. Leeds, of Atlantic City, New Jersey, also bought many of these over a period of time. Henry Chapman sold the Leeds Collection on November 27-28, 1906, noting at that time: "For many years he was an ardent collector, turning his attention to accumulating all the examples he could of certain dates, his especial hobby being 1856 Eagle cents of which he had 109 specimens, the greatest collection ever offered of this very rare cent. Mr. Leeds was a firm believer in the rarity and value of this coin, and bought all that he could for many years past. The advance of the past 10 years has proved his judgment to have been correct" (numismatic accumulation).

1857 Flying Eagle cents: Commodore W.C. Eaton gathered 115 specimens of 1857 (mostly) and 1858 Flying Eagle cents in the 1910s and early 1920s. These were sold as Lot 547 in Henry Chapman's sale of May 7, 1929, to Floyd Starr. Sold by Stack's in October 1992 and January 1993 as part of the Floyd Starr estate (numismatic accumulation).[2]

1858 Flying Eagle cents: Dealer Richard Snow has told of a hoard of 30 or so 1858 Large Letters pieces that came to light many years ago in Upstate New York. These were sold as "Proofs" a leading dealer, and, apparently, closely resembled the Proof product. By now the hoard is widely distributed. While the die characteristics were not recorded, they may be from the Large Letters die with a tiny crack extending downward to the rim from near the right tip of the eagle's tail.

1861 Indian cents: John Dannreuther commented:[4] "There was a small hoard of 15 to 30 pieces, I believe, of very choice Mint State coins several years ago. In fact, there was a MS-68 (the only copper-nickel cent ever graded this high by PCGS) and several MS-66 and MS-67 pieces."

1862 Indian cents: On January 25 and 26, 1918, Thomas L. Elder conducted an auction featuring the Robert Hewitt and B.C. Bartlett collections. Lot 318 was described: "1862 C. Nickel. Bright. Unc. 125 pcs." This was followed by lots 319 to 323, each described as "Bright Unc." and each containing 100 coins. Then came Lot 324, also of 100 coins, "Unc. red." Apparently, these were toned. Lot 325 featured 50 specimens, "Unc. Bright." To this point 775

---

[1] James C. Gray, letters, August and September, 1996, and various *Gobrecht Journal* Collective Volumes, Dr. John McCloskey, editor, various as cited, were useful in regard to Liberty Seated coins.

[2] Eaton is discussed at length under 1857 Flying Eagle cents in Q. David Bowers, *A Buyer's and Enthusiast's Guide to Flying Eagle and Indian Cents,* 1996.

[3] Letter, April 10, 1996; modified by letter, May 3, 1996; quoted in Bowers, *Flying Eagle and Indian Cents,* 1996.

[4] Letter, May 13, 1996; quoted in Bowers, *Flying Eagle and Indian Cents,* 1996.

pieces of Mint State 1862 cents had been offered. Then followed three lots of 100 coins each, described as containing mixed cents dated from 1857 to 1862, each including "many" 1862 cents, but without the number specified. Accordingly, it is probable that the Elder hoard consisted of about 1,000 specimens of this date.[1]

Another hoard: In his *Encyclopedia of Proof Coins* Walter Breen tantalizingly mentioned, "a hoard [of Proofs] is known," without elucidating; apparently, this referred to a small group, estimated to have been as high as 200 or more, but possibly only a few dozen, that turned up at the Mint in the late 1870s.[2]

1872 Indian cents: Numismatist Carl Herkowitz began in the 1980s to save business strike examples of this scarce date, and by September 1996 he had 151 coins. This "keeps hoarders from getting them," he observed whimsically (numismatic accumulation).[3]

1886 Indian cents, Type II obverse: On June 4, 1994, a farmer from Southbury, Connecticut, stopped by to visit Bill Wright, who had set up a display of coins for sale at a flea market.[4] Taking a coin from a bag, he quickly showed it to Bill, said it was an 1884 Indian cent, and that he had 32 pieces that with some other coins he had found in a bottle buried in the ground. Bill, who was more interested in selling coins than buying them, said that such a coin might be worth $50 or so. The visitor also related that he had nine "new 1883 V nickels" and two silver dollars with a CC on each. After viewing some coins in the case, including a trade dollar, the farmer allowed that what he had were two trade dollars. On July 2 the farmer came back with the Indian cents, all 32 of them, and this time let Bill inspect them carefully, upon which inspection it was found that they were not 1884s at all, but were of the 1886 Type II variety. He reported that the nickels were no longer available as his wife had sold them to their television cable installer. Bill bought the Indian cents. They later graded mostly MS-63 and MS-64, red and brown.

1909 V.D.B. Lincoln cents: Released on August 2, 1909, these coins were an immediate sensation, as just about everyone had spent a lifetime seeing nothing but Indian cents or, for old-timers, large cents years earlier. The Lincoln cents were widely hoarded. Today in the 1990s rolls sometimes still come on the market. The writer recalls seeing an account of thousands of these coming to light in the 1960s or 1970s when loot from a train robbery was found, but as this book goes to press the specific clipping could not be located.

1909-S V.D.B. Lincoln cents: In addition to the alleged hoard once owned by John Zug, there have been other accounts of groups of this low-mintage cent. Arthur M. Kagin related:[5] "In early 1952 I received an inquiry from a California collector asking for an offer on an Uncirculated roll of 1909-S, V.D.B. cents, I offered him $500 per roll. Each roll had 50 coins in it. About 10 days later five rolls arrived. About two weeks after sending him the check another five rolls arrived. In sending him the check I stated that I would buy all he had at the same price as I didn't want him to break the market by offering a large quantity at one time. About four or five months later a number of ads appeared in the *Numismatic Scrapbook Magazine* offering Uncirculated 1909-S V.D.B. cents at $12 to $15 each. Apparently, he had sold more rolls to other people."

1914-D cents: In the 1970s two rolls of Uncirculated coins, 100 pieces total, turned up in Hawaii (another account says the Philippine Islands). The writer examined several pieces said to have been from that source, and they were spotted red and brown. Walter Breen writes that a "hoard of at least 700 Uncirculated specimens existed until the early 1950s."[6]

1922-D Lincoln cents: Maurice Scharlack of Corpus Christi, Texas, loved 1922-D cents, and over a long period of years in the 1930s through the 1950s accumulated thousands of them, mostly in worn grades (numismatic accumulation).

1931-S Lincoln cents: In the 1930s when it was reported that only 866,000 pieces were coined of this date and mint, there ensued a scramble to hoard them. Walter Breen reported that the Maurice Scharlack hoard contained "over 200,000 red Uncirculated specimens, many weak."[7] As late as the 1950s it was not unusual to see these traded by the roll at coin conventions. Later, most were broken up.

1955 Doubled Die cents: In the late 1950s the writer and his partner, James F. Ruddy, ran advertisements in upstate New York and Massachusetts newspapers offering to buy these coins, which had originally been distributed in those areas. At one time 800 pieces were on hand, all mounted in large-size Raymond "National" album pages—what a sight! Only a small percentage could be described as brilliant Uncirculated. Over a period of time these were sold to various collectors and dealers.

1972 Doubled Die cents: John Hamrick, well-known Georgia dealer and partner in WorldWide Coin Investments,[8] found thousands of these in bags of 1972 cents he had obtained earlier. Other numismatists made discoveries as well. Probably fewer than 20,000 came on the market totally.

The Hamrick coins were found in a very interesting manner. WorldWide desired to keep a stock of current coins on hand, and ordered some Mint-sealed $50 bags of cents from Philadelphia dealer partners Harry J. Forman and Ruth Bauer. When these bags arrived in Atlanta, John Hamrick tossed them into the trunk of his car and left them there, as they

---

1 Catalogue copy furnished by Frank Campbell, American Numismatic Society, New York City; hoard quoted in Bowers, *Flying Eagle and Indian Cents,* 1996.

2 Richard Snow, letter, April 10, 1996 (higher estimate); R.W. Julian, letter, April 24, 1996 (lower estimate); here adapted from Bowers, *Flying Eagle and Indian Cents,* 1996.

3 Letter, September 10, 1996.

4 William M. Wright, Jr., letter, August 1995.

5 Letter, August 24, 1996.

6 *Encyclopedia,* 1988, p. 228.

7 *Ibid.*, p. 230.

8 WorldWide, located in Atlanta, offered its stock to the public. It may have been the first rare coin firm to install a large computer (Burroughs make) in house.

had no premium value, and he was busy with other things. Later in the year he heard about the 1972 Doubled Dies, remembered the bags in his trunk, searched through them, and became thousands of dollars richer![1]

1995 Doubled Die cents: In 1995 there was a free-for-all in the coin hobby when it was discovered early in the year that some Lincoln cents were slightly doubled on the obverse, particularly at LIBERTY. Many advertisements for these appeared in popular periodicals, and one dealer, Rich Stiles, seemed to be at the center of activity and sold thousands of them, including some that his clients found in bulk, unsorted bags of cents he had sold.

1873 silver three-cents: A holding of several dozen of these was stolen in the 1930s. Walter Breen stated: "The Mint's publicity agent, Arthur Madsen Smith, had a hoard of at least 300."[2] However, numismatic historian Pete Smith, who has studied Smith's activities in detail, says the Breen comment "is curious since Smith did not move to Philadelphia until 1876, and it took him a while to establish Mint connections."[3] If Smith had such pieces, he must have acquired them from secondary sources.

1883 Liberty nickels without CENTS: These were widely hoarded at the time of issue, and quantities still remain in the hands of the public. It is not unusual for these pieces to come on the market a few dozen at a time. In fact, the Louis E. Eliasberg, Sr. Collection sale of May 1996 included among the duplicates over 100 sparkling Uncirculated pieces. At one time in the 1950s a rare coin dealer put a basket full of these—grades ranged from Extremely Fine to Mint State—in his shop window.

1939 Jefferson nickels with doubled MONTICELLO: Boston dealer Malcolm O.E. Chell-Frost discovered this dramatic variety about 1939, and forthwith began searching for them in circulation. Others were advised to keep on the lookout, and from these and other sources more were acquired, until he had several hundred pieces. Virtually all of these—95% or more—were worn.

It was not until the 1960s that collecting these and other doubled die varieties became popular in a large way. As time went on, such numismatists as Frank Spadone, James Johnson, Bill Fivaz, and J.T. Stanton did much to publicize these nickels and dozens of other interesting varieties, with the result that today there is a strong demand for some of the more notable ones. The 1939 nickel with doubled MONTICELLO remains quite elusive, and the Chell-Frost hoard has long since been dispersed.

1848 Liberty Seated half dimes, Large Date variety: In the 1970s dealer Bill Grayson had a group of about 75 pieces (numismatic accumulation).[4]

1863-S to 1872-S Liberty Seated half dimes: Quantity of several hundred pieces found in Hong Kong in the 1950s. Each had some silver scraped away at the center of the Liberty Seated figure on the obverse, a location where its removal would not be immediately noticed.[5]

1844 Liberty Seated dimes: Scarce, low-mintage issue sometimes referred to as the "Orphan Annie Dime." One West Coast numismatist took a fancy to this particular variety in the 1980s and acquired over 200 of them (numismatic accumulation).

1856 Liberty Seated dimes, Small Date variety: Gerry Fortin acquired a hoard of about 70 pieces in the 1980s (numismatic accumulation).[6]

1860-O Liberty Seated dimes: Sometime before autumn 1990 a relic hunter found four examples, each now grading AU-58, at a former Confederate States of America camp site in Warrenton, Virginia.[7]

1869-S Liberty Seated dimes: Several dozen or more of these turned up in the early 1990s in Europe in a former communist country. One piece examined by the author was choice Mint State.

1877-S Liberty Seated dimes: In the 1980s Gerry Fortin had a hoard of 25 pieces (numismatic accumulation).[8]

1898-S Barber dimes: Quantities of 1898-S, 1899-S, and 1900-S dimes were sent to the Philippine Islands at or near the time the coins were minted. Years later many pieces were found, mostly in EF and AU grades and mostly cleaned.[9]

1899-S Barber dimes: Known from the Philippines. See entry under 1898-S dimes.

1900-S Barber dimes: Known from the Philippines. See entry under 1898-S dimes.

1942/1 Mercury dimes: It is said that four rolls of Uncirculated coins (equal to 200 specimens) were found in 1954.[10] The writer recalls no such group coming on the market, but they could have been parceled out one at a time.

1876-CC 20-cent pieces: This is one of the most remarkable finds in the American series. In the late 1950s, Baltimore dealer Tom Warfield found a group of seven, eight, or possibly nine splendid Mint State coins in his home town. Each piece was a lustrous gem, delicately toned, and virtually perfect. It is my opinion that these may have come from someone who once served on the Assay Commission which in 1877 reviewed the prior year's coinage. The genesis of

---

1 John Hamrick, conversation, circa 1972.
2 Breen, ***Encyclopedia,*** 1988, p. 375. Also see A.M. Smith entry in the preceding chapter.
3 Letter, September 8, 1996.
4 Dr. John McCloskey, letter, September 28, 1996.
5 Personal experience; coins purchased and resold.
6 Dr. John McCloskey, letter, September 28, 1996.
7 Bill Bugert, ***Gobrecht Journal,*** November 1990.
8 Dr. John McCloskey, letter, September 28, 1996.
9 David Lawrence, ***The Complete Guide to Barber Dimes,*** 1991, p. 117.
10 Breen, ***Encyclopedia,*** 1988, p. 328.

this cache was never revealed, but was variously thought by others to have been T. Harrison Garrett (who died in 1888, had a fabulous collection, but did not seem to have acquired many mintmarked issues; in my opinion, he can be eliminated as a possibility), Waldo C. Newcomer, or Frank G. Duffield. Even the name of super-collector Louis E. Eliasberg, Sr., was mentioned.

Four of these coins were sold to the author, who subsequently distributed them into as many different collections.[1] Several more were sold to John J. Ford, Jr., of New Netherlands Coin Co., who recalls showing one to Morton Stack, who expressed great surprise and admiration, then quickly showing him a second coin, and selling him both.[2]

The 1876-CC 20-cent piece is one of the most formidable rarities in the Liberty Seated series, and it is believed that fewer than 20 are known. Thus, the "Baltimore Hoard" was and still is of incredible significance.

1852-O Liberty Seated quarters: According to a report, a steamship wreck salvaged in the lower Mississippi River was recovered in the 1980s. Four or five Mint State, but oxidized, quarter dollars were found.[3] Separately, Larry Briggs reported: "Three hoards of 1852-O quarters are known totaling over 120 pieces" (numismatic accumulations).[4]

1854-O Liberty Seated quarters with "Huge O" mintmark: In the 1970s it is believed that a dealer had accumulated a hoard of over 50 examples of this variety by placing advertisements to buy them (numismatic accumulation).[5]

1877-CC Liberty Seated quarters: Hundreds of these came onto the coin market in the 1950s and 1960s, many if not most with the bottom tips of the 77 digits doubled. All were frosty, lustrous examples of great aesthetic appeal. The writer has never been able to learn their source.

1898-S Barber quarters: EF and AU, mostly cleaned. Known from the Philippines. See entry under 1898-S dimes.

1899-S Barber quarters: EF and AU, mostly cleaned. Known from the Philippines. See entry under 1898-S dimes.

1900-S Barber quarters: EF and AU, mostly cleaned. Known from the Philippines. See entry under 1898-S dimes.

1926-D Standing Liberty quarters: Of all quarter dollars of this design type, more 1926-Ds were set aside as bank-wrapped rolls than were any others. However, roll quantities were known of all quarters after about 1924, with the possible exceptions of 1926-S and 1927-S. However, by the end of the 1960s nearly all such holding had been widely dispersed.

1929-S Standing Liberty quarters: A hoard of 100 is said to have been found in California in 1975.[6] Such a group would not have been unusual 20 years earlier in 1955, but by 1975 it was worth noting.

1932-D and S Washington quarters: A New Jersey numismatist took a fancy to these two scarce dates and saved many dozens of Mint State coins, primarily 1932-S. These were sold to Bowers and Merena Galleries in the 1980s and early 1990s (numismatic accumulation).

1842-O Small Date Liberty Seated half dollars: A group of 31 coins was assembled from 1976 to 1983 by Roy Pohler of Cameron, Louisiana. Mr. Pohler also accumulated 1855-S and 1870-CC halves (see below; many of these were acquired for him by dealer Bill Grayson).[7] The finest coin was described as AU, followed by four at the EF level, eight VF coins, and on down to three at the Abt. Good level (numismatic accumulation).[8]

1855-S Liberty Seated half dollars: Accumulated by Roy Pohler of Cameron, Louisiana, from 1976 to 1983, this group contained 87 coins when examined by Randy Wiley in April 1986. The finest was a Mint State (from Steve Ivy's Stanford Sale in 1976) followed by four at the AU level, nine EF coins, on down to 15 that were Abt. Good to Good (numismatic accumulation).[9]

1870-CC Liberty Seated half dollars: Accumulated from 1976 to 1983 by Roy Pohler of Cameron, Louisiana, this group contained 90 coins, the three finest of which were AU, followed by nine at the EF level (numismatic accumulation).[10]

1898-S Barber half dollars: EF and AU, mostly cleaned. Known from the Philippines. See entry under 1898-S dimes.

1899-S Barber half dollars: EF and AU, mostly cleaned. Known from the Philippines. See entry under 1898-S dimes.

1900-S Barber half dollars: EF and AU, mostly cleaned. Known from the Philippines. See entry under 1898-S dimes.

1919-S Liberty Walking half dollars: Arthur M. Kagin, long-time dealer, related this:[11] "In the 1940s or 1950s (some things become a little hazy with time) I bought a roll of 20 Uncirculated halves of 1919-S from a California collector,

---

[1] For listing of these four see Breen, *Encyclopedia,* 1988, p. 335.
[2] Recollection of John J. Ford, Jr., telephone conversation, October 11, 1996.
[3] James C. Gray, letter, September 1996; he purchased one of these coins in 1988.
[4] *The Comprehensive Encyclopedia of United States Liberty Seated Quarters,* 1991, p. 79.
[5] Dr. John McCloskey, letter, September 28, 1996.
[6] Breen, *Encyclopedia,* 1988, p. 365.
[7] Dr. John McCloskey, letter, September 28, 1996.
[8] Randy [Randall] Wiley and Bill Bugert, *The Complete Guide to Liberty Seated Half Dollars,* 1993, p. 64; also see the *Gobrecht Journal,* November 1977, "The Louisiana Hoard," Randall E. Wiley.
[9] Wiley-Bugert, 1993, p. 112. Separately, James C. Gray, letter, August 1996, reported: "I got the pick of that hoard. The coin that I selected was a pristine, almost fully struck, EF-45. A couple of pieces had a slightly higher technical grade but were not nearly as choice as this piece."
[10] Wiley-Bugert, 1993, p. 169.
[11] Letter, August 24, 1996.

who, I found out later, had also sold a roll to Bebee's."

1872-S Liberty Seated silver dollars: A member of the Liberty Seated Collectors Club had 78 pieces which he had purchased over a span of years. This may include about 70 pieces owned in the 1970s by dealer Bill Grayson. These averaged Very Fine to Extremely Fine grade.[1]

1873-CC Liberty Seated silver dollars: Walter Breen stated unequivocally that "three Uncirculateds turned up in a Carson City cornerstone in 1873,"[2] but the author has never been able to find any confirmation of this.

1875 $2.50 gold. Among quarter eagles the 1875 Philadelphia Mint issue is one of the rarest in the series. A Long Island, New York, collector is said to have amassed 18 or more examples of this issue, ranging in grade from Very Good to Mint State.[3]

1878 $3 gold: Dealer Bill Mertes had an original group of 50 pieces in the 1950s and displayed it here and there at coin shows. It is said that later the coins were stolen. The John A. Beck estate sold by Abner Kreisberg and Jerry Cohen ("Quality Sales") contained over 30 pieces. Walter Breen reported seeing a roll of 20.[4] Today, the 1878 is the most often seen Mint State $3 after 1854.

1883 $3 gold: Walter Breen reported that a small hoard was found about 1968; no quantity was given.[5]

1889 $3 gold: It has been reported that in 1889 collector Virgil M. Brand bought 50 of these from the Mint.[6] These would have been dispersed into numismatic circles after his death in 1926.

1853 $10 gold: A few Uncirculated pieces are said to have turned up in a hoard in North Carolina before 1973.[7]

1898-S $10 gold: A few Uncirculated pieces are said to have been found in a "tiny hoard" in 1977.[8]

1908-S $10 gold: A hoard of "at least 20" is said to have been found in the 1940s and a smaller hoard in the 1970s, the latter from Europe.[9] Today, this low-mintage date is a highly prized rarity, and any such hoard coins have been widely distributed.

1909-S $10 gold: A hoard of "about 70 to 90 in all?" is said to have been found in South America about 1977.[10]

1911-S $10 gold: A hoard of 60 is said to have been found in the Philippine Islands circa 1976, transshipped to Spain, and then to New England Rare Coin Galleries.[11]

---

1 Dr. John McCloskey, letter, September 28, 1996.
2 Breen, *Encyclopedia,* 1988, p. 443.
3 Mark Van Winkle, letter, October 3, 1996.
4 Breen, *Encyclopedia,* 1988, p. 508.
5 *Ibid.*, p. 509.
6 *Ibid.*, p. 509.
7 *Ibid.*, p. 553.
8 *Ibid.*, p. 557.
9 *Ibid.*, p. 560.
10 *Ibid.*, pp. 560-561.
11 *Ibid.*, p. 561.

Artist's conception of what it might have been like during one very special day in 1904 in an Irish farmhouse. (Sandy Martin illustration)

CHAPTER 21

Interesting Single-Coin Finds

Assorted Finds and Discoveries

While a "hoard" probably should include at least two coins, there are many single-coin finds that are worth mentioning, at least in passing. Several interesting ones are delineated in this chapter.

The possibilities are virtually endless, as just about every coin that is worn and rare was at some time found by someone. Thus, this is but a sampler:

"A Queer Piece of Money"

Hidden or lost: 17th century
Found: 1893
Treasure: Willow Tree shilling

This account appeared in H.E. Morey's *Numismatic Quarterly and Catalogue,* January 1894:

> While digging a cellar on the Deacon Faulkner estate in Malden [Massachusetts], an Irishman found a queer piece of money. A gentleman passing by offered the Irishman a quarter for it. Pat accepted at once, pleased at getting something he could spend, while the gentleman added a fine Willow Tree shilling to his collection.[1]

Not so fortunate was the real (apparently) find of some unreal (apparently) coins reported in the same journal:

> A portion of the famous buried treasure of the late Captain Kidd [*very* late!] was found in Malden recently, or rather that is what a workman thought while digging on Hawthorne Street when he struck a two-quart pail filled with shining metal coins. He was an employee of Lyman B. Jordan and was digging a post-hole when he struck a metallic substance.
>
> Investigation proved the find to be a pail containing coins of the denominations of dollars, halves, and quarters. They were new and were dated 1860 and 1863. The man's dream of wealth was shattered, however, after he had them tested, for they proved counterfeit. How or when they were buried there is a mystery.

In an Irish Farmhouse

Lost: 18th or 19th century
Found: 1904
Treasure: 1787 Clinton copper and other coins

In Rural Ireland

Sometime before early 1905, presumably in the warmer months of the preceding year, 1904, an American numismatist made a tour of Ireland.[2]

Stopping at a rural farmhouse the collector engaged its owner in conversation. Finally, the topic turned to old coins, and "the farmer said he had a few stowed away somewhere that he had no use for."

---

[1] There is the possibility this might have been a joke rather than a legitimate report, as it was common at the time to poke fun at the innocent nature of Irishmen, and "Pat" was sometimes used as a generic name in this regard.

[2] From an account, "Europe Hunting Place For Coins," in the *Boston Sunday Herald,* April 30, 1905, furnished by David Sundman, Littleton Coin Co.

After duly rummaging around he brought forth a small box that appeared to be filled with old Roman coins of low value, perhaps from the time centuries earlier when Romans occupied Britain. Glancing quickly over the lot, the visitor saw nothing of value, offered a couple of dollars, consummated a transaction, and put the coins in his trunk.

After returning to the United States the collector opened the box:

> Upon examining the coins he was surprised to find a beautiful specimen of a New York cent of the date of 1787, one of the rarest of the colonial coins. This coin is known as the Clinton cent, having been issued when George Clinton was governor of New York, and bearing his portrait. The coin was worth up in the hundreds of dollars, but just how much no one knows, for there are only four of them known.

The 1787 copper Clinton cent is indeed a major rarity, and today in the 1990s it is believed that only 10 to 12 are known. Whether the Irish find was one of these, or was a copy (such as made by James Bolen) that was "laundered" through this tale, is not known. If the latter, it would still be collectible today, but would be worth but a tiny fraction of the price of an original.

A Find in France

Exported: 19th century
Found: Circa 1904
Treasure: $50 gold "slug"

A remarkable "find" was made in Europe by a "millionaire collector from one of the New England states," who visited the head of one of the larger French financial institutions. This account appeared in a 1905 newspaper story: [1]

> The banker said that in one of their branch banks was a $50 gold piece which he could have at face value, and welcome.
>
> Of course, the collector could not eat or sleep until he had located the coveted coin. It was found to be just as represented, in splendid condition. The new owner now says that $500 would not buy it.
>
> And there are hundreds of other chances awaiting the lucky man in the thousand and one old shops in European cities.

One can but speculate if the aforementioned $50 piece was one that had been part of a $200,000 shipment of coins of this denomination—some 4,000 pieces!—from New York City to Liverpool on the steamer *Asia,* cited in a newspaper account on January 13, 1853.[2]

A Great Rarity, This

Hidden or lost: 17th century
Found: 1910
Treasure: Pine Tree shilling

The earlier accounts in Chapter 1, including one of 6,000 shillings, differ dramatically in the quantity of pieces from a newspaper story of years later, October 24, 1910, concerning another find, this being but a single piece:[3]

> Coin Made in 1652 Found in Field
>
> Cassius D. Phelps, a South Williamstown merchant, while plowing in a field, found one of the rarest of American coins, a Massachusetts Pine Tree shilling, for which he has refused $300. It is one of the first coins which was minted in the Massachusetts Bay Colony and is dated 1652, 32 years after the landing of the Pilgrims at Plymouth.
>
> There are only two others like it in existence, and neither is as good a specimen as this one. One is owned by a Boston collector and cost him $212, and the other is owned in Albany, and no price will be placed upon it.

As is true of many, indeed most accounts of coin finds in the popular press, the preceding yields virtually nothing in the way of numismatic information. At the time an ordinary Massachusetts 1652 Pine Tree shilling would have been worth just a few dollars.

---

1 From an account, "Europe Hunting Place For Coins," in the *Boston Sunday Herald,* April 30, 1905, furnished by David Sundman, Littleton Coin Co.

2 Mentioned by Edgar H. Adams, *Private Gold Coinage,* 1912, p. 51.

3 As quoted in the *American Journal of Numismatics,* 1910, p. 178.

An 1804 Dollar in a Pot of Coins

Hidden: 19th century
Found: December 26, 1913
Treasure: 1804 dollar (or was it?)

"The King of American Coins"

In the annals of American numismatics no coin has received as much coverage as the legendary 1804 silver dollar.[1] Indeed, the 1804 has been called "The King of American coins." The facts, summarized, are these:

Although Mint records state that 19,570 silver dollars were minted in calendar year 1804, nowhere is it stated that the coins actually bore the 1804 date. At the time it was Mint practice to keep using dies of earlier dates until they broke or wore out. Sometimes these older dies were overdated (the 1802/1 dollar is an example), but often the original dates were retained as made, quite probably because the dies had already been hardened for use, and the overpunching (overdating) procedure required that the dies be heated to a high temperature, cooled, and cleaned, a painstaking process. Thus, it is believed that the "1804" dollars struck in 1804 bore earlier dates such as 1803 and possibly earlier dates as well.

Numismatic knowledge was scarce in America in the early 1830s. The first specialized book on United States coins had yet to be written, and the Mint's own collection—the Mint Cabinet—would not be formed until June 1838, although "master coins" (Proofs) of certain issues had been saved for a number of years in anticipation of the establishment of a collection within the Mint.[2]

These coins were to be fitted in special cases and to contain one coin of each denomination made by the United States. On November 11, 1834, the Department of State ordered two special sets of United States coinage to be made up by the Philadelphia Mint for presentation to the King of Siam and the Imam of Muscat, the latter being active in world commerce (especially opium) and with whose country it was anticipated there would be opportunities for trade.[3]

At the time the currently-produced coins included the half cent, cent, half dime, dime, quarter, half dollar, gold quarter eagle, and gold half eagle. Proofs dated 1834 were made of each of these. A search of Mint records revealed that two other denominations were still authorized, but had not been struck for many years. Silver dollars had been last struck in 1804 and $10 gold eagles were last struck in that year as well. What the coiners of the Mint had no way of knowing in 1834, as no numismatic check list had ever been printed, was that while $10 gold coins struck in 1804 were dated 1804, the silver dollars minted in that year were of earlier date(s).

Seeking to present coins that were historically accurate, the engraver and coiner at the Mint simply made up new silver dollar and $10 gold dies bearing the 1804 date, to illustrate these coins of yesteryear, believed to have been made, but for which no specimens were on hand. This was done in all good faith, and in 1834, for the first time 1804-dated silver dollars were struck. There was no intent to deceive anyone or make any kind of misrepresentation.

As years went on, Mint officials such as Jacob R. Eckfeldt and William E. DuBois became more numismatically knowledgeable. In time, the Mint Cabinet became a reality, and an invitation was extended to coin collectors to make exchanges with the Mint. This cordial, open-handed practice was continued until at least 1859, as evidenced by Mint Director (1853-1861) James Ross Snowden issuing a printed circular inviting trades.

On May 9, 1843, Matthew A. Stickney visited the Mint and obtained an 1804 silver dollar in an open exchange documented by letters, a coin which was to grace several illustrious cabinets later, including that of Louis E. Eliasberg, Sr., the well-known Baltimore numismatist.

---

[1] Citations furnished by David Sundman, Littleton Coin Co. The illustration is of an authentic Class III 1804 dollar from the Garrett Collection and is not the specimen found in the pot. The numismatic background of the 1804 dollar is adapted from Bowers, *Louis E. Eliasberg, Sr.: King of Coins,* 1996; this account, in turn, was based upon *The Fantastic 1804 Dollar,* by Eric P. Newman and Kenneth E. Bressett, 1962, and Bowers, 1992, *Silver Dollars and Trade Dollars of the United States: A Complete Encyclopedia.* The Eliasberg Collection contained a prize authentic 1804 silver dollar tracing its pedigree to the U.S. Mint, where a previous owner, Matthew A. Stickney, obtained it in trade in 1843.

[2] James Ross Snowden, *A Description of Ancient and Modern Coins in the Mint Cabinet,* 1860, p. iii.

[3] A trade agreement with Muscat was concluded in 1835, and a few years later the *Sultanée* arrived in the port of New York City laden with coffee, indigo, and other goods. A contemporary view is provided by "Our Trade With the Imam of Muscat," *The Merchants' Magazine and Commercial Review,* 1840, p. 61.

The philosophy was to change. Apparently, an element of cupidity entered the equation by the late 1850s during a rapid growth stage in numismatic interest and a corresponding rise in market values. Certain Mint employees realized that the 1804-dated dollar was a rare and valuable coin indeed, and that it would be profitable to strike more examples and sell them privately, rather than in open exchange for the benefit of the Mint Cabinet.

It seems that at this time, circa the late 1850s, the reverse die used to produce earlier versions of the 1804-dated dollar could not be found, and a hitherto unused reverse die of the same design, but differing in minor details, was employed. Coins from this new combination were made and sold secretly. Some of these were brought by collectors back to the Mint to be authenticated, and on several occasions various Mint officials were all too happy to pronounce them to be genuine original coins actually made in the year 1804. In time, various stories were devised by collectors and romanticists to explain why only a dozen or so examples were known of the 1804 silver dollar, in spite of the Mint report that 19,570 were made.

Varieties of 1804 Dollars

Today in the 1990s, the following sequence of production is believed by numismatists to be accurate:

> VARIETIES OF 1804 DOLLARS:
>
> For many years 1804 dollars were called "originals" or "restrikes," depending upon which reverse die was used. Today, the following classifications are employed:
>
> Class I 1804-dated dollars: Reverse die with E in STATES over a cloud. "Original" dollars of the first type, first coined in 1834 for diplomatic presentation purposes, and perhaps continued to be coined through the mid-1850s. Eight specimens are known to exist, several of which are in museums. The Eliasberg Collection coin, earlier from the Stickney Collection, is a Class I.
>
> Class II 1804-dated dollars: Reverse die with E in STATES over junction between two clouds. Plain edge. "Restrike." Made in 1858. Only one known, struck over a Swiss dollar-sized silver coin. In the National Coin Collection in the Smithsonian Institution.
>
> Class III 1804-dated dollars: Reverse die as preceding. "Restrike." Lettered edge. Made circa late 1850s onward, last date of manufacture unknown, but possibly into the late 1860s or early 1870s. Six specimens are known to exist.

From the mid-nineteenth century to the present time, more columns of print have been devoted to the 1804 silver dollar in the pages of *The Numismatist* than to any other single United States rarity. The *Guide Book of United States Coins* currently gives more space to the 1804 dollar than to any other coin and has done so for many editions. Walter Breen's 1988 *Encyclopedia* devotes three pages to it.

For well over a century the possession of an 1804 silver dollar in a collection has bestowed an aura of glory upon its owner. More than any other single coin the 1804 dollar has attracted a lot of attention in numismatic circles. A book has been written about it and posters have featured its image. From time to time specimens on display at museums such the Smithsonian Institution (Washington, D.C.), the American Numismatic Association (Colorado Springs), and the Museum of Western History (Omaha) have drawn thousands of visitors.

Often, the significance and excellence of an old-time collection or catalogue of that collection has been judged, rightly or wrongly, by whether it contained a specimen of the hallowed 1804. Ever since the true history of the "King of United States Coins" has been recorded in the Newman-Bressett book, this coin has been in greater demand and has brought higher prices.

All Eyes on New Haven

With the preceding background in mind, today's reader in the 1990s can well imagine the excitement that this news article, datelined December 27, 1913, New Haven, Connecticut, caused among collectors at the time:

> Numismatists flocked to this city today in an effort to get possession of the 1804 silver dollar which was found in a pot of coins and old documents unearthed at the excavation for the Yale hockey rink in this city yesterday.
>
> Col. J.P. Hart of Philadelphia, representing a wealthy collector of that city, was early on the ground with an offer of $2,000 for the coin and obtained permission to take it to New York to further its authenticity. Other offers, one of $1,200 for the coin, have already been received.

On January 8, 1914, a further account emanated from New Haven:

> The 1804 silver dollar found several weeks ago at the excavating for the Arena-Centerfreeze Company's hockey rink is still undisposed of, and the numismatists have not completed their examination of it. It has been pronounced genuine, but there is some question as to whether it was issued in 1804, or is one of the few struck off the die in 1858.
>
> The coin was found by William Sullivan, an assistant foreman of the work of excavation. Under the Connecticut law the property found belongs to the Arena-Centerfreeze Company.

What happened to this "1804 silver dollar" is not known, but even if it had been a circa 1858 striking (today known as the Class III 1804 dollar) it would have had great value. More likely, it was adjudged spurious. In any event, the ardor for its possession seems to have subsided by two weeks after its discovery.

What about the "pot of coins" of which this fabled

1804 was a part? Sorry, but there seems to be no information about those pieces either.

The 1804 dollar seems to be a mother lode for coin stories, and over the years many have appeared in print, including this one of a special Mint visitor (shades of Sir Rowland Winn; see Chapter 18):[1]

Édouard Frossard in his house organ, *Numisma,* May 1884, told of a "perfectly struck, brilliant, nearly Proof, almost high relief, sharp, strong dollar of 1804" in an oval morocco presentation case, with this inscribed in gold lettering on the outside cover:

> Presented to Frank S. Houghton, Esq're, on the occasion of his visit at the National Mint in Philadelphia July 4th 1804, his fortieth birthday, Elias Boudinot, Director.

In their 1962 book on the 1804 dollar, Eric P. Newman and Kenneth E. Bressett lamented that "it is disillusioning that the Mint has not kept up such a pleasant custom of giving birthday presents on a national holiday when it was closed."

Other tales relate to 1804 dollars lost at sea (near China, Central America, or Africa) or seized by pirates, or even swiped by a tramp, as in this caper:

Another 1804 Dollar Comes to Light

It must have been a slow day for news on July 22, 1895, when *The New York Daily Tribune* informed its readers of two men named Schultz and a great rarity:[2]

> Judge Fitzgerald, sitting Sessions, the other day had before him a man named Charles Schultz, who was arraigned for theft. The complainant was one Felix Schultz, who said he had recently been appealed to for assistance by a stranger, who gave his name as Charles Schultz. It was evident from his appearance that he was in hard luck. Felix Schultz was moved by the sad story told by Charles to take him into his house, where food and a night's lodging were generously provided.
>
> The next morning Charles had gone and so had Felix's new trousers, his grandfather's gold watch and chain and some money and coins that were in the pockets. The police were promptly informed of the case, and Charles was arrested and arraigned before Judge Fitzgerald. T.F. Gibbons, a lawyer, of No. 105 West Tenth Street, appeared for Felix Schultz. During the examination it was discovered that Charles had Felix's trousers on, and he admitted that he had pawned the jewelry.
>
> As Judge Fitzgerald was about to sentence Charles to Sing Sing, Felix importuned him to mitigate the sentence if Charles would tell what he had done with a pocket-piece, a silver dollar of the coinage of 1804, that he prized from the fact it had been in his family for three generations.
>
> Judge Fitzgerald asked the prisoner what he had done with the coin. The prisoner said he had tried to pass it in a saloon, but the proprietor refused to take it because it was so old. He then, on the advice of the bartender, took the coin to a dealer in old coins in Broadway, who offered him $75 for it. He concluded to try other dealers in coins. He named the Scott Stamp and Coin Company (Ltd.), in East Twenty-Third Street, who, he asserted, purchased it for $90.
>
> "We have begun a suit against the Scott Company, of East Twenty-Third Street, for the recovery of this coin," said Mr. Gibbons, "and the case is to be tried before Judge Roesh on the 30th inst. The Scott Company have made a general denial of ever having purchased the coin."
>
> Of the 1804 dollars, all but 12 that were issued were returned to the Mint owing to an omission in stamping them. Of the 12 outstanding, 11 have been accounted for and this coin which is dispute is supposed to be the missing one.
>
> Mr. Gibbons said he had demanded $5,000 from the Scott Company. He also said that an uptown dealer catalogued the coin as being worth from $600 to $2,400.

The Ultimate Rarity!

As a parting commentary on rare 1804 dollars it is perhaps significant, certainly interesting, to reprint this news clipping dated Bunkie, Louisiana, March 4, 1930:[3]

> The proverbial end-of-the-rainbow story came true yesterday for Forest Normand, Avoyelles Parish farmer, when he plowed up a pot of silver coins on his farm near here. While plowing, he noticed a few coins turned up, and upon closer investigation, unearthed an old iron pot, rusty with age, containing more than 3,000 pieces of Spanish silver, coins from 1763 to 1805. Included in the find was an American silver dollar bearing the date 1804 with the likeness of George Washington.

Presumably, this is the ultimate United States rarity, an 1804 silver dollar showing the Father of Our Country rather than Miss Liberty!

A Long-Lost Proof Set

Lost or saved: 19th century
Found: 1940s
Treasure: 1842 Proof set

In the 1930s and 1940s, Oscar G. Schilke used to advertise in newspapers to buy coins. In addition, he had an arrangement with certain banks in Connecticut and New York whereby he would visit their lobbies and conduct free coin appraisals for bank clients.

---

1 Adapted from Eric P. Newman and Kenneth E. Bressett, *The Fantastic 1804 Dollar,* 1962, Chapter III, "Disappearance Stories."
2 Citation furnished by Wayne Homren.
3 Quoted by Lyle Saxon, *Lafitte the Pirate,* 1930, p. 296.

Over a period of time he acquired many interesting things.

One of his prize finds was brought to him by a Connecticut lady who found a group of copper and silver coins in a small case stored under some other things in a bedroom chest of drawers. Oscar could hardly believe his eyes as he contemplated a glittering United States Proof set of the year 1842, containing one each of the half cent, large cent, half dime, dime, quarter dollar, half dollar, and silver dollar.

While such a set is exceedingly rare and of immense value, this particular 1842 group contained a special rarity: the Liberty Seated quarter dollar was of the variety with Small Date numerals. In that year, all quarter dollars made at the Philadelphia Mint for circulation in commerce had the date in larger numerals. A few presentation Proof sets—probably not more than a dozen or two—contained quarters from the special Small Date die. This was one of them.

Today, fewer than 10 1842 Small Date quarters are known, and the Schilke Collection specimen, which later appeared in the Century Collection Sale (1965) may be the finest of these.

A "Little Princess" Makes Her Debut

Lost: 19th century
Found: Circa 1960
Treasure: 1841 quarter eagle

In the early 1960s a lady who lived near Hamilton, New York—a quiet little town best known as the home of Colgate University—found an old gold coin among her family heirlooms. Taking it to a rare coin dealer, she was delighted to find that it was no ordinary gold coin, but was one of the very rarest dates in the $2.50 series, the 1841.

Known as "The Little Princess," an appellation given to it years earlier by Abe Kosoff, this particular Philadelphia Mint variety was struck to the extent of just a few pieces—perhaps fewer than a couple dozen. By 1960 fewer than 10 were known to exist.

Finding an 1841 quarter eagle "in the woodwork" was virtually unheard of, and it was mandatory that the piece be checked for authenticity. Quite possibly it might be an 1841-C (with a tiny mintmark C on the reverse, for Charlotte, North Carolina) or an 1841-D (with a D for Dahlonega, Georgia), but with the C or D mintmark cleverly removed. The 1841-C and D coins were scarce and worth over $100 each at the time, but an 1841 struck at Philadelphia and without a mintmark was worth thousands of dollars.

James F. Ruddy and the author, owners at the time of the Empire Coin Company, checked it carefully and then showed it to several other numismatists including John Jay Pittman (of Rochester, New York) and John N. Rowe III (of Dallas, Texas). All agreed that it was, indeed, a genuine 1841 "Little Princess," and this new discovery was added to the short roster of the pieces known. Soon thereafter it was sold to a gold coin specialist.

If You Find Just One Large Cent...

Hidden or lost: Late 18th or 19th century
Found: 1974 or earlier
Treasure: 1793 Chain large cent rarity

If you find *just one* old large cent, if it is a 1793 you've struck the jackpot![1]

---

1 Information from David E. Tripp, letter, September 13, 1996, and Sotheby's catalogue description. Tripp, on the staff of Sotheby's in the 1970s, is presently an independent numismatic consultant and does expert cataloguing for several clients including Sotheby's. The American branch of Sotheby's (which began in England) was known as Sotheby Parke Bernet in the 1970s, Parke Bernet Galleries before that, and traces its origins to earlier firms including Anderson-American Art Association, and in the nineteenth century, Bangs, Merwin & Co.

There were three major designs of cents this year: the Chain, the Wreath, and the Liberty Cap types. The earliest was the Chain style, so-called from the continuous chain of 15 (one for each state) links on the reverse. Among Chain cents there are several die varieties, the most famous of which is that with the name of our country abbreviated as AMERI.[1] The engraver probably believed that the full word AMERICA would not fit comfortably on this particular die (but was able to include it on later dies).

One day in June 1974, a lady walked into the New York City office of the Sotheby Parke Bernet auction house. She showed to the coin expert David E. Tripp a leather pouch which held some poorly preserved English copper pieces of the late eighteenth century, pieces of no numismatic account or monetary importance. Then there was one more coin: a gorgeous 1793 United States cent, a Chain AMERI!

Tripp accepted the coin for a forthcoming auction sale. Seeking to share his excitement he took it to the Park Avenue office of Lester Merkin, who carefully treated it with a badger's[2] hair brush and, with the agreement of David Tripp, assigned the quite conservative (in the opinion of certain later viewers) grade of EF-45, with traces of mint lustre, to it. The coin crossed the auction block and fetched $13,000, the buyer being Maryland professional numismatist Julian Leidman.[3]

The story of a "penny selling for $13,000" hit the news wire services, but there was a little problem: the date was transposed, and articles were published about Sotheby's selling a *1973* cent, a coin worth just face value, for $13,000! "As a result, I was deluged with letters and calls to the extent that I dreaded coming to the office," Tripp later recalled.

Such is the life of a rare coin dealer!

Subsequently, the prized 1793 Chain AMERI cent was acquired by large cent connoisseur Herman Halpern (and was sold at auction by Stack's), later going to Bowers and Merena Galleries and other owners, finally into a spectacular type set of United States coins formed by a Southern California physician. By that time it was generally regarded as a candidate for Mint State honors.

Such is the life of a rare coin when graded by various observers!

A Very Special Necklace

Set aside: Circa 1907-1908
Found: 1975
Treasure: MCMVII $20 gold piece

In 1974 General Mills, Inc., of Minneapolis was in an acquisitive mode. The internationally known cereal firm had been diversifying, and in recent years had acquired many non-food divisions. Among these were Parker Brothers (maker of Monopoly and other games), Kenner Toys (the world's largest maker of toys), Eddie Bauer sporting goods, Monet costume jewelry, Foot-Joy golf shoes, David Crystal knitwear, and a host of others amounting to several dozen in all.

Along the way General Mills decided to enter the field of collectibles. Its first acquisition was the H.E. Harris Stamp Company, the world's largest stamp firm. Then in a stock swap in 1974, General Mills acquired a controlling interest in Bowers and Ruddy Galleries, Inc., owned by James F. Ruddy and the author.

By the early 1980s, General Mills changed its corporate direction, diversified itself of all non-food divisions, and returned to its core business. The author and Raymond N. Merena acquired the assets of the former Bowers and Ruddy Galleries and from this transaction Bowers and Merena Galleries was born. But, that is another story.

In 1975 an executive with General Mills at its Minneapolis headquarters telephoned me at Bowers and Ruddy Galleries to see if an old gold $20 piece mounted in a necklace might have any value. It had descended in his wife's family. Apparently, the one-ounce gold coin was a bit too heavy to comfortably wear, and the necklace remained unused in a drawer.

"Yes, *any* $20 gold coin has value," I replied, at the same time envisioning a typical necklace in which a

---

1 Variety Sheldon-1 as described in William H. Sheldon's *Early American Cents* (1949) and *Penny Whimsy* (1958).

2 Many numismatists use camel's hair; Dr. William H. Sheldon, *Penny Whimsy,* 1958, p. 45, suggested goat's hair; Merkin preferred the hair of the badger (cf. David E. Tripp, letter, October 2, 1996). Brushing an old copper coin gently is a time-honored tradition employed by many advanced collectors.

3 Sotheby Parke Bernet sale of November 20, 1974, Lot 59.

common-date $20 had been soldered in a frame, and over the years polished to keep it "bright." Typically, such $20 coins were worth little more than the bullion price for an ounce of gold.

A few months later the General Mills executive visited the coin company office and brought the old necklace with him. You can imagine my surprise when I saw that it was no ordinary $20 gold coin, but a rare MCMVII (1907) with Roman numerals in the date, a coin worth thousands of dollars! Moreover, the coin had been mounted carefully years ago in an easily removable bezel that did not damage the coin at all.

My visitor did not know the coin's specific history. We both mused that, perhaps, when this new and beautiful MCMVII design appeared in late 1907, it was recognized for its artistry, and a specimen was obtained for face value from a bank and made into a necklace.

If You Find Just One $20 Piece...

Hidden or lost: Late 19th century
Found: 1977
Treasure: 1870-CC $20 gold rarity

Variation on a theme: If you find *just one* old gold $20 double eagle, if it is an 1870-CC you've hit the jackpot![1]

One day at his desk at Sotheby Parke Bernet in spring 1977, David E. Tripp received a coin in the mail from Nevada. Upon inspection it proved to be somewhat worn and not particularly attractive. No matter. It was the most highly prized of all $20 gold coins made at the short-lived Carson City Mint, an 1870-CC!

In Tripp's words:

> I called the man to discuss his good luck, but he was too poor to own a telephone. I wrote him and suggested he call me collect. When I told him what he had, he was astonished.
>
> It is probably the lowest-grade piece among the few known 1870-CC double eagles, but when it sold it fetched $10,000!

A Hitherto Unknown Half Dime

Saved or hidden: Circa 1870s
Found: Circa 1977
Treasure: Unique 1870-S half dime

One of the most significant numismatic discoveries of our era took place in the 1970s. Rarcoa, the Chicago coin dealer, dazzled the hobby by announcing that an 1870-S half dime had come to light.[2] The coin had previously been purchased over the counter at a suburban Chicago coin shop as a common date coin, and only later was the S mintmark on the reverse noticed! The coin was then sold to Rarcoa. The remarkable new discovery was exhibited at several conventions. I had the privilege of examining it closely. The coin had not been listed in the *Guidebook, The Standard Catalogue of United States Coins,* or any other references, nor had it been mentioned in any official Mint Reports. Indeed, not only was the coin not known, but the very fact that it was ever made was not known either.

Shortly after the announcement, John Abbott, a well-known Michigan coin dealer, sought to buy the piece. What was it worth? The thought went through the mind of Ed Milas, the owner of Rarcoa. It was decided that when Bowers and Ruddy Galleries auctioned the Garrett Collection 1804 silver dollar as a part of a series of sales we were conducting for The Johns Hopkins University, the selling price of that rarity, plus $25,000, would be a reasonable figure for the unique 1870-S.

In a fantastic "fight" among enthusiastic bidders on the auction floor, the 1804 silver dollar broke all past records and soared to $400,000, thus setting the auction sale record for any United States silver coin!

---

1 Information from David E. Tripp, letter, September 13, 1996, and Sotheby Parke Bernet catalogue description, sale of September 27, 1977, Lot 175: "Weakly struck on left side, obverse and reverse, dig through T of TRUST, otherwise Fine and exceptionally rare."

2 Certain information courtesy of Dennis Forgue and Thomas K. DeLorey, communication, October 11, 1996.

This was Lot 698 on the evening of March 26, 1980. As agreed beforehand $25,000 was added to the price, and $425,000 became the transaction basis by which John Abbott acquired the 1870-S half dime.

As it turned out, the Garrett Collection was sold at the very height of the market at the time, and the general price level subsided. This also affected the 1870-S half dime, and when it was again sold, crossing the auction block as Lot 174 in our auction of September 9, 1985, it fetched $176,000, the buyer being Martin Paul of Massachusetts. He held the coin for some time, then sold it, and, years later it appeared in the stock of Jay Parrino, trading as The Mint, Kansas City. It is rumored that around 1995 the coin changed hands privately for in the $1 million range.

The coinage of 1870-S has been partially an enigma, inasmuch as the silver dollar of that date is a great rarity—about a dozen are known—but there are no mintage reports in government records. Similarly, it is believed that of the 1870-S $3 piece, two examples were struck, of which just one is known to exist. The San Francisco kept sloppy or incomplete records at the time.

No "Small Potatoes" Here!

Hidden or lost: 17th century or later
Found: February 1990
Treasure: NE silver sixpence

Still another variation on a theme: If you find *just one* old American colonial coin, if it is a New England (Massachusetts) silver sixpence minted in 1652 you've hit the jackpot![1] While some Massachusetts silver varieties are a bit rarer, the NE sixpence is certainly in the front row and commands a lot of attention!

On one cold February night in 1991, in a potato field in East Hampton, New York, Lillian P. Rade and her coin-collecting husband Ron were looking for coins. Lillian's metal detector gave off a delightful buzz, indicating that something was in the offing. Using an ice pick to probe the frozen earth, a small hole was dug and a little silver disc was found. Then, in Mrs. Rade's words: "When I first saw it, I thought the coin was junk."

Hardly any markings could be seen, except for "NE" on one side and "VI" on the other. That evening the Rades looked through Ron's numismatic library to see if anything matched the little silver piece they had unearthed. Aha! It seemed to be a rare New England shilling!

The Rades took it to New York dealer Stack's, who advised them to send it to the American Numismatic Association Authentication Bureau in Colorado Springs. After due inspection, J.P. Martin of ANAAB, working with consultants including Michael Hodder, pronounced it to be absolutely genuine and thanked the Rades "on behalf of coin collectors everywhere for bringing this numismatic rarity to light."

Subsequently, the coin was given to Sotheby's for auction and crossed the block in November 1991, in which catalogue description David E. Tripp, drawing upon the notes of Michael Hodder, suggested that it was one of just eight specimens of the NE silver sixpence known to exist. When the dust settled in the sale room, the Rades were $32,000 richer, less a modest commission to the auction house. No "small potatoes" this!

---

1 Information from David E. Tripp, letter, September 13, 1996, and Sotheby's catalogue description, sale of November 21, 1991, Lot 108. This coin was also featured in *The Numismatist,* September 1991, pp. 1385-1386 (source of the Rade quotation).

CHAPTER 22

Undiscovered Treasures

(coming attractions)

Waiting to be Found

There are many stories of railroad and stagecoach holdups, but most leave the reader in suspense. Was the loot ever recovered? Probably yes in many instances and no in many others.

This chapter includes stories of coin hoards, holdup booty, and other potential treasures believed to be largely lost, perhaps awaiting discovery—and new stories.

Samples:

Pine Tree Shillings if You Can Find Them

Hidden: 1751
Treasure: Massachusetts and other coins

In 1751 the main structure for the Pennsylvania Hospital was built.[1] Benjamin Franklin was its first superintendent. The edifice still stands today. Numismatist Henry Stevens recently wrote:

> The first job I had after separating from the Army in February 1966, was employment at the Pennsylvania Hospital in Philadelphia. Pennsylvania Hospital, at 8th and Spruce streets was our budding country's first hospital. The main structure, still standing and in use today, was constructed in 1751. Indeed, no less than Benjamin Franklin himself was its first superintendent! The motto of the hospital was that of the Good Samaritan, "Take care of him and I will repay thee."
>
> An old account of the hospital's history suggests that among items put in the cornerstone were Massachusetts Pine Tree shillings and other circulating coins of the era. In later years a numismatist sought to learn more, but after some searching the cornerstone could not be located. While it would most logically be at the location of the Philadelphia Hospital on 8th Street, there was a story that it had been moved generations ago several miles to the west when the Philadelphia Hospital Institute branch was built on 49th Street.

What happened to the cornerstone? To the coins in it? No one seems to know.

The Lost Coins of R. Coulton Davis?

Acquired: 1870s and 1880s
Dispersed: Unknown
Numismatic hoard: Patterns, rarities

In the 1940s Neil Shafer (born 1933), then of Phoenix, Arizona, had a high school chum named Don

[1] Information from Henry Stevens, Ph.D., letter, August 1996.

Davis.[1] Shafer, whose interest in coin collecting was just beginning, visited Davis' home and saw many impressive early issues including several 1797 copper large cents in AU or finer grades, eight to 10 Randall Hoard cents of 1819 and 1820, a lustrous and especially beautiful AU 1798 dime, an exceedingly rare 1774 silver Virginia "shilling," and other things.[2] His friend gave him a copy of George G. Evans' *Illustrated History of the U.S. Mint,* 1892 edition, and some nineteenth-century auction catalogues published by the Chapman brothers of Philadelphia.

This material had descended in the Davis family, presumably from a serious numismatist active many years earlier, quite possibly in the Philadelphia area. In later years Neil Shafer lost contact with his boyhood friend and was not able to locate him, despite several attempts. Endeavoring to locate old-time numismatists with the Davis surname, Shafer quickly encountered information about R. Coulton Davis (born circa 1813, died August 25, 1888), a prominent Philadelphia pharmacist and active collector of coins, specializing in patterns and other rarities. The presence of the 1774 silver Virginia "shilling," a great rarity, seemed to indicate that the Davis ancestor was very seriously involved, perhaps with interest later continued by other family members (as with the acquisition of the 1892 Evans book). Davis' main collection was sold at auction by the New York Coin and Stamp Co., January 1890, but perhaps some delicacies were retained by his heirs. The coins Neil Shafer viewed in the 1940s remain unlocated to this day.

Mormon Gold Coins

Dispersed: 1877
Treasure: Brigham Young's coins

The following excerpt is from an article which appeared in the *Salt Lake Tribune* and was subsequently reprinted in *The Granite State News,* December 13, 1898. Can any of the gold coins belonging to Brigham Young be specifically traced today?

> The ancient coinage of Utah, the period when the glittering particles of yellow gold from California were minted in a little adobe building in Salt Lake, has been half forgotten. The written and printed records of that time, by a strange oversight, throw no light on the subject.

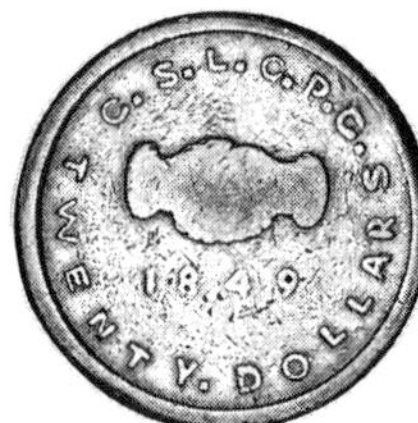

> Those Utahans whose memory dates back to 1849 remember the establishment of the mint, but the exact dates are confused. It was some time toward the close of 1849 that the mint was inaugurated as a measure of public convenience. Brigham Young was the instigator of the coinage system and exercised a personal supervision over the work....
>
> The mint ceased operations in 1860 because of the appearance in sufficient quantities of United States gold and silver coins.... Few of the [Mormon] coins are known to be in existence today. Because of their purity they were rapidly worn, and as a consequence deteriorated in value by erosion.
>
> Many of them were remelted and made into necklaces, chains and other articles of jewelry. Apostle Brigham Young has a watch chain that was made from two of the $20 pieces. He had the chain made in Switzerland while in that country some years ago. E.H. Pierce has one $20 coin, and several others are in possession of Salt Lakers.
>
> When President Brigham Young died in 1877, his executors, in going over his personal property, found a locked strong box. On forcing the lid a number of the coins of the period described were found. They covered all the denominations, and were sold at auction, bringing a premium over their face value. President Young's son, Apostle Brigham Young, at that time secured six of the $5 denomination, which he still has. The others were scattered in such a way as to make it impossible to trace them....[3]
>
> The California slug circulated also very freely here and was used for other purposes besides money. Apostle Brigham Young said recently that as a boy he had frequently seen men pitching quoits with California slugs. [Just imagine!]

Will They Ever Be Found?

Lost or hidden: Early 20th century
Treasure: Scarce U.S. coins

James Riggs related a story of a hoard of United States coins started in the nineteenth century by a

[1] Recollections provided by Neil Shafer, August 14, 1996, from the manuscript of his unpublished personal numismatic history. Shafer's contributions to numismatics over the years have been immense and have touched many specialties, especially paper money. In 1990 he was a recipient of the ANA Medal of Merit.

[2] The 1774 silver coinage (unresolved as to whether the pieces were intended as pattern shillings or were silver strikings of a proposed 1773 copper halfpenny) is discussed at length in Eric P. Newman, *Coinage for Colonial Virginia,* 1956, pp. 37 ff. He noted that he knew of only four examples: the F.C.C. Boyd, Garrett, and Norweb coins plus an example in his own cabinet.

[3] In Salt Lake City, in the president's vault in the Church of Latter Day Saints, the original dies for the Mormon coinage are said to be preserved to the present day. It is further said that some coins are there also.

German immigrant who had settled in a small American town of about 7,000 people and started his own business.[1] Being sort of a collector at heart, but not a numismatist, he determined to set aside interesting coins as he encountered them in his trade. In eight glass canning jars various pieces were saved over a long period of years. One had old copper large cents and many Indian cents; another was for Shield, Liberty, and Buffalo nickels; the third jar contained silver coins from half dimes to early Mercury dimes; the fourth and fifth jars were filled with quarter dollars through the early 1930s; and the sixth jar had nineteenth- and early twentieth-century half dollars and silver dollars. Then came the two final jars which Riggs, who saw them as a child, remembers most: one with odd denominations and items including two-cent and three-cent pieces and tokens, and the last with gold coins.

The German emigrant, who had three sons, lived to the age of 98. One son took an interest in the coins and was told that he would be the heir to them. Meanwhile, his father was still alive. Seeking to secure them, the son sealed them in a brick wall under his father's home. By a curious turn of events, the house was sold to strangers, and despite the son's desire to re-enter the home and retrieve the coins, no way has been figured out to do this, and they remain there to this day.

Twice-Told Treasure Tales

Lost or hidden: 18th and early 19th centuries
Treasure: Gold and silver coins and more

The American West is rich with folklore (and, here and there, some facts) about stagecoach and bank robberies, lost mines, and other caches, check lists of which appear in several commentaries. Although the West is usually associated with treasure stories, there is probably no part of the United States without caches of one sort or another said to be awaiting lucky finders.

Along the Atlantic coast there is hardly a worthwhile stretch of sand without its tale of Captain Kidd's or Blackbeard's treasure being buried there. In fact, such names as Kidd, Lafitte, and Blackbeard recur in the names of islands, restaurants, lodging facilities, and other places in the Atlantic and Gulf coastal areas. Nor did the pirates stop hiding treasure when they reached the end of the Maine coast and came to the Canadian border. If this book were a hundred pages longer, tales could be told of caches in Nova Scotia and other provinces to the north of Maine.[2]

In the Midwestern states such as Oklahoma, bandits seem to have outnumbered law-abiding citizens at one time, if holdup stories are any indication. When the gang went "thataway," they were taking their ill-gotten $100 bills and $20 gold coins to secret hiding places, or so it has been said. Accounts would have one believe that robbers always hid their money and never had time to enjoy it. Perhaps so in some instances.

Down in the South during the Civil War it was popular to hide the family fortune in the plantation yard before the cussed Yankees descended upon the old homestead. In border states, Johnny Reb was a threat to those with leanings toward the northern view.

Along the Ohio River, any boatman reading a sign which beckoned, "Wilson's Liquor Vault & House for Entertainment," would have had a rude awakening. This, too, is part of a treasure tale—see below.

While most entries in treasure guides refer to presently unlocated mines, prospects, and raw gold or silver, some of the many allusions to United States coins and related numismatic material—and a few other topics as well—include those given below. There seems to be "treasure in them thar hills," no matter where the hills are located!

Quite probably, many if not most of the following accounts contain a generous amount of wishful thinking. In virtually all stories of bank robbers, stagecoach bandits, and pirate treasures such caveats as "alleged to have been," "perhaps," "possibly," etc., should be

[1] Letter, August 1996.

[2] Arguably, the most famous of all pirate treasure sites is Oak Island in Mahone Bay near Lunenberg, Nova Scotia, which is beyond the geographical scope of this book. Over the years multiple expeditions have spent millions of dollars exploring what seems to be an underground network of tunnels and platforms, but to date no numismatic treasure has been found.

inserted. Also remember this: if a treasure were easy to find, it would have been found by now.

Here we go, state by state:[1]

ALABAMA TREASURES WAITING TO BE FOUND:

• The Nuñez family treasure is said to be buried near an old river ferry site at Seminole, Baldwin County.

• Along the Alabama seacoast pirate treasures may be buried, including some caches by Jean Lafitte at Bayou Batre and elsewhere.

• On the shore of Bay Minette in Baldwin County some Spanish-American gold may have been cached. Nearby and not far from Fort Morgan pirates may have buried some treasure.

• C.E. Sharps, a wealthy mill owner in Alabama, liked to keep his money in gold coins, and hidden, according to one account. In June 1899 he drowned, taking the secret of his "huge cache of gold" to the grave.[2]

ALASKA TREASURES WAITING TO BE FOUND:

• There are scattered reports of missing gold in the Yukon. Doubtless, nuggets were cached here and there, but probably few minted coins were involved.

• A safe deposit box in Juneau is said to contain a number of rare national currency $10 notes from that city, put away long ago by a mine owner in the district.

• In Stevens Passage between Admiralty and Douglas Islands in the southern reaches of the state's Pacific coast the steamer *Islander* went down on August 15, 1901, with a reported $3,000,000 in gold and $400,000 in currency aboard. Forty people lost their lives.[3]

ARIZONA TREASURES WAITING TO BE FOUND:

• Bars of gold remain hidden in the San Francisco Mountains in Coconino County. If stamped with the markings of territorial assayers they would have significant numismatic value.

• Bandits' loot from a train robbery secreted near Bisbee Junction has never been found.

• Treasure from a holdup at Canyon Station. Will C. Barnes commented:[4] "A large natural cave on Posta Quemada Canyon, eight miles off the Tucson-Douglas highway and 19 miles east of Tucson. On south slope of Wrong Mountain in the Rincon range. Owned by the state. First discovered by a man named Rolls, 1879. A Southern Pacific Railroad train was robbed in 1884, and the robbers trailed to this cave. One man was found dead. The others escaped. On Christmas, 1902, some Tucson people found some old Wells-Fargo sacks which proved to be part of the 1884 holdup upon identification in San Francisco."

• Hashknife Charley's missing 38 gold bars, near Sononita, Santa Cruz County may have assayers' stamps on them, but no one will know until they are found.

• A safe and its contents proved to be missing after a flash flood in Fools Gulch northeast of Wickenburg. Possibly, the treasure remains today underground in some dry stream bed.

• Treasure taken by pirates from the steamer *Gila* near Crescent Spring, Mohave County. (This sounds like a very interesting story!)

• A thousand pounds of silver dollars taken in a train robbery in the Dos Cabezas Mountains near Willcox remains unaccounted for. At 56 pounds per $1,000 face value, this would amount to close to 20,000 coins.

• In addition to coin accounts, stories abound of lost silver (mostly) and gold mines in Arizona. The legend of the Lost Dutchman Mine at Superstition Mountain is a staple item in thefolklore of the state.

ARKANSAS TREASURES WAITING TO BE FOUND:

• The fortune of a mill owner (assuming that mill owners have fortunes; they recur in treasure accounts) is said to have been buried near Huntsville, Madison County, and partially recovered at a later date.

---

[1] Over two hundred books, pamphlets, treasure guides, maps, pirate accounts, tourist guides, etc., including the following were reviewed in the search for stories: Nina and William Anderson, *Southern Treasures,* 1987; Norman Carlisle and David Michelson, *The Complete Guide to Treasure Hunting,* 1973; Robert M. Coates, *The Outlaw Years: The History of the Land Pirates of the Natchez Trace,* 1930 (also gives many accounts of river pirates along the Ohio in particular); F.L. Coffman, *1001 Lost, Buried, or Sunken Treasures,* 1957 (a generous part of the 1,000 figure is a long list of sunken ships without details as to what they contained); W.C. Jameson, *Buried Treasures of the South,* 1992; Michael P. Henson, *A Guide to Treasure in Virginia and West Virginia,* 1982; Charles D. Miller, *Encyclopedia of Buried Treasure,* 1965; Thomas Penfield, several titles including *Wild Bill Hickok Guide to Lost Treasures,* Rand McNally, 1952; Thomas Probert, *Lost Mine and Buried Treasures of the West,* 1977; *Directory of Buried or Sunken Treasures and Lost Mines of the United States,* and *A Guide to Treasure in Arkansas, Louisiana, and Mississippi;* Harry E. Rieseberg, *Fell's Complete Guide to Buried Treasure on Land and Sea,* 1970; Robert Ellis Cahill, *New England's Pirates and Lost Treasures,* 1987.

[2] W.C. Jameson, *Buried Treasures of the Ozarks and the Appalachians,* 1993.

[3] Adrian L. Lonsdale and H.R. Kaplan, *A Guide to Sunken Ships,* 1964, p. 177.

[4] *Arizona Place Names,* 1988 reprint, p. 105.

German immigrant who had settled in a small American town of about 7,000 people and started his own business.[1] Being sort of a collector at heart, but not a numismatist, he determined to set aside interesting coins as he encountered them in his trade. In eight glass canning jars various pieces were saved over a long period of years. One had old copper large cents and many Indian cents; another was for Shield, Liberty, and Buffalo nickels; the third jar contained silver coins from half dimes to early Mercury dimes; the fourth and fifth jars were filled with quarter dollars through the early 1930s; and the sixth jar had nineteenth- and early twentieth-century half dollars and silver dollars. Then came the two final jars which Riggs, who saw them as a child, remembers most: one with odd denominations and items including two-cent and three-cent pieces and tokens, and the last with gold coins.

The German emigrant, who had three sons, lived to the age of 98. One son took an interest in the coins and was told that he would be the heir to them. Meanwhile, his father was still alive. Seeking to secure them, the son sealed them in a brick wall under his father's home. By a curious turn of events, the house was sold to strangers, and despite the son's desire to re-enter the home and retrieve the coins, no way has been figured out to do this, and they remain there to this day.

Twice-Told Treasure Tales

Lost or hidden: 18th and early 19th centuries
Treasure: Gold and silver coins and more

The American West is rich with folklore (and, here and there, some facts) about stagecoach and bank robberies, lost mines, and other caches, check lists of which appear in several commentaries. Although the West is usually associated with treasure stories, there is probably no part of the United States without caches of one sort or another said to be awaiting lucky finders.

Along the Atlantic coast there is hardly a worthwhile stretch of sand without its tale of Captain Kidd's or Blackbeard's treasure being buried there. In fact, such names as Kidd, Lafitte, and Blackbeard recur in the names of islands, restaurants, lodging facilities, and other places in the Atlantic and Gulf coastal areas. Nor did the pirates stop hiding treasure when they reached the end of the Maine coast and came to the Canadian border. If this book were a hundred pages longer, tales could be told of caches in Nova Scotia and other provinces to the north of Maine.[2]

In the Midwestern states such as Oklahoma, bandits seem to have outnumbered law-abiding citizens at one time, if holdup stories are any indication. When the gang went "thataway," they were taking their ill-gotten $100 bills and $20 gold coins to secret hiding places, or so it has been said. Accounts would have one believe that robbers always hid their money and never had time to enjoy it. Perhaps so in some instances.

Down in the South during the Civil War it was popular to hide the family fortune in the plantation yard before the cussed Yankees descended upon the old homestead. In border states, Johnny Reb was a threat to those with leanings toward the northern view.

Along the Ohio River, any boatman reading a sign which beckoned, "Wilson's Liquor Vault & House for Entertainment," would have had a rude awakening. This, too, is part of a treasure tale—see below.

While most entries in treasure guides refer to presently unlocated mines, prospects, and raw gold or silver, some of the many allusions to United States coins and related numismatic material—and a few other topics as well—include those given below. There seems to be "treasure in them thar hills," no matter where the hills are located!

Quite probably, many if not most of the following accounts contain a generous amount of wishful thinking. In virtually all stories of bank robbers, stagecoach bandits, and pirate treasures such caveats as "alleged to have been," "perhaps," "possibly," etc., should be

[1] Letter, August 1996.

[2] Arguably, the most famous of all pirate treasure sites is Oak Island in Mahone Bay near Lunenberg, Nova Scotia, which is beyond the geographical scope of this book. Over the years multiple expeditions have spent millions of dollars exploring what seems to be an underground network of tunnels and platforms, but to date no numismatic treasure has been found.

inserted. Also remember this: if a treasure were easy to find, it would have been found by now.

Here we go, state by state:[1]

ALABAMA TREASURES WAITING TO BE FOUND:

• The Nuñez family treasure is said to be buried near an old river ferry site at Seminole, Baldwin County.

• Along the Alabama seacoast pirate treasures may be buried, including some caches by Jean Lafitte at Bayou Batre and elsewhere.

• On the shore of Bay Minette in Baldwin County some Spanish-American gold may have been cached. Nearby and not far from Fort Morgan pirates may have buried some treasure.

• C.E. Sharps, a wealthy mill owner in Alabama, liked to keep his money in gold coins, and hidden, according to one account. In June 1899 he drowned, taking the secret of his "huge cache of gold" to the grave.[2]

ALASKA TREASURES WAITING TO BE FOUND:

• There are scattered reports of missing gold in the Yukon. Doubtless, nuggets were cached here and there, but probably few minted coins were involved.

• A safe deposit box in Juneau is said to contain a number of rare national currency $10 notes from that city, put away long ago by a mine owner in the district.

• In Stevens Passage between Admiralty and Douglas Islands in the southern reaches of the state's Pacific coast the steamer *Islander* went down on August 15, 1901, with a reported $3,000,000 in gold and $400,000 in currency aboard. Forty people lost their lives.[3]

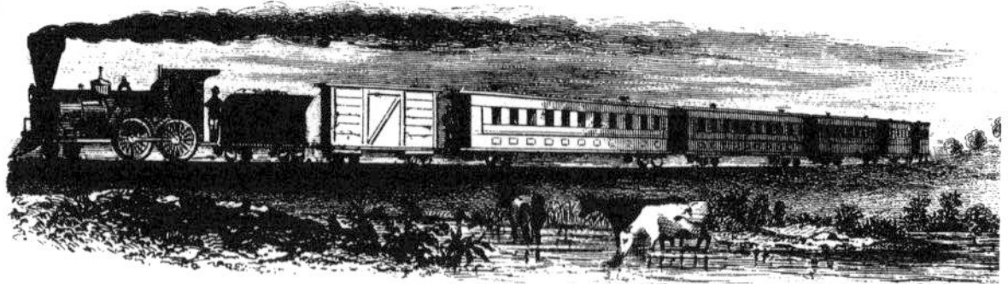

ARIZONA TREASURES WAITING TO BE FOUND:

• Bars of gold remain hidden in the San Francisco Mountains in Coconino County. If stamped with the markings of territorial assayers they would have significant numismatic value.

• Bandits' loot from a train robbery secreted near Bisbee Junction has never been found.

• Treasure from a holdup at Canyon Station. Will C. Barnes commented:[4] "A large natural cave on Posta Quemada Canyon, eight miles off the Tucson-Douglas highway and 19 miles east of Tucson. On south slope of Wrong Mountain in the Rincon range. Owned by the state. First discovered by a man named Rolls, 1879. A Southern Pacific Railroad train was robbed in 1884, and the robbers trailed to this cave. One man was found dead. The others escaped. On Christmas, 1902, some Tucson people found some old Wells-Fargo sacks which proved to be part of the 1884 holdup upon identification in San Francisco."

• Hashknife Charley's missing 38 gold bars, near Sononita, Santa Cruz County may have assayers' stamps on them, but no one will know until they are found.

• A safe and its contents proved to be missing after a flash flood in Fools Gulch northeast of Wickenburg. Possibly, the treasure remains today underground in some dry stream bed.

• Treasure taken by pirates from the steamer *Gila* near Crescent Spring, Mohave County. (This sounds like a very interesting story!)

• A thousand pounds of silver dollars taken in a train robbery in the Dos Cabezas Mountains near Willcox remains unaccounted for. At 56 pounds per $1,000 face value, this would amount to close to 20,000 coins.

• In addition to coin accounts, stories abound of lost silver (mostly) and gold mines in Arizona. The legend of the Lost Dutchman Mine at Superstition Mountain is a staple item in thefolklore of the state.

ARKANSAS TREASURES WAITING TO BE FOUND:

• The fortune of a mill owner (assuming that mill owners have fortunes; they recur in treasure accounts) is said to have been buried near Huntsville, Madison County, and partially recovered at a later date.

---

[1] Over two hundred books, pamphlets, treasure guides, maps, pirate accounts, tourist guides, etc., including the following were reviewed in the search for stories: Nina and William Anderson, *Southern Treasures,* 1987; Norman Carlisle and David Michelson, *The Complete Guide to Treasure Hunting,* 1973; Robert M. Coates, *The Outlaw Years: The History of the Land Pirates of the Natchez Trace,* 1930 (also gives many accounts of river pirates along the Ohio in particular); F.L. Coffman, *1001 Lost, Buried, or Sunken Treasures,* 1957 (a generous part of the 1,000 figure is a long list of sunken ships without details as to what they contained); W.C. Jameson, *Buried Treasures of the South,* 1992; Michael P. Henson, *A Guide to Treasure in Virginia and West Virginia,* 1982; Charles D. Miller, *Encyclopedia of Buried Treasure,* 1965; Thomas Penfield, several titles including *Wild Bill Hickok Guide to Lost Treasures,* Rand McNally, 1952; Thomas Probert, *Lost Mine and Buried Treasures of the West,* 1977; *Directory of Buried or Sunken Treasures and Lost Mines of the United States,* and *A Guide to Treasure in Arkansas, Louisiana, and Mississippi;* Harry E. Rieseberg, *Fell's Complete Guide to Buried Treasure on Land and Sea,* 1970; Robert Ellis Cahill, *New England's Pirates and Lost Treasures,* 1987.

[2] W.C. Jameson, *Buried Treasures of the Ozarks and the Appalachians,* 1993.

[3] Adrian L. Lonsdale and H.R. Kaplan, *A Guide to Sunken Ships,* 1964, p. 177.

[4] *Arizona Place Names,* 1988 reprint, p. 105.

• John Murrel (also spelled as Murrell), notorious bandit, buried treasures on Stuart Island near Lake Village in Chicot County. Murrel made many depredations in the Mississippi River watershed area and is said to have had "HT," for "Horse Thief," branded on a thumb as part of his conviction for that crime. Loot from his various robberies is said to have been buried in different places in Arkansas, Mississippi, Louisiana, and elsewhere. Murrell also engaged in nefarious activities along the Natchez Trace.

• Many Spanish-American gold coins brought overland from Texas and Mexico are said to have been hidden here and there around the state—not much to go on with information as vague as this!

• On or near the land once owned by John Avants along the Cosatot River is a vast fortune transported overland from Mexico in several wagons.

CALIFORNIA TREASURES WAITING TO BE FOUND:

• $200,000 in gold coins may be hidden near Scotty's Castle in Death Valley, today a tourist attraction. Scotty is mentioned in many stories published over the years. He may have had lots of money or he may have had none, depending upon what you read. Scotty was certainly a fascinating character.

• The fortune of a French saddle maker (as we asked about mill owners, did saddle makers accumulate fortunes?) is concealed on the Rancho Santa Teresa near San Jose.

• In the Trinity Mountains near Cecilville in Siskiyou County $80,000 in stolen money was hidden by "Rattlesnake Dick."

• Loot from the Bentz Company robbery hidden near Biggs in Colusa County has never come to light.

• Treasure from the holdup of the Bodie stage north of Bodie in Mono County and also a strongbox from the Bodie stage at Freeman Junction about 60 miles east of Bakersfield remain who knows where.

• Famous bandit Joaquin Murietta hid some loot in Arroyo Cantoova and Hornitos, among many other places.

• In Mokelumne Hill in along Route 49 in the Mother Lode country, a cache of $50 gold coins is said to be in an old foundation wall.

• $30,000 in hijackers' loot was once stashed at Camp Oak Grove, San Gabriel Mountains, Los Angeles County, and may still be there.

• A bandits' underground hiding place near Avila, San Luis Obispo County, is said to have been the depository for much loot, but how can one locate the cave?

• In Los Angeles a pirate treasure is said to have been buried where Elysian Park is now. If so, this might be a tough one to spirit away without notice, for the Los Angeles Police Department has a training site there.

• Treasure taken from a Death Valley wagon train that was burned is, perhaps, somewhere in that vast desert area.

• Treasure from the Fallbrook stage coach on the Butterfield line between Temecula and Pala in San Diego County is among the missing.

• Gold bars from the Freemont (or Frémont) Mine near Amador City are said to have been hidden in the area. One cannot help but wonder if they have anything to do with Felix Grundy Hoard (see Chapter 12).

• Gold coins were lost in Horse Canyon near Tehachapi.

• Treasure belonging to an innkeeper at the old Warner Ranch at Aguana in San Diego County awaits discovery.

• Coins hidden in the hills near Isabella, Kern County, have never been found.

• Dr. John Marsh's cache of $40,000 in gold coins, Marsh Creek, east side of Mount Diablo, near Brentwood, Contra Costa County, would be worth many multiples of that figure if it were found today.

• Lieutenant Jonas Wilson's poker winnings—no description at hand—are said to be hidden somewhere in Hoaglin Valley at the foot of Haman Ridge, Trinity County.

• Coins lost near Ventucopa, Santa Barbara County are still lost.

• Gold "slugs" and coins, the treasure of the Mariposa tax collector, remain unlocated on Deadman's Creek near Agua Fria, Mariposa County.

• Loot from the Needles bank robbery, near Oro Grande, San Bernardino County, is supposedly still missing.

• The *S.S. Mollie Stevens* laden with gold bullion, was lost on Owens Lake in the Owens Valley in May 1882, according to one account.[1] Another account is more mundane and noted that after the *Mollie Stevens* had served well on the lake from about 1874, she was beached alongside the *Bessie Brady* so that parts from her including the steam engine could be used in the latter vessel.[2] During the process, the *Mollie Stevens* caught fire and was destroyed.

• Gold "slugs" hidden at the old Forty Mile House near Shingle Springs near El Dorado County have never come to light.

• A lost cache of "octagonal gold coins" in the Panamint Mountains remains unaccounted for. Alert readers will realize the numismatic implications of this. The only trouble is that one could spend a lifetime poking around this particular mountain group and still not cover every outcrop and gully. By the way, the name is from a good wish expressed to gold miners: "I hope you pan a mint."

• The "Rifle Barrel payroll" hidden near French Gulch, Shasta County, has been missing for many years.

• Treasure taken by the Ruggles brothers (who were subsequently hanged) from the Redding stage and buried near Middle Creek about six miles from Redding, Shasta County, is nowhere to be found.

• Assets of a saloonkeeper hidden at the junction of Greenhorn Gulch and Freeman Gulch, Kern county, await the lucky finder.

• "Treasure of the San Francisco Mint" at Shelter Cove near Point Delgado, Humboldt County, no doubt would prove interesting if found.

• Loot from the Sonora stage was hidden near Snelling, Merced County.

• A tub filled with gold coins was hidden at Yankee Hill (old mining town) near Sonora, Tuolumne County. A washtub? Bathtub?

1 Thomas Probert, 1977.

2 Don B. Marshall, *California Shipwrecks,* 1978, p. 15.

A train of freight wagons heads through Ute Pass on the eastern slope of Pikes Peak, possibly taking goods to Leadville, Aspen, or another mining camp. "Land pirates" often ambushed such processions.

• In addition, just about all of the old Spanish missions along the coast have treasure tales connected with them. Stories of lost mines in the Sierras and Mother Lode country also abound.

COLORADO TREASURES WAITING TO BE FOUND:

• $100,000 stolen by bandits was hidden east of Clifford, Lincoln County.

• The site of Bent's Fort on the old Santa Fe Trail is supposed to be where much treasure is buried.

• "Treasure of the Denver Mint," apparently including silver dimes, was concealed in a chasm on the Gunnison River between Crawford and Montrose.

• At Robbers' Roost near Fort Collins a lot of stagecoach holdup loot is said to have been hidden.

• Treasure of the paymaster of Fort Garland was stashed on Trinchera Creek, Costilla County.

• Two barrels of coins belonging to Henry Sefton were lost at the Gomez Ranch, Sangre de Cristo Mountains, Huerfano County. Sounds interesting!

• Some of Jesse James' treasure is said to have been cached in Half Moon Gulch, southwest of Leadville. (Accounts of his hidden loot abound and are ascribed to many different western states.)

• $100,000 in gold hidden by outlaws near Manitou Springs at the foot of Pikes Peak has never been found. "Near Manitou Springs" covers many square miles of territory.

Manitou Springs at the base of Pikes Peak (snowy outcrop in the distance) not far from Colorado Springs. Could there be gold hidden here?

• The "Bloody Espinosas," obviously an unsavory group, buried treasure near the present-day town of Cascade in Ute Pass in the late 1860s; this is on the slopes of Pikes Peak not far from Colorado Springs or, for that matter, Manitou Springs, or for that matter, where A.J. Mitula built his "nickel house" (see Chapter 19).

• A chest filled with gold was hidden on Ralston Creek Road between Central City and Denver.

• Coins hidden by the Reynolds gang near Hand Cart Gulch, Park County, have never turned up.

• Train robbery loot hidden near Grand Valley, Garfield County, remains undiscovered.

• Near Monument, between Colorado Springs and Denver, the Butch Cassidy gang is said to have stashed $100,000 from bank robberies. Monument, which a few years ago was nothing but a small roadside stop along the Interstate is now a teeming community, probably making it difficult to seriously prospect for hidden gold and silver.

• Treasure from a wagon train, hidden near La Junta, Otero County, has never been found.

CONNECTICUT TREASURES WAITING TO BE FOUND:

• Tuxis Island off Milford is said to have yielded "a great quantity of eighteenth-century coins" for a group of campers in 1903. Perhaps more remain.[1]

• The beach at Penfield Reef near Fairfield may be worthwhile, as in 1888 George Hawley found a cache of gold and silver coins all dated 1795.[2] If, perchance, these were United States coins, this has to be one of the most interesting finds around. Too bad we don't have more details.

DELAWARE TREASURES WAITING TO BE FOUND:

• The Atlantic coastal areas of Delaware have yielded many coins over the years, numerous examples of which have washed up on the shore. The salvage of the *DeBraak* and an account of the *Faithful Steward* are given in Chapter 10. Many other ships have been wrecked off Delaware and in her inlets and bays, and doubtless there is treasure waiting to be found. Most such coins are probably Spanish-American or British.

DISTRICT OF COLUMBIA TREASURES WAITING TO BE FOUND:

• A private residence once occupied by the commandant of the United States Marine Corps is said to have $25,000 hidden within.

• Who knows what may be cached in the Treasury Building on Pennsylvania Avenue. Old coins? Old currency? What

1 Cahill, 1987, p. 58.

2 *Ibid.*

we need is a numismatic detective with a license to snoop, to spend a week or two looking around!

FLORIDA TREASURES WAITING TO BE FOUND:

• Stories of Florida treasures are dominated by accounts of buried pirate treasure and sunken Spanish galleons, both of which largely antedate indigenous American coinage. Chapter 10 discusses several important finds made from the 1960s to date, but undoubtedly there are more to be located. Nearly all finds have been associated with Spanish treasure fleet wrecks and not with pirates. The treasure-hunting community is particularly active along the Florida coast, and numerous shops offer Scuba equipment, electronic treasure detectors, guidebooks, and other useful items.

• Fowler's Bluff on the Gulf Coast may be a productive site for the seeker of pirate treasure.

• At the headwaters of Carter's Mill Creek in the northern part of the state, Indians may have cached a fortune in gold coins received from the British as payment for their depredations on settlers.

• At Amelia Island there may be much buried pirate treasure.

• F.L. Coffman reported that "an old treasure hunter, Bill Sneed," found $625,000 in gold bullion and coins at the mouth of the Suwanee River, a part of a treasure of gold coins valued at $5,000,000. The present writer knew Bill Sneed, who in the 1950s operated the Wilmary Motel in Lakeland, Florida, and recalls that he enjoyed regaling his acquaintances with tall tales, but had relatively few rare coins as evidence to verify his finds.

• José Gaspar, better known as Gasparilla the pirate, is said to have buried many treasures along the Gulf Coast. In modern times his name has been given to an annual festival in the Tampa-St. Petersburg area.

• Near Fort Walton on Choctawhatchee Bay on the Gulf Coast, pirate Billy Bowlegs may have cached many gold and silver coins.

• On the bottom beneath the sparkling waters of Silver Springs, near Ocala, are coins tossed by tourists including, perhaps, some dating from the 1920s and 1930s or even earlier.

• In his *History Under the Sea,* 1965, Mendel Peterson gave advice concerning potentially profitable sites for undersea treasure exploration, noting: "The reefs of the Florida Keys and coast of Florida north to Cape Kennedy [Cape Canaveral], which is one of the richest spots." Further: "Almost any bar lying near harbor approaches on the Atlantic coast will yield sites. On the eastern side of the Florida Passage to the Bahamas formed a dangerous barrier for ships, and these reefs and keys are littered with sites."

GEORGIA TREASURES WAITING TO BE FOUND:

• A certain Mr. Duncan, a prosperous businessman who lived in Griffin, Georgia, did not trust banks, but kept coins and bills stored here and there around the house. His wife feared for his and her safety, as his wealth was well known,

and someone might break in. At her insistence, he consolidated all of this money—said to amount to at least $100,000—and said he would take it to a bank. However, he had second thoughts and buried it in a peach orchard instead. Some months later, Duncan was disabled by a heart attack. While bedridden he attempted to gesture as to where the trove was hidden, but could not make himself understood. He died shortly thereafter, taking the secret of the location with him.[1]

• The old Lions House on Third Street, Columbus, is supposed to contain hidden treasure.

• At Blackbeard's Island the treasure of you-know-who is said to have been buried. More of his chests (or whatever he used for storage) may be on Ossabaw Island.

• Various citizens of the state buried coins and other treasures to prevent capture by William Tecumseh Sherman during his famous (or infamous) march through the countryside, in which his troops pillaged and burned everything in sight.[2] A psychologist might find that he did this because he had failed in banking, lawyering, and a few other endeavors before the military provided him with the proper emotional outlet.

• Near LaGrange a wealthy plantation owner named Lipscomb accumulated about $100,000 in silver and gold coins and buried the treasure in two places near his house just before the Civil War. He enlisted the aid of a faithful servant whenever he dug up the ground to make a "deposit" or simply to review what he had stored. One day he wanted to visit his coins, but his servant was not around, and Lipscomb could not locate the sites. Forewarned, he later recorded directions to the spots. Lipscomb died, and his widow was not able to locate the directions. Today the treasure is still missing.[3]

• At Milledgeville, Baldwin County, a treasure of remarkable proportions is said to be hidden under a house.

• In Savannah the pirate treasure of John Flint may be concealed in or near a house he once occupied on Broad Street.

• Many gold and silver coins that were once a part of the Confederate States of America Treasury may be hidden on the south bank of the Savannah River (or near Washington, Georgia; or Abbeville, Georgia; or near Richmond, Virginia; or in the false bottom of a horse-drawn coach; or divvied up among trusted officers, who each did their own hiding; or in a railroad car, etc.), while other narratives relate that military payrolls from both sides were hidden on various occasions when their security became endangered.

IDAHO TREASURES WAITING TO BE FOUND:

• Multiple possibilities: Booty from a stagecoach holdup was hidden on the south side of the Boise River near Boise, another stagecoach stash may still be secreted near Camas

---

[1] W.C. Jameson, *Buried Treasures of the South,* 1992, pp. 48-51.

[2] Sherman had intended to follow a career in finance, but he suffered greatly in the Panic of 1857 and its immediate antecedents (see note under the account of the *S.S. Central America* in Chapter 11). Thus, the Union eventually gained one of its foremost heroes.

[3] W.C. Jameson, *Buried Treasures of the South,* 1992, pp. 58-62.

Creek in Jefferson County, and yet another near Grimes Creek in Boise County awaits discovery.

• Robbers hid $75,000 in loot ("cold cash"?) near the Shoshone Ice Caves in Lincoln County.

• North of Boise a strongbox with $50,000 in stagecoach loot is hidden.

• A robber's treasure secreted near Lewiston, if discovered, will be found by accident, as the territory described covers a very large area—a common theme for many "clues" to such caches.

• Treasure, possibly from a Wells Fargo stage holdup, may still be at Mud Lake southwest of Idaho Falls.

• The Lewis and Clark Expedition in the early 1800s took with it many Washington Season medals[1] for distribution as peace medals to Indians in the north central and northwest sections of America. Only a few of these are accounted for today.

• In McCammon, Bannock County, about $100,000 taken from an 1865 stagecoach heist is hidden. The bandits were chased by a posse and killed. Obviously, driving a stagecoach or being a bandit in Idaho was dangerous business!

• Money taken from a pack train by robbers between White Bird and Dixie, Idaho County, has never been accounted for.

• $118,000 stolen by bandits is buried in the area of Humphrey in Clark County.

• Loot of the Henry Plummer gang, hidden in Beaver Canyon near Spencer, Clark County, likewise remains unlocated.

• Virgil Brumbach's Gold Certificates are said to be lost in Soldier's Canyon east of Saint Maries, Shoshone County.

ILLINOIS TREASURES WAITING TO BE FOUND:

• In the late 1860s in the 1200 block of North State Street in Chicago, Felix and Ellen Conway spent their married years, but were not on friendly terms with each other. Felix, upon being diagnosed with an incurable illness, dug deeply in his backyard and buried $250,000 in gold coins. He told his doctor of the cache, and suggested that after he died and after Ellen also had passed to her reward, he could recover it. The doctor himself became ill and neared death, at which time he told his son of the fortune in store. As it turned out, the doctor's son died, while Ellen Conway continued to live, until at the age of 92 she passed away. Today, the exact location of the gold coins is not known, and they are presumed to still be there.[2]

• Near old John Hill's Fort at Carlyle, Clinton County, a buried fortune remains for the lucky finder.

• Cave In Rock in Hardin County was long used as a hideaway by many robbers and other unsavory characters including the Harpes Gang and the notorious Wilson, and it is said much loot remains secreted there. Robert M. Coates has written:[3] "From Red Bank [on the Ohio River] on down to the town of Smithland, the river traversed its most dangerous section. Shoals abounded, sand bars lay just below the ripple of the surface, islands split the channel.... Landsmen most of the travelers were, as they came poling down in their barges.... A whole hierarchy of piracy had arisen to prey on them. The first of these was a man named Wilson.... He took his stand at a cave in the bluff along shore, a cave with deep chambers and hidden recesses. He posted a sign on the river bank: 'Wilson's Liquor Vault & House for Entertainment.' The cave was known as the Cave Inn, later twisted to Cave-In-Rock. It had a long chapter in the history of river piracy. Boat-wreckers waited along the bank. Watching a boat pass, they would offer to pilot it through the channel. If the unskilled steersman chose to run the rapids unaided, it was more than likely he would run aground. If he hired a pilot, the chance of his grounding became a certainty. Once beached, the boat and its occupants fell easily before the attack of Wilson's gang."

INDIANA TREASURES WAITING TO BE FOUND:

• In or near Rockford, Jackson County, $98,000 taken in a train robbery is buried. Could this be related to the following account?

• On May 22, 1868, the Reno gang (Clinton, Frank, John, Simon, and William) held up the J.M. & I. Railroad train at Marshfield, Indiana, about 20 miles south of Seymour, and escaped with $90,000 cash described as being in "new notes." After another escapade or two, the brothers were tossed into jail in New Albany in December of the same year. On December 11 a group of do-gooders went to New Albany, entered the jail, seized the prisoners, and hanged them. What happened to the stolen currency was not stated.[4]

• In the mid-1820s one of Marquis de Lafayette's carriage drivers stashed $8,000 in gold in the ground in Connelton, Perry County. Lafayette, French hero of the American Revolution, revisited the United States in 1824-1825 and was declared by Congress to be "The Nation's Guest."

IOWA TREASURES WAITING TO BE FOUND:

• Near Redfield in Dallas County a gang of outlaws buried their ill-gotten coins.

• A long time ago outlaws gathered in Bellevue, Jackson County, and buried treasure in the area.

• At Kelly's Bluff in Dubuque a well-to-do miner buried his personal fortune. Some of it was later discovered, but more remains to be found.

• Horse thieves buried their treasure near Sabula, Jackson County.

---

1 Dies by Conrad Küchler for the Soho Mint, Birmingham. The set of medals consisted of three different obverse designs depicting as many aspects ("seasons") of American life. Examples were struck in silver and copper.

2 Coffman, pp. 99-101.

3 *The Outlaw Years: The History of the Land Pirates of the Natchez Trace,* 1930; account occupying many pages and most of two chapters; this book contains many dramatized accounts of the Natchez Trace (which went from eastern Tennessee, up through Kentucky, through the middle of Tennessee, the northwest corner of Alabama, continuing through Mississippi to the city of Natchez on the Mississippi River). Also, Otto A. Rothert, *The Outlaws of Cave-in-Rock,* 1924.

4 James Mitchell Guthrie (editor), *Indiana Sesquicentennial Commission,* 1966 anthology of newspaper articles, pp. 76-78. Sent by Mark B. Wolf.

KANSAS TREASURES WAITING TO BE FOUND:

• Treasure of an Army paymaster was lost near Lawrence, Douglas County.

• Wells Fargo treasure was hidden west of Dodge City, Ford County.

• Bandit loot hidden at Point of Rocks northwest of Elkhart, Morton County, remains concealed.

• Treasure from a wagon train of Forty Niners headed to California was hidden southwest of Offerle, Edwards County.

• Near Point of Rocks some other wagon trains headed for California—or perhaps this is another version of the preceding story—were plundered by outlaws who buried their loot in the area.

• Yet another wagon train treasure is said to have been concealed near old Fort Dodge.

• Similarly, a wagon train from Mexico with a vast fortune aboard was attacked by Indians. Some travelers survived with their money and buried it in the area.

• A group of Forty Niners returning from California with $50,000 in a buckskin bag buried their treasure near Offerle, Edwards County, before being killed by Indians.

KENTUCKY TREASURES WAITING TO BE FOUND:

• Just before the Civil War, William Pettit hid treasure at Alleghany Hall, south of Lexington.

• Indians are said to have buried an immense treasure including many coins (some of which have been found now and then) in the Winchester area.

• In Hueysville, Thayer County, a well-to-do landowner buried a large quantity of gold coins around the turn of the twentieth century.

• Contents of a chest of silver and gold coins stolen from a bank in Nicholasville, Kentucky, may lie on the bottom of King's Mill Pond, although a few coins were recovered by a fishing guide in 1910. [1]

LOUISIANA TREASURES WAITING TO BE FOUND:

• Stories of the treasure buried in Louisiana and other Gulf of Mexico places by pirate Jean Lafitte have filled several books. Lafitte, who is alternately viewed as a hero or a scoundrel, and who was of help to the government during the War of 1812, plundered many ships. Quite possibly within his buried strongboxes and chests are many United States coins, although probably most are Mexican or from other Spanish-American mints. Within Louisiana such places as near Shell Beach Drive in Lake Charles, Opelousas in St. Landry Parish, an island in Lake Borge (such island, like Lake Wobegon, having eluded mapmakers), the banks of the Mississippi River upstream from New Orleans, Caillou Island, the LeBleu plantation site in Calcasieu Parish, Pecan Island near Westwego in Jefferson Parish, Kelso's Island, Isle Dernier, and Jefferson Island near Lafayette are said to be especially good possibilities for the location of Lafitte's gold and silver.

• Marsh Island may be where coins salvaged at an early date from Spanish wrecks off Padre Island (Texas) were brought for safekeeping. [2]

• Marie Laveau, the beautiful "Voodoo Queen," offered fortune telling and consultation to various clients and in time became wealthy, so much so that she built a fine home, Maison Blanche, on Lake Pontchartrain near New Orleans. When she passed from this earthly sphere in 1881, her fortune estimated at $2 million could not be located.

• Honey Island in St. Tammany Parish may be one of many places in the Mississippi River area where John Murrel hid his loot (see entry under Arkansas above). Outlaw James Copeland may have cached coins on this island as well as along many other coastal areas.

• The Parlange Plantation treasure, near New Roads, Pointe Coupee Parish, is part of a cache originally comprising nearly a half million dollars' ($300,000 appears in several accounts, $500,000 in another) worth of silver and gold coins stored in three metal strongboxes or chests and buried early in the Civil War. The owner, Madame Virginie Parlange, feared that Union soldiers would ravage the mansion, which had been built by Marquis Vincent de Ternant in 1750. The Yankee troops arrived in due course, but were friendly to the owner after she greeted them in a warm fashion and even invited them to dinner. After the war, her son followed his mother's instructions and unearthed two of the chests, but the third could not be found. It was presumed that the two slaves who had helped bury the chests and who had since decamped to Texas had unearthed the coins and had reburied them elsewhere. Although several attempts were made to locate the treasure, the coins remain missing to this very day.[3]

• The Gabriel Fuselier plantation in St. Landry Parish is believed to be the site for coins buried during the Civil War era.

• In Magnolia Cemetery in East Baton Rouge Paris there may be something buried besides bodies, that being gold

---

[1] W.C. Jameson, *Buried Treasures of the Ozarks and the Appalachians,* 1993.

[2] Nina and William Anderson, p. 17.

[3] W.C. Jameson, *Buried Treasures of the South,* 1992, pp. 87-89; other sources.

The rocky outcrops and islands off the coast of Maine were fraught with dangers that claimed many ships.

and silver coins. One might imagine that modern digging there would be discouraged, however.

• An entire "shipload of gold" (Penfield, 1952) may be at the bottom of the Amite River near the site of where Galvez Town used to be, near present-day Oak Grove in West Carroll Parish.

• The site of an old French settlement, Fort Iberville, in Plaquemines Parish, is said by some to be where $160,000 in gold treasure is buried. [1]

• Various plantations on inland waterways are said to be very rich possibilities for very rich treasures. Of the over 1,000 large plantations in operation along the Mississippi River and elsewhere in the states along the lower reaches of the river, only a few hundred remained active after the Civil War.

• In Natchitoches Parish at an old landing on the Red River, hidden treasure worth several thousand dollars has been found over the years, and its is said that this is just the beginning. Good luck!

• In Hulls Lake at Selma, Grant Parish, the loot from a bank robbery was hidden, never to be found, at least not yet.

• On the banks of the Red River near Acme, many gold coins are said to have been buried circa 1861.

• In a bayou near the Chretien Plantation a large quantity of coins is said to have been hidden prior to the Civil War. Some of this treasure may have been from pirates who had some sort of an arrangement with the owner of the estate.

MAINE TREASURES WAITING TO BE FOUND:

• The coast of Maine is said to have been an especially popular place for such pirates as Captain Kidd, Captain Bellamy, and their ilk to have buried treasure. All of Bellamy's gold and silver may have been hidden near the coastal town of Machias, but, on the other hand, it may have been buried elsewhere (such is the nature of pirate treasure accounts, and if enough of them are read, the reader comes back full circle to the starting place). If and when any such treasure is found, most probably it will consist primarily of Spanish-American coins, although there is the possibility that some Massachusetts silver could be included. In addition, the "stern rockbound coast" (as one poet put it) of New England, and of Maine in particular, spelled disaster to many coastwise ships who became lost in fog or darkness. Many of their hulks remain today at the bottom of the sea, some with rare coins scattered in the sand nearby.

• All along the Maine coast are more islands than can be counted, and many of these have been suggested as burial sites for buccaneers and privateers. Deer Isle, Vinalhaven and North Haven (constituting the main part of the Fox Islands group), Fort Popham (built in 1861 as a deterrent should the Confederacy invade the Pine Tree State), Reef Ram Island, Mount Desert Island (a vast acreage now a national park; Ship Bottom Bay is there), Monhegan Island, Elm Island, Bailey Island, and Money Cave (sounds particularly interesting!) on Isle du Haut are among the sites reflected in treasure lore.

• Pirates aside, the coastal areas of Maine have yielded their share of Massachusetts Pine Tree shillings and related pieces over the years, as related in Chapter 1. At the very least, any treasure hunter who pokes around the Maine coast will see a lot of great scenery even if he or she doesn't find

[1] Nina and William Anderson, p. 19.

any Pine Tree shillings or Spanish-American gold doubloons.

• At Cedar Ledges east of Ram Island in Casco Bay, three kettles of gold coins were found on Thanksgiving Day, 1852, and more may still be there.[1]

• On Richmond Island, offshore from Cape Elizabeth, a vast treasure of Spanish-American and other gold and silver coins was found in 1855. Many of the pieces were given to the Maine Historical Society.

• Maine is one of only a few states for which the population 150 years ago was a substantial fraction of what it is today. This means that old sites have not been overwhelmed by new construction, developments, etc. Thus, certain areas may yield treasures. In general, wealth was concentrated along coastal areas rich with sea commerce, shipbuilding, etc. Inland activities were mainly agrarian.

MARYLAND TREASURES WAITING TO BE FOUND:

• A French immigrant is said to have buried $100,000 in coins near Catonsville.

• At or near the old Croissant Mansion in California, St. Mary's County, a treasure is said to be hidden.

• Near Salisbury, about $30,000 in treasure had already been found by the early 1950s, and legend has it that more awaits lucky searchers.

• Maryland coastal areas are said to conceal some of Captain Kidd's treasure, some of which may be inland near the old Mansion House in northwest Baltimore.[2]

• Maryland has a rich colonial history, and without doubt many town and commercial sites conceal coins awaiting seekers using electronic detectors.

• Chesapeake Bay has had its share of ship losses, but any coins remaining on the sea bottom are probably the personal property of passengers rather than lost treasure cargo.

MASSACHUSETTS TREASURES WAITING TO BE FOUND:

• In Salisbury, Essex County, $175,000 in buried treasure has never been found.

• Nantucket and Martha's Vineyard, both offshore south of Cape Cod, are said to have been favorite roosts for buccaneers.

• Cape Cod (in particular) and other coastal regions are said to have been a popular place for secreting pirate gold and silver. Captain Kidd's name is often associated with such accounts. Anyone wanting to read exciting tales of Massachusetts ship losses, disasters, and pirates need but acquire several of the books written by the late Edward Rowe Snow, who for many years was the prime American chronicler of sea lore. Snow related that it was common practice for pirates to be tried (loose interpretation of this judicial term) in Boston and their corpses put in shackles and chains and taken to islands in Boston harbor to be strung up from a gibbet in full view of passing ships—a warning to what happens to buccaneers when they are caught. Among those so displayed was Jack Quelch, who often operated out of Marblehead; his corpse put in chains and strung up at Nix's Mate, a small island in Boston harbor, where it rotted away, although some remains could be viewed for several years thereafter.[3]

• In and around Marblehead harbor various pirates, most especially the aforementioned Jack Quelch, are believed to have hidden treasure.

• Snake Island, offshore from Marblehead, is supposed to have been a hiding place for pirate loot. Ditto for Plum Island near Newburyport, today a popular seaside nature conservancy and tourist destination.

• The banks of the Parker River near Byfield may be a worthwhile site for treasure hunting, including over $200,000 worth of gold and silver in a chest.[4]

• At Dalton in Berkshire County loot stolen by Hessian mercenary soldiers during the American Revolution is said to be buried. Doubtless, such coins as Pine Tree shillings would have been included.

• Near old Tenney Castle at Methuen, Essex County, two eccentric brothers are said to have hidden a fortune.

• At Deer Island near Winthrop, 1,200 Mexican 8-reals were dug up in 1906, and who knows how many more there might be. The beaches at Ipswich and Salisbury are said to frequently yield 8-real Mexican silver coins dated circa 1715. Short Beach and Grover's Cliff as well as nearby Nahant and Revere were used as cache sites for pirate silver and gold.[5]

MICHIGAN TREASURES WAITING TO BE FOUND:

• A fortune belonging to François Fontenay is said to be buried on Presque Isle near Detroit.

• Many treasures are said to be aboard sunken ships off the shores of Michigan. Over the years many thousands of ships have gone down in Lake Michigan and the other Great Lakes.

MINNESOTA TREASURES WAITING TO BE FOUND:

• In a stand of trees at Henderson, Sibley County, a treasure is buried.

• In the woods near Wadena a group of bandits buried their loot and were killed shortly thereafter by a posse.

MISSISSIPPI TREASURES WAITING TO BE FOUND:

• Near the old Gore mansion in Calhoun City valuable treasure was hidden in the earth.

• Bandit James Copeland is said to have hidden gold coins in coastal areas in the 1840s and 1850s.

• Pirate Patrick Scott is said to have buried some treasure in the early nineteenth century near Ocean Springs, Jackson County.

• A treasure of gold coins may have been buried at Beaux Bridge in St. Martin's Parish in the early nineteenth century by the slaves of Narcisse Thibodeaux.

• The Pirate's House near Bay St. Louis is said to offer obvious possibilities including the finding of underground tunnels facilitating the clandestine transfer of gold and silver from shore to the house.

• The treasure of merchant Gaines is said to have been hidden in Greene County, and although quite a bit of it was recovered in the late nineteenth century, much remains undiscovered

1 Cahill, 1987, p. 58.
2 Penfield, 1952.
3 Cahill, 1987, p. 45
4 *Ibid.*, pp. 56-57.
5 *Ibid.*, p. 53.

• Just before the Civil War the Pickett family buried its fortune near the edge of Vicksburg.

• Two kegs of gold are said to have been buried near Greenwood in 1865 by robbers.

• At Mathiston in Choctaw County many buried gold coins are supposedly waiting to be found.

• Joe Hare, a bandit who once operated in the area, may have buried his treasure in Fayette, Jefferson County.

• At Pass Christian in Harrison County the old oak tree beneath which Captain Dane is supposed to have buried $200,000 may not still be there, but the treasure near it has never been discovered. The money, in Spanish-American gold coins, belonged to a lady passenger of the *Nightingale,* who in the aftermath of a love triangle, was locked in a cabin when the ship sank. Great material for a novel, it would seem!

• The Copeland gang looted the Bay St. Louis area in the early nineteenth century and buried their treasure in Catahoula Swamp.

MISSOURI TREASURES WAITING TO BE FOUND:

• Near Waynesville in Pulaski County a wealthy Forty Niner is said to have buried $60,000 in the hills.

• In the river areas near St. Louis there are said to be several coin-laden steamship wrecks.

MONTANA TREASURES WAITING TO BE FOUND:

• Much Plummer gang (also active in Idaho) loot was hidden near Sun River, Cascade County, and several other specified areas.

• The Horsethief Cache near Billings is said to be where cattle rustlers hid treasure (presumably coins, not cows or horses).

• Robbers' Roost at Sheridan, Madison County, is where thieves secreted their plunder.

• At Drummond in Granite County a Chinese miner is said to have buried five pounds of gold (coins? nuggets?) in a can under a tree.

• Treasure taken from Gen. Custer's troops after his "last stand" in Big Horn County is said to have been hidden in the area (although one can only with great difficulty imagine Army troops having much treasure). Separately, a few scattered coins such as Shield nickels have been found on the site in recent decades and, called "half dimes," were shown in an issue of *National Geographic Magazine* a few years ago.

• Virginia City, Montana (named after Virginia City, Nevada), was the site of extensive gold discoveries in the 1860s. It is said that much treasure is still hidden in the region.

NEBRASKA TREASURES WAITING TO BE FOUND:

• Jesse James is said to have hidden loot here and there, such as at Devil's Nest near Crafton, Knox County.

• $40,000 stolen from a bank in Kearney is believed to be hidden near Sargent, Custer County.

• Gold miners returning from California were robbed near Lexington, Dawson County, and their treasure buried in the area.

• Robbers' Cave near Macy, Thurston County, may contain much treasure.

NEVADA TREASURES WAITING TO BE FOUND:

• Loot of highwaymen: Stagecoach robbery loot hidden near Columbus, Esmeralda County; Wells Fargo treasure from the Empire Stage, near Carson City; stagecoach coins

Miners and local ladies dancing at the Hurdy-Gurdy House, Virginia City, Montana, circa 1867.

hidden north of the ghost town of Jarbridge, Elko county; tens of thousands of dollars in takings known as the stage-coach treasure of Williams Station on Harrison Creek near Hill Beacher Road, Elko County; and another stagecoach treasure hidden near Genoa, Douglas County, remains to be found.

• The payroll intended for workers at the Candaleria Mines was stolen and is said to be hidden near Mina, Mineral County.

• Lost gold from the Mormon caravan, between Cave Valley and Ash Meadows near Carp, Lincoln County, has never been located.

• Money left behind in the winter of 1846-1847 by the ill-fated Donner expedition in the High Sierras may still be hidden somewhere, perhaps in the region of Shafter, Elko County (also see account in Chapter 2 of a find from the Donner Party).

• A miser's fortune was hidden near the old Pogue Station southeast of Eureka, White Pine County.

• A bank robber's treasure was hidden near Six Mile Canyon near the road from Carson City to the ghost town of Ramsey.

• As is the case with many western states, most treasure stories concerning Nevada have to do with lost silver (mostly) or gold mines, not coins.

NEW HAMPSHIRE TREASURES WAITING TO BE FOUND:

• Near Colebrook in Coos County, far in the northern regions of the state and quite distant from the sea, some of Captain Kidd's treasure is said to have been buried, and "old coins have been found." If so, there is a remote possibility that such a cache could have or still does include Massachusetts silver coins. However, it is difficult to imagine that Captain Kidd would have spent a week or more journeying to this remote inland location after he anchored his ship on the New Hampshire coast.

• In Dublin a treasure buried in the 1940s has never been found.

• Governor John Wentworth is said by some to have buried $25,000 in coins and silverware near Portsmouth, presumably before fleeing to the north during the parlous times of the Revolutionary War. It is known that Wentworth was a man of considerable wealth. Separately, the site of his summer home on the shore of the body of water that today bears his name, Lake Wentworth, in Wolfeboro, New Hampshire, has been a prime archaeological focal point for many years, various small British coins and numerous artifacts have been located there, and today a small local association supports its heritage. Despite reading several accounts, the author has never located any reliable reports of his having hidden any treasure, but anything is possible.

• The Isles of Shoals off the coast of New Hampshire and just about every landing along the state's short (about 17 miles) seacoast have been long regarded as prime sources for hunting pirate treasure, although little has actually been found there. This offshore group includes Smuttynose Island, said to be a particularly rich possibility, for many pirates, including in particular Jack Quelch, thought this was a great location to bury silver and gold (if after a search there, a treasure seeker is in need of a libation, some Old Brown Dog Ale made by the Smuttynose Brewing Co. in nearby Portsmouth can offer succor). Ned Low and William Fly were two other pirates who liked the area. Cotton Mather, the Massachusetts diarist and prominent justice, recorded that Fly's career was especially bloodthirsty, but lasted only 35 days before he was tried and hanged in Boston, where Fly helped the hangman tie the knot for his neck. Appledore Island, not far away, is said to be laden with treasure just waiting to be found, although a lot of people have tried. Ditto for Star Island. Londoner Island, later called Lunging Island, is where Blackbeard is said to have buried treasure, on the side of the island facing the Star Island Hotel across the water; Blackbeard is said to have had 14 wives and a bevy of concubines, apparently a treasure of another sort.

• The lower reaches of the Piscataqua River, which empties into the Atlantic at Portsmouth, are said to be where Samuel Bellamy cached some supplies and possibly coins.

NEW JERSEY TREASURES WAITING TO BE FOUND:

• With all of its shoreline, New Jersey was an enticing place for pirates to bury treasure, and some of them did. However, very few American coins would have been included. It is not unusual for old coins to wash up on beaches, particularly after storms and high tides or, especially, after a combination of both of these events. Asbury Park, Stone Harbor, Beach Haven, and other coastal sites have been mentioned in this regard. Pirate gold is said to be secreted at several places including Perth Amboy and Cape May.

• Near Colt's Neck and near Farmingdale, both in Monmouth County, robbers who terrorized the pine barrens are said to have buried their loot.

• Near Caldwell a German naval officer is said to have secreted a treasure before he was killed.

NEW MEXICO TREASURES WAITING TO BE FOUND:

• Money from the Cooney stagecoach, hidden near Cooney, Grant County, has never been found.

• Stagecoach treasure hidden in Doubtful Canyon near Steins Peak, Hidalgo County, is unlocated.

• Lost treasure of Fort Bayard, Grant County, remains unfound.

• At Devoy's Peak near Mount Dora much outlaw loot is hidden.

• $100,000 in missing cash from train robbery(ies) believed hidden near the Lava Beds southeast of Grants, Valencia County, is still hidden.

• A Texas outlaw's stash may still be concealed at Pump Canyon, San Juan County.

• Seventeen to 20 tons of gold ingots believed by some to be hidden near Shiprock, San Juan County, and believed by others to be imaginary, makes an interesting story.

• Gold bars have been missing for many decades at Tres Piedras in the San Juan Mountains, Taos County.

• $40,000 in gold coins from a wagon train, hidden about

25 miles east of Springer, Colfax County, may still exist.

• In addition to coin stories, there are many tales of lost silver and gold mines in this state, with one particularly interesting account telling of a hill near Pinos Altos being made of nearly pure gold.

NEW YORK TREASURES WAITING TO BE FOUND:

• At the old Jeffery Amherst Fort site at Crown Point, Essex County, treasure may have been buried.

• In the Montezuma Swamp near Seneca Falls the Loomis gang is said to have buried much loot.

• At Grand Island in Lake Erie, not far from Niagara Falls, a fortune is said to have been hidden by an early resident.

• Near Hell's Gate in the East River a ship carrying a vast fortune was lost many years ago, and although the area is not large, the hulk of the ship in question has never been found.

• The west shore of Lake Champlain is said to offer possibilities for electronic metal detector use, and quite a few old coppers have turned up.

• The notorious Captain Kidd is said to have buried much treasure in coastal areas, especially at Gardiners Island. Most probably, if such still exists it includes few American coins. There are numerous accounts of lost chests, sunken ships, etc., near Manhattan in the East River, Hudson River, and New York harbor areas. Long Island, with its extensive sandy beaches, is said to offer many possibilities.

NORTH CAROLINA TREASURES WAITING TO BE FOUND:

• A stranger is said to have buried a bag filled with gold near the old Brummels Inn at High Point.

• In the early twentieth century some old Spanish-American coins—including some dated 1788—were found on the James Robert Thomas property in Waynesville.

• On the bottom of the Pamlico River an old brick vault is said to have been found by fishermen, and within were several kettles and over 200 Spanish-American gold coins. For reasons hard to figure out, the fisher folk are said to have reburied the treasure on a nearby shore, where it was lost track of, as flooding changed the profile of the river bank.

• Near Chimney Rock, Round Top mountain, which forms one side of Hickory Nut Gap, is said to be the burial site for a pot of gold put there by a group of six Englishmen over 250 years ago. A copy of a map indicating the site is in the Library of Congress. Several explorations have been made, but no success has been reported.[1]

• Off Cape Hatteras, the "Graveyard of the Atlantic," countless ship hulls litter the sea bottom—so many, in fact, that they are beyond counting. Presumably, many contain at least a few United States coins. Shoreline areas—such as near Okracoke Inlet—are said to have been an especially popular place for Blackbeard (who seems to have frequented the place) and other pirates to bury chests of treasure.

• Near Wrightsville Beach there is a place aptly named Money Island.

• Plum Point in Beaufort County was a burial spot for pirate booty, and to prove the contention, some has already been recovered (so they say).

• The Great Dismal Swamp may be where Frenchmen, fleeing a British warship, hid gold during the early days of colonization.

Stagecoach being held up by Indians as depicted in a nineteenth-century engraving. In reality, the typical bandit was a white man.

NORTH DAKOTA TREASURES WAITING TO BE FOUND:

• Along the Missouri River near Bismarck, Forty Niners laden with gold from California are said to have buried treasure worth $90,000 to prevent its capture by Indians.

• At Rolla in Rolette County, bank robbers hid loot in the foothills of Turtle Mountain.

• The paymaster for Hudson's Bay Company buried $40,000 in the area of Lignite, Burke County, just before an attack by robbers.

OHIO TREASURES WAITING TO BE FOUND:

• The Bridge family pot of gold was buried near Eaton, Preble County, in the early nineteenth century and has never been recovered.

• At Rockford, Mercer County, loot of bank robbers has been found, but more is believed to be in the area.

OKLAHOMA TREASURES WAITING TO BE FOUND:

• Gold belonging to an Atoka cattleman is believed to be lost.

• Half a bushel of silver coins hidden by bandits on Holsum Valley road, Le Flore County, has never been found.

---

[1] Nina and William Anderson, p. 16.

A nineteenth-century shootout with robbers and other desperadoes.

• At Roman Nose State Park, near Watonga, Blaine County, the loot of several old-time outlaw gangs is said to be buried.

• Robber's Cave State Park, near Wilburton, Latimer County, offers obvious possibilities.

• An outlaw's treasure on Boggy Creek near Boswell, Choctaw County, awaits a lucky searcher.

• Treasure formerly the property of California emigrants, is supposedly hidden on Fish Creek near the old Edwards Post south of Holdenville, Hughes County. One cannot help but wonder how much "treasure" the average person going from the East to seek wealth in the West actually carried. Probably not much.

• Charles ("Pretty Boy") Floyd's loot hidden near Sallisaw, Sequoyah County, may still be there.

• Treasure from Captain Golden's wagon train was hidden at Big Caney Creek south of Artillery Mound near Boulanger, Osage County.

• Loot of the Dalton gang was hidden in various locations around the state including in caves at Sand Springs. Dozens of rumors exist, but little in the way of facts.

• Dick Estes' outlaw gold treasure on Panther Creek about 10 miles north of Cache, Comanche County, has not been found.

• The lost gold of Fort Arbuckle, on or near the old Fort Sill Military Reservation, is still missing.

• Glass jars containing $58,000 or more in coins was secreted near Sulphur Canyon Bridge near Clayton, Pushmataha County. (Anyone writing a history of glass jars may well want to include a chapter on coin caches, for such tales recur!)

• Robber Henry Starr's ill-gotten gains may be cached near Rose and Pryor, Mayes County.

• Treasure in the ghost town of Ingalls east of Stillwater, Payne County, awaits the discoverer.

• The Dillon gang is said to have buried treasure in and around Mannford, Creek County.

• Joe Vann's treasure on the site of his old mansion, Webbers Falls, Muskogee County, has been talked about, but not found.

• Kenton, Cimarron County, was once a center for banditry, and stolen treasure is still hidden in the area.

• $50,000 in gold coins is said to be hidden near Rattan at Seven Devil Mountain, this being from the loot of a bank robbery. The bandit was hanged, but not before giving directions to where the coins were cached. However, later attempts to locate the coins proved futile.[1]

• The safe taken from the Kosoma train on Buck Creek near Antlers, Pushmataha County; has been missing for a long time.

• Silver dollars were lost near Summerfield, Le Flore County.

• An Army paymaster's cache may be hidden at Twin Mounds near Jennings, Pawnee County. Similarly, an Army

[1] Coffman, pp. 80-81.

payroll was hidden at Cache, Comanche County, to prevent capture by Indians.

• In addition, there are many stories of Jesse James' loot being hidden in the state.

OREGON TREASURES WAITING TO BE FOUND:

• A buried fortune may or may not be on the Baker Ranch on Birch Creek south of Pilot Rock, Umatilla County.

• At Mount Hood in the area of Government Camp, Clackamas County, stolen treasure was buried.

• Pirate treasure is said to be buried near Cascade Head, Lincoln County.

• In Baker City, some of the two-ounce gold "buttons" made in 1907 may be in safe deposit boxes or elsewhere. Only three or four are known today from an original production of many dozens.

• Many ships in the coastwise trade have been wrecked off the coast, and it is said that some contain money from passengers' purses and from safes, although factual accounts of coins are scarce.

• At Horse Thief Meadows near Parkdale, Hood River County, $25,000 from a stagecoach robbery is believed to be hidden.

PENNSYLVANIA TREASURES WAITING TO BE FOUND:

• Many Indian peace medals were given out by early settlers, but only a few of these are known to numismatists today. Medals were given out in many other eastern and midwestern areas as well.

• At a place called Asylum on the upper reaches of the Susquehanna River, escapees from the French Revolution (and some displaced Frenchmen from the West Indies as well) are said to have concealed their wealth during the mid-1790s.

• Near Mount Carmel $250,000 is missing from the site of a 1948 airliner crash.

• Pithole City on Pithole Creek where it joins the Allegheny River, was a boom town beginning with the discovery of oil there in 1865. Within a year or two there was so much business going on there that the incoming and outgoing mail at the Post Office was third in volume only to Philadelphia and Pittsburgh in the state. "Fortune seekers from all parts of America and Europe were attracted. On every train they came rushing to the land of derricks." The population grew to 12,000 to 15,000 inhabitants. Alas, it was not to last. Most oil claims petered out. The Oil City & Pithole Branch Railroad banked the fires in its locomotives, and the Reno, Oil Creek & Pithole Railroad was never completed beyond the grading and tie-laying process. No one checked in anymore at the four-story hotel in the center of town. By 1870 Pithole City was no more, and it was not even mentioned in the federal census of that year.[1] Today the site may furnish interesting opportunities for electronic treasure detection.

• The Doone Gang of Tories stashed $100,000 in loot near Wernersville, Bucks County.

• For such a big state with such a long history, there are not many treasure tales to relate. Not enough pirates or stagecoach robbers in this area, I suppose.

• In a home on the south side of a country road near Carverton, Luzerne County, a cigar box filled with old Indian cents is believed to exist.

• Money gathered by settlers at the communal settlement of Ephrata Cloisters is said to be concealed somewhere in that area.

RHODE ISLAND TREASURES WAITING TO BE FOUND:

• There are lots of pirate treasure stories associated with the beaches and inlets of this seacoast state.

• Pirates' Cave on the southern reaches of Conanicut Island in Narragansett Bay may or may not be aptly designated.

SOUTH CAROLINA TREASURES WAITING TO BE FOUND:

• Most treasure stories relating to this state concern pirate loot, such as treasure hidden at the appropriately named Pirate House on Church Street, Charleston; the site of old Fort Randall; Tilghman's Point on Little River; and Murrell's Inlet in Georgetown County.

• Hampton Plantation, located northeast of Charleston, is where Edgar Allan Poe is said to have written his "Gold Bug" story in the 1840s, obviously an excellent omen for a place said by later generations to conceal treasures. George Washington is said to have slept there, too. Archibald Rutledge (life dates: 1883-1973) once owned the place, and when there he found 198 gold coins hidden during the Civil War, no numismatic description of which has been encountered. Could there be more waiting to be found? If so, midnight might be the best time to look—because the place is now owned by the state and operated as a tourist attraction—but this brings up the problem of a ghost which is said to haunt the place. Beware!

SOUTH DAKOTA TREASURES WAITING TO BE FOUND:

• Money may still be hidden on the site of a burned ranch near Redfern, Pennington County.

• Loot from the holdup of the "Old Ironsides" Canyon Springs stagecoach is believed to be hidden near the junction of Prairie and Rapid creeks near Rapid City. One might imagine that the robbers of this and other stagecoaches made off with their ill-gotten gains and spent it, rather than burying the treasure and never coming back to claim it.

• Buried treasure of the Gordon Stockade, French Creek, Lawrence County, remains lost.

• Fruit jars filled with cash, the Mexican Ed Sanchez treasure, is hidden on Dirty Woman Creek near the old town of Grinston, Custer County.

• Loot from the Sidney Stage may still be buried or stashed near Hat Creek near Ardmore, Fall River County.

• Stagecoach holdup loot was buried near French Creek near Fairburn, Custer County.

• Loot amounting to $140,000 was taken in a stagecoach holdup in 1878, hidden along a creek near Fairburn, Custer County, and never found. The treasure was being sent from a mining camp to a bank. The bandits were chased by a posse and killed.[2]

• Near Hat Creek, Rumford, Fall River County, a strongbox taken in a stagecoach robbery in 1877 remains missing.

---

1 John T. Faris, *The Romance of Forgotten Towns,* 1924, pp. 305 ff.

2 Coffman, p. 179, and other sources.

This may be the same as $30,000 in gold coins in a treasure chest reported taken in a train robbery.[1]

• A steamboat was lost near Riverside Park, Pierre, in the 1860s, with much gold aboard. To this day it has not been located.

• At the bottom of Long Lake near Lake City, Marshall County, a "flour sack full of gold" is said to be hidden.

• Miners returning from the Virginia City, Montana, area in the 1860s, laden with gold, buried their treasure near Deadwood before being killed by Indians.

TENNESSEE TREASURES WAITING TO BE FOUND:

• The Touhy gang from Chicago stashed $60,000 near Newport.

• Wartburg in Morgan County is where much gold brought back from California in the 1850s remains buried.

• The parts of the Natchez Trace that wound through the forested areas of the state are said to offer many possibilities for robbers' loot including some from notorious Samuel Mason and his son.

• John Murrel, a bandit in early times, is said to have cached up to $1,000,000 worth of treasure near Denmark, Madison County.

• During the Civil War much treasure was buried near Dover, Stewart County.

TEXAS TREASURES WAITING TO BE FOUND:

• Gold bars were lost in Paisano Pass near the Brewster-Presidio county line, Brewster County.

• Coins taken by Emperor Maximilian from the Mexican treasury may have been spirited off to Texas and hidden there.

• Notorious Texas outlaw Sam Bass spent time in the 1870s robbing stagecoaches including several near Deadwood in the Dakota Territory. Seeking other opportunities, Bass and his sidekick Joel Collins went to Big Springs, Nebraska, and there held up the Union Pacific Railroad, escaping with a payroll of 3,000 freshly-minted 1877 $20 gold pieces in a trunk. Although $25,000 worth of coins and jewelry (this would have been 1,250 $20 gold coins if the jewelry had been minimal) was recovered, Collins and Bass died without revealing where the rest of the loot was. It is said that Bass had hidden his part in Cove Hollow about 30 miles from Denton, Texas, where, who knows, it may still be today.[2]

• In spring 1894 four men held up the First National Bank in Bowie, Texas, and rode away with 500 $20 gold pieces ($10,000) and $18,000 in currency. Considering that the bank, chartered in 1890, issued its own $10 and $20 notes, could there have been any of these among the bills taken? Before crossing the flooded Red River they decided to bury the heavy coins as they might impede their crossing, but it seems highly unlikely that at the rate of 125 coins per man, each coin weighing about one ounce, that they would really have been a problem. Anyway, as the story goes, the men were later captured and hanged, but not before one of the desperadoes confided to lawman Palmore that the gold was buried beneath a large tree, supposedly in a stand of cottonwoods near where the Red River meets the Little Wichita River.[3]

• A cache of coins hidden by robbers near or on Biloxi Creek near Lufkin, Angelina County, has never been discovered.

• At Castle Gap, about 15 miles east of Horsehead Crossing, the gold and other treasure of Emperor Maximilian may be buried. A 15-wagon caravan was ambushed circa 1866 by ex-Confederate soldiers and other opportunists. Does this treasure exist. If so, does it include gold coins?[4]

• Treasure of the Forty Niners hidden at Buffalo Gap south of Abilene remains unfound.

• In Illinois a gang of desperadoes held up a train, escaped with $350,000 in loot, and for some reason took it to near San Antonio, Texas, to hide it, apparently so well that it has never been found.

• Butterfield Stage treasure was hidden at Castle Gap near King Mountain, Upton County.

• Loot hidden by an Illinois train robber near San Antonio remains unlocated to this day.

• A lost cache of $20 gold coins in Palo Duro Canyon, Armstrong County, will certainly yield surprises if found.

• A Missouri wagon train treasure, possibly as much as $30 million, was hidden near Willow Springs northeast of Monahans, Winkler County.

• Forty Niners laden with gold from California, on their way back east, buried gold in Buffalo Gap, Taylor County, when ambushed by Indians.

• The missing Musgraves treasure of gold coins is said to be near Cotulla, La Salle County.[5]

• Stagecoach robbery loot was hidden in Rattlesnake Cave, a.k.a. Skeleton Cave (for one of the bandits' remains are supposed to still be there), near old Fort Concho west of San Angelo, Tom Green County.

• The missing $100,000 on the old Riddles Ranch near Fort Worth has never turned up.

• The Sanderson train robbery loot, near Sue Peak, Brewster County, remains missing. More loot from another train holdup is believed to be hidden at the southwest edge of Stanton, Martin County.

• Stories abound of pirate Jean Lafitte's treasures hidden at various places along the Gulf of Mexico coast and of gold and other treasures brought to Texas from Mexico, only to meet various fates. Similarly, Mexican troops involved in various battles (the Alamo, for example) are said to have hidden coins in various places.

UTAH TREASURES WAITING TO BE FOUND:

• An Army payroll treasure remains missing near Castle Dale, Emery County.

• Train robbers' loot hidden near Bear River City, about four miles north of Corinne, Box Elder County; has never been found. Ditto for the take from the Corinne stagecoach robbery believed to be concealed near Corinne.

• Caleb Rhodes, of Mountain Home, Duchesne County, had much wealth from an unknown source. Some of this, or perhaps a secret gold mine, awaits discovery.

---

1 *Ibid.*, p. 178.

2 W.C. Jameson, *Buried Treasures of Texas,* 1991.

3 *Ibid.*

4 Coffman, pp. 83-84.

5 The name is reminiscent of the treasure hunt mentioned in the fictional Sherlock Holmes detective story by A. Conan Doyle, "The Musgrave [*sic*] Ritual."

• Members of the Donner Party (also see Nevada entry above and Donner information in Chapter 2) on the way to California are said to have hidden valuable coins near Silver Island Mountain near Wendover, Tooele County, Utah, in autumn 1846.

• The Castlegate payroll treasure near Hanksville, Wayne County, has been missing for a long time.

• Robbers' loot from an Emery bank holdup was hidden at Hondo Arch near Emery.

• The Mountain Meadow Massacre treasure is said to be hidden about 30 miles south of Cedar City, Iron County. This dreadful encounter has been written about by Mark Twain and others, and it seems unlikely that any treasure was actually left behind by the perpetrators of this sad event, a very dark chapter in the history of Utah.

• Mormon gold coins are said to be stored in a vault in Salt Lake City.

• The "Wild Bunch treasure," about $28,000, was secreted at a cabin near Brown's Hole, San Juan County.

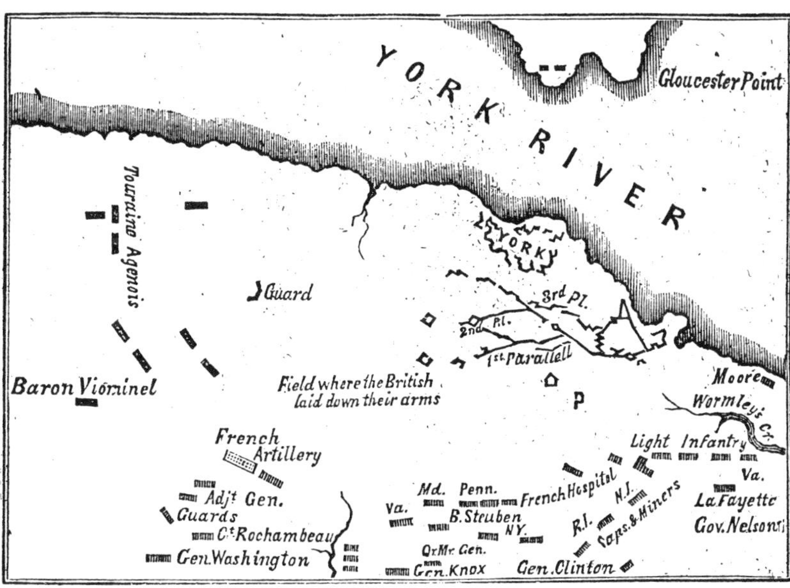

VERMONT TREASURES WAITING TO BE FOUND:

• One does not usually associate Spanish explorers and expeditions with the Green Mountain State, but Tom Penfield (1952) told of two treasures buried by Spaniards, one of gold on the slopes of Ludlow Mountain.

• One often sought "treasure" is the original wooden mint building used by Reuben Harmon and his associates in the coining of Vermont coppers circa 1785-1786. In the 1960s, when poking around Pawlet in search of clues, I was shown not one but two candidates for the structure, both moved from the original site along a brook. Too bad that Sylvester S. Crosby (*Early Coins of America,* 1875, p. 90) gives a fairly detailed account of the building's loss when it collapsed in a windstorm in the winter of 1855-1856.

VIRGINIA TREASURES WAITING TO BE FOUND:

• On a hill near McGaheysville, Rockingham County, a treasure was buried, according to local accounts.

• In Fauquier County, William Kirk amassed a large fortune by the late eighteenth century, and is said to have hidden it on the grounds of his estate, thus accounting for various scattered discoveries of coins in later years. However, the bulk remains unlocated.

• Major General George Cornwallis, whose surrender effectively ended the Revolutionary War, is said to have cached his own coins plus those captured during his earlier forays, to prevent seizure by the American troops. These coins and other precious items may still be found in or around Yorktown, if you are lucky enough to look in the right place.

• On or near Chincoteague Island, on a wooded knoll overlooking the water, 10 strongboxes filled with treasure may have been buried by pirate Charles Wilson.

• In Prince William County, Confederate raider John S. Mosby captured a troop of Union forces who had in their possession many coins, jewels, and other items pilfered from Virginia homes. Mosby hid these items in the area, and they still may be there.

• In 1794 the family of Baron François Pierre de Tubeuf, who lived in Washington County, was killed by outlaws, who may have hidden the baron's money nearby, for when they were captured there were no coins in their possession.[1]

• Near Richmond $10,000,000 or more in gold coins, part of the much-discussed "Treasure of the Confederacy," a loan from England, is said to be buried. This can be discounted as fiction, according to most modern scholars of the subject. The tale is probably derived from an account in the *New York Times,* October 31, 1947, "British Loan to Confederacy Thought Buried in Virginia:" It was related that Virginia Governor William M. Tuck had recently received a letter from F.L. Weathers, of Greenville, South Carolina, who related that his grandfather, a Confederate soldier, had helped bury $10 to $11 million in gold, a loan from the British government, in an iron box and burying it. "I know the exact location in Virginia where the money is buried," Mr. Weathers wrote. "Some time ago I talked with a resident of that area, who said that the place I have mentioned has remained undisturbed since the close of the Civil War." Governor Tuck told reporters that in view of the state's annual budget he would be grateful if such a treasure could be found. Apparently, Weathers declined the governor's invitation to come to Virginia and act upon his information.

• On an old plantation near Front Royal, somewhere along where a tree-lined drive was once located in front of the mansion's portico, a pot of silver coins may have been buried in 1861.

• Roanoke comprised many wealthy families before the Civil War. Many treasures of these people were hidden in and around the city, where they may remain to the present day.

• In Saltville, Abraham Smith and his sons are said to have buried $46,000 worth of silver and gold coins under a

[1] Nina and William Anderson, p. 22.

View of the old Moore house at Yorktown, Virginia, as photographed in May 1862. Gen. Cornwallis surrendered his British troops near here. Today the Yorktown area is said to be a fertile field for coin discoveries.

roadbed during the Civil War to prevent them from falling into the hands of Union soldiers.

• Thomas Jefferson Beale may or may not have deposited hundreds of thousands of dollars' worth of gold and silver coins and gold nuggets somewhere in the state in the early nineteenth century, in a location described in a cipher message, but many believe the whole story is just a hoax.

• In Page County, Edwin Powell is believed to have buried a large quantity of silver coins in the early eighteenth century. The site may be under a rock into which the design of a horseshoe is carved. Powell is believed to have been a counterfeiter, so there is no guarantee that, if found, the treasure will consist of genuine Spanish-American silver coins or whatever else may have been circulating in the area at the time.[1]

• One of the more fanciful tales holds that Charles II of England, who was on the throne from 1660 to 1685, was fearful of being deposed, and in an early-day version of what many dictators and their kin would do to national treasuries years later—even now in the twentieth century—he sent some trusted aides with a large holding of coins to be secreted in the colony of Virginia. Part of this treasure may even include some ancient Roman coins.[2]

• The coastal areas of the state are rich hunting grounds for anyone equipped with an electronic metal detector, and many old coins have been found, usually one at a time.

WASHINGTON TREASURES WAITING TO BE FOUND:

• Captain Johnson's cache of gold may still be at the old Johnson home site, Ilwaco, Pacific County.

---

[1] *Ibid.*, p. 19.
[2] *Ibid.*, pp. 20-21.

• On Vashon Island in Puget Sound a logger buried gold in 1877, and it remains unlocated.

• The treasure of Capt. James Scarborough is believed to be hidden at Fort Columbia.

• Sarah Smith Collard of Seattle traveled widely and is said to have hidden money in out of the way places on her journeys, including $500,000 in an old clock and several $1,000 bills in another location. In the 1950s the administrator of her estate was seeking clues as to where some of the money was.[1]

• Robbers' Roost (several different places bear this name in the American West) near Fruitland is the site of buried loot.

WEST VIRGINIA TREASURES WAITING TO BE FOUND:

• Dennis Adams buried his wealth in Kermit in the early twentieth century. It has never been found.

• Near Chapmanville a payroll in coins destined for Union troops may be buried on the west bank of the Buyandotte River, while an even larger payroll may be secreted in Upshur County near or in Rock Cave.

• In 1758 a group of Shawnee Indians attacked a settlement in this remote area, captured those who lived there, and took their coins and other possessions away. These have never been found and may have been buried on the slopes of South Fork Mountain.

• The outlaw sons of John Jennings may have buried loot in and around Wetzel County.

• In Jefferson County, Virginia, later a part of West Virginia (as of October 20, 1863), Rezin Davis Shepherd may have buried coins on his land in the 1850s and early 1860s.

• Near the Buckhannon River in Randolph County two separate hoards of coins may be hidden.

• Around 1820, Col. Joseph Van Swearingen, a Revolutionary War veteran, is said to have buried much of his fortune about a half mile north of Shepherdstown in Jefferson County, Virginia, in a district which later became part of West Virginia when it separated during the Civil War.

• In 1917 a draft evader is said to have buried $150,000 in the vicinity of Marlowe, Berkeley County.

WISCONSIN TREASURES WAITING TO BE FOUND:

• Near Antigo a bunch of bank robbers hid their loot, but were never able to come back to get it.

• The Dillinger gang hid $250,000 in currency in the woods near Mercer in 1934.

• Outlaws considered Bogus Bluff near Gotham, Richland County, to be a good hiding place for coins, many of which remain there today.

• On Stockton Island (one of the Apostle Islands near Bayfield) treasure is supposed to have been hidden by British soldiers.

WYOMING TREASURES WAITING TO BE FOUND:

• Bandits' loot hidden near old Fort Laramie has never been found.

• The Jack Slade gang hid treasure in Slade Canyon near Sunrise, Platte County.

• $37,000 in stagecoach holdup loot was hidden in 1878 near Newcastle, Weston County, and remains missing.

• The coins of an Army paymaster were buried at Smoot, Lincoln County, to avoid capture by Indians.

• "Teton" Jackson buried his loot at Cache Creek near Jackson Hole, possibly the same treasure as given in a report of $150,000 in stolen gold hidden in the area.

• In the vicinity of Baggs, Carbon County, outlaw treasure is hidden.

• Gold coins were found at Rock River, Albany County, in 1916, but are believed to be just a small part of a treasure that is still unlocated.

• Train holdup booty secreted near Rock Springs, Sweetwater County, remains untraced.

• Stagecoach treasure near Newcastle, Weston County, has been lost for decades.

Challenges

What better way to end the present chapter than to suggest that while the over hundreds of treasure stories and finds related in these pages each have their unique aspects, perhaps even more exciting narratives are ahead of us as treasure-detecting equipment, undersea exploration devices, and other technology improves. On the terrestrial front I read of a radar device that can "see" through 20 to 30 feet of sand or loose soil. What undiscovered treasures await searchers of old caves, mansion and plantation sites, bank foundations, and other locations?

The $50,000 in coins aboard the *Vineyard* may be discovered in whole or in part, possibly deteriorated by seawater as in the 1652-dated Massachusetts silver coins found in Boothbay, Maine. Or, perhaps they will be nearly pristine as with many of the gold coins recovered from the *S.S. Central America*. The coins of the *Republic, Lexington,* and many other ships await recovery. And, perhaps, some Wild West accounts of stagecoach robberies and Civil War stories of hidden army payrolls have an element of truth, and some numismatic artifacts will be found—much as the 1854 and 1855 Kellogg $20 coins were found near a cave entrance as secreted by victims of an Indian attack.

With *tens of thousands* of ships awaiting discovery and salvage, and who knows how many buried treasures on land, safe deposit box caches, cornerstones, and other hiding places waiting to be found accidentally or by trained treasure seekers, we await news with anticipation—with a few grains of salt at hand to sprinkle here and there if needed.

---

[1] Coffman, pp. 103-104.

APPENDIX I

Pseudo Hoards and Amazing "Finds"

(various dates)

This category includes items that have been questioned by numismatists or which contain restrikes or fantasies made later than the dates they bear. Other "finds" relate to the American series and have been attributed to old-time hoards or discoveries, but more likely were assembled in later times. In addition, several "theories" and "facts" presented to account for the rarity of certain issues are recited, some of which are quite amusing to read today.

Mention also should be made of the process of "laundering" coins, these being fakes, copies, fantasies, and other items that appear on the numismatic market backed by "pedigrees," sometimes impressive. Innovation and imagination know no bounds when it comes to bringing questionable coins to market. According to what some would have their victims believe, these "rarities" have been found by metal detectors, or have descended in the families of former Mint engravers or employees, or have been located in old safe deposit boxes, or in barns, pirate chests, or woodpiles. Old ranches and grist mills make convincing pedigrees.

Some particularly enterprising owners of spurious items have consigned them to auctions overseas, so the coins can be "discovered" by Americans who believe they have a chance to secure bargains that few other stateside numismatists know about. In another instance (not given in this book) a would-be salvor of undersea wrecks sprinkled some modern fake Spanish-American coins on the sea bottom, "discovered" them, and sold them to eager buyers.

It is worth noting that the same sort of laundering of fakes and the creation of phony pedigrees exists in other fields. For example, the art world was startled in 1996 to learn that art forgers of paintings were "found to have doctored the archives at the Tate Gallery [in London] so that when consulted by a prospective buyer of a painting or sculpture, the record shows that the fake is authentic."[1] The Tate, one of the world's most respected art museums, discovered the fraud in September 1995, and an investigation was begun at that time. An account in the *International Herald Tribune* further noted that apart from the Tate situation, "Investigators have reportedly discovered that, in some cases, forgers went so far as to print bogus catalogues and place them in museum libraries." In the 1950s a wealthy Texas collector of art was sold many rarities that were illustrated in beautiful catalogues; the only problem was that separate new pages featuring color illustrations of the fakes were printed and inserted in standard works of the artist in question. History made to order, it seems!

The desire to create worth from worthlessness is hardly new. The numerous accounts of alchemy attempted by advisors to the courts of medieval Europe make fascinating reading today. Many scientists were able to transmute lead into gold, it was said. Of course, their secret processes were never revealed.

A handy rule for numismatists: A phony coin accompanied by an elegant pedigree or story is still a phony coin.

If anything, the accounts given below have a great measure of entertainment value:

1854. The Boscawen Hoard: In 1854 a Mr. Getchell advised numismatist Dr. Ammi Brown that he had some *1650*-dated Massachusetts silver Pine Tree shillings as well

[1] Reference: *International Herald Tribune,* June 20, 1996, p. 1, "Setting the Records in Art Forgery," by Alan Riding.

as some with the normal 1652 date that he had obtained from an old man in Boscawen, N.H. The 1650-dated pieces were later adjudged counterfeit.[1]

1856. The Chelsea Hoard: In Chelsea, Massachusetts, near Boston, a reporter for the *Boston Journal,* issue of June 16, 1856, had this experience:

"We had the pleasure of seeing today some of the Pine Tree money of Massachusetts, which was dug up some time since at Chelsea. There were a shilling, sixpence, threepence, and twopence, dated 1652, in almost as good preservation as if they had been coined one year [ago] only, every letter and figure upon them being perfectly clear and distinct; they probably have been entombed for more than 150 years. The bottle in which they were found, and several of the coins, were purchased by a gentleman to be presented to the British Museum."

This notice caught the eye of reader "Nummus," who hastened to pen a commentary for the *Boston Transcript,* August 16, 1856, noting in part:

"It is remarkable to observe how many different means unprincipled people resort to replenish their empty purses. Too proud to work for an honest livelihood, and too indolent to engage in some legitimate pursuit, their wits are constantly at work devising new ways to fatten themselves upon the industry of others....

"A few weeks since a paragraph appeared in several of our papers, stating that a large number of Pine Tree coins had been recently dug up in this vicinity. No sooner had this announcement been made than complete sets of this coinage poured into our city. NE shillings and sixpence, before so rare, together with some other pieces never before seen, were to be found exposed for sale in this city.... It has, however, turned out that all of these pieces are counterfeit, and made by a man in New York City, who represents them to be originals...."

The perpetrator was one Thomas Wyatt, who lived on Mercer Street, New York City, circa 1840-1860. A knowledgeable numismatist, he wrote *A Description of the National Medals of America, Presented to the Officers of the Wars of the Revolution and 1812* (New York, 1854) and once assisted Prof. Daniel E. Groux[2] in the making of reproductions of rare U.S. medals. His interests were varied and also included natural history, religion, military history, conchology, and other fields. Circa 1856 Thomas Wyatt struck or had made to his order a dozen "sets" of Massachusetts silver coins, each containing one each of the NE shilling and sixpence; an Oak Tree shilling and twopence; a Pine tree sixpence, threepence, and hitherto unknown one pence; and a Good Samaritan shilling.[3]

1880. To find treasure, go to Africa: Dr. Ivan C. Michels' 1880 (and other editions) book, *The Current Gold and Silver Coins of All Nations,* included helpful information about the history and rarity of many United States issues. While much if not most of the entries were accurate or were reflections of scholarship at the time, some included tales, today considered to be fanciful, to explain the rarity of certain issues. The reader of the following might well come to the conclusion that a trip to Africa would yield a numismatic bounty. Samples:

What with pirates, the "Millions for defense, not one cent for tribute" slogan, and tales of adventure, Tripoli, shown here under bombardment by United States naval forces, was a logical focal point for rumors of missing 1804 silver dollars said to have been cargo aboard ships such as these.

The mysterious 1801 $5 gold coin (today in the 1990s none are known to exist): "Considerable dispute has been advanced among collectors of coins as to the issue of the half eagle of 1801. The United States Mint report for that year returns a coinage of 26,006 pieces. James Ross Snowden, Esq., one of the directors of the U.S. Mint, and author of *A Description of Ancient and Modern Coins in the Cabinet Collection of the Mint of the United States,* published in 1860, states the number of half eagles coined in 1801 as aforementioned. In the *Annual Report of Director of U.S. Mint,* 1879, to the Secretary of the Treasury, on page 45, the coinage of half eagles of 1801 is stated at their value of $130,030.00. Per contra William S. Appleton, of Boston, in his summary of U.S. coins, ignores the half eagle of 1801. In the Coin Cabinet of the U.S. Mint in Philadelphia, no specimen is to be found. Dr. M.W. Dickeson, in his *American Numismatic Manual,* says: "26,006 pieces were coined, as per report of the U.S. Mint, and yet every piece has escaped the eagle eyes of numismatologists: Not a single piece having been seen by them.... There is a mystery connected with it wholly inexplicable to us." Diligent inquiry establishes the fact that a half eagle of 1801 is in the coin collection of Edward Wood, Esq. Dr. M.W. Dickeson admits, in a footnote in his publication to have seen two specimens of the half eagle of 1801. For the seeming total disappearance of this coin, a theory—and only a theory can be advanced, namely: On the 10th of June 1801, the Bashaw of Tripoli, a petty prince of the Barbary States, in the north of Africa, declared war against the

[1] Cf. *Sylvester S. Crosby, Early Coins of America,* 1875, pp. 62-67; Sydney P. Noe, *Pine Tree Coinage of Massachusetts,* 1952, pp. 42-42; Don Taxay, *Counterfeit, Mis-Struck and Unofficial U.S. Coins,* 1963, pp. 133-135. Two of these 1650 shillings later went into the Charles I. Bushnell Collection.

[2] Seemingly a remarkable person on the collecting scene, in the mid-1850s Groux announced that he would soon publish a three-volume set of books on American numismatics. Apparently, he ran out of steam, for after a flurry of activity including visiting collectors up and down the Atlantic Seaboard, nothing further happened.

[3] Cf. Richard D. Kenney, *Struck Copies of Early American Coins,* 1952, pp. 1-2; *Sylvester S. Crosby, Early Coins of America,* 1875, p. 74 (silver penny

United States. Ships of Algiers, Tunis, Tripoli, and Morocco captured American vessels; and, not satisfied with ordinary piratical plundering, they reduced the crew and passengers of the captured vessels to a condition of servitude. Captain Bainbridge was dispatched to cruise in the Mediterranean in order to protect American commerce. Before leaving the U.S. shores it is surmised that the purser of his vessel was provided with half eagles of that year's coinage; if so, it is but probable that only a few coins ever reached our shores again."

The actions of the Barbary pirates and their request for money to persuade them to stop their operations led to the rousing cry attributed to American diplomat Charles Cotesworth Pinckney, "Millions for defense, not one cent for tribute," which years later (circa 1837 and again circa 1863) was widely used on cent-size tokens.

The rare 1804 dollar is the subject of a related theory as expressed by Michel: "1804 dollar—similar to the dollar of 1803. This dollar has become exceedingly scarce, and the last sale of a fine specimen was made at $1,000. Of this dollar, according to returns of the United States Mint records, 19,570 pieces were struck, and, with the exception of a few, were all exported to Africa to pay the sailors and soldiers engaged in the war against Tripoli. On the 10th of June 1801, the Bashaw of Tripoli declared war against the United States; but no further notice was taken of the declaration until 1803, when Commodore Preble was sent to Tripoli with a large squadron. On the 31st of October 1803, Captain Bainbridge was sent into the harbor of Tripoli to reconnoiter. His vessel, the *Philadelphia,* of 44 guns, advanced too far in eager pursuit of a small Tripolitan gunboat, and struck on a rock. The officers were treated as prisoners of war, but the crew were made slaves. In 1804, Lieutenant Stephen Decatur was ordered to recapture the *Philadelphia*, which he promptly accomplished. As it was impossible to take her out, she was set on fire and abandoned. Soon after, Tripoli was bombarded several times by the U.S. ships of war. In 1804, an expedition was started from the United States against Tripoli, headed by Captain Eaton and Hamet Carmanly, exile and elder brother of the Bashaw of Tripoli. Their march lay across a thousand miles of desert; yet it was accomplished, with indescribable fatigue and suffering, in 50 days. To pay the expenses of this little army of mounted Arabs and 70 American seamen, these 1804 dollars were shipped to the coast of Africa, and only very few of them, if any, were brought back by the returned victors. A few years ago 10 pieces of 1804 dollars were struck from the old original dies at the U.S. Mint in Philadelphia and distributed. All but two or three were afterwards called in by order of our government, and to this day the coin cabinet of the Philadelphia Mint exhibits one 1804 dollar struck in 1804, and another with the same date, but of the latter issue."

The rare 1799 cent: "This cent, owing to a heavy export of the same by a New England merchant in 1799, to the coast of Africa, has become very scarce, and when in find condition sells at a heavy premium.

Perhaps it is appropriate at this point to comment upon various rumors, unrelated to the preceding, relative to the rarity today of the 1844 Liberty Seated dime. In actuality, today it is fairly scarce, but probably no more elusive than its mintage of 72,500—one of the lowest of the era—would suggest. Numismatic writer C. Frank Ross, Jr., apparently coined the name "Orphan Annie Dime" for this issue, possibly because he considered it to be "alone" in the scale of rarity among dimes of its time. He and others devised stories about the 1844 dime. To quote the mention of these tales by historian Pete Smith in his biography of Ross,[1] "They were hijacked by Indians on their way across the West, they were lost in the Johnstown flood [1889], burned in the Chicago fire [1871]," etc.

1890. Imagination rampant in Dedham: In 1890 the various Boston newspapers carried accounts of a fabulous hoard of "ancient" coins found when an old well was examined on Two Elms Farm in nearby Dedham. A seal was removed from an old iron pot, and Spanish, British, French, Irish, and other coins were revealed, including a "United States coin of 1795." Trouble was that the entire matter was a hoax.[2]

1890s. Kroll hoard of California gold: Herman Kroll, a jeweler with premises at 37 John Street, New York City, apparently produced large quantities of Liberty Head "California gold coins," mainly of the 25¢ and 50¢ denominations, octagonal and round shapes. Although these are believed to have been made sometime between the 1880s and the early 1900s, they bear earlier dates in the 1850s and 1860s.[3]

Many of these coins were sold to pioneer gold specialist A.C. Nygren, and nearly a thousand appeared in Henry Chapman's sale of the Nygren Collection, April 29, 1924. Certain of Kroll's dies survived to a later date and were used after the early 1960s to strike additional pieces.

Opinion as to the original intent of the Kroll pieces has been divided. Specialist and author Kenneth Lee considered them to be controversial as to authenticity and did not integrate them into his book on California gold. On the other hand Walter Breen and Ronald Gillio featured and illustrated them in their 1983 work, *California Pioneer Fractional Gold,* relating much of preceding and assigning them and others to Period Three (1883 onward) issues.

1900s. Stephen K. Nagy productions: Nagy, a well-known Philadelphia dealer and one-time business associate of J.W. Haseltine, is believed to have caused certain pieces to have been struck around the turn of the present century. Examples include Templeton Reid "trial pieces" of gold coins

illustrated from a 1763 work by Martin Folkes, "Tables of English Silver and Gold Coins," which may have been Wyatt's inspiration; in 1856 there were no American numismatic references in print concerning the series); Sydney P. Noe, *New England and Willow Tree Coinages,* 1943, pp. 50-55; Noe, *Pine Tree Coinage of Massachusetts,* 1952, p. 47 and other citations; Don Taxay, *Counterfeit, Mis-Struck and Unofficial U.S. Coins,* 1963, pp. 137-139; also Eric P. Newman, *The Secret of the Good Samaritan Shilling,* 1959, various pages; p. 43 includes biographical notes on Wyatt; the Newman plates illustrate Wyatt and other copies/forgeries. Wyatt copies were first illustrated in the Clay Collection sale catalogue, 1871.

1 *American Numismatic Biographies,* p. 202.

2 *American Journal of Numismatics,* October 1890, p. 48. "The discovery so minutely [*sic*] described never took place; the whole story is the work of some reporter's imagination." The "minute descriptions" were mainly listings of dates, but with no information about denominations or varieties.

3 Backdating small denomination California gold coins was not an unusual procedure, and numerous other, earlier, coiners did it. Kroll's productions were late in the game and were considered more as tokens or souvenirs than as pieces made for use as small change.

struck on U.S. large cents, typically of the Draped Bust type.[1] These were "laundered," presumably by Nagy, through various dealers with no mention being made of their non-contemporary origin. Today, such fantasies are highly collectible in their own right.

1923, August. The Hauser gold coin find: On August 23, 1923, Lee Hauser, a 23-year-old laborer on a road project near Hagerstown, Maryland, located a $20 gold piece.[2] This was the prelude to a major find: a tin container the size of a large cigar box, stuffed with gold coins which was soon unearthed! Apparently, his co-workers gathered around, and his employer, George W. Ingram, also gazed upon the scene, generously stating that the coins belonged to the finder. At this point the story becomes complicated. The Department of Justice sent four agents to investigate—on the theory that the coins could have been part of a cache hidden by Grover Cleveland Bergdoll, who was described a World War draft evader and German sympathizer. Grover and his brother Erwin were said to have operated from a hotel in Hagerstown, and possibly in exchange for certain illegal information, received as payment five valises filled with money, which was taken by Bergdoll to Germany, America being neutral at the time. Excitement prevailed as news of the gold treasure spread. Lee Hauser then disclaimed finding any such cache of gold coins, and his sister Esther told the press that the entire story was a hoax. No more questions, no more publicity was wanted by the finder. Whether it was a hoax or not remains the subject of conjecture. In any event, Uncle Sam's agents went away coinless.

1940s-1960s. Numismatic fantasies and daydreams: Someone with a barely passing grasp ("a little knowledge is a dangerous thing") of history and a good measure of imagination is believed to have created in the 1950s a group of large cents, half dollars, and other coins counterstamped with modern-style letters with variations on the Wells Fargo name including WELLS FARGO / U.S. / R.W.P.O / EXPRESS (probably intended to represent "Railway Post Office") and the even more improbable WELLS FARGO / BONDED / LEWIS & CLARKE.

The large cents were said to have been used in Nevada as chits or receipts by Wells Fargo on its Pony Express stagecoaches. Trouble is that large cents were never used in the American West, that the Pony Express (which employed single riders, not stagecoaches) was not established until 1860 by which time large cents were obsolete, the correct spelling is Lewis and Clark (and their expedition took place in the first decade of the nineteenth century, decades before Wells, Fargo & Co. was formed by Henry Wells and William Fargo in 1852), etc.

Related in concept are coins with large, modern-style letters counterstamped with LOUISIANA / 4 BITS and TEXAS / 4 BITS.[3] As if these were not enough, circa 1958 and especially circa 1970, groups of early nineteenth-century coins crudely counterstamped UNION MINE / 5 Dol. / OREG. / TERR came on the market. "They should fool no one except the most uninitiated," token specialist Alan V. Weinberg advised token expert Russell Rulau.[4]

Michael Hodder reported this:[5] "On the same general subject, something called a 'Texas dollar' does exist, a Mexican silver 8-real piece counterstamped with TEXAS 8 BITS. I know of only one such piece, that shown by an eastern numismatist at the March 31, 1950, meeting of the Brooklyn Coin Club."

Further from Michael Hodder: "I have seen at least two Spanish colonial 8-escudo gold pieces with a plug in the center which has been counterstamped '16.' One was on a 1761 Santiago Mint coin, while the other was on a 1778 Popayan Mint piece. I have no idea what these were, although I do not believe them to have been contemporary. These, occasionally, have been called Texas or California 16 dollar pieces, akin to the Moffat $16 gold bars."

1950s. The secret of an old mill: In the early 1950s a young couple—we'll call them Rick and Stephanie for purposes of telling of this remarkable treasure—bought a property in rural Connecticut. An old grist mill built in the 1790s was on the land. Its water wheel had long ceased turning, and the snows and rains of many seasons had penetrated the loose wooden siding. Derelict probably since the last century, the structure seemed to be on the verge of collapse.

The husband and wife decided to explore it. Who knows, perhaps something interesting could be found—perhaps some old newspapers, record books, or other artifacts from the long-ago time when the mill was important in local agricultural commerce.

Hours were spent poking about in nooks and crannies until darkness gathered. Early the next day they continued their search, encouraged by finding an old almanac, an Indian penny, and a few old books.

Aha! At last, something worthwhile: Behind a loose board in a storeroom a cavity was found. Quickly, other boards were pried away to reveal a metal-banded wooden keg filled to the brim with old pennies. Picking one up, Rick noted that it had a lady's head on one side and the date 1793. On the back side was a chain design and some lettering. He then reached in for a generous handful, then a double handful. All of the pennies looked the same and all were made in 1793. Gosh, there must be thousands of them!

Could these have any value to a collector?

Determined to find out, the husband and wife took one of the copper pennies with them the next time they visited New York City. Showing it to a coin shop owner and telling of the thousands more left at home, they were told, in effect, "Yes, these old coins could have value—not a great amount, but enough to make it worthwhile for you to bring in the whole batch for my offer. Right now, could I buy the sample you brought with you?"

"What would you offer?"

---

[1] Several different $10 and $25 pieces are described and illustrated by Donald Kagin, *Private Gold Coins and Patterns of the United States,* p. 378; it being his opinion that the dies were original as made for Reid in the 1830s, but not used until many decades later when Nagy had impressions struck.
[2] B.A. Tompkins, *Treasure,* p. 110, citing the August 25, 1923, issue of the *New York Times,* "Hauser Hoax" and other sources.
[3] Cf. *American and Canadian Countermarked Coins,* Dr. Gregory G. Brunk, p. 188 (Wells Fargo). Also p. 110 (Louisiana) and p. 174 (Texas). Description of history of these pieces from a western numismatist having some for sale (letter to author, 1980s).
[4] Rulau described the UNION MINE pieces on pp. 245-246 of *Standard Catalogue of United States Tokens,* 1700-1900, 1993, pp. 245-246. Also Alan V. Weinberg, note, October 16, 1996.
[5] Communications, July 1 and 7, 1996.

An old mill in New England.

"How much do you want for it?"

"You are the expert. You tell us. That is why we brought it here."

"How about ten dollars?"

"Wow! That sounds great! We never thought it would be worth that much! However, we don't want to sell it right now, but we will be back soon, now that we know they are so valuable and you want to buy them."

A nice story, but without a word of truth.

The tale had its genesis when a knowledgeable old-time collector of United States large cents connived with a young coin dealer and decided to use a high-grade 1793 Chain cent from the former's collection to play a joke on a coin shop owner they both knew. They enlisted two friends in their 20s to carry it out.[1]

1950s. Scrooge McDuck: For comic relief, mention should probably be made of Walt Disney's cartoon character, Scrooge McDuck, uncle to ducklings Huey, Dewey, and Louie. McDuck loved money had had three *cubic acres* of the stuff, in which he enjoyed cavorting, diving, etc. At one time he took a fancy to 1916 Standing Liberty quarter dollars and tried to hoard every one in existence, which he almost did.

1950s to date. Great "numismatic rarities" are found: In the 1950s and 1960s copies of many thousands of American rarities were cast in base metals and were at one time sold by a company (not a regular coin dealer) in Yonkers, New York, for $2 each, with price lists being sent to dealers. These included copies of the 1783 Nova Constellatio 1000 units or one mark piece (the copy was cast from a nineteenth-century copy, not from the original), 1776 Continental "dollars," 1776 New Hampshire pattern coppers, and others. In addition, and possibly by another distributor, large numbers of 1855 Blake & Company pieces in imitation of a $20 gold coin, but in base metal washed with a gold-colored substance, were sold. Also common was a forgery purporting to be a $20 gold ingot issued by Parsons & Co. in Colorado and gold-colored base metal copies of the 1787 Brasher doubloon.

All of these things contributed to give legitimate coin dealers countless headaches as phones jangled with people thinking they had found a fortune, and who did not want to be told that what they had was a worthless fake. Later, the Hobby Protection Act required that copies be marked as such, but enough earlier copies remain that these pieces will deceive for centuries to come. Even if a copy were to be marked COPY, a determined person can remove or fill in the lettering.

1950s. Republic of Texas gold coins: These pieces are authentic Spanish-American gold coins of the 1830s, but with modern fantasy counterstamps. On the obverse a star surrounded by a wreath has the outer legend REPUBLIC OF TEXAS. On the reverse a liberty cap (such as found on early nineteenth-century Mexican coins) is surrounded with the legend HOUSTON TREAS. DEPT. 16 D. 8 E. 21 C.

In his book, *American and Canadian Countermarked Coins,* p. 147, Dr. Gregory Brunk illustrated a specimen and commented: "These pieces were discovered in the early 1960s, and they appear to be struck from coin dies. Their origin is uncertain. Some think they are recent fantasies."

Walter Breen related to the author that in the 1950s he was enlisted to help create the designs for these, based upon historical records. New dies for the counterstamps were made in Milan, Italy, and impressions were struck on authentic 8-escudos (equivalent to about $16 U.S.) Spanish-American gold coins plus at least one trial striking in lead or white metal.

Breen was told that F.C.C. Boyd had conceived the idea as a prank, possibly to see what a well-known Eastern dealer would say when he was shown a handful. However, the pieces seem to have been suppressed.

1960s. Mormon gold coin "patterns": In the early 1960s a large group of Mormon "pattern" coins surfaced and were represented as being from an old Ohio hoard, where the coins had been for many decades. All were one-sided (uniface), and some had wire shanks attached to their backs. The designs were those used on the Salt Lake City coinage of the Mormons, circa 1849-1860.

Opinion as to the authenticity of these was mixed at the time, with some numismatists calling them modern counterfeits and others considering them to be rare patterns. Years later in his 1981 book, *Private Gold Coins and Patterns of the United States,* pp. 368-369, Donald H. Kagin described them thus: "All restrikes probably made during the 50-year anniversary in 1898."

1960s to date. Colorado bordello tokens, Coca-Cola memorabilia, and more: In the 1960s collectors of tokens were delighted to find that a bordello in a Colorado mining camp in the Rockies west of Denver had issued tokens redeemable by its patrons during the nineteenth century. What a great new discovery! What a pedigree! Certainly, tokens from a madam in a red light district were more interesting to own than those issued by dry-goods merchants or livery stables.

Then it developed that not just one, but several Rocky Mountain bordellos issued brass tokens. Many additional

1 Recollection of the former "young coin dealer," who shall remain nameless at present, to the author, circa 1958.

pieces came on the market, obviously from an old hoard. Then more appeared. And still more. Before long, such tokens—often lightly etched, worn, or weathered—became common in Colorado souvenir shops. It developed that they had been made in recent times by a Chicago manufacturer of tokens.

In more recent times, token makers have incorporated other flights of numismatic imagination. In an article in *Numismatic News,* July 9, 1996, token specialist David E. Schenkman described two tokens. One was marked DRINK COCA-COLA, GOOD ONLY AT 1904 WORLD'S FAIR, FREE, and the other had the inscription U.S. DEPT. OF INDIAN AFFAIRS / VALUE $10 / HAY, GRAIN, FARM GOODS. Schenkman commented: "Fantasies such as this have plagued the antique, collectibles, numismatic markets for more than 20 years, and during that time many people have paid good money for worthless pieces of metal."

In the *Token and Medal Society Journal,* August 1996, Schenkman described a few more: Copper octagonal token marked FORT WAGNER / SOUTH CAROLINE / 1863, etc. • Brass token marked EMPIRE CITY MINE / 1876 / EMPIRE, COLO. Reverse inscribed COLORADO GOLD / 5 / DOLLARS. • Brass token marked THE TOPIC SALOON / 1890 / LEADVILLE / COLO.

Typically, "research" for such a token-making project involves checking old newspapers, directories, and other old sources for the names and specialties of merchants, tradesmen, and others. Then a sketch or design is made of a token of the type that *might have been* issued by such an establishment, the wording on the token matching known genuine tokens produced by other firms of the same era or locality. Then the services of a die shop or token-making enterprise are enlisted, with privacy requested, and fantasy coins are created.

1960s. Dozens of missing 1916 Standing Liberty quarters: In the Pennsylvania Dutch area of Pennsylvania in the 1950s an enthusiastic numismatist was fond of displaying *one* of his treasures: a gem Uncirculated 1916 Standing Liberty quarter, a classic rare issue worthy of the admiration of just about anyone.

During a period of time this single coin generated several stories of its being taken from an original bank-wrapped roll of 40 coins still in existence and, better yet, from one of four original rolls. When asked about the veracity of such rumors, the numismatist simply gave a knowing wink. The man died, and his children became embroiled in a big squabble with each other when only a single rare 1916 quarter could be found, as they just "knew" that their dad had owned dozens more—and couldn't find which of the siblings had pilfered them, but wasn't telling. In actuality, probably there was only a single coin to begin with.

1960s to date. Misuses of Mint medals: The Philadelphia Mint maintains on sale many back-dated medals, some of which were first made in the early nineteenth century. Some pieces are from original dies, others are from modern copy dies, but none bear any notation such as "copy" or "restrike," federal law and the Hobby Protection Act notwithstanding (although it can be argued that a modern "restrike" from copy dies may not be a copy).

As one of many examples, such were described in detail in the 1972 work, ***Medals of the United States Mint Issued For Public Sale, Department of the Treasury,*** published by the Government Printing Office. The foreword noted in part: "All of the medals listed in this catalogue are offered for purchase by the public. Order forms appear in the appendix."

Although the Treasury Department and Bureau of the Mint had no intention to deceive, many of these restruck and copy medals were later offered by others as originals.

In a typical scenario, someone with a silver-plated copper restrike (or, infrequently, a silver restrike) of a nineteenth-century Indian Peace medal, an original of which would be worth thousands of dollars, will give it the appearance of having been used by an Indian years ago, by tumbling it in a machine to give it the appearance of wear, and drilling a hole at the top for suspension. Hundreds of these have been so altered, and typically sold at "bargain" prices at gun shows and antiques shows. A sales pitch goes something like this: "I bought this medal, don't know what it is worth, but as I didn't pay much for it, you can have it for only $300." The seller does not represent that it was a fake and later can claim that he sold it "as is." Every so often a small group or "hoard" of such restrikes comes on the market, usually accompanied by a tale of the pieces having been found by a metal detector in territory once occupied by Indians, or something along this line. All professional numismatists who specialize in tokens and medals have heard many such stories of elation, then woe, by people who have bought these "bargains."

1970s. The Indian and Lincoln cent rarities hoard: In the mid-1970s a man in the San Francisco Bay area of California visited Los Angeles dealers and had with him hundreds of 1877 and 1909-S Indian cents, 1909-S V.D.B. cents, and other rare issues, most of which were lustrous brown Uncirculated with somewhat pinkish edges. The pieces were said to have been put away years earlier.

An alert professional called in the Secret Service and, after questioning, the owner of the coins confessed to making them. However, he was of an innovative turn of mind and claimed that he did nothing wrong, as he had acquired very worn specimens of these varieties and by a casting process had simply "augmented" them by adding more metal. The final disposition of the case is not known.

1970s. $1,000 for a worthless dime. Thomas K. DeLorey recalled this:[1] "While I was working at ANACS, we had a middle-aged man come in one day with an rare 1894-S dime he had just purchased on a vacation to the Philippines. The coin might be worth many tens of thousands of dollars, and he wanted us to authenticate it. Unfortunately, it was a Philadelphia Mint coin with an added S, very professionally done. It seems that the man, a collector, had been in the habit of inquiring in small towns if anybody had any old coins, and in one town a storekeeper said he knew an old man who had a rarity. He closed his shop and drove the collector on a circuitous route up in the hills, and introduced him to the old man, who said that during the war he had rescued an American pilot and hidden him from the Japanese, and in gratitude the pilot had given him this very valuable rarity. Now that he was old, he wished to sell

---

[1] Letter, September 29, 1996.

the coin. Eventually they settled upon a price of $1,000, which the American paid quickly, concealing his excitement at obtaining such a bargain.

"Upon returning to the U.S. the collector rushed to Colorado Springs, where I examined the coin and gave him the bad news. He was angry he had been duped (and, I guess, because he was not going to make the huge profit he was anticipating!) and was prepared to fly back to the Philippines to try to get his money back when I convinced him he had been had by professional con men and his money was gone. Since then I have heard a similar story from a dealer, involving another 1894-S. These con men, or others, may be spreading the rumors about rare coins to lure in other suckers. Of course, there is not much an American can do after the fact if he is cheated in a foreign country and buys 'bargain' coins for cash."

Stories such as this abound and often involve eager collectors shelling out cash while on trips a long way from home to buy "rarities" at below-wholesale prices from sellers who want the matter kept secret from relatives (or business partners etc.), or, don't want Uncle Sam (or the French customs agents, or the British tax authorities, etc.) to know about it, etc. Reasons are many and diverse. Days, weeks, and thousands of miles later, the coins are offered to rare coin dealers or are submitted for authentication or grading, and are found to be worthless fakes.

Circa 1976: "Mystery tokens" found on Long Island: The September 6, 1994, issue of *Numismatic News* contained an article by Christopher Batio, "Mystery 'tokens' Dug Up on Long Island Shore," which told of what was viewed by some as a fabulous find. Working with a metal detector, a treasure hunter "dug up more than 100 roughly round chunks of what looked like copper and pewter....that look like tokens that would have been meant to circulateduring the Revolutionary War.... More than 10 different types [were found]. All but one is dated between 1774 and 1779, yet none of them corresponds with any known tokens of the colonial or Revolutionary period. This fact makes them immediately suspect to numismatists. What are they then? Fantasy issues produced sometime after the Revolution? Someone's experiments, as old as the Revolutionary period? Unfinished buttons?"

The pieces were said to have been found on the shore of Long Island Sound near Fort Salonga, New York. Inscriptions on the pieces included UNITE OR DIE, UNITY, CONTINENTAL CENT OR PENCE, ONE CENT, PASS AS ONE PENCE, and PLATT'S TAVERN / HUNTINGTON. On October 24, 1994, Russell Rulau, well-known token expert and author, corresponded with Rufus B. Langhams, local (Huntington, New York) historian who had been called upon to research the pieces and, in fact, had written a monograph on them, *Long Island Revolutionary Coins, Patterns & Tokens 1774-1779,* which was offered for sale by the town of Huntington. Rulau stated that there was no historical backing to support these having been made in the 1770s.

Further: "The items are, on their face, too good to be true and thus suspect. They could have been made a century ago for some personal whim; a number of Americans overcome by nostalgia made their own coin-like items in the 1850-1880 period and these are pretty well documented, but new ones may turn up.:..."[1] It should be further noted that a correct rendering of the denomination of one penny would be PENNY, for pence is the plural term. Further, the first American coin denominated ONE CENT was the Massachusetts cent of 1787. The decimal system of coinage, with cents, was not used in America until long after 1774-1779; Continental Currency notes of the 1770s are denominated in Spanish milled dollars (divisions of which were reals, not cents).

1980s. The Philippines hoard: An American stationed or living in the Philippines wrote many detailed letters to rare coin dealers describing a vast treasure of United States coins buried circa 1940 to prevent capture by the Japanese. The story grew in the telling, and after a while the hoard was said to have included an 1804 silver dollar, Proof trade dollars of 1884 and 1885, and a bag of 1933 $10 gold pieces! Although the prospect seemed to be quite exciting at first to those contacted, no coins are known to have materialized, and as more and more classic rarities were added to the list, skepticism grew until further letters on the subject went directly to the wastebasket.

1980s. Hoards of "1911-D" $5 and other fake gold coins: In 1996, Michael Fahey, authenticator for the ANACS grading service, reported that he had recently inspected a hoard of counterfeit 1911-D half eagles. Further, "This counterfeit has been in our photomicrograph files since the 1970s and was most likely first introduced in the 1960s. When I first started working as an authenticator for ANACS in the early 1980s, this counterfeit turned up at coin shows and then dried up, but now it appears to be back."[2]

As the leading grading services (ANACS, NGC, and PCGS), and possibly some others as well, guarantee the authenticity of the gold and other coins they encapsulate, the threat of counterfeits to knowledgeable buyers in the numismatic community has lessened greatly in recent years. However, in bullion exchanges, flea markets, antique shops, and other places they are still encountered with frequency and are often offered at "bargain" prices.

The writer recalls a swing through Europe in 1978 during which bullion exchanges (not staffed by professional numismatists) were visited in Greece, France, England, and elsewhere, and virtually all $1 and $3 coins seen were struck counterfeits, as were many of other denominations.

1980s. The Chapman pedigrees: Often when a coin can be pedigreed to a well-known numismatist its value and desirability are enhanced. Of old-time dealers, the name of Philadelphia dealer Henry Chapman (1859-1935) ranks especially high, for he and his brother S. Hudson Chapman (1857-1931) handled many really outstanding coins and collections in their time.

An enterprising Californian in the 1980s acquired some old, unused Henry Chapman coin envelopes and used them to store recently-acquired inventory items from various sources, thus giving his stock the appearance of a long-forgotten holding. In short order the deception was discovered, and the "Henry Chapman pedigree" idea came to a quick end.

---

1 Copies of correspondence with Rufus B. Langhans furnished to the author by Russell Rulau.

2 *Coin World,* October 7, 1996, p. 32.

In the 1960s another inventive numismatist did the same thing with B. Max Mehl (life dates: 1884-1957) envelopes.

1980s-1990s. The Wells Fargo coin hoard: In this era a story made the rounds that a vast hoard of mint-sealed bags of gold and silver coins put away years ago by Wells Fargo & Co. had been discovered in a Chicago (or San Francisco) bank vault, and a Southern California (or Chicago or New Hampshire) dealer had an agreement to buy it. Bags of rare 1927-D $20 pieces and 1919-S Liberty Walking half dollars were just two of many treasures therein, the aggregate of which was said to total many tens of millions of dollars in numismatic value. After a year or two, rumors subsided, and so far as is known, no newly-found 1927-D $20 or other rarities in quantity came on the market.

In 1996 the author saw an inventory said to have been made of the hoard, which was different in its composition from some of the accounts heard earlier (for example, the inventory showed just a single 1927-D $20 coin, but it did include 4,000 1919-S halves). This delineation occupied many pages and, at the very least, would have required a lot of effort to create. The list began with early half cents and ended with late-date double eagles.

Among single coin rarities were gold Proofs more or less continuous from the 1850s onward and an 1884 trade dollar (highly unusual as numismatists believe that all 10 pieces released are presently accounted for), a choice Uncirculated 1871-CC dime, an 1873-S half dollar *without* arrows (no others known to exist), and many other delicacies. The composition was that of a very large and impressive numismatic collection plus unbelievable quantities of certain rare as well as common date coins. The numerous great rarities such as the 1884 trade dollar, Carson City coins by date sequence (the 1870-CC $20 is EF), and the run of early gold Proofs, would have to indicate that this was formed by a numismatist who was prescient enough in the nineteenth century to acquire many fine items, in combination with someone with the financial wherewithal to store huge quantities face-value wise of $20 gold coins and other items for many decades, in combination with someone else who kept adding to the collection through the 1930s. And, this string of events would have had to have been accomplished without a peep about this activity appearing in any numismatic catalogues or magazines over a period of nearly a century.

Highlights of items present in very large quantities in the revised inventory included:

10¢: 1877-CC, 348 pieces, AU to Uncirculated.
10¢: 1878-CC, 42 pieces, grades as preceding.
10¢: 1896, 4,115 pieces, Uncirculated.
10¢: 1904-S, 5,000 pieces, Uncirculated.
10¢: 1917-D, 10,000 pieces, Uncirculated.
10¢: 1920-D, 4,284 pieces, Uncirculated.
25¢: 1860-O, 1,553 pieces, Uncirculated.
25¢: 1872-CC, 1,100 pieces, Uncirculated.
25¢: 1892-O, 4,000 pieces, Uncirculated.
25¢: 1904-O, 8,000 pieces, Uncirculated.
25¢: 1907-D, 8,000 pieces, Uncirculated.
50¢: 1877-CC, 2,000 pieces, Uncirculated.
50¢: 1893-O, 1,080 pieces, Uncirculated.
50¢: 1894-O, 560 pieces, Uncirculated.
50¢: 1894-S, 1,579 pieces, Uncirculated.
50¢: 1895-O, 2,000 pieces, Uncirculated.
50¢: 1900-S, 1,840 pieces, Uncirculated.
50¢: 1904-O, 6,000 pieces, Uncirculated.
50¢: 1907-D, 6,000 pieces, Uncirculated.
50¢: 1913-S, 2,000 pieces, Uncirculated.
50¢: 1918-D, 4,000 pieces, Uncirculated, weakly struck.
50¢: 1920-D, 1,980 pieces, Uncirculated.
50¢: 1920-S, 2,474 pieces, Uncirculated.
50¢: 1923-S, 1,680 pieces, Uncirculated.
50¢: 1929-D, 1,280 pieces, Uncirculated.
50¢: 1929-S, 2,869 pieces, Uncirculated.
50¢: 1933-S, 2,100 pieces, Uncirculated.
$1 silver: 1879-CC, 140 pieces, Uncirculated.
$1 silver: 1884-O, 30,000 pieces, Uncirculated.
$1 silver: 1888-O, 20,000 pieces, Uncirculated.
$1 silver: 1894-S, 1,000 pieces, Uncirculated.
$1 silver: 1895-O, 1,000 pieces, Uncirculated. [Highly unusual; this would be the first Treasury sealed bag confirmed to exist in modern times].
$1 silver: 1901-O, 4,550 pieces, Uncirculated.
$1 silver: 1903-O, 6,450 pieces, Uncirculated. [Highly unusual as until the Treasury release of autumn 1962, fewer than a dozen Uncirculated coins were known to exist in all of numismatics.]
$1 silver: 1904-O, 35,560 pieces, Uncirculated.
$1 silver: 1922-S, 43,000 pieces, Uncirculated.
$1 silver: 1923-D 12,000 pieces, Uncirculated.
$1 silver: 1923-S, 18,000 pieces, Uncirculated.
$1 silver: 1924-S, 2,000 pieces, Uncirculated.
$1 silver: 1925-S, 19,000 pieces, Uncirculated.
$1 silver: 1928-S, 1,000 pieces, Uncirculated.
$1 silver, other Morgan issues: Many 1,000 coin bags of various dates.
$1 trade: 1877-CC 1,000 pieces, Uncirculated. [Highly unusual as trade dollars were demonetized after July 22, 1876, quantities were not kept by United States banks, none were placed in American circulation, and examples were struck only for export purposes.]
$1 gold: 1853, 653 pieces, Uncirculated.
$1 gold: 1853-O, 643 pieces, Uncirculated.
$1 gold: 1854-S, 967 pieces, Uncirculated.
$1 gold: 1855-O, 3,785 pieces, Uncirculated. [Highly unusual for a quantity of these to exist—ditto for any other quantity of Uncirculated $1 gold coins of this era—as gold dollars of the 1850s were not bullion coins and tended to be spent.]
$1 gold: 1862, 6,797 pieces, Uncirculated.
$2.50 gold: 1831 342 pieces, Uncirculated [Highly improbable that these would have survived the vast melting of such coins circa 1833-1834 when their bullion value exceeded their face value.]
$2.50 gold: 1843-O 3,743 pieces, Uncirculated.
$2.50 gold: 1861-S 431 pieces, Uncirculated.
$2.50 gold: 1914-D 4,000 pieces, Uncirculated.
$3 gold: 1878 987 pieces, Uncirculated.
$5 gold: 1843-O 1,988 pieces, Uncirculated.
$5 gold: 1885-S 2,000 pieces, Uncirculated.
$5 gold: 1914-S 2,483 pieces, Uncirculated.
$10 gold: 1843-O 2,001 pieces, Uncirculated.
$10 gold: 1854-S 987 pieces, Uncirculated.
$10 gold: 1909-S 198 pieces, Uncirculated.
$10 gold: 1914-D 2,984 pieces, Uncirculated.
$10 gold: 1915-S 1,735 pieces, Uncirculated.
$20 gold: 1860-S 321 pieces, Uncirculated.
$20 gold: 1861 269 pieces, Uncirculated.

$20 gold: 1861-O 53 pieces, Uncirculated.
$20 gold: 1861-S 546 pieces, Uncirculated.
$20 gold: 1865-S 800 pieces, Uncirculated.
$20 gold: 1874-CC 1,000 pieces, Uncirculated.
$20 gold: 1904-S 1,000 pieces, Uncirculated.
$20 gold: 1907-S Liberty Head, 1,000 pieces, Uncirculated.
$20 gold: 1907 Saint-Gaudens, 1,000 pieces, Uncirculated.
$20 gold: 1914-D 1,841 pieces, Uncirculated.
$20 gold: 1916-S 1,001 pieces, Uncirculated.
$20 gold: 1927 1,000 pieces, Uncirculated.
$20 gold: 1930-S 640 pieces, Uncirculated.
$20 gold: 1931 329 pieces, Uncirculated.
$20 gold: 1854 Kellogg & Co., 34, VF to Uncirculated.
$20 gold: 1855 Kellogg & Co., 41, EF to Uncirculated.
$50 gold: 1855 Wass, Molitor & Co., EF to Uncirculated, 4 pieces.
And the list goes on....

Now, I am the first to hope that this hoard exists. If it does, certainly the schedule of rarity of certain things we now know would be altered, and in the process the publicity the hobby would be vastly expanded—just as the Treasury release in 1962-1964 of previously-rare silver dollars gave the hobby a tremendous boost.

Pardon me if I am skeptical. However, I am not the only one. In reviewing this list, professional numismatist Thomas K. DeLorey mused that it was unusual that the Ark of the Covenant and the Holy Grail were not also included in the hoard![1]

1996. Bag of 1889-CC Morgan dollars (for starters): The story sounded good enough: In a bank vault in Southern California a man, now quite old, put away many numismatic treasures years ago, among which was an original 1,000-coin bag of rare 1889-CC Morgan silver dollars. Desirous of selling these and other rarities, the man had his attorney contact various rare coin dealers from California to New England.

Eager to get the inside track on this cache, the dealers kept their own counsel, until they began comparing notes after no 1889-CC dollars or other coins materialized and they became suspicious. One had even given the old gent $5,000 worth of Canadian "maple leaf" one-ounce gold coins—obviously the old man had great assets, but wanted to diversify—and had received a bad check in payment.[2]

---

1 Letter, September 29, 1996.
2 David Hall comment to author, August 29, 1996; D.H. had not been involved, but related two accounts of other dealers who were. An Eastern dealer also had this experience.

APPENDIX II

Numismatic Index to Coins Mentioned

A cross-reference in numismatic order (denomination and date), by page(s) listed, of the various early American, federal, territorial, and related coins of which 10 or more were found as part of hoards and finds.

Silver Dollars

Trade Dollars

Gold Dollars

Quarter Eagles

Index

(Listings in bold represent references found in footnotes.)

C

D

E

I

J

K

L

M